THE INTERNATIONAL HANDBOOK
OF PUBLIC ADMINISTRATION AND
GOVERNANCE

The International Handbook of Public Administration and Governance

Edited by

Andrew Massey

Professor, University of Exeter, UK

Karen Johnston

Professor, Glasgow Caledonian University, UK

Edward Elgar
PUBLISHING

Cheltenham, UK • Northampton, MA, USA

Published by
Edward Elgar Publishing Limited
The Lypiatts
15 Lansdown Road
Cheltenham
Glos GL50 2JA
UK

Edward Elgar Publishing, Inc.
William Pratt House
9 Dewey Court
Northampton
Massachusetts 01060
USA

A catalogue record for this book
is available from the British Library

Library of Congress Control Number: 2014957084

This book is available electronically in the **Elgar**online
Social and Political Science subject collection
DOI 10.4337/9781781954492

ISBN 978 1 78195 448 5 (cased)
ISBN 978 1 78195 449 2 (eBook)

Typeset by Servis Filmsetting Ltd, Stockport, Cheshire
Printed and bound in Great Britain by T.J. International Ltd, Padstow

Contents

Contributors

Perri 6 is Professor in Public Management at Queen Mary University of London, UK. He has published extensively on executive government, neo-Durkheimian institutional theory, organizational processes, public policy, inter-organizational relationships, networks and joined-up government in public services. His recent books include *Explaining Political Judgement* (Cambridge University Press, 2011) and *Principles of Methodology* (with C.A. Bellamy, Sage, 2012).

J. Theodore Anagnoson is Professor Emeritus of Political Science at California State University, USA, where he researches and teaches courses on public policy and administration and American politics. He is also a visiting professor at the University of California, Santa Barbara, where he teaches courses on American politics and public policy. His research interests are the politics of federal policy making and implementation. He is the author, most recently, of 'The United States civil service', a book chapter in *The International Handbook on Civil Service Systems* (Cheltenham, UK and Northampton, MA, USA: Edward Elgar Publishing), and co-author of *Governing California in the 21st Century* (4th edn, New York: Norton, 2013).

Greg Andranovich is Professor of Political Science at California State University, Los Angeles, where he teaches public administration and urban politics courses. His research interests are the urban impacts of the Olympic Games, and the challenges of collaborative public decision making. He has authored and co-authored numerous books and journal articles in the area of public administration and urban governance.

Ahmed Badran is Assistant Professor of Public Policy at Mohammed Bin Rashid School of Government, Dubai. He holds a PhD degree in Politics (Public Policy) from the University of Exeter, UK. His research expertise is on public policy, public administration and regulatory processes. Dr Badran's research interests cover regulatory governance and politics of regulation in liberalized public utilities, including telecoms, water and energy sectors, particularly in transition and developing economies.

Geert Bouckaert is Professor at the Faculty of Social Sciences at the Katholieke Universiteit Leuven Public Governance Institute, Leuven, Belgium. He is coordinator of the Policy Research Centre – Governmental

Organization – Decisive Governance and president of the International Institute of Administrative Sciences (IIAS). He is an internationally respected academic with research expertise in public administration, performance management, financial management and trust, with extensive publications in these research areas.

Robert Cameron is Professor of Public Administration at the University of Cape Town, South Africa. His research interests include public administration, local government politics and reorganization and public sector reform. His published research, in numerous journals and books, is highly regarded. Professor Cameron is a member of the Board of the Comparative Local Government and Politics panel at the International Political Science Association.

Stanka Setnikar Cankar is Professor at the University of Ljubljana, Slovenia. Her areas of research expertise are public administration, economics and finance. Since 2000, Professor Cankar has been a member of the Senate of the University of Ljubljana. She has published a number of highly regarded journal articles and books in public administration, public economics and finance, and is a member of various editorial boards, chief editor of *Administration* magazine and a member of the Board NISPAcee.

Guillermo M. Cejudo is provost at the Center for Research and Teaching on Economics, CIDE, in Mexico City, where he has been professor at the Public Administration Department since 2006. He is the author of several government reports, and also of various books on Mexican state governments, accountability, public management, transparency, evaluation and public policy analysis. He has published in the *International Review of Administrative Sciences*, *International Public Management Journal*, *International Public Management Review*, and *Public Administration Review*. He holds a PhD in Political Science from Boston University. His research interests are quality of government in new democracies, accountability, local governance and policy analysis.

Dion Curry is a lecturer in public policy in the Department of Political and Cultural Studies at Swansea University, Wales, UK. Dr Curry's research focuses on devolution and regionalization, EU public policy and governance and multi-level governance in EU and comparative contexts.

Wolfgang Drechsler is Professor and Chair of Governance at Tallinn University of Technology, Estonia (TUT), and Vice Dean for International Relations of the Faculty of Social Sciences. As a respected academic he has served as Advisor to the President of Estonia, as Executive Secretary with the German Wissenschaftsrat during German Reunification, and, as an APSA Congressional Fellow, as Senior Legislative Analyst in the United

States Congress, and has been a consultant to several international organizations and countries. Professor Drechsler's areas of interest are non-Western, especially Chinese and Islamic, public administration; public administration, technology and innovation; and public management reform.

Ricardo Corrêa Gomes is Associate Professor in Public Management at Universidade de Brasilia, Brazil, and is the Coordinator of the Public Administration and Government division of the Associação Nacional de Pesquisa e Pós-Graduação em Administração – ANPAD. Dr Gomes has published extensively in the area of public management and is a member of the editorial board of scientific journals such as *Public Management Review*, *International Journal of Public Sector Management*, *Financial Accountability & Management*, and *The International Journal of Public and Private Healthcare Management and Economics*.

John Halligan is Professor of Public Administration, Institute for Governance and Policy Analysis, University of Canberra, Australia. His research interests are comparative public management and governance, specifically public sector reform, performance management and government institutions. He specializes in the anglophone countries of Australia and New Zealand, and, for comparative purposes, Canada and the UK. His current studies are corporate governance in the public sector, performance management, and a comparative analysis of public management. Professor Halligan, as a distinguished academic and adviser to government, has published numerous books and articles in these research areas.

Gerhard Hammerschmid is Associate Dean and Professor of Public and Financial Management at the Hertie School of Governance, Berlin, Germany. He is Program Director for the Hertie School's Executive Master of Public Management (EMPM). His research focuses on public management (reform), performance management, comparative public administration, personnel management/HRM, public service motivation and organization theory. Professor Hammerschmid has published several books on public management reform and in various international, peer-reviewed journals.

Brian W. Head is Professor at the Institute for Social Science Research, University of Queensland, Australia. He has held senior roles in government, universities and the non-government sector. He is the author and editor of several books and numerous articles on public management, governance, social issues and environmental policy. His major interests are evidence-based policy, program evaluation, early intervention and prevention, collaboration and consultation, service delivery, accountability and leadership.

Sebastian Jilke is a PhD candidate at Erasmus University Rotterdam, Department of Public Administration, and is a research associate and administrative manager within a major European research project, 'Coordinating for Cohesion in the Public Sector of the Future'. His research interest lies at the intersection of public administration and political science, and the introduction of choice and competition into public services.

Karen Johnston (*née* Miller) is Professor of Politics and Public Policy and Associate Dean (Research) at Glasgow Caledonian University, UK. She has extensive academic and research experience, having worked in leading universities in South Africa, the USA and the UK. In addition to her academic career she has worked with and for public sector and civil society organizations to improve public service delivery, and has worked for a donor organization to promote democratic development on an international scale. Professor Johnston's research expertise includes public policy, political–administrative leadership, public governance, public management and gender equality, and she has published numerous peer-reviewed journal articles and books in these areas.

Andrew Massey is Professor of Politics and Head of Department at the University of Exeter, UK. His research areas of expertise include UK, European, and US policy and politics. His main areas of research include comparative public policy, public administration and issues around the reform and modernization of government and governance at all levels in the UK, the USA, the EU and globally. He has published extensively in these areas, and as a respected academic has been an adviser to government, serves on executive boards of a number of scholarly organizations such as the European Group of Public Administration, and on editorial boards. Professor Massey is currently the editor of *Public Money and Management* and the *International Review for Administrative Sciences*.

Duncan McTavish is Professor of Public Policy and Management at Glasgow Caledonian University, UK. He has a wide range of experience and expertise as an academic, practitioner and consultant in public and private sectors. His track record is national and international in scope, and in academia he has worked in a number of universities and in a range of countries. He has a wide range of highly regarded publications, edits a leading academic journal, has taught undergraduate, postgraduate and professional-level programmes and has led and managed major research and consultancy projects.

Janine O'Flynn is Professor of Public Management at the University of Melbourne. Her expertise is in public sector management, particularly in the areas of public sector reform and relationships. Professor O'Flynn is an editor at the *Australian Journal of Public Administration*, and is an editorial board member for *Public Administration*, *Journal of Management & Organization* and *Canadian Public Administration*. She was awarded the 2013 Best Book Award in the Public Non-profit stream by the United States Academy of Management for *Rethinking Public Service Delivery: Managing with External Providers* (Routledge; with John Alford), and was part of the research team that received both the Charles H. Levine and the Carlo Masini Award (2013) and was nominated for the Carolyn Dexter Award (2014).

Veronika Petkovšek is an assistant in Public Sector Economics at the Faculty of Administration, University of Ljubljana, Slovenia. Her research interests include public sector reform, health care in Slovenia, evaluation of effectiveness and efficiency in public administration, public procurement and cross-border cooperation in the Alps–Adriatic region.

Robert Pyper is Professor of Government and Public Policy at the University of the West of Scotland, UK. His research interests include national and international trends in civil service policy and management; aspects of accountability in public policy and management; modernization and reform agendas in the British civil service; public services reform and modernization; and public policy in the devolved polities. His books, book chapters and journal articles cover topics including UK governance, the British civil service, devolution, and public services modernization.

R.A.W. Rhodes is Professor of Government (Research) at the University of Southampton, UK, and at Griffith University, Brisbane, Australia; and Emeritus Professor of Politics at the University of Newcastle, UK. He is life Vice President and former Chair and President of the Political Studies Association of the UK; a Fellow of the Academy of the Social Sciences in Australia; and a Fellow of the Academy of Social Sciences, UK. He has also been a Fellow of the Royal Society of Arts, editor of *Public Administration* from 1986 to 2011, and Treasurer of the Australian Political Studies Association, 1994–2011. He is an internationally respected scholar in public administration with an extensive publication record (see http://www.raw-rhodes.co.uk/).

Donald J. Savoie holds the Canada Research Chair in Public Administration and Governance at the University of Moncton, New Brunswick, Canada. He is a former civil servant and has extensive work experience in both government and academia. He has been an adviser to federal, provincial and territorial governments, the private sector, the World Bank and the United Nations. He is a highly respected academic and has authored and co-authored numerous books and journal articles.

Leonardo Secchi is Professor at the Universidade do Estado de Santa Catarina, Brazil. He has extensive research experience and publications in the area of public administration, bureaucracy, administrative reform, public policy and studies of local government. He was President of PVBLICA – Institute for Public Policy – is Director of Events of the Brazilian Society of Public Administration (SBAP) and Professor of Undergraduate and Master's Degrees from the State University of Santa Catarina (UDESC/ESAG), where he teaches Public Policy.

Anne Tiernan is a Professor at the School of Government and International Relations, Griffith University, Australia, where she is Director of postgraduate and executive programs in policy analysis and public administration. Dr Tiernan's research interests include: policy advice, executive governance, policy capacity, federalism and intergovernmental coordination. She has authored numerous books and articles, including, most recently, *Lessons in Governing: A Profile of Prime Ministers' Chiefs of Staff* and *The Gatekeepers: Lessons from Prime Ministers' Chiefs of Staff* (both with R.A.W. Rhodes, Melbourne University Publishing, 2014). Dr Tiernan is a member of the Public Records Review Committee of the Queensland State Archives and has served on the Board of Queensland's Public Service Commission. She consults regularly to Australian governments at all levels.

Krishna K. Tummala is Professor Emeritus, and was Director of the Graduate Program in Public Administration, Kansas State University, Manhattan, KS, USA. He served on the governing bodies of the American Society for Public Administration and the National Association of School of Public Affairs and Administration, and was President of the public administration honour society, Pi Alpha Alpha. Among the several awards he received are: Paul H. Appleby Award for 'Distinguished Service to Indian Institute of Public Administration (IIPA) and Public Administration, 2011'; Fred Riggs award for 'Lifetime Scholarly Achievement in the Field of Comparative and International Administration', SICA/ASPA, 2008; and 'Don Stone' award from the American Society for Public Administration for 'Outstanding Services', 2005. He has published extensively in various national and international journals in his areas of competence.

Steven Van de Walle is Professor of Public Administration at Erasmus University Rotterdam, the Netherlands. He is Fellow of the Public

Management Institute at the Katholieke Universiteit Leuven, and a senior member of the Netherlands Institute of Government. His research and teaching covers the role of public administration in societies and in the state, and specific research interests include citizens' perceptions of the public sector, government–citizen relations, public sector performance, corruption, trust in government, satisfaction surveys, comparative public administration and governance indicators. Professor van de Walle's research has been published in books and in leading public administration journals.

Zhichang Zhu is a Reader in Strategy and Management at the University of Hull Business School, UK and holds visiting professorships in China, Japan and the USA. Dr Zhu researches and teaches in corporate and reform strategy from an institutional, comparative and complexity perspective. His work has been listed as *Strategy+Business* Best Business Books of the Year (2012).

Introduction

Andrew Massey

Omnia mutantur, nos et mutamur in illis.
(All things are in the process of change; we also are in the process of change among them.)

We must all obey the great law of change. It is the most powerful law of nature.
Edmund Burke (1991)

Nascentes morimur.
(From the moment of being born, we die.) Manilus, *Astronomica* iv.16

We all live continually in a time of change, whether in an age of innovation or in a period of decay. This is the natural ebb and flow of the human condition, and likewise that of all the institutions created and staffed by people. Even those venerable customs and structures such as the civil and administrative organizations in old countries are constantly being reinvented and reformed (Kuhlman and Wollman, 2014). Change also affects newly formed countries, even as they emerge star-like from the flux of war or civil strife; or simply because their citizens no longer wish to be linked to an autocratic regime, another nation or group of nations. Some of these resurrect ancient borders and long-smothered nations; others challenge the colonial borders bequeathed by retreating empires (Vidmar, 2012). In all these examples the core structures of the state and the way in which these link to the populace are integral to understanding the delivery of basic services such as law and security, and more sophisticated services such as higher education and innovative medicine. There is a mix of levels, from global governance and supranational, legal organizations (such as the International Court of Justice and International Court of Arbitration) through to myriad local government structures around the globe. Understanding this multi-level governance and the differentiated forms it and the constituent polities take, through surveying public administration, is a core aim of this book.

The transformation of public administration around the globe in the last 30 years shows no sign of abating and remains driven by the powerful dynamics of technical innovation, political development, globalization and economic necessity. Our understanding of how we make sense of these changes also fluctuates, as does our use of language to describe these phenomena. For example, this volume explores the concepts and

1

practicalities of both public administration and governance. But these remain contested in many respects. This was epitomized in a 2013 debate over the nature of 'governance', as considered by a group of leading scholars via the blog of the eponymous journal (http://governancejournal.net). Francis Fukuyama set that debate in motion with a paper that called for better measures to assess governance, while noting that these did not necessarily need to include democratic aspects of accountability and liberal-democratic notions of what is meant by good governance (Fukuyama, 2013). In other words, as he, scholars and political leaders from various parts of the world and different ideological traditions have argued (in different ways), good governance does not need to be democratic governance. Indeed, it may be the case that authoritarian governments can deliver good governance in the sense that it is efficient, effective and delivers good-quality public services. This perspective is anathema to those who argue that good governance is synonymous with liberal-democratic notions of accountability and transparency (Fraser-Moleketi, 2005; Halabi, 2004). Yet there are many in the global South (and elsewhere) who, while they call for public administration to deliver good governance on precisely those utilitarian grounds of efficient and effective services that have the alleviation of human misery as their desired outcome, eschew a call for Western-style democracy.

For example, since it was established in 1944, as one of the so-called Bretton Woods institutions, the World Bank's stated mission has been to help to establish 'a world free of poverty'. Indeed, this aim is carved in stone in the organization's Washington headquarters and features on the Bank's website, and many of its publications over the years state boldly (and in several different ways) that

> This mission underpins all our analytical, financial and convening work in more than 145 client countries that strive to end extreme poverty and promote shared prosperity. The developing world has already attained the first Millennium Development Goal target – to cut the 1990 poverty rate in half by 2015. The 1990 extreme poverty rate – $1.25 a day in 2005 prices – was halved in 2010, according to estimates. According to these estimates, 21 percent of people in the developing world lived at or below $1.25 a day. That's down from 43 percent in 1990 and 52 percent in 1981.This means that 1.22 billion people lived on less than $1.25 a day in 2010, compared with 1.91 billion in 1990, and 1.94 billion in 1981. Notwithstanding this achievement, even if the current rate of progress is to be maintained, some 1 billion people will still live in extreme poverty in 2015 – and progress has been slower at higher poverty lines. In all, 2.4 billion people lived on less than US $2 a day in 2010, the average poverty line in developing countries and another common measurement of deep deprivation. That is only a slight decline from 2.59 billion in 1981. (World Bank, 2014)

The situation is, however, more complicated than simply listing statistics that show the poverty levels of different countries. The Bank itself notes that in 'some developing countries, we continue to see a wide gap – or in some cases – widening gap between rich and poor, and between those who can and cannot access opportunities' (ibid.). That is, the comparative rates of poverty within developing countries vary enormously, but then they do also in many developed countries. The UK's Office of National Statistics produces annual tables and reports on comparative wealth and deprivation, such as the *Atlas of Deprivation* (2011), and similar studies in the USA demonstrate that in both of those countries the gap between a small number of wealthy individuals and a much larger proportion of poorer people is widening (United States Census Bureau, 2014). This leads to a series of rhetorical questions:

1.   What is good governance?
2.   What is the purpose of good governance and how do we recognize it?
3.   Can we measure it?
4.   What is the purpose and role of public administration?
5.   Is it to simply carry out the wishes of the government and control the delivery of services deemed necessary by the government?
6.   Or is it to establish institutions and procedures to alleviate inequalities of wealth and power, and deliver services that ameliorate the deprivation of poverty?
7.   Can we plan these things strategically in terms of policy-making and public administration (Lusk and Birks, 2014)?
8.   Or is public administration something more than any of this? Is it fundamental to the understanding of a nation's role and status, and does it reflect the broader social and political context?

In terms of question 6, it is worth recalling the statistic that Europe, with just over 7 per cent of the world's population and about a quarter of its economy, accounts for half the global spending on welfare; in many of the poorer member states of the EU welfare is being paid for only by virtue of the largess (or self-interest) of the richer Northern countries (Hillman, 2014). In such a scenario, when combined with the statistics on global poverty, the many and varied answers to the questions listed above incite contention.

The International Handbook of Public Administration and Governance is intended to provide a guide to and explanation of the concepts of and influences on governance and public administration. It cannot provide definitive answers to the above-listed questions, but it does offer a series of perspectives and observations to enable readers to evolve their own perceptions of what these concepts mean and what the institutions of government and governance are for. It is an ambitious volume replete with contributions from eminent scholars that address the key questions of how governments, nationally and internationally, can tackle public administration and governance challenges in an increasingly globalized world. The international coverage of perspectives, including those from Africa, Asia, Europe, Australia, North and South America, is a distinctive feature of this book. It adopts contemporary perspectives of governance, including public policy capacity, 'wicked' policy problems, public sector reforms, the challenges of globalization and managing complexity. The book is in two parts.

Part I is largely theoretical and addresses 'Public Administration, New Public Management and Governance: Concepts and Contestabilities'. It begins with a scene-setting chapter by Robert Pyper that introduces and contextualizes public administration, public management and governance as key concepts. There is no attempt here (or anywhere in the volume) to create a general theory of public administration, as has been done elsewhere (Lalor, 2014); rather, Pyper provides a careful explanation and exploration of the historical and academic context. This leads into the original and theory-building chapter by Bouckaert. He opines that 'governance' as a word does not travel well between languages, but he builds a new and beautifully constructed typology to explore the culturally defined nature of the concept. In this he confronts some of the issues raised in this introduction, namely: whether there can be good governance without democracy; the extent of governance without government; and the role of governance in different degrees of development. Perri 6 (Chapter 3) lays down a challenge to much of the existing usage of the term 'governance' as applied to public administration. He argues that governance theories are a merger basis for normative analysis of institutions, and that government institutions do not govern alone, with command being a blunt and often crude instrument. He wants to move public administration beyond governance theory. In Chapter 4 Rhodes and Tiernan (the former of whom 6 had disagreed with in terms of multi-level governance and other concepts) look again at the different approaches to executive government, teasing out where the study of executive government in political science intersects with the study of governance in public administration. The authors question the capacity of government by concentrating on what they refer to as four puzzles: predominant or collaborative leadership; central capability or implementation; formal or informal coordination; and political accountability or webs of accountability. Part I concludes with the chapter by Wolfgang Drechsler (Chapter 5), which offers a glimpse into the paradigms of non-Western public administration and governance, a glimpse that develops into a more sustained scrutiny in Part II. Drechsler explores non-Western public administration, in particular the Islamic and Chinese paradigms, arguing that we can arrive more easily at good public administration if we accept that there are different contexts and (legitimately) different goals. He wrestles with the kind of issues raised by the questions posed in this introduction, and concludes that perhaps we can best advance by accepting that different places have different narratives; we can progress through different paths with different goals and (perhaps) different destinations.

Part II, 'International Perspective of Public Administration, New Public Management and Governance', delivers a series of country and regional specific analyses of governance and public administration, drawing upon the issues and perspectives outlined in Part I. In particular, the chapters look at change and challenges, with Robert Cameron (Chapter 6) charting the journey in South Africa from the apartheid regime to the successive administrations under the African National Congress and that movement's embrace of new public management (NPM). As he notes, the 'major challenge was to move from a state that provided services predominantly to a small white constituency to one that also provided decent services to the disadvantaged black majority'. The South African government opted to adopt administrative delegation, performance management and corporatization, but Cameron's analysis suggests that these NPM techniques have not travelled particularly well and we require a more nuanced approach rooted in the domestic context of the nation to effect reform that delivers positive outcomes. Ahmed Badran (Chapter 7) takes readers to the other end of the African continent and examines public administration reform and governance in Egypt. Here, as in other emerging economies, he argues, 'reforming state machinery and public bodies has been regarded as a means for achieving broader social and economic developmental goals'. In a strategic review of the Egyptian public sector from a political-economy perspective, he charts its development through the various welfarist and regulatory phases up to and beyond the 2011 revolution, noting the difficulties associated with meeting the competing demands upon it and the power of the elite to frustrate change. We cross continents with Donald Savoie (Chapter 8) to explore the impact of globalization and the desire of Canadian politicians to 'grab hold of the policy-making levers and to become less dependent on career public servants for policy advice'; he notes that 'the push to have public sector managers emulate their private sector counterparts has knocked the public service off its traditional moorings'. The impact of these reforms on Canada's public administration has been to try to emulate the private sector, but this has not been entirely successful. This is unsurprising because, as Pyper points out in Chapter 1, the whole purpose of public administration is to do different things at different levels of transparency and accountability from private companies.

Crossing the border, Andranovich and Anagnoson (Chapter 9) deliver a magisterial review of the issues and challenges to public administration and governance in the USA. The role of the executive, contested throughout US history, its relationship to the other parts of government and to the citizenry, is explored through the prism of public administration and governance. The authors map the changing size and structures of the US public administration, focusing on the pinch points dealing with various 'wicked' issues. They conclude that 'the reasons why the public sector is not functioning well in the USA are not fundamentally administrative – they are political. With the country roughly equally divided between Republicans and Democrats, between those seeking a significantly smaller government with fewer services as opposed to a larger government with a significant array of services, public administrators and executive branches are caught in the middle.' Traversing the Darien Gap to reach Brazil, the chapter from Gomes and Secchi (Chapter 10) demonstrates again the issues confronting a country with a large public sector, a large population and huge disparities of wealth and power. But they remind us that, although much of Brazil may look like a developing or emergent economy, it is the world's seventh-largest economy and is set to continue to grow quickly. In that sense Brazil is grappling with the challenges of economic success combined with continuing poverty. The country's public administration is central to addressing these issues. The authors demonstrate the intricacies of a public sector that, like the country itself, is large and diverse. Unlike the policy transfer of NPM ideas in other countries, though, some of the experiments in wider public participation in policy-making and service delivery are genuinely novel. The 'Brazilian participation experiences are unique – born, tested and improved locally. There was no inspiration from foreign literature or foreign experiences of public governance, or policy networks or co-production.' Guillermo Cejudo (Chapter 11) takes a broader perspective and assesses public administration more regionally from a wide Latin American perspective. He explores the different trajectories that countries in the region have followed since emerging from dictatorship. The chapter debates why some democracies find it difficult to reform their public administration in ways that deliver efficient services to the widest possible clientele, while other 'third-way' democracies have been relatively more successful in transforming government and creating professional bureaucracies. The author provides illuminating case studies evaluating these issues, concentrating on Mexico, Chile and Argentina. His analysis again demonstrates the importance of political structures and, more significantly, political constraints in delivering positive reforms.

Krishna Tummala delivers a review of and explanation for developments in Indian public administration (Chapter 12). Like Brazil, India is huge, accounting for 1.2 billion people and an economy that is the world's fourth largest and still growing. It is diverse (22 constitutionally recognized languages) in terms of ethnicity, religion and geography. Yet, despite having concentrations of wealth and power, it also has deep and abiding poverty. The colonial civil service inherited from the British was transformed in the years following independence and used to construct and attempt to implement a series of five-year plans under the direction of Indian socialism. The chapter charts the development of the modern Indian public administration, but does not shrink from exposing the bleak picture framed by corruption and the illegal activities of politicians, activities that have stunted and blunted reform. Suggestions for further reform and shafts of administrative 'sunshine' conclude the chapter. We then cross the Himalayas for a review and analysis of the second Asian giant in the chapter by Zhichang Zhu on China (Chapter 13). This chapter resonates with the issues raised by Drechsler, with Zhu exploring the Chinese bureaucratic tradition and the impact of the historical legacy of centralized authoritarianism. Inherent to the modern reforms is the tradition, current throughout ancient and modern history, that the role of government had no boundaries. Zhu concludes by analysing the reasons for the post-Mao reforms and their mixed success, noting that, even when China borrows an idea from elsewhere, it adapts it for the specific Chinese context. This means that 'China's reform has displayed historical continuity as well as skilful learning from the West'.

John Halligan begins his chapter (Chapter 14) on public sector reform in Australia by noting that developing 'government capacity to address complex and intractable problems has become increasingly a priority for Australian central government'. Australian federal and state governments have been innovative in the measures and structures developed over the last 30 years, and have been at the forefront of developing new institutions and procedures to deliver services and achieve a set of desired national outcomes from the country's public administration. As one of the anglophone countries, Australia was quick to adapt its administrative structures during the fashion for NPM, but it was also in the lead to move on from these structures and reform them to develop capacity to deliver modern services through collaboration and shared outcomes. The second of our Australian chapters takes many of the points raised by Halligan and develops them to explore how Australia's innovative approach to bureaucratic reform developed capacity to address and manage 'wicked issues', including the disadvantage experienced by Indigenous peoples. In this chapter (Chapter 15), Brian Head and Janine O'Flynn argue that the reforms led to great tensions at the heart of Australian governance, with increased contestability in terms of the sources of policy advice. One of the lessons learned (and there have been many) is the need for coordination and something of a return (where applicable in a federal system) to central government exercising strategic direction.

Dion Curry, Gerhard Hammerschmid, Sebastian Jilke and Steven van de Walle contribute a chapter (Chapter 16) that examines European public sector reform via an overview of public administration in Europe. The second half of the chapter discusses key trends such as outcome/result orientation, downsizing, contracting out, transparency, openness, e-government and citizen participation, among others. The authors highlight the similarities and differences regarding these issues across European countries, pointing out the diversity of public administration origins across the continent: Anglo-Saxon, Scandinavian, Roman and Napoleonic. To illustrate these points they use several case countries: Norway, Estonia, Hungary, the Netherlands, Italy, France, Germany, Austria, Spain and the UK. Based on extensive original research, the authors chart and analyse the reforms across Europe and conclude that the nature and extent of public administration reforms vary greatly. Some of these variations follow traditional North/South, East/West divides, but since the fall of the Berlin Wall and the expansion of the EU, such distinctions are much less marked than before. The context of reform remained the most important factor, reflecting the robustness of each country's political system in terms of good governance and also the way in which they were affected by the global financial crisis. Chapter 17, by Stanka Setnikar Cankar and Veronika Petkovšek, focuses on one of the world's newer countries, Slovenia, which emerged from the breakup of the former Yugoslavia. As a member of the EU, Slovenia has benefited from EU assistance and has received guidance on reconfiguring its public sector, but the impact of the financial crisis had a highly damaging impact on the country and the most recent reforms have demonstrated the way in which a small country with a vulnerable economy has acted in concert with EU institutions to rebuild confidence and competitiveness. Nearly all recent reform has been driven by the belief in the need for austerity measures. Duncan McTavish (Chapter 18) outlines the traditional configuration of UK public administration before assessing the impact of NPM reforms and the development of regulatory audit and inspection regimes. He concludes by evaluating the UK's public administration within the new complexity of devolved administrations, the impact of the EU and broader global dynamics. The UK adoption of NPM was 'more systemic and thorough than in other countries, and the ideational and ideological drive was clear: the accentuation of management, often transferred in from the business sector; cost control and discipline; competition; privatization and use of market mechanisms; efficiency and modernization leading to a separation of policy and management of delivery through agencies and arm's-length bodies'. But, as he makes clear, there has been very little systematic evaluation of the success of the reforms in terms of their stated intention: value for money; greater efficiency; effectiveness; and economy. In short, we know there has been transformative change, but we do not know if it has worked according to its original criteria, let alone more up-to-date measures, however defined.

This returns us to our original questions at the beginning of this chapter. We conclude the book (Chapter 18) with a summary of its main points and lessons to be drawn from our global journey. We draw out examples, as we see them, of good practice and good governance. While the book does not amount to a paean in praise of bureaucracy *per se*, we are supporters of good bureaucracy: good in terms of efficiency, effectiveness, professional merit-based appointments and, above all, integrity and broad accountability to citizens. Indeed, good governance necessitates good administrative and political institutions serving its citizenry. That is, after all, the basis of good governance and, without that, civilization, indeed humanity, cannot flourish.

REFERENCES

Burke, E. (1991), *The Enlightenment and Revolution*, ed. Peter Stanlis, New Brunswick, NJ: Transaction Publishers.

Fraser-Moleketi, G. (2005), *The World We Could Win: Administering Global Government*, Amsterdam: IOS Press.

Fukuyama, F. (2013), 'What is governance?', *Governance*, **26**(3), 347–68.

Fukuyama, F. (2014), http://governancejournal.net.

Halabi, Y. (2004), 'The expansion of global governance into the Third World: altruism, realism, or constructivism?', *International Studies Review*, **6**, 21–48.

Hillman, N. (2014), 'Debate: reforming state welfare', *Public Money and Management*, **34**(3), 159–61.

Kuhlman, S. and Wollman, H. (2014), *Introduction to Comparative Public Administration: Administrative Systems and Reforms in Europe*, Cheltenham, UK and Northampton, MA, USA: Edward Elgar Publishing.

Lalor, S. (2014), *A General Theory of Public Administration*, Dublin: Lalor.

Lusk, S. and Birks, N. (2014), *Rethinking Public Strategy*, Basingstoke: Palgrave.

Office of National Statistics (2011), http://www.ons.gov.uk/ons/dcp171780_239839.pdf.

United States Census Bureau (2014), https://www.census.gov/prod/2014pubs/p60–248.pdf.

Vidmar, J. (2012), 'South Sudan and the international legal framework governing the emergence and delimitation of new states', *Texas International Law Journal*, **47**(3), 547–59.

World Bank (2014), http://www.worldbank.org/en/topic/poverty/overview.

PART I

PUBLIC ADMINISTRATION, NEW PUBLIC MANAGEMENT AND GOVERNANCE: CONCEPTS AND CONTESTABILITIES

1. Public administration, public management and governance

Robert Pyper

This chapter introduces and contextualizes public administration, public management and governance as key concepts with fundamental structural and operational implications for government and public policy. It sets out a historical perspective on the paradigm shifts encapsulated in the movement from public administration to (new) public management to governance, while arguing for the continued importance of public administration as an overarching paradigm. It summarizes the consequences and implications of these shifts, and categorizes the major academic and political critiques of the theory and practice contained within the paradigms. The need for caution regarding uncritical acceptance of supposed international ubiquity, or even national consistency, is stressed and significant divergence from assumed 'norms' in certain parts of the globe and, over time, within certain states, is noted. Finally a series of 'sub-concepts' is examined in order to determine the extent to which they represent significant refinements and developments of the major themes, or have the status of passing fads and fashions.

KEY CONCEPTS, HISTORICAL CONTEXT AND PARADIGM SHIFTS

In one simple and straightforward form of analysis, it is possible to view the key concepts that form the subject of this chapter as stages of linear development in a chronological and historical context, and also in terms of paradigmatic shifts. Thus, to coin a phrase, public administration begat public management, which in turn begat governance. The weaknesses of such a sweeping generalization are immediately apparent, however. In the real world of government, there are major overlaps between developmental phases, and, in practice, there is no neat and clean succession of modes or regimes. Additionally, the academic paradigms are significantly more complex than these shifts would suggest, and, in particular, it can be argued that, depending upon the prevailing mode of analysis, governance is both an element within public administration and public management, and also one among several possible 'successors' to the latter (as discussed below).

An alternative, and more useful, approach is to view public administration not merely as a description of a rather traditional, historic mode of government whose time has come and gone, but as an overarching paradigm within which we can locate subsequent developments, including public management and governance. This can help us come to terms with the continued deployment of the term 'public administration' as a working description of the organizational settings for government. Public administration continued to be the default description of the central and local structures, systems and processes established for the creation of policy and the delivery of public services in many parts of the globe, long after the apparent embrace of (new) public management by the Anglo-Americans. However, the persistence of the term can be seen even in states such as the UK, where it is often assumed that public administration has been superseded by public management and its new variants. To cite one example: the existence of a select committee of the UK Parliament with a focus on public administration is indicative of something more than a reluctance to rename the body; this speaks to the continued utility of the concept.

Some critics have argued, convincingly, that the new public management (NPM) was really a sub-species of public administration, and its effects were restricted due to, *inter alia*, the relative poverty of its conceptual and theoretical bases, the weaknesses of its claims of novelty, and the lack of evidence to support its prescriptions for improved organizational and societal outcomes (see, e.g., Pollitt, 1990; Frederickson and Smith, 2003).

Public administration is a multifaceted concept, with some key features at its core. As a discipline, it encompasses, *inter alia*:

- administrative theories
- the history of public sector bodies
- biographical studies of civil servants and other public officials
- organizational and institutional arrangements for service delivery
- relationships between officials and politicians, and between both of these and the public
- modes of accountability and control
- citizens' rights of access to public bodies and the information they hold
- policy making and implementation
- public finance and budgeting
- public sector performance (and the measurement and evaluation thereof)

- management and leadership in public sector organizations
- human resource management and labour relations in the public sector
- professional development, education and training for public officials
- national and international comparative studies of governmental organizations
  (adapted from Caiden et al., 1983: xiv–xv and Massey, 1993: 9–10).

Traditionally, much of the focus of public administration was on the workings of government departments at central and local levels, and state-run entities including nationalized industries. The hierarchical, rule-bound public administration systems favoured by Max Weber and Woodrow Wilson as a means to insulate officialdom at central and local levels from the corruption of raw politics evolved over time to become more fluid and flexible, and increased recognition came to be given to the subtleties of systems within which the exercise of significant, though accountable, influence could be wielded by 'street-level bureaucrats'. However, notwithstanding this evolution, in the historical context, as the boundaries between the public and private sectors became increasingly blurred (due in part to increased interdependencies and privatizations of some state entities), and as the influence of private sector business approaches to management and organization increased, public administration came to be viewed in some quarters as a somewhat outdated concept. In this perspective, it was seen as rule-bound and inflexible, paying insufficient attention to the attractions of new modes of thinking and approaches to the practice of running large and complex organizations.

These developments brought challenges to, and refinements of, public administration. The reaction to three successive, yet overlapping, challenges brought about significant changes. The first challenge dated from the late 1950s and early 1960s, and had as its main focus the need to modernize systems and processes, particularly in relation to budgeting, policy making and analysis, and the associated managerial imperatives. The new, modern approaches often required new types of people in government, and in the USA, the appointment to the Kennedy administration of Robert S. McNamara as Defense Secretary was indicative of this. McNamara brought into government a combination of systems analysis based on his statistical work in the US Airforce during the Second World War, and finely honed business and management skills from his work as president of the Ford Motor Company. Despite his Republican background, his modern managerial credentials meant that he was 'on everybody's list of candidates' for a job in the administration of the new Democrat president, and he was considered suitable for either the Treasury or Defense (Dallek, 2003: 312). Under McNamara, the US Defense Department's internal processes rapidly became a model of modernization in public administration (see Shapley, 1993). In the UK, at the same time, the Plowden Report (Plowden Committee, 1961) examined new systems for the control of public expenditure in the broader context of modernizing management in government, and the latter theme was picked up subsequently in the Fulton Report (Fulton Committee, 1968) and the Heath government's White Paper, *The Reorganisation of Central Government* (HM Government, 1970). During this phase, the challenge associated with adopting more rational and strategic approaches to policy making and evaluation

> coincided with, and was part of, a period of 'high modernism' when rapid advances in science and technology, combined with a huge growth in the university-based study of the social sciences, seemed to hold out the promise of a more rational 'designed' set of public policies and institutions. (Pollitt and Bouckaert, 2011: 6)

In the second phase, broadly spanning the late 1960s to the late 1970s, the challenge was to produce new ways of organizing and managing the business of the state in the face of socioeconomic crises and apparent 'overload' and 'ungovernability' (the title and content of King, 1976, although UK focused, spoke to a global malaise). The reaction to this challenge saw serious concerns arise in relation to the 'machinery of government', and the launch of waves of structural and managerial reforms, many of which continued well into the 1980s and beyond. In the UK and the USA, the search for greater coordination of policy making and implementation and economies of scale saw moves to create 'giant' government departments (in the UK context, typified by the huge Department of the Environment), and the spread of 'rational' approaches to policy analysis and budgeting (including the proliferation of planned, programmed budgeting systems (PPBS) and the search for value for money (VFM)). As the vogue changed, structural 'giantism' gave way to a new preference for discrete organizational units with their own performance regimes and specific service delivery foci. The creation of multiple executive agencies, influenced significantly by the Swedish model of government (although always with specific local variations), could be seen throughout the globe as the 1980s progressed. In the UK context, this process was encapsulated within the 'Next Steps' initiative (Efficiency Unit, 1988).

Christopher Hood captured the meaning and impact of this second phase in his seminal work charting the impact of the new managerialism on public administration, and setting out the fundamental changes taking place in the functioning of public service organizations. *Inter alia*, there would be increased emphasis on the disciplined use of resources, greater managerial autonomy and 'flexibilities', competition via tendering and contractualization, disaggregation through structural change and privatization, and the application of performance standards and measurement (Hood, 1991: 4–5). Public management, or new public management (NPM), had become the titular embodiment of the paradigm shift that encapsulated the approaches taken by the Thatcher and Reagan governments in the UK and USA respectively in the early 1980s, spread to Australia and New Zealand by the middle of that decade, and then became current across the globe (although see below for a cautionary note regarding assumed ubiquity),

> driven partly by the forces of globalization and by international organizations dominated by the same countries, but also nationally by conservative and neo-liberal parties, in some cases in collaboration with mainstream social democratic parties. (Christensen and Lægreid, 2010b: 1)

Even as this happened, however, the third challenge had emerged, and from the mid-1980s onwards the reaction to this led to a new phase of development for public administration. As the mix of public, private and 'third sector' bodies and agencies with an involvement in policy making and delivery expanded and developed, so the complexities associated with coordination, 'joining up' and securing adequate accountabilities, regulation and control became increasingly acute. Influenced to some extent by the elements of the international relations literature, which sought to make sense of the 'complex interdependencies' in that sphere (e.g. the work of Keohane and Nye on power and interdependence – see 4th edn, 2011), public administration analysts began to stress the importance of understanding the interactions between governmental and non-governmental organizations in terms of networks (an early theoretical exposition of networks can be found in Knoke and Kuklinski, 1982, and a useful summary of the development of the theory in Enroth, 2011). Networks could be relatively closed (the 'iron triangles' in the USA, wherein government departments or agencies, Congressional committees and dominant lobbies or interest groups effectively incorporated key policy spheres) or open (wide and shifting arrays of departments, formal and informal interest groups from the public, private and third sectors). The literature on network theory and practice expanded beyond its US base, reflecting the increasing utility of the concepts (in the UK context, see, e.g., Jordan, 1990; Rhodes, 1990; Marsh and Rhodes, 1992).

The diffusion and fragmentation seen as a consequence of the increased significance of networks led to further theoretical and conceptual insights, including the 'hollowing-out' thesis. This saw governments 'lose' policy functionality 'upwards' (to state and transnational organizations, including foreign powers, the World Bank and multinational corporations), 'downwards' (to privatized and contractualized elements of the system), and 'outwards' (to arm's-length bodies such as executive agencies – key sources on all of this are Rhodes, 1994, 1997). The 'differentiated polity' thesis focused on the effect of decentralization, subsidiarity and devolution on policy making and delivery, again adding to the impression of functional disaggregation and fragmentation (see Rhodes et al., 2003).

These theoretical and analytical approaches were closely associated with the broader governance paradigm. Influenced by the analyses of Kooiman (1993) and Pierre and Peters (2000) (their 2000 work best captures the development of their ideas), Rhodes (1997) summarized the shift from 'government' to 'governance' in terms of a new focus on the network interactions between politicians and officials ('government') and the non-governmental actors. The increased importance of networks, reduced role for government in some spheres, proliferation of managerial initiatives, and continuing programmes of organizational and institutional reform were key features of the new mode. Within this developmental phase of public administration, the concept of governance emerged as a response to the challenge of increasingly complex governmental and societal interactions. There was a perceived need to 're-engineer' or 'reinvent' government. These concepts initially assumed particular significance in the USA following the publication of work by public management consultants David Osborne and Ted Gaebler (Osborne and Gaebler, 1992). Their definition of 'governance' was broad. It was

> the process by which we collectively solve our problems and meet our society's needs. Government is the instrument we use. The instrument is outdated and the process of reinvention has begun. (Ibid.: 24)

Their work both reflected changing realities in the practice of governance at all levels of the USA, and also influenced policy makers in the Clinton administration (see Aberbach and Rockman, 2001). The 'reinventing government' agendas spread rapidly beyond the USA, with the core idea from Osborne and Gaebler that the fundamental role of government should be to 'steer' policy delivery rather than attempt to do the 'rowing' itself. This built upon the basic theses of NPM, recognized the vital importance of networks, and aligned with the increasing emphasis being given to service performance comparisons, competition among service providers, optimizing managerial practices, treating service users as customers with rights and expectations, decentralizing decisions on delivery mechanisms and modes, enhancing accountability for outcomes, and, of course, the perennial search for the 'right' organizational structures.

Governance theory became increasingly complex, as it moved beyond a 'first wave' with its focus on networks, to a 'second wave' of 'metagovernance' (see Jessop, 2011) in which the state seeks to secure 'coordination in governance ... [by] its use of negotiation, diplomacy and more informal modes of steering' (Bevir and Rhodes, 2011: 206), and on to the 'third wave' of the 'stateless state ... a decentred approach [which] focuses on the social construction of patterns of rule through the ability of individuals to create meanings in action' (ibid.: 209). Curiously, and slightly confusingly, one of the proponents of the deconstructed, decentred 'third wave' that has supposedly superseded the phases of governance in which networks and the 'steering state' existed also argues, separately, that networks and steering have a continuing currency in 'global governance' ('the management of transnational issues by international organisations and other non-state actors as well as by sovereign states' – Bevir and Hall, 2011: 352). Does the post-structuralist, postmodern, quasi-Foucaultian search for meaning in social constructs within a 'stateless state' apply only at national level?

Notwithstanding this, the novelty of governance as a fresh feature of public administration could be overstated. Arguably, 'good governance', in the specific, focused sense of proper decision-making procedures, recognized standards of conduct for politicians and officials, and robust mechanisms of accountability and control had always been a key element of sound public administration. The ubiquity of this application of the term has been noted:

> The World Bank and the International Monetary Fund make loans conditional on 'good governance'. Climate change and avian flu appear as issues of 'global governance'. The European Union issues a White Paper on 'Governance'. The US Forest Service calls for 'collaborative governance'. (Bevir, 2011b: 1)

For the United Nations (United Nations Economic and Social Commission for Asia and the Pacific, 2006) the eight key features of good governance were accountability, orientation in consensus, efficiency and effectiveness, equitability and inclusivity, participation, respect for the rule of law, responsiveness and transparency.

THE PERSISTENCE OF PUBLIC ADMINISTRATION

Beyond this, even in the context of the wider application of the governance concept, to encapsulate the complex interdependencies of networks, some analysts argued that the era of 'traditional government', with its emphasis on 'rowing' as well as 'steering', could be seen as something of an aberration, with the historical norm actually being much closer to the modern governance mode than might be assumed. Thus, for example, in the UK context, observers charting the renewed emphasis on governance in Whitehall in the late 1990s (Lowe and Rallings, 2000) noted that the role and functioning of government in the UK in the post-Second World War period could be viewed as an exception: the importance of networks and complex interactions between officials at different levels of the system of government, and across sectors, could be discerned in the public administration of the early part of the twentieth century, and was now being given renewed life.

Even in the context of the post-Second World War growth of the central state, it could be argued that the public administration systems this engendered were replete with examples of organizational innovation and working across complex networks. As one proponent of the values of bureaucracy within public administration has pointed out:

> establishing the National Health Service, a new social security system, the expansion of education at all levels and the nationalization of the major public utilities could hardly be considered to lack the qualities of managerial initiative and enterprise. (Du Gay, 2005: 4)

The continuing importance and value of bureaucracy, as a feature of public administration can be used to place the NPM and governance developments in context. While it is 'almost unimaginable for a politician . . . to stand for re-election on a pro-bureaucracy ticket' and 'contemporary public administrators found it very difficult to give voice to the values of Weberian public bureaucracy without appearing to be old fashioned, anachronistic and irrelevant' (du Gay, 2005: 2), it can be argued that there has been a growing recognition of the risks associated in particular with NPM's focus on specific, limited aspects of the challenges of governing and delivering services. Rhodes (1994: 151) had predicted some 'returns to bureaucracy':

> Bureaucracies have demonstrable advantages, including reliability, predictability, probity, cohesion and continuity. Above all, they provide direct, hands-on control of services through the hierarchical, rule-based, disciplinary structure. These characteristics favour intervention. Should any future government rail against the constraints of fragmented service delivery systems and seek to steer, the tool it will turn to will be bureaucracy. A government with redistributive aims will have obvious incentives to intervene but if there is the potential for catastrophe then the political complexion of the government will be irrelevant. Needs must where the devil drives, and foundering service delivery systems carry a high electoral penalty.

Rhodes's prediction became particularly apposite as governments searched for coordinated, joined-up approaches as means to overcome the challenges resulting from disaggregation and fragmentation. In some cases the value of bureaucracy was reasserted as coordinating mechanisms struggled with the task of asserting control and order over increasingly complex policy fields. There was a renewed interest in the policy contexts of bureaucracies, exemplified in the UK context by the work of Page and Jenkins (2005). Peters (2004) recognized the attraction for governments of the idea of 'rebuilding the state' and reasserting the values of centralism in a more traditional public administration framework. The dangers of an unthinking attempt to resurrect a supposed golden age were recognized, however. Taking an example of sound practice from Finland, where the 2004 'Government Programme' system attempted to deploy a civil service reform programme as a means to reassert control over fragmented departments and create 'horizontal governance', Lodge and Kalitowski (2007: 29) identified a range of evidence of alternative approaches in which civil service systems

> are looking for ways to improve central governance capacity and to reassert some control and coherence over the state. The tricky part is to develop a strategy that does not simply see them returning to the status quo ante. A return to the . . . days of hierarchical and rigid government is not the answer. Nor, indeed, should the quest for greater coherence result in over-centralisation. Instead, civil services need to rethink the role of the centre and the part civil services should play.

The fluid nature of public administration can be illustrated with reference to the shifts over time between private and public sector ownership. In the UK context, for example, during the 30 years following the end of the Second World War, the iron and steel industry shifted from one sector to the other and back again. State ownership of the major public utilities was secured in the 1940s, but while the superficial impression might be that large elements of the former public sector were transferred permanently into the hands of the private sector during the 1980s and early 1990s, the reality was much more complex. The model of privatization deployed involved creating an enhanced role for government through the expansion in the numbers of regulatory agencies overseeing the former public utilities. As the sands continued to shift, UK Treasury civil servants found themselves involved in the running of new 'nationalized industries'. Reflecting on the nationalization of the failing bank, Northern Rock, in February 2008, Simon Jenkins pointed to other examples in this countervailing trend:

> Railtrack plc was nationalised by Labour as Network Rail in 2001 and the Tube firm Metronet was nationalised last year at a cost of £1.7 billion . . .

they were unequivocally private companies and they are now unequivocally nationalised enterprises. (Jenkins, 2008)

In the UK (and in other states facing the consequences of the post-2008 global financial meltdown), the move to large or majority government shareholding in banks and effective renationalization of rail routes in the face of financial crises and failed privatizations demonstrated that 'returns to bureaucracy' could and would happen at times of acute governmental and societal crises. Beyond this, in a demonstration of the inherent linkages between the concepts and paradigms, as we note below when citing the work of Pierre and Rothstein (2011), there is some evidence to suggest that early, Weberian forms of public administration, with their emphasis on rules and hierarchies, can be important (but all too often ignored) foundations for the successful implementation of NPM reforms.

THE DANGERS OF ASSUMED UBIQUITY

When discussing changes to the meaning and understanding of public administration, it is important to stress that caution is required in making assumptions about the broad or even universal application of the changes falling under the headings of public management and governance.

It is also sensible to exercise some caution in relation to the degree of intentionality behind such changes. Analysts have emphasized the key roles played by elites in public service reform processes. The composition of the elites (broadly defined as political executives and senior officials) may alter, they are often influenced by external factors ('ideas' and 'pressures', including, in recent times, globalization and the international financial crises), and their plans are subject to unintended consequences and distortions during implementation within the structures and substructures of the political system. However, reform 'tends to begin in the upper, rather than the lower reaches of governance' (Pollitt and Bouckaert, 2011: 33). Citing the work of Goodin (1996) on the theory of institutional design, Pollitt and Bouckaert argue that:

> it is the exception rather than the rule for reform schemes to be comprehensive, even in intent. Reformers try to improve this or that institution or programme, or sometimes a whole sector (health, education), but they seldom attempt to remodel the entire sweep of public sector institutions in one go. (Pollitt and Bouckaert, 2011: 34)

This is debatable, however, as it might be argued that, for example, in the UK the Blair administration's 'Modernising Government' programme represented an attempt (albeit flawed) to produce a sector-wide blueprint for reform (Prime Minister Blair, 1999), and the post-2010 UK coalition government's *Open Public Services* White Paper (HM Government, 2011) was a similar (and arguably similarly flawed – see Painter, 2013) attempt to provide an overarching statement of intent. Even where there is no comprehensive plan *per se*, there is usually at the minimum a broad guiding outlook or philosophy. None the less, as Pollitt and Bouckaert rightly point out,

> it is easy to exaggerate the degree of intentionality in many reforms . . . although . . . intentional acts of institutional redesign have been crucial . . . this should not be read as an elevation of organizational elites into God-like designers who are routinely able to realize bold and broad schemes of improvement. (Pollitt and Bouckaert, 2011: 34)

As the NPM and governance ideas spread, particularly during the third developmental phase discussed above, claims of ubiquity, occasionally accompanied by understated qualifying statements, became increasingly common. For example, Karmarck (2003) argued that the degree of global convergence with NPM norms was remarkable, and the publications of the OECD (see, e.g., 2005) appeared at times to assume a universal applicability for the tenets of NPM.

For Kettl (2000), public management reform was a worldwide phenomenon of 'revolutionary' proportions, while Lodge and Kalitowski (2007: 5) explicitly connected civil service reform programmes to what they saw as the global influence of NPM and modernization. Drawing on his work as Director General of the International Institute of Administrative Sciences, Duggett (2007: 19) was convinced that NPM and its associated 'modernization' and reform agendas had come by the 1990s to represent 'a kind of global debate where a theory . . . was in fact being tested'. Duggett further argued that a subsequent reaction against NPM orthodoxies in the early 2000s saw the concept subjected to 'a full-frontal assault . . . launched by a wide range of scholars and practitioners' (ibid.). He believed that this process had led to agreement on a new 'way forward' that was taking the form of 'contextualized' NPM, geared to local circumstances and needs.

Notwithstanding this, another group of analysts (see, e.g., Kickert, 1997; Pollitt, 2001; 2007; Pollitt and Bouckhart, 2011) challenged the case that NPM and 'modernization' had ubiquitous status. They argued that there had never been a single 'NPM model', and the design and implementation of governmental reforms across the globe during the 1990s and after were characterized by significant degrees of variation. Developing this argument, Massey (2007: 20) pointed out that 'the near-universal acceptance of "new public management" was never as universal or as accepted as Michael Duggett . . . suggests'. Bevir and Rhodes (2003: 83) focused on limitations to the spread of NPM and pointed out its lack of coherence and consistency:

> the similarities in NPM are superficial, masking significant underlying differences. The trend to NPM is not universal. Rather, traditional public administration persists in places such as the EU Commission and Germany. What is more, the aims and results of NPM differ. In Britain, NPM aimed to create the minimalist state. In Denmark, it aimed to protect the state. The language of NPM obscures differences; for example, NPM covers agencification in Britain but not in Australia . . . Several of the individual parts of NPM are not new: for example, performance measurement. The distinctiveness of NPM could lie in the package not the parts, but there is no uniform, agreed package. Finally, the meaning of NPM has changed; for example, in Britain the early focus was on cost-cutting and efficiency but later the main concern was for the consumer.

Pollitt had been sceptical about the claimed universality of NPM from the outset, and he re-emphasized his argument in 2002 (275–6, 277):

> For some years now there has been a powerful story abroad. It tells that there is something new in the world of governance, termed 'the New Public Management', 'reinvention', re-engineering' or given some equally dynamic title. This is generally presented as a formula for improving public administration . . . From this perspective particular governments or public services can be seen as being 'well ahead' or 'lagging behind' along what is basically a single route to reform. [But significant studies show] a world in which, although the broad aims of producing efficient, effective and responsive public services may have been widely shared, the mixtures of strategies, priorities, styles and methods adopted by different governments have varied very widely indeed.

In subsequent work, Pollitt also warned of the dangers of accepting a new orthodoxy – 'contextualization' as 'the continuation of NPM with a few of the rough corners sanded down for those cultures where the pure form might cause too much abrasion' (Pollitt, 2007: 22).

Agreeing in general terms with Pollitt's critique, Massey (2007: 20) was none the less more sympathetic towards the idea of 'contextualization' provided it did not become a new dogma its own right: 'in the modern, post-NPM world of public administration, there is no Stalinist one-size-fits-all; context is everything'. This approach chimed with the revisionist perspective of Christopher Hood. Moving on from his seminal early 1990s analysis of NPM (Hood, 1991), and revisiting his initial analysis of the concept (Hood, 1995), he was clear that the view that NPM was a global paradigm had been overstated.

The importance of avoiding assumptions of ubiquity and understanding the significance of contextualization can be seen even in those states that were the early adopters of NPM. The nuanced nature of specific states' embrace of public management can be seen in the UK context, where the period since the mid-1970s saw public service reform agendas driven by a confluence of ideas. In broad terms, it has been argued that these stemmed from three schools of thought (Chicago – Friedmanite; Austria – Hayekian; Virginia – public choice theorists including Niskanen), and formulated into the 'reinvention' of government around the practices of the NPM, which were, in turn, moulded during the 1990s and 2000s into a specifically UK reform context (described as 'modernization', and encapsulating within it new concepts of 'governance'), which incorporated elements of European policy making and governance, as well as features of bureaucratic statism seen most obviously in the regimes of 'performance targets' (for a detailed discussion of these reform trajectories, see Massey and Pyper, 2005: 27–39). The post-2010 Conservative–Liberal Democrat coalition has attempted to stake out new reform territory that would open public services to an increasingly varied range of providers and lead to a new configuration of relationships between the state and the networks of civil society and the free market, as an explicit reaction to the perceived bureaucratic centralism of New Labour (see HM Government, 2011). However, early analysis of this approach suggests that the 'bottom–up narrative cannot disguise the fact that the Coalition partners were not averse to top–down hierarchical governance when politically expedient', and there is evidence of reform synergies and continuities across the New Labour and Coalition periods framed around 'a curious hybrid of bureaucratic control and market competition' (Painter, 2013: 7; 15). Overall, therefore, this emphasizes the importance of avoiding over-sweeping generalizations about the adoption of 'global phenomena', and the need to look within states to identify the particular facets and features of public administration reform programmes.

Halligan's comparative analysis (Halligan, 2011) of the 'Anglo-Saxon countries' (the UK, New Zealand, Australia and Canada) gives further emphasis to the importance of understanding the specific features and characteristics of reform processes within states. New Zealand's approach from the 1980s gave particular emphasis to the deployment of executive agencies, but the challenges associated with, *inter alia*, fragmentation and variations in the quality of service delivery led to 'system rebalancing' by the 2000s, and NPM continued to be 'adapted and modified' while key features were retained (Halligan, 2011: 87–8). In Australia, the reform waves saw an embrace of managerialism, organizational decentralization, and then a move to an enhanced role for the centre within an 'integrated governance' approach (ibid.: 88–9). As with the other states, the Canadian experience was coloured by path dependency (particularly the historic mix of the Westminster model and the influences from the USA), and in this case there was evidence of a less systematic approach to the implementation of managerial and structural reforms, with the result that there was greater opportunity for localized initiatives (ibid.: 89–91).

Halligan's overview of the systems he examined indicates that there has been a move to more integrated forms of governance as a successor to the original brand of NPM, but the key NPM features, and particularly the performance management element, remain strong as the 'divergence and convergence' across the countries continues, amidst the 'rediscovering' of 'old values' (ibid.: 95). The latter we could see as referring to the continuing importance of public administration as the overarching paradigm.

Examining the experiences of a cluster of continental European states (France, Germany, the Netherlands, and Southern European countries collectively), Kickert (2011) also emphasizes the importance of history and constitutional arrangements in determining the nature and form of the varied approaches to public management reform. He argues that it is misleading to make claims of relative 'success' in the adoption of key elements of NPM by, on the one hand, the Anglo-Saxon countries, and, on the other, the continental Europeans. While the legalistic administrative systems of Germany, the tradition of the strong central state in France, and the overriding concerns with securing the democratic rule of law in the Southern states with relatively recent histories of dictatorship all meant that managerial reforms were placed in different contexts, this did not mean that the reforms did not take place, in one form or another. In some cases, the changes would be more obvious at the substate levels, and in all cases, the pace and shape of the reforms would be influenced by particular, specific circumstances (see Chapter 16). Similarly, generalizations about the experience of the Scandinavian countries are problematic. In Norway, Sweden and Denmark,

> there are similarities but also many differences. Historical differences in the organization of central government, different administrative cultures, different challenges met at different points in time, as well as differences in political constituencies in power have all shaped public sector reforms in different ways. Each country has developed its own reform profile with different combinations of reform components. (Hansen, 2011: 129)

The very particular nature of the reform agenda in Denmark was captured by Greve (2006), who described the successive waves of public sector modernization initiatives launched by successive governments from the early 1980s onwards. These reform programmes featured the familiar themes of contracting out, privatization, deregulation, performance management and marketization. Structural reorganizations also featured as part of the modernization drives, with the whole balance of responsibilities between central, regional and local government affected by the most recent reform. By the mid-2000s, the implementation of public management reform in Denmark was based on guidance and exhortation rather than formal power:

> Because each ministry is headed by a cabinet minister, the responsibility for modernization lies with the individual minister in his or her own organization ... The constitutional-based autonomy of each ministry means that the implementation of public management reform remains uneven as government departments to some extent are free to determine their own public management profile. (Greve, 2006: 167–8)

Looking beyond Europe, Australasia and the USA, NPM reforms designed to enhance drives to democratization, economic growth and modernized public services became key features of changing systems of public administration in developing countries. Turner's (2006) analysis of reform in parts of Southeast Asia confirmed the significance of local circumstances in determining outcomes. From 1991 onwards, three states with a history of centralized government systems, the Philippines, Indonesia and Cambodia, successively embraced programmes of decentralization with the aim of improving service delivery (Turner, 2006: 265). These states had quite different experiences, however.

> What is evident in all cases is that there has not been significant policy transfer in the initial design of decentralisation. Domestic policy actors have determined the structures of central–local relations and then invited eager donors to contribute funding and expertise to implement their designs. Donors strongly support decentralisation because of its association with good governance. (Ibid.: 270)

Interestingly, the external donors saw 'decentralization' as an understood, and inherently 'good', aspect of global NPM, while in practice the local interpretations of decentralization were based on a range of internal factors, including 'culture, history, finance, time, the relative power of different political interests, the existing nature of subnational territories, ethnic diversity and the orientations and skills of the designers' (ibid.). Once again, the local context was vitally important, and the results of the reform initiatives were 'in large part determined by complex constellations of country-specific factors. There is no regional model and no coercive transfer of decentralisation policy. Indeed there is little if any policy transfer and certainly no copying or emulation' (ibid.: 271).

This comparative analysis concluded that the decentralization programmes had improved the chances of citizens engaging with the democratic process, and brought about some marginal improvements in service delivery systems. However, these improvements were limited, and decentralization could not be seen as 'a magic bullet for service delivery'.

The conclusion of another analysis of Asian experiences also emphasizes the importance of scepticism regarding ubiquity, and a healthy respect for contextualization. Cheung's account of the impact of NPM and governance on Asian countries sees responses in these states as

> shaped by domestic conditions and institutional dynamics. Asian public sector reforms, even if donning imported NPM or 'good governance' clothing, or subscribing to the language and rhetoric of global reform fashions, are still essentially policy instruments to shore up and sustain the existing pro-state, and very often also pro-bureaucracy regime. The lack of a major ideological or paradigm break with the past means that governance reform or the reinvention of public administration is pursued only to the extent of preserving pre-existing interests and institutions. (Cheung, 2011: 143)

The continuing resonance of 'traditional' public administration and the importance of local contextualization are given further emphasis in the analysis of Pierre and Rothstein (2011). They note that the 'good governance' prescriptions of international organizations, including the World Bank, the European Union and the United Nations, are at their core 'Weberianism-oriented' because they stress the importance of, *inter alia*, 'precise and unambiguous rules; merit-based recruitment; . . . public officials less susceptible to bribery; and a transparent system of responsibility' (Pierre and Rothstein, 2011: 409). While recognizing that the Weberian model of public administration reflected an earlier developmental stage of the paradigm, during which it was important for trust to be built in institutions and public officials by creating a focus on responsible hierarchies, legal norms and impartiality, and effectively limiting the scope for significant discretion on the part of particular administrators, Pierre and Rothstein argue that the attempts by international bodies to steer developing and failed states down the path of NPM are inherently problematic. This is due to the emphasis within NPM on 'decentralisation, managerial autonomy and clear separation of policy and operations' (Pierre and Rothstein, 2011: 414), all of which can work effectively only if there is inherent trust in the system of government and public administration. It may be that NPM-style reforms can work only if they are layered upon a state that has as its *modus operandi* a Weberian understanding (universalism, impersonality, impartiality) of 'how the state should behave' (ibid.: 416).

CONCLUDING THOUGHTS ON SUB-CONCEPTS AND 'NEW PARADIGMS'

Just as it might be argued that the 'parent', overarching paradigm of public administration spawned public management and governance, so the latter two can also be seen to have produced variants, sub-species and a series of sub-concepts. Occasionally, the proponents of these sub-concepts seem to be arguing that they are, in fact, new paradigms, which have superseded the extant regimes of thought and practice. Such claims should be treated with caution. The fundamental argument of this chapter has been that the overarching paradigm of public administration continues to resonate and have meaning even as, under its wide umbrella, the variants of public management and governance continue to evolve. Space does not allow us to discuss all of the sub-concepts, but it is possible to touch on some of them.

Stephen Osborne has argued that public management, or specifically NPM, 'has actually been a transitory stage in the evolution from traditional public administration to . . . New Public Governance' (Osborne, 2011: 417). He acknowledges the coexistence of these paradigms, and elements of overlap between them, but argues that there is sufficient evidence to support the case that 'the time of NPM has . . . in fact been a relatively short-lived and transient one between the statist and bureaucratic tradition of PA and the embryonic and pluralist tradition of NPG' (ibid.: 419). For Osborne, the key features of NPG are: 'socio-political governance'; 'public policy governance'; 'administrative governance'; 'contract governance'; and 'network governance' (ibid.: 421–2). This is effectively a synthesis of the various theoretical and conceptual perspectives that emerged within, and as offshoots from, public administration and public management. Osborne argues that NPG is 'neither a normative new paradigm to supersede PA and NPM nor as "the one best way" [citing the work of Alford and Hughes] . . . rather it is . . . a conceptual tool with the potential to assist our understanding' (ibid.: 420–21). Slightly confusingly, he then goes on to make the major claim that

> from being an element within the PA and NPM regimes of public policy implementation and public services delivery, public governance has become a distinctive regime in its own right that captures the realities of public policy implementation and public services delivery within the plural and pluralist complexities of the state in the twenty-first century. (Ibid.: 422)

Successive waves of governance forms and types are deployed by Janet Newman (2011) as a means of imposing coherence and order on what she sees as the line of succession from public administration through NPM to governance. Thus she describes the regimes of 'hierarchical', 'managerial' and 'network' governance (Newman, 2011: 356–7) leading on to the challenge of 'self-governance', which is

> paradoxical in its political orientation, being associated both with the empowered discourse of public participation and with the responsible discourse: in offering empowerment it simultaneously responsibilises citizens to take action on their own (and others') behalf rather than to rely on the state. (Ibid.: 357)

Within this, the ideas of empowerment and participation, previously examined by Newman in the context of a 'remaking of the public sphere' (Newman, 2005), provide a link to the concept of public value (see Moore, 1995; Bennington and Moore, 2011; Coats and Passmore, 2008), which incorporated within public administration and public management the strategic imperative to enhance value in a fashion similar to that found in the private sector, where the addition of 'shareholder value' is an intrinsic objective (although it should be noted that Newman's work is not concerned with the public value concept *per se*). Moore's work laid the foundations for the development of thinking and practice around the concept of public value. Within this, the importance of governments creating understandings of public values and value systems, responsible stewardship of public assets by public managers, and the incorporation of stakeholders within each stage of the policy process, all loom large (Burnham and Horton, 2013: 42 effectively summarize the key features of Moore's prescription). The vision here is of a key role being performed by entrepreneurial public officials. Interestingly, this was a breed identified by Osborne and Gaebler (1992), which perhaps proves once again that there is nothing new under the sun. Critics of the public value concept (see, e.g., Rhodes and Wanna, 2007) have argued that the applicability of these ideas in the US context does not guarantee transferability to other public administration systems, where the political autonomy of public officials is more circumscribed. Notwithstanding this, public value has attained a certain currency, and Bennington and Moore (2011) have attempted to make the case for transferability across systems. Stripped down to its basic elements,

> Public value argues that public services are distinctive because they are characterised by claims of rights by citizens to services that have been authorised and funded through some democratic process . . . It is designed to get public managers thinking about what is most valuable in the service that they run and to consider how effective management can make the service the best that it can be . . . engaging with citizens is not an exercise in giving the public what they want or slavishly following the dictates of public opinion polls. Public value offers a framework for how the information gathered using these processes should be used to improve the quality of the decisions that managers take. It

calls for a continuing dialogue or conversation between public managers and citizens. (Coats and Passmore, 2008: 4)

While it is clear that public value can represent a reasonable refinement and development of an evolving approach to public management and governance, there would appear to be nothing in this prescription, as set out above, that would fail to fit within a modernized approach to these concepts within the overarching paradigm of public administration. Public value itself certainly adds to our understanding of the complexities and challenges associated with modern public administration. It is not a successor paradigm in its own right.

It makes sense to view the 'next-stage' developmental issues for public administration and its component elements, including public management and governance, in terms of the particular challenges associated with the complications flowing from the need for enhanced integration and coordination of policy making and service delivery in a world of complex interdependencies, sometimes confused accountability lines, increased demands from citizens, and acute financial pressures. Is this a 'post-NPM' or 'post-governance' regime? Academics are particularly attached to the idea that an all-encapsulating title is needed to describe any particular developmental phase, although, as this chapter has tried to illustrate, there are serious pitfalls associated with the use of catch-all terminology. Perhaps the name we attach to this is less important than our attempts to grapple with the realities of the situation. Our present preoccupation with what Christensen and Lægreid (2011c) describe as the 'whole of government' reform movement (this might be broadly interpreted as encapsulating most if not all of the 'post-NPM/governance' trajectories) needs to be viewed in a longer-term perspective within which such movements can 'gradually fade away and be supplemented or replaced by new reform initiatives' (Christensen and Lægreid, 2011c: 403).

NOTE

The third section of this chapter draws significantly on elements of Robert Pyper (2011), 'Decentralisation, devolution and the hollowing out of the state', in Andrew Massey (ed.), *International Handbook of Civil Service Systems* (Cheltenham, UK and Northampton, MA, USA: Edward Elgar Publishing).

REFERENCES

Aberbach, Joel and Rockman, Bert (2001) 'Reinventing government, or reinventing politics?', in B. Guy Peters and Jon Pierre (eds), *Politicians, Bureaucrats and Administrative Reform*, London: Routledge, pp. 24–334.

Bennington, John and Moore, Mark H. (eds) (2011) *Public Value: Theory and Practice*, Basingstoke: Palgrave Macmillan.

Bevir, Mark (ed.) (2011a) *The Sage Handbook of Governance*, London: Sage.

Bevir, Mark (2011b) 'Governance as theory, practice and dilemma', in Mark Bevir (ed.), *The Sage Handbook of Governance*, London: Sage, pp. 1–16.

Bevir, Mark and Hall, Ian (2011) 'Global governance', in Mark Bevir (ed.), *The Sage Handbook of Governance*, London: Sage, pp. 352–65.

Bevir, Mark and Rhodes, R.A.W. (2003) *Interpreting British Governance*, London: Routledge.

Bevir, Mark and Rhodes, R.A.W. (2011) 'The stateless state', in Mark Bevir (ed.), *The Sage Handbook of Governance*, London: Sage, pp. 203–17.

Burnham, June and Horton, Sylvia (2013) *Public Management in the United Kingdom*, Basingstoke: Palgrave Macmillan.

Caiden, G.E., Lover, R., Sipe, L.F. and Wong, M.M. (eds) (1983) *American Public Administration: A Biographical Guide to the Literature*, New York: Garland Publishing.

Cheung, Anthony B.L. (2011) 'NPM in Asian countries', in Tom Christensen and Per Laegreid (eds), *The Ashgate Companion to New Public Management*, Farnham: Ashgate.

Christensen, Tom and Lægreid, Per (eds) (2011a) *The Ashgate Companion to New Public Management*, Farnham: Ashgate.

Christensen, Tom and Laegreid, Per (2011b) 'Introduction', in Tom Christensen and Per Lægreid (eds), *The Ashgate Companion to New Public Management*, Farnham: Ashgate, pp. 1–13.

Christensen, Tom and Laegreid, Per (2011c) 'Beyond NPM? Some developmental features', in Tom Christensen and Per Lægreid (eds), *The Ashgate Companion to New Public Management*, Farnham: Ashgate, pp. 391–404.

Coats, David and Passmore, Eleanor (2008) *Public Value: The Next Steps in Public Service Reform*, London: The Work Foundation.

Dallek, Robert (2003) *John F. Kennedy. An Unfinished Life 1917–1963*, London: Allen Lane.

Du Gay, Paul (2005) 'The values of bureaucracy: an introduction', in Paul du Gay (ed.), *The Values of Bureaucracy*, Oxford: Oxford University Press, pp. 1–13.

Duggett, Michael (2007) 'A new world order', *Public*, May, 19–20.

Efficiency Unit (1988) *Improving Management in Government: The Next Steps*, London: HMSO.

Enroth, Henrik (2011) 'Policy network theory', in Mark Bevir (ed.), *The Sage Handbook of Governance*, London: Sage, pp. 19–35.

Frederickson, H.G. and Smith, K. (2003) *The Public Administration Primer*, Boulder, CO: Westview Press.

Fulton Committee (1968) *The Civil Service* (The Fulton Report), Cmnd 3638.

Goodin, R. (1996) *The Theory of Institutional Design*, Cambridge: Cambridge University Press.

Greve, Carsten (2006) 'Public management reform in Denmark', *Public Management Review*, **8**(1), 161–9.

Halligan, John (2011) 'NPM in Anglo-Saxon countries', in Tom Christensen and Per Lægreid (eds), *The Ashgate Companion to New Public Management*, Farnham: Ashgate, pp. 83–96.

Hansen, Hanne Foss (2011) 'NPM in Scandinavia', in Tom Christensen and Per Lægreid (eds), *The Ashgate Companion to New Public Management*, Farnham: Ashgate, pp. 113–30.

HM Government (1970) *The Reorganisation of Central Government*, White Paper, Cmnd 4506.

HM Government (2011) *Open Public Services*, London: Stationery Office.

Hood, Christopher (1991) 'A public management for all seasons', *Public Administration*, **69**(1), 3–19.

Hood, Christopher (1995) 'Contemporary public management: a new global paradigm?' *Public Policy and Administration*, **10**(2), 104–17.
Jenkins, Simon (2008) 'The state is utterly clueless on the public–private divide', *The Guardian*, 20 February: 29.
Jessop, Bob (2011) 'Metagovernance' in Mark Bevir (ed.), *The Sage Handbook of Governance*, London: Sage, pp. 106–23.
Jordan, A.G. (1990) 'Sub-governments, policy communities and networks: refilling the old bottles?', *Journal of Theoretical Politics*, **2**(3), 319–38.
Karmarck, E. (2003) *Government Innovation Around the World*, Cambridge, MA: Ash Institute for Democratic Governance and Innovation, John F. Kennedy School of Government.
Keohane, Robert and Nye, Joseph (2011) *Power and Interdependence*, 4th edn, London: Pearson.
Kettl, D.F. (2000) *The Global Public Management Revolution*, Washington, DC: Brookings Institution Press.
Kickert, W. (ed.) (1997) *Public Management and Administrative Reform in Western Europe*, Cheltenham, UK and Lyme, USA: Edward Elgar Publishing.
Kickert, Walter J.M. (2011) 'Public management reform in continental Europe: national distinctiveness', in Tom Christensen and Per Lægreid (eds), *The Ashgate Companion to New Public Management*, Farnham: Ashgate, pp. 97–112.
King, Anthony (1976) *Why Is Britain Becoming Harder to Govern?* London: BBC Books.
Knoke, D. and Kuklinski, J. (1982) *Network Analysis*, Beverly Hills, CA: Sage.
Kooiman, Jan (1993) *Modern Governance*, London: Sage.
Lodge, Guy and Kalitowski, Susanna (2007) *Innovations in Government. International Perspectives on Civil Service Reform*, London: Institute for Public Policy Research.
Lowe, R. and Rallings, N. (2000) 'Modernising Britain, 1957–64: a classic case of centralisation and fragmentation?', in R.A.W. Rhodes (ed.), *Transforming British Government*, London: Macmillan, pp. 99–118.
Marsh, David and Rhodes, R.A.W. (1992) *Policy Networks in British Government*, Oxford: Clarendon Press.
Massey, Andrew (1993) *Managing the Public Sector: A Comparative Analysis of the United Kingdom and the United States*, Aldershot, UK and Brookfield, USA: Edward Elgar Publishing.
Massey, Andrew (2007) 'Context is everything', *Public*, July, 20.
Massey, Andrew and Pyper, Robert (2005) *Public Management and Modernisation in Britain*, Basingstoke: Palgrave Macmillan.
Moore, Mark H. (1995) *Creating Public Value: Strategic Management in Government*, Cambridge, MA: Harvard University Press.
Newman, Janet (2005) 'Participative governance and the remaking of the public sphere', in Janet Newman (ed.), *Remaking Governance. Peoples, Politics and the Public Sphere*, Bristol: The Policy Press, pp. 119–38.
Newman, Janet (2011) 'Serving the public? Users, consumers and the limits of NPM', in Tom Christensen and Per Laegreid (eds), *The Ashgate Companion to New Public Management*, Farnham: Ashgate, pp. 349–60.
OECD (2005) *Modernising Government*, Paris: OECD.
Osborne, David and Gaebler, Ted (1992) *Reinventing Government: How the Entrepreneurial Spirit is Transforming the Public Sector*, New York: Plume.
Osborne, Stephen (2011) 'Public governance and public services: a "brave new world" or new wine in old bottles?', in Tom Christensen and Per Lægreid (eds), *The Ashgate Companion to New Public Management*, Farnham: Ashgate, pp. 417–30.
Page, Edward C. and Jenkins, Bill (2005) *Policy Bureaucracy. Government With a Cast of Thousands*, Oxford: Oxford University Press.
Painter, Chris (2013) 'The UK Coalition government: contrasting public service reform narratives', *Public Policy and Administration*, **28**(1), 3–20.
Peters, B. Guy (2004) 'Back to the centre? Rebuilding the state', in Andrew Gamble and Tony Wright (eds), *Restating the State*, Oxford: Blackwell, pp. 130–40.

Pierre, Jon and Peters, B. Guy (2000) *Governance, Politics and the State*, London: Macmillan.

Pierre, Jon and Rothstein, Bo (2011) 'Reinventing Weber: the role of institutions in creating social trust', in Tom Christensen and Per Lægreid (eds), *The Ashgate Companion to New Public Management*, Farnham: Ashgate, pp. 405–16.

Plowden Committee (1961) *Control of Public Expenditure* (The Plowden Report), Cmnd 1432.

Pollitt, Christopher (1990) *Managerialism and the Public Services: The Anglo-American Experience*, Oxford: Basil Blackwell.

Pollitt, Christopher (2001) 'Clarifying convergence: striking similarities and durable differences in public management reform', *Public Management Review*, 3(4), 471–92.

Pollitt, Christopher (2002) 'The New Public Management in international perspective. An analysis of impacts and effects', in Kate McLaughlin, Stephen P. Osborne and Ewan Ferlie (eds), *New Public Management. Current Trends and Future Prospects*, London: Routledge, pp. 274–92.

Pollitt, Christopher (2007) 'One size does not fit all', *Public*, June, 22.

Pollitt, Christopher and Bouckhaert, Geert (2004) *Public Management Reform: A Comparative Analysis*, 2nd edn, Oxford: Oxford University Press.

Pollitt, Christopher and Bouckaert, Geert (2011) *Public Management Reform. A Comparative Analysis – New Public Management, Governance and the Neo-Weberian State*, Oxford: Oxford University Press.

Prime Minister Blair (1999) *Modernising Government*, Command Paper 4310 Session 1998–99.

Rhodes, R.A.W. (1990) 'Policy networks: a British perspective', *Journal of Theoretical Politics*, 2(3), 293–317.

Rhodes, R.A.W. (1994) 'The hollowing out of the state: the changing nature of the public services in Britain', *Political Quarterly*, 65(2), 138–51.

Rhodes, R.A.W. (1997) *Understanding Governance: Policy Networks, Governance, Reflexivity and Accountability*, Buckingham: Open University Press.

Rhodes, R.A.W., Carmichael, P., McMillan, J. and Massey, J. (2003) *Decentralizing the Civil Service: From Unitary State to Differentiated Policy in the United Kingdom*, Buckingham: Open University Press.

Rhodes, R.A.W. and Wanna, J. (2007) 'The limits to public value, or rescuing responsible government from the Platonic Guardians', *Australian Journal of Public Administration*, 66(4), 406–21.

Shapley, Deborah (1993) *Promise and Power. The Life and Times of Robert McNamara*, Boston, MA: Little, Brown.

Turner, Mark (2006) 'From commitment to consequences. Comparative experiences of decentralisation in the Philippines, Indonesia and Cambodia', *Public Management Review*, 8(2), 253–72.

United Nations Economic and Social Commission for Asia and the Pacific (2006) *What is Good Governance?* www.unescap.org/huset/gg/governance.htm.

2. Governance: a typology and some challenges
Geert Bouckaert

'Governance' as a word does not travel well between languages. In several non-English languages the English word is used for convenience. This probably proves that the concept of 'governance' is culturally defined. This is even more the case if the qualification 'good' is added. 'Good governance' is supposed to be opposed to 'bad governance', just as in Lorenzetti's *Allegory of Good and Bad Government* fresco in Siena's town hall that he painted between 1337 and 1339 (Drechsler, 2001). Governance is therefore not only a scientific and descriptive term, but can also be a normative concept.

Governance also emerges in the scientific community in different ways as an agenda. Conference themes are labeled under this umbrella (ASPA 2013: Governance & Sustainability: Local concerns, Global challenges; IPSA/AISP 2014: Challenges of Contemporary Governance), master's degrees are relabeled, institutes are (re)named (KU Leuven Public Governance Institute, Leuven, Belgium; Hertie School of Governance, Berlin, Germany), and journals are created around this concept (*Governance*). 'Governance' becomes a general and generic thought frame with a functional ambiguity, perhaps even with a 'flou académique' (academic fog), or it becomes a 'magic' concept (Pollitt and Hupe, 2011).

This chapter is about a typology of 'governances' defined as a 'span of governance' that immediately affects definitions and content, but also reform projects, their measurement and assessment. Within this 'span of governance', changing positions are taken as priorities for reform, resulting in trajectories to improve the span of control of governance, within and outside the public sector, at different levels. This 'span of governance' results in a range of positions that serve the purpose of Ashby's law of 'requisite variety'. It provides a span of controls resulting in different 'governances' for different purposes (see also Andrews, 2010).

In all fields of society, governance is and will remain a crucial topic for several reasons. First, crises require that resources, especially if they are shrinking, should be allocated in a way that guarantees results; the 2007–08 financial and economic crisis has affected national and

European governance (Ongaro, 2014; Ploom, 2014). Second, increasingly, partnerships, collaboration, joint or even co-production are ways to pool efforts to deliver services and to realize effective policies (Verhoest et al., 2012); this requires adjusted governance. Third, activities are shifting locations, from public to private and sometimes vice versa, from public to not-for-profit and sometimes vice versa, within the public sector from central to local or to Europe, or vice versa. In this context it is crucial that the capacity for governance is guaranteed. For this reason, it is important to identify the weakest part of the span of governance in a specific society. It is certainly crucial to identify the weakest part within the public sector: what level of government, what type of governance, which organization?

This span should become the context (Pollitt, 2013) for guiding a governance reform strategy that may include three different ideal types, such as new public management (NPM), neo-Weberian state (NWS) and new public governance (NPG) (Pollitt and Bouckaert, 2011). For all these reasons, public governance and a 'logic of governance' will remain on the reform agenda, and therefore on the research agenda (Lynn et al., 2001). A systematic overview of the span of governance allows one to identify five types to focus on (see Figure 2.1):

1. corporate governance is about the management of public sector organizations. The question here is to what extent, or under what

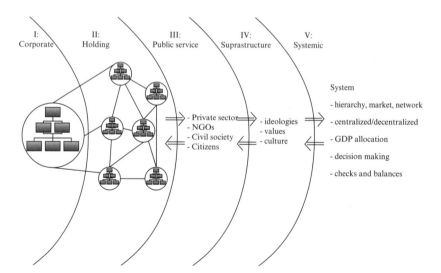

Figure 2.1   Span of governance: five types

conditions, private sector corporate governance can be transferred in order to build a solid public sector management system. Solid corporate governance is necessary but not sufficient in practice and for our research agenda;

2. holding governance is about managing a range of organizations that belong together and need a consolidated governance. The 'togetherness' of these public sector organizations might be due, for example, to reasons to do with territory, function, policy field, service delivery and so on, so they need to be looked at from the point of view of the uniqueness of their corporate governance, as well as regarding their togetherness. Their connectedness will contribute to efficiency and effectiveness. Solid holding governance is necessary but not sufficient in practice and for our research agenda;

3. public service governance includes service delivery by the public service, in collaboration with the private and not-for-profit sectors, which must therefore have sufficient governance. Solid public service governance is necessary but not sufficient in practice and for our research agenda;

4. suprastructure governance refers to what is beyond institutional infrastructure governance. Ideas, ideologies, values and culture must be equally part of the governance agenda. This implies a two-way interaction between the hardware of organizations and institutions and their software in terms of ideas, values and culture. Suprastructure governance is necessary but not sufficient in practice and for our research agenda;

5. systemic governance refers to the system design at the state level. This type of macrogovernance includes the major checks and balances, the key allocation mechanisms within a country, the core decision making, and the distribution of power in society. Under this systemic governance debate, three additional agendas have been added: first, governance without democracy; second, governance without government; and third, the effect of (economic) development on governance. Systemic governance at the state level is certainly necessary in practice and for our research agenda.

All these components of this span of governance are relevant and necessary for all public spheres in all countries, whatever the degree of development, culture and history. In the following, we discuss these five types of span of governance.

CORPORATE GOVERNANCE IN THE PUBLIC SECTOR

Corporate governance is about the management of public sector organizations as single and autonomous entities. One of the first references in the shift from public administration to public management was based on the assumption that public management is about transferring private sector techniques to public sector organizations. As Perry and Kraemer (1983: x) put it, '[p]ublic management is a merger of the normative orientation of traditional public administration and the instrumental orientation of general management'. The logic is very simple, and in its simplicity very powerful. General management applies to the private and the public sector. It suffices to transfer those general management principles that are already applied in the private sector to the public sector, and we have public management. It is not a coincidence that this idea of general 'common' management is readily accepted in 'common' law countries where a system of general legal principles applies to the private and the public sector. This debate on general management has generated a wide-ranging discussion on the differences and commonalities between public and private management.

Many management systems are subject to transfers from the private to the public sector. This applies to very technical management systems such as ICT, inventory management, accounting, business process engineering or re-engineering, or certain elements of personnel management, such as how to use function descriptions.

The literature on corporate governance is itself predominantly focused on specific topics such as ownership structure, executive compensation, boards of directors (their roles, duties and responsibilities), and different cultures (Boubaker et al., 2012). The related research agenda is about shareholders and shareholder activism, roles of directors and their compensation schemes, international corporate governance with elements of cross-border, cross-country and different cultures of political economies (Bebchuk and Weisbach, 2012).

> Good governance is defined as the ability or organizations in the private, public and non-profit sectors to achieve their purpose in the most efficacious manner while minimizing the need for laws, regulations, regulators, courts or codes of so called 'best practices' to protect and further the interests of their stakeholders and society. (Turnbull, 2012: 347)

At the same time, it is clear that some elements of management in the public sector are quite distinct and different from those in the private sector. This literature is at a significant distance from the public sector, except for public companies, public agencies and some public–private partnerships. In some cases this generic vision of governance, where corporate governance applies to all types of organizations, is also very ideological. The conclusion may be that private and public governance may be alike in all unimportant matters (Allison, 2012; Boyne, 2002).

The whole process of budgeting, the need for evaluation of policies, the administrative and political leadership, the additional requirements of accountability, the need to distinguish rights and duties of citizens and users of public services, are some examples of why public management needs to be different from private management, even if some general managerial principles can be shared. This also applies to the corporate governance codes in the public sector, which, certainly in continental European systems, are straightforwardly embedded in administrative and public law systems.

As noted at number 1 above, a key question is to what extent private sector corporate governance can be transferred, or under what conditions it could be transferred, to a solid public sector management system. A recent example is the case of internal audit, a rather new phenomenon in the public sector, which takes a specific position to support internal control systems of the executive, but which also needs to be a complement to external audit, which is a constitutional requirement supporting the legislative. Simple copy-pasting of private sector techniques on to the public sector is not always possible; nor is it in many cases desirable. Adjusting methods and techniques to develop and strengthen internal control systems should be high on the agenda to improve public governance. There are some fine examples of this, such as quality models, but also cost accounting or agency design.

Creating quality models in the public sector was significantly inspired by the private sector. It is interesting to see that the transfer of the value of quality of service delivery to the public sector resulted not only in applying private sector techniques in the public sector (such as ISO, or the first generation of EFQM (European Foundation of Quality Management)), but also triggered specific public sector quality models (such as the European CAF or Common Assessment Framework, or the Canadian MAF (Management Accountability Framework) as developed by the Treasury Board Secretariat. This even pushed private sector models to adjust to become more generic and therefore to become applicable to the public sector as well (such as EFQM second generation) (see Bouckaert and Halligan, 2008).

Finally, private sector ideas and practices flow to the public sector, but the reverse is also the case. General models of budgeting, but also more detailed planning techniques such as developed by operational research, have been exported from the public to the private sector (e.g. PERT – Program Evaluation and Review Technique).

Corporate Governance Reform Programs

From the above it is possible to derive a clear reform program consisting of concrete reform projects to upgrade corporate governance within the public sector by improving all aspects of its management: personnel, finance (budgeting, accounting, auditing), stock-keeping, strategy, organization, communication, leadership and so on. Implementing these projects is already a major reform challenge in many countries.

Measuring corporate governance in the public sector

Measuring corporate governance is not straightforward, not even in the private sector. In many cases market mechanisms, borrowing capacity and stock exchange positions are measures of private corporate governance, mostly including corporate governance and finance. As Shleifer and Vishny (1996: 55) state in their corporate governance survey, 'In the course of surveying the research on corporate governance, we tried to convey a particular structure of the field. Corporate governance deals with the agency problem: the separation of management and finance.' Within the public sector, many corporate governance score cards have been developed. Most of them are converging, some of them have real scores, and sometimes there are awards. Most organizations have one or more models to monitor, guide and upgrade their governance, such as ISO, Balanced Score Cards, EFQM and CAF, or the Canadian MAF, or some *sui generis* models.

In conclusion, strong corporate governance for the public and the private sector implies that there are transfers of ideas from the private to the public sector and vice versa, taking the features into account. Second, our academic research should not just follow realities by explaining and understanding them, but should also lead to new practices and result in innovations. Finally, it is clear that a solid corporate governance in the public sector is necessary but not sufficient. The public sector is not just a set of disconnected single organizations. It is a connected family of organizations with a shared objective. Therefore there is a need for holding governance.

HOLDING GOVERNANCE IN THE PUBLIC SECTOR

Holding governance is about managing a range of organizations that belong together and need a consolidated approach. According to Metcalfe and Richards (1987: 73–5),

[t]he critical area of public management is the management of organizational interdependence, for example, in the delivery of services or in the management of the budgetary process. Public management is concerned with the effective functioning of whole systems of organizations . . . What distinguishes public management is the explicit acknowledgement of the responsibility for dealing with structural problems at the level of the system as a whole.

Therefore holding governance implies the responsibility for the performance of a system of organizations. The key words are: responsibility, performance, system. Taking or getting responsibility implies being immediately accountable. In several languages it is not straightforward to translate the double set of words 'responsibility/accountability'. This is certainly the case in Latin languages, but also in some others. Responsibility refers to a grantor that allocates resources and competencies to a grantee. Accountability refers to a grantee that provides accounts, in the broadest meaning – financial, legal and performance. Performance has a double meaning. It is not just about results, but also about putting something on the stage, presenting results. In this sense, it is also about the performance of the performance, the presentation of the results. There could be a broad span of performance that needs a broad span of control to deliver: not just inputs and activities (or throughput), but also output and outcome, and ultimately trust. The broader this span of performance, the greater the need for a broader span of control to realize it. This brings us to the third key word: system, as a coherent set of organizations in the public sphere and under the holding as a formally recognized set of public sector organizations. This is more than the summation of the single organizations. Holding governance includes interactions, synergies, collaboration, coordination and division of labor. Autonomy of single organizations makes sense only if there is sufficient coordination. The more autonomy, the more coordination is needed. The performance of the system depends on the performance of individual organizations, but perhaps even more, it depends on the coordination of these organizations. This requires consolidation at the level of a holding.

The togetherness of these public sector organizations could have different reasons. The holding could be on a clearly defined territory, for example all municipal public organizations. There could also be a functional approach. The holding could be a clearly defined policy field, for example schools and related organizations in education, or hospitals and related organizations in health, or police and related organizations in security. It is more difficult to have programs that are problem related and contribute to solving a policy problem, for example fighting poverty. Equally difficult could be a chain of service delivery, for example food safety (from production to consumption), or a clustering of service delivery around shared data sets that contribute to this service delivery, for example in social security, or around geo-data with GIS (Geographic Information Systems), or a financial system at a country level (Cagniano, 2013).

The connectedness of these organizations will contribute to efficiency and effectiveness. Different types of coordination will make a difference: joined-up policies, horizontal and vertical coordination, transversal policies, cross-border collaboration are all variations on the general theme of coordination. Different mechanisms are used to coordinate a range of organizations. Hierarchy-type mechanisms (HTM), market-type mechanisms (MTM), and network-type mechanisms (NTM) are very different but share an objective to coordinate (Verhoest et al., 2012; Bouckaert et al., 2010).

Holding governance involves being responsible and accountable for the performance of the holding system, for example in a territorial definition. The mayor of a city is responsible and accountable, not just for the municipal organization in the strictest sense, but for all public organizations under the municipal umbrella. Difficulties arise for a functional holding, such as education or health, and for a policy program holding. In all cases the issue of leadership, especially political leadership, is crucial. It could be useful to develop the CAF, the Common Assessment Framework, not just at the level of individual organizations, but also at the level of holdings, territorial and functional. Finally, it will also be useful to develop strong evaluations and audits at the level of these holdings. Leadership, quality models, and evaluation and audit are all subject to development and improvement, and could benefit from serious academic research.

There is a temptation to call this type 'network governance', even in the private sector:

> Examples of organizations with over a hundred boards show how network governance provides: (a) division of powers; (b) checks and balances; (c) distributed intelligence; (d) decomposition in decision making labor; (e) cross checking communication and control channels from stakeholder engagement; (f) integration of management and governance to further self-regulation and self-governance with: (g) operating advantage and sustainability. (Turnbull, 2012: 347)

But holdings are more than just networks, even if there are strong and weak holdings.

Holding Governance Reform Programs

The content of a holding governance reform program consists of choosing and implementing concrete mechanisms of HTM (e.g. input budgets, top–down instructions and control lines), MTM (output budgets, tendering, vouchers), and/or NTM (knowledge and personnel exchange, sharing corporate identities, pooling resources) (Bouckaert et al., 2010: 52–4, 73–4). The interesting part of the reform question is finding the optimal combination of HTM, MTM and NTM. There is a general impression that HTM is still very effective, even if MTM could be used in specific task contexts, while NTM remains attractive and appealing. Holding governance reform programs are about ensuring governance readiness to create capacities for single and clustered sets of public sector organizations (Lodge and Wegrich, 2014: 152–67).

Measuring Holding Governance

Verhoest et al. (2012) have mapped the dynamics of numbers of agencies that to an extent suggest fragmentation and centrifugal tendencies within the national public sectors, followed by a reduction in those numbers, suggesting a higher level of coherence. Bouckaert and Halligan (2008) have mapped for some countries the intensities and dynamics of these numbers and their degree of consolidation, and the (changing) range of mechanisms used to govern this organizational population. Mapping coherence and togetherness of holdings remains a difficult exercise in practice and in theory. Solid holding governance is necessary but not sufficient. At this stage, the individual organization and the holding remain within the public sector. It is public service governance that is needed, and that includes the private and the not-for-profit sectors.

PUBLIC SERVICE GOVERNANCE AND THE PUBLIC SECTOR

Public sector delivery is part of public service delivery, which includes the interaction with the not-for-profit and the private sector, and the citizens. According to Pierre (1995: ix), '[w]e conceive public administration as the key output linkage of the state towards civil society. However, the interface between public administration and civil society is a two-way street, including public policy implementation as well as policy demands from private actors towards policy-makers.'

Public service governance refers to the premise that the public sector delivery is part of the public service delivery. Most of the services delivered will be effective only in collaboration with the private sector, the not-for-profit sector, and the citizens. This implies that for public service delivery the functioning of the public sector itself is necessary but not sufficient.

There is also a need to manage the interfaces with the private sector and the third sector, and to make sure there is sufficient governance capacity in the private and in the third sectors. The whole policy cycle, its design, its implementation and its evaluation, happens in an open system of government. Implementation will be more successful if stakeholders are involved from the beginning. Because of ownership, there will be a higher chance of civic behavior. If evaluations take stakeholders' opinions into account, there is a higher chance of a trusting population (OECD, 2011).

Obviously, in the implementation stage there is contracting out, partnerships, delegation to the private sector, to the third sector and to citizens. Within the OECD, there is a general recommendation to use these partnerships with the private sector, the not-for-profit sector, with citizens, and for central government with local government, to guarantee service delivery in times of crisis and when dealing with public investment money.

Public service governance means that this two-way traffic of ideas and involvement is well organized. This interface needs to be governed in a transparent, legal and functional way, since it could also be a source of corrupted interfaces. This means that the public sector needs to invest in solid governance models in the private sector, in the third sector, and in citizen initiatives, since this is part of public service governance (Pierre and Peters, 2000; Bovaird and Löffler, 2009). One element of this public service governance is clearly defining responsibilities and accountabilities in situations of contracting out, partnerships and delegations. In addition, mechanisms and rules of the game for these interfaces should be defined: should it be more hierarchical, or more marketized, or more networked? Weak or bad public service governance results in high risk of corruption, or capture, or a situation where the cost is to the public sector and the benefits to the stakeholder.

Public Service Reform Programs

Most projects in public sector reform programs are related to supporting, regulating and ensuring that markets, non-profit or non-governmental organizations, and citizen participation work properly. Investing in the quality of private sector governance and third sector governance is essential for a solid public service delivery as delegated or contracted out by the public sector. A second major cluster of projects is to guarantee capacity within the public sector to create sustainable exchange of activities with the private sector (market and not-for-profit). This implies capacity to know the field and to create partnerships. There also needs to be a solid, transparent and competent capacity to contract out, including monitoring, inspecting and evaluating these partnerships and contracts. Public service reform programs recognizing and pushing interdependence, positive-sum solutions, multilateralism and collaboration are means to ensure public service governance (Anheier, 2013: 149–59).

Measuring Public Service Governance

The significant literature on public service motivation and its measurement through surveys gives a first idea of the importance of motivation for governance (Perry, 2000; Perry and Hondeghem, 2008). According to Vandenabeele (2007: 552), 'this means that civil servants will only demonstrate public service behavior to the extent that their organization embraces public service values as a principle'.

Developing indicators is another approach to measuring public service governance, also in a context of public sector governance or quality of government. The OECD initiative 'Government at a Glance' includes explicitly public services that are not provided (but budgeted and paid for) by the public sector (OECD, 2013). Similar efforts to develop indicators to measure, map and assess governance or quality of government indicators are made within private foundations (e.g. Bertelsmann Stiftung, 2014) or for example the University of Gothenburg (Quality of Government Institute, 2010).

Solid public service governance is necessary but not sufficient. All governance so far, corporate, holding or public service, is about organizational and institutional infrastructures with mechanisms, tools and instruments. The drivers of governance are ideas, cultures and values. Therefore there is a need for suprastructure governance.

SUPRASTRUCTURE GOVERNANCE IN THE PUBLIC SECTOR

Suprastructure governance feeds the software of the machinery. According to Clarke and Newman (1997: ix), '[w]e talk about the *managerial* state because we want to locate managerialism as a cultural formation and a distinctive set of ideologies and practices which form one of the underpinnings of an emergent political settlement'.

Suprastructure governance refers to what is beyond institutional infrastructure governance. It is essential that ideas, ideologies, values and culture are equally part of the governance agenda. This implies a two-way interaction between the hardware of organizations and institutions and their software in terms of ideas, values and culture. This is not just, as some argue (Rothberg, 2014), about a governance 'logic of consequences', where inputs ultimately generate outputs and outcomes (Bouckaert and Halligan, 2008), but also about a governance 'logic of appropriateness', with key concepts for governance such as values, integrity, transparency (Hood and Heald, 2006), ideas, and a culture of responsibility and accountability (Huberts et al., 2008). This may contribute to legitimacy (Dilulio, 2012). A governance 'logic of *in*appropriateness' would then be defined by corruption, fraud, lack of transparency, a culture of irresponsibility and absence of accountability.

There is a large literature about public value, but also about its operationalization. However, the first line should be about the value of the public as such, in an open society. The agenda here is to increase public value to legitimize the public sphere. Like justice, where the statement is that justice should not only be done, but should be *seen* to be done, one could say that public value should not only be generated, but should be *seen* to be generated. This has to do with perception, but also with expectations that lead to satisfaction and ultimately to trust.

Change will happen if elites think that reforms will be desirable and feasible. It helps if change is necessary and impossible to escape, like a burning platform. But it also requires a private sector, a not-for-profit sector and citizens to make this change happen. This raises the problem of causality. Do we first change the infrastructure, that is, the institutions and organizations, the legislation, and then the practices will effectively change since the ideas, the values and the culture will have changed? Or do we first change the values, the ideas, the culture, and then it will be easier to change practices and institutions and legislation? Obviously, both causalities are needed. And in many cases there is also a need to replace people and to have sufficient time to change and reform.

Culture is also a crucial term, such as in cultures of openness and transparency, of fairness, of justice, of absence of corruption. Even in the private sector it is recognized and accepted that 'national culture is an essential for the design of corporate governance systems' (Breuer and Salzmann, 2012: 394). This is even more the case for the public sector. In the literature, several schools discuss culture and also measure it. The crucial point of this literature is to make the connection with management, administration and governance (Schedler and Pröller, 2007).

Suprastructure Reform Programs

Much research demonstrates the importance of leadership to boost suprastructure governance. Developing leadership programs therefore becomes a crucial type of project in suprastructure reform programs (Kaptein et al., 2005). Even if it is accepted that cultural change takes a long time and is difficult, and given that removing people is not always possible or easy, training and education becomes a valid type of project to change governance logics of appropriateness in society at large. It would be useful for each reform project to have an *ex ante* evaluation of what impact the project will have on infrastructure and suprastructure. Projects could be infrastructure oriented (like making legislation or creating an anti-corruption organization), they could be suprastructure oriented (training), or they could be both.

Measuring Suprastructure Governance

The measurement of suprastructure governance includes two major types of perception measurement. There is measurement of 'corruption' and of 'transparency'. These international and diachronic measures are developed by international NGOs. Even if there is significant criticism of the methodological basis, there is a general understanding and intuition of the indicators, and the suggested levels of corruption and transparency. Suprastructure governance is necessary but not sufficient. Ultimately, there is a macro-governance level, at the level of the state, where the major societal mechanisms should come together. There is a need for systemic governance.

SYSTEMIC GOVERNANCE IN THE PUBLIC SECTOR

Systemic governance is at the level of the state itself and encompasses micro- and mesogovernances. According to König (1996: 4; 59),

> [p]ublic administration may be interpreted as a social system existing and functioning in accordance with its own order but, on the other hand, it also depends on environmental conditions in a complex and changing society . . . In the light of the modern society's functional differentiation, state and market are notable for their own characteristic strategies to control the supply of goods. The type, scope, and distribution of private goods are decided on by harmonizing the individual preferences within the market mechanism; decisions on the production of public goods, on the other hand result from a collective, i.e. politico-administrative, development of objectives.

Systemic governance refers to the system design at the state level. A basic framing document for this macro-systemic governance is the Constitution as guardian of the state of law, referring to common law or to public and administrative law. This also includes the 'checks and balances' in the system.

A first key element is the proportion of the division of GDP for the market, for the public and for not-for-profits; this immediately implies the weight of the different allocation mechanisms of price, budget and negotiated transfers. A second element is the degree of centralization and decentralization, with strong cities, or federalism with strong regions, as an expression of autonomy (Conteh, 2013; Ongaro et al., 2011). A third element is how societal, political and administrative elites are connected, related and shaped. Another element is the way participation is organized (Hoffmann-Martinot, 2013), including choice of voting system, where some countries have moved to more proportional systems. These are some key components of a systemic macrogovernance. Vincent Ostrom (2014: 238) describes the two tendencies of, on the one hand, 'the manifestation of a "natural" tendency in any system of government to move to a single center of ultimate authority that would exercise a position of absolute supremacy in the governance of society', and, on the other, 'the equilibrating tendencies of a federal system of governance constituted on principles of opposite and rival interests where power is used to check power' (ibid.).

It is clear, as Figure 2.2 demonstrates, that the so-called third sector and

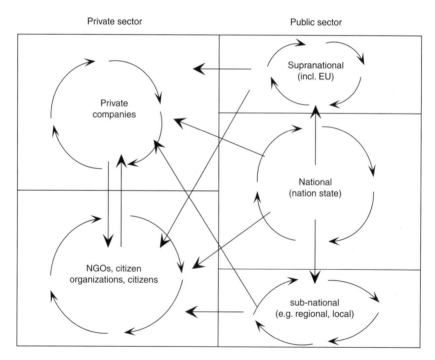

Figure 2.2   Systemic governance

a related resource allocation and governance mechanism are crucial and indispensable in the governance of states. According to Elinor Ostrom (2014: 167), '[c]ontemporary research on the outcomes of diverse institutional arrangements for governing common-pool resources (CPRs) and public goods at multiple scales builds on classical economic theory while developing new theory to explain phenomena that do not fit in a dichotomous world of "the market" and "the state"'.

Figure 2.2 shows the dynamics and the complexity of systemic governance at the state level. It includes the private sector with the market-based organization and the not-for-profit, non-governmental organizations. It obviously includes the entire public sector. But it also includes the interactions, interfaces and shifts between all these components, changing their importance. Shifts between these boxes sometimes just happen ('It's the economy, stupid'), sometimes they need to happen (as in saving the banks that were too big to fail), or sometimes it is actively organized (privatization; decentralization within the public sector). This all adds to the complexity of regimes in governance (Moynihan et al., 2011).

Whole-of-government (WG) is one version of a consolidated, joined-up, or integrated vision of systemic governance. According to Christensen and Lægreid (2007: 1060),

> [t]he scope of WG is pretty broad. One can distinguish between WG policy making and WG implementation, between horizontal linkages and vertical linkages . . . WG activities may span any or all levels of government and involve groups outside government. It is about joining up at the top, but also about joining up at the base, enhancing local level integration, and involving public–private partnerships.

Systemic Governance Reform Programs

Projects covering a systemic governance reform program include rewriting the constitution and legislation to decentralize generally, to actively decentralize resources (HR and budgets), to regulate political party financing, to approve institutions and legislation promoting an open society (ombudsman, audit, open data etc.), to define and change election types (proportional, majoritarian), to develop NGO legislation and so on. This results in system transformation such as in Central and Eastern Europe after the fall of the Berlin Wall (Bouckaert et al., 2009). Changing the nature of a system to become more marketized, or participatory, or decentralized, or transparent and so on requires a long-term, coherent and sustainable vision of a whole societal elite.

Measuring Systemic Governance

Measuring progress or change in systemic governance requires long-term data sets on key issues such as participation, decentralization, marketization, transparency and the like. This is not straightforward, but these data and indicators are necessary to assess long-term transformations and transitions.

To this systemic governance debate, three additional agendas have been added: first, what about governance without democracy?; second, what about governance without government?; the third is that of governance and countries' degrees of development.

GOVERNANCE WITHOUT DEMOCRACY?

According to Fukuyama (2013: 4), governance is 'a government's ability to make and enforce rules, and to deliver services, regardless of whether that government is democratic or not'. From this controversial point of view, 'governance is about the performance of agents in carrying out the wishes of principals, and not about the goals that principals set' (ibid.). In this context Fukuyama refers to Weber's bureaucracy as an ideal type. In a reaction, Kishore Mahbubani points out that what Fukuyama actually says is that 'democracy is neither a necessary nor a sufficient condition for good governance' (29 March 2013, comments on the Governance website). And he continues, 'yes, it is possible to have good governance without democracy'. According to the five levels that have been developed above, a technocratic vision of governance is possible, and it, too, is necessary but certainly insufficient.

The five levels need to be taken into account to be able to talk in a sustainable way about governance. In the EU institutional context, it is certainly true that improving governance and upgrading the democratic level of the EU are seen as a pair, especially in periods of crisis (Habermas, 2013). But in developing countries also, this connection is valid. According to Huque and Zafarullah (2014: 19),

> [a]n inclusive state will have much better prospects of success in making reforms effective . . . it guides our thinking toward the establishment of an open and transparent political system that allows various groups in society to contribute to governance. This will facilitate free and open communication, resulting in citizen input in political and administrative decisions. The inclusive state will thus have a participatory and democratic environment that has the potential to overcome the restrictions found in exclusive states.

Democracy is not just about electing representatives every four or five years. It is about participation, transparency, open society, due process in decision making, responsibility and accountability, legitimacy and trusting systems. Most of these key words are related or are present in the definition of the concept of governance.

GOVERNANCE WITHOUT GOVERNMENT?

The second debate, which arose in the Belgian case when there was no federal government for 590 days (until 6 December 2011), about one and a half years, raised the question 'Governance without government?' Five lessons could be derived from this situation (Bouckaert and Brans, 2012). First, caretaker conventions and routines guarantee the continuity of government operations; second, when the terms of contracts of top civil servants exceed the term of government, this contributes to stability and continuity; third, in mature democracies, a power vacuum is taken care of in a constructive, creative and responsible way; fourth, the multilevel governance of regions, caretaker government and the EU is robust; fifth, there is no 'normal' length of time in taking crucial political decisions.

The issue was already raised by Peters and Pierre (1998). On the one hand it is possible to define governance without government in a positive sense as governance consisting of networks, partnerships and markets, including international markets. In this sense, governments are not able to govern globalized and international markets, especially if they are disconnected from the private market. There could also be a negative definition, where 'hollow' states emerge. In these cases, markets and society fill the vacuum, and perhaps also local communities and/or criminal organizations.

GOVERNANCE AND DEGREES OF DEVELOPMENT

In general, it is unwise to blindly copy-paste the solutions of others. This is particularly true for developing countries looking at developed countries, since solutions do not travel well (Schick, 1998). Nevertheless, governance for development and excellence in public service do happen in practice (G4D, 2014).

According to Conteh and Huque (2014: 5), '[d]eveloping countries were both obliged and compelled to adjust to the trend that began in the developed world'. The trends within the public sector are participation, flexibility, deregulation, performance focus, decentralization, responsibility/

accountability for results and contracting. Trends outside the public sector are privatization and the generalized use of market-type mechanisms and partnerships with the private sector.

A crucial element of governing a developing country's state will be its inclusiveness:

> An inclusive state will have a much better prospect of success in making reforms effective ... In most developing countries, the state is authoritarian and exclusive ... the success of public management reforms in developing countries is closely related to the transformation of the nature of the state. (Huque and Zafarullah, 2014: 19–20)

Conteh emphasizes explicitly two elements in his appraisal of new public governance in Africa. State building and systemic governance are both essential, especially for developing countries: 'effectiveness of public management and service delivery in the context of fragile post-conflict states is fundamentally about restoring the legitimacy of the state as the appropriate conduit for pursuing society's collective development aspirations' (Conteh, 2014: 32). The second condition is a systemic approach:

> 'Systems thinking' focuses on developing a shared vision of governance between public agencies. A systems approach to public management serves a tension management, both as a concept and a practice, is nested within the institutions of the state, and serves as the main vehicle for accomplishing public policy goals. (Ibid.)

CONCLUSION

We have looked at the five types within the broadest span of governance resulting in related reform programs. Depending on the priorities of a country, these priorities change. Ultimately all five types need to be governed. A society cannot afford to have weak links within this span of governance. This governance debate becomes more complex when issues of public and private, and key concepts such as democracy, government and development, are added.

REFERENCES

Allison, Graham T. (2012) 'Public and private management: are they fundamentally alike in all unimportant respects?', in G.M. Shafritz and A.C. Hyde (eds), *Classics in Public Administration*. Belmont, CA: Wadsworth, Cengage Learning, pp. 395–411.

Andrews, Matt (2010) 'Good government means different things in different countries', *Governance*, **23**(1), 7–35.

Anheier, Helmut K. (2013) 'Recommendations and conclusions' in Hertie School of Governance, *The Governance Report 2013*, Oxford: Oxford University Press, pp. 149–61.

Bebchuk, Lucian A. and Weisbach, Michael S. (2012) 'The state of corporate governance research', in Sabri Boubaker, Bang Dang Nguyen and Duc Khuong Nguyen (eds), *Corporate Governance: Recent Developments and New Trends*, Berlin and Heidelberg: Springer Verlag, pp. 325–46.

Bertelsmann Stiftung (2014) *Policy Performance and Governance Capacities in the OECD and EU: Sustainable Governance Indicators*, Gutersloh: Bertelsmann Stiftung.

Boubaker, Sabri, Nguyen, Bang Dang and Nguyen, Duc Khuong (eds) (2012) *Corporate Governance: Recent Developments and New Trends*, Berlin and Heidelberg: Springer Verlag.

Bouckaert, Geert and Brans, Marleen (2012) 'Commentary: governing without government: lessons from Belgium's caretaker government', *Governance*, **25**(2), 173–6.

Bouckaert, Geert and Halligan, John (2008) *Managing Performance, International Comparisons*, London: Routledge.

Bouckaert, Geert, Nemec, Juraj, Nakrosis, Vitalis, Hajnal, Gyorgy and Tonnisson, Kristiina (eds) (2009) *Public Management Reforms in Central and Eastern Europe*, Bratislava: NISPAcee Press.

Bouckaert, Geert, Peters, B. Guy and Verhoest, Koen (2010) *The Coordination of Public Sector Organizations: Shifting Patterns of Public Management*, Basingstoke: Palgrave Macmillan.

Bovaird, Tony and Löffler, Elke (eds) (2009) *Public Management and Governance*, 2nd edn, London: Routledge.

Boyne, George A. (2002) 'Public and private management: what's the difference?', *Journal of Management Studies*, **39**(1), 97–122.

Breuer, Wolfgang and Salzmann, Astrid Juliane (2012) 'National culture and corporate governance', in Sabri Boubaker, Bang Dang Nguyen and Duc Khuong Nguyen (eds), *Corporate Governance: Recent Developments and New Trends*, Berlin and Heidelberg: Springer Verlag, pp. 369–97.

Cagniano, Marco (ed.) (2013) *Public Financial Management and Its Emerging Architecture*, Washington, DC: International Monetary Fund.

Christensen, Tom and Laegreid, Per (2007) 'The whole-of-government approach to public sector reform', *Public Administration Review*, November/December, 1059–66.

Clarke, J. and Newman, J. (1997) *The Managerial State*, London: Sage.

Conteh, Charles (2013) *Policy Governance in Multi-level Systems: Economic Development & Policy Implementation in Canada*, Montreal and Kingston: McGill-Queen's University Press.

Conteh, Charles (2014) 'An appraisal of the new public governance as a paradigm of public sector reform in Africa', in Charles Conteh and Ahmed Shafiqul Huque (eds), *Public Sector Reforms in Developing Countries: Paradoxes and Practices*, London: Routledge, pp. 23–35.

Conteh, Charles and Huque, Ahmed Shafiqul (2014) 'Paradoxes in public management reform in developing countries: introduction', in Charles Conte and Ahmed Shafiqul Huque (eds), *Public Sector Reforms in Developing Countries: Paradoxes and Practices*, London: Routledge, pp. 3–9.

Dilulio, John J. Jr (2012) 'James Q. Wilson: "The Legitimacy of Government Itself"', *Public Administration Review*, **72**(4), 485–6.

Drechsler, Wolfgang (2001) 'The contrade, the palio, and the ben comune: lessons from Siena', *TRAMES*, **10**(2), 99–125, at www.ceeol.com.

Fukuyama, Francis (2013) 'What is governance?', *Governance*, **26**(3), 347–68.

G4D (2014) *Governance for Development: Towards Excellence in Global Public Service*. Cambridge: Nexus Strategic Partnerships Ltd.

Habermas, Jürgen (2013) 'Democracy, solidarity and the European crisis', Lecture delivered at the K.U. Leuven, 26 April 2013.

Hoffmann-Martinot, Vincent (2013) 'Challenges of contemporary governance', *Participation*, **37**(1), 2.

Hood, Christopher and Heald, David (eds) (2006) *Transparency: The Key to Better Governance, Proceedings of the British Academy* 135, Oxford: Oxford University Press.

Huberts, W.J.C., Maesschalck, Jeroen and Jurkiewicz, Carole L. (eds) (2008) *Ethics and Integrity of Governance: Perspectives Across Frontiers*, Cheltenham, UK and Northampton, MA, USA: Edward Elgar Publishing.

Huque, Ahmed Shafiqul and Zafarullah, Habib (2014) 'Public management reform in developing countries: contradictions and the inclusive state', in Charles Conteh and Ahmed Shafiqul Huque (eds), *Public Sector Reforms in Developing Countries: Paradoxes and Practices*, London: Routledge, pp. 10–22.

Kaptein, Muel, Huberts, Leo and Avelino, Scott (2005) 'Demonstrating ethical leadership by measuring ethics: a survey of U.S. public servants', *Public Integrity*, **7**(4), 299–311.

König, K. (1996) 'On the critique of New Public Management', *Speyer*, **155**, Speyer Forschungsberichte.

Lodge, Martin, and Wegrich, Kai (2014) 'Enhancing administrative capacities for better governance: seven recommendations', in Hertie School of Governance, *The Governance Report 2014*, Oxford: Oxford University Press, pp. 151–70.

Lynn, Laurence E. Jr, Heinrich, Carolyn and Hill, Carolyn J. (2001) *Improving Governance: A New Logic for Empirical Research*, Washington, DC:

Georgetown University Press.

Mahbubani, Kishore (2013) 'Comment on Fukuyama', *Governance*, 29 March; also published in *Singapore Straits Times*.

Metcalfe, L. and Richards, S. (1987) 'Evolving public management cultures' in J. Kooiman and K.A. Eliassen (eds), *Managing Public Organizations: Lessons from Contemporary European Experience*, London: Sage.

Moynihan, Donald P., Sergio, Fernandez, Soonhee, Kim, Kelly, M. LeRoux, Suzanne, Piotrowski, J., Wright, Bradley E. and Yang, Kaifeng (2011) 'Performance regimes amidst governance complexity', Special Issue. *J-PART*, **21**(1), 141–55.

OECD (2011) *The Call for Innovative and Open Government*, Paris: OECD.

OECD (2013) *Government at a Glance 2013*, Paris: OECD.

Ongaro, Edoardo (2014) 'The relationship between the new European governance emerging from the fiscal crisis and administrative reforms: qualitative different, quantitative different, or nothing new? A plea for a research agenda', *Administrative Culture*, **15**(1), 10–20.

Ongaro, Edoardo, Massey, Andrew, Holzer, Marc and Wayenberg, Ellen (eds) (2011) *Policy, Performance and Management in Governance and Intergovernmental Relations: Transatlantic Perspectives*, Cheltenham, UK and Northampton, MA, USA: Edward Elgar Publishing.

Ostrom, Elinor (2014) 'Beyond markets and states: polycentric governance of complex economic systems', in Filippo Sabetti and Paul Dragos Aligica (eds), *Choice, Rules and Collective Action: The Ostroms on the Study of Institutions and Governance*, Colchester: ECPR Press, pp. 167–209.

Ostrom, Vincent (2014) 'A conceptual–computational logic for federal systems of governance', in Filippo Sabetti and Paul Dragos Aligica (eds), *Choice, Rules and Collective Action: The Ostroms on the Study of Institutions and Governance*, Colchester: ECPR Press, pp. 227–41.

Perry, James L. (2000) 'Bringing society in: toward a theory of public-service motivation', *J-PART*, **10**(2), 471–88.

Perry, James L. and Hondeghem, Annie (eds) (2008) *Motivation in Public Management: The Call of Public Service*, Oxford: Oxford University Press.

Perry, J. and Kraemer, K. (eds) (1983) *Public Management: Public and Private Perspectives*, Palo Alto, CA: Mayfield.

Peters, B. Guy and Pierre, John (1998) 'Governance without government? Rethinking public administration', *J-PART*, **8**(2), 223–43.

Pierre, J. (ed.) (1995) *Bureaucracy in the Modern State: An Introduction to Comparative Public Administration*, Aldershot, UK and Brookfield, US: Edward Elgar Publishing.

Pierre, J. and Peters, G. (2000) *Governance, Politics and the State*, Basingstoke: Macmillan.

Ploom, Illimar (2014) 'Towards neoliberal imperialism? Discussing implications of the new European governance emerging from the fiscal crisis and administrative reforms for the identity of the EU', *Administrative Culture*, **15**(1), 21–38.

Pollitt, Christopher (ed.) (2013) *Context in Public Policy and Management: The Missing Link?*, Cheltenham, UK and Northampton, MA, USA: Edward Elgar Publishing.

Pollitt, Christopher and Bouckaert, Geert (2011) *Public Management Reform: A Comparative Analysis – NPM, Governance and the Neo-Weberian State*, Oxford: Oxford University Press.

Pollitt, Christopher and Hupe, Peter (2011) 'Talking about government: the role of magic concepts', *Public Management Review*, **13**(5), 641–58.

Quality of Government Institute (2010) *Measuring the Quality of Government and Subnational Variation. Report for the European Commission*, Stockholm: University of Gothenburg, Sweden.

Rothberg, Robert I. (2014) 'Good governance means performance and results', *Governance*, **27**(3), 511–18.

Schedler, Kuno and Pröller, Isabella (eds) (2007) *Cultural Aspects of Public Management Reforms*, Amsterdam: Elsevier.

Schick, Allen (1998) 'Why most developing countries should not try New Zealand reforms', *The World Bank Research Observer*, **13**(1), 123–31.

Shleifer, Andrei and Vishny, Robert W. (1996) 'A survey of corporate governance', NBER Working Paper Series, Working Paper 5554, Cambridge, MA: National Bureau of Economic Research.

Turnbull, Shann (2012) 'A sustainable future for corporate governance: theory and practice', in Sabri Boubaker, Bang Dang Nguyen and Duc Khuong Nguyen (eds), *Corporate Governance: Recent Developments and New Trends*, Berlin and Heidelberg: Springer Verlag, pp. 347–68.

Vandenabeele, Wouter (2007) 'Toward a public administration theory of public service motivation', *Public Management Review*, **9**(4), 545–56.

Verhoest, Koen, Van Thiel, Sandra, Bouckaert, Geert and Laegreid, Per (eds) (2012) *Government Agencies: Practices and Lessons from 30 Countries*, Basingstoke: Palgrave Macmillan.

3. Governance: if governance is everything, maybe it's nothing[1]
Perri 6

For almost a generation, debates in public administration, policy studies, international relations and development studies have centred upon claims about a supposed rise of 'governance'. Definitions of the term vary. Nor do researchers agree about what is supposed to have changed, when or what caused the change. But there are common themes. Chhotray and Stoker (2009: 3) define governance as 'rules of collective decision-making . . . where there is a plurality of actors or organisations and where no formal control system can dictate the terms of the relationship between these actors and organisations'. Bevir (2011: 2) characterizes governance as 'complex processes and interactions that constitute patterns of rule . . . phenomena that are hybrid and multijurisdictional with plural stakeholders'. Bevir and Rhodes (2003: 55) list resource interdependence, trust, reciprocity and diplomacy as defining features of governance. Similarly, van Kersbergen and van Waarden (2004: 151–2) claim that all the usages they review across disciplines share an understanding of governance as 'pluricentric', based on 'networks' among relatively autonomous but interdependent actors, with an emphasis on process of negotiation and accommodation rather than formal structure, in order to find ways to reduce uncertainty and thereby strengthen reasons for cooperation. Rosenau (1992) defined governance as

> activities backed by shared goals that may or may not derive from legal and formally prescribed responsibilities and that do not necessarily rely on police powers to overcome defiance and attain compliance . . . subsum[ing] informal non-governmental mechanisms . . . dependent on inter-subjective meanings . . . that work . . . only if [they are] accepted by . . . the most powerful of those [they] affect.

Peters and Pierre (2000) allowed governance to encompass coordination by any of the now conventional trichotomy of markets, hierarchies and networks (Thompson et al., 1991) and for good measure added a fourth category of 'communities'. They even insisted on the continuing centrality of public authorities in all forms of governance. By contrast, Bevir and van Kersbergen and van Waarden insist that only 'networks' and not hierarchical forms constitute governance, in which state bodies have no privilege. Kooiman's (2003) theoretical treatment similarly emphasized diversity in 'interactive' structures among many actors and organizations, but did allow public authorities some weaker instruments for persuasive and indirect influence under the rubric of 'metagovernance'.

By comparison with the state of the public administration literature in the 1970s, debates about 'governance' have raised the quality of analysis and explanation. They have fostered closer attention to governments' relations with, and even dependence on, other agencies domestically and internationally in the making of policy, to its implementation and coordination, to sustaining legitimacy with individual clients and the wider citizenry and with powerful interests, and even to the elementary processes of gathering information. Claims about the efficacy of constitutional presumptions have been subjected to more extensive empirical analysis than was the case in the writings of the 1960s and 1970s. Debates about governance helped to make the study of public management more outward-looking and better integrated with organizational sociology. Those debates led public management scholars to pay more attention to theoretical micro-foundations. This prompted creative work on types of institutions, relations among them, on ways in which policy instruments shape relations between agencies and on their capabilities and limitations, and is in turn shaped by institutional and technological change.

Yet, this chapter argues, many of these theories of governance now seem overstated at best. As is the fate of most fashionable social science concepts, 'governance' has suffered increasingly from concept stretching (Sartori, 1970). The claim no longer seems so convincing that there has been a grand historical discontinuity in recent decades. The typologies of institutional forms used by most governance theorists now seem theoretically weak, and they provide a poor basis for normative analysis of institutional design. The chapter makes each of these critiques in turn, before concluding that more nuanced and sophisticated micro-foundational frameworks will be required than those that underpinned the mainstream theories of governance.

WHAT IS NOT GOVERNANCE?

If claims about the rise, prevalence or centrality of governance are to have any purchase, they must be falsifiable. Therefore we need to know what might be excluded by these definitions, and what arrangements we should expect to find in decline, either in the attempt or in their effectiveness.

Chhotray and Stoker (2009: 4) suggest that the opposite of governance is 'monocratic government – governing by one person'. If that is all that is excluded, then it is difficult to find empirical cases. Certainly, historical dictatorships usually rested on complicated mutual dependency and accommodation within ruling elites and beyond. Simple fiat and credible threat of force were never the principal means by which twentieth-century dictators or seventeenth-century absolute monarchs achieved such influence as they did over their bureaucratic or military apparatus. Persuasion, incentives and the building of shared identities, beliefs or norms are always necessary to motivate supporters among those asked to exercise domination and to secure sufficient acquiescence and supply of information from those over whom power is exercised for the system to maintain itself at feasible cost. Perhaps governance theorists would regard their conception of monocratic rule as an ideal type, never actually realized. If so, then these theories' capacity to distinguish trends towards 'more' governance become markedly weaker, for they must thereby concede that there is governance everywhere, and that most of political and administrative history consists in variations on governance.

Although Peters and Pierre (2000) and even Kooiman (2003) allow 'hierarchy' as one form of governance, many governance theorists suggest that hierarchy is inimical to governance as they understand it. Bevir and Rhodes (2003: 55–6) specifically insist that 'governance as networks' is to be contrasted with hierarchy. They define hierarchy as authority, rules, commands and subordination, and a system in which the direct employment relationship is the basis of organization. Again, though, most organizational settings either conventionally described or properly understood as hierarchical both lack one or more of these features, but may be characterized as hierarchical on the basis of features not mentioned in Bevir and Rhodes's list. However, as we shall demonstrate in a later section, this is a theoretical misunderstanding of hierarchy that mis-describes the cases commonly used to anchor the concept. Some hierarchical systems have no single centre of authority. Many hierarchies make little use of prior command and detailed control. Hierarchical ordering is often sustained with neither direct employment nor vertically integrated formal organization; indeed, it often works through systems of negotiated contracts.

Rhodes's (1997) early accounts of 'governance' claimed that states now exhibited a 'hollow centre', so suggesting that a key opposite form from governance would be centralization. His critics replied that, even under Thatcher, to whose period in power Rhodes had originally traced the rise to dominance of 'governance', and to a greater degree under Blair, there were major investments in central capacities for oversight over and intrusion into departmental and local decision-making, by no means all of which were merely ineffective, straightforwardly frustrated or else empty symbolic shams (Marsh et al., 2003). If centralization suggests a unitary state and if 'governance' is anything else, then the UK was always subject only to governance, never having been a unitary state but a structure of three mainland jurisdictions, several others for the Channel Islands, the Isle of Man and assorted self-governing overseas territories, to say nothing of the sequence of structures used in Northern Ireland since 1922.

For Rhodes (e.g. 2011; Bevir and Rhodes, 2010: 164), a key opposite case for 'governance' is 'the Westminster model'. That term of art is generally understood to mean principles of the sovereignty of the elected house, the power of ministers who are themselves accountable to Parliament to require a politically neutral civil service to carry out lawful instructions after hearing advice. As an empirical account of how the British, let alone Canadian or Australian or any other government worked, the 'model' would be entirely inadequate for any period since 1688. It functions, if it functions at all, as a guiding and legitimating myth rather than as a description. Yet self-organizing, horizontal networks without authority are not the only alternative to such a 'model'. Today, Rhodes (2011) freely concedes the first point. Moreover, his anti-foundationalist shift to documenting contrasting 'narratives' (Bevir and Rhodes, 2010; Rhodes, 2011) has forced him to concede that his own conception of governance, too, has only the same status of being a legitimating myth. This move drastically weakens the claims originally made for governance and indeed it undermines the interest of governance as a substantive theory.

In international relations, the opposites of governance are typically claimed either to be 'the Westphalian system' of monadic nation states in zero-sum competition or else 'inter-governmentalism' in which nation states cooperate without conceding powers to supranational bodies or to any cross-national concertation among subnational ones. A weakness of the same type arises here. As critics such as Osiander (2001) have shown, even the supposed high point of monadic nation states in zero-sum competition in the seventeenth century following the Treaty of Westphalia was no such thing. Extensive cooperation and coordination through trade arrangements, joint dynastic strategy and occasional grand treaty-making among states were necessary to sustain the commitment to state sovereignty in religious matters (see also Krasner, 1995; Teschke, 2003). In mediaeval times, a much more fragmented order operated that encompassed supranational tiers of authority in papal and imperial structures and greatly fragmented authority within kingdoms and republics (Caporaso, 2000). Osiander shows that the period of nearly genuinely general sovereignty for nation states in Europe arose much later, in the nineteenth century, and was transitory and atypical precisely because it was not sustainable. 'Westphalia' serves as a legitimating myth, although the treaty of 1648 both attempted and achieved much less than the subsequent ideal type of national sovereignty implies. Moreover, even twentieth-century international relations were marked not by anarchy but by hierarchical ordering (in both the strict and loose senses) based on authority rather than simple force, both within alliances and in international structures (Lake, 2009).

Each of the proposed opposite forms for governance turns out not to be empirically realized. At most, each is an ideal type. Empirical cases of supposed opposites turn out to exhibit many features claimed for governance. Reliance on ideal-typical contrast might not be catastrophic for falsifiability, if we had clear means of scaling cases as showing more or less governance or some opposite form (Page, 2008). But it is clear that this cannot be done, because each opposite ideal type turns out, for reasons that become clear in examination of empirical cases, to be unsustainable unless some of the features claimed for governance are granted to it. Therefore the contrast between governance and its opposites is not a comparison of similarly specified concepts – a condition that clearly indicates concept stretching.

THERE HAS BEEN NO GRAND, RECENT HISTORICAL DISCONTINUITY

Public administration theories of governance typically claim that there has been a recent grand historical transition towards governance, from whatever converse condition they particularly emphasize. For example, although his subsequent work (e.g. 2011) has retreated from this view, Rhodes (1997a) summarized his claims, made in a series of studies, that in the 1980s there was a major shift in Britain away from hierarchy towards networks and fragmentation arising from contracting out of public services and lobby mobilization within central government. In similar vein, Sørensen and Torfing (2005) repeatedly emphasized the 'new and distinctive' configuration that they detect in 'network governance'. They were less interested than Rhodes in purchase-of-service arrangements, and more concerned with consultation and negotiation with and participation by private and voluntary organizations in decision-making. Although its constituent chapters did not bear out this part of its argument, the premise of Salamon's (2002) volume was that 'the new governance' consisted in a recent once-for-all shift from reliance on direct government provision to the use of other policy instruments ranging from tax incentives through purchase-of-service contracting to vouchers by way of regulation. This section shows that these claims are unsustainable.

Reviewing historical studies of policy-making in British central government since the 1980s – the period that Rhodes regarded as marked by declining central capability and growing influence of autonomous networks – Bellamy (2011) shows that, on the contrary, there was a continuous process over a much longer period of reconfiguration from informal to more formal hierarchy: attempts to 'fill in' were more consequential than processes of 'hollowing out'. Within central governments, central oversight capacity over spending departments has been strengthened in a great many countries in the past two decades (Dahlström et al, 2011; Holliday, 2000). Rhodes argues that these central agencies have disappointed the hopes invested in them. Certainly, there have been unintended consequences of tight central performance management (Peck and 6, 2006; Bevan and Hood, 2006). But all forms of social organization risk futility, jeopardy or perversity (Hirschman, 1991): no one has shown that central oversight is more vulnerable to them than is (for example) consensual negotiation, or vice versa (6, 2014b).

Moreover, hierarchy in its proper sense has not declined in central government departments, below the core executive. For example, Page and Jenkins's (2005) detailed study of middle-ranking civil servants' roles in rule-making and developing policy detail within broad parameters set by ministers shows that hierarchical ordering remains secure in British government. Page's (2012) subsequent cross-national comparative programme reinforced the finding. Scholars emphasizing roles for private sector agencies in rule-making now acknowledge that much of that work is done in the 'shadow of hierarchy' – meaning that agencies act under state licence, with state enablement, or under threat of 'last resort' action by states (Héritier and Lehmkuhl, 2008).

The governance theorists' implied claim that before the 1980s governing was typically organized around tight, command-based and explicit rule-based central authority is as poorly founded as their claims of a drastic shift since then. Indeed, the reverse is closer to the truth. In the 1950s and 1960s in Britain's nationalized health care system, often supposed to have been the apogee of authority, and in the central–local relations that ordered primary and secondary schooling, central influence was often indirect. It was exercised through guidance and funding approvals rather than by commands, reliant on few performance controls of any quantitative kind. Inspectorates were typically bodies exercising professional rather than managerial judgement, and exercised largely consensual regulation. Governance theorists ought to recognize this pattern as showing much of the self-organizing, partly horizontal, negotiated order that they claim to be absent in this period and supposedly only ascendant from the 1980s. Yet examination of central government confirms the pattern observed in health and education. British governments from 1945 through to the end of the 1970s had to engage in frequent negotiations with trades unions, which limited their authority to exercise direct control over policy, industries and public service configuration in sharp contrast with their successors. Pemberton (2004) demonstrates that cliques, claques and clusters of individuals and interest groups typically defined by governance theorists as 'networks' exercised huge influence within the machinery of the core executive and with spending departments, and not only in externally convened 'iron triangles', during the 1960s, in precisely the way that governance theorists have wanted to claim as a novelty of post-1980s governing. As far as self-organizing groups are concerned, the Treasury's 1960s Economic Policy group enjoyed professional autonomy greater than any Treasury team would have now (Cairncross, 1997).

The same critique can be made of services and operations, over both the long and recent history of governing, as Bellamy makes for policy-making. For most of the history of government, states have purchased both inputs and services for citizens from external bodies. A canonical study of the Roman republic showed that external procurement from contractors was the principal policy instrument of that sophisticated state (Badian, 1972). Core functions of European absolutist states, including the collection of taxes, were 'farmed' by private contractors. Defence procurement of uniforms, small arms and battleships has been by contract with private suppliers ever since standing armies and navies replaced militias and feudal levies that had to supply their own matériel. Indeed, by comparison with the period between 1916 and 1919, when Britain's Ministry of Munitions represented the fastest growth in public expenditure on purchase of goods and services in modern times (Adams, 1978), any recent shifts seem very modest. Regulation goes back to the first controls of weights and measures in ancient Sumer. Independent arm's-length regulatory bodies were established for occupational health and safety and then for railways in many countries in the nineteenth century. There has been innovation in all these policy instruments, but that process has been continuous throughout the history of governing. True, government insurance for priority services was hardly used until the early twentieth century, but this only extended export guarantee schemes used by early modern mercantilist states. Vouchers for public services in their present form were not widely used until the twentieth century. Yet even these only extend the individualized hypothecated financial support that Lloyd George introduced in 1911 for health insurance (Grigg, 1978). Just when tax reliefs were first used to stimulate priority services depends on definition. Yet they were already well established when Gladstone made them a central tool of micro-economic management by introducing them for life insurance (Zimmeck, 1985). On the measure of concertation between voluntary bodies and government in welfare, Dutch 'pillarization' developed from roots in sixteenth-century denominational organization into a system in concertation with state guidance, persuasion and consultation after 1918 (e.g. van Kersbergen and Becker, 1988).

Those who claim that something new has occurred recently sometimes suggest that the proportion of governing activity on which these tools are used is greater than before, say, the 1980s. The claim does not withstand much scrutiny. Today, the biggest single item of public expenditure in most European states is that for old age pensions. In many countries pensions are still administered by directly employed agencies (save in countries where pensions were always administered by social insurance funds anyway). Contracting-out and public–private partnerships are limited in pension administration to inputs such as information technology and construction for buildings. Most countries eliminated tax farming for many taxes by the nineteenth century in favour of directly administered collection; this method still dominates. Self-assessment, compliance and the dance between avoidance and evasion is as much a matter of negotiated relations with companies and their tax advisers over tax liabilities and just as delicate as it ever was. Indeed, recent concerted inter-governmental pressure on tax havens has arguably strengthened the power of states to exercise some degree of tighter rule-based control, after many decades of what many ministers regard as too little government and too much governance. Conversely, Jordan et al. (2005) found that there is little evidence of a major recent shift in tool selection in environmental policy towards weaker or more consensual instruments.

In countries with national health service (NHS) systems, it is true that, by comparison with the high tide of social democracy in the 1970s, there has been subsequently much more contracting-out and use of public–private partnerships for capital finance in everything from hospital cleaning (although worries about hospital-acquired infection in the 2000s led to many such contracts being taken back in house) to construction, IT and clinical services such as elective surgery. Yet the British NHS, supposedly the apogee of direct government, was built entirely on self-employment because general practitioners in primary care and consultants in the secondary sector were always independent. Social care for older people in the UK was never fully municipalized: voluntary and small-scale commercial provision of residential, nursing and domiciliary services was an important part of the mix from the 1940s.

Some might argue that the quality of strategic, ideological commitment to these tools rather than direct government provision has grown significantly in many countries since the 1980s. Yet if governance were now to be redefined as a normative ideology rather than a measure of empirical inter-sectoral relations in, for example, welfare state services, then we should not emphasize any discontinuity in the 1980s. Britain's 'new Liberal' and then coalition governments from 1909 until 1945 mainly used the private and voluntary sectors to develop welfare services and did so in significant part from ideological commitment. Lloyd George's reforms achieved in 1911 set the pattern in which the state assumed responsibility for both financing from taxes and administering the payment of cash benefits such as pensions, while health and what could now be called social care, were organized through a mix of taxpayer-subsidized insurance or vouchers and municipal arrangements in strategic partnership with charities. Rather, it would be more candid to acknowledge that the period between 1945 and 1980 was the aberration from a longer-run trend that drove developments, in Britain's case, from the 1906 general election. The important discontinuity would therefore be the 1945 election, not that of 1979.

Far from the period since the 1980s having seen a decline in tight rule-based control, there has been sustained innovation since then in instruments of tight rule-bound control over provision of public services across sectors, especially in the UK, Australia, New Zealand and the Netherlands, but in many European countries too. True, few services previously run by private companies and voluntary bodies have been taken over by direct government organization, except in emergencies such as the post-2007 financial crisis when many countries found no alternative to nationalizing banks to prevent systemic risk. Yet in all other respects, the growth of regulation of everything from the prohibition of sole practitioner surgeries in primary care after the Shipman murders to requirements to publish 'kill rates' for surgeons has greatly increased government control over these professionals, who for decades operated with professional autonomy in the NHS on a scale to which their contemporary epigones cannot aspire. Performance management and regulation in policing, education, health, social care, local government (Hood et al., 1999; Barber, 2007; Boyne et al., 2006), computer-based workflow control, ballooning detail in contracts and soaring expenditure in procurement oversight have been extended to areas previously subject to discretion and professional autonomy or guidance and persuasive norm-setting. New regulatory agencies setting both price and output quality targets for public transport and essential utilities were established early in the period, followed by others for schools, hospitals, care homes and other bodies. Integration of performance management systems with payment systems advanced steadily during the 1990s and 2000s. Retrospective oversight for control using financial review through audit was extended, with new roles for supreme audit institutions in the assessment of 'value for money' (Power, 1999, 2000). In the process of substituting first general management authority for collegial professional domination of management in hospitals and then centrally specified target-based control for staff, professional autonomy in both its individual and its informal collegial forms has been directly challenged and steadily eroded, while formal collegial professional organization has increasingly become co-opted into the administration of performance management through peer review in clinical governance in health care (Harrison, 2002).

Greater use of private companies and voluntary organizations to provide public services does not mean that relations between these agencies and their public sector funders and regulators are any more 'horizontal', 'collaborative', based on 'trust', or any less ordered around the exercise of control (both effectively and ineffectively), than were previous relations with direct service-providing bodies. Rather, the means by which tight vertical control is sustained have shifted from reliance on informal internal influence to formal external influence, as major recent empirical studies on domestic services have shown (Bell and Hindmoor, 2009; Laffin, 2013; Laffin et al, 2013; Davies, 2005, 2011; Whitehead, 2003). The argument is reinforced by theoretical arguments from positions as diverse as those of Larsson (2013) and Papadopoulos (2010). Interestingly, the empirical finding is accepted both by Davies (2011), who disapproves of tight control, and Provan (Kenis and Provan, 2006; Provan and Kenis, 2008), who welcomes central authority structures in local service provision systems as essential for improved performance. Similar findings have been reported on supranational decision-making processes sometimes supposed to be egalitarian (Börzel, 2010).

The financial crisis and general economic depression since 2007 have shifted patterns of formal public regulation away from 'light-touch' oversight of procedures and process towards more prescriptive controls of substantive risks in financial services. In other policy fields, too, many countries have been tightening regulation. In several countries sanctions for breaches of data protection and privacy regulators' investigatory powers have been increased. Following major crashes in several countries in the 1990s and early 2000s, passenger rail safety regulation has been tightened. After failures of social work oversight led to deaths of children known to social services in England, Scotland, Belgium and elsewhere, and after abuse scandals in care homes and geriatric wards and other hospital services, regulation has been tightened in the social services. In general, therefore, regulatory stances have grown more prescriptive and inspection more onerous.

Internationally, alongside the decay of older centrally led structures such as the Western Alliance under US leadership and the Warsaw Pact, there has been a steady wave of innovation in new forms of rule-based authority of both formal and informal kinds. This has not occurred only through formal treaty structures or courts with powers over national jurisdictions such as the International Criminal Court. It has also flowed through bodies without legal authority but able to use standard-setting on an authoritative basis in banking under the Basel system, international accounting standards, World Trade Organization dispute resolution mechanisms, ICANN and other Internet rule-making bodies, and a plethora of sectorally specific bodies (Dunoff and Trachtman, 2009; Avant et al., 2010) and many standard-setting organizations (Brunsson et al., 2000). Indeed, few of these bodies are free from informal and backstairs influence by the major national powers. The USA, China and the EU exercise informal influence and control in many global institutions (Stone, 2011; Lake, 2009). But this only reinforces the point that, far from the last two decades seeing a general decline in authority-based systems of control and rule-making that sustains differences of status (although not necessarily hierarchy in the true sense), the period has been one of intensive and constant innovation in formal authority and informal influence within the enduring imperative of hierarchy.

The claim that the 1980s represent a grand discontinuity in the history of public administration is, at best, greatly exaggerated and, at worst, false; indeed, the reverse may be closer to the truth. There has been no general shift from tight rule-based central control to more horizontal, self-organized relations. Central governments are not now weaker in relation to other interests and organizations than they were in the 1970s. In many ways tight, rule-based central control has seen increasing investment, innovation and formalization in the very period when governance theorists suppose it to have been in decline.

GOVERNANCE THEORIES MISUNDERSTAND INSTITUTIONAL FORMS

Governance theorists did not develop their own theory of variety in institutional forms. Instead, they borrowed an approach that was fashionable in late 1980s organizational sociology, dividing institutions into hierarchies, markets and networks (Thompson et al., 1991: for borrowing in public administration governance literature, see, e.g., Kickert, 1997; Lowndes and Skelcher, 1998). Unfortunately, the trichotomy is not well formed. The three supposed types are not of the same order. As standardly defined, they are neither mutually exclusive nor jointly exhaustive. Many governance theorists' claims about them have been undermined by subsequent empirical research or theoretical developments.

As used by governance theorists, the trichotomy misunderstands hierarchy. Some hierarchical systems have no single centre of authority. Simon (1996: 185) insisted that systems with single centres of authority are at most a special subcategory of hierarchy: for him, hierarchy consisted essentially in partitioning of subsystems – a structured 'division of labour'. In the classic anthropological study of hierarchy, '*Homo hierarchicus*', Dumont (1980) explained how the nineteenth-century Hindu caste system sustained hierarchical ordering precisely without a single centre of authority. Dumont argued that multiple centres of authority operating contrapuntally provided a suppleness that enabled the caste system to survive, despite the evident disadvantages and even oppression that it brought.

Hierarchy is not just any kind of inequality – after all, free markets and competition produce quite different kinds of inequality, based on power and control of resources rather than on status. Nor is hierarchy the same as domination: indeed, it is the opposite case, for domination is arbitrary, not rule-based. Hierarchy is that design principle which sustains stability in status ranking without needing to resort to domination. Hierarchy recognizes and indeed institutionalizes diversity without imposing simple unity, let alone uniformity. Hierarchy consists in asymmetric, reciprocal but restricted roles for superiors in an ordered division of labour, and a recognized contrapuntal relation between contrasting principles of organization. Although the socio-legal theorist Damaška (1986) defined hierarchy as requiring rule-based superiority, he argued that it is a procedural system of appeal through stages in executive as well as in judicial contexts, not a system of prior substantive command by superiors: for him, in hierarchy each tier legitimately possesses its proper sphere of professional action. The possibility of these features is best explained by defining hierarchy using Durkheim's (1951) elementary dimensions of variation in institutional forms, by the combination of strong social regulation with strong social integration (Douglas, 1982).

For example, Britain's National Health Service before the 1983 reforms was organized contrapuntally around dual authority structures of profession and organization working in both tension and loose collaboration, yet exhibited many other characteristics of hierarchy such as layered status systems on both the professional and organizational sides of the structure. Although many scholars write loosely of the NHS in those decades as a 'command and control system', Le Grand (2003: 48–9) correctly pointed out that there were 'rather few commands and precious little control'. Both professional authority and hospital management were largely conducted by guidance, expectation and integration into a common community of membership rather than by fiat, let alone orders simply backed by threats. Although financial discipline in the NHS in the 1970s (but not in the 1950s or even the 1960s) was weak by contemporary standards, professional control of clinical organization was rather tight (cf. Gorsky, 2008). In a rather different fashion, it would be fair to describe the English secondary school system of the 1950s and early 1960s as genuinely hierarchical in its status system, in its recognized roles for head teachers, local education authorities, the inspectorate, the national peak associations (such as the Association of Education Committees) and professional bodies and for the department. Yet the department issued very few commands, relying instead on guidance, standard setting, oversight of local planning and incentives through support for capital finance. Schools and the Department of Education were both strongly integrated into the 'education world', as British professionals and politicians of the 1950s and 1960s called it. That 'world's' local education authorities, professional institutions and leading academics had to be consulted before any major central guidance could be finalized and agreed. Secretaries of state for education were strongly expected not to interfere in curriculum matters, while their counterparts at health did not involve themselves in decision-making over the approval of particular expensive new health technologies or hospital management, just as classical Hindu Brahmin castes did not intrude on matters properly reserved for other castes just because their status was greater. These self-denying ordinances, recognizing the scope for lower tiers' roles, were not simply, as later reformers implied, lax or lazy. Rather, they were part of the integument of a genuinely hierarchical order. This feature is entirely obscured by Bevir and Rhodes's and most 'governance' theorists' account of hierarchy.

Nor is hierarchy the same thing as bureaucracy. Some hierarchical systems – such as the caste system – are not very bureaucratic. Some bureaucratic organizations are despotic (as the Nazi and Stalin-era Soviet state bureaucracies were). Others are ordered around informal cliques or 'clubs' (Moran, 2003) rather than being hierarchical.

Hierarchy, properly understood, is not necessarily admirable (although du Gay's 2000 one-sided normative case for bureaucracy as impartial and independent would have been better presented as one for hierarchy). It has deformations, excesses, inherent incapabilities and dangers, like any other way of organizing. But the idea of a general opposition between coordination, which recognizes difference and which does not rely on command, and supposedly homogenizing and authoritarian hierarchy, is misconceived.

Understood in this way, hierarchy is an underlying institutional ordering that can be realized in a variety of empirical arrangements, of which a genuinely hierarchical bureaucracy is but one family of many. Governance theorists risk treating single-organization bureaucracies with directly administered provision, inter-organizational arrangements marked by regulation by law-bound dedicated agencies, fields in which ministers have almost unfettered powers to regulate by issuing directives, national and local monopsony purchasing systems, performance management schemes, and settings where the informal power of a rich nation to strong-arm others could prevail, as if they all exhibited the same ordering principle, which they do not. Coercion and rule-based authority are fundamentally contrasting institutional orders, creating quite different types of inequality.

A market – the second term in the trichotomy – is not a single institutional ordering. There are monopolistic, monopsonistic, competitive, fragmented, regulated and deregulated markets, weakly structured informal markets and markets with highly legalistic contract systems. Just like 'bureaucracy' but precisely unlike 'hierarchy', the term 'market' does not pick out a single elementary institutional form. A market is any empirical arrangement in which purchasers give providers some form of consideration (even if only in the long run) in exchange for provision; this is consistent with several kinds of basic institutional ordering.

The notion that use of voluntarily negotiated and priced contracts constitutes an institutional form that is necessarily non-hierarchical is a canard. As long ago as the 1980s, Stinchcombe and Heimer (1985; Stinchcombe, 1990) demonstrated with careful and detailed analysis that a complex system of hierarchical tiers, powers, controls, authority and statuses can be and often is constructed through a nexus of individually negotiated contracts between multiple organizations, not only along a conventional vertical supply chain but in a complex web: Weber himself anticipated the argument (Page, 2008). The term 'market' was at first distinguished from 'quasi-markets' (Le Grand and Bartlett, 1993) on the basis that the latter described government monopsony procurement of services for third-party citizens. Yet quickly public administration scholars dropped the qualifying term. Although Rhodes (1997b) makes much of the fact that government purchasers need providers of services and that there is resource dependence between them, it does not follow that public purchasers are always the weaker party in any such transaction. There are indeed examples of catastrophic failure of hierarchical control by government purchasers, of which some of the most egregious and best-documented fiascos arose in US procurement in Iraq and Afghanistan after the overthrow of Saddam Hussein's and the Taliban's regimes (Commission on Wartime Contracting in Iraq and Afghanistan, 2011). In many fields, public procurement agencies can achieve effective discipline over providers on many aspects of provision: not all contracts are failures. The relevant point is not that contracting can fail generally and so too can hierarchical ordering through contract, both from insufficient commitment and from the deformations of overly tight design (Bevan and Hood,

2006) – after all, so do direct government provision, private markets and charity. Rather, what matters is that since the 1980s there has been continuous innovation in the design of tight controls in government contract specification, in post-contracting inspection and oversight, in the design of performance incentives and the exercise of regulation, to the point that government procurement across the range of domestic public services is as hierarchical as it has ever been and probably more than it used to be, even in defence procurement during the great wars of the twentieth century (Bertelli, 2012: 123–45; Alford and O'Flynn, 2012).

Third, the term 'network' has suffered catastrophic concept stretching (Sartori, 1970). Its clearest, most rigorous and most valuable meaning is as a method of mathematical description and analysis of sets of ties between nodes (which might be individuals, organizations or even documents) (Wasserman and Faust, 1994). The method can be used to describe hierarchical structures that may be procurement markets too (as in Provan and Milward's studies – e.g. 1995 – of city and state purchasing of mental health services and linkages of subcontracting, referral and information exchange among providers), and to describe highly individualistic and instrumental tie-formation and exploitation (Granovetter, 1995; Burt, 1992), Alternatively, as in many studies of 'policy networks', it can be used to describe the precise opposite case of tightly bounded, club-like groups with strong bonds. The term 'network' certainly does not, either as a method of description or in its practical usage in social science, capture any single institutional form that could be contrasted with hierarchy.

Powell's (1990) and Bradach and Eccles (1989) began the romanticization of anything that could be called a network, as if networks were things, and claimed that they had a monopoly on trust and self-organization, as if markets too are not based on trust and self-organization and as if bureaucracies could run without trust. Powell's own subsequent work heavily qualified these exaggerated ideas, but they have become accepted wisdom among many 'network governance' theorists. 6 et al. (2006) showed, on the contrary, that quite different kinds of trust are cultivated in different fully institutional settings, which can be realized in empirical arrangements as diverse as markets, quasi-markets, bureaucracies, communities and families.

Worse, much of the 'network governance' literature indiscriminately lumps together competitive systems of service providers, collaborative joint working in large clubs, instrumental bilateral strategic alliances, lobbying coalitions and even interpersonal ties among civil servants within the executive all as 'networks'. Too often, studies from the late 1990s and early 2000s on 'joined-up government' (e.g. 6 et al., 2002) were simply assumed to be about 'networks', even though most of the joint arrangements established under that rubric by the Blair government were mandated rather than self-organizing, were subject to tight performance management and central funding, and quite unlike the other phenomena already lumped together under the term 'network'. The result was both conceptual muddle and empirical error.

Because the trichotomy is not made up of three elements of the same kind but of a fundamental institutional ordering, a cluster of empirical settings and a method of description, the idea that there could have been a general transition from one form to another is unsound. Indeed, when governance theorists such as Kooiman (2003) and Sørensen (2006) used the loose notion of 'metagovernance' to capture direct influence by public authorities over other organizations as well as such institutionally diverse methods of regulation, norm-setting, persuasion, efforts to use condition-ality and changing financial incentives, they implicitly acknowledged that hierarchical and individualistic as well as other institutional orderings con-tinue to be fundamentally important, and that the term 'network' does not capture any single distinctive institutional ordering. The arguments about 'metagovernance' amount to a tacit admission that conflation and concept stretching under the rubric of 'networks' have gone too far for the notion to hold any explanatory force. Yet 'metagovernance' itself remains so loose and baggy a category that it hardly represents significant progress.

Progress in understanding diversity in institutional forms will not be made until the distinction is clearly drawn between elementary or underly-ing institutional imperatives, empirical settings and methods of descrip-tion, and quite different conceptual machinery developed at each of these levels of analysis. This means abandoning the trichotomy of markets, hierarchies and networks entirely in favour of better-specified theory and method. In some ways, progress will require returning to older approaches developed as far back as Durkheim's (1951, 1995) analysis of elementary forms of institutions, as recast by mid-twentieth-century anthropologists such as Douglas (1982) and to Simmel's analysis of ties (1955) as devel-oped in sociometric analytic method. One advantage of, for example, neo-Durkheimian institutional approaches (6, 2004, 2011, 2014a) is that they provide a clear account of elementary institutional imperatives and structures that can be realized in a variety of empirical settings. Another advantage is that the neo-Durkheimian account of institutional variation can demonstrate that there are forms of great importance in politics and public administration – such as isolate ordering (6, 2011, 2012, 2014a) – that are not encompassed in the conventional trichotomy at all. The advantage of sociometric mathematical network analysis is that it enables the examination of various measures (at the level of patterns of ties among nodes) of centrality, density, structural holes, transitivity and nodes with spanning ties, to construct proxy measures for some of the key symptoms of all those elementary institutional forms, including hierarchical ones (6 et al., 2006).

GOVERNANCE THEORIES ARE A POOR BASIS FOR NORMATIVE ANALYSIS OF INSTITUTIONAL DESIGN

The only strand of theory using the term 'governance' that offers extensive normative argument has been the 'good governance' tradition in development studies (e.g. World Bank, 1992, 1997). Ironically for the public administration governance theorists' claims about the decline of tight rule-based controls in favour of self-organizing structures, work on 'good' governance has been preoccupied with the need for tight legal control over the public sector in accountability and transparency rules, systems of redress for citizens and business, and tightly specified laws controlling property rights and human rights, and the use of rule-based and enforced conditionality by donors on aid and development investment to buttress these commitments. As one would expect, those who are sceptical on normative grounds of the value or the sufficiency or feasibility of tight rule-based controls generally have not been convinced by the 'good governance' arguments in development either (Doornbos, 2001; Weiss, 2000).

In public administration traditions, there is rather less convergence on any scheme of normative claims. True, there continues to be a strain of writing paeans about 'trust' and democratic participation in praise of 'networks' (e.g. Sørensen and Torfing, 2005; Torfing et al., 2012). Other governance theorists such as Stoker (1998) have been willing to celebrate some aspects of what he then diagnosed as a shift towards self-organizing, decentralized horizontal structures. More stridently, Rhodes (2000) stressed risks of unintended consequences, unaccountability, blame-shifting, and incoherence in systems where public authorities have weak capacities to exercise tight control over self-organizing groups and clusters of commercial and voluntary organizations, sub-national authorities and links among individuals, some of whom may be public servants. Kenis and Provan (2006, 2008) argue for the normative superiority of such hierarchical structures in performance. By contrast, governance theorists Sørensen and Torfing (2005), arguing normatively against state pre-eminence in rule-making, are more interested in political acceptability and in values such as participation (e.g. Eversole, 2011) than in performance in respect of service effectiveness or efficiency.

Unfortunately, the forms of normative analysis of institutional analysis available to governance theorists are altogether too simple. Stoker (1998) confined his normative considerations to listing advantages and correlative disadvantages. The concluding chapter of Chhotray's and Stoker's (2009) extensive review and synthesis of governance theories provides a similar kind of offsetting analysis. Rhodes (1997b), working with the market–hierarchy–network trichotomy, simply says that 'it's the mix that matters', but provides no way of telling what would be a better or a worse mix in any particular condition. A second approach is merely to encourage the use of multiple criteria for evaluating institutional forms in particular empirical cases and to forgo any aspiration for generalization (Hertting and Vedung, 2012). A third approach is that of 'horses for courses'. In this approach, scholars try to identify contingencies with respect to conditions of resources, risks and the legacy of social organization on which inter-organizational arrangements are to be established, which might argue for the conditional superiority of particular forms (Herranz, 2010). A grander, cross-nationally comparative version of this approach is suggested by Skelcher et al. (2011). They find fairly coarse contrasts in styles of inter-organizational arrangements, among countries with consensual rather than majoritarian democracies and with greater or less buttressing of any independence in power base for voluntary associations. The authors appear to infer that the context-dependence of forms at their very high level of aggregation may be normatively appropriate for each of the 'democratic milieux' defined by the intersection of those two dimensions.

More promisingly, Chhotray and Stoker (2009) also draw on the neo-Durkheimian institutional framework (esp. from Rayner, 1999, derived from Douglas 1982; cf. 6, 2014a) for comparative analysis of the viability (although Chhotray and Stoker do not use this term) of institutional forms and mixes (6, 2003: Thompson et al., 1990). Those institutional dynamics rest on trajectories of positive and negative feedback in elementary forms of institutions (Thompson, 1982, 1992, 2008; 6, 2003). Lacking a theory of institutional dynamics of this kind and relying on the static and ill-formed market–hierarchy–network trichotomy, governance theories have been unable to develop frameworks for analysing viability of institutional forms in ways that can examine rigorously how – for example – legitimacy deficits can in some settings feedback negatively on performance very quickly, while in other settings may not do so for some time. That trichotomy cannot sustain a coherent theory of dynamics because it mixes one of several underlying elementary institutional forces with one cluster of empirical settings with a third category of conflation of descriptive and analytic method with a very wide range of empirical forms. For the same reason, the static approach offered by Herranz and others to identifying contingencies has severe limitations: without a theory of institutional dynamics, it becomes impossible to think through just how stable or unstable any given empirical context might be, which supposedly conduces to the superiority of a particular institutional form.

Viability analysis using theories of institutional dynamics must be conducted before normative evaluation. Until we know what organizational arrangements might be feasible, risky, costly, or in dynamic tension with other institutions, in the short, medium and longer terms it is futile to attempt to prescribe policy design on normative grounds. Viability analysis does not simply identify prudential risks of cost-ineffectiveness, a variety of side-effects, political justice risks of illegitimacy or of political risks of unpopularity common types of unintended consequences and so on. Rather, it examines how these risks either reinforce or offset each other, in a range of plausible scenarios (6, 2014b), Without first undertaking this kind of viability analysis, attempts to examine trade-offs between rival normative criteria become either *ad hoc* or dependent on dogmatic insistence on the superiority of one criterion, come what may.

CONCLUSION

Governance theory served as a useful reminder of some truisms that were well known to political scientists such as Neustadt (1990) and to the social administration tradition of analysis of implementation (Pressman and Wildavsky, 1984; Hjern and Porter, 1981) that government does not govern alone but in inter-organizational arrangements, and that command is a rarely needed and often blunt instrument. A generation ago, its valuable corrective to some of the inward-looking and descriptive work in the field in the 1970s and 1980s was welcome.

Now, it is time for public administration to move beyond governance theory. Even though the volume of output from governance theorists continues to grow and new adjectives (participatory, network, interactive etc.) continue to be added and new refinements developed, its positive contribution to the field is largely exhausted. Unfortunately, governance theorists allowed their central concepts of governance and networks to undergo concept stretching to the point that it became difficult to discern what would not fall within their scope. They resorted to claims of historical trends that do not bear scrutiny, and that misrepresented systems of rule in both the post-war decades and in more recent times. The theory helped itself to a badly formed typology of forms, which mixed levels of analysis and therefore proved neither jointly exhaustive nor mutually exclusive, and which could not provide the basis for understanding institutional dynamics either for explanatory work or for pre-normative appraisal. Its best known empirical claims have failed. 'Hollowing out' proved a poor prediction. The notion of a general shift away from rule-based authority is now as clearly threadbare as the implication that the post-war years exhibited the zenith of tight control by command and control – indeed, in many ways this is the reverse of the truth. Normatively, the romanticization of 'trust' and 'reciprocity', which governance theory perpetuated long after the organizational sociologists who first published those ideas had drawn back from them, now seems quaint at best. At worst it appears to gloss over special pleading for entrenching the special interests of particular voluntary organizations or joint boards.

Public administration now requires frameworks of institutional analysis that provide rigorous modelling of positive and negative feedback dynamics of institutional change as well as of continuity, rather than looking for another static approach such as that offered by the trichotomy. It requires understandings of institutional diversity that avoid mixing elementary and empirical levels, are not subject to concept stretching, are more comprehensive than the trichotomy, but can readily be integrated with sociometric analysis. Normatively, the field now requires frameworks that do not claim automatic superiority for any particular institutional form, but can diagnose weaknesses and risks to viability in each basic institutional form and might suggest approaches to designing combinations that might at least offset and constrain the limitations of each form using relations with the others. I have suggested that the neo-Durkheimian institutional tradition can offer one account that meets these standards (6, 2013). Whether or not others find its account persuasive, it seems clear that only approaches that meet these standards can provide the intellectually progressive content (Lakatos, 1970) that governance theories no longer have.

NOTE

1. After deciding on this title, I discovered that, in a book review, Boyne (2005, 515) once also used the same adaptation of Wildavsky's (1973) title. I am grateful to Chris Bellamy, Ed Page, Jonathan Davies and the editors for comments on an earlier draft, but all remaining mistakes are entirely my own responsibility.

REFERENCES

6, P (2003) 'Institutional viability: a neo-Durkheimian theory', *Innovation: the European Journal of Social Science Research*, **16**(4), 395–415.

6, P (2004) *E-governance: Styles of Political Judgement in the Information Age Polity*, Basingstoke: Palgrave Macmillan.

6, P (2011) *Explaining Political Judgement*, Cambridge: Cambridge University Press.

6, P (2012) 'Explaining styles of political judgement in British government: comparing isolation dynamics between administrations, 1959–74', paper presented at the Political Studies Association annual conference, Belfast, 3–5 April 2012.

6, P (2014a) 'Explaining decision-making in government: the neo-Durkheimian institutional framework', *Public Administration*, **92**(1), 87–103.

6, P (2014b) 'Unintended, unanticipated or unexpected consequences of policy: understanding how bias and process shape causation: comparing British governments, 1959–74', *Public Administration*, **92**(3), 673–91.

6, P, Goodwin, N., Peck, E.W. and Freeman, T. (2006) *Managing Networks of Twenty First Century Organisations*, Basingstoke: Palgrave Macmillan.

6, P, Leat, D., Seltzer, K. and Stoker, G. (2002) *Towards Holistic Governance: The New Reform Agenda*, Basingstoke: Palgrave Macmillan.

Adams, R.J.Q. (1978) *Arms and the Wizard: Lloyd George and the Ministry of Munitions*, London: Cassell.

Alford, J. and O'Flynn, J. (2012) *Rethinking Public Service Delivery: Managing with External Providers*, Basingstoke: Palgrave Macmillan.

Avant, D.D., Finnemore, M. and Sell, S.K. (eds) (2010) *Who Governs the Globe?*, Cambridge: Cambridge University Press.

Badian, E. (1972) *Publicans and Sinners: Private Enterprise in the Service of the Roman Republic*, Ithaca, NY: Cornell University Press.

Barber, M. (2007) *Instruction to Deliver: Tony Blair, Public Services and the Challenge of Achieving Targets*, London: Politico's.

Bell, S. and Hindmoor, A. (2009) *Rethinking Governance: The Centrality of the State in Modern Society*, Cambridge: Cambridge University Press.

Bellamy, C. (2011) 'The Whitehall Programme and after: researching government in time of governance', *Public Administration*, **89**(1), 78–92.

Bertelli, A.M. (2012) *The Political Economy of Public Sector Governance*, Cambridge: Cambridge University Press.

Bevan, G. and Hood, C. (2006) 'What's measured is what matters: targets and gaming in the English public health care system', *Public Administration*, **84**(3), 517–38.

Bevir, M. (2011) 'Governance as theory, practice and dilemma', in M. Bevir (ed.), *The Sage Handbook of Governance*, London: Sage, pp. 1–16.

Bevir, M. and Rhodes, R.A.W. (2003) *Interpreting British Governance*, London: Routledge.

Bevir, M. and Rhodes, R.A.W. (2010) *The State as Cultural Practice*, Oxford: Oxford University Press.

Börzel, T. (2010) 'European governance: negotiation and competition in the shadow of hierarchy', *Journal of Common Market Studies*, **48**(2), 191–219.

Boyne, G. (2005) 'Review of Ingraham PW and Lynn LE, eds, 2004, The art of governance: analyzing management and administration, Washington DC: Georgetown University Press', *Local Government Studies*, **31**(4), 514–16.

Boyne, G.A., Meier, K.J., O'Toole, L.J. and Walker, R. (eds) (2006) *Public Service Performance: Perspectives on Measurement and Management*, Cambridge: Cambridge University Press.

Bradach, J.L. and Eccles, R.G. (1989) 'Price, authority and trust: from ideal types to plural forms', *Annual Review of Sociology*, **15**(1), 97–118.

Brunsson, N., Jacobsson, B. and Associates (2000) *A World of Standards*, Oxford: Oxford University Press.

Burt, R.S. (1992) *Structural Holes: The Social Structure of Competition*, Cambridge, MA: Harvard University Press.

Cairncross, A. (1997) *The Wilson Years: A Treasury Diary, 1964–66*, London: Historian's Press.

Caporaso, J.A. (2000) 'Changes in the Westphalian order: territory, public authority, and sovereignty', *International Studies Review*, **2**(2), 1–28.

Chhotray, V. and Stoker, G. (2009) *Governance Theory and Practice: A Cross-disciplinary Approach*, Basingstoke: Palgrave Macmillan.

Commission on Wartime Contracting in Iraq and Afghanistan (2011) *Transforming Wartime Contracting: Controlling Costs, Reducing Risks*, Arlington, VA: Commission on Wartime Contracting in Iraq and Afghanistan.

Dahlström, C., Peters, B.G. and Pierre, J. (eds) (2011) *Steering from the Centre: Strengthening Political Control in Western Democracies*, Toronto: University of Toronto Press.

Damaška, M.R. (1986) *The Faces of Justice and State Authority: A Comparative Approach to the Legal Process*, New Haven, CT: Yale University Press.

Davies, J.S. (2005) 'Local governance and the dialectics of hierarchy, market and network', *Policy Studies*, **26**(3–4), 311–35.

Davies, J.S. (2011) *Challenging Governance Theory: From Networks to Hegemony*, Bristol: Policy Press.

Doornbos, M. (2001) '"Good governance": the rise and decline of a policy metaphor?', *Journal of Development Studies*, **37**(6), 93–108.

Douglas, M. (1982) 'Cultural bias', in M. Douglas (eds), *In the Active Voice*, London: Routledge & Kegan Paul, pp. 183–254.

du Gay, P. (2000) *In Praise of Bureaucracy: Weber, Organisation, Ethics*, London: Sage.

Dumont, L. (1980) *Homo Hierarchicus: The Caste System and its Implications*, rev. edn, trans. M. Sainsbury, L. Dumont and B.Gulati, Chicago, IL: University of Chicago Press.

Dunoff, J.L. and Trachhtman, J.P. (eds) (2009) *Ruling the World? Constitutionalism, International Law and Global Governance*, Cambridge: Cambridge University Press.

Durkheim, É. (1951) *Suicide: A Study in Sociology*, trans. J.A. Spaulding and G. Simpson, London: Routledge.

Durkheim, É. (1995) *Elementary Forms of Religious Life*, trans. K. Fields, New York: Free Press.

Eversole, R. (2011) 'Community agency and community engagement: retheorising participation in governance', *Journal of Public Policy*, **31**(1), 51–71.

Gorsky, M. (2008). 'The British National Health Service 1948–2008: a review of the historiography', *Social History of Medicine*, **21**(3), 437–60.

Granovetter, M.S. (1995 [1974]). *Getting a Job: A Study of Contacts and Careers*, Chicago, IL: University of Chicago Press.

Grigg, J. (1978) *Lloyd George: The People's Champion 1902–1911*, Harmondsworth: Penguin.

Harrison, S. (2002) 'New Labour, modernisation and the medical labour process', *Journal of Social Policy*, **31**(3), 465–85.

Héritier, A. and Lehmkuhl, D. (2008) 'Introduction: the shadow of hierarchy and new modes of governance', *Journal of Public Policy*, **28**(1), 1–17.

Herranz, J. Jr (2010), 'Network performance and coordination: a theoretical review and framework', *Public Performance and Management Review*, **33**(3), 311–41.

Hertting, N. and Vedung, E. (2012) 'Purposes and criteria in network governance evaluation: how far does standard evaluation vocabulary takes us?', *Evaluation*, **18**(1), 27–46.

Hirschman, A.O. (1991) *The Rhetoric of Reaction: Perversity, Futility, Jeopardy*, Cambridge, MA: Belknap Press of Harvard University Press.

Hjern, B. and Porter, D.O. (1981) 'Implementation structures: a new unit of administrative analysis', *Organisational Studies*, **2**(3), 211–27.

Holliday, I. (2000) 'Is the British state hollowing out?', *Political Quarterly*, **71**(2), 167–76.

Hood, C., Scott, C., James, O., Jones, G.W. and Travers, T. (1999), *Regulation Inside Government: Waste-watchers, Quality Police and Sleaze-busters*, Oxford: Oxford University Press.

Jordan, A., Wurzel, R.K.W. and Zito, A. (2005), 'The rise of "new" policy instruments in comparative perspective: has governance eclipsed government?', *Political Studies*, **53**(3), 477–96.

Kenis, P. and Provan, K.G. (2006) 'The control of public networks', *International Public Management Journal*, **9**(3), 227–47.

Kickert, W.J.M. (1997) 'Public governance in the Netherlands: an alternative to Anglo-American "managerialism"', *Public Administration*, **75**(4), 731–52.

Kooiman, J. (2003) *Governing as Governance*, London: Sage.

Krasner, S.D. (1995) 'Compromising Westphalia', *International Security*, **20**(3), 115–51.

Laffin, M. (2013) 'A new politics of governance or an old politics of central–local relations? Labour's reform of social housing tenancies in England', *Public Administration*, **91**(1), 195–210.

Laffin, M., Mawson, J. and Ormston, C. (2013) 'Public services in a "post-democratic age": an alternative framework to network governance', *Environment and Planning C*.

Lakatos, I. (1970) 'Falsification and the methodology of scientific research programmes', in I. Lakatos and A. Musgrave (eds), *Criticism and the Growth of Knowledge*, Cambridge: Cambridge University Press, pp. 91–196.

Lake, D.A. (2009) *Hierarchy in International Relations*, Ithaca, NY: Cornell University Press.

Larsson, O.L. (2013) 'Sovereign power beyond the state: a critical reappraisal of governance by networks', *Critical Policy Studies*, doi:10.1080/19460171.2013.784624.

Le Grand, J. (2003) *Motivation, Agency and Public Policy: Of Knights and Knaves, Pawns and Queens*, Oxford: Oxford University Press.

Le Grand, J. and Bartlett, W. (eds) (1993) *Quasi-markets and Social Policy*, Basingstoke: Macmillan.

Lowndes, V and Skelcher, C.K. (1998) 'The dynamics of multi-organizational partnerships: an analysis of changing modes of governance', *Public Administration*, **76**(2), 313–33.

Marsh, D., Richards, D. and Smith, M. (2003) 'Unequal plurality: towards an asymmetric power model of British politics', *Government and Opposition*, **38**(3), 306–32.

Moran, M. (2003) *The British Regulatory State: High Modernism and Hyper-innovation*, Oxford: Oxford University Press.

Neustadt, R.E. (1990) *Presidential Power and the Modern Presidents: The Politics of Leadership from Roosevelt to Reagan*, New York: Free Press.

Osiander, A. (2001) 'Sovereignty, international relations, and the Westphalian myth', *International Organization*, **55**(2), 251–87.

Page, E.C. (2008) 'Farewell to the Weberian state? Classical theory and modern bureaucracy', *Zeitschrift für Staats- und Europawissenschaften*, **1**(4), 485–504.

Page, E.C. (2012) *Policies without Politicians: Bureaucratic Influence in Comparative Perspective*, Oxford: Oxford University Press.

Page, E.C. and Jenkins, B. (2005) *Policy Bureaucracy: Government with a Cast of Thousands*, Oxford: Oxford University Press.

Papadopoulos, Y. (2010) 'Accountability and multi-level governance: more accountability, less democracy?', *West European Politics*, **33**(5), 1030–49.

Peck, E.W. and 6, P (2006) *Beyond Delivery? Policy Implementation as Sense-making and Settlement*, Basingstoke: Palgrave Macmillan.

Pemberton, H. (2004) *Policy Learning and British Governance in the 1960s*, Basingstoke: Palgrave Macmillan.

Peters, B.G. and Pierre, J. (2000) *Governance, Politics and the State*, Basingstoke: Palgrave Macmillan.

Powell, W.W. (1990) 'Neither market nor hierarchy: network forms of organisation', *Research in Organisational Behaviour*, **12**, 295–336.

Power, M. (1999) *The Audit Society: Rituals of Verification*, Oxford: Oxford University Press.

Power, M. (2000) 'The audit society – second thoughts', *International Journal of Auditing*, **4**, 111–19.

Pressman, J.L. and Wildavsky, A. (1984) *Implementation: How Great Expectations in Washington are Dashed in Oakland*, 3rd edn, Berkeley, CA: University of California Press.

Provan, K.G, and Kenis, P. (2008) 'Modes of network governance: structure, management, and effectiveness', *Journal of Public Administration Research and Theory*, **18**(2), 229–52.

Provan, K.G. and Milward, H.B. (1995) 'A preliminary theory of network effectiveness: a comparative study of four community mental health systems', *Administrative Science Quarterly*, **40**(1), 1–33.

Rayner, S. (1999) 'Mapping institutional diversity for implementing the Lisbon principles', *Ecological Economics*, **31**(2), 259–74.

Rhodes, R.A.W. (1997a) *Understanding Governance: Policy Networks, Governance, Reflexivity and Accountability*, Buckingham: Open University Press.
Rhodes, R.A.W. (1997b) 'From marketisation to diplomacy: it's the mix that matters', *Australian Journal of Public Administration*, 56(2), 40–53.
Rhodes, R.A.W. (2000) 'The governance narrative: key findings and lessons from the ESRC's Whitehall programme', *Public Administration*, 78(2), 345–63.
Rhodes, R.A.W. (2011) *Everyday Life in British Government*, Oxford: Oxford University Press.
Rosenau, J.N. (1992) 'Governance, order and change in world politics', in J.N. Rosenau and E.-O. Czempiel (eds), *Governance without Government: Order and Change in World Politics*, Cambridge: Cambridge University Press, pp. 1–29.
Salamon, L.M. (ed.) (2002), *The Tools of Government: A Guide to the New Governance*, New York: Oxford University Press.
Sartori, G. (1970) 'Concept misformation in comparative politics', *American Political Science Review*, 64(4), 1033–53.
Simmel, G. (1955) *Conflict and the Web of Group-affiliations*, trans. K.H. Wolff and R. Bendix, New York: Free Press.
Simon, H.A. (1996) *The Sciences of the Artificial*, 3rd edn, Cambridge, MA: MIT Press.
Skelcher, C., Klijn, E.-H., Kübler, D., Sørensen, E. and Sullivan, H. (2011) 'Explaining the democratic anchorage of governance networks: evidence from four European countries', *Administrative Theory and Praxis*, 33(1), 7–38.
Sørensen, E. (2006) 'Metagovernance: the changing role of politicians in processes of democratic governance', *American Review of Public Administration*, 36(1), 98–114.
Sørensen, E. and Torfing, J. (2005) 'The democratic anchorage of governance networks', *Scandinavian Political Studies*, 2(3), 195–218.
Stinchombe, A.L. (1990) *Information and Organisations*, Berkeley, CA: University of California Press.
Stinchombe, A.L. and Heimer, C.A. (1985), *Organisational Theory and Project Management: Administering Uncertainty in Norwegian Offshore Oil*, Bergen: Norwegian University Press.
Stoker, G. (1998) 'Governance as theory: five propositions', *International Social Science Journal*, 50(155), 17–28.
Stone, R.W. (2011) *Controlling Institutions: International Organisations and the Global Economy*, Cambridge: Cambridge University Press.
Teschke, B. (2003) *The Myth of 1648: Class, Geopolitics and the Making of Modern International Relations*, London: Verso.
Thompson, G., Frances, J., Levačić, R. and Mitchell, J. (eds) (1991) *Markets, Hierarchies and Networks: The Coordination of Social Life*, London: Sage.
Thompson, M. (1982) 'A three-dimensional model', in M. Douglas (ed.), *Essays in the Sociology of Perception*, London: Routledge and Kegan Paul, pp. 31–63.
Thompson, M. (1992) 'The dynamics of cultural theory and their implications for the enterprise culture', in S. Hargreaves Heap and A. Ross (eds), *Understanding the Enterprise Culture: Themes in the Work of Mary Douglas*, Edinburgh: Edinburgh University Press, pp. 182–202.
Thompson, M. (2008) *Organising and Disorganising: A Dynamic and Non-linear Theory of Institutional Emergence and its Implications*, Axminster: Triarchy Press.
Thompson, M., Ellis, R.J. and Wildavsky, A. (1990) *Cultural Theory*, Boulder, CO: Westview Press.
Torfing, J., Peters, B.G., Pierre, J. and Sørensen, E. (2012) *Interactive Governance: Advancing the Paradigm*, Oxford: Oxford University Press.
Van Kersbergen, K. and Becker, U. (1988) 'The Netherlands: a passive social democratic welfare state in a Christian Democratic ruled society', *Journal of Social Policy*, 17(4), 477–99.
Van Kersbergen, K. and van Waarden, F. (2004), '"Governance" as a bridge between disciplines: cross-disciplinary inspiration regarding shifts in governance and problems

of governability, accountability and legitimacy', *European Journal of Political Research*, **43**(2), 143–71.

Wasserman, S. and Faust, K. (1994) *Social Network Analysis: Methods and Applications*, Cambridge: Cambridge University Press.

Weiss, T. (2000) 'Governance, good governance and global governance: conceptual and actual challenges', *Third World Quarterly*, **21**(5), 795–814.

Whitehead, M. (2003) '"In the shadow of hierarchy": meta-governance, policy reform and urban regeneration in the West Midlands', *Area*, **35**(1), 6–14.

Wildavsky, A. (1973) 'If planning is everything, maybe it's nothing', *Policy Sciences*, **4**(2), 127–53.

World Bank (1992) *Governance and Development*, Washington, DC: World Bank.

World Bank (1997) *The State in a Changing World*, Washington, DC: World Bank.

Zimmeck, M. (1985) 'Gladstone holds his own: the origins of income tax relief for life insurance policies', *Historical Review*, **58**(138), 167–88.

4. Executive governance and its puzzles
R. A. W. Rhodes and Anne Tiernan

The phrase 'executive governance' refers to the merger of two discrete bodies of work, the study of executive government in political science and the study of governance in public administration. We focus on their intersection – on common ground and shared puzzles. We start with a brief account of the several approaches to executive studies in political science, and of the various waves in the study of governance. We cover the core executives of Westminster and Western Europe parliamentary polities. After this conspectus of the literature, we devote most of our attention to the shared puzzles where executive studies and governance intersect. We focus on four puzzles: predominant or collaborative leadership; central capability or implementation; formal or informal coordination; and political accountability or webs of accountabilities. We conclude with some suggestions about directions for future research under the headings of the interpretive turn, court politics and presidential studies.

APPROACHES TO EXECUTIVE GOVERNMENT

This section introduces briefly the main approaches to the analysis of executive government that are directly relevant to the study of governance. We focus on: formal institutional analysis; modernist empiricism; political biography; the core executive; and the predominant prime minister. We realize that this listing is not exhaustive. It omits, for example, rational choice analysis and the psychology of political leadership because they do not engage with the literature on governance (but see Rhodes, 2006a).

Formal Institutional Analysis

Eckstein (1963: 10–11) points out that

> If there is any subject matter at all which political scientists can claim exclusively for their own, a subject matter that does not require acquisition of the analytical tools of sister-fields and that sustains their claim to autonomous existence, it is, of course, formal-legal political structure.

(See also Rhodes, 2006b.) Perhaps the most famous example of this approach is the work on Westminster polities. This notion is remarkably diffuse but commonly refers to a family of ideas that includes: parliamentary sovereignty; strong cabinet government; ministerial responsibility, where ministers are individually and collectively accountable to parliament; a professional, non-partisan public service; and a legitimate opposition (Rhodes et al., 2009: ch. 1).

Most relevant for our discussion is the notion of the 'efficient secret' of 'the closer union, the nearly complete fusion, of the executive and legislative powers' (Bagehot, 1963: 65). In the 2000s, parliamentary government continues to be defined by this buckle. For Shugart (2006: 348), the executive arises out of the legislative assembly, and can be dismissed by a vote of 'no confidence' by that legislature. So, the party or parties with a majority in parliament form the executive, defined by key positions (that is, prime minister and cabinet). The cabinet is collectively responsible for its decisions, and its members (or ministers) are individually responsible to parliament for the work of their departments. The Westminster approach also assumes that power lies with specific positions and the people who occupy those positions. Examples of work in this tradition include Birch (1964), Jennings (1959) and Wheare (1963).

Modernist Empiricism

Modernist empiricism (sometimes labelled positivism or behaviouralism) treats institutions such as legislatures, constitutions and executives as discrete, atomized objects to be compared, measured and classified. It adopts comparisons across time and space as a means of uncovering regularities and probabilistic explanations to be tested against neutral evidence (see Bevir and Rhodes, 2006: ch. 5). The favoured method is the survey. For example, Blondel and Müller-Rommel's (1993: 15) work on Western Europe studies the 'the interplay of one major independent variable – the single-party or coalition character of the cabinet – with a number of structural and customary arrangements in governments, and of the combined effect of these factors on decision making processes' in 12 West European cabinets. It is 'a fully comparative analysis' with data drawn from a survey of 410 ministers in nine countries; and an analysis of newspaper reports on cabinet conflicts in 11 countries. Similarly, Aberbach et al. (1981) conducted a survey of politicians and bureaucrats in seven countries, exploring their social origins, their roles and styles in policy making, their ideology, their commitment to democratic principles, and the interactions between politicians and bureaucrats.

Political Biography

'Life history' refers to auto/biography and the collection and use of personal documents – memoir, diary, oral history, and other personal documents and stories – to write 'a life' (Denzin, 1989: ch. 2, Roberts, 2002: ch. 3). Marquand's (2009: 189) appellation 'tombstone biography' remains apt. It refers to 'an ingrained centuries-old habit of mind' in which 'biographers take it for granted that their task is to portray their subject as more worthy than she or he might otherwise be thought to be' (Pimlott, 1994: 157). For all the dangers of becoming 'valets to the famous' (ibid.: 159), this tradition has produced many accomplished life histories. The volume of 'private information' reported in the work of biographers is impressive, and will bear such secondary analysis as mapping the membership of the prime-ministerial courts (see the section on 'Court Politics' below).

Life history can be a tool for answering broader questions in the study of politics that go beyond the life itself; they are not just chronological narratives (Walter, 2002; Rhodes, 2012a). Often the uses of biography are cast in general terms. Thus Pimlott (1999: 39, 41) writes about 'a character in an environment' because it 'illuminates a changing environment'. He wrote about Harold Wilson 'as a way of assessing the change of attitudes that swept Britain in the post-war period, and especially in the 1960s'. So, political scientists writing life history can and do apply insights from the academic study of politics.

Core Executive

The core executive approach was developed in the analysis of British government by Dunleavy and Rhodes (1990), but it has travelled well (Elgie, 1997, 2011). It defines the executive in functional terms. So, instead of asking which position is important, we can ask which functions define the innermost part or heart of government. For example, the core functions of the British executive are to pull together and integrate central government policies and to act as final arbiters of conflicts between different elements of the government machine. These functions can be carried out by institutions other than prime minister and cabinet; for example the Treasury and the Cabinet Office. But power is contingent and relational; that is, it depends on the relative power of other actors and events. Ministers depend on the prime minister for support in getting funds from the Treasury. In turn, prime ministers depend on their ministers to deliver the party's electoral promises. Both ministers and prime ministers depend on the health of the global economy for a stable currency and economic growth to ensure the necessary financial resources are available. This power-dependence approach focuses on the distribution of such resources as money and authority in the core executive and explores the shifting patterns of dependence between the several actors. Power relations vary because all core executive actors have some resources, but no one consistently commands all the resources necessary to achieve their goals. So they exchange such resources as, for example, money, legislative authority or expertise. These exchanges take the form of games in which actors manoeuvre for advantage. The term 'core executive' directs our attention, therefore, to the key questions of 'who does what' and 'who has what resources' (for examples of work in this idiom see: Elgie, 1997, 2011; Rhodes, 1995; Smith, 1999 and their citations).

Prime-ministerial Predominance

This thesis is associated with the work of Richard Heffernan. He argues that the proposition that power is relational and based on dependency is

> only partially accurate. Power is relational between actors but it is also locational. It is dependent on where actors are to be found in the core executive, and whether they are at the centre or the periphery of key core executive networks. (Heffernan, 2003: 348)

Power-dependence characterizes core executive relationships, so Heffernan focuses on the distribution and dispersal of resources and shifting patterns of dependence between multiple actors. Prime ministers command many 'institutional resources', including patronage, prestige, authority, political centrality and policy reach, knowledge, information and expertise, control of the agenda, and Crown Prerogative, for example to delegate powers and responsibilities to ministers and departments (ibid.: 356–7). They also have 'personal resources' such as reputation, skill and ability; association with political success; public popularity; and high standing in their party (ibid.: 351; Heffernan, 2005: 16). It follows that the more resources prime ministers have, or can accumulate, the greater their potential for predominance. But many ministers also have resources that are not necessarily available to prime ministers. They can include 'a professional, permanent and knowledgeable staff, expert knowledge and relevant policy networks, time, information, and, not least, an annual budget' (ibid.: 614). There is much variation between countries but the minister without resources is the exception rather than the rule.

From the start, Heffernan's (2003: 350) argument about predominance had many qualifications. He suggested that prime-ministerial authority is 'contingent and contextual'. Prime ministers have the 'potential' to be predominant 'but only when personal resources are married with institutional power resources, and when the prime minister is able to use both wisely and well'. So the prime minister's personal resources are 'never guaranteed. They come and go, are acquired and are squandered, are won and lost' (ibid.: 356). Later versions of the prime-ministerial dominance argument also make significant qualifications (Heffernan, 2005: 616–17). In short, contingency, or one damned thing after another, means that predominance is transient.

So we read the later Heffernan (2005) and Bennister and Heffernan (2011) as an important set of qualifications to the prime-ministerial pre-dominance argument. It is significant that they wrote their first version during the heyday of the Blair 'presidency', while their qualifications reflect his later decline. In his most recent article, in reply to Dowding (2013), Heffernan (2013: 642, 643) emphasizes that prime ministers can have 'more or less political capital' and their 'power waxes and wanes'. These qualifications downplay prime-ministerial predominance and bridge the gap between their approach and proponents of the core executive (see the section on 'Predominant or Collaborative Leadership').

APPROACHES TO GOVERNANCE

The literature on governance is large and scattered (see Kjær, 2004; Pierre, 2000). We describe the main waves of governance in the study of public administration: network governance and metagovernance (and for more detail see Rhodes, 2012b).

Network Governance

The network governance literature has been reviewed and classified many times (Börzel, 1998, 2011; Klijn, 1997, 2008; Rhodes, 1990, 2006c). We offer only a brief recap of the several strands (see the section on 'The Interpretive Turn' below).

In Britain, the first wave of governance narratives is referred to as the 'Anglo-governance school' (Marinetto, 2003). It starts with the notion of policy networks or sets of organizations clustered around a major government function or department. Central departments need the cooperation of such groups to deliver services. For many policy areas, actors are inter-dependent and decisions are a product of their game-like interactions, rooted in trust and regulated by rules of the game negotiated and agreed by the participants. Trust and reciprocity are essential for cooperative behaviour and, therefore, the existence of the network. These networks are a distinctive coordinating mechanism different from markets and hierarchies and not a hybrid of them. Such networks have a significant degree of autonomy from the state – they are self-organizing – although the state can indirectly and imperfectly steer them (Rhodes, 1997: 53). In sum, for the 'Anglo-governance school', governance refers to governing with and through networks (see Rhodes, 2007).

In Germany, there is the work of Renate Mayntz, Fritz Schapf and their colleagues at the Max Planck Institute on *Steuerungtheorie* (see, e.g., Marin and Mayntz, 1991; Scharpf, 1997). They were among the first to treat networks, not as interest-group intermediation, but as a mode of governance. In the Netherlands, scholars at the Erasmus University focused on more effective ways of steering networks; see, for example, Kickert et al. (1997); Koppenjan and Klijn (2004). Such ideas caught on rapidly and mutated to embrace working in partnerships and collaborative management (see the section on 'Predominant or Collaborative Leadership' below).

Most recently, attention turned from describing the growth of networks to the normative implications of that growth and the questions of how to find ways of participating in networks that preserve legitimacy and accountability, and how to hold networks to account (see the section on 'Political Accountability or Webs of Accountabilities'). The search was on for new forms of democratic governance and new mechanisms of accountability (see, e.g., Bevir, 2010).

Finally, America caught up with Europe and brought its characteristic modernist-empiricist skill set to bear on networks and governance. If European scholars favoured case studies, their American colleagues combined 'large N' studies of networks (for a survey of this work see Meier and O'Toole, 2005) with an instrumental view that sought to make the study of networks relevant to public managers (see, e.g., Agranoff, 2007; Goldsmith and Eggers, 2004).

Metagovernance

Critics of the first wave characteristically focus on the argument that the state has been hollowed out. For example, Pierre and Peters (2000: 78, 104–5, 111) argue that the shift to network governance could 'increase public control over society' because governments 'rethink the mix of policy instruments'. As a result, 'coercive or regulatory instruments become less important and . . . "softer" instruments gain importance'. In short, the state has not been hollowed out, but has reasserted its capacity to govern by regulating the mix of governing structures such as markets and networks and deploying indirect instruments of control (see, e.g., Bell and Hindmoor, 2009; Jessop, 2000, 2003; Kooiman, 2003; Sørensen and Torfing, 2007).

Metagovernance refers to this new mix – to the state's use of nego-tiation, diplomacy and more informal modes of steering to secure coordination. As with network governance, metagovernance comes in several varieties (Sørensen and Torfing, 2007: 170–80). However, these approaches share a concern with the varied ways in which the state now steers organizations, governments and networks rather than directly providing services through state bureaucracies, or rowing. These other organizations undertake much of the work of governing: they imple-ment policies, they provide public services, and at times they even regulate themselves. The state governs the organizations that govern civil society; 'the governance of government and governance' (Jessop, 2000: 23). Moreover, the other organizations characteristically have a degree of autonomy from the state: they are often voluntary or private sector groups or they are governmental agencies or tiers of government separate from the core executive. So the state cannot govern them solely by the instruments that work in bureaucracies (see the section on 'Central Capability or Implementation' below).

THE PUZZLES

According to the literature on executive studies, we have witnessed the emergence of the predominant prime minister. According to the 'Anglo-governance school', the core executive's capacity to steer is reduced or hollowed out from above by international interdependencies such as mem-bership of the EU, from below by marketization and networks, and from within by the competing agendas and ambitions of ministers and agencies. As Helms (2012: 2) argues:

> The 'governance turn' in political science moved the focus of political analy-sis on decision making and problem solving but at the same time cultivated strongly sceptical views about the possible relevance of individual political leaders.

We unpack this broad characterization of the relationship between the two fields of study by focusing on four 'puzzles' (Heclo, 1974: 305–6): predominant or collaborative leadership; central capability or implemen-tation; formal or informal coordination; and managerial accountability or webs of accountabilities. We have devised these puzzles to encompass and systematize the diverse debates in executive governance. In particular, we focus on shared puzzles – on the intersection of executive studies and governance.

Predominant or Collaborative Leadership

The classic debate in the Westminster formal institutional tradition (see above) concerned the relative power of prime minister and cabinet (see Blick and Jones, 2010: chs 1 and 2), Latterly, the presidentialization thesis took over from this debate. For Poguntke and Webb (2005: 5, 7), presidentialization has three faces: the executive face; the party face; and the electoral face. Presidentialization occurs when there is a shift of 'political power resources and autonomy to the benefit of individual leaders' along each face and a corresponding loss to such collective actors as cabinet (see also Foley, 2000: ch. 1). The problem with this argument is that it was both mislabelled and overstated. We do not have the space (or indeed inclination) to rehash the debate (see, e.g., Dowding, 2013, and the several replies in *Parliamentary Affairs*, 66 (3), 2013). We restrict ourselves to three comments.

First, in the electoral arena, personalization is a prominent feature of media management in all countries and has a significant if small electoral effect in most. If we must use presidential language, it is here in the electoral and party arena that it is most apt. We live in an era of spatial leadership in which prime ministers cultivate selective political detachment or distance from their party and their government, especially their problems (Foley, 2000: 31).

Second, in the policy-making arena, there is some truth to the claim of a centralization of policy making on the prime minister. However, this claim applies to selected policy areas, with the equally important qualification that the prime minister's attention is also selective (see the section on 'Central Capability or Implementation' below).

The prime minister's influence is most constrained in the policy implementation arena. This arena is conspicuous by its absence from the presidentialization thesis. It is central to the network governance narrative. In this account, other senior government figures, ministers and their departments, and other agencies are key actors. Much goes on in government about which the prime minister knows little and affects even less. Many of these policy arenas are embedded in dependent relationships with domestic and international agencies and governments, making command-and-control strategies counterproductive. So there is another story of prime-ministerial power that focuses on the problems of governance and sees the prime minister as constantly involved in negotiations and diplomacy with a host of other politicians, officials and citizens.

We accept that prime ministers can be predominant, but few control and then only for some policies, some of the time. At this point, the argument can be helpfully recast taking account of the network literature. Burch and

Holliday (1996, 2004) see the prime minister as the core, or nodal point, of the networks supported by enhanced central resources that increase his or her power potential. However, 'the enhancement of central capacity within the British system of government reflects contingent factors, including the personalities of strategically-placed individuals (notably, but not only, the PM)'. They note that such changes are 'driven by prime ministerial whim' and 'if they so desire, [prime ministers] try to shape the core in their own image'. However, their ability to manage these core networks 'depends on the motivation and skill of key actors, and on the circumstances in which they find themselves at any given moment in time' (Burch and Holliday, 2004: 17, 20). Similarly, Helms's (2005) comparative study accepts that resource exchange is central to analysing executive leadership (see Elgie, 2011 for further comparative citations). The shared meeting ground for all sides in this debate is the idea that the prime minister is the 'principal node of key core executive networks' (Heffernan, 2005: 613).

We can now introduce a second strand to the network governance literature. Accepting that central actors depend on subnational and other actors for the delivery of key services, the network governance literature explores the limits to command-and-control strategies and explores other cooperative leadership styles. The literature on collaborative governance will serve as an example.

Ansell and Gash (2008: 544) define collaborative governance as a collective decision-making process 'where one or more public agencies directly engages non-state stakeholders' in the 'formal, consensus oriented, and deliberative' implementation of public policy or management of public programmes. The key question is whether opposing stakeholders can work together in a collaborative way. The answer is a 'cautious yes', and a key part of that answer is leadership, which is 'crucial for setting and maintaining clear ground rules, building trust, facilitating dialogue, and exploring mutual gains' (ibid.: 12–13). Such leadership is variously described as hands-off, soft, integrative, facilitative or diplomatic. The shared feature is that it is not directive, hands-on, or command and control. There is also a related literature on how to manage networks that focuses on steering, not rowing (see, e.g., Agranoff, 2007; Goldsmith and Eggers, 2004; Huxham and Vangen, 2005).

Central Capability or Implementation

With the perceived centralization of policy making, the executive studies literature focused on central capacity or central capability. Political leaders are constantly searching for tools that will deliver better coordination and regulation in a governance environment seen as more pluralized, fragmented and contested. This environment continually exposes their dependency and the inability to exert control and influence.

The literature on Westminster governments notes the pluralization of advice, the growth of central advisory units, and the attendant challenges for coordination and in managing new dependencies. Among Westminster governments, prime ministers and ministers traditionally looked to the career public service for policy advice and for structures and routines to support their decision-making. Under the pressures of governance they have relied increasingly on staff in their private offices. The task of supporting ministers is now shared between partisan personal staff, non-partisan career officials, external consultants and others. Ministerial support arrangements have become more varied, requiring someone to manage them.

A growing body of literature documents the growth of staffing and support units in the core executive throughout advanced industrial democracies. Peters et al. (2000: 15) note that 'growth, institutionalization, as well as politicization and hybridization are common features of the staffing of summits'. The pressures fuelling this growth are said to include: the 24/7 news cycle and the personalization of politics; the exigencies of the war on terror; increasing demands for domestic policy coordination; and the pluralization of policy advice (ibid.: 6–11). The emergence and growing importance of political staff is a response to these pressures and the need to coordinate inputs from multiple sources, referred to as the pluralization of advice (Blick, 2004; Eichbaum and Shaw, 2010; Tiernan, 2007). The consequences of this trend are a matter of dispute. For proponents of the presidential and predominance theses, this growth of staff support has strengthened prime ministers at the expense of ministers, cabinet and other players, allowing them to become predominant (Bennister, 2007; Walter and Strangio, 2007).

Proponents of the governance narrative observe that this growth seeks to sustain a command-and-control prime minister when governance is characterized by 'rubber levers'. They observe, for example, that the continuous reform of the British centre speaks of the failure of centralized interventions (rarely control). Also, despite a large and growing prime-ministerial office with its many advisers, the experiences of the Rudd and Gillard governments in Australia are not obvious examples of clear, central political direction. None the less, political advisers are now an essential 'third element' in the core executives of most parliamentary governments (Eichbaum and Shaw, 2010; Tiernan, 2007).

As well as pointing to the limits to centralizing strategies, the meta-governance literature also argues for a new toolkit for central agencies. Its proponents argue that there are several ways in which the state can steer, rather than command, the other actors involved in governance (see, e.g., Jessop, 2000: 23–4; 2003). First, the state can set the rules of the game for other actors and then leave them to do what they will within those rules; they work 'in the shadow of hierarchy'. Thus it can redesign markets, reregulate policy sectors or introduce constitutional change. Second, the state can try to steer other actors using storytelling. It can organize dialogues, foster meanings, beliefs and identities among the relevant actors, and influence what actors think and do. Third, the state can steer by the way in which it distributes resources such as money and authority. It can play a boundary-spanning role, alter the balance between actors in a network; act as a court of appeal when conflict arises; rebalance the mix of governing structures; and step in when network governance fails.

Finally, a central image in the governance narrative is of a pendulum swinging from centralization to governance and back. Against the centralizing strategies of the core executive networks, it argues for a bottom–up, not a top–down, view of government. The focus is implementation, yet for many the study of implementation is one of 'yesterday's issues' (Hill, 1997) and an 'intellectual dead end' with 'lots of leads, little results' (deLeon and deLeon, 2002). The governance narrative revives the topic, highlighting that implementation is mediated through the actions of front-line workers whose perspectives reflect local conditions, local knowledge and professional norms. Thus Maynard-Moody and Musheno (2003: ch. 12) argue that street-level bureaucrats 'actually make policy choices rather than simply implement the decisions of elected officials'. They fix client identities, often stereotyping them, which, in turn, fixes the occupational identity of the street-level bureaucrat as, for example, bleeding heart or hardnosed, which, in turn, sets the decision premises for the street-level bureaucrat's judgements. They manage the 'irreconcilable' dilemmas posed by clients' needs, administrative supervision (of rules and resources), and the exercise of state power. They are not heroes, but they are an example of bottom–up leadership of the complexities of network governance.

Executive studies may pay little attention, but implementation remains a critical issue for governments of all persuasions and a central concern of the governance narrative. When service provision spans governmental jurisdictions, and the public and private sectors, it involves markets or contracts and patient choice, hierarchy or bureaucracy, and networks or partnerships. Not only does each implementation structure have its own set of strengths and weaknesses, but mixing these structures can be like mixing oil and water. Implementation studies dramatize the dilemmas of core executives confronted by network governance.

Formal or Informal Coordination

The spread of network governance also undermines coordination. Despite strong pressures for more coordination, the practice is 'modest'. It is negative, organized by specific established networks; it is rarely strategic, intermittent, selective, sectoral, politicized, issue-oriented and reactive (Wright and Hayward, 2000: 33). For example, John Howard (Prime Minister of Australia) described 'a whole of government approach' as a key challenge to the Australian Public Service (APS). The APS aim was to encourage public service agencies to work, formally and informally, across portfolio boundaries to achieve a shared goal (MAC, 2004: 1). There were problems. Departments are competing silos. The rewards of departmentalism are known and obvious. For interdepartmental coordination, it is the costs that are known and obvious! Coordination costs time, money and staff; whole-of-government is a sideshow for most managers. Above all, coordination was seen as applying to central agencies, serving their priorities, not those of the departments.

These problems arise before we introduce networks into the equation. Staying with our Australian example, federalism is a major check on the ambitions of national governments. The Commonwealth does not control service delivery. It has limited reach, so it has to negotiate. For example, a major review of school funding initiated by the Rudd–Gillard Labor government, proposed a new, 'needs-based' funding model for the nation's schools. The Labor government promised significant funding increases for public schools, but these schools are mainly funded and run by state governments. So, although the relevant legislation was passed, the plan foundered when state premiers objected to the terms of the new funding arrangements. Despite intense bilateral negotiations and offers of additional funding, the Commonwealth succeeded in securing the agreement of only four states (of six) and one territory (of two) before the federal election in 2013, when Labor was defeated. In short, central coordination presupposes agreement with the priorities of central agencies when it is the lack of such agreement that created many of the problems – a genuine Catch 22 situation.

Networks make the goal of coordination ever more elusive. As Peters (1998: 302) argues, 'strong vertical linkages between social groups and public organizations makes effective coordination and horizontal linkages within government more difficult'. Once agreement is reached in the network, 'the latitude for negotiation by public organizations at the top of the network is limited'. However, these remarks presume that hierarchy is the most important or appropriate mechanism for coordination. Many years ago, Lindblom (1965) persuasively argued that indirect coordination or mutual adjustment was messy but effective. Public transit in the San Francisco Bay Area is a multi-organizational network, and Chisholm (1989: 195) shows that only some coordination can take place by central direction, so 'personal trust developed through informal relationships acts as lubricant for mutual adjustment'.

Core executives confront two broad tasks in such multi-organizational networks. They not only have to manage individual networks, but they also confront a portfolio of networks. Central agencies are the nodal points for both the portfolio and individual networks. Each central agency belongs to, and seeks to manage, a group of networks – its 'multi network portfolio' (Ysa and Esteve, 2013). Managing the network portfolio has its own distinct challenges. The most obvious challenge is to find out which networks the agency is trying to manage. All too often, an agency has no map of its own networks, let alone the networks of other central agencies. There will be no mechanisms for coordinating the responses of a central agency to either the portfolio or individual networks. Networks are messy. There are no guarantees of successful results, only the relentless pressure from the sour laws of network governance and the imperatives of constant nurturing. The role of any central agency is to manage their network portfolio, and to provide collaborative leadership.

In sum, coordination is the holy grail of modern government, ever sought, but always just beyond reach, and networks bring central coordination no nearer. However, they do provide their own informal, decentralized version, as long as the core executive can tolerate the mess.

Political Accountability or Webs of Accountabilities

A central theme in executive studies that follows logically from the claim of a predominant or presidential prime minister is the loss of accountability. Thus Savoie (2008: 232) argues that centralization suits prime ministers because they can set aside formal processes and get things done more quickly. But there are significant costs. Savoie (2008: 230, 339) argues that the key adverse consequences are centralization and the collapse of accountability. When there are few if any veto points, a powerful centre can act with impunity, acknowledging no other authority. An Australian example again is instructive. The 2001 political controversy known as the 'Children Overboard' affair arose from the allegation that refugees, also known as boat people, threw their children overboard to gain entry to Australia. The allegation was untrue but government ministers deliberately ignored 'inconvenient information'. Political staffers and public servants provided 'plausible deniability' for ministers in parliament and the media (for the relevant sources see Tiernan, 2007: 171–2). Veteran political journalist Paul Kelly (2009: 611–12) concludes that the case exposes a 'profound failure of accountability' that was exploited for the political benefit of the government of the day.

Proponents of the governance narrative also argue that there has been a breakdown of accountability, but for different reasons. They argue that conventional notions of accountability do not fit when authority for service delivery is dispersed among several agencies. Bovens (1998: 46) identifies the 'problem of many hands', where responsibility for policy in complex organizations is shared and it is correspondingly difficult to find out who is ultimately responsible. He also notes that fragmentation, marketization and the resulting networks create 'new forms of the problem of many hands' (ibid.: 229). These dilemmas are often laid bare in the 'accountability and blame' phase that follows natural disasters. The police and fire services would seem to be archetypal command-and-control bureaucracies, but responding to disasters involves many interlaced networks able to react rapidly to changing local conditions (Arklay, 2012). So, who is to blame when something goes awry – the bureaucracies or the networks? The inevitable inquiries after disasters struggle with the messiness. Such inquiries call for clarity of organization when redundancy, or overlap and duplication, is strength (Landau, 1979).

As Mulgan (2003: 211–14) argues, buck-passing is much more likely in networks because responsibility is divided and the reach of political leaders is much reduced. It is common for network governance to be closed to public scrutiny, a species of private government. The brute conclusion is that we face a crisis of accountability because centralization weakens traditional accountability to parliament and the multiple accountabilities of networks erode central control.

WHITHER THE STUDY OF EXECUTIVE GOVERNANCE?

Finally, we identify likely trends in the study of executives. We focus on: the interpretive turn; court politics; and presidential studies.

The Interpretive Turn

First-wave narratives of the changing state focus on issues such as the objective characteristics of policy networks and the oligopoly of the political marketplace. They stress power-dependence, the relationship between networks and policy outcomes, and the strategies by which the centre might steer networks. The second-wave narratives focus on the mix of governing structures, such as markets and networks, and on the various instruments of control, such as changing the rules of the game, storytelling and changing the distribution of resources. In contrast, the third wave of interpretive analysis focuses on the social construction of patterns of rule through the ability of individuals to create meanings in action. An interpretive approach highlights the importance of beliefs, practices, traditions and dilemmas for the study of the changing state. It represents a shift of topos from institutions to meanings in action. It explains shifting patterns of governance by focusing on the actors' own interpretations of their beliefs and practices. The everyday practices arise from agents whose beliefs and actions are informed by traditions and expressed in stories. It explores the diverse ways in which situated agents are changing the boundaries of state and civil society by constantly remaking practices as their beliefs change in response to dilemmas. It reveals the contingency and contestability of narratives. It highlights a more diverse view of state authority and its exercise.

There are many routes to this 'constructed' state and governance (see, e.g., Bevir and Rhodes, 2010; Dean, 2007: ch. 2; Hay, 2011; and Miller and Rose, 2008: ch. 3). Its singular advantage is that it is 'edifying'; it is a way of finding 'new, better, more interesting, more fruitful ways of speaking about' executive governance (Rorty, 1980: 360). Thus Bevir and Rhodes (2010) discuss some of the distinctive research topics that spring from an interpretive approach under the heading of the '3Rs' of rule, rationalities and resistance. Interpretive theory suggests that, under rule, political scientists should ask whether different sections of the governing elite draw on different traditions to construct different narratives about the world, their place within it, and their interests and values (see the section on 'Court Politics' below). An interpretive approach draws attention to the varied rationalities that inform policies across different policy arenas. Britain, like much of the developed world, has witnessed the rise of neoliberal managerial rationalities and the technology of performance measurement and targets (see the section on 'Political Accountability or Webs of Accountabilities' above). Finally, politics and policies do not arise exclusively from the strategies and interactions of elites. Other actors can resist, transform and thwart the agendas of elites. An interpretive approach draws attention to the diverse traditions and narratives that inform actors at lower levels of the hierarchy, and citizens – for example, the role of street-level bureaucrats (see the section on 'Central Capability or Implementation' above).

Court Politics

Court politics have existed throughout the ages in the Manchu Court, Imperial Rome, and the English Court during the Wars of the Roses. It is the stock of fiction, whether the faction of The White Queen or the fantasy of The Game of Thrones (see Campbell, 2010). In its current reincarnation, the idea marries the core executive to the analysis of prime-ministerial predominance (Rhodes, 2013). Also known as high politics, the approach builds on the notions of interdependence and the bargaining games of elite actors. For Cowling (1971), the high politics approach meant studying the intentions and actions of a political leadership network that consisted of 'fifty or sixty politicians in conscious tension with one another whose accepted authority constituted political leadership'. High politics was 'a matter of rhetoric and manoeuvre' by statesmen (ibid.: 3–4). For Savoie (2008: 16–17), the court encompasses 'the prime minister and a small group of carefully selected courtiers'. It also covers the 'shift from formal decision-making processes in cabinet . . . to informal processes involving only a handful of actors'. This conception is too narrow. We accept that there is often an inner sanctum, but participants in high politics are rarely so few. We prefer Cowling's more expansive definition, allied to Burch and Holliday's (1996) notion that the centre is a set of networks. These networks are still exclusive. The number of participants is still limited. But, as well as the core network or inner circle, we can also talk of circles of influence (Hennessy, 2000: 493–500) – a use that resonates with political folklore and practice.

There is an increasing number of ethnographic fieldwork studies of governing elites and their courts (see Rhodes, 2011). Also, the information in biographies, autobiographies, memoirs and diaries can be treated as raw data for this approach (see the section on 'Political Biography'). There are too many items of journalists' reportage, auto/biographies, memoirs and diaries for a comprehensive listing. Recent examples for Australia include Blewett (1999) and Watson (2002). Recent examples for the UK include Blunkett (2006) and Rawnsley (2001, 2010).

Such courts matter. They are key parts of the organizational glue holding the centre together. They coordinate the policy process by filtering and packaging proposals. They contain and manage conflicts between ministerial barons. They act as the keeper of the government's narrative. They act as the gatekeeper and broker for internal and external networks. The notion also directs our attention to the analysis of rival courts in departments and in other levels of government. Baronial politics live inside and outside the heart of government (see the section above on 'Predominant or Collaborative Leadership').

Presidential Studies

Scholars of executive governance are often sceptical about the utility of concepts and ideas drawn from presidential studies, believing that the differences between presidential and parliamentary government are too great. However, many argue that parliamentary governments are increasingly characterized by the fragmentation of executive authority, the growth of the core executive, the pluralization of advice and the increasingly personal and leader-centred nature of prime-ministerial leadership. So we ask: what lessons can we learn from the presidential literature?

Political Leadership

Theakston (2011: 79) argues that the presidential studies literature holds significant promise for executive studies scholars seeking ways of 'understanding and analysing the components of prime ministerial style and skills, within a framework permitting comparison, generalization and evaluation'. He draws particularly on Greenstein's (2004) six-point framework for analysing the political and personal qualities and skills of US presidents. They cover: skill as public communicators; organizational capacity; political skills; policy vision; cognitive style; and emotional intelligence. Theakston (2002, 2011) adapts this framework to the Westminster context, arguing that most analyses of the core executive pay too little attention to the individual characteristics and skills of prime ministers (see also Verbeek, 2003).

The style and skills of individual prime ministers are indeed significant, but only as part of a broader analysis of relationships and dependencies – the 'court politics' of the core executive. The presidential studies literature has long recognized the need also to understand the leader's operating context, notably the 'bargaining uncertainty' inherent in their role when there is a separation of powers (Neustadt, 1991[1960]).

Institutionalization

In the USA, the concept of the 'institutional presidency' is well established (Burke, 2000). It recognizes that 'leadership in the modern presidency is not carried out by the president alone, but rather by presidents with many associates'. Scholars of the institutional presidency have described the development of the staffing structures and advisory arrangements that support the president. They chart the growth in size and organizational complexity of the 'presidential branch'. This descriptive literature contains few lessons of wider applicability (see the section on 'Central Capability or

Implementation'). Of greater interest are the consequences of this growth. First, it creates new dependencies, pathologies and transaction costs that have not been documented (see the section on 'Court Politics'). Second, it provides contending explanations of this growth. For many, it is a consequence of presidential overload (Ragsdale and Theis, 1997). Others, however, argue that

> White House staff growth is largely driven by successive presidents' search for assistance in managing interactions with Congress, the media and the public, as well as by the long-term rivalry between the president and Congress, and only marginally by an expansion in the size or workload of the federal government. (Dickinson and Lebo, 2007: 207)

Presidents have responded to 'a more fluid, less stable and distinctly more partisan bargaining environment' by 'embracing tactics formerly restricted to political campaigns'. So executive growth is a response to, and fuels, executive bargaining. It can be seen as creating a presidential court with all the interpersonal conflicts and politicking such a phrase implies.

CONCLUSIONS

Executive studies and the governance narrative may interweave but they have distinct and distinctive foci. Executive studies focuses on prime-ministerial predominance, building central capacity, formal top–down coordination and traditional mechanisms of accountability. The governance narrative sees networks of dependencies, disconnected implementation structures, informal coordination and webs of accountabilities.

There are connections. Executive studies incorporates the insights of network governance. The prime-ministerial predominance argument sees the prime minister as the node of the core executive networks. We suggest a focus on court politics – on the inner circle and its circles of influence – and Bennister (2007: 337) agrees. There are shared concerns. There is agreement on an accountability deficit, even if the accounts of its causes differ. The two literatures are the opposite sides of the same coin. The governance narrative explores the limits to executive intentions and practices. There is a plethora of shorthand phrases seeking to capture these differences: hands-on or hands-off, top–down or bottom–up, and rowing or steering, to mention only three. They all tackle the puzzles we have discussed.

Our puzzles are best likened to anomalies or incongruities. As Thomas Kuhn (1996: 62–4, 67, 76, 82) argues, anomalies 'appear against the background provided by the paradigm' of normal science. However, when 'normal technical puzzling-solving activity breaks down' and 'the tools a paradigm supplies' are no longer 'capable of solving the problems it defines', then the accumulating anomalies will lead to a crisis and the transition to a new paradigm. The command-and-control paradigm of executive government confronts at least four anomalies. We are left puzzling about these shared puzzles and the biggest puzzle of all: whether the interpretive paradigm offers greater edification.

ACKNOWLEDGEMENT

The authors acknowledge funding support provided by the Australia and New Zealand School of Government (ANZSOG).

REFERENCES

Aberbach, J., Putnam, Robert D. and Rockman, Bert A. (1981), *Bureaucrats and Politicians in Western Democracies*. Cambridge, MA: Harvard University Press.

Agranoff, R. (2007), *Managing Within Networks: Adding Value to Public Organizations*. Washington, DC: Georgetown University Press.

Ansell, Chris and Gash, Alison (2008), 'Collaborative governance in theory and practice', *Journal of Public Administration Theory and Practice*, **18** (4), 543–71.

Arklay, T. (2012), 'Queensland's State Disaster Management Group: an all agency response to an unprecedented natural disaster', *Australian Journal of Emergency Management*, **27** (3), 9–19.

Bagehot, W. (1963 [1867]), *The English Constitution*, with an introduction by R.H.S. Crossman. London: Fontana.

Bell, S. and Hindmoor, A. (2009), *Rethinking Governance: The Centrality of the State in Modern Society*. Port Melbourne, Victoria: Cambridge University Press.

Bennister, M. (2007), 'Tony Blair and John Howard: comparative predominance and institution stretch in the UK and Australia', *The British Journal of Politics and International Relations*, **9** (3), 327–45.

Bennister, M. and Heffernan, R. (2011), 'Cameron as Prime Minister: the intra-executive politics of Britain's Coalition Government', *Parliamentary Affairs*, **65** (4), 778–801.

Bevir, M. (2010), *Democratic Governance*, Princeton, NJ: Princeton University Press.

Bevir, M. and Rhodes, R.A.W. (2006), *Governance Stories*. Abingdon: Routledge.

Bevir, M. and Rhodes, R.A.W. (2010), *The State as Cultural Practice*. Oxford: Oxford University Press.

Birch, A.H. (1964), *Representative and Responsible Government*, London: Allen & Unwin.

Blewett, N. (1999), *A Cabinet Diary: a Personal Record of the First Keating Government*. Kent Town, South Australia: Wakefield Press.

Blick, A. (2004), *People who Live in the Dark: the Special Adviser in British Politics*, London: Politico's.

Blick, A. and Jones, G. (2010), *Premiership*. London: Imprint Academic.

Blondel, J. and Müller-Rommel, F. (1993), 'Introduction', in J. Blondel and F. Müller-Rommel (eds), *Governing Together. The Extent and Limits of Joint Decision-Making in Western European Cabinets*. Basingstoke: Macmillan, pp. 1–19.

Blunkett, D. (2006), *The Blunkett Tapes. My Life in the Bear Pit*. London: Bloomsbury.

Börzel, T.J. (1998), 'Organizing Babylon: on the different conceptions of policy networks', *Public Administration*, **76** (2), 253–73.

Börzel, T.J. (2011), 'Networks: reified metaphor or governance panacea?', *Public Administration*, **89** (1), 49–63.

Bovens, M. (1998), *The Quest for Responsibility: Accountability and Citizenship in Complex Organizations*. Cambridge: Cambridge University Press.

Burch, M. and Holliday, I. (1996), *The British Cabinet System*. Englewood Cliffs, NJ and Hemel Hempstead: Prentice Hall/Harvester Wheatsheaf.

Burch, M. and Holliday, I. (2004), 'The Blair Government and the core executive', *Government and Opposition*, **39** (1), 1–21.

Burke, J.P. (2000), *The Institutional Presidency*. 2nd edn. Baltimore, MD: The Johns Hopkins University Press.

Campbell, J. (2010), *Pistols at Dawn. Two Hundred Years of Political Rivalry from Pitt & Fox to Blair & Brown*. London: Vintage.

Chisholm, D. (1989), *Coordination without Hierarchy. Informal Structures in Multiorganizational Systems*. Berkeley, CA: University of California Press.

Cowling, M. (1971), *The Impact of Labour 1920–1924*. Cambridge: Cambridge University Press.

Dean, M. (2007), *Governing Societies*. Maidenhead: Open University Press.

deLeon, P. and deLeon, L. (2002), 'Whatever happened to policy implementation? An alternative approach', *Journal of Public Administration Research & Theory*, **12** (4), 467–92.

Denzin, N.K. (1989), *Interpretive Biography*. London: Sage.

Dickinson, M.J. and Lebo, M.J. (2007), 'Re-examining the growth of the institutional presidency, 1940–2000', *Journal of Politics*, **69** (1), 206–19.

Dowding, K. (2013), 'The prime ministerialization of the British Prime Minister', *Parliamentary Affairs*, **66** (3), 617–35.

Dunleavy, P. and Rhodes R.A.W. (1990), 'Core executive studies in Britain', *Public Administration*, **68** (1), 3–28.

Eckstein, H. (1963), 'A perspective on comparative politics, past and present', in H. Eckstein and D.E. Apter (eds), *Comparative Politics: A Reader*. London: The Free Press of Glencoe, pp. 3–32.

Eichbaum, C. and Shaw, R. (eds) (2010), *Partisan Appointees and Public Servants: An International Analysis of the Role of the Political Adviser*. Cheltenham, UK and Northampton, MA, USA: Edward Elgar Publishing.

Elgie, R. (1997), 'Models of executive politics: a framework for the study of executive power relations in parliamentary and semi-presidential regimes', *Political Studies*, **45** (2), 217–31.

Elgie, R. (2011), 'Core executive studies two decades on', *Public Administration*, **89** (1), 64–77.

Foley, M. (1993), *The Rise of the British Presidency*. Manchester: Manchester University Press.

Foley, M. (2000), *The British Presidency*. Manchester: Manchester University Press.

Goldsmith, S. and Eggers, W.D. (2004), *Governing by Networks*. Washington, DC: Brookings Institution Press.

Greenstein, F. (2004), *The Presidential Difference: Leadership Style From FDR to George W. Bush*. 2nd edn. Princeton, NJ: Princeton University Press.

Hay, C. (2011), 'Interpreting interpretivism, interpreting interpretations: the new hermeneutics of public administration', *Public Administration*, **89** (1), 167–82.

Heclo, H. (1974), *Modern Social Politics in Britain and Sweden*. New Haven, NJ: Yale University Press.

Heffernan, R. (2003), 'Prime ministerial predominance? Core executive politics in the UK', *British Journal of Politics and International Relations*, **5** (3), 347–72.

Heffernan, R. (2005), 'Exploring and explaining the British prime minister', *British Journal of Politics and International Relations*, **7** (4), 605–20.

Heffernan, R. (2013), 'There's no need for the "-ization": the prime minister is merely prime ministerial', *Parliamentary Affairs*, **66** (3), 636–45.

Helms, L. (2005), *Presidents, Prime Ministers and Chancellors. Executive Leadership in Western Democracies*. London: Macmillan.

Helms, L. (2012), 'Introduction: the importance of studying political leadership comparatively', in L. Helms (ed.), *Comparative Political Leadership*. Basingstoke: Palgrave Macmillan, pp. 1–14.

Hennessy, P. (2000), *The Prime Ministers*. London: Allen Lane, The Penguin Press.

Hill, M. (1997), 'Implementation theory: yesterday's issues?', *Policy and Politics*, **25** (4), 375–85.

Huxham, C. and Vangen, C. (2005), *Managing to Collaborate: The Theory and Practice of Collaborative Advantage*. London Routledge.

Jennings, I. (1959 [1936]), *Cabinet Government*. Cambridge: Cambridge University Press.

Jessop, B. (2000), 'Governance failure', in G. Stoker (ed.), *The New Politics of British Local Governance*. Basingstoke: Macmillan, pp. 11–32.

Jessop, B. (2003), 'Governance and metagovernance: on reflexivity, requisite variety, and requisite irony', in H.P. Bang (ed.), *Governance as Social and Political Communication*. Manchester: Manchester University Press, pp. 101–16.

Kelly, P. (2009), *The March of Patriots: The Struggle for Modern Australia*. Carlton, Victoria: University of Melbourne Press.

Kickert, W.J.M., Klijn, E.-H. and Koppenjan, J.F.M. (eds) (1997), *Managing Complex Networks: Strategies for the Public Sector*. London: Sage.

Kjær, A.M. (2004), *Governance*. Cambridge: Polity.

Klijn, E.-H. (1997), 'Policy networks: an overview', in W.J.M. Kickert, E.-H. Klijn and J.F.M. Koppenjan (eds), *Managing Complex Networks: Strategies for the Public Sector*. London: Sage, pp. 14–61.

Klijn, E.-H. (2008), 'Governance and governance networks in Europe: an assessment of 10 years of research on the theme', *Public Management Review*, **10** (4), 505–25.

Kooiman, J. (2003), *Governing as Governance*. London: Sage.

Koppenjan, J.F.M. and Klijn, E.-H. (2004), *Managing Uncertainties in Networks: A Network Approach to Problem Solving and Decision Making*. London: Routledge.

Kuhn, T. (1996 [1970]), *The Structure of Scientific Revolutions*. 3rd edn. Chicago, IL: Chicago University Press.

Landau, M. (1979), *Political Theory and Political Science: Studies in the Methodology of Political Inquiry*. Brighton: Harvester Press.

Lindblom, C.E. (1965), *The Intelligence of Democracy*. New York: The Free Press.

MAC (Management Advisory Committee) (2004), *Connecting Government. Whole of Government Response to Australia's Priority Challenges*. Canberra: Australian Public Service Commission.

Marin, B. and Mayntz, R. (eds) (1991), *Policy Network: Empirical Evidence and Theoretical Considerations*. Frankfurt am Main: Campus Verlag.

Marinetto, M. (2003), 'Governing beyond the centre: a critique of the Anglo-Governance School', *Political Studies*, **51** (3), 592–608.

Marquand, D. (2009), 'Biography', in M. Flinders, A. Gamble, C. Hay and M. Kenny (eds), *The Oxford Handbook of British Politics*. Oxford: Oxford University Press, pp. 187–200.

Maynard-Moody, S. and Musheno, M. (2003), *Cops, Teachers, Counsellors: Stories from the Front Lines of Public Service*. Ann Arbor, MI: The University of Michigan Press.

Meier, K.J. and O'Toole, L.J. (2005), 'Managerial networking: issues of measurement and research design', *Administration & Society*, **37** (5), 523–41.

Miller, P. and Rose, N. (2008), *Governing the Present: Administering Economic, Social and Personal Life*. Cambridge: Polity.

Mulgan, R. (2003), *Holding Power to Account. Accountability in Modern Democracies*. Basingstoke: Palgrave Macmillan.

Neustadt, R.E. (1991 [1960]), *Presidential Power and the Modern Presidents: The Politics of Leadership from Roosevelt to Reagan*. Rev. edn. New York: The Free Press.

102 The international handbook of public administration and governance

Peters, B.G. (1998), 'Managing horizontal government: the politics of coordination', *Public Administration*, **76** (2), 295–311.
Peters, B.G., Rhodes, R.A.W. and Wright, V. (eds) (2000), *Administering the Summit: Administration of the Core Executive in Developed Countries*. Basingstoke: Macmillan.
Pierre, J. (ed.) (2000), *Debating Governance*. Oxford: Oxford University Press.
Pierre, J. and Peters, B.G. (2000), *Governance, Politics and the State*. Basingstoke: Macmillan.
Pimlott, B. (1994), 'The future of political biography', in *Frustrate Their Knavish Tricks. Writings on Biography, History and Politics*. London: HarperCollins, pp. 149–61.
Pimlott, B. (1999), 'Is contemporary biography history?', *Political Quarterly*, **70** (1), 31–41.
Poguntke, T. and Webb, P. (eds) (2005), *The Presidentialization of Politics*. Oxford: Oxford University Press
Ragsdale, L. and Theis, J.J. (1997), 'The institutionalization of the American presidency: 1924–92', *American Journal of Political Science*, **41** (4), 1290–318.
Rawnsley, A. (2001), *Servants of the People: The Inside Story of New Labour*. Rev. edn. London: Penguin Books.
Rawnsley, A. (2010), *The End of the Party. The Rise and Fall of New Labour*. London: Viking.
Rhodes, R.A.W. (1990), 'Policy networks: a British perspective', *Journal of Theoretical Politics*, **2** (3), 292–316.
Rhodes, R.A.W. (1995), 'From prime ministerial power to core executive', in R.A.W. Rhodes and P. Dunleavy (eds), *Prime Minister, Cabinet and Core Executive*. London: Macmillan, pp. 11–37.
Rhodes, R.A.W. (1997), *Understanding Governance*. Buckingham, UK and Philadelphia, PA: Open University Press.
Rhodes, R.A.W. (2006a), 'Executive government in parliamentary systems', in R.A.W. Rhodes, S. Binder and B. Rockman (eds), *The Oxford Handbook of Political Institutions*. Oxford: Oxford University Press, pp. 324–45.
Rhodes, R.A.W. (2006b), 'Old institutionalisms', in R.A.W. Rhodes, S. Binder and B. Rockman (eds), *The Oxford Handbook of Political Institutions*. Oxford: Oxford University Press, pp. 90–118.
Rhodes, R.A.W. (2006c), 'Policy network analysis', in M. Moran, M. Rein and R.E. Goodin (eds), *The Oxford Handbook of Public Policy*. Oxford: Oxford University Press, pp. 423–45.
Rhodes, R.A.W. (2007), 'Understanding governance: ten years on', *Organization Studies*, **28** (8), 1243–64.
Rhodes, R.A.W. (2011), *Everyday Life in British Government*. Oxford: Oxford University Press.
Rhodes, R.A.W. (2012a), 'Theory, method and British political "life history"', *Political Studies Review*, **10** (1), 161–76.
Rhodes, R.A.W. (2012b), 'Waves of governance', in David Levi-Faur (ed.), *The Oxford Handbook of Governance*. Oxford: Oxford University Press, pp. 33–48.
Rhodes, R.A.W. (2013), 'From prime ministerial leadership to court politics', in P. Strangio, P. 't Hart and J. Walter (eds), *Prime Ministerial Leadership: Power, Party and Performance in the Westminster System*. Oxford: Oxford University Press, pp. 318–33.
Rhodes, R.A.W., Wanna, J. and Weller, P. (2009), *Comparing Westminster*. Oxford: Oxford University Press.
Roberts, B. (2002), *Biographical Research*. Buckingham: Open University Press.
Rorty, R. (1980), *Philosophy and the Mirror of Nature*. Oxford: Blackwell.
Savoie, D. (2008), *Court Government and the Collapse of Accountability in Canada and the United Kingdom*. Toronto: University of Toronto Press.
Scharpf, F.W. (1997), *Games Real Actors Play. Actor-centred Institutionalism in Policy Research*. Boulder, CO: Westview Press.
Shugart, M. (2006), 'Comparative executive–legislative relations', in R.A.W. Rhodes, S. Binder and B. Rockman (eds), *The Oxford Handbook of Political Institutions*. Oxford: Oxford University Press, pp. 344–65.
Smith, M.J. (1999), *The Core Executive in Britain*, London: Palgrave Macmillan.
Sørensen, E. and Torfing, J. (2007), 'Theoretical approaches to metagovernance',

in E. Sorsensen and J. Torfing (eds), *Theories of Democratic Network Governance*. Basingstoke: Palgrave Macmillan, pp. 169–82.

Theakston, K. (2002), 'Political skills and context in prime ministerial leadership in Britain', *Policy & Politics*, **30** (2), 284–323.

Theakston, K. (2011), 'Gordon Brown as prime minister: political skills and leadership styles', *British Politics*, **6** (1), 78–100.

Tiernan, A. (2007), *Power without Responsibility: Ministerial Staffers in Australian Governments from Whitlam to Howard*. Sydney: University of New South Wales Press.

Verbeek, B. (2003), *Decision Making in Great Britain during the Suez Crisis: Small Groups and a Persistent Leader*. Farnham, Surrey: Ashgate Publishing.

Walter, J. (2002), 'The solace of doubt? Biographical methodology after the short twentieth century', in P. France and W. St Clair (eds), *Mapping Lives: The Uses of Biography*. Oxford: Oxford University Press, pp. 321–35.

Walter, J. and Strangio, P. (2007), *No, Prime Minister: Reclaiming Politics from Leaders*. Sydney: University of New South Wales Press.

Watson, D. (2002), *Recollections of a Bleeding Heart: A Portrait of Paul Keating PM*. New York: Knopf.

Wheare, K.C. (1963), *Federal Government*, 4th edn. Oxford: Oxford University Press.

Wright, V. and Hayward, J.E. (2000), 'Governing from the centre: policy coordination in six European core executives', in R.A.W. Rhodes (ed.), *Transforming British Government. Volume 2. Changing Roles and Relationships*. London: Macmillan, pp. 27–46.

Ysa, Tamyko and Esteve, M. (2013), 'Networks never walk alone: the governance of network portfolios'. Paper to the Global Governance Club, Netherlands Institute for Advanced Study in the Humanities and Social Science (NIAS), Wassenaar, The Netherlands, 29 May–1 June 2013.

5. Paradigms of non-Western public administration and governance
Wolfgang Drechsler

This chapter argues that there are different paradigms of governance and especially public administration, including the Chinese, Western and Islamic ones. This means that there is not one global best public administration, but that what we call global public administration is actually Western public administration – and, today, that means to a large extent Anglo-American public administration. Paradigms comprise first of all the potentiality and theory of forms of what we can call non-Western public administration (NWPA), rather than reality and practice as we observe it today. Including a discussion of the recent contributions of the work of Francis Fukuyama regarding public administration, governance and the specific case of China, this chapter's guiding question is whether we arrive more easily at good public administration if we realize that there are different contexts and thus either different ways thither, or even legitimately different goals.

THE PROBLEM AND THE THREE PARADIGMS

The title of this chapter is programmatic: I will suggest and tentatively conceptualize that there are different paradigms of governance and especially public administration. This means that there is not one global best (practice of) public administration, but that what we call global public administration is actually Western[1] public administration – and, today, that means to a large extent Anglo-American public administration (cf. Raadschelders 2013, pp. ix, 216–17; de Vries 2013b, pp. 108, 123) If public administration (PA) has two dimensions, ethics (goals) and performance (mechanics), linked though they may often be, 'good PA' both works well and is ethical by its own standards. With paradigms, I mean not only real, existing, but also potential, historical or theoretical forms of what we can call non-Western PA (NWPA) – we may also say possible epistemes.

In most social sciences and humanities, to say something like that would hardly be novel, and even in economics, amazingly enough, globalization has apparently not led to convergence (classically Boyer 1994). It may do so at some point, as even key protagonists of non-Western paradigms, such as Kishore Mahbubani (2013a), argue, but certainly cultural–ethical 'differences will remain for a long time' (ibid., p. 259). In many areas of scholarly inquiry, especially in the humanities, the opposite attitude of 'one-Western-size-fits-all' prevails, perhaps even to the point of what has been called 'Occidentalism' (Buruma and Margalit 2004).

But in PA, this is certainly not the case – here, it is generally, if tacitly, assumed that there is one good PA, and that this is global-Western PA; it is certainly the case in scholarship (see *Public Administration Review* 2010; Raadschelders 2013, p. ix), but even more so in PA reform (cf. most recently Andrews 2013, *passim*). In other words, countries and places that do not adhere to or fail at least to move towards the global-Western standard (even if this is understood to include significant regional variations, which is not always the case) are somehow remiss: they do not provide optimal PA and thus governance. The only excuse they may have is that they are laggards, they are in transition, but they are expected to eventually arrive at global-Western PA.

Contrary to this, what I would like to suggest is that, while there are indeed PA solutions to problems that arise from the nature of PA itself, in turn based on the fact that more human beings live in society than can be coordinated personally and directly, the following can be assumed:

A. In different contexts, there are also solutions to common problems that are different, but not worse; at least some of them are very probably even better;

B. There are adequate, good, indeed excellent solutions that completely depend on context – understood here as *Lebenswelt*[2] – which are neither necessarily worse than the solution proposed by Western PA, nor move in this direction (never mind the genuine phenomenon, on many but not all levels of life, of globalization); and

C. The debate whether, for all human beings in time and space, there is or should be one set of ethics; that is, whether there is a cohesive, unitary set of universal human values and thus also rights that applies to everyone, everywhere, at all times, is – although largely the purported view of international organizations – not really closed and is in fact the 'elephant in the room'; much depends on the answer, for PA as well.[3]

In 2013, this differentiation moved briefly to the centre of attention of the scientific community of governance and, though to a lesser extent, of PA because of Francis Fukuyama's widely distributed and discussed essay, 'What is governance?' (2013a). Against prevailing global Western orthodoxy, and following some earlier recent work of his on this issue (2011, 2012), Fukuyama looks for ways to 'better measure governance' (2013a, p. 1). Although highly instructive as such, what is important for the present context is that Fukuyama defines 'government's ability to make and enforce rules, and to deliver services, *regardless of whether the government is democratic or not*' (p. 3, my emphasis). Governance is 'not about the goals' – 'governance is thus about execution, or what has traditionally fallen within the domain of public administration, as opposed to politics' (p. 4; see Rothstein 2013 for a traditional critique of this perspective). According to Mahbubani, this is 'a distinction which is almost inconceivable in Western minds', most of which 'cannot conceive of "good governance" as an independent and desirable goal' (2013b). And while we do not need to follow Fukuyama in making governance part of PA rather than the other way round, as is usual,[4] the differentiation between goals and means is key here, because, as Fukuyama says, the entire point is to study the connection between the two, rather than simply to assume it (2013a, pp. 3–4).[5] He himself had earlier claimed that 'the rule of law and democratic accountability are important to high-quality state performance' (2012, p. 23), but this is just that: a claim.[6] As recent studies show, the connection of accountability and performance is at best non-linear (de Vries 2013b; Christensen and Lægreid 2013), and as Mahbubani (2013b) says in his comment, 'to put it bluntly, democracy is neither a necessary nor a sufficient condition for good governance'. Altogether, Fukuyama himself underlines that he is more interested in what I have above labelled B, rather than C.

The two most obvious potential partners, or challengers, of global-Western PA as largely independent paradigms are, I would suggest, first Chinese and second Islamic PA (cf. Painter and Peters 2010, pp. 3, 19). For the few people dealing with this issue, it is contentious whether there may be more, and what the other paradigms might be,[7] but I would single out these two for now because they, and I think only they, share a few significant advantages for such a comparison:

- a large body of theoretical literature
- centuries of practice
- strong relevance today
- a convincing carrier country
- a largely non-derivative system.

This is most clearly the case with *classical* Chinese, that is, largely Confucian, and *classical* Islamic, that is, what one could perhaps call caliphate, PA. Because of the 'classical' part, we will have to look more at history than is usual in PA – not because of simple notions of legacy and context,[8] but because our concern, as indicated, must be potentiality rather than current realization and recognition in contemporary scholarship, which certainly is global-Western (see Raadschelders 2013). The argument is, basically, about an honest basis for a convincing narrative, or convincing narratives; regarding contemporary empirics, it is therefore more of an agenda, rather than being based on previous research.

But why would that be interesting to begin with? The abovementioned equation, global = Western = good, can be extended by the addition of 'modern'; that is, global = Western = good = modern. Thus modernization would equal Westernization, which would be a good thing. But, first, the suggestion that modernization, that is, any improvement, automatically means Westernization actually delegitimizes the former in those contexts in which Westernization is at least an ambiguous concept for many. Assuming that, often, these are contexts that could really benefit from it, to show that the improvement of PA does not automatically mean Westernization, in other words, that modernization is not necessarily Westernization, would be a major accomplishment (assuming that the goal is not Westernization *per se*). It may then easily be that countries that do not follow the global-Western model are not laggards but rather pursue their own path towards good PA.[9] In that case, policy recommendations (often linked to financial incentives) to move towards Western PA benchmarks might be not only misguided, but may even turn out to be highly counterproductive.

This brings us to the second point: if the large-scale global effort to improve the world by improving governance and PA were to be an overwhelming success, some serious arguments would be needed that would speak against such an effort. However, as Matt Andrews has argued in an important recent book on development (2013), to the contrary, there is 'mounting evidence that institutional reforms in developing countries do not work. Case studies and multicountry analyses show that many governments in developing nations are not becoming more functional, even after decades and hundreds of millions of dollars of externally sponsored reforms' (p. xi). Andrews proposes a new, highly contextualized way of implementing public sector reform (pp. 227–31), stopping short, however, as Fukuyama does, of suggesting that there may be different goals altogether (point C above). In fact, as Andrews shows, even if one uses the indicators rightly derided by Fukuyama (2013a), fewer internationally funded development-based public sector reform programmes were successful than not (Andrews 2013, pp. 13–15), and according to a World Bank (2008) evaluation, 'civil service reforms led to improved quality of public administration in 42 percent of countries borrowing for such interventions' (p. 213), meaning that in 58 per cent of these cases, there was no improvement at all.

Interest vested in the global-Western paradigm is none the less very substantial, both in policy and in scholarship, and always has been. However, during the last half-decade or so, three phenomena have weakened the assuredness in and of the West that its solutions are the global ones wherever one goes, and this has slowly reached PA as well. One is the global financial crisis, which has called the Western system into question both as regards setup and performance, including PA (see Drechsler 2011). Another is the awareness, in West and East, of the apparently sustainable (re-)emergence of the largely Confucian Southeast and East Asian 'tiger states', about which more below.

Specifically for PA, third, all this occurs at a time at which it is difficult to offer a cohesive (global-Western) PA paradigm, because one no longer exists. After the demise of the NPM as the ruling model (see Drechsler 2009b, 2009c; Drechsler and Kattel 2009), what we are facing is a post-NPM *Unübersichtlichkeit* (fuzziness) with several 'paradigmettes', such as the old NPM and the new one (a response to the global financial crisis), traditional Weberianism, NPM-plus concepts such as new public governance and its varied permutations, as well as public value, and Weberian-plus ones, such as the Neo-Weberian state (see Pollitt and Bouckaert 2011). Some beliefs that were held to be true until very recently have become highly volatile – privatization, say – and some others have recently become very questionable – transparency as a goal may come to mind (see Han 2012). So, what is it that the West can responsibly sell?

THREE WAYS OF LOOKING AT PA

But even if there is such a thing as non-Western PA, and even if this can be good; that is, it works well and is ethical PA, not an aberration or an atavism, there seems to be also a core of good PA that all systems share, and there are plenty of grey zones in between (see points A and B above). In order to clarify this vague-sounding scenario, I would at this point preliminarily propose three possible models of trajectories to good PA: Western, multicultural and contextual.

The first is what I have described as the global-Western mainstream: global = Western = good (= modern). All other traditions, including Chinese and Islamic, would eventually have to converge on the development trajectory of this or else be not just different but worse. One may or may not allow contextual variations, but, in principle, the idea is that we know what good PA is, that it is universal, that by and large this is Western PA, and will remain so for the foreseeable future.[10]

If one does not buy into this narrative, or at least would like to question it, then the second model would seem to be the obvious, or logical, counter-alternative. This, which we may call multicultural PA, would hold – it is a theoretical model – that there is no such thing as ideal PA as such, that good PA depends entirely on culture and context, never mind at which level, and that the ways to reach it are also entirely context-dependent and generally not linked to one another. Multicultural public administration has the advantage of being politically correct in many contexts (outside of PA); it is *prima facie* a good alternative to the erroneous simplicities of global-Western PA. However, the problems with this approach are manifold as well, and perhaps first of all, as mentioned and as any NWPA research will very quickly show, there are actually both problems and solutions that are germane to PA, no matter where one looks, and solutions may be sometimes different across time and space but sometimes very, indeed strikingly, similar (see Drechsler 2013c regarding neo-Confucian China).

The third model, the contextual one, would say that the key to good PA is to realize where one is coming from at the moment and to be in synch with that, and that means to realize what the context actually is. Of course, one can look at other systems and learn from them, but in this context, that would necessarily be policy learning, not mere policy transfer (see Randma-Liiv and Kruusenberg 2012; a recent empirical case study in line with this is Christensen et al. 2012). But first, 'good' in PA means primarily 'fulfilling its purpose in a given context' – PA is good when it does what it is supposed to do; like the market in an economy, it does not come *prima facie* with values attached, as we have gathered from the Fukuyama debate mentioned above (certain forms of PA have certain effects that from certain perspectives have normative connotations, but not more than that).

Yet this is not significantly different for ethics, especially when we are looking for truly *good* governance – a cliché term that clearly begs the question, 'Good for whom?' (see Drechsler 2004). It is pivotal to realize this, not least for policy. When de Vries sums up an empirical study of Central and Eastern Europe (CEE) by stating, 'Bad governance seems to do as good as, and in times of economic crisis even better than, good governance' (2013b, p.122), what meaning does the 'good' in 'good governance' possibly retain?

> The Hatter . . . had taken his watch out of his pocket, and was looking at it uneasily . . . 'Two days wrong! . . . I told you butter wouldn't suit the works!' he added, looking angrily at the March Hare.
> 'It was the best butter,' the March Hare meekly replied.

As Peter Heath explained this passage from Lewis Carroll's *Alice in Wonderland* (1865),

> 'Good', like its superlative, is often a relative term, meaning 'good of its kind', or for its standard purpose, whatever that may be. Failing such a reference, the judgment of goodness is indeterminate, and cannot be applied or debated without risk of confusion. [Thus the March Hare's statement is right in that the butter was best as butter goes, no doubt, but not as a mechanical lubricant.] (Heath 1974, pp. 68–9)

Aristotle, one of the most quintessentially, definitively Western philosophers, '*the* philosopher' in fact, and the father, one could say, of ethics, makes almost exactly this point in his political *magnum opus*, the *Politika* (*Politics*), when listing the necessary qualifications for members of a government or administration:

> First, sympathy for the constitution as it actually exists; second, competences that are in line with the tasks of their specific office; third, a sense of virtue and justice that matches exactly those of the state in which they live – because, if the concept of justice is not the same in every state, it is obvious that there must be different kinds. (Arist. Pol. 1309a; V 9)

How to metaphorize good, primarily effective, PA in context? Let us say that all paradigms as proposed participate in some solutions that can be said to form 'good PA' in the sense that it does its job in a decent, primarily in an effective and secondarily in a contextually ethical, way, that it fulfils its standard purpose on any possible level, including institutions, people and concepts, but that, in general, these are adapted to context. That means that there may be:

(a) a small nucleus of effective PA that almost always works, tiny because it must match all performance and all ethics – and (a) is a purely empirical, not a normative concept; then
(b) a larger one in which such generally valid principles are adapted to the context and thus work; and
(c) a third level where solutions work well within a given paradigm but not (necessarily) in any other, which, given the high requirements, would be expected to be the most common case.

For our limited model of three paradigms, this would, again tentatively and subject to review, look as in Figure 5.1.

Now, (a) is what is generally assumed to be good PA, and the contextualized second nucleus (b) is what the more sophisticated PA research supports today (although it is not the common view), but our

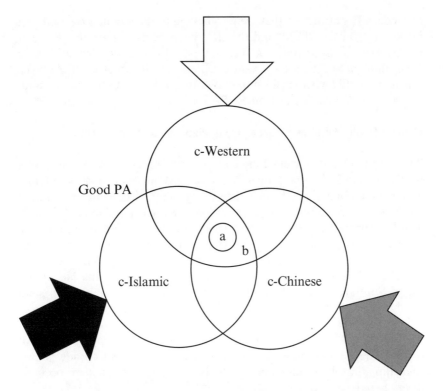

Figure 5.1   Three paradigms of public administration

focus is on (c), the postulated spheres of good PA, each with(in) a certain paradigm that does not work well, nor does it have to, in any other. If this is even partially true, then it indeed means that one should not judge, and try to improve, PA on the basis of and towards the outer (b), let alone the inner nucleus (a), but just ask whether, under the given circumstances, PA does its job, or is moving in the right direction.

CHINESE AND ISLAMIC PA ILLUSTRATED

One could actually end at this point, but, even in the current context, a few brushstrokes sketching out the alternatives to Western PA, of classical Chinese and Islamic PA and governance, are in order because, otherwise, the thesis may remain too abstract, and also because much of this is so counter-epistemic for PA that some examples of both ethics and performance might be helpful. I have recently described both the Chinese roots of modern PA principles that seem to belong to the second and even first nucleus (Drechsler 2013c) and the effective aspects of Ottoman PA that belong specifically to its own, Islamic, paradigm (Drechsler 2013b), so I will limit myself to a few examples, partially drawn from these texts. The issue is only whether we should discuss Islamic or Ottoman PA, and, respectively, Confucian or Chinese PA.

Chinese Public Administration or Confucian Public Administration

So, should one talk about Chinese or about Confucian PA? What speaks for Confucian PA is that it includes, next to Mainland China (with Hong Kong, which previously belonged to this group as well, and to an extent still does), also Taiwan, Singapore, South Korea and Japan. Of these, Taiwan carries on the Confucian legacy of the Chinese Empire in the most direct way, after it was destroyed several times during the twentieth century, the last time during the Cultural Revolution (see Berman 2010; Jan 2010; Suleski 2008, pp.267–70). Of these, as Fukuyama has noted, Japan, South Korea and Taiwan were 'checked by the international system (in the guise of the U.S. military)' (2012, p.16), whereas Singapore was voluntarily Western, and thus strong enough to take its own path, rather than obeying Western advice and fashion (Andrews 2013, pp.190–91). All of them are among the great success stories of the recent decade or two (including, in spite of all its problems, Japan, since the problems occur at a very high level). And

> one of the reasons that the Chinese-influenced parts of East Asia have had a big leg up in terms of development outcomes is their inheritance of Chinese traditions of stateness. China, Japan, Korea, and Taiwan have been able to take a functioning state for granted in a way that countries in other regions could not. (Fukuyama 2013b)

Of these, next to Taiwan, it may be especially tempting to speak about the hugely successful and explicitly Confucian Singapore when discussing contemporary Confucianism. After all, the father of Singapore's success, Lee Kuan Yew, is a self-professed Confucian, and it does not matter in the least whether there may be doubts about how academically valid his principles are deemed to be (cf. Bell 2011, p.97; see Lord 2003, pp.101–5; Suleski 2008, pp.272–5). Fukuyama's important point regarding ethics, that 'contemporary comparative politics has largely lost sight of the Aristotelian distinction between kingship and tyranny, and has no good way of categorizing nondemocratic regimes that nonetheless can be said to serve a broader public interest' (2012, p.18), is very clear in Singapore, and Singapore would easily compare favourably in most important categories with many Western countries.

But we will look at Mainland China generally, because this is what gives Confucianism its main global eminence, and because classical China was essentially Confucian (in spite of all nuances, including the important legacy of legalism and considerable variations of the domination of schools and religions over the centuries; on legalism versus Confucianism, see Tan 2011), just as Confucianism is essentially Chinese. Most importantly, however, for the reasons mentioned above, using China makes the non-Western alternative more obvious than any other country could demonstrate.

On the other hand, in many respects China is easy to present as an alternative to the Western way: classical China is no longer much of a 'hard sell' in the West. It hardly ever was, for those aware of the sophistication of the culture, perhaps even less than the legacy of Confucian thought, but, coupled with the economic and political eminence of China today, it is quite difficult, the more one knows, to relegate China to an inferior global position – let alone that of a 'developing country', and never mind the less than 250-year dip in dominance from which it has just emerged. If we look at the last period when China arguably 'led the world', its name-giver, the Qianlong emperor (1711–99), following great emperors as son and grandson, was not only seen as the most powerful, but also as the most wise, artistically gifted and last but not least just ruler of his time, even by many in the West (see Elliott 2009; Berliner et al. 2010).

For PA specifically, it is worth recalling the features in which China was clearly leading. We can assume that the modern state itself started in China and not in the West (Fukuyama 2011, p.18); that this is a state understood very differently from the Western model (Jacques 2011) makes it even more interesting.

> China alone created a modern state in the terms defined by Max Weber. That is, China succeeded in developing a centralized, uniform system of bureaucratic administration that was capable of governing a huge population and territory ... China had already invented a system of impersonal, merit-based bureaucratic recruitment that was far more systematic than Roman public administration. (Fukuyama 2011, p.21; see Jacques 2011, p.2)

And this state was enormously successful – so successful that it was not challenged until the mid-nineteenth century as regards organization (Fukuyama 2011, p.93). 'It is safe to say that the Chinese invented modern bureaucracy, that is, a permanent administrative cadre selected on the basis of ability rather than kinship or patrimonial connection' (ibid., p.113). What is hard to fathom, even for someone with a Weberian or

French-style *étatiste* background, is the importance the state and thus PA had in the people's mind and understanding – something that is, though in weaker form, still present in all Confucian countries today.

At the core of the Chinese PA system is the Imperial civil service – and, as the Qianlong emperor used to say, and as we now again realize, 'There is no governing by laws; there is only governing by people' (Elliott 2009, p. 152). This is a Confucian point: 'In Confucian political philosophy, it is more important to have virtuous people in government than to have a good system of laws' (Tan 2011, p. 470; see *passim*). The – not always positive, but generally very respected – image of the Chinese civil servant lives on in his specific Western designation, 'Mandarin', a term that also entered Western PA parlance for its own independent, highly competent scholar-bureaucrat, especially in the Anglo-American context, generally – until very recently – with a slightly negative if awe-inspiring connotation ('Sir Humphrey Appleby').

As economic history and to some extent the present show, the dominance of the civil service in the economy was not harmful to the economy, nor to technological innovation – maybe because innovation flourishes best within a regulated framework rather than in a free-for-all situation, although how one judges that depends on one's own economic faith. And that even pertains to creativity in the wider sense – MacGregor (2011), in the context of describing the creation of a Han Dynasty lacquer cup, even speaks of Chinese Imperial 'bureaucracy as a guarantee of beauty' (p. 219; see Tan 2008a on the general cliché of anti-creative Confucianism and how to overcome it).

The civil service was created by the famous civil-service exam, the longest-continuing PA exam or probably educational institution generally in the history of humankind and the first large-scale competence-based test for anything, which was abolished in 1904, after altogether 13 centuries, 'in the name of "Westernization"' (Elman 2000, p. xxxv; see Miyazaki 1981, p. 125; in modified form, however, it lives on, for example, in the Taiwanese Examination Yuan and its Civil Service Examination; see Jan 2010). The civil-service exam largely consisted of a very open written exam, radically narrowing the group in different stages, which entailed the formal discussion of the great Confucian classics; it remained largely stable over the centuries and is thus often seen as too formal and abstract. (On the exam, see briefly and accessibly Miyazaki 1981; also now Elman 2000, with a strong sociological bias.)

How important the civil-service exam was in China can be seen from the high esteem in which it, and success in it, was held in Chinese life. This is because becoming a civil servant was simply the highest position one could aspire to – 'the one and only career that mattered in imperial

China' (Elliott 2009, p. 4), one that granted prestige and wealth both to the individual and to his family, even to his place of origin. That the examination was done with the personal involvement of the emperor himself, who personally graded the final top essays (see Miyazaki 1981, pp. 81–3), unthinkable in the West, shows its centrality in the state system and the esteem in which the process, and thus civil-service selection, was held.

And the exam had its very good sides: it objectivized and was much better than nothing; it was a meritocratic test and thus potentially the only way to counteract the nepotism that has always been seen as a problem in China and that is, so to speak, a collateral of strong family ties, which in turn is one of the deciding features of the Chinese context. As Fukuyama says, 'the natural human propensity to favour family and friends – something I refer to as patrimonialism – constantly reasserts itself in the absence of countervailing incentives' (2011, p. 17; see Michels 1911, pp. 13–14). In China, this seems to be the case more than elsewhere – today especially as compared to the West. The standard canon also means that passing the exam was possible by everyone, at least in principle (meritocracy is a Confucian virtue; Suleski 2008, p. 256); it contributed to the state being perceived as an 'us' and not a 'them'; in its objective continuity and transparency, it communicated that the process and thus the state was basically not corrupt; and last but not least, it meant that there was no recruitment problem for the Chinese civil service, on which the country so much depended.

If there had to be standard texts on which to base the exam, the neo-Confucian *Four Books* was not the worst choice. The potentially quite subversive nature of these texts in respect of any oppressive, irresponsible regime is very clear even for the casual reader – especially in Mencius, the second-generation Confucian who focused more than the Master on 'the individual's role in society' (Suleski 2008, p. 259) and thus also in governance and PA (see Gardner 2007 for a useful selection; regarding Mencius, first of all Book 1B6, 1B8 [Mencius 2008, pp. 24, 26]; Suleski 2008, pp. 259–62).

This reflects, not coincidentally but precisely, the strong Chinese tradition, at the very core of Confucianism, that the ruler must deliver, that is procure, at least peace and food for his people – if not, he does not have the 'Mandate of Heaven' (that is the significance of this concept) and can be replaced, even legitimately killed (see MacGregor 2011, p. 151 for a nutshell definition, and the Mencius references above). Further, 'though not commonly practiced, the Chinese, including many Confucians over the centuries, have had the ideal that when the "son of heaven" breaks a law, he should be punished in the same way as the common people' (Tan 2011, p. 472). That the bureaucracy actually shared the power, in a sense, of the emperor and the court (Cheung 2010, pp. 38–40), and that, over time, ministerial councils established themselves and bureaucratized decision-making (Bartlett 1991, esp. pp. 270–78) is neither surprising nor specific – it is what one would expect in any PA context. 'This was the essence of Confucianism: . . . This moral system was institutionalized in a complex bureaucracy whose internal rules strictly limited the degree to which emperors, whose authority was theoretically unlimited, could act' (Fukuyama 2012, p. 19).

Corruption, as was mentioned, has always been an issue in China, and remains so (Osnos 2012 is a good example; see also Fukuyama 2012, pp. 20–21); it is often seen as one of the main obstacles to effective party rule and thus governance of China today. And while corruption is a cultural–contextual phenomenon, the definition of which cannot be easily transferred from one paradigm to another (cf. Urinboyev 2011; Wade 2013), and while, again, in China it is partially the dark side of close family ties, corruption as such is by definition a problem, because it means that things are not done as they should be done. But it is a problem that permeates all PA systems, and those we think of as historically particularly non-corrupt – the Venetian Republic, Prussia around 1900 – had to pay a price for it. The point in our context is that corruption in China is not something that has just been noted from the outside; it has always been recognized as an issue, and thus it is something that can be managed and contained from the inside, both regarding equity and performance, ethics and mechanics – the civil-service exam being the primary example. Introducing a system that would just 'outlaw' family responsibility would hardly be very promising.

In spite of all tradition and tradition-mindedness of which classical China has so often been accused, not least by its own Young Turks, as in all PA paradigms, PA reform is a red ribbon going through Chinese history. Wang Anshi (1021–86), well known as one of the greatest statesmen of classical China and one of the leading neo-Confucians, with his 1058 *Wan Yan Shu* (*Memorandum of a Myriad Words*; 1935), is one of the first public management authors in the modern sense, if not the first. This is so because Wang addresses current concerns of the civil service – selection, training, motivation, remuneration – often by presenting solutions that are completely in line with today's perspective, discussing questions, *inter alia* of performance pay, benchmarking and managerial trust. But this text is a PA reform programme, including large segments criticizing the too impractical civil-service exam. Many of Wang's changes were implemented, many rolled back, as is usual in PA reform. For the current general argument, it is especially important that he presents an excellent corpus of neo-Confucian PA, mostly human resource management, on a theoretically justified, empirically sound, and realistic, contextualized level that penetrates all three spheres of good PA mentioned above (Drechsler 2013c).

But finally, how important is Confucianism in China today? Is it the key to understanding the country or just folklore for ill-informed Westerners? Is there even something we can call Confucianism, or are there so many interpretations and hybrids that we cannot responsibly even use the label? 'If one understands Confucianism as a broad stream of thought to which numerous individuals have contributed by studying the writings associated with the tradition, thinking about Confucius' teachings in relation to important problems, and using them as a guide in life' (Tan 2008b, p. 140), then there certainly is. On a second level, 'the significance of Confucius's teaching can perhaps be best seen in its unconscious manifestation in Chinese society today' (Jones 2008, p. xix); 'for many, many Chinese, the Confucianism they adhere to is an inarticulate Confucianism' (Suleski 2008, p. 281).

The scope of Confucianism for current Chinese governance is perhaps best symbolized by the Confucius statue in, or near, Tiananmen Square. Facetiously speaking, sometimes it is there in front of the new museum, sometimes inside in a courtyard; it depends which faction in the government is exercising its will at the moment, and for some old-line communists, Confucius is still reactionary and even anathema (Siemons 2010, 2011; Fähnders 2011). The real Westernizers do not like him very much either, and never did – Max Weber, the most important public administration scholar ever, belonged to those who blamed, and continue to blame, China's 'backwardness' on his 'reactionary' philosophy (1986, pp. 430–58).

But importantly, there is a sufficiently cohesive 'third' intellectual movement in China and also beyond, usually and best called new Confucianism (to differentiate it from the millennium-old neo-Confucianism; like all such movements, naturally, books about how cohesive it actually is abound, or at least exist). New Confucianism emerged as a 'conservative' reaction to Chinese modernization in the early twentieth century and moved to the Chinese diaspora after the communist takeover – Hong Kong and Taiwan first of all; also, regarding theory, the USA; and, because of its practice, later increasingly Singapore. It has been gaining in importance in Mainland Chinese academe, society and certainly also in governance, including politics during the last two decades, probably not least because of the rapprochement with Taiwan and the re-inclusion of Hong Kong. New Confucianism is the main intellectual worldview that makes Confucianism applicable, and applies it to Chinese individual life, society and state today, and it entails a response to the West, with the idea that learning should go both ways (Tan 2008b, p. 142; generally, see 2008b, esp. pp. 141–53, as an overall introduction; Bell 2010 is excellent as regards governance). In that sense, it may be the most convincing alternative to the 'consumerist patriotism' (Zarrow 2008, p. 44; see Suleski 2008, pp. 270–71) that is more or less the quasi-official line of Chinese development today.

As regards the aforementioned, allegedly untimely anti-creativity, anti-economic aspect of Confucianism, as we have seen, the achievement of bureaucracy in neo-Confucianism is inextricably linked with (economic) performance, that is, output orientation, and that remains very strong in Mainland China, certainly at the local level (Fukuyama 2012, p. 22), maybe – as most non-Chinese China observers would probably argue – even too strong.[11] What new Confucianism, neo-Confucianism and Confucianism (at least in the Mencian version) certainly (try to) create is what Mahbubani has credited, in his comments on Fukuyama, the civil service of Singapore with: it 'has performed brilliantly . . . because it has imbibed a culture which focuses the minds of civil servants on improving the livelihood of Singaporeans' (2013b; cf. Louie 2008, p. 13, on China).

Nonetheless, what can be said is that the relevance of Confucian governance in Mainland China, as well as in all the Confucian countries of Asia, is infinitely larger than that of Confucian PA as embodied by, for instance, Wang Anshi. However, there is no reason for Confucian PA not to be rediscovered and redeployed. A convincing narrative can certainly be developed from a genuine basis, and from a practice that in many respects is quite close to it – a living legacy, so to speak, that needs only to rediscover its own theory. The dynamics of global as well as local circumstances surely appear to point in this direction.

Islamic Public Administration or Ottoman Public Administration

Even more immediate in Europe, and that means towards the traditional and maybe also future core of the West (see Kimmage 2013) is Islamic PA and governance, because of both legacy and presence, although it is *prima facie* less convincing an alternative than its Chinese or Confucian counterpart. And yet, although a significant part of Europe shares an Islamic, and that means Ottoman, PA legacy, studying the context and practice of Islamic PA in this region is almost totally neglected. If it is mentioned, then usually Islamic times and institutions, indeed the entire context, are seen as obstacles to modern PA and to Europeanization, as stumbling blocks on the way to good PA; usually, they are dismissed in a cavalier footnote (Drechsler 2013b).

Ironically, for those who see a relevant topic here: as with Confucianism, yet even more strongly, the first question raised is: is there such a thing as Islamic PA; is it not already Orientalism to suggest that there might be? Experts are split on this issue, and many good reasons argue against describing as Islamic anything except Islam itself.[12] We could bypass this issue elegantly by addressing only Ottoman PA in the current context. And yet, for our current concern, the third paradigm of PA and govern-ance, and to show the uniqueness and specific quality of Islamic PA, to first talk about Islam as such might do less harm than good because of its larger scope and, if to a lesser extent, because of its applicability to the non-Ottoman sphere.

One aspect that argues for Islamic PA as such is that the people in the Islamic countries themselves would overwhelmingly say that Islam – Islam as such, whatever their own tradition – matters, and that it matters very much – often to the chagrin of Western observers who want to bring Western-style democracy to these countries and then note that elec-tion victories go to Islamic parties, not to people who think as they do (cf. Lerch 2012; Bauer 2011, pp. 401–4). The hypothesis would thus be that Islam – being such a strong determinant of context, of the world in which people live and of the systems that they build there and that emerge – has had, and still has, a non-incidental, important and actually crucial impact on how the public sphere is organized and managed. Thus one of the most important variables for PA – not just governance – in Islamic countries would probably be Islam, not just the national tradition, even (albeit less so) if the society in question is quite secular.

Regarding the substance of Islamic PA and governance, there is cer-tainly a large traditional and still viable literature on the governance aspect. For instance, Nizām al-Mulk (1018–92) and his *Siyāsatnāma* (*The Book of Government*) (1960) present us with a specific, workable concept of state administration that may be as different from the usual Western recommendations for improving the governance of the Central Asian and Middle Eastern countries as it may be superior in realism and applicabil-ity. One important example regarding both equity and performance is the strong emphasis on the absolute non-delegatability of responsibility for those over whom one rules (1960, II, IV, VI). This was seen as a key feature also of Islamic PA, even in the West, for many centuries, although today it is generally forgotten (cf. Hebel in Stolleis 2003, pp. 81–5). Its importance today lies in creating direct responsibility of the ruler for his subjects, crucial for him and his record, and for how he will be judged. The idea is the same as in Confucianism: 'an ethical doctrine designed to moderate the behaviour of rulers and orient them towards the interest of the ruled' (Fukuyama 2012, p. 19).

For the purposes of this chapter, however, I will now focus specifically on the Ottoman Empire, although this is a somewhat historical institution.

But only somewhat: even beyond the current search for potentiality, Ottoman PA as Islamic PA is a central PA narrative that is about history, but not in itself historical at all (cf. Sindbaeck and Hartmuth 2011). And there are many good reasons for this: because of its centrality for much of what is now a Western region (CEE), especially in its Western Muslim part, but also in the countries it formerly fought and often conquered, such as Hungary or Romania; because of its sophistication in PA and public policy, especially on the practical level; because its successor, modern Turkey, is again becoming, or actually has become, the power-house in the former Imperial region (see Aras 2012) and is to a large extent the main carrier country of Islamic PA; because of the centuries-long, at best questionable, track record of Westernization as well as Western inter-ventionism in the region and in Turkey itself (see Schulz 2011, esp. p. 487); and also because today's radical Islamicism is to a large extent based on a fundamentalist movement against the Ottomans (see Kadri 2011, pp. 123–5; Finkel 2007, pp. 411–12; for the opposite of a radical Islamic theology, see Khorchide 2012).

Especially in the last decade or two, the Ottoman Empire has been reassessed by historians and sociologists as 'not so bad' in many ways, quite contrary to the clichés that various legacies – self-interested, more often than not – have so far promulgated (see, e.g., Finkel 2007). And these reassessments have occasionally included governance (see, e.g., Barkey 2008; Hanioğlu 2008). To use Weber's words, ironically enough, the Sultan's rule was not 'sultanistic', a form of rule that is '*nicht sachlich ratio-nalisiert, sondern es ist in ihr nur die Sphäre der freien Willkür und Gnade ins Extrem entwickelt*' (not objectively rationalized, but the sphere of arbitrari-ness and grace is developed here to an extreme) (Weber 1922, p. 134; and see pp. 133–4; Chehabi and Linz 1998, pp. 4–7). In addition, shifts in how we see governance and PA generally have also contributed to new pos-sibilities in assessing Osmanian rule and administration. Merilee Grindle's concept of 'good enough governance' (2004, 2007; see de Vries 2013a for a PA perspective) is one of the most important ones in this context, underlin-ing that, very often, governance is about achieving minimal workability of a system against the odds of heavy policy constraints.

Like its Chinese counterpart, Ottoman PA was constantly under reform, too – perennially modernizing at least since the late eighteenth century (see Findley 1980; Heper 2001, esp. pp. 1021–2) – and perhaps the ideal case study for such an effort under such circumstances. The key Westernizing variant of this modernization effort, known as the Tanzimat reforms or the Tanzimat era (1839–76), was, however, also a reaction to Western pressure, which partially contributed to its illegitimacy in the eyes of many citizens (Ansary 2009, pp. 285–8). Thus to see the successor paradigm, Hamidism (1876–1908), the governance reforms and reactions to exterior and interior pressure by the last powerful sultan, Abdülhamid II, as a less Western but more contextual form of modernization (see Hanioğlu 2008, pp. 123–9; Finkel 2007, pp. 488–501) is one of the more recent and controversial trends in Ottoman governance re-evaluation and, I think, very likely correct (to be 'controversial', after all, is a good thing). (Examples include the refocus on the sultan's role as caliph, the dexterous use of media and communication technology, the emphasis on personal loyalty and the purposeful creation of the ideology of Ottomanism; see Haslip 1973 [1958]; and, generally, Reinkowski 2005, pp. 14–29).

These newly apparent aspects of the Ottoman Empire, however, have not yet made it into PA history, let alone PA studies generally. To the contrary: basically, as mentioned earlier, the Ottoman and thus Islamic legacy is always seen as bad, because the fight against the Ottomans is an – often the central – identity-creating myth of many CEE countries. Differences in administrative and life quality are still accounted for today by saying that one part was Western and the other Turkish (cf. Sindbaeck and Hartmuth 2011, pp. 1, 5).

In addition, Islamic–Ottoman PA shares with Confucian–Chinese PA two crucial features for re-evaluation today, one for and one against: its promotion primarily via the economic success of the main carrier country; and its less than complete enthusiasm for this legacy by the elites in that country. Among the three main intellectually significant Turkish political groupings, extreme Westernizers, Kemalite modernizers and AKP followers, praise of the governance aspects of the Ottoman Empire, let alone of Hamidism, usually meets with incredulity at best. And, while there are some tendencies to a re-evaluation of Ottoman history as such among the latter group (cf. briefly Bilefsky 2012; Reinkowski 2011), current Turkish PA and PA reform is not Ottoman at all – structurally, it is basically still Kemalite with the AKP reform efforts on top, to the extent that they are geared towards modernization (whether in the sense of 'reactionary modernism' or not), following old-fashioned NPM tenets (see Filkins 2012, esp. p. 43; Tuğal 2009, pp. 55–6; Sezen 2011, esp. p. 339).[13]

Principally, however, Turkey is an example of the 'three paradigms' model in practice. In spite of the 2013 crackdowns on the Taksim Square/ Gezi Park demonstrations against the Erdoğan-AKP government, seen as undemocratic and un-Western by many observers from the West and beyond, although the prime minister, while losing popularity, was seen as potentially winning re-election should there be an election at that stage (cf., e.g., *New York Times* 2013; Peter 2013), Istanbul remains the largest, most dynamic and most innovative city in Europe. Indeed, it is one of the three largest municipalities in the world (a fact rarely realized in the West), and the Turkish economic miracle only occurred after post-Ottoman Kemalism was realigned with Islam (see Lerch 2012; Gülen 2012; Tuğal 2009). The Islamic–Ottoman case is weaker than the Confucian-Chinese one, however, because, first, Turkey is not as directly the successor of the Ottoman Empire as today's China is of Confucianism, and, second, beyond folklore and imagery, there is very little of a serious, intellectual 'new Ottoman' movement in Turkey and among Turks as compared to new Confucianism.

So why would this case be important? The reassessment of the Ottoman Empire is an ideal case study of the potential policy relevance of what looks like merely a shift in academic conceptualization. Once we appreciate that Constantinople had and has a legacy in the governance and PA of CEE that may be different from others, but not necessarily worse, this may eventually give the Muslim-majority Balkan countries a freer hand to deal with the possibilities of PA development towards genuine modernization. In her excellent case study of Albania, Cecilie Endresen has shown how a positive Ottoman discourse can and does legitimize even global-Western-style progress (2011, pp. 48–50).

Of course, such a way of thinking comes with costs. For Europe and PA, it goes against the principles of the European administrative space; it goes against the mind-set that still, even from a liberal and not just from a right-wing perspective, defines Europe as 'non-Turkey' (see Böckenförde 2011). It is clear that the Turkish government's handling of the Taksim Square demonstrations has brought this sentiment to the forefront of the European *juste milieu* once again, to the point of wanting to exclude Turkey from the Europe of the EU (see, e.g., Bilefsky 2013; Martens 2013). And that is the general tradition, of course: not only CEE, but also Europe as such is historically often defined by the struggle against the Turks, and against Islam generally, and this 'othering' continues with a vengeance. The Ottomans are still the 'quintessentially other', and Muslims, it sometimes seems, as well – not only in Europe, but in the West generally, especially in the last decade or so, from 9/11 to the Boston Marathon bombings of 2013.

There is one ironic yet profound effect, however, of defining Europe, and by extension the West, by excluding and contrasting it with Turkey, the Ottoman Empire and Islam: if this is so, then surely it is much more likely that there is indeed something like non-Western and something we can call Islamic PA, because there must then be something specifically Western, rather than global, in our current system. And that, in turn, does much to confirm the three paradigms thesis, and thus the feasibility of NWPA.

WHAT IS WESTERN?

To sum up, the question here is: do we arrive more easily at good, meaning effective, PA if we realize that there are different contexts and thus, potentially at least, different ways to it; indeed, are there legitimately different goals? If we condemn certain places, as is so often the case, for not living up to the standards of globalized–Western PA, is this necessarily the problem of the countries in question, or might it also be the problem of asking the wrong questions and setting the wrong targets? This is where the debate on goals (point C above) comes in, and it is a hard one inasmuch as telling non-Western nations that freedom and democracy, Western-style, are not for them because they have their own traditions may be as wrong, and indeed as post-colonialist, as trying to impose Western values, by calling them human, global or universal, on others. This is a debate that is nowhere near resolved.

However, it is easier to discuss this matter in PA, ironically because, here, the debate basically does not happen – in PA, as I have pointed out, the discussion begins and ends with an unjustified, tacit, implicit assumption in favour of the global-Western solution, and that, again, works only as long as this solution is clearly superior, both in ethics and in performance. Yet, even if this were the case, this should give PA scholarship reason for doubt, this being the nature of scholarship; but right now, when dusk seems to settle (perhaps for real, perhaps just due to some temporary darkness), the Owl of Minerva may again spread her wings more easily. What the current situation implies is that simple assumptions, intellectually and policy-wise, are clearly no longer good enough. The Confucian challenge to the global-Western model, to seek 'harmony over freedom, consensus over choice, intimacy over integrity, and communitarianism over individualism' (Jones 2008, p.ix), is a choice that can and may be contested. But can it still be cavalierly dismissed, especially when those who do the dismissing are really no longer cavaliers, or indeed, if the age of cavaliers is coming to an end?

This is all the more important if we look at the context of development. The Western countries were, until very recently, undoubtedly more successful, which means that the non-Western ones were, and to a great extent still are, less successful and, thus, in need of development. The fact that administrative capacity, institutionally as well as personally, is a *conditio sine qua non* for development is clear (Nurkse 1952, 1964; see Drechsler 2009a). That too many developing countries do not have it, yet need it – indeed that this could even define 'developing' (whatever that means) – is likewise obvious (cf. http://www.unpan.org/, if only for the problem, not necessarily for the remedy). This changed for the reasons mentioned above, especially in the context of the emergence of the non-Western 'tigers' and the re-entry into the West, even into the EU, of some countries that one would have to call 'developing' by several criteria. In addition, these days many of us see that

> problems of implementation are at the root of poor economic and social outcomes all over the world. Governments routinely fail to deliver basic services like education, health, security, macroeconomic stability, or fail to deliver them in a timely, impartial, and cost-effective manner. This is as true of the United States as of any developing country. (Fukuyama 2013b; see also Mahbubani 2013b)

Now, one could interpret it either way: developing countries do not have sufficient administrative capacity and thus need to be motivated or forced to move towards global-Western public administration, or – either for now or in general – developing countries, seeing that this ostensibly does not work (in many places at least) or that it may not even be necessary or desirable, need to develop optimal capacity according to their own governance system and general context. And what speaks for the latter, even if one believes in common goals, is that the track record of Westernization, especially of Islamic countries, and societies, in PA and otherwise, has not exactly been universally excellent. As pointed out above, in PA today, this is even more the case because the goals of good global-Western PA are moving as well.

But even if we pursue global-Western values, should we not at least look into whether they are perhaps global but not exclusively Western, and whether they could not just be promulgated in a way that is easier to swallow than Western triumphalism, especially as the present makes the latter sound quite hollow (cf. Steiner et al. 2007, pp. 517–40; Maier 1997, pp. 48–50)? In other words, should we not ask whether different narratives are possible, even if we believe in common goals and even some common best practices?

And yet, in the end, we will always return to the question: is it not a betrayal of humankind, especially of that outside the West, to even question the universality of ethical goals, and of all the great Western accomplishments such as 'separation of power, sovereignty of the people, representative democracy' (Winkler 2011; cf. Diamond 2013)? Is it true that part of the Western legacy is to absolutize oneself and proclaim the universality of one's achievements? As we have seen, and as can be observed daily, in too many places this leads to inverted, paradoxical results; there is more than just a whiff of post-colonialism in this position; and to question oneself is not only, but decidedly, Western, as is trying to understand the other, at least as an initial move.

To allow different places and different narratives is, I think, in the end more Western than not to do so. And whatever the possible outcome of the general debate, in PA this debate is generally not even taking place. Therefore, regarding international PA, following the governance discourse, the truly Western position right now, and the heuristically best position for non-Western stakeholders as well, is to question the orthodoxy that global = Western = good, and to discuss what the NWPA alternatives, regarding both goals and performance, are or could be – in other words, whether one can progress towards the good at least via different paths and perhaps even with different goals, rather than via one way to one destination only.

ACKNOWLEDGEMENTS

This chapter develops Drechsler (2013a), and thus many passages have been incorporated. For friendly review of the current version, I thank Rainer Kattel, Olga Mikheeva and Ingbert Edenhofer.

NOTES

1. By 'West' and 'Western', I mean Europe, North America, and Australia and New Zealand, with its Greco-Christian-Enlightenment-Scientism legacy plus both production and consumer capitalism.
2. *Lebenswelt*, 'life-world', in the sense of the existence of the human person in a phenomenological, Continental-idealist or semiotic sense, is 'the sum of non-inheritable information' (Lotman 1971, p. 167) in which individual persons, and by extension groups of persons, live by their own, however evolving and latent, self-definition, and through which they operate – what defines people is what they let define them. According to Nicolai Hartmann (who talks about *Geist*, which arguably is the manifestation of context), 'Nobody invents his own language, creates his own science; the individual, rather, grows into what is existing, he takes it over from the common sphere, which offers it to him' (1949, p. 460; for a general philosophical discussion of this question, see Drechsler 1997, pp. 67–9).
3. That the most serious external challenges to the view that universal human rights are at least to some extent a Western construct, legacy or view (Kühnhardt 1987, p. 301: 'The human rights topos in the sense of inviolable and innate human rights is not part of the inventory of the history of ideas of non-Western political thinking') comes mainly from Chinese and Islamic sides is *prima facie* hardly grounds for dismissal.
4. But see also Raadschelders (2013, p. 218); on Governance, see Drechsler 2004; and critically about this discussion, Hajnal and Pál 2013.
5. Fukuyama discusses 'procedural measures, input measures, output measures, and measures of bureaucratic autonomy' (2013a, p. 5; see pp. 5–13 for the discussion), suggesting, partially, for reasons of measurability, as a result an optimal combination of autonomy and quality of governance (= administrative capacity) (pp. 11–16).
6. Cf. however Fukuyama (2012, p. 24), where he states that the connection between democracy and bureaucratic quality (in this case, in East Asia) has not yet been sufficiently studied.

7. The usual contenders would be Russian/Soviet, Hispanic/Latin, Indian or Japanese PA (see also Painter and Peters 2010, pp. 19–30). Even though this will not be acceptable to all readers, I will suggest that the first three are basically Western; the last is partially Chinese, partially Western.
8. Going beyond these, see Painter and Peters (2010, pp. 3–16, 237); Yesilkagit (2010), with a very nice heuristic distinction between legacy ideas and legacy structures.
9. A parallel is the European countries, which some ten or 15 years ago were still judged according to how close they were 'already' to the New Public Management (NPM) (a good example is Bossaert and Demmke 2003), but which, according to Pollitt and Bouckaert (2004), did not follow the NPM at all but rather their own, perhaps even (and in my opinion certainly) better, model, that of the Neo-Weberian state (NWS) (see ibid., pp. 99–100). Observing this phenomenon gave rise to the concept of the NWS to begin with, which later partially transformed from an empirical to a normative model (see Drechsler and Kattel 2009).
10. *Public Administration Review* (2010), in spite of much sophistication of some of the contributions, and recently Gulrajani and Moloney (2012), basically make this point, both for science and for policy; the latter also provides a handy summary of the theory and practice of comparative 'third-world' PA scholarship during the last few decades from an Anglo-American mainstream perspective.
11. It is interesting that Fukuyama dismisses output measures because they are complex and difficult to measure (2013, pp. 8–9); however, this is valid only for (precisely, 'scientific') measurement, not for the criterion as such. Therefore, though coming from another perspective, Christopher Pollitt has pointed out 'the magnitude of the loss if one abandons any attempts to measure the impact of government actions and settles for just input and process matters' (2013).
12. For example, Thomas Bauer has recently attacked this position with verve as an 'Islamicization of Islam', as pretty much the root, and a primary tool, of all evil in misunderstanding both Islam and the countries where this is the predominant faith (2011, esp. pp. 192–223).
13. Even Arab PA, that is, PA as practised and discussed in the countries of the Arabian peninsula, where much of the funding to promote Islam globally comes from and which, partly for this reason, and partly because it is the place of origin and thus the original context of Islam, dominates both Islamic discourse and the perception of Islam in the West, is largely Westernized today, as opposed to the culture and governance discourse. For a recent snapshot, see the programme and abstracts of the IIAS-IASIA joint congress in Bahrain in June 2013, http://iias-iasia-congress2013.org/.

REFERENCES

Note: Pure web-based information is not repeated here; all websites are valid as of 1 July 2013.

Andrews, M. (2013), *The Limits of Institutional Reform in Development: Changing Rules for Realistic Solutions*, Cambridge: Cambridge University Press.

Ansary, T. (2009), *Destiny Disrupted: A History of the Islamic World through Islamic Eyes*, New York: Public Affairs.

Aras, B. (2012), 'Turkey and the Balkans: new policy in a changing regional environment', *German Marshall Fund on Turkey Analysis*, 31 October.

Barkey, K. (2008), *Empire of Difference: The Ottomans in Comparative Perspective*, Cambridge: Cambridge University Press.

Bartlett, B.S. (1991), *Monarchs and Ministers: The Grand Council in Mid-Ch'ing China, 1723–1820*, Berkeley, CA: University of California Press.

Bauer, T. (2011), *Die Kultur der Ambiguität: Eine andere Geschichte des Islam*, Berlin: Verlag der Weltreligionen/Insel.

Bell, D.A. (2010), *China's New Confucianism: Politics and Everyday Life in a Changing Society*, 4th edn, Princeton, NJ etc.: Princeton University Press.

Bell, D.A. (2011), 'Singapore: the city of nation building', in D.A. Bell and A. de-Shalit (eds), *The Spirit of Cities: Why the Identity of a City Matters in a Global Age*, Princeton, NJ: Princeton University Press, pp. 78–110.

Berliner, N. with Mark C. Elliott and Liu Chang, Yuan Hongqi, and Henry Tzu Ng (eds) (2010), *The Emperor's Private Paradise: Treasures from the Forbidden City*, New Haven, CT and London: Peabody Essex Museum/Yale University Press.

Berman, E.M. (2010), 'Public Administration in East Asia: Common Roots, Ways and Tasks', in E.M. Berman, M. Jae Moon and Heungsuk Choi (eds), *Public Administration in East Asia: Mainland China, Japan, South Korea, Taiwan*, Boca Raton, FL: CRC Press, pp. 2–32.

Bilefsky, D. (2012), 'As if the Ottoman period never ended', *The New York Times*, 29 October.

Bilefsky, D. (2013), 'A potential casualty of Turkey's crackdown: European Union membership', *The New York Times*, 13 June.

Böckenförde, W. (2011), 'Europa und die Türkei [2005]', in *Wissenschaft, Politik, Verfassungsgericht*, Berlin: Suhrkamp, pp. 281–98.

Bossaert, D. and C. Demmke (2003), *Civil Service in the Accession States: New Trends and the Impact of the Integration Process*, Maastricht: EIPA.

Boyer, R. (1994), 'The convergence thesis revisited: globalization but still the century of nations?', in S. Berger and R. Dore (eds), *National Diversity and Global Capitalism*, Ithaca, NY: Cornell University Press, pp. 29–59.

Buruma, I. and A. Margalit (2004), *Occidentalism: A Short History of Anti-Westernism*, London: Atlantic Books.

Chehabi, H.E. and J.J. Linz (1998), 'A theory of sultanism 1: a type of nondemocratic rule', in H.E. Chehabi and J.J. Linz (eds), *Sultanistic Regimes*, Baltimore, MD: Johns Hopkins University Press, pp. 3–25.

Cheung, A.B.L. (2010), 'Checks and balances in China's administrative traditions: a preliminary assessment', in M. Painter and B.G. Peters (eds), *Tradition and Public Administration*, Basingstoke: Palgrave Macmillan, pp. 31–43.

Christensen, T. and P. Lægreid (2013), 'Performance and accountability – a theoretical discussion and an empirical assessment', Uni Rokkan Centre Working Paper 3/2013.

Christensen, T. Lisheng Dong, Martin Painter and Richard M. Walker (2012), 'Imitating the West? Evidence on administrative reform from the upper echelons of Chinese provincial government', *Public Administration Review*, **72** (6), 798–806.

De Vries, Michiel (2013a), 'The challenge of good governance', *The Innovation Journal: The Public Sector Innovation Journal*, **18** (1).

De Vries, Michiel (2013b), 'Out of the box: CEE and CA transitions and PA paradigms', in M. Vintar, Allan Rosenbaum, György Jenei and Wolfgang Drechsler (eds), *The Past, Present and Future of Public Administration in Central and Eastern Europe: Twenty Years of NISPAcee, 1992–2012*, Bratislava: NISPAcee Press, pp. 108–24.

Diamond, L. (2013), 'Why wait for democracy?', *The Wilson Quarterly*, Winter.

Drechsler, W. (1997), 'On German *Geist*', *Trames*, **1** (2), 65–77.

Drechsler, W. (2004), 'Governance, good governance, and government: the case for Estonian administrative capacity', *Trames*, **8** (4), 388–96.

Drechsler, W. (2009a), 'Towards the law & economics of development: Ragnar Nurkse (1907–1959)', *European Journal of Law and Economics*, **28** (1), 19–37.

Drechsler, W. (2009b), 'The rise and demise of the New Public Management: lessons and opportunities for South East Europe', *Uprava – Administration*, **7** (3), 7–27.

Drechsler, W. (2009c), 'Towards a neo-Weberian European Union? Lisbon Agenda and public administration', *Haldus-kultuur – Administrative Culture*, **10**, 6–21.

Drechsler, W. (2011), 'Public administration in times of crisis', in R. Kattel, Witold Mikulowski and B. Guy Peters (eds), *Public Administration in Times of Crisis*, Bratislava: NISPAcee Press, pp. 15–25.

Drechsler, W. (2013a), 'Three paradigms of governance and administration: Chinese, Western, and Islamic', *Society and Economy*, **35** (3), 319–42.

Drechsler, W. (2013b), '"Islamic" public administration: the missing dimension in NISPAcee public administration research?', in M. Vintar, Allan Rosenbaum, György Jenei and Wolfgang Drechsler (eds), *The Past, Present and Future of Public Administration in Central and Eastern Europe: Twenty Years of NISPAcee, 1992–2012*, Bratislava: NISPAcee Press, pp. 57–76.

Drechsler, W. (2013c), 'Wang Anshi and the origins of modern public management in Song Dynasty China', *Public Money and Management*, **33** (5), 353–60.

Drechsler, W. and R. Kattel (2009), 'Conclusion: towards the neo-Weberian state? Perhaps, but certainly adieu, NPM!', *The NISPAcee Journal of Public Administration and Policy*, **1** (2), 95–9.

Elliott, M. (2009), *Emperor Qianlong: Son of Heaven, Man of the World*, New York: Longman.

Elman, B.A. (2000), *A Cultural History of Civil Examinations in Late Imperial China*, Berkeley, CA: University of California Press.

Endresen, C. (2011), 'Diverging images of Ottoman legacy in Albania', in T. Sindbaeck and M. Hartmuth (eds), *Images of Imperial Legacy: Modern Discourse on the Social and Cultural Impact of Ottoman and Habsburg Rule in Southeast Europe*, Münster: Lit, pp. 37–51.

Fähnders, T. (2011), 'Welcher Konfuzius darf es sein?', *Frankfurter Allgemeine Zeitung*, 1 April.

Filkins, D. (2012), 'The deep state. The prime minister is revered as a moderate, but how far will he go to stay in power?', *The New Yorker*, 12 March, 38–49.

Findley, C.V. (1980), *Bureaucratic Reform in the Ottoman Empire: The Sublime Porte, 1789–1922*, Princeton, NJ: Princeton University Press.

Finkel, C. (2007), *Osman's Dream: The Story of the Ottoman Empire 1300–1923*, New York: Basic Books.

Fukuyama, F. (2011), *The Origins of Political Order: From Prehuman Times to the French Revolution*, New York: Farrar, Straus and Giroux.

Fukuyama, F. (2012), 'The patterns of history', *Journal of Democracy*, **23** (1), 14–26.

Fukuyama, F. (2013a), 'What is governance?', Center for Global Development Working Paper 314, January. Also in *Governance*, **26** (3), 347–68.

Fukuyama, F. (2013b), 'Fukuyama replies', The GOVERNANCE blog, available at http://governancejournal.net.

Gardner, D.K. (ed.) (2007), *The Four Books: The Basic Teachings of the Later Confucian Tradition*, Indianapolis, IN: Hackett.

Grindle, M.S. (2004), 'Good enough governance: poverty reduction and reform in developing countries', *Governance*, **17** (4), 525–48.

Grindle, M.S. (2007), 'Good enough governance revisited', *Development Policy Review*, **25** (5), 533–74.

Gülen, F. (2012), 'Islam und Moderne stehen nicht im Widerspruch', interview with R. Hermann, *Frankfurter Allgemeine Zeitung*, 6 December.

Gulrajani, N. and K. Moloney (2012), 'Globalizing public administration: today's research and tomorrow's agenda', *Public Administration Review*, **72** (1), 78–86.

Hajnal, G. and G. Pál (2013), 'Some reflections on the Hungarian discourse on (good) governance', MTA TK Politikatudományi Intézet Working Papers in Political Science 2013/3.

Han, B.-C. (2012), *Transparenzgesellschaft*, Berlin: Matthes & Seitz.

Hanioğlu, M.Ş. (2008), *A Brief History of the Late Ottoman Empire*, Princeton, NJ: Princeton University Press.

Hartmann, N. (1949), 'Nikolai Hartmann', in *Philosophen-Lexikon: Handwörterbuch der Philosophie nach Personen*, 1, Berlin: de Gruyter, pp. 454–71.

Haslip, J. (1973 [1958]), *The Sultan: The Life of Abdul Hamid II*, London: Weidenfeld & Nicolson.

Heath, P. (ed.) (1974), *The Philosopher's Alice*, New York: St Martin's Press.

Heper, M. (2001), 'The state and bureaucracy: the Turkish case in historical perspective', in A. Farazmand (ed.), *Handbook of Comparative and Development Public Administration*, 2nd edn, New York: Dekker, pp. 1019–28.

Jacques, M. (2011), 'How China will change the way we think: the case of the state', TransAtlantic Academy Paper Series, February.

Jan, C.-Y. (2010), 'History and context of public administration in Taiwan', in E.M. Berman, M. Jae Moon and Heungsuk Choi (eds), *Public Administration in East Asia: Mainland China, Japan, South Korea, Taiwan*, Boca Raton, FL: CRC Press, pp. 497–516.

Jones, D. (ed.) (2008), *Confucius Now: Contemporary Encounters with the Analects*, Chicago and La Salle, IL: Open Court.

Kadri, S. (2011), *Heaven on Earth: A Journey Through Shari'a Law*, London: Bodley Head.

Khorchide, M. (2012), *Islam ist Barmherzigkeit: Grundzüge einer modernen Religion*, Freiburg: Herder.

Kimmage, M. (2013), 'The decline of the West: an American story', Transatlantic Academy Paper Series 2012–2013, 4.

Kühnhardt, L. (1987), *Die Universalität der Menschenrechte*, Bonn: BzfpB.

Lerch, W.G. (2012), 'Die Wende', *Frankfurter Allgemeine Zeitung*, 23 July.

Lord, Carnes (2003), *The Modern Prince: What Leaders Need to Know Now*, New Haven, CT and London: Yale University Press.

Lotman, J.M. (1971), 'Problema "obushenya kulture" kak yeo tipologisheskaya harakteris-tika', *Semeiotiké*, **5**, 167–76.

Louie, K. (ed.) (2008), *The Cambridge Companion to Modern Chinese Culture*, Cambridge: Cambridge University Press.

MacGregor, N. (2011), *A History of the World in 100 Objects*, London: Allen Lane.

Mahbubani, K. (2013a), *The Great Convergence: Asia, the West, and the Logic of One World*, New York: Public Affairs.

Mahbubani, K. (2013b), 'Reply to Fukuyama 2013a', The GOVERNANCE blog, available at http://governancejournal.net.

Maier, H. (1997), *Wie universal sind die Menschenrechte?* Freiburg: Herder.

Martens, M. (2013), 'Erdogans Kettenhund', *Frankfurter Allgemeine Zeitung*, 23 June.

Mencius (2008), *Mengzi: With Selections from Traditional Commentaries*. B.W. Van Norden (tr. and ed.). Indianapolis, IN: Hackett.

Michels, R. (1911), *Zur Soziologie des Parteiwesens in der Modernen Demokratie: Untersuchungen über die oligarchischen Tendenzen des Gruppenlebens*, Leipzig: Klinkhardt.

Miyazaki, I. (1981), *China's Examination Hell: The Civil Service Examinations of Imperial China*, New Haven, CT: Yale University Press.

New York Times (2013), 'Turkey in Turmoil' (editorial), 19 June.

Nizām al-Mulk (1960), *The Book of Government or Rules for Kings. Syiāsát-nāma or Siyar al-Mulk*. H. Drake (trans.), London: Routledge & Kegan Paul.

Nurkse, R. (1952), 'Trade fluctuations and buffer policies of low-income countries', *Kyklos* **12** (3), 141–54; Epilogue: 244–65.

Nurkse, R. (1964 [1953]), *Problems of Capital Formation in Underdeveloped Countries*, 9th impr., Oxford: Basil Blackwell.

Osnos, E. (2012), 'Boss Rail: the disaster that exposed the underside of the boom', *The New Yorker*, 22 October.

Painter, M. and B.G. Peters (eds) (2010), *Tradition and Public Administration*, Basingstoke: Palgrave Macmillan.

Peter, Tom A. (2013), 'Poll shows Erdogan's popularity has taken a hit: could he lose his mandate?', *The Christian Science Monitor*, 18 June.

Pollitt, C. (2013), 'Reply to Fukuyama 2013a', The GOVERNANCE blog, available at http://governancejournal.net.

Pollitt, C. and G. Bouckaert (2004), *Public Management Reform: A Comparative Analysis*, 2nd edn, Oxford: Oxford University Press.

Pollitt, C. and G. Bouckaert (2011), *Public Management Reform: A Comparative Analysis: New Public Management, Governance, and the Neo-Weberian State*, 3rd edn, Oxford: Oxford University Press.

Public Administration Review (2010), eds R. O'Leary and D.M. Van Slyke, *Special Issue on the Future of Public Administration in 2020*, **70** (Supplement s1).

Raadschelders, J.C.N. (2013), *Public Administration: The Interdisciplinary Study of Government*, Oxford: Oxford University Press.

Randma-Liiv, T. and R. Kruusenberg (2012), 'Policy transfer in immature policy environments: motives, scope, role models and agents', *Public Administration and Development*, **32** (2), 154–66.

Reinkowski, M. (2005), *Die Dinge der Ordnung: Eine vergleichende Untersuchung über die osmanische Reformpolitik im 19. Jahrhundert*, München: Oldenbourg.

Reinkowski, M. (2011), 'The Ottoman Empire and South Eastern Europe from a Turkish perspective', in T. Sindbaeck and M. Hartmuth (eds), *Images of Imperial Legacy: Modern Discourse on the Social and Cultural Impact of Ottoman and Habsburg Rule in Southeast Europe*, Münster: Lit, pp. 21–36.

Rothstein, B. (2013), 'Reply to Fukuyama 2013a', The GOVERNANCE blog, available at http://governancejournal.net.

Schulz, O. (2011), *Ein Sieg der zivilisierten Welt? Die Intervention der europäischen Großmächte im griechischen Unabhängigkeitskrieg (1826–1832)*, Münster: Lit.

Sezen, S. (2011), 'International versus domestic explanations of administrative reforms: the case of Turkey', *International Review of Administrative Sciences*, **77** (2), 322–46.

Siemons, M. (2010), 'China und der Konfuzianismus: Kotau mit Krawatte', *Frankfurter Allgemeine Zeitung*, 1 November.

Siemons, M. (2011), 'Zum Denken bitte in den Hinterhof', *Frankfurter Allgemeine Zeitung*, 26 April.

Sindbaeck, T. and M. Hartmuth (eds) (2011), *Images of Imperial Legacy: Modern Discourse on the Social and Cultural Impact of Ottoman and Habsburg Rule in Southeast Europe*, Münster: Lit.

Steiner, H.J., Philip Alston and Ryan Goodman (2007), *International Human Rights in Context*, 3rd edn, Oxford: Oxford University Press.

Stolleis, M. (2003), *Der menschenfreundliche Ton: Zwei Dutzend Geschichten von Johann Peter Hebel mit kleinem Kommentar*, Frankfurt/Main: Insel.

Suleski, R. (2008), 'Confucius: the organization of Chinese society', in D. Jones (ed.), *Confucius Now: Contemporary Encounters with the* Analects, Chicago and La Salle, IL: Open Court, pp. 253–90.

Tan, S.-h. (2008a), 'Three corners for one: tradition and creativity in the *Analects*', in D. Jones (ed.), *Confucius Now: Contemporary Encounters with the* Analects, Chicago and La Salle, IL: Open Court, pp. 59–77.

Tan, S.-h. (2008b), 'Modernizing Confucianism and "new Confucianism"', in K. Louie (ed.), *The Cambridge Companion to Modern Chinese Culture*, Cambridge: Cambridge University Press, pp. 135–54.

Tan, S.-h. (2011), 'The *Dao* of politics: li (rituals/rites) and laws as pragmatic tools of government', *Philosophy East and West*, **61** (3), 468–91.

Tuğal, C. (2009), *Passive Revolution: Absorbing the Islamic Challenge to Capitalism*, Stanford, CA: Stanford University Press.

Urinboyev, R. (2011), 'Law, social norms and welfare as means of public administration: case study of Mahalla institutions in Uzbekistan', *NISPAcee Journal of Public Administration and Policy*, **4** (1), 33–57.

Wade, R.H. (2013), 'Poverty, corruption, and the changing world, 1950–2050', *Triple Crisis* blog, 17 June, available at http://triplecrisis.com/poverty-corruption-and-the-changing-world-1950-2050/.

Wang Anshi (1935), *The Wan Yen Shu, or Memorial of a Myriad Words* [1058], in H.R. Williamson, *Wang An Shih: A Chinese Statesman and Educationalist of the Sung Dynasty* 1, London: Probsthain, pp. 48–84.

Weber, M. (1922), *Grundriß der Sozialökonomik* 3: *Wirtschaft und Gesellschaft*, Tübingen: Mohr Siebeck.
Weber, M. (1986), *Gesammelte Aufsätze zur Religionssoziologie* 1, 8th edn, Tübingen: Mohr Siebeck.
Winkler, H.A. (2011), 'Wo fängt der Westen an, wo hört der Osten auf?', interview with C. Seidl, *Frankfurter Allgemeine Zeitung*, 24 December.
Yesilkagit, K. (2010), 'The future of administrative tradition: tradition as ideas and structure', in M. Painter and B.G. Peters (eds), *Tradition and Public Administration*, Basingstoke: Palgrave Macmillan. pp. 145–57.
Zarrow, P. (2008), 'Social and political developments: the making of the twentieth-century Chinese state', in in K. Louie (ed.), *The Cambridge Companion to Modern Chinese Culture*, Cambridge: Cambridge University Press, pp. 20–45.

PART II

INTERNATIONAL PERSPECTIVES OF PUBLIC ADMINISTRATION, NEW PUBLIC MANAGEMENT AND GOVERNANCE

6. Public service reform in South Africa: from apartheid to new public management
Robert Cameron

INTRODUCTION

Public service reform in South Africa has entailed the transition from an apartheid-based, public service to a more democratic administration. The major challenge was to move from a state that provided services predominantly to a small white constituency to one that also provided decent services to the disadvantaged black majority. The post-apartheid state is pursuing the provision of services to all its constituents, thus increasing its target group from approximately 4 million to 50 million.

The public service was not only apartheid based; it was also outdated by international standards. Sanctions and boycotts had contributed to an isolated public service that in some respects was run on scientific management lines. The new South African government introduced new public management (NPM) reforms in order to modernize the public service, although there has been some debate about how extensively they have been implemented (Cameron, 2009).

This chapter plans to examine the three main components of NPM that were adopted in South Africa. First, there is administrative decentralization (or delegation), which aimed to give line managers greater managerial authority and responsibility. The second component of NPM that is of relevance is performance management. If managers are to be given greater autonomy, they need to be held accountable through performance standards. Explicit standards and measures of performance require goals to be defined and performance targets to be met. This can take the form of using performance indicators and setting targets. The third element is that of corporatization. This involves breaking up central government departments into corporatized units around services that can then deal with each other on an arm's-length basis. There is a split between a small strategic policy core and large operational arms of government, which have increased managerial autonomy to promote efficient service delivery (Hood, 1991).

This chapter examines how deeply NPM reforms have entrenched themselves into the South African public service. This case study will be examined in terms of a comparative, developing-country lens.

NEW PUBLIC MANAGEMENT

In the 1980s, the traditional bureaucratic public administration model of Max Weber was challenged in anglophone countries such as the United Kingdom, Australia and New Zealand. A new model of public sector management emerged in these countries called new public management (NPM). It involved the use of private management ideas, such as greater autonomy and flexibility for managers, contract appointments, performance management and new financial techniques. NPM was seen as a way of cutting through the red tape and rigidity associated with old-style public administration and providing more efficient service delivery (Hood, 1991; Pollitt, 1993; Minogue, 1998; Hughes, 2003).

The evidence on the success of NPM in developed countries is sparse and indifferent. Frederickson and Smith (2003: 14), in an overview of NPM literature, state that the application of these principles can result in selective and short-term increases in efficiency; is negatively related with fairness, equity and justice; seldom reduces costs; and has produced innovative ways to accomplish public purposes. McCourt (2001: 113) points out that it is difficult to demonstrate that the much-touted NPM service delivery reforms have led to significant improvements, although there is sufficient negative evidence to refute some of the more extravagant claims.

A recent study has thrown doubt on the applicability of NPM, even in its OECD heartland. Meier and O'Toole (2008), in a study of Texas school data sets, found that there is weak support for many of the nostrums of public management; for example, contracting out is less about efficiency and more about dumping problems. The evidence-based conclusion of this study led the authors to term their article 'The proverbs of public management', which is of course a new take on the title of Herbert Simon's classical critique of scientific public administration (Simon, 1952). Thus the question remains: how transferable and suitable is NPM to developing countries?

TRANSFERABILITY OF NPM TO DEVELOPING COUNTRIES

NPM reforms have spread through many developing countries, including much of anglophone Africa. The suitability of such NPM reforms for developing countries is a matter of conjecture. McCourt (2013: 2) concludes that context is more important than international best practice, which cannot be transplanted uncritically from one environment to another. There are, however, subtle variants of this proposition.

Schick (1988) argues that developing countries are characterized by informality rather than formal bureaucratic rules and contracts. A discussion of performance contracts and decentralized authority is characteristic of a more formal world. He attests that developing countries need old-style public administration with a framework of rules and a culture of implementing them before NPM reforms can be introduced. Weakening already weak procedures by giving managers 'the right to manage' aggravates the various problems that NPM tries to ameliorate (see also McCourt, 2013).

There is some evidence to support Schick's position. Larbi (1999: 26–7), in a review of performance contracting in developing countries, suggests that its successful implementation requires certain preconditions. Capacity issues range from managers' autonomy through to effective management information systems and a well-staffed and well-equipped monitoring agency. These factors are not always present in developing countries. Hughes (2003: 231–2) points out that NPM is based on applying market principles to public administration. This entails reducing government and developing markets. The problem in developing countries is that there is often little experience in the operation of markets and a range of factors is required before markets can be effective, such as the rule of law to ensure contracts. Notwithstanding this, he cautiously suggests that NPM may be no worse than previous experiences with traditional public administration.

Polidano (1999: 23–4) disputes Schick's stage-of-development thesis, arguing *inter alia* that there is no single historical path towards a professionalized bureaucracy. He states that the outcome of reforms, rather than any preconceived arguments, should be the defining issue when judging NPM. He concludes that the evidence on the impact of NPM is 'perplexingly equivocal' (Polidano, 1999: 26). He emphasizes the importance of contingency factors, arguing that there are few generalizations. Prichard and Leonard (2010), drawing on multiple data sets on African governance, argue that 'pockets' of effectiveness are likely to exist even in the public administrations of states that are generally known for poor governance. This is an implicit critique of Schick's position.

Manning (2001: 301–3) appears to support aspects of Schick's argument but he has a more nuanced position. He advances a few reasons why NPM has delivered less in developing countries than initially claimed. First, public expectations of government in developing countries are fundamentally different from those found in the OECD. NPM in developed countries was built on the expectation that citizens were increasingly becoming 'angry customers' who wanted better-quality services. Conversely, public expectations of service quality from government in many developing countries are understandably low, with the consequence that citizens are unlikely to feel that complaints are worth the effort. Furthermore, from the government perspective, donor conditionalities are a far greater factor than nascent consumer discontent. Second, some old public disciplines remained important in the NPM era. For example, there was the assumption that the budget was the defining statement of mutual expectations between the central agencies and the line departments. It was assumed that the budget constrained line departments to a particular business area, while holding the central agencies to the provision of a certain level of funding. Similarly, the NPM debate assumed that staff, although prone to self-interest, were largely constrained by some clear standards of behaviour. It also assumed that policy was authoritative; for example, streams of conflicting or inconsistent ministerial decrees did not undermine the credibility of government policy.

Data on the effect of NPM reforms on service delivery in developing countries are sketchy. McCourt (2001: 166) states that such evidence as there is is anecdotal and fragmentary, but there have been very few cases of recorded service improvement. Manning (2001) suggests that the effects of NPM in developing countries have been modest, with some improvements in efficiency and mixed effects on equity. He argues that NPM was no more able than old public administration to provide governments with the incentives and the capacity to address poverty and provide better services.

THE RISE OF NEW PUBLIC MANAGEMENT IN SOUTH AFRICA, 2009

During the apartheid era, South African public service was isolated and out of touch with international developments (Thornhill, 2008). Subsequently, during the transition in the early 1990s, very little work was done by the African National Congress (ANC) on the nature of post-apartheid administrative change. The nature of the political economy was a far more important priority. After the 1994 elections, the ANC became the majority party in parliament and had to apply its mind to public service reform. There were two major tasks that had to be undertaken. First, there had to be a transformation from an apartheid-driven bureaucracy towards a more democratic public service that provided services to the entire population, not merely to a minority group. Second, there had to be modernization of the public sector. In the early 1990s, NPM was in its heyday and its tenets had a certain amount of appeal to the new government.

The *White Paper on the Transformation of the Public Service* laid down the national policy framework for the transformation of the public service (RSA, 1995). Many of its recommendations were in line with 'international best (NPM) practice', although the *White Paper* warned against the uncritical adoption of a NPM framework (Bardill, 2000: 105). Many of the goals of the *White Paper* were further entrenched in the Constitution (Ncholo, 2000: 88).

The Presidential Review Commission of Inquiry on Transformation and Reform in the Public Service (PRC) was set up to evaluate the public service. It made a number of wide-ranging recommendations, some of which were implemented by the new government (PRC, 1998). The Commission had international advisers who were steeped in NPM. The role of PSR in the Commonwealth Secretariat more generally was also influential. Gasper (2002: 19) states that NPM was promoted in lower-income countries by the Commonwealth Secretariat (see also Kaul, 1996). Gasper (2002: 19) also points out that management consultancy groups were influential in spreading NPM throughout Africa.

It is generally accepted that NPM reforms were influential in South Africa. Miller (2005: 70) states that 'much of the reforms (in South Africa) paralleled those which were implemented in other countries, in particular Britain and the USA'. The then Director General for the Department of Public Service and Administration (DPSA), Richard Levin (2004: 12–13), argued that public sector reform in South Africa has been shaped by the tenets of NPM, including a strong focus on decentralized management of human resources and finance (see also DPSA, 2008a: 16). The ex-Minister for Public Service and Administration, Geraldine Fraser-Moleketi, stated in a 2008 interview that the reforms were not influenced significantly by NPM ideology. The government wanted to borrow NPM skills and techniques to modernize the public service without buying into the ideological framework. There was, however, the acknowledgement that some NPM reforms had been introduced. She stated that there were a number of measures that had been introduced that would not be adopted now (Cameron, 2009: 915).

STRUCTURE AND FUNCTION OF THE SOUTH AFRICAN PUBLIC SERVICE

In terms of the 1996 Constitution (RSA, 1996), parliament consists of the National Assembly and the National Council of Provinces (NCOP). There are nine provincial governments. The legislative authority of a province is vested in the elected provincial legislature. Provinces can pass legislation with regard to any matter within a functional area listed in Schedule 4 (Functional Areas of Concurrent National and Provincial Legislative Competence) and Schedule 5 (Functional Areas of Exclusive Provincial Legislative Competence), and other matters assigned to provinces by national legislation.

Strong local government is an integral part of South Africa's new democracy. The Constitution states that a municipality has the right to govern, on its own initiative, the local government affairs of its community, subject to national and provincial legislation. National or provincial government may not compromise or impede a municipality's right or ability to exercise its powers or perform its functions. There are currently 278 municipalities.

The public service consists of national and provincial government. Local government is separate and each local government is a distinct public employer, subject to national framework legislation such as labour law and collective bargaining. In December 2010 there were 1 283 636 public servants, excluding local government employees, estimated at 203 734 (DPSA, 2010).

The cornerstone of the Constitution is a progressive, human-rights-orientated Constitution that includes a Bill of Rights giving citizens the right to have access to a number of services, including housing, health care and water. The Constitution makes specific reference to public administration. Section 195 (1) states that public administration must be governed by democratic values and principles, including the following:

(a)   A high standard of professional ethics must be promoted and maintained.
(b)   Efficient, economic and effective use of resources must be promoted and maintained.
(c)   Public administration must be development-oriented.
(d)   Services must be provided impartially, fairly, equitably and without bias.
(e)   People's needs must be responded to, and the public must be encouraged to participate in policy-making.
(f)   Public administration must be accountable.
(g)   Transparency must be fostered by providing the public with timely, accessible and accurate information.
(h)   Good human-resource management and career-development practices, to maximize human potential, must be cultivated.
(i)   Public administration must be broadly representative of the South African people, with employment and personnel practices based on ability, objectivity, fairness, and the need to redress the imbalances of the past to achieve broad representation.

The Constitution also provides for an independent Public Service Commission (PSC) (Section 196 [1]) whose powers include promoting the Section 195 values and principles and investigating, monitoring and evaluating the organization and personnel policies and practices of the public service.

ADMINISTRATIVE DECENTRALIZATION

Before examining administrative decentralization in South Africa we must look at the political–administrative context within which it occurs.

During the negotiation phase in the early 1990s, the major political parties agreed on a 'sunset clause' that guaranteed the jobs of public servants who were employed before the 1994 elections (Miller, 2005). This meant that, once in power, the ANC was faced with bureaucrats who had implemented apartheid policies – there was genuine concern that old-guard bureaucrats would thwart the implementation of the policies of the new government. A survey conducted by the Human Sciences Research Council in August 1991 showed that the top echelons of the civil service still strongly supported apartheid laws and practices (DPSA, 2008a: 56).

This led the ANC, once in government, to start appointing people who shared its ideological values to senior positions in the public service. The former Minister for the Public Service and Administration, Geraldine Fraser-Moleketi, explained that 'you brought in people you could trust, namely old comrades from the years of struggle' (Cameron, 2010: 12).

In 1997, the ANC introduced its Cadre Policy and Deployment Strategy, which advocated political appointments to senior positions in the public service. It emphasized recruitment from within parties, and potential deployees were made to understand and accept the basic policies and programmes of the ANC (Mafunisa, 2003; Maserumule, 2007). The strategy made no reference to the need for administrative competence. Similar deployment structures exist at provincial level in respect of provincial and local management appointees, although there is some doubt about whether deployment committees function in a systematic way at sub-national level.

The overall picture is one of high political involvement in appointments, and significant control over promotion, transfer and performance (Matheson et al., 2007; Cameron, 2010). This procedure ensures that the directors general are appointed largely on the basis of political affiliation. As one senior government minister said, 'If any of the top two levels of appointees have expertise, it is a bonus' (Cameron, 2009: 926). The PSC (2008a: 38) points out that the British system of professional career heads of department has largely been replaced by a combination of political and contract-based appointments (also see Naidoo, 2013).

We now explore administrative decentralization, which is an important part of NPM. It means giving line managers in government departments and agencies greater managerial authority and responsibility (Polidano, 1999: 19). Hood (1991: 4–5) describes this perspective as hands-on professional management: let the managers manage. Devolving human resource and management functions to managers is an important component of NPM.

This can be distinguished from devolution of political power to lower levels of government, generally elected local authorities. These two types of decentralization are referred to as administrative decentralization and political decentralization respectively (Polidano, 1999: 19–20). In practice these different types of decentralization are often conflated. This chapter focuses on NPM-inspired administrative decentralization.

Whether administrative decentralization in developing countries leads to better performance is a moot point. Schick (1998) points out that it would be foolhardy to entrust public managers with complete freedom over resources when they have not yet internalized the habit of spending public money according to prescribed rules. Weakening already weak procedures by giving managers 'the right to manage' aggravates the various problems that NPM tries to ameliorate. In practice there is also limited delegation in developing countries. McCourt (2013: 6) states that civil service management remains highly centralized in developing countries. The reasons are that patronage pressures can be controlled more easily from a single point, and central bureaucrats are reluctant to delegate power.

The counter-argument is that of Grindle (1997), quoted in Minogue (1998: 288), who points out that, while management decentralization is inextricably linked with the Balkanization of the public sector, it may also be the only hope of improving the performance of sluggish public organizations.

Before 1994 the public service was highly centralized. The Commission for Administration (the predecessor of the PSC) had extensive powers. These included the setting of wages and salaries, responsibility for disciplinary authority, pensions, leave, promotions, and evaluating staff qualifications and requirements. It was also responsible for grading posts and regulations of conditions of work (DPSA: 2008b: 2; Picard, 2005: 59; Ncholo, 2000: 89). According to Ncholo (ibid.), then Director General for DPSA, this was in conflict with international best practice. To rectify this, human resource functions were transferred to the line departments (DPSA, 2008b: 53–4).

The Public Service Laws Amendment Act 47 of 1997 made the Minister for the Public Service and Administration responsible for, *inter alia*, policy on the functions of the public service; the determination of policy on conditions of service, salary scales, wages and allowances according to class, rank and grade; employment policy; internal organization; organizational structure; and the transfer of functions, post establishment, the creation, grading and abolition of posts and appointments, promotions and transfers.

The Act also made provision for the transfer of a number of human resources functions formerly administered by the PSC to executing authorities (EAs, ministers in charge of departments), which could, in turn, delegate these to either directors general, provincial heads of department (HoDs) or departmental managers. These included the organization of staff issues; the appointment, promotion and transfer of members of staff; performance management; and the obligations, rights and privileges of officers and employees. EAs may delegate to HoDs, and HoDs in turn may delegate to other employees. The Act confers some broad powers directly on HoDs, such as the broad responsibility for the efficient management of their departments, but, given their lack of original human resources management powers, they are quite limited. In practice this means that an EA may appoint all staff to the lowest level, unless this function has been delegated to the HoD (Ncholo, 2000: 89–90; DPSA, 2008b).

A further amendment to the Public Service Act (PSA) in 1998 led to the structure of provincial departments mirroring that of national departments. The members of the provincial executive councils (MECs) responsible for these newly created provincial departments now had the managerial authority to organize their departments and hire and dismiss their employees. This meant that there was decentralization of human resources powers to provincial politicians and not to provincial managers.

During the apartheid era, there were detailed public service staff codes that tended to be highly regulatory. New Public Service Regulations (PSR) introduced in July 1999 were intended to repeal the detailed human resources provisions contained in the then Public Service Staff Code. These new regulations were intended to promote the decentralization of human resources powers to managers (RSA, 2001; Adair and Albertyn, 2000: 116).

To what extent have decentralization and delegation to managers occurred in practice? There is an argument that decentralization has been a failure. Levin (2004: 13) argued that decentralization has not really empowered managers, as they have been granted delegation without being equipped with the necessary resources to utilize it effectively. For example, the decentralization to managers of the authority to manage leave, sick leave, discipline, recruitment and retention has been less than satisfactory. The PSC (2004: 4, 34) came to a similar conclusion, stating that many public service organizations were struggling to meet the required standards in crucial areas.

An empirical survey conducted by the DPSA (2008b) came to a different conclusion. The study found that, while a framework for decentralization had been put in place, there had been limited delegation in practice. The survey requested all national and provincial departments to provide a list of delegation of powers and duties in terms of the PSA and PSR. Of the 73 departments that responded (out of a total of 151), 33 per cent had limited delegation from EAs to HoDs, 39 per cent had average delegation, 18 per cent had above average delegation, and 10 per cent had extensive delegation. Further data indicated that delegation to officials lower in the hierarchy was even more limited. A survey of the PSR alone indicated that 56 per cent of EAs had not delegated powers, while in 72 per cent of cases, powers had not been delegated to officials further down the hierarchy by either EAs or HoDs. This trend was repeated when the PSA was analysed separately (DPSA, 2008b: 4–8).

These findings show that most departments are still centralized, with only 28 per cent of HoDs exercising reasonable degrees of delegation. The data revealed the beginning of a trend according to which departments that were performing well were more likely to have delegated a fair proportion of powers and duties to HoDs. Rather than 'let the managers manage', in line with international good practice, it was a case of 'let the politicians manage' (Cameron, 2009). The Presidency (2013: 27–9) undertook a more recent study of management practices in the public sector. This included updated data on, first, approved EA delegations in terms of the PSA and the PSR, and, second, approved delegations in terms of the Public Finance Management Act (PFMA). The standard in terms of approved EA and delegations in terms of the PSA and PSR covers how EAs delegate decision-making authority for their PSA powers to various levels in their departments. The standard requires that the delegated functions be clear, with conditions, and be signed off on each assigned delegation to minimize the risks. Forty-seven per cent of departments met the legal/regulatory requirements for public administration delegations. Thirty-four per cent of departments had delegations in place that were compliant with the PSA and PSR and consistent with the DPSA framework. Thirteen per cent of departments, in addition to the minimum requirements of the DPSA delegations framework, demonstrated effective use of delegations to appropriate levels in the organization and to regional offices. Thirty-six per cent of departments did not provide evidence of having any delegations in place.

Seventeen per cent of departments' delegations did not comply with the PSA and PSR. In the case of one province (Northern Cape), no EAs had delegated powers to their HoDs as all delegations had been withdrawn by the Office of the Premier. A common problem with delegations was that departments did not document or capture them in a delegations register, and the conditions of the delegation were not always specified. Other challenges related to delegations not being signed off by the EA and the Accounting Officer failing to make such delegations legally binding. Some delegations as signed by predecessors were in former names of departments and they were not reviewed.

The report stated that departments, by not delegating authority to the appropriate levels, experienced delays in decision-making, as decision-making becomes over-centralized. The absence of delegations, especially of those matters pertaining to human resources, has a major impact on departments' ability to recruit and fill vacancies.

The results for delegations in terms of the PFMA were marginally better than the results for PSA delegations. Fifty-four per cent of departments met the legal/regulatory requirements for delegations for financial administration. Thirty-five per cent had financial delegations in place that were aligned to Treasury guidelines and the approved departmental structure. Their delegations register was approved and there was evidence of delegation from the Accounting Officer to the Chief Financial Officer and to other officials. Nineteen per cent of departments demonstrated that delegations were made at the appropriate level. The Presidency study used a different methodology to that of the DPSA study, which makes it difficult to compare systematically the respective results. Having said that, the trends are broadly the same – poor levels of delegation. Forty-seven per cent of departments met the legal/regulatory requirements for public administration delegations and 54 per cent of departments met the legal/regulatory requirements for delegations for financial administration.

The lack of delegations is not only due to the intransigence of politicians. There is evidence to suggest that managers are not willing to manage. According to the PSC (2008b: 7–8), some EAs believe that HoDs needed to exercise good judgement in relation to which areas they needed to consult on, even if powers had been delegated. The Cameron study (2009) showed that one of the reasons why delegation was limited was that managers were not prepared to make tough decisions. Ministers often have to make the tough decisions, and delegation to managers will not prevent corruption and patronage. There was a need for managers to provide better leadership. In a similar vein, McLennan (2007: 14–15) states that many institutions formed under apartheid were used to working under bureaucratic line authority. This meant that officials were unwilling to take on the responsibility or consequences of more independent decision-making.

PERFORMANCE MANAGEMENT

The second relevant component of NPM is performance management. If managers are to be given greater autonomy, they need to be held accountable through performance standards (Minogue, 1998: 26; United Nations, 2005: 55). Hood (1991: 4–5) points out that explicit standards and measures of performance require that goals are defined and performance targets are met. This can take the form of using performance indicators and setting targets. Hughes (2003: 54–5) points out that NPM entails moving from inputs to outcomes or outputs. There is a need for a performance appraisal system to measure both individual and organizational performance. There is a trade-off between giving managers greater autonomy and performance management. In return for being allowed greater autonomy, managers must be accountable for their performance through performance targets (Minogue, 1998: 26; United Nations, 2005: 55).

While performance management has in some cases led to improved service delivery, its efficacy has been questioned, even in developing countries. Talbot (2005) points out, *inter alia*, that performance measurement is about trying to put quantitative values on to many aspects of public services that are difficult to quantify; that a consequence of the rewards and sanctions, coupled with the problems associated with measuring complex areas of professional practice, may result in changes in behaviour in which performance is not optimized and, drawing on Lindblom, that public systems are dominated by politics, which inevitably leads to instability, incrementalism, muddling through, messy compromises and value judgements that fatally undermine all attempts at rational decision-making. Hood (2007: 100) argues that gaming, namely the deliberate massaging or outright fabrication of numbers collected with the intention of improving the position of an individual or organization, is widespread in British government. He also states that, where performance is accurately reported and organizations are genuinely improving their performance, it can lead to a focus on narrow outcomes or outputs for one agency to the detriment of other wider policy and programme objectives. Pollitt (2006) states that there is little evidence that in the USA and in Dutch local government performance information is actually used in the process of making budget decisions.

In the literature on the applicability of performance management to developing countries, there are similar constraints. Larbi (1999: 26–7), in a review of performance contracting in developing countries, suggests that its successful implementation requires certain preconditions. Capacity issues range from managers' autonomy through to effective management information systems and a well-staffed and well-equipped monitoring agency. These factors are not always present in developing countries. Talbot (2004a: 312–13), in a review of performance management in Jamaica, states that there is a tendency to adopt a 'scatter-gun' approach, measuring everything and anything that comes into view. Many of the indicators were operational rather than strategic. This was translated into vague and imprecise policy indicators.

Conversely, Verheijen and Dobrolyubova (2007), in an analysis of public management reform process in Latvia, Lithuania and Russia, reach a different conclusion. They argue that the introduction of such reforms can be successful even in public management systems that are not 'advanced'. This contradicts the widely held notion that performance-based public management systems are not suitable for 'developing' countries. The article concludes that, if sufficient political support and a dedicated reform team in the civil service are present, and performance management systems are introduced in a step-by-step manner, significant improvement in the effectiveness and efficiency of public management systems can be achieved.

In South Africa the Public Service Laws Amendment Act introduced performance management. The PSR of 1999 gave performance management more flesh (Miller, 2005: 86–9). It was originally for directors and above. A senior manager who was not an HoD would enter into a performance management contract with his or her immediate supervisor, while in the case of a director general it would be with his or her minister.

Miller (2005: 191) provides three main reasons why performance management was introduced. The first was to provide an objective measure to assess managers' performance. The second was to determine whether they were performing their functions effectively. The third was to improve the political–administrative interface.

There are two main official documents that look at organizational performance management. First, the National Treasury (2007) has published *Framework for Managing Programme Performance Information*. Of importance is its assertion that budgets are developed in relation to inputs, activities and outputs, while the aim of management is to achieve the outcomes and impacts. Second, The Presidency (2009) issued a report entitled *Improving Government Performance*, which looks at ways of improving government's organizational performance. There is now an emphasis on the outcomes performance management system. The starting point of this process is the Medium-Term Strategic Framework (MTSF). It is a five-year plan arising from the government's Vision 2025 and other issue-specific policy research. The MTSF is converted into the main outcome indicators, approved by Cabinet. They are a simple and clear way of expressing government's mandate.

The Presidency plays a supporting role in establishing performance agreements with ministers and in sectoral delivery agreements, focusing on a small set of outcomes and a selected group of outputs. Ministers will cascade results-focused lines of accountability down to senior officials.

The DPSA has produced two main documents dealing with individual performance management. One is the *Senior Management Service (SMS) Handbook* (DPSA, 2003) and the other is the *Performance Management Development System* (PMDS) document for salary levels 1–12 (DPSA, 2006). While the framework for performance management is contained in Chapter 4 of the *SMS Handbook*, aspects of this PMDS are also applicable to SMS members. The documents are very similar in performance management processes, although the SMS requirements are more specifically linked to competency requirements.

The following five categories of individual performance are used for the purpose of performance rating, review and the annual assessment of employees:

- unacceptable performance (rating 1);
- performance not fully effective (rating 2);
- performance fully effective (rating 3);
- performance significantly above expectations (rating 4); and
- outstanding performance (rating 5).

Performance bonuses and pay progression are given to those who get a 4 or 5 rating. Ratings of 1 and 2 do not get performance bonuses or pay progression. A 3 rating gets a pay progression only. The Minister of Public Service and Administration has determined that only 1.5 per cent of the departmental remuneration budget can be allocated to performance bonuses.

Studies have shown that there are substantive problems of implementation and compliance in respect of both the signing of individual performance agreements and of evaluation (Maphunye, 2001; Miller, 2005; Cameron, 2009, 2012). A case study of the Department of Labour (DoL, Cameron, 2012) pointed to a lack of coordination between individual and organizational performance. This enables the gaming of the system, through which non-performers still get performance bonuses. A major problem was that organizational performance is set by the Treasury and the Presidency, while individual performance is guided by the DPSA's framework. There were also different provincial approaches to measuring data and a lack of capacity at many labour centres.

There were concerns about the low level of compliance in the signing of performance agreements by senior officials (Public Service Commission

(PSC), 2007: 45–6). The government releases an annual programme of action that includes a set of top priorities, which it calls 'Apex priorities' (now called Government Programme of Action). One of the Apex priorities in 2008 was to ensure that all SMS members signed performance agreements in a timely manner (DPSA, 2008b). As at November 2008, 83 per cent of managers in the public service had done so (DPSA, 2008a). However, in 2010 this dropped to 65 per cent, which was partly due to the fact that the 2009 elections had brought in new ministers who were still familiarizing themselves with their new portfolios (PSC, 2010: 52). The most recent data on the compliance rate for the filing of performance agreements of HoDs of 78 per cent was obtained for both the National and Provincial departments for the 2009/10–2011/12 financial years (PSC, 2011: 34–5).

There is also the possibility that poorly formulated performance agreements may result in appraisal outcomes that are biased, either towards or against the HoD. These are performance appraisals that fail to show an adequate correlation between the individual performance of the HoD and the overall performance of the department (PSC, 2008a: 18). There are a number of reasons for non-compliance with performance management regulations, ranging from unforeseen emergencies, work pressures and restructuring to the frequency of political and administrative leadership changes, which creates organizational instability (DPSA, 2008b). The PSC (2011: 35) also stated that the filing of performance agreements had been delayed because of new appointments. Mechanisms need to be put in place to ensure that the filing takes place in a timely manner as performance agreements and evaluation of the performance of the incumbent of the key post of HoD are important accountability mechanisms.

The PSC also raised problems of performance evaluation in a number of its reports. In 2004 (PSC, 2004: 16, 34) it pointed out that performance management was still a major challenge facing the public service and described compliance with guidelines as erratic and inconsistent. In 2005/06 it got worse, with 50 per cent of HoDs at national level and 44 per cent at provincial level not being evaluated (PSC, 2008b: 66). More recent research by the PSC (2011: 33–4) indicates that during the 2008/09 financial year, of the 31 HoDs in national departments who qualified to be evaluated, only four were in fact evaluated. In the 2009/10 financial year at national level, there were 16 HoDs who qualified to be evaluated. As at end October 2011, only two performance assessments were held for the 2009/10 financial year. The technical brief states that this is the worst non-compliance rate the PSC has ever reported since the inception of the HoD evaluation framework during the 2001/02 financial year. At provincial level 72 HoDs qualified to be evaluated for the 2008/09 financial year, of whom only 29 (40 per cent) were evaluated.

A final indicator was whether departments have established performance management systems. The PSC (2011: 35–6) found that the overall average performance score obtained by the 51 evaluated departments in the 2009/10 and 2010/11 cycle is 75 per cent. Of the 51 departments, 21 (41 per cent) obtained an excellent score between 81 and 100 per cent. It has also been noted that 92 per cent of departments have put in place performance management systems for all departmental programmes.

The fact that a performance management system is in place says nothing, however, about the quality of the performance information. The finding of the Attorney General in this regard was illuminating in that 25 out of 35 national departments' performance information did not comply with regulatory requirements and was not useful or not reliable. The same finding applied to 72 per cent of provincial departments.

It can be seen that the signing of performance agreements is less than optimal and performance evaluation was on the low side. A cynical interpretation is that there is no need to game the system – if the building blocks of the performance management system are not in place, it is not necessary to manipulate the numbers! Furthermore, the quality of performance information is also inadequate. It appears that this NPM-driven reform is only skin deep. The evidence suggests that there is not a substantive performance culture in the South African public service. However, these problems of implementing performance management are not unique. These findings are consistent with evidence on performance-related pay in other countries that is inconclusive and ambiguous (United Nations, 2005: x; Bourgon, 2007: 49–50).

CORPORATIZATION

The third relevant element of NPM is that of corporatization. Hood (1991: 4–5) refers to this as the disaggregation of units in the public sector. This involves breaking up central government departments into corporatized units around services. These units deal with each other on an arm's-length basis. There is a split between the small strategic policy core and the large operational arms of government, which have increased managerial autonomy to promote efficient service delivery. These arm's-length agencies have greater managerial flexibility in the allocation of human resources in return for greater accountability for results (also see Larbi, 1999). Bouckaert and Peters (2004: 46) point out that the rationale of removing programmes from political organizations is that it enables decisions to be based on economic and efficiency criteria rather than on political considerations.

Talbot (2004b: 5) distinguishes between agencies within departments or the public service, such as Next Steps agencies in the UK, and those outside the public service, which are commonly called quasi-autonomous non-governmental organizations (quangos). This categorization is broadly used in South Africa (DPSA/Treasury, 2005). Pollitt (2004), in a case study of Latvia, draws a number of lessons for developing countries about the Anglo-American model of performance agencies. He states, *inter alia*, that this model can be successful only when contextual prerequisites are met. For example, agencies can only be steered by their parent ministries if the latter bodies have information, appropriate skilled staff and appropriate levers by which to steer. He concludes that 'agencification' is premature. He argues that giving public agencies greater freedom carries a substantial risk that the autonomy will be exercised for corrupt means and that the frequent absence of clear policy objectives means that the missions of agencies remain vague. Talbot (2004a), in a case study on Jamaica, points out that the executive agencies programme there has made some progress but warns against large-scale autonomization, stating that a 'soft state' can lead to large-scale corruption.

There has been limited research on corporatization in South Africa. Most of the research has been on public entities that exist outside the public service. A DPSA/Treasury report (2005: 10–11) concluded that there was no policy framework in place to guide the process of establishing and reviewing public entities. This had led to a lack of performance culture in public entities, and performance targets and review periods are often not clear. Johannesburg municipality created a number of corporatized structures to deliver services, but this system has been criticized for lack of coordination and fragmentation (South African Cities Network, 2007). A study in Tshwane (Pretoria) municipality came to a similar conclusion by pointing to ambiguous reporting lines and coordination (HSRC, 2009).

A study by Cameron (2012) examined performance management in a Next Steps agency in the South African DoL, looking at the roles of the national office, provincial offices and labour centres. Labour centres form a government agency that can be defined as an autonomous organizational component in the public service (DPSA/Treasury, 2005: 5). Policy making resides in a relatively small national government department and implementation is the responsibility of labour centres, which have a degree of autonomy in providing certain labour services. There are also provincial offices of the DoL whose function is to support labour centres. The article examined the two main components of the DoL, namely the Public Employment Services (PES) and Inspection Enforcement Services (IES).

The findings were, *inter alia*, that, despite pockets of excellence, there was limited evidence to suggest that the agency model has led to more efficient service delivery. This finding conforms to previous studies (Schick, 1998; Larbi, 1999; Pollitt, 2004), which suggest that the Next Steps agencies model is perhaps not appropriate for developing countries. Pollitt's (2004: 293) conclusion on the Latvian case study was that 'decentralising many functions to autonomous agencies was trying to run before the public service could walk'. This is equally valid for the South African case. The DoL case study showed that autonomous labour centres have contributed to poorly skilled and patronage appointments and, consequently, to poor performance. Not only are many labour centres characterized by poor performance, but there is little that the national department can do to intervene because of the autonomy given to these Next Steps agencies. Furthermore, although the national DoL staff are responsible for targets, they have no say over performance at labour centres, which are headed by regional managers and are accountable to the respective Chief Director: Provincial Operations in the respective provinces. The NPM assumption that removing decisions from direct political control will lead to decisions being made on efficiency grounds rather than being based on political criteria is not borne out by this case study. Perhaps a merit-based public service is a precondition for the introduction of Next Steps agencies in developing countries.

A final point is that the next-step NPM structure of the department, which splits functions into policy and implementation arms, does not lend itself particularly well to countries where there are three different structures, namely head office, provincial offices and labour centres. It is cumbersome and has led to unclear reporting lines. In particular, there appeared to be overlap between the national and provincial government roles. Both provide support and capacity building to labour centres.

CONCLUSION

This chapter looked at how deeply three key NPM reforms, namely administrative delegation, performance management and corporatization, have worked themselves into the South African public service.

While a framework for administrative decentralization has been put in place, in practice there has not been as much decentralization as is normally presumed. There has been limited delegation to managers by ministers. There is a view among politicians that delegation has been limited because managers do not provide proper leadership. There appears to be a paradox. On the one hand, politicians want improved service delivery by the public service, yet on the other hand they do not trust senior bureaucrats, many of whom are political appointees, to perform this implementation role (Cameron, 2012).

Performance management is a major component of public service reform in South Africa. Although there are well-developed performance management frameworks, they have been applied only erratically and inconsistently. The quality of performance information is inadequate, while the signing of performance agreements and performance evaluation is on the low side. There is also a major disjuncture between individual and organizational performance. A major problem was that organizational performance is set by the Treasury and the Presidency, while individual performance is guided by the DPSA's framework. There were also different provincial approaches to measuring data, and a lack of capacity.

Limited literature is available on the performance of corporatized agencies. What the available documentation suggests is that the corporatized agency model has not necessarily led to more efficient service delivery. A case study of the DoL pointed out that autonomous labour centres have contributed to patronage appointments, which are not based on skill and have consequently led to poor performance. There is little that the national office can do to intervene because of the autonomy given to these agencies. Attempts to generalize from a single case study must obviously be treated with caution. Notwithstanding this, the study does suggest that there is a need to strengthen the core of the public service in developing countries before creating arm's-length Next Steps agencies.

These findings confirm the view that NPM techniques do not travel particularly well to developing countries. Whether this is primarily due to Schick's argument that 'you need to crawl before you walk' or to contingent factors is not entirely clear. More research is needed in this regard.

What about the future direction of the public service? The National Planning Commission published its National Development Plan (NDP), which set out the country's vision for 2030. Chapter 13 of its diagnostic report looked at improving the capacity of South Africa's state institutions/bureaucracy. It made a number of recommendations to stabilize the political–administrative interface. These included:

- ensuring that the public service is immersed in the development agenda but insulated from undue political interference;
- strengthening the oversight role of the PSC departments to respond to the PSC proposals and giving greater force to PSC recommendations;
- creating an administrative head of the public service with responsibility for managing the career progression of HoDs, including convening panels for recruitment processes, performance assessments and disciplinary procedures. At provincial level, the same role should be played by the director general in the Office of the Premier;

- using a selection panel convened by the chair of the PSC and the administrative head of the public service to draw up a shortlist of suitable candidates for top posts. The selection panel should make use of competency tests and other assessment mechanisms;
- moving towards long-term contracts for HoDs and reducing the use of three-year contracts;
- amending the Public Service Act to locate responsibility for human resources management with the HoD.

The report did not say anything about improving performance management and the efficiency of Next Steps agencies, which, certainly in the case of the former, was surprising. What is of relevance for this chapter is its suggestion that human resource management be located with the HoD. While the government is committed to implementing the NDP, there is evidence that it is less than keen to lose control of human resource management.

In summary, while it is true that there are elements of NPM in the public service reform programme, they have not been systematically applied nor are they likely to be implemented rigorously in the future. As Polidano (1999: 3) remarks, 'NPM initiatives may be little more than a minor strand of reform, the froth at the top of the glass'.

REFERENCES

Adair, B. and Albertyn, C. (2000), 'Restructuring management in the public service: implications for new legislation', in G. Adler (ed.), *Public Service Labour Relations in a Democratic South Africa*, Johannesburg: Wits University Press, pp. 110–25.
Bardill, J.E. (2000), 'Towards a culture of good governance: the Presidential Review Commission and public service reform in South Africa', *Public Administration and Development*, 103–18.
Bouckaert, G. and Peters, G.B. (2004), 'What is available and what is missing in the study of quangos', in C. Pollitt and C. Talbot (eds), *Unbundled Government. A Critical Analysis of the Global Trend to Agencies, Quangos and Contractualisation*, London: Routledge, pp. 22–49.
Bourgon, J. (2007), 'Responsive, responsible and respected government: towards a new public administration theory', *International Review of Administrative Sciences*, 73(1), 5–26.
Cameron, R. (2009), 'New Public Management reforms in the South African public service: 1999–2009', *Journal of Public Administration*, 44(4.1), 910–42.
Cameron, R. (2010), 'Redefining political–administrative relationships in South Africa', *International Review of Administrative Sciences*, 76(4), 676–701.
Cameron, R. (2012), 'Performance management and corporatisation in a developing country: the case of the South African Department of Labour', paper presented at the 5th International SPMA Conference, University of Pretoria, 16–17 November.
Department of Public Service and Administration (DPSA) (2003), *Senior Management Service Handbook*, Pretoria: DPSA.
DPSA (2006), *Performance Management and Development System for Salary Levels 1–12*, Pretoria: DPSA.

DPSA (2008a), *15 Year Review. A Review of Changes in the Macro-Organisation of the State: 1994–2008*, Pretoria: DPSA.

DPSA (2008b), *Summary Report to the July 2008 Lekgotla. Status regarding HR delegations from EAs to HoDs in the public service*, Pretoria: DPSA.

DPSA (2008c), *Cabinet Lekgotla Report APEX Project 15: Regularise Employment and Performance Employment and Performance Agreements at Designated Levels*, Pretoria: DPSA.

DPSA (2010), *Personnel Statistics*, Pretoria: DPSA.

DPSA and National Treasury (2005), *Policy Framework for the Governance and Administration of Public Sector Institutions*, Pretoria: DPSA.

Frederickson, H.G. and Smith, K.B. (2003), *The Public Administration Theory Primer*, Boulder, CO: Westview Press.

Gasper, D. (2002), 'Fashion, learning and values in public management: reflections on South African and international experience', *Africa Development*, **27**(3–4), 17–47.

Hood, C. (1991), 'A public management for all seasons', *Public Administration*, **69**(1), 3–19.

Hood, C. (2007), 'Public service management by numbers: why does it vary? Where has it come from? What are the gaps and the puzzles?', *Public Money and Management*, **27**(2), 95–102.

Hughes, O.E. (2003), *Public Management and Administration. An Introduction*, 3rd edn, New York: Macmillan.

Human Sciences Research Council (HSRC) (2009), 'Analysing institutional blockages to service delivery in the city of Tshwane', unpublished paper, Pretoria: HSRC.

Kaul, M. (1996), 'Civil service reforms: lessons from commonwealth experience', *Public Administration and Development*, **16**(2), 131–50.

Larbi, A. (1999), 'The New Public Management approach and crisis states', UNRISD Discussion Paper No. 112, Geneva: United Nations Research Institute for Social Development.

Levin, R. (2004), 'Building a unified system of public administration', speech delivered at the 2nd Public Service Conversation, Gordons Bay.

Mafunisa, J. (2003), 'Separation of politics from the South African public service: rhetoric or reality?', *Journal of Public Administration*, **38**(2), 85–101.

Manning, N. (2001), 'The legacy of new public management in developing countries', *International Review of Administrative Sciences*, **67**(2), 298–312.

Maphunye, K.J. (2001), 'The South African senior public service: roles and structures in post-1994 departments', *Journal of Public Administration*, **36**(4), 312–23.

Maserumule, H. (2007), 'Conflicts between directors-general and ministers in South Africa: a "postulative" approach', *Politikon*, **34**(2), 147–64.

Matheson, A., Weber, B., Manning, N. and Arnould, E. (2007), 'Study on the political involvement in senior staffing and on the delineation of responsibilities between ministers and senior civil servants'. OECD Working Papers on Public Governance No 6. Paris: OECD Publishing.

McCourt, W. (2001), 'The NPM agenda for service delivery: a suitable model for developing countries?', in W. McCourt and M. Minogue (eds), *The Internationalisation of Public Management. Reinventing the Third World State*, Cheltenham, UK and Northampton, MA, USA: Edward Elgar Publishing, pp. 107–28.

McCourt, W. (2013), 'Models of public service reform: a problem solving approach', Washington, DC: World Bank Working Paper 6428.

McLennan, A. (2007), 'Unmasking delivery: revealing politics', *Progress in Developmental Studies*, **7**(1), 5–20.

Meier, K.J. and O'Toole, L.J. (2008), 'The proverbs of New Public Management: lessons from an evidence-based research agenda', *The American Review of Public Administration*, 4–22.

Miller, K. (2005), *Public Sector Reform: Governance in South Africa*, Aldershot: Ashgate.

Minogue, M. (1998), 'Changing the state: concepts and practice in the reform of the public sector', in M. Minogue, C. Polidano and D. Hume (eds), *Beyond the New*

Public Management: Changing Ideas and Practices in Governance, Cheltenham, UK and Northampton, MA, USA: Edward Elgar Publishing, pp. 17–37.

Naidoo, V. (2013), 'Cadre deployment versus merit? Reviewing politicisation in the public service', in D. Pillay, J. Daniel, P. Naidoo and R. Southall (eds), *New South African Review 3: The Second Phase – Tragedy or Farce?* Johannesburg: Wits University Press, pp. 261–77.

National Planning Commission (2012), *National Development Plan 2030. Our Future – Make it Work*, Pretoria: NPC.

National Treasury (2007), *Framework for Managing Programme Performance Information*, Pretoria: Treasury.

Ncholo, P. (2000), 'Reforming the public service in South Africa: a policy framework', *Public Administration and Development*, **20**, 87–102.

Picard, L.A. (2005), *The State of the State: Institutional Transformation, Capacity and Political Change in South Africa*, Johannesburg: Wits University Press.

Polidano, C. (1999), 'The New Public Management in developing countries', IDPM Public Policy and Management Working Paper No. 13.

Pollitt, C. (1993), *Managerialism and the Public Services: Cuts or Cultural Changes in the 1990s*, 2nd edn, Oxford: Basil Blackwell.

Pollitt, C. (2004), 'Castles built on sand? Agencies in Latvia', in C. Pollitt and C. Talbot (eds), *Unbundled Government. A Critical Analysis of the Global Trend to Agencies, Quangos and Contractualisation*, London: Routledge, pp. 283–96.

Pollitt, C. (2006), 'Performance information for democracy. The missing link?', *Evaluation*, **12**(1), 38–55.

Presidential Review Commission (PRC) (1998), *Developing a Culture of Good Governance. Report of the Presidential Review Commission on the Reform and Transformation of the Public Service in South Africa*, Pretoria: PRC.

Prichard, W. and Leonard, D.L. (2010), 'Does reliance on tax revenue build state capacity in sub-Saharan Africa?', *International Review of Administrative Sciences*, **76**(4), 653–75.

Public Service Commission (PSC) (2004), *State of the Public Service Report*, Pretoria: PSC.

PSC (2007), *State of the Public Service Report*, Pretoria: PSC.

PSC (2008a), *The Turnover Rates of Heads of Department and Its Implications for the Public Service*, Pretoria: PSC.

PSC (2008b), *A Report on Strategic Issues Emanating from the Evaluation of Heads of Department*, Pretoria: PSC.

PSC (2010), *State of the Public Service Report 2010. Integration, Coordination and Effective Service Delivery*, Pretoria: PSC.

PSC (2011), *Fact Sheet on the State of Public Service*, Pretoria.

Republic of South Africa (RSA) (1995), *White Paper on the Transformation of the Public Service*, *Government Gazette* **365**(16838) of 1995, Pretoria.

RSA (1996), *The Constitution of the Republic of South Africa Act No. 108 of 1996*, Pretoria: Government Printer.

RSA (2001), *Public Service Regulations. 2001 Government Gazette*, No. R. 1 of 5 January 2001 as amended, Pretoria.

Schick, A. (1998), 'Why most developing countries should not try New Zealand reforms', *The World Bank Research Observer* **13**(1), 123–31.

Simon, H. (1952), 'Development of theory of democratic administration: replies and comments', *American Political Science Review*, **46**(2), 494–503.

South African Cities Network (2007), *State of City Finances Report 2007*. Cape Town.

Talbot, C. (2004a), 'A radical departure? Executive agencies in Jamaica', in C. Pollitt and C. Talbot (eds), *Unbundled Government. A Critical Analysis of the Global Trend to Agencies, Quangos and Contractualisation*, London: Routledge, pp. 297–315.

Talbot, C. (2004b), 'The agency ideas: sometimes old, sometimes new, sometimes borrowed, sometimes untrue', in C. Pollitt and C. Talbot (eds), *Unbundled Government. A Critical Analysis of the Global Trend to Agencies, Quangos and Contractualisation*, London: Routledge, pp. 3–21.

Talbot, C. (2005), 'Performance management', in E. Ferlie, L. Lynn and C. Pollitt (eds), *The Oxford Handbook of Public Management*, Oxford: Oxford University Press, pp.491–517.

The Presidency (2009), *Improving Government Performance: Our Approach*, Pretoria.

The Presidency (2013), *State of Management Practices in the Public Service. Results of Management Performance Assessments for the 2012/13 Financial Year*, Pretoria.

Thornhill, C. (2008), 'Research in South Africa: some South African developments', *Administratio Publica*, 1–18.

Verheijen, T. and Dobrolyubova,Y. (2007), 'Performance management in the Baltic States and Russia: success against the odds?', *International Review of Administrative Sciences*, **73**(2), 205–15.

United Nations (2005), *Unlocking the Human Potential for Public Sector Performance. World Public Sector Report*. New York: Department of Social and Economic Affairs.

7. The political economy of administrative reforms in Egypt: governance, reforms and challenges
Ahmed Badran

INTRODUCTION

This chapter focuses on public administration reforms and governance in Egypt. As was the case with many other emerging economies, reforming state machinery and public bodies has been regarded as a means for achieving broader social and economic developmental goals in Egypt. Consequently, the Egyptian administrative system has been subject to different reform initiatives aiming at changing structures, functions and cultures of Egyptian public organizations. The features and main characteristics of each administrative reform programme were greatly shaped by the overall socioeconomic and political context, as well as the prevailing vision and ideological views about the role of the state in the society.

The state–society relationship, in terms of the role of the state in social and economic spheres, has been redefined several times since the revolution of 1952, based on the dominant political ideology. At least three different models can be identified in the modern history of Egypt: a welfare state model in 1952–70; a mixed state–market model in 1970–81; and a regulatory state model from 1981 to the present. The socialist era of President Nasser, 1952–70, was characterized by an ever-growing role of the state in economic and social domains. The function of the state at that time was defined as to re-engineer and restructure the Egyptian society in order to achieve social equity and economic development. All means of production have come under the direct control of the state and its apparatus, following a wide movement of nationalization for the main industrial and economic projects. The state has become the major producer of goods and the main provider of a wide range of social and economic services via public sector organizations. The Egyptian state has become the principal agent for redistributing wealth among the different groups in the society, and has presented itself as the grantor for the rights of weak and disadvantaged Egyptians.

President Sadat, the successor of President Nasser from 1970 to 1981, did not believe as strongly in the role of the public sector and state machinery in modernizing the Egyptian state and achieving the hoped-for economic growth. He was more inclined to accept the notion of liberal markets and focused his reform efforts on giving more space to the participation of the private sector in service provision under what was known as the 'open door' policy. None the less, Sadat's regime was not able to completely undo Nasser's policies, particularly as regards the role of the state in social services provision, including education, employment and health care. Therefore the best way to describe the state–society relationship under his leadership is by presenting it as a hybrid model that included a major role of the state and the public sector, and a relatively limited and minor role of the private sector.

During the 1980s and throughout the 1990s the consecutive Egyptian governments have been forced to rethink and reconsider the role of the state in a society driven by accumulated foreign debts and a huge deficit in public budgets. The Egyptian welfare state has gone through a crisis as it did not keep its promises in social and economic areas. The performance record of public sector organizations was poor and the quality of provided goods and services was even poorer. These worsened economic conditions paved the way in 1991 to the intervention of the global financial institutions, including the International Monetary Fund (IMF) and the World Bank (WB), which gave Egypt a ready-made prescription to reform its deteriorating economy via what is known as stabilization and structural adjustment programmes (Alissa, 2007). The reform prescription was long and included many reforms. Chief among these were the privatization of state enterprises, the liberalization of economic sectors and the downsizing of public sector organizations. The introduction of new liberal economic reforms and the growing role and importance of private sector organizations in production and service provision have denoted the emergence of a new model of state–society relations; that gave rise to the birth of the Egyptian regulatory state (Badran, 2013).

The discussion in this chapter is based on the changes in the major contours of the role of the Egyptian state and its institutions in society. The chapter focuses primarily on the political economy of the administrative reform in an attempt to underline the dynamics between the bureaucrats and politicians, and the ways in which such dynamics have been reflected in reform initiatives. For contextualization purposes, the institutional and legal foundations of the Egyptian administrative governance system will be discussed in the next section. The third section focuses on the politics of the administrative reform processes and the changing role of the Egyptian state in society. The following sections discuss the persistent reform issues and the initiatives to address the problems of the Egyptian bureaucracy.

CONTEXTUALIZING ADMINISTRATIVE GOVERNANCE IN EGYPT: INSTITUTIONAL AND LEGAL FOUNDATIONS

Before going into a detailed discussion of the administrative reform and modernization processes of the Egyptian bureaucracy, it might be useful to shed some light on the main characteristics of the broader institutional and legal context. As per the Egyptian Constitution, the political system in Egypt is based on the notion of republicanism, with a wide range of authorities given to the president of the state. In that sense, the political system in Egypt is normally described as a hybrid system with semi-presidential features. From an institutional perspective, the Constitution identifies the main players, roles and responsibilities as well as relationships and interaction mechanisms among those players. Considering the focal analytical point of this chapter, a brief description of three main players will be provided: the presidency, the Cabinet and the legislative.

Under the 1971 Constitution, the president of Egypt enjoyed many powers, and many authorities were at his disposal. As head of state, the president is expected to span the boundaries of different institutions to guarantee the full functioning of the different parts of the system (Constitution of the Arab Republic of Egypt, 1971, article 73). At the executive level, 'The President of the Republic shall assume executive power and shall exercise it in the manner stipulated in the Constitution' (article 137). In that sense, the president is expected to work in collaboration with the Egyptian government to form and implement public policies. To this end, the president has been granted many executive powers, including appointing and removing the prime minister (article 141), as well as dealing directly with the council of ministers in terms of calling meetings, presiding at the council's meetings and asking for reports (article 142). Additionally, the president has the power to appoint and dismiss public and military officials, and to issue disciplinary and legal enforcement regulations (articles 43–45). He also has the right to take decisions regarding the creation and organization of public services, and to issue decrees that have the force of law when the parliament is not in session. Many of these powers have not been used following the revolution of January 2011. New restrictions in the draft constitution of 2012 have none the less been imposed on the way in which the president exercises these powers, with more authority given to the parliament in supervising the government's activities (Kirkpatrick, 2012).

The Egyptian Cabinet represents the supreme executive and administrative body of the state, and consists of the prime minister, the cabinet ministers and their deputies (Constitution of the Arab Republic of Egypt,

1971, article 153). Unlike in parliamentary systems, the Egyptian prime minister plays a supervisory role as the actual executive powers are in the hands of the presidents. The Cabinet has considerable influence on shaping the agenda for the parliament through proposing public policies and new legislation. It also has a great impact on the implementation of policies as it has the power to control and coordinate the work of the ministries and streamline the activities of executive authorities in order to meet policy goals and objectives. The hierarchy of the Egyptian Cabinet includes six levels: the prime minister; the ministers; the ministers of state; the ministers without portfolio; the chairmen of departments; and the ministers' delegate. Since the revolution of 2011, consecutive short-term governments have been formed to lead the country through such a critical and sensitive transitional period. The task nevertheless seemed to be so challenging that we have witnessed three governments in fewer than three years. At the time of writing, the existing Cabinet has been working under the leadership and supervision of Hazem Al Beblawi since July 2013, with a composition of 34 members (Ahram Online, 2013).

The legislative function in Egypt is exercised by a bi-cameral parliament encompassing two chambers: the upper chamber known as the Consultative Council or *Maglis El-Shura*; and the lower chamber, the People's Assembly or *Maglis El-Shaab*. It is worth mentioning in this regard that the composition of the legislative branch is under consideration at the time of writing from the 50-member committee responsible for the revision and redrafting of the 2012 Constitution, and that the abolition of *Maglis El-Shura* is highly likely. Those who oppose *Maglis El-Shura* (54 per cent of the committee members) claim that its legislative role is considerably limited and the cost for running the council adds to the burden of the exhausted public budget. They also argue that the creation of the council by President Sadat in 1981 has had a specific purpose: to keep an eye on the national press and not to play a major role in making legislation. On the other hand, those who support the existence of *Maglis El-Shura* argue that the abolition of the council will result in a great loss of expertise. It will also cede new legislative power to the president of the state, particularly in the case of the absence of *Maglis El-Shaab*. From this angle, adding more powers to the president contradicts the goal of limiting presidential powers in the new constitutions and giving more authority to the parliament (AllAfrica, 2013).

Compared with the executive branch, namely the presidency, the Egyptian parliament appears to have limited power and authority over the activities of the government authorities. Although the constitutions of 1971 and 2012 have given the Egyptian parliament the right to hold ministers to account using different tools, including voting a motion of censure, the utilization of such tools and their influence were quite limited and in most of the cases superficial. This deficiency in the relationship between the executive and legislative branches of government is being addressed in the redrafting of the Constitution of 2012, which aims to establish a balance between the two branches, with more powers given to the parliament to effectively supervise, control and hold to account government ministers (Kirkpatrick, 2012).

THE POLITICS OF ADMINISTRATIVE REFORMS IN EGYPT: THE ROLE OF THE STATE

Bureaucracy is a long-standing and deeply rooted phenomenon in Egypt: it is as old as the notion of the state itself in ancient Egypt. The very first idea of a unified central state in Egypt was achieved by King Menes, who unified the northern and the southern parts of Egypt under his reign more than 7000 years ago (Ayubi, 1991). At that time, the establishment of a central state was regarded as a necessity for controlling the River Nile and for organizing farming and irrigation activities (CIPE, 2010). Modern Egypt as a sovereign nation state can, however, be traced to the reign of Mohammed Ali Pasha (1805–48), who attempted to build up a modern army and to develop an educational system that served his ambitions to modernize the Egyptian state socially and economically. The efforts to modernize the Egyptian state under Mohammed Ali Pasha were not fruitful for internal and external reasons. Internally, the lack of accountability and the absence of control and monitoring mechanisms were among the chief shortcomings of the modernization project. At the external level, the pressures, particularly from the European countries, which regarded the rise of modern Egypt as a threat to their interests in the region, ended the developmental plans of Mohammed Ali. The collapse of the modernization project paved the way to the British occupation in 1882.

Mohammed Ali's successors ruled the country under the British occupation until 1952. During this period none of the kings of Egypt presented a comprehensive reform project to modernize the Egyptian state similar to that put forward by Mohammed Ali. They were much less ambitious and in many situations they had to consult the British authorities before taking any decisions. Foreign debts have accumulated in Egypt because of the irresponsible borrowing of the rulers, and corruption has become the norm at different personal and administrative levels. The gap between the poor and the rich has increased and wealth concentration has reached its peak. The lack of social justice, in addition to the spread of corruption in the monarchy, was among the prime drivers for the revolution of 1952, which abolished the monarchy in Egypt and established republicanism.

The Interventionist State of Egypt: Nasser's Welfare Model

The revolution of 1952 marked a new episode in the history of modern Egypt, with new ideological and political orientations. The role of the state in Egyptian society was redefined and more responsibilities and tasks were assigned to the state apparatus. As reported by CIPE (2010: 16),

> The government's responsibility expanded after the Egyptian Revolution of 1952 and it began to assume new roles such as direct investment in the industrial, agricultural and commercial public sectors, offering basic services to its citizens in the fields of health, education, housing, and transport among other sectors.

A comprehensive developmental project was launched under the notion of Arab nationalism, with an eminent role assigned to the Egyptian bureaucracy in leading the transformation process. The role of the private sector in the economy was limited to commercial activities and small business with no role to play in the grand scheme of re-engineering society. This limited role became even more restricted following the large-scale nationalization programme in 1961. As noted by Alissa (2007: 2), 'At the time, feudal and semi-feudal relations ruled over rural areas, while the private sector dominated commerce and small industries'. Direct government interventions were planned and designed to lead and protect the infant national industry and to keep control over foreign currencies.

The interventionist role of the state during President Nasser's reign was manifested in the growing size of public sector organizations as a result of the establishment of new projects and industries, in addition to the nationalization of many private industries at the end of the 1950s (Ayubi, 1991). Added to this, the central tendency of the state during the 1950s and the 1960s, as well as the obligation of the state at that time to achieve full employment via what were called *Tawzeef* policies, have also contributed to the expansion of the public sectors. As noted by Sayed (2004: 10), 'the 1961 "graduate policy" of the interventionist socialist state took upon itself to employ all university graduates to match the enlarged role of the state'. The aim at that time was to fill the gap created by the departure of expatriates who occupied different positions in the Egyptian bureaucracy. The Ministry of Labour Force has played a major role in *Tawzeef* policies as a central agency responsible for recording and allocating university graduates to the different ministries and bureaucratic units. One major shortcoming of these policies was that the distribution of the graduates was undertaken on a quantitative and not qualitative basis. This means that graduates were employed based on the needs of public organizations regardless of their area of specialization. At later stages, the enormous bureaucratic organizations thus created have developed survival strategies and have defended their existence against any attempts to reform, modernize or change their status quo (Ayubi, 1991).

Consequently, a new bureaucratic elite from the well-educated upper and middle classes started to emerge and to gain importance in delivering the intended developmental goals identified by the regime. The composition of the elite has changed at different stages of the implementation process, however. The regime relied at the beginning on the military elite to run the state apparatus; however, this trend changed in later stages to rely more on technocrats, namely engineers and economists. This shift from 'militocracy' to technocratic governments was needed to provide the expertise and specializations for mega-projects initiated at that time, including the high dam and the steel complex (Ayubi, 1991). The pre-eminence of the newly emerged bureaucratic elite became quite obvious, with the Egyptian bureaucracy growing and becoming an integrated part of the state machinery. In this regard, Ayubi (1991: 7) has noted that 'there was certainly an element of charismatic leadership, mass agitation, and socialist rhetoric but the actual running of the regime remained firmly in the hands of the bureaucrats: firstly military and then increasingly technocrats'. State monopolies were extended to include many strategic sectors such as the banking sector, public utilities and the trade sector. The expansion of state ownership in these areas resulted in a sharp decline in private projects and investments, which were basically restricted to agriculture, real estate and the informal economy (Alissa, 2007). The government used the public budget to subsidize a wide range of services and basic goods, accompanied by a noticeable increase in military expenditure.

Despite every effort to establish an effective and specialized bureaucratic regime in order to achieve economic and social goals, the performance record of the Egyptian bureaucracy at that time was not so impressive. As reported by CIPE (2010: 16), 'As the government began to establish public facilities and to administrate them, bureaucratic diseases began to intensify'. On the one hand, joining the civil service at that time was a means to gain social status and to be a part of the developmental trajectory of the state. A wide range of services in areas such as education, health and social security was provided via public organizations. The public sector was seen as a vehicle for social mobility and as an arena that would reach full employment and hire new graduates. On the other hand, many complaints about the red tape and routine in delivering governmental services have been documented, in addition to many other problems related to coordination and cooperation among the gigantic body of government in relation to implementing economic and social reforms. Furthermore, the overstaffing of public organizations has also contributed to the deterioration of public sector performance and created a new form of unemployment known as disguised unemployment, wherein new graduates were hired for no reason or need but to fulfil employment obligations by the state. Many of these issues have become chronic maladies in the body of the Egyptian administrative system until the time of writing (2013).

From Bureaucracy to Oligarchy: Sadat's Technocratic State

By the end of the 1960s it was quite clear that the Egyptian bureaucratic leviathan had become too big to perform efficiently. Therefore President Sadat started to change the orientation of the economic and social compass to focus more on the private sector and less on public organizations for delivering public services and goods. Ayubi (1991) none the less has rightly noted that it would be inaccurate to attribute the ideological changes at this stage solely to the change in leadership. The Egyptian bureaucratic elite, the most beneficial party from the creation of the public sector and the expansive role of the state, found itself at a cross-roads. On the one hand, Egyptian bureaucrats realized that it was almost impossible to carry on working with existing structures with all their shortcomings, particularly the financial losses of the public sector. But, at the same time, they were reluctant to accept drastic changes that might affect their privileges and the benefits they receive because of their positions. Three main trends can be identified among Egyptian bureaucrats at that time in relation to how to reform the administrative systems. A conservative group of bureaucrats were in favour of continuing to do business as usual through public sector organizations. Another group of civil servants preferred a full shift to a capitalist economic system and a move from public to private forms of organization. The third group of bureaucrats tried to find a middle ground and was more pragmatic, starting to think about how to benefit from their positions in the public sector when doing business with the private sector.

A new pattern of relations between bureaucrats and private investors emerged: the least that can be said about it is that it was corrupt. The revolving-door effect was quite evident, with many senior civil servants and ex-military personnel leaving the public sector to join the vibrant and lucrative private sector at that time. Ayubi (1991: 14) has commented on this phenomenon:

> From the late sixties and early seventies ex-army officers and high government officials were moving consistently into private business . . . among the

prominent businessmen in 1976 one could count two ex-premiers, twenty-two ex-ministers, dozens of ex-chairmen of public enterprises, undersecretaries of state and governors.

Public managers and senior government officials started to think of ways in which they could utilize their networks and connections, in addition to the wealth they accumulated over the years, to benefit from the new shift in state ideology to focus more on the private sector. Some of them started their own private businesses while in public office and entered into different forms of transactions and deals that benefited their private businesses at the expense of the public organizations they ran. Other forms of misconduct have also been reported, wherein the private sector has exploited public organizations using different methods, including commissions and bribes to public managers in return for contracts to supply their organizations with products from private companies. The prices of the supplied material and goods were of course much higher than their market value (sometimes 400 per cent higher). The facilities of public sector organizations, including personnel and means of transportation, were used in ways that benefited the private businesses of public managers or their relatives. The lack of effective internal monitoring plus the absence of accountability mechanisms facilitated the misconduct undertaken by bureaucrats and resulted in a situation in which the private sector flourished at the expense of the public sector.

The victory of the Egyptian army in 1973 in its war against Israel gave President Sadat and his regime more legitimacy and boosted his policies, particularly on the economic front. The new orientation towards capitalism and the increasing role of the private sector materialized on the ground in the form of what was known as the 'open-door policy' or *Infitah*. The blueprint of this policy was the October paper in which President Sadat called for 'Opening up the Egyptian economy to foreign investment and inter-Arab joint investment projects, as well as promoting the role of the private sector in the economy' (Alissa, 2007: 3). This policy orientation was translated into concrete terms with the promulgation of Law No. 43 of June 1974. The law encouraged private investments, including foreign investment, by granting investors tax holidays and exemptions.

The 'open-door policy' was justified on different grounds; nevertheless, its overall rationale is still quite vague. For some, *Infitah* was more than an economic policy; it represents a master policy with implications in different socioeconomic and administrative areas. The idea was to combine Egyptian human capital with the know-how of the Western countries, namely the USA and Japan, and the surpluses of oil revenues in the Gulf to achieve economic development in Egypt. The newly emergent class of businessmen (former state bureaucrats and military officials) acted as a catalyst for such a transformation. By doing so, they have turned against the very administrative system that benefited them the most. The new business elite also rejected any etatist policies or social rhetoric and called for cutting down the public sector and lifting existing limitations on wealth.

By the end of the 1970s and during the early 1980s the public sector in Egypt was in an awkward position. At the outset, the open-door policy pursued by President Sadat limited but did not put an end to the interventionist state created by President Nasser. As noted by Sayed (2004: 3), 'Even though Sadat attempted to give more space to market economy through the open door policy, he did not alter the interventionist functions of the state'. Consequently, Egypt ended up with a public sector that was competing unfairly with a young and fast-growing private sector while being totally isolated from any grand political ideology and any clear idea about its role in society compared with the economic enterprise. Additionally, the public sector was run by experts who lacked public spirit and had little belief in the value of public organizations. Economic burdens that resulted from the wars Egypt was involved in, particularly the defeat of 1967, also contributed to the problems of the public sector alongside the different forms of corruption and exploitation by the private sector. All these shortcomings and symptoms have paved the way for another reconsideration and redefinition of the role of the Egyptian state and public administration in Egyptian society. The emphasis this time was on the state as a regulator and rule-maker rather than as a direct service provider or producer.

The Regulatory State of Egypt

Following the assassination of President Sadat in October 1981, President Mubarak came to power to continue what Sadat had started. No big ideological changes took place, as more emphasis was put on the importance of the private sector in leading the economy and the urgency of addressing the shortcomings of the public sector in order to minimize its negative impacts on the economy and the public budget. In this regard, Vignal (2010) has noted that the first step to reform the Egyptian economy was taken by the former president Sadat, who initiated the open-doors policy in 1974. This policy gave some fresh impetus to the private sector; however, in terms of economic development it remained far too modest in scope and ambition to make any real difference.

The emphasis on the significance of private investments was welcomed and encouraged by the WB and the IMF as they agree with their prescription presented in the form of the Structural Adjustment Plan in 1991 to reform and revitalize the Egyptian economy (Alissa, 2007). In that sense, the reform process has been associated from the very beginning with the deteriorated economic conditions and the intervention of the international monetary institutions to structurally reform the Egyptian economy. The economic reform programme has included a major component of privatization in terms of selling state-owned enterprises and liberalizing the utility sectors. The idea was to roll back the frontiers of the Egyptian state and to encourage the retreat of the state from many economic and social fields in order to allow more space for the private sector to take the lead in the area of production and service provision. Contrary to what was expected, liberalization and privatization during the 1980s and 1990s have led to a vast growth in the state's regulatory obligations and marked a new age of the Egyptian state: the age of the Egyptian regulatory state (Badran, 2013).

The emergence of the regulatory state in Egypt was quite evident given the number of independent regulatory authorities created as part of liberalization in many utility sectors. The telecoms sector in Egypt is a case in point. Driven by the need to make credible policy commitments to private investors domestically and internationally, the Egyptian government created the National Telecommunications Regulatory Authority (NTRA) as an independent sector regulator. That was a necessary step for liberalizing the sector, given the long history of state monopoly in this area. The creation of the NTRA was instrumental in that it was devised to encourage participation of the private sector in service provision but without harming the interests of the incumbent Telecom Egypt, which acted for years as the sector's sole service provider and regulator at the same time (Badran, 2011).

The economic reforms enacted by the consecutive governments under Mubarak's regime had deep social and economic impacts on the majority of the population in Egypt. As was the case during President Sadat's era, few businessmen have succeeded in forging strong ties with the ruling National Democratic Party (NDP) and the political leadership in the country. Many of them have occupied influential positions in the parliament, government and the NDP that enabled them to benefit the most from the reform process and to maximize their personal profits and revenues at the expense of the masses. A quick look at some of those figures clearly illustrates how corrupt and unfair the system was. In 1989 Ahmed Ezz, an Egyptian businessman and the Secretary of Organization in the former NDP, had $300 000. After joining Mubarak's administration, this figure grew to $3 billion. The many different positions occupied by Ezz in the party, parliament and government enabled him in a relatively short period of time to control over 60 per cent of the steel market in Egypt. Other ministers, including former Minister of Housing Ahmed al-Maghraby, former Tourism Minister Zuhair Garrana, and former Minister of Trade and Industry Rashid Mohamed Rashid have had their fortunes estimated at almost $2 billion (Ramstack, 2011).

In addition to their very close ties with the regime, many businessmen have also benefited from the way in which the reform process was undertaken. The implementation of unpopular privatization programmes in particular was full of deficiencies, corrupt practices and a great lack of transparency with regard to the ways in which public assets were evaluated and sold to private investors. The revenues from the process of selling state assets were not used efficiently in investment projects but most probably used to finance current government activities, which means the loss of those revenues. Additionally, many employees and workers lost their jobs because of the downsizing programmes, and joined the long queue of the unemployed. In short, the rich have become richer and the poor have become poorer. Under such worsened economic and social conditions, the Egyptian people revolted against Mubarak's regime and asked primarily for bread, social justice, human dignity, and better standards of living.

The Impact of the January 2011 Revolution: Back to the Welfare State Model?

Mubarak's regime was unexpectedly brought down by protesters in February 2011. On 25 January 2011, millions of Egyptians, fuelled by anger and driven by the regime's corrupt practices at all social, economic, and political levels, went out into the streets of Egypt, calling first for radical changes and reforms, and eventually for the overthrow of the regime. The success of the revolution took everybody by surprise and the question became: what to do next? People held great expectations and high hopes, as is the case with any country after a revolution. Much was going on in Egypt: vibrant debates about the new Constitution and the role and responsibilities of different authorities, as well as about individual freedoms and rights. Presidential elections resulted in the selection of Dr Mohammed Morsi, the first civilian president of Egypt since 1952, and a new parliament with a majority of the seats went for the first time to the Islamists, namely the Muslim Brotherhood.

Because of the incompetence of Morsi's administration, as it failed to address the most pressing economic and social issues facing the country, people went out into the streets again on 30 June and 3 July 2013, but this time they were backed by the military institution. President Morsi was ousted from office and a new interim government was selected to run the country during the transitional phase. Since the January 2011 revolution and throughout the rule of the Muslim Brotherhood the economic situation moved from bad to worse. At the time of writing, the interim government is running an economy with alarming indicators: a budget deficit that has soared to about $3.2 billion per month; a gross domestic product (GDP) of 2.2 per cent per year, while a 6 per cent GDP rate is required to absorb those who search for jobs; a drastic decline in revenues from oil and gas exports, which have been redirected to meet domestic demand for energy; an inefficient system of subsidization that costs the government millions of dollars; a lack of cooperation from the IMF, which again asked for more reforms that will negatively impact on the already deteriorated socioeconomic conditions (Werr and Torchia, 2013).

The interim government does not have a clear strategy on how to address these economic problems. One possible explanation for this is that the ministers are aware that they do not have a complete mandate from the people to proceed with radical policies that may backfire on them. Another possible explanation could be that the interim government try to avoid unpopular policies which may have negative impacts on the people. For example, a decision to cut subsidization on fuel will result in a rise in fuel prices which in turn may push people to protest against the government. From this angle, the interim government preferred to throw the ball into the next elected government's court. That means, they have decided to use the easy money they received from the Gulf countries namely Saudi Arabia, UAE, and Kuwait to provide people with pressing needs in a welfare form of solution to the persistent economic problems. This strategy might work in the short run, nonetheless, in the long run that is not a sustainable way to deal with the weakened economy of Egypt. Most of the aids that Egypt has received from the Gulf States come in the form of loans which have to be paid back with the required interest. That means more economic burdens in the medium and long run. At the same time, going back to the welfare state model with a centralized economy and a state-led public sector does not appear to be a plausible option.

The discussion so far has indicated that the perceived role of the state and in turn public administration in the Egyptian society has changed at different points in history in an attempt to respond to ideological shifts and sometimes changes in the political leadership. The common denominator among all political regimes even since the creation of the first central state in Egypt was the instrumental utilization of public administration and the intertwining of administrative reforms and reforms in other areas, especially the economy. To put it another way, the Egyptian public administration has always been regarded as a means for delivering broader socioeconomic reforms in society and not as an end in itself. Regardless of the ideological orientation of the political regime, the role of the Egyptian bureaucratic elite and public organizations in realizing the intended developmental goals was highly emphasized by the political leadership. Therefore developing and reforming bureaucracy in Egypt was a means to facilitate capital accumulation and development as well as improving the competitiveness of the entire economy (CIPE, 2010).

THE EGYPTIAN BUREAUCRACY: DIAGNOSING THE MALADIES

Examination of the Egyptian bureaucracy reveals that since the very beginning of the central state in Egypt the performance record of the bureaucratic units was not very impressive. The administrative system in Egypt has shown symptoms of numerous managerial maladies that can be described as chronic. The reason for this is that, in spite of the different initiatives to reform and modernize the Egyptian public administration, the results of such reforms in terms of their ability to address managerial and administrative problems of the public sector in Egypt were quite modest. Discussing the problems of the public sector in Egypt in detail goes beyond the scope of this chapter. Therefore, in this section the major problems will be briefly highlighted as an introduction to the discussion of reform initiatives in the section to follow.

From a structural point of view, the way in which the administrative apparatus in Egypt is organized has greatly contributed to the problems and shortcomings highlighted in this section. The main characteristics of the Egyptian bureaucracy are summarized by Sayed (2004) as being hierarchical, centralized and mechanistic. Rigid hierarchical relationships exist among the different levels of the bureaucratic machine, with decision-making authority at the top managerial levels. As mechanistic entities, public organizations in Egypt include top–down communication channels to transfer orders from the central authority with clearly defined rules and standard operating procedures. As put by Lunenburg (2012: 50), mechanistic organizations are characterized by 'a rigid hierarchy; high levels of formalization; a heavy reliance on rules, policies, and procedures; vertical specialization; centralized decision making; downward communication flows; and narrowly defined tasks'. Although they are designed to be efficient, these organizational features of mechanistic organizations have resulted in practice in many shortcomings and problems.

A major issue for running hierarchical, centralized and mechanistic bureaucracies is the lack of coordination and the inevitable overlapping between administrative units. Structural overlapping can be noted among different ministries and governmental units in Egypt. For instance, the Ministry of Irrigation and Water Resources intersects with the Ministry of Agriculture and Land Reclamation. The same can be said about the Ministry of Petroleum and the General Authority of Petroleum, as well as the Ministry of Manpower and Immigration and the Ministry of Administrative Development. Added to this, the existence of different supreme monitoring and supervisory bodies with reporting requirements and mechanisms from lower-level organizations has added to the complexity and rigidity of the Egyptian administrative system and made the task of coordinating its activities almost impossible (Sayed, 2004).

Composition-wise, as is the case in various countries, the government of Egypt is the largest employer in the country. According to the Central Agency for Public Mobilization and Statistics (CAPMAS), the number of public sector employees reached 5.1 million in the 2011/12 fiscal year (CAPMAS, 2013, www.capmas.gov.eg). This fairly large number of employees has always been an obstacle in the face of any reform efforts. As public employees, those who work for the public sector in Egypt are very well protected by different laws and regulations that guarantee their prerogatives and make them untouchable in many situations. This has influenced the way in which those employees perceive their role in relation to the public they are supposed to serve. They are most likely to look at themselves as masters who rule through their public offices and bureaux. They are the people with power who can make things happen; they are in office for life, regardless of their performance, and they work for the government and not for citizens or anyone else.

This understanding of the role of public administration has resulted in the creation and reinforcement of authoritarian organizational culture wherein public employees normally look up to their superiors in the hierarchy and try superficially to comply with their orders. Such a negative attitude has been reinforced by the central and hierarchical nature of the bureaucracy and the overall authoritarian and paternalistic nature of Egyptian society. In this context, Sayed (2004: 12) has noted that

> In a large bureaucracy with a promotion system based on seniority rather than performance, basic monthly salaries ranging from USD 35 to USD 70, and supplementary payments controlled by senior management, employees are encouraged to be in the good books of their superiors.

Employees must show respect to their superiors, who in turn have the right to decide on their remuneration and also have the authority to deprive them of other privileges. There is no place for consumers or citizens in this obedience chain, simply because citizens have no power to harm public employees' status or to hold them accountable for their misconduct. Obedient employees always receive the support of their managers, even if they were wrong or delivered poor services to the citizens.

Such an authoritarian organizational culture, along with the absence of accountability mechanisms and the lack of transparency, has made corruption and favouritism the name of the game in the Egyptian public sector. Inefficient delivery of public services and the image of the all-powerful public employee have forced many people to engage in corrupt practices such as bribes in order to get their jobs done properly. Despite the difficulty of measuring the exact degree of corruption in the Egyptian administrative system, given the secretive nature of corrupt practices, international organizations, including Transparency International, Global Integrity and the Heritage Foundation, have acknowledged the widespread corruption in Egypt, particularly over the last two decades (OECD, 2009). The 2013 annual Corruption Perceptions Index issued by Transparency International indicated that Egypt dropped six places (118 out of 176 countries) as levels of bribery, abuse of power and secret dealings remain high in the Egyptian administrative system (Transparency International, 2013). Most of the corrupt practices, however, take place in the low-level bureaucracy, with a noticeable decline in high-level corruption among ministers and senior civil servants (Aziz and Clinger, 2013).

Petty corruption among public employees has been facilitated by the lack of democratic governance and the absence of internal monitoring and accountability mechanisms. As reported by CIPE (2010: 19), 'The absence of democracy, public scrutiny, properly qualified civil servants, and increasing centralization has made corruption rampant'. A major contributing factor to the spread of corruption at that level is the jungle of laws and regulations resulting from the accumulative reform efforts and initiatives. Many archaic laws and regulations are in place, which add to the ambiguity of the legal and regulatory environment of the Egyptian public sector. To give an example, there are more than 40 different laws and regulations and no fewer than 55 decrees regulating the government employees' pay system (El-Baradei and Abdelahmid, 2010: 62). Such an ambiguous legal and regulatory environment gives corrupt employees the opportunity to twist and manipulate laws and regulations in a way that complicates the administrative processes and the processes of service delivery. The regulatory burden goes directly to citizens, who have to pay bribes to get their work done.

In addition to the absence of good governance, in terms of accountability and transparency in the processes of public administration, which greatly contribute to the spread of corrupt practices, other important factors should also be underlined in this respect. Chief among these is the low salary and low remuneration scale of public employees. This is not to say that receiving a low salary justifies corrupt practices, but it is important to refer to that issue as an explanatory factor in why public employees seek benefits from public office. Although minimum wages are guaranteed by law, public employees' payments do not allow them to meet their basic needs as they are most likely to fall under the national poverty line. In this regard, the CIPE (2010: 16) has reported that 'civil servants suffer from extremely low salaries compared to the constant growth in prices of products and services'. In the same vein, El-Baradei and Abdelahmid (2010: 63) have stated that 'the lower bound entry salary for a civil servant at grade 6 is LE 35 per month in 2008'. After adding bonuses, this figure jumps to LE 289 per month; nevertheless, the growing inflation rates in addition to the devaluation of the Egyptian pound and the continued increase in prices reduce the purchasing power of public employees and flatten their real wages (Sayed, 2004).

This issue becomes more complicated if one considers the difference between the minimum and the maximum levels of income in the public sector; it can be complicated even more if we look at the discrepancies among public organizations and across sectors. Just comparing the payments received by public employees working for central ministries such as the Ministry of Finance with what local authority employees might get can highlight a huge gap in incomes (CIPE, 2010). Addressing the low salary of public employees has always been an issue for the consecutive governments of Egypt. Because of the large size of the public sector, initiating any shape of reform in this area will definitely have a detrimental impact on the public budget. A one-pound monthly increase in public employees' salaries means an increase of over 5 million pounds per month in the public budget, as mentioned by Zaki Abu-Amer, the former minister of administrative development (Abu-Amer, 2001).

The low salary and low remuneration scales of public employees have been worsened by the deteriorated physical working environment of public organizations. A visit to one of the public organizations, particularly in rural areas and districts other than Cairo and Alexandria, can tell an analyst a great deal about the shortage of resources, in the physical sense, of those organizations. Old furniture, antique computers, if any, overstaffed offices, and of course unsatisfied employees, is the norm in public offices in Egypt. As reported by Sayed (2004: 9), in Upper Egypt '16% of office buildings are considered hazardous, 18% do not have telephone connections, and 6% do not have access to water, sanitation or electrical energy'. The poor working environment and lack of resources affect the way in which public employees deal with the citizens and the way they deliver their services.

Combined with low salaries, poor working conditions have resulted in a deterioration of the social status of the public employees in society. Although it is prohibited by law to combine public employment with any other work during non-working hours unless permitted (Law 47, 1978:

articles 11–12), it is quite common to find a public employee who drives a taxi or works in a restaurant or in any other private venue in order to earn extra money to compensate for the low salary received from the government. In this context, an analysis of the responses of 100 employees interviewed by El-Baradei and Abdelahmid (2010: 68) indicated that 82 per cent of respondents were not staisfied with their monthly pay and 97 per cent thought that monthly pay is not compatible with the market value of wages and salaries. Any explanation of the demoralization of public values and low productivity of the Egyptian civil service should underline these factors.

Another human resources issue in Egyptian public organizations is related to the appraisal system and the way in which employees' performance is evaluated. In this regard, Maher (2011: 399) has noted that 'the whole evaluation system is highly subjective, since 99% of employees receive "excellent" grades regardless of their performance which may lead to the deterioration of the performance system among government employees'. According to Maher, the assessors themselves lack the very basic skills required for conducting performance evaluation and appraisal. Added to this, seniority and not necessarily performance is the major factor to be taken into account when promoting public employees. Sayed (2004) has attributed the existence of such a flawed evaluation and appraisal system to the weak financial incentives and rewards in the public sector. From her perspective, the assessors try to compensate public employees for the absence of substantial financial rewards for their achievements by grading them 'excellent' or giving a score of 90 per cent or above in order to facilitate their promotion to higher positions.

The negative organizational culture of the Egyptian public sector has also been reflected in the lack of trust among the different levels of the organizational pyramid. Those at the bottom of the pyramid do not trust senior civil servants and top bureaucrats who, according to their view, treat them as scapegoats to cover their failures and incompetence in running their organizations. In this regard, Sayed (2004) has mentioned that middle and junior staff always cast doubt on the intentions of top management and their reform initiatives. They normally look at them as the sole beneficiary of these reforms. Additionally, the close relationships between top management and senior civil servants on the one hand and politicians on the other increase such doubts and make public employees suspicious about the real intent and goals of reform.

Having identified and briefly discussed what can be described as the chronic maladies of the Egyptian bureaucracy, and without making any claim that what has been debated so far provides an exhaustive list of public sector problems in Egypt, the next section will focus on the reform initiatives and the government's efforts to address the highlighted issues.

THE EGYPTIAN BUREAUCRACY: REFORM INITIATIVES

Administrative reform in Egypt has been launched under different slogans such as 'an administrative revolution', 'shaking up the government institutions', or 'demolishing the failing routine' (CIPE, 2010). As indicated above, the reform of public administration should be regarded as a part of an overall reform project to improve social and economic conditions in Egypt. The message was pretty clear that the bureaucratic body of the state suffers from different illnesses and there is a pressing need to find a remedy in order to treat these problems. The implementation of the reform, none the less, as well as the delivery methods, results and outcomes, were controversial issues, as will be indicated later in this section.

Given the complex and overlapping nature of the problems facing public sector organizations, it would be an oversimplification to expect that there is a medicine that can cure all these long-standing illnesses at once. A gradual approach has been followed by different consecutive governments in an attempt to solve the problems of the public sector. Different reform initiatives have been launched and efforts have been made to improve the structural as well as the functional aspects of the Egyptian public administration. At the structural level, the OECD (2010) has reported that Egypt has taken important steps towards solving the issue of overlap among public organizations. According to the report, a programme has been launched to review the functions of existing public administration units in order to assess the roles they play and the functions they deliver to society. Redundant functions and duplication are to be eliminated in order to improve coordination and cooperation among public organizations as well as to enhance complementarity among their activities. The report also underlined efforts to simplify administrative procedures and create a good legal and regulatory environment.

The Egyptian Regulatory Reform and Development Activity (ERRADA) is a case in a point in this regard. This initiative started in 2008 in an attempt to open a dialogue between public and private organizations in order to come up with an effective regulatory framework. To this end, ERRADA has undertaken different activities to address the issues related to the multiplicity of complex and overlapping regulations: lack of clarity of valid regulations; absence of a system to identify implicitly repealed decrees; overlap of authorities issuing regulations; inconsistency in the regulation drafting cycle across ministries; and the lack of specific mechanisms to study the economic impact of new regulations (ERRADA, www.errada.gov.eg). Despite the good efforts exerted by the initiative to improve the regulatory environment, the scope of this exercise is still considerably limited given the size of the Egyptian bureaucracy. Only ten ministries were involved at the initial stage; however, it would be good practice to extend the activities of ERRADA to other ministries and administrative units.

The Egyptian government has also embarked on a programme to improve the process of service delivery and the quality of provided services using e-governance. The idea was to promote innovative solutions to service delivery problems, to achieve customer satisfaction internally and externally, and to improve decision-making capacity by providing solid and up-to-date evidence to decision-makers. As reported by the Ministry of State for Administrative Development (MSAD) (2010: 9),

> ICT is the main tool that is used to develop the two dimensions of government services 'front and back ends'. Using ICT enables better efficiency and simple government services, and allows for 24 hours services throughout the country via various delivery channels and models.

Different models of e-government have been communicated and several international agreements have been signed with countries such as France, South Korea, Slovenia, Malaysia and India to learn from their experiences in e-governance. The Egyptian Government Services Portal was launched in 2004, supported by an advanced search engine that allows bilingual search and provides access to 700 informational and 100 transactional services. For better usability purposes, a new version of the portal was launched in 2008. Following a citizen-centric approach, the government established a Citizens Relationship Management (CRM) system in 2009. The system aims at maintaining and managing citizens' complaints, suggestions and inquiries. The efforts of e-government applications can also be seen in creating electronic databases and smart cards in order to deal with problems in areas such as intergovernmental cooperation and subsidization policies.

Despite such efforts to integrate ICT in service delivery and the businesses of government institutions in general, the overall proration of government organizations using ICT is still low. A quick look at the e-Government Readiness Index 2004, which underlines the 'generic capacity or aptitude of the public sector to use ICT for encapsulating in public services and deploying to the public, high quality information (explicit knowledge) and effective communication tools that support human development' (DPADM, 2004: 15), reveals that, in comparsion with other countries in the region such as Algeria, Tunisia and Morocco, Egypt's efforts in this area look pretty humble; see Figure 7.1.

In response to such a limited utilization of ICT by government

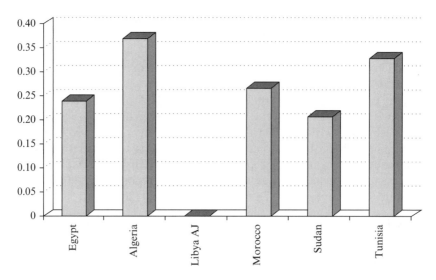

Source: United Nations (2003).

Figure 7.1   e-Government Readiness Index

institutions, MSAD has started an awareness campaign to educate public managers about the usefulness of using such technologies and the positive impacts of their utilization on customer satisfaction and organizational performance. Thanks to such efforts, in addition to improvements at the infrastructure level and in relation to citizens' participation, the rank of Egypt has improved in the 2012 index, in which Egypt was ranked second after Tunisia; see Figure 7.2.

A comparison of Figures 7.1 and 7.2 indicates that between 2004 and 2012 Egypt succeeded in closing the gap separating its e-government from the leading North African countries. In fact, it succeeded in coming before Algeria and Morocco and very close to Tunisia. Another major component in the reform initiatives focuses on creating a more account- able, more transparent and less corrupt public sector through embracing the notion of good governance. As reported by Egypt Independent (2012), 'Corruption ranging from the petty to the grand scale was one of the main grievances that toppled Mubarak'. Despite the fact that Egypt has more or less succeeded in stabilizing its economy during the last two decades, very little has been done to fight corruption and promote good govern- ance (see Alissa, 2007). A gap could be spotted in this regard between the official positions of the consecutive governments, which have all been in favour of more transparency and less corrupt practices in the

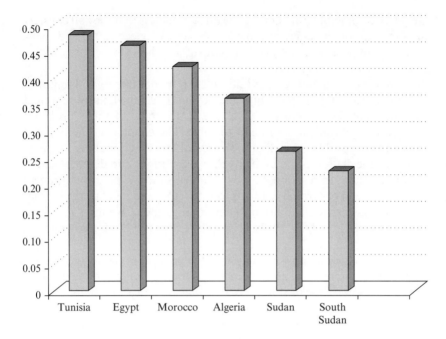

Source: Based on the UN 2012 e-Government Readiness Index.

Figure 7.2 E-government development

public sector, and what was going on on the ground as different forms of corruption were taking place at different levels.

CONCLUSION

In this chapter, the process of administrative reform in Egypt has been analysed from a political-economy perspective in an attempt to underline the major changes in the role of the Egyptian state in society and the associated changes in the role of public administration. Three main models have been identified: the welfare; mixed-economy; and regulatory. Under each model the role of the state has been redefined in the light of the ideological orientation of the political regime. In turn, the role of the public sector has also changed from being the leading driver of economic development under the welfare-state model to becoming one among other non-state actors involved in forming and implementing public policies under the mixed-economy model and to a greater extent under the regulatory model. A common feature among the three models is that they all consider the Egyptian bureaucracy as a means for achieving economic and social ends. Consequently, the Egyptian bureaucracy has always been at the centre of any reform project.

In spite of the many reform initiatives to modernize Egyptian public administration, the Egyptian bureaucracy has developed many persistent maladies that defied reforms. Over the years, some of those problems have become chronic and difficult to solve. The chapter has highlighted some of those problems, including structural and functional overlapping, as well as the deterioration in the working conditions and demoralization of public values. In response to those problems the Egyptian government initiated several programmes to improve the legal and regulatory environment for businesses, in addition to developing innovative ways to deliver better services at higher levels of quality using ICT and e-government applications.

Overall, the discussion and analysis of the political economy of administrative reform initiatives in Egypt indicates that the Egyptian bureaucracy does not lack expertise or skills, given the high qualifications of most of the public employees, particularly those who occupy senior positions. Added to this, senior managers have always welcomed reform initiatives and supported innovative practices. The problem, however, springs from the way in which public sector reform initiatives have been implemented. The ability of senior civil servants to communicate the reform messages and to emphasize the importance of reforms and their positive impacts to middle and front-line managers, let alone the rest of the employees, was limited.

Furthermore, most of the reform initiatives come from the senior civil servants and top bureaucrats and follow a top–down approach without real participation from middle and lower management. This top–down approach to enacting public sector reforms, in addition to the exclusion of employees from decision-making processes, normally results in lack of ownership of the reform project. In this context, public employees tend to perceive reform initiatives as benefiting senior managers and politicians while adding to the burdens of employees. They also look at such reforms as cosmetic and as not resulting in real change on the ground.

REFERENCES

Abu-Amer, Z. (2001). Development not unemployment. *Ahram Weekly Online*: http://weekly.ahram.org.eg/.
Ahram Online (2013). Egypt's interim president is swearing in first government, 16 July.
Alissa, S. (2007). *The Political Economy of Reform in Egypt: Understanding the Role of Institutions*. Carnegie Middle East Centre.

AllAfrica (2013). Egypt: Shura Council cancelled in New Constitution. http://allafrica.com/stories/201311081787.html.

Ayubi, N.N. (1991). *The State and Public Policies in Egypt Since Sadat*. Reading: Ithaca.

Aziz, S. and Clinger, D. (2013). Egypt's corruption woes. CNNWORLD: http://globalpublicsquare.blogs.cnn.com/2013/02/08/egypts-corruption-woes/.

Badran, A. (2011). *The Regulatory Management of Privatised Public Utilities: A Network Perspective on the Regulatory Process in the Egyptian Telecommunications Market*. VDM Verlag Dr. Müller.

Badran, A. (2013). Understanding the Egyptian regulatory state: independent regulators in theory and practice. In N.K. Dubash and B. Morgan (eds), *The Rise of the Regulatory State of the South: Infrastructure and Development in Emerging Economies*. Oxford: Oxford University Press, pp. 55–87.

Central Agency for Public Mobilization and Statistics (CAPMAS) (2013). http://www.capmas.gov.eg/.

CIPE (2010). *Tackling the Leviathan: Reforming Egyptian Bureaucracy for Improved Economic Growth*. Cairo: CIPE.

Constitution of the Arab Republic of Egypt (1971). Retrieved from http://www.sis.gov.eg/En/Templates/Articles/tmpArticles.aspx?CatID=208.

DPADM (2004). *The Arab Republic of Egypt Public Administration Country Profile*. UN: Division for Public Administration and Development Management (DPADM).

Egypt Independent (2012). Egypt slips in corruption index despite Arab Spring. http://www.egyptindependent.com/news/egypt-slips-corruption-index-despite-arab-spring.

Egyptian Regulatory Reform and Development Activity (ERRADA) (2013). Retrieved from http://www.errada.gov.eg/index_en.php?op=about_us_en, 11 December.

El-Baradei, L. and Abdelahmid, D. (2010). Reforming the pay system for government employees in Egypt. *International Public Management Review*, 59–87.

Kirkpatrick, D. (2012). Egyptian Islamists approve draft constitution despite objections. *The New York Times*, 29 November.

Lunenburg, F. (2012). Mechanistic–organic organizations – an axiomatic theory: authority based on bureaucracy or professional norms. *International Journal of Scholarly Academic Intellectual Diversity*, 50–62.

Maher, A. (2011). Reforming government employees' performance appraisal system in New Egypt. *Journal of Emerging Trends in Economics and Management Sciences*, 399–401.

MSAD (2010). *Ministry of State for Administrative Development 2010–2012 Work plan*. Cairo: MSAD.

OECD (2009). Business climate development strategy. http://www.oecd.org/daf/psd/46341460.pdf.

OECD (2010). *Background note on the state of economic and governance reforms*. http://www.oecd.org/countries/egypt/40252444.pdf.

Ramstack, T. (2011). Obama optimistic about Egypt as negotiators make concessions. *All Headline News*: http://archive.is/g47JZ.

Sayed, F. (2004). *Innovation in Public Administration: The Case of Egypt*. New York: UN DESA.

Transparency International (2013). Corruption perceptions index. http://www.transparency.org/research/cpi/overview.

Vignal, L. (2010). Reforming Egypt? Fifteen years of EU–Egypt cooperation from the Association Agreement to the European Neighbourhood Policy. RAMSES working papers: http://www.sant.ox.ac.uk/esc/ramses/ramsespaperVignal.pdf.

Werr, P. and Torchia, A. (2013). New Egypt government may promote welfare, not economic reform. REUTERS: http://www.reuters.com/article/2013/07/17/us-egypt-economy-policy-analysis-idUSBRE96G0IP20130717.

8. The Canadian public service: in search of a new equilibrium

Donald J. Savoie

INTRODUCTION

The Canadian public service has been buffeted about in recent years by a variety of forces. Globalization, the desire of politicians to grab hold of the policy-making levers and to become less dependent on career public servants for policy advice, and the push to have public sector managers emulate their private sector counterparts have knocked the public service off its traditional moorings. Politicians in Canada, like those in other Anglo-American democracies, have and continue to run against the status quo, entrenched government and whatever else stands in the way of change. Bureaucracy has often been the target.

It is against this backdrop that this chapter takes stock of the state of the Canadian public service. In Canada, the public service has been asked to keep pace with the private sector, as it struggles to compete in an increasingly competitive environment. At the same time, the government has introduced one measure after another and one oversight body after another to ensure greater transparency in government operations. As mentioned above, the Canadian public service has been knocked off its traditional moorings in recent years. Canadian politicians, like their other Anglo-American counterparts, decided some 30 years ago to grab hold of the policy-making levers and to push public servants to become better managers and to look to the private sector for guidance. The rise of the global economy and the politics of fiscal squeeze have had a profound impact on the work of Canadian public servants. The chapter reviews the ambitious reform measures and other developments that have reshaped the Canadian public service. It seeks to answer a number of questions – what role does the public service play in shaping new policy; what has been the impact of various management reform efforts; and how have public servants been able to square various contradictory messages directed at them? It concludes with an assessment of what now and how the Canadian public service, as an institution, can move towards a new equilibrium.

RUNNING AGAINST THE STATUS QUO

Margaret Thatcher's election victory in 1979 proved to be a seminal moment in the development of Western bureaucracies. The election of other right-of-centre politicians, Ronald Reagan in 1980, and Brian Mulroney in Canada in 1984, sent a clear signal that the status quo was no longer acceptable. Thatcher once declared that she disliked public servants as a breed; Reagan said that he was going to Washington to drain the swamp; and Mulroney pledged that, if elected, he would give pink slips and running shoes to the bureaucrats (Savoie, 1994).

They had an agenda – cut government down to size, bring a distinct Conservative agenda to policy making, hold the upper hand in shaping new policies and direct senior public servants to concentrate their efforts on the boiler room of government operations. They set out to turn government administrators into public sector managers with a bias for action. If senior public servants could not come up with ways to become better managers, then they should look to their private sector counterparts for inspiration and guidance. If there was no bottom line in government, then public servants were told to come up with one.

The notion that government managers should emulate their private sector counterparts has not lost its political currency in recent years. It will be recalled, for example, that Tony Blair made it clear, time and again, that the private sector was key to improving management in government.[1] In Canada, prime ministers Jean Chrétien, Paul Martin and now Stephen Harper have all sung the praises of private sector management practices and said that government managers should borrow best practices from business (Savoie, 2013).

The above makes the point that the Canadian public service has been buffeted by several powerful forces. They include: politicians determined to take charge of policy making and to put public servants in their place; a new approach to management; globalization and sustained efforts to make government operations more transparent.

GLOBALIZATION

Jan Aart Scholte (1997: 439) explains that one consequence of globalization has been the "detachment of money from territorial space". It is now widely accepted that those national economies that do not adjust to the requirements of the global economy will suffer. National governments protect their home businesses at their peril, making them uncompetitive over time. In brief, globalization has "deterriolized" economic power (Beck, 2007).

Globalization has also been felt in the public sector. Ideas on new approaches to management move around quickly and national governments will latch on to them for fear of being left behind. New public management (NPM) is a case in point. It started in Britain and within several years had spread to the other Anglo-American democracies. Underpinning NPM is the view that private sector management practices are superior to those found in government.

With the rise of globalization came the notion that the private sector knows best. Henry Mintzberg (1996) summed it up well when he observed that "Capitalism has triumphed". He added: "that was the pat conclusion reached in the West as, one by one, the Communist regimes of Eastern Europe began to fall. It has become such an article of faith that we have become blind to its effects" (Mintzberg, 1996: 75). Mintzberg's point was that too many lumped everything together and concluded that the collapse of communism showed that capitalism and the private sector were superior in every way to the public sector and government (Mintzberg, 1996).

The business community may well see merits in globalization and applaud efforts to "deterriolized" economic power. However, national politics remains essentially about space. Tip O'Neill's often-repeated quote, "all politics is local", rings as true today as it did when he first made the observation after he ran for a Cambridge Council seat in 1935 (Farrell, 2001: 21). Public administration is also defined by space but it is essentially about organizations, hierarchy, sectors and programs. Though they are still left to pick up the pieces when things go wrong, presidents and prime ministers understand better than anyone how and why political power has drifted downward and outward from national governments. They have first-hand knowledge that there is less "loose" power around national governments than was the case 30 years ago. More to the point, power inside national governments is not as evident as it once was.

The above explains, at least in part, why presidents and prime ministers have come to believe that the levers of political power do not work as well as they would like or as they once did. It may well also explain why they want to centralize power in their own hands. In any event, they reason that it is the only way to get things done in modern government. It may also explain why British, Australian and Canadian prime ministers have put in place two policy processes – one for themselves and another for everybody else. When they take an interest in a policy initiative, things get done, but when they do not, an elaborate and consultative policy process takes over and it takes an inordinate amount of time to strike a decision. The same can be said for the French and the US presidents (Dahlström et al., 2011).

ON POLICY: WHEN 2 + 2 CAN EQUAL 5

The market for policy advice in government in the post-positivism era is not nearly as clear as it was 30 to 40 years ago (see, e.g., Fischer, 2003). The market for policy analysis, where public policy problems could be reviewed scientifically (positivism) and where hypotheses could be prepared and tested through rigorous statistical analysis, has been on the defensive since the 1980s.

Public servants brought to Canada's national capital the knowledge they had acquired in the social sciences. They emphasized empirical research designs, the use of surveys and sampling techniques, proper data-gathering procedures and they produced input–output studies, cost–benefit analyses, and developed socioeconomic models with predictive power (see, among others, Weiss, 1990). If politicians and politics could not understand this, then politics itself was seen as the problem. The Thatcher era, the rise of neoconservatism, and the determination of politicians to grab the policy agenda and shape it to their wishes put senior public servants and their more formal policy-making processes on the defensive. Today, politicians, when developing public policy, take into consideration ideology, partisan concerns, the pressures of the day and the ever-watchful media. One senior Industry Canada official explained, "We have reached the point where two plus two can now make five."[2]

Senior public servants have adjusted. Canadian political scientist Peter Aucoin wrote about their habit of "demonstrating enthusiasm" for the government's agenda, either as a tactic to advance their own personal careers or in the mistaken notion that neutral public servants should all be, as one British scholar put it, "promiscuously partisan" – that is, partisan to the government of the day but willing to change when a different party takes over (Aucoin, 2004). They are more likely to do this if they have served in various central agencies and departments rather than in a single department, where they are able to gain a thorough understanding of a sector or policy field.

Don Drummond, a former senior government of Canada public servant, praised former clerk of the Privy Council Jocelyne Bourgon for rebuilding the policy units in departments after they had been "weakened" in the 1994–97 program review exercise. The policy units, together with program evaluation and internal audit units, were indeed rebuilt between 2000 and 2010, when a substantial number of new positions was added to them. But this did not prevent Drummond in 2011 from writing about the government's dismal policy capacity (Drummond, 2011: 345). Drummond (ibid.: 337) wrote about the loss of the "analytical discipline" in government that "combined rigour in theory and quantitative methods". He maintains that important policy shifts in recent years on such policy issues as immigration and environment have not been accompanied by policy analyses of the kind produced for the Canada–US Free Trade Agreement and the introduction of the goods and services tax (ibid.: 338).

The high-profile Munir Sheikh case speaks to the new order in the Canadian public service. Sheikh, the former chief statistician for Canada, fell on his sword over the government's decision to cancel the long-form census and replace it with a voluntary survey. Shortly after the government announced that the 2011 census would include only the short form, a chorus of protests erupted from 370 groups across Canada opposed to the decision. The government responded by arguing that it did not wish to secure information by threatening to send Canadians to jail for failing to fill out the census. The minister responsible for Statistics Canada explained that the government wanted to strike a proper balance in getting the needed data and the citizens' desire to maintain privacy.[3] Sheikh later pointed out that Statistics Canada had worked well with the Office of the Privacy Commissioner and there were no issues of violating privacy in gathering census data.[4]

Sheikh resigned after the minister announced that the quality of the voluntary survey data would be as good as that of the long-form census and that both he and Statistics Canada were behind this decision. Sheikh felt that media stories on the matter were damaging the reputation of Statistics Canada and that they cast doubt on his own integrity.[5] He later was adamant that a voluntary survey and a short form can never be a substitute for a mandatory long-form census.[6]

Sheikh has recently asked a number of questions that remain unanswered. The questions go to the heart of post-positivism and the loss of influence of senior public servants in shaping public policy. They include: did the government analyse carefully the consequences of a loss in data quality as a result of the voluntary survey? Did it consider how this loss in quality would affect the data needs of users? Did it examine the negative consequences of this on policy development, including that at the federal level? In undertaking such an analysis, why did the government not consult with data users? Did it compare these consequences from the loss of data quality against any privacy gains?[7] In a world where 2 + 2 can equal 5, there is little need to answer these questions. Sheikh is still waiting for answers.

Research institutes, think-tanks and lobby groups have also had a profound impact on the policy work of public servants. Politicians can now turn to a host of research institutes to get the answers they are looking for on any policy issue. These cover the full political spectrum, from left to right. Should this tactic fail, politicians can turn to the 2000 or so lobbyists working in the national capital who are always at the ready to promote their clients' perspective. There are even lobbyists working to promote the interests of the tobacco industry. If policy truths are not absolute, elected politicians now have any number of sources to consult to establish truths as they wish to hear them (Savoie, 2008: 156).

The role of permanent career officials in policy making some 30 years ago was to search for relevant information, analyse it, and provide advice to politicians on the government side. Information and data were not then readily accessible (see, e.g., Fischer, 1998: 129–46). Today, one can Google any policy issue and quickly obtain the relevant information. If policy making in a post-positivism world is a matter of opinion, where 2 + 2 can equal 5, Google searches may well provide any answer a politician is looking for.[8]

Google search is a profoundly democratic instrument. It opens up the policy-making field to anyone who is interested. Allan Gregg (2011) put it very well when he wrote,

> Feeling more knowledgeable, connected and in control of our personal lives has also directly reduced our reliance on authority. As a result, we have little incentive to uncritically swallow the claims of political leaders who don't seem to understand our concerns, share our experiences or speak in a way we find authentic. Our political leaders have not only failed to adjust to this new reality, they also avoid honestly and directly engaging on our most pressing issues.

He could have added that senior public servants have also failed to adjust or have not been allowed to adjust.

Still, old habits die hard in government, as students of institutionalism and path dependency have often observed. Public servants who wish to make it to the top know that the ability to avoid controversy and negative attention to their ministers and their departments, combined with a capacity to promote the policy preferences of the prime minister's court and to defend their department's interest – or, more often, that of central agencies in interdepartmental committee meetings – are what truly matters. In brief, the ability to work the "thick" process-oriented Ottawa system is what counts for the ambitious public servant. Management is still left to the less gifted, to those not able to make it to the top (Savoie, 1994: 175).

General Lewis MacKenzie claims that the ability to work the Ottawa system has now become a major factor for promotion, even within the military:

> Regrettably, the mastery of the Ottawa game became one of the criteria, if not the key criterion, for selection as the Chief of Defence Staff. This reinforced the opinion of field soldiers that senior field command was not the route to follow if one aspired to be CDS – a most unfortunate and uniquely Canadian development. (*Globe and Mail*, 1996: A17)

Working well with the centre of government and other departments requires wide experience in the system and an ability to think in political (albeit not necessarily partisan) terms and to navigate the upper echelons of the political–bureaucratic world.

Deputy ministers (i.e. the equivalent of permanent secretaries) in the government of Canada now spend one hour out of every three on inter-departmental issues. It is interesting to note that they typically allocate nearly twice as much time to meetings with their peers as to matters involving their own ministers (Bourgault, 1997: 21–2). Avoidance of embarrassing disclosures and the ability to manage a controversy have ramped up spin operations to the point that spin is now central to government operations and management. Spin is about survival, and surviving in government is of course highly valued in both the political and the bureaucratic worlds (ibid.).

Cyberspace, the social media, 24-hour news channels, "gotcha" journalism, the never-ending call for greater transparency, and the work of officers of Parliament (the blame generators) all make it extremely difficult, if not impossible, to have centralized control of sensitive or embarrassing information (Hood, 2011: 635–8). The solution: beef up the government's spin operations to deal with any fallout. Today, there are an estimated 3824 spin specialists or communications staffers in the federal government, including about 100 in the Prime Minister's Office and the Privy Council Office. Growth in the number of communications specialists began in earnest in the early 1980s and has shot up in recent years. There has been an increase of over 700 positions in the last six years alone.[9] Scott Reid, former director of communications to Prime Minister Paul Martin, explains:

> At the political level, there really were no formal positions known as director of communications in the early '90s. By 2003, every minister had both a communications director and a press secretary . . . you saw changes of that kind happen, all of which are clear indications that the emphasis on communications was increasing at both the political and bureaucratic level. (Martin, 2011: 33)

No issue is too trivial for senior government officials to ignore in managing blame avoidance. Some observers, including Ralph Heintzman, have pointed to the "growing involvement of public servants in communications", suggesting that they are crossing the line at the highest level, putting "loyalty to the government of the day above loyalty to the public interest, and far above loyalty to the values of the very institution they were charged with leading" (Heintzman, 2010: 6).

MANAGEMENT: EMULATING THE PRIVATE SECTOR, UP TO A POINT

As noted, regaining the upper hand in shaping policy was only part of the agenda. Politicians also wanted to transform public service administrators into strong managers and, as noted, they looked to the private sector for inspiration. It is no exaggeration to state that politicians, on both the political right and left, have for the past 30 years sought to make the public sector look like the private sector.

It is a rare document indeed in which the Privy Council Office or the Treasury Board Secretariat does not employ a business-inspired vocabulary when dealing with management practices in government. Like deputy ministers, they refer to their "lines of business", their "business plans" and their "bottom line". Starting at the very top, with the clerk of the Privy Council, we increasingly hear about the "business of government" and "integrated business plans".[10] They are not alone. In its fifth annual report, the Prime Minister's Advisory Committee on the Public Service, co-chaired by former clerk Paul Tellier and former Cabinet Minister David Emerson, employed the word "business" on 14 occasions in their 11-page report. Among other things, the committee urged the public service to "transform the way it does business", arguing that the "current business model of fragmented administrative services is inefficient and costly" and that government operates in "a long-cycle business".[11] In its sixth annual report, the committee urged the government to pursue "a new business model".[12]

The desire to look to the private sector for inspiration now permeates the political and bureaucratic worlds in Ottawa. Indeed, a former senior federal public servant thinks that things have got out of hand. It is worth quoting him at length:

> Without blushing or even without a second thought, we now talk about our 'customers' or 'clients' in a way that would not have occurred to public servants three or four decades ago. And this is just the tip of the iceberg . . . Sometimes the results of this attempt to reinvent the public sector into the private sector are quite bizarre. I recently visited a well-meaning colleague who proudly presented to me the organizational renewal efforts of a high-priced foreign consultant that consisted in, among other things, the translation of all terms of public administration and parliamentary democracy into private sector equivalents, including the reinvention of members of Parliament as the shareholders of the corporation and Cabinet as the Board of Directors.

In the early 1990s, when NPM came into vogue, a deputy minister explained at some length what he believed to be the renewal and transformation of his department. "This is really serious stuff," he exclaimed proudly. "It's just like the private sector" (Heintzman, 1999: 7–9).

Table 8.1   Public administration and new public management

Public administration	New public management
Old culture	*New culture*
Controlling	Empowering
Rigid	Flexible
Suspicious	Trusting
Administrative	Managerial
Secret	Open
Power based	Task based
Input/process oriented	Results oriented
Preprogrammed and repetitive	Capable of purposeful action
Risk averse	Willing to take intelligent risks
Mandatory	Optional
Communicating poorly	Communicating well
Centralized	Decentralized
Uniform	Diverse
Stifling creativity	Encouraging innovation
Reactive	Proactive

Source: Public Service 2000 Secretariat, Government of Canada (1990).

NPM, it will be recalled, also sought to empower managers by removing red tape. Red tape, it is argued, belongs to a different era, not to a modern machinery of government that looks to the private sector for inspiration. If the private sector can run operations efficiently with a minimum of red tape, why not the public sector? The Public Service 2000 exercise, which squared nicely with NPM, urged departments to launch reviews to identify "useless" red tape (Tellier, 1990: 123–32). It produced a table that compared NPM with "old" public administration (see Table 8.1).

The table addresses what is wrong with public administration in a fast-changing global economy. In the eyes of the political leadership, the public sector had to shed its risk-averse culture and the heavy bureaucratic hand that inhibited creativity. The public sector had to learn from the private sector to become more task based and results oriented, and to instil in its managers a bias for action. By the 1990s, red tape became the symbol of bureaucratic inefficiencies and had to be attacked.

Red tape is not without some value, however, at least in the public sector; there was a time when career officials saw a great deal of merit in it and in due process. Given recent developments, it is worth quoting how a former deputy minister saw things in 1961:

The Civil Service Commission may be slow and meticulous in the recruitment of staff, but this is because parliament rightly insists upon every citizen having an equal right to try for a job. Appropriation and allotment controls may impose on field workers certain delays, but parliamentary control over expenditures is much more important than these minor inconveniences. The same applies to controls over individual expenditures: these must be reported in the Public Accounts in order that parliament might review them, and a good deal of book-work is justified in making this possible. (Johnson, 1961: 367)

The former deputy minister pointed out that government "supervisors" have no profit motive to encourage them to streamline work, simplify performance standards and so on; nor should they (ibid.). No deputy minister would make such a statement today.

To remove red tape at the same time that organizational boundaries are collapsing is not without implications for the machinery of government, particularly for accountability in managing the expenditure budget. Red tape has served several purposes, including a check on political and bureaucratic miscues and abuses, as well as numerous checks on the spending of public money.

DIFFERENT IN BOTH IMPORTANT AND UNIMPORTANT WAYS

Attempts to make the public sector look like the private sector have been misguided and costly to taxpayers. The genius of the private sector is its capacity to generate creative destruction where innovation and new firms attract resources from old ones. The private sector has a clear bottom line that tells essentially all that needs to be told about a firm's success. The genius of the public sector is that it is inclusive and that it gives life to democracy (Jacobs, 1992).

In short, the main difference between the public and private sector is that the private sector manages to the bottom line, while the public sector manages to the top line (Wilson, 1989). Government agencies – to a far greater degree than private businesses – must serve goals or purposes that are not always the preferences of the agency's senior administrators. Wilson explains, "control over revenues, productive factors and agency goals are all vested to an important degree in entities external to the organization – legislatures, courts, politicians, and interest groups" (ibid.). The result is that government officials will often look to the demands of the "external entities" rather than down the organization. It is for this reason, Wilson argues, that government managers are driven by the constraints on the organization, not by its tasks, and that public sector managers will invariably manage to the top line.

It does not matter much in the private sector if you only get it right 60 percent of the time, provided you secure a larger share of the market and you are able to turn a handsome profit. It does not matter much in government if you get it right 99 percent of the time if the 1 percent entails high-profile negative media attention for the government for an extended period of time. Efforts to borrow management practices from the private sector overlook the reality that public and private sectors are fundamentally different in both important and unimportant ways. Management in the private sector is about competition, securing a larger market share and the bottom line. Management in the public sector is in large measure about blame avoidance.

There are two management cultures currently in play in the Canadian government, and they view the world from vastly different perspectives. One looks up and is concerned primarily with the policy process, with ministers, central agencies, Question Period, and the senior public service. The other looks down and out – to citizens, clients, programs, program delivery, levels of services, and the managing of staff and financial resources. The managing-up culture is preoccupied with process, with protecting the prime minister and ministers, and with managing the media and their "gotcha" bias. Its emphasis is on blame avoidance. The managing-up culture is the one that matters most, and it is expensive to operate. The managing-down culture has little choice but to tolerate the managing-up culture and try to work around it. To challenge the managing-up culture by pointing to its flaws, even internally, is a sure way for public servants to stunt their careers (Savoie, 2013).

To be sure, central agencies have delegated considerable management authority to line departments to staff, classify or reclassify positions and to manage financial resources. Deputy ministers now hold authority to reclassify positions and to hire consultants to prepare the paperwork to produce the reclassification. Until a few years ago, deputy ministers and senior departmental officials also had the authority to move funds from programs to operating expenses to meet funding demands for reclassifications or establishing new positions. However, delegation of authority has been accompanied with a requirement to produce one evaluation and performance assessment report after another. Managers have never been able to make results-based accountability work. Year after year, the auditor general points out that the capacity to measure performance in government departments is inadequate and urges that more resources and greater efforts be earmarked to that end. Year after year, the Treasury Board Secretariat makes the case that line departments need to do better at program evaluation. The Treasury Board now produces an annual report on the "Health of the Evaluation Function", and it introduced in 2007–08 a central funding initiative worth $10.7 million per year to increase government-wide allocation to evaluation functions. Its 2010 annual report pointed to several weaknesses, including the need to emphasize "the use of evaluations to support a broader range of decisions" (Government of Canada, 2010). Yet year after year, the efforts still come up short. Other than the Treasury Board Secretariat and the Office of the Auditor General – which have done a very poor job at assessing their own performances or having independent, arm's-length evaluation of their performance carried out – it is not at all clear that there is a market for such performance evaluation reports.[13]

Members of Parliament have shown precious little interest in the reports. The former chair of the Public Accounts Committee explains that they are "lacking in credibility and objectivity and are basically self-serving and congratulatory fluff" (Murphy, 2010: 37). If there is one parliamentary committee that should have some interest in these reports, it is the Public Accounts Committee. The media, MPs and voters also pay scant, if any, attention to the volumes and volumes of reports submitted to Parliament every year.

The point is that one can fudge reports but one can hardly fudge centrally prescribed policies, rules and regulations. The former behaviour is associated with new public administration, the latter with the old public administration. One needs to look no further than the work of public and private sector unions to see the stark difference between the two sectors.

FABRICATING A BOTTOM LINE

For management in the public sector to emulate private sector management, a bottom line had to be fabricated. This has been the driving force of management reform in the Canadian government since the 1980s.

On management, senior public servants concluded that producing more evaluation and performance reports and responding to the Office of the Auditor General's latest fashion would somehow be seen as making public sector management look like that in the private sector. The result is that government departments in Ottawa are now top heavy, with overhead units producing all manner of reports, from risk management to evaluation and performance-pay schemes. One suspects, however, that many senior public servants would agree with the findings of Julian Le Grand on motivation in the public sector when he concluded that it is "difficult, if not impossible" to construct a viable measuring and monitoring system to indicate better performance (Le Grand, 2003: 47). No matter; it is in their interest to produce such reports if only to show politicians that management in government can be as strong as that found in the private sector. No one in line departments is in a position to stand up and say that these costly initiatives are leading nowhere and that the notion that one can transform public sector management to look like that of the private sector is misguided.

NOT ALL IS WELL

Yet there are signs that not all is well in the Canadian public service. Surveys reveal a stubborn morale problem that will not go away, and the federal public service has in the past few years been plagued by "soaring disability claims".[14] According to a report from the Public Service Alliance of Canada (PSAC), nearly 4000 public servants – a record – filed disability claims in 2010. Mental health disorders, led by depression and anxiety, accounted for nearly 50 percent of the claims. In 1991, only 23.7 percent of the claims were for mental health disorders. Bill Wilkerson, co-founder of the Global Business and Economic Roundtable on Addiction and Mental Health, described the government workplace as "an emotionally airless environment" and an "almost uninhabitable workplace".[15]

Statistics Canada reported in 2009 that "low morale was prevalent among executives and knowledge workers", and that in the federal public service "many employees felt that workplace conditions were not conducive to confidence in management, job satisfaction and career advancement" (Government of Canada, 2009). A number of observers have also written about a "serious morale challenge" in the federal public service (see, among others, Winsor, 2010: 8).

WHAT TO DO?

Unless one is able to disconnect the work of public servants from a highly charged political environment – which is unlikely – one should look to the past for the way ahead. The argument here is that public sector administration remains joined at the hip to the country's political institutions. Ambitious public service reforms are unlikely to have much success without correspondingly ambitious reforms to the political institutions. Waiting for such a development is like waiting for the Greek month of calends.

If anything, our political institutions are less tolerant of administrative miscues than they were 40 years ago. Permanent election campaigns, tied to the rise of the new media and "gotcha" journalism, along with access to information legislation, have had a profound impact on public sector management at about the same time that politicians decided to look to the private sector for inspiration on how to fix bureaucracy. Thus, precisely at the point when politicians, the media and taxpayers sought more clarity on how government spends, and looked for ways to ensure that public servants could not squirm out of their Weberian apparatus, centrally pre-scribed rules and processes were substantially reduced in a fruitless search for a bottom line in government operations. The verdict? We have wit-nessed in the last decade, in particular, a tremendous growth in the cost of government operations, and, as Chris Pollitt and Geert Bouckaert argue in their widely read *Public Management Reform*, we have seen, after 30 years of public sector reform efforts, "falling civil service prestige" (Pollitt and Bouckaert, 2000: 92).

We now need to promote the idea of a public service with a distinctive status, culture, terms and conditions (Lynn, 2006). We need to reaffirm both the role of representative democracy and the central position of statutes in defining the role of policy makers and decision makers. The thinking here is that rediscovering roots will rescue the public administra-tion from simple assumptions tied to economic self-interest and deductive models, and release it from the mantra that reforms inspired by the private sector can drive productive change in the public sector.

The goal should be to place renewed emphasis on procedural controls and rules, on the distinctiveness of the public sector, and on rediscovering the public service's sense of frugality (Hood, 1994). This calls for an over-haul of the work of agents of Parliament, the machinery of government, and rebuilding the relationship between politicians and public servants. It calls on politicians to see merit in evidence-based policy advice.

Paul Tellier, former Cabinet Secretary to the Mulroney government, told the media that senior public servants need to rediscover the capacity to "say no to ministers when required" (Tellier, 2006: A1). This will not happen just because we wish it to happen or because a former Cabinet Secretary suggests that it should. We need to give public servants a statu-tory capacity and duty to perform in this manner. If this is not possible, citizens will have to accept that their public service will never measure up to expectations. It will remain riddled with inefficiencies and will be far more costly to taxpayers than necessary. And retaining the best and the brightest in the public service will become increasingly difficult, despite generous salaries and highly attractive employment benefits.

How deputy ministers are appointed needs an overhaul. It is no longer appropriate for the prime minister and the clerk of the Privy Council to hand-pick appointees from a limited pool of candidates from central agencies who have little experience in actually delivering programs and services to Canadians. Other Westminster-style parliamentary systems and some provincial governments in Canada have opened up the appointment process to competition (see, among others, Aucoin and Jarvis, 2005; Government of Canada, 2005). It is considerably easier to speak truth to power and to be fearless in providing advice when a public servant's appointment is supported by formal processes and structures, rather than leaving such officials on their own to deal with two powerful individuals – the prime minister and the clerk – who have all the power to decide who makes it to the top and who stays there.

Simplicity, formal rules, formal processes, a recognition that the public sector has its own intrinsic characteristics, along with the promotion of a parsimonious culture in government operations, a streamlined hierarchy, transparency and a three-way moral contract, can rebuild the federal public service's credibility with Canadian taxpayers and politicians. This will assist members of Parliament and Canadians in general to gain a better understanding of government operations and a greater ability to determine "who gets the most of what there is to get" (Lasswell, 1990).

NOTES

1. See, for example, "The Two Tonys", *New Yorker*, 6 October 1997 and the UK document *Modernising Government*, presented to Parliament by the prime minister and the minister of the Cabinet Office, 1999, p.11.
2. Consultation with a senior Industry Canada official, Moncton, 23 December 2011.
3. See, among others, "Tony Clement clears the air on census", www.theglobeandmail.com, 21 July 2010.
4. Sheikh (2011), pp.305–35.
5. Ibid., p.329.
6. *Globe and Mail* (2010).
7. Sheikh (2011), p.327.
8. "Making copyright work better online: a process report", Google Public Policy Blog-blogspot.com, 2 September 2011.
9. Based on information from the Treasury Board Secretariat as reported in Steve Maher, "Harper's PR obsession fostering paranoia and paralysis in public service", www.canada.com, 30 November 2011.
10. Government of Canada (2007), pp.4 and 9.
11. Government of Canada (2011).
12. Government of Canada (2012), p.4.
13. The office argues that it has called for an international peer review of its performance. The most recent was conducted by a team of like-minded auditors from the Australian National Office in 2009. See Government of Canada, *External Reviews* (Ottawa: Office of the Auditor General, 2010).
14. "PS disability claims soaring", www.ottawacitizen.com, 28 June 2011. See also "Depression in PS a public health crisis", www.ottawacitizen.com, 10 January 2010.
15. Quoted in "PS disability claims soaring".

REFERENCES

Aucoin, Peter (2004) "Influencing public policy and decision-making: power shifts", notes for presentation to the 2004 APEX Symposium, "Parliament, the People, and Public Service", Ottawa, 6–7 October.

Aucoin, Peter and Jarvis, Mark D. (2005) *Modernizing Government Accountability: A Framework for Reform*, Ottawa: Canada School of the Public Service.

Beck, Ulrich (2007) *Power in the Global Ages: A New Global Political Economy*, trans. Kathleen Cross, Cambridge: Polity Press, p. 52.

Bourgault, Jacques (1997) "De Kafka au Net: la lutte incessante du sous-ministre pour contrôler son agenda", *Gestion*, **22**(2): 21–2.

Dahlström, Carl, Peters, B. Guy and Pierre, Jon (2011) *Steering from the Centre: Strengthening Political Control in Western Democracies*, Toronto: University of Toronto Press.

Drummond, Don (2011) "Personal reflections on the state of public policy analysis in Canada", in Fred Gorbet and Andrew Sharpe (eds), *New Directions for Intelligent Government in Canada: Papers in Honour of Ian Stewart*, Ottawa: Centre for the Study of Living Standards, pp. 328–41.

Farrell, John A. (2001) *Tip O'Neill and the Democratic Century*, Boston, MA: Little Brown and Company.

Fischer, Frank (1998) "Beyond empiricism: policy inquiry in postpositivist perspective", *Policy Studies* **26**(1): 129–46.

Fischer, Frank (2003) *Reframing Public Policy: Discursive Politics and Deliberative Practices*, Oxford: Oxford University Press.

Globe and Mail (1996) "Lewis Mackenzie: on choosing a Chief of Defence Staff", *Globe and Mail* (Toronto), 27 May, A17.

Globe and Mail (2010) "The inconvenient truth in Mr. Sheikh's resignation", www.theglobeandmail.com, 22 July.

Government of Canada (2005) Commission of Inquiry into the Sponsorship Program and Advertising Activities, Toronto roundtable.

Government of Canada (2007) *Fourteenth Annual Report to the Prime Minister on the Public Service of Canada*, Ottawa: Privy Council Office.

Government of Canada (2009) *Public Service Employee Survey*, Ottawa: Statistics Canada.

Government of Canada (2010) *Annual Report on the Health of the Evaluation Function*, www.tbs-sct.gc.ca/report.

Government of Canada (2011) *Fifth Report to the Prime Minister: A Public Service for Challenging Times*, Ottawa: Prime Minister's Advisory Committee on the Public Service.

Government of Canada (2012) *Sixth Report of the Prime Minister's Advisory Committee on the Public Service: Moving Ahead – Public Service Renewal in a Time of Change*, Ottawa: Privy Council Office.

Government of Canada Secretariat (1990) *Public Service 2000*, Ottawa: Privy Council Office.

Gregg, Allan (2011) "Telling the naked truth is good politics", www.theglobeandmail.com, 19 December.

Heintzman, Ralph (1999) "The effects of globalization on management practices: should the public sector operate on different parameters?" Paper presented to the Institute of Public Administration of Canada (IPAC) National Conference, Fredericton, NB, 31 August, pp. 7–9.

Heintzman, Ralph (2010) "Loyal to a fault," *Optimum Online*, **40**(1): 6.

Hill Times (Ottawa) "PM Harper takes communications strategy to a whole new level", *Hill Times* (Ottawa), 21 November, 33.

Hood, Christopher (1994) *Explaining Economic Policy Reversals*, Buckingham: Open University Press.

Hood, Christopher (2011) "From FOI world to WikiLeaks world: a new chapter in the transparency story?", *Governance*, **24**(4): 635–8.

Jacobs, Jane (1992) *Systems of Survival*, New York: Random House.

Johnson, Al (1961) "The role of the Deputy Minister: III", *Canadian Public Administration*, **4**(4): 367.
Lasswell, Harold (1990) *Politics: Who Gets What, When, How*, Gloucester, MA: New Edition.
LeGrand, Julian (2003) *Motivation, Agency, and Public Policy: Of Knights and Knaves, Pawns and Queens*, Oxford: Oxford University Press.
Lynn, Lawrence E. (2006) *Public Management: Old and New*, London: Routledge.
Martin, Paul (2011) *Hell or High Water: My Life in and out of Politics*. Toronto: McClelland and Stewart.
Mintzberg, Henry (1996) "Managing government, governing management", *Harvard Business Review*, May–June, 75.
Murphy, Shawn (2010) Quoted in "Annual departmental performance reports lack credibility, objectivity", *Hill Times*, 18 October, p. 37.
Pollitt, Christopher and Bouckaert, Geert (2000) *Public Management Reform: A Comparative Analysis*, Oxford: Oxford University Press.
Savoie, Donald J. (1994) *Thatcher, Reagan, and Mulroney: In Search of a New Bureaucracy*, Pittsburgh, PA: University of Pittsburgh Press, ch. 4.
Savoie, Donald J. (2008) *Court Government and the Collapse of Accountability in Canada and the United Kingdom*, Toronto: University of Toronto Press.
Savoie, Donald J. (2013) *Whatever Happened to the Music Teacher: How Government Decides and Why*, Montreal: McGill-Queen's University Press.
Scholte, Jan Aart (1997) "Global capitalism and the states", *International Affairs*, **73**(3), 427–39.
Sheikh, Munir (2011) "Good data and intelligent government", in Fred Gorbet and Andrew Sharpe (eds), *New Directions for Intelligent Government in Canada: Papers in Honour of Ian Stewart*, Ottawa: Centre for the Study of Living Standards, pp. 305–35.
Tellier, Paul (1990) "Public Service 2000: the renewal of the public service", *Canadian Public Administration*, **33**(2): 123–32.
Tellier, P. (2006) "Stop talking about fixing government, just do it, public says", *Citizen* (Ottawa), 14 August.
Weiss, Carol (1990) "Policy research data, ideas or arguments?", in Peter Wagner, Carol H. Weiss, Björn Wittrock and Hellmut Wollmann (eds), *Social Sciences and Modern States*, Cambridge: Cambridge University Press.
Wilson, James Q. (1989) *Bureaucracy: What Government Agencies Do and Why They Do It*, New York: Basic Books, chs 7 and 11.
Winsor, Hugh (2010) "A new style for the public service", Kingston: Queen's University News Centre.

9. Public administration and governance in the USA

Greg Andranovich and J. Theodore Anagnoson

INTRODUCTION

The relationship between public administration and governance in the USA has shifted dramatically in the period since the 1960s. On the surface, the 1960s represented a decade of growth of government, expanding the reach of the administrative state beyond the nation's economy and into areas of social regulation. Beneath the surface, however, questions about power in America, and the relationship between the American people and their government, were being revisited as authority was shifted from governmental organizations to the people through, for example, the early community action programs in the War on Poverty. A number of new programs were developed to lift the American people out of poverty and to provide more access to a better life, and many of these programs required the people directly, or community organizations as a proxy, to be involved in their design and implementation. The idea that government was a necessary, but not sufficient, instrument to authoritatively allocate values (that is, to make and implement public policy) ultimately led to an exploratory journey back into the nature of American public administration and governance. In 1972, two of our colleagues taking that journey wrote a short book, *From Amoral to Humane Bureaucracy*, critically analyzing executive power and bureaucratic institutions (Dvorin and Simmons, 1972). Rereading that book today is a reminder that the struggles to achieve better governance cannot be found in the routine application of our existing 'models of administration'. Dvorin and Simmons were concerned with the effects of efficiency and triangular hierarchy in the exercise of anonymous bureaucratic power as it ground down concerns for human dignity, and how this affected public policy making and its implementation. They wrote,

> Contemporary studies abound that document the plain fact the few Americans can ever realize what they have been indoctrinated to believe it is their right to expect. The gap between anticipation and realization is no longer a characteristic uniquely attributable to the less developed Third World. (Ibid., p. 67)

Events and activities regarding public administration and the search for better governance in the summer and autumn of 2013 illustrated how many of the concerns noted by Dvorin and Simmons 40 or more years ago remain the challenges facing us today and tomorrow. Three episodes in particular showed the face of public administration and the challenges of governance in the USA. The first was the Bradley Manning espionage trial, in which military intelligence analyst Manning, who in 2010 leaked classified Iraq and Afghanistan war logs, video logs, US State Department cables and other documents before being arrested and interrogated in a Marine Corps brig in Quantico, Virginia, USA, was given a 35-year sentence for sharing classified material with the press. The second event involved the most secret of the intelligence agencies in the USA – the National Security Agency (NSA) – becoming an almost daily news story around the world following the revelations of a massive domestic and international spying operation, leaked by a defense contractor who fled Hawaii to Hong Kong before divulging the details of NSA programs to a British journalist living in Brazil. In addition to the general architecture of the telecommunications spying were the revelations that the US Congress was sloppy in its oversight of this spying operation in the post-9/11 world. The clumsy posturing regarding 'who knew what when' in the American government, and then in several European governments, followed by the 'grounding' of the Bolivian president's airplane in Spain and the detention of a Brazilian journalist (partner of the journalist who reported the NSA leaks) in London's Heathrow Airport for eight hours could only be topped by this: the American defense contractor Edward Snowden, whose requests for political asylum were turned down while he was stranded in the transit zone of Moscow Airport after the US government cancelled his passport, was finally given political asylum in . . . Russia! The third event was the shutdown of the American government by the US House of Representatives, where the Republican majority fractured over demands to not fund access to healthcare (Obamacare) through a tax on medical devices (among other things), and the American government shut down its operations for 16 days, initially furloughing 800 000 federal workers on 1 October 2013, the start of the new federal fiscal year. That the US government does not have a fallback position to counter the effects of partisan political bickering led the Chinese government news agency to speculate that perhaps it was time to look for a de-Americanized global economy.

These three episodes, and many others, demonstrate the changed nature of governance today and how the role of public administration in governance has become far more complex in the USA of the early twenty-first century. Upon his exit from the presidency, D. Eisenhower warned America to beware the military–industrial complex, and his words were prescient. The rise of the military–industrial complex signaled both a major shift in our understanding of how public policy decisions were made and that the gaze of American government extended toward broader horizons. In short order, the level of administrative complexity increased as the scope of decisions expected of government agencies expanded beyond national defense and the American economy into regulatory arenas involving the environment, the workplace and the home. In these new functional arenas, the intersections of policy substance and political process led to tension, conflict and opportunity: which knowledge was relevant, how certain were we, what level of risk was acceptable, which organization or organizations were involved in implementation, and how advances in technology affected governance illustrated the administrative management challenges facing decision makers in the agencies of the administrative state. These tensions certainly are reflective of value differences, but also how these values (and their differences) are contextualized in decision making.

Our examination of American public administration and governance addresses the public administration challenges in a changed decision-making environment. We begin with a discussion of the unique context of public administration in the USA, continue with an examination of governance issues today before examining different reform ideas, and then we conclude with the challenges of managing in a more complex world. Although we are using the term 'governance' confidently, we note that the conditions surrounding it – ranging from its full description, to its operation, to its consequences – are not yet fully established in public administration theory. What we can say about governance is that a number of trends have evolved that depict the shift from the state, as the primary actor in making and implementing public policy, to a more complex institutional environment that incorporates multiple scales (from the supranational to the local) and involves not only the public sector but also contractors, private and nongovernmental institutions whose involvement includes limited oversight and monitoring while working through markets and networks in the search for solutions to a number of interrelated problems and challenges. As was the case in the 1960s (and earlier, we should add), there are both surface-level explanations and deeper questions about the balance of power in America, and the role of government in supporting, mediating or breaking down entrenched private interests.

PUBLIC ADMINISTRATION AMERICAN STYLE

In the beginning (1789), the issues of greatest importance in American government were representation of citizens and the separation of powers to prevent tyranny, and these twin forces, preserving liberty and limiting government, have informed most discussions of American government organization and governing ever since that time. The focus on representation and the separation of powers led to a government that represents Americans based on geography and provides for several competing branches and levels of government. This combination of geographic representation and competing power centers ensures that a certain level of conflict and competition will always be present in American government, and that power will always be 'moving' in our governing system. The federal structure of our political system ensures that both the national and state governments have constitutional powers; some powers are national, some are state and some are shared powers. Local governments are not mentioned in the US Constitution, but local government became an increasingly important player in national and state politics as the national government implemented programs focused on the local level, particularly since the 1960s. And for American public administration, this captures the essence of the dilemma: developing a theory or theories that guide the actions of the administrative state in a context in which the functional actions of the administrative state are not deemed as important as the issues of representation, and the administrative state has evolved in response to political changes. So, to begin to understand the role of government is to look at what government 'is'. Table 9.1 shows changes in units of American government over the past 60 years.

Table 9.1 shows that the policy-making context in the USA is extremely fragmented, with overlapping geographies of jurisdiction that have been structurally fluid through history. While the federal government and state governments have remained consistent in number, at the substate level changes are constant, with nearly 2500 units of government added in the decade 2002–12. The sheer number of these governments can be seen as either an impediment to action, or providing multiple avenues for participation. What Table 9.1 does not show is where power is located in the federal system. Until the economic recession of the 1930s most functions of government were carried out at the state and local levels, and the federal government exercised limited domestic powers. In fact, in the early periods of American history a doctrine of 'dual federalism' was practiced, and the powers of the federal government and the states were seen as distinct and almost mutually exclusive (Rivlin, 1992). After the Great Depression of the 1930s spread throughout the economy, when it became evident that the

Table 9.1   Number of governmental units by type, 1952–2012

Type	1952	1962	1972	1982	1992	2002	2012
US government	1	1	1	1	1	1	1
State government	48	50	50	50	50	50	50
Local governments	116756	91186	78218	81780	84955	87525	90056
Counties	3052	3043	3044	3041	3043	3034	3031
Municipal	16807	18000	18517	19076	19279	19429	19519
Township/town	17202	17142	16991	16734	16656	16504	16360
School district	67355	34678	15781	14851	14422	13506	12880
Special district	12340	18323	23885	28078	31555	35052	38266

Sources: US Census Bureau, Statistical Abstract of the United States, 2008, Table 414; US Census Bureau, Census of Governments, Volume Vol. 1, No. 1, Government; Organization Series GC02(1)-1; US Census Bureau, Census of Governments: Organization Component Preliminary Estimates, 2012; data are not subject to sampling error, but for information on nonsampling error and definitions, see http://www.census.gov/govs/cog2012.

states and local governments could not adequately respond to the effects of economic devastation, the people elected a president who promised that the national government would take action to resolve the economic crisis. It was evident that, if the economy had become a national economy, America's federal government needed to be able to act nationally since the states could not act beyond their borders. In this new environment, the USA created social security, unemployment insurance, strengthened banking and credit institutions and practices, and began more extensive economic regulation, including putting in place the infrastructure for future economic development; all of this required specialized government agencies for implementation. In these early days of federal government expansion, the perceived role of public administration in governance was simply to implement policies made in the elected branches of government – the Congress or through presidential actions. Implementation focused on administrative techniques grounded in scientific rationality in search of efficiency, and displayed through the narrow span of control in hierarchical organizations to ensure accountability (Wilson, 1887).

The American states continued to play an important part in the expansion of the federal government in the aftermath of World War II. However, in large part the role played by the states was a negative one: they were limited in resources, and state politics reflected America's pre-recession past in legislatures dominated by rural interests and without professional staff. This combination often led to outcomes that today we call 'bad governance': entrenched interests directing public policy that was not responsive to the increasing urban populations that included racial and ethnic minorities who, in many cases, were prohibited (either legally or by cultural practice) from participating in politics. By the 1960s there was a new call for the federal government to increase its spending in functions that were previously the domain of the states: housing, education, job training and health services. With this came an interest in incorporating new groups – racial and ethnic minorities, women and young people – into the political process, broadening the empirical boundaries of the public interest. In this environment, expansionary federal programs became the jurisdiction of a renewed public administration where the role of the administrative state was not simply to manage implementation efficiently, but instead became enmeshed in the politics of expansion and political incorporation. In what Patterson (2012) describes as the pivotal year for change, 1965, all of these challenges came together in the transformation of American society and culture. From civil rights violence perpetrated by local police in the American South to the expansion of the Vietnam War, the political and administrative repercussions resulted in a more measured, emergent conservative politics.

Table 9.2 shows the size of the American government in terms of the personnel employed. What is clear is that the size of federal government exploded during the years of World War II, and then again in the 1960s; it peaked in 1990, which led President Clinton to proclaim in his 1996 state of the union address, 'the days of big government are over'. In terms of personnel employed by the federal government, this seems to be the case as public sector employment has declined since 1990. Table 9.2 does not show the increased responsibilities of 'big' government, or that these responsibilities are increasingly met by a large contingent of contractors who are not government employees, or the fact that American government is not that big (as a percentage of the American economy, compared to governments in other developed nations), or that 'big' American government has not abridged the civil liberties or civil rights of the American people by abusing and usurping the people's rights to voice opinions or participate in democracy. The challenge today is fitting the government, and the administrative state in particular, to the requisites of governing. This is no easy task in the American political environment, which is notoriously anti-government in its rhetoric, and often anti-democratic in its public policy. As Neiman (2000, pp. 3–4) points out, a significant challenge lies in the way in which rhetoric shapes governance:

> the language of antigovernment sentiment and the accompanying political success of antigovernment politicians have produced an interpretation of

Table 9.2 Number of federal, state and local civil servants, per 100000 population (numbers in thousands)

Year	All levels of government			Federal government			State governments			Local governments			Resident pop. of the US
	Number	Per 1000 pop.	% change	Number	Per 1000 pop.	% change	Number	Per 1000 pop.	% change	Number	Per 1000 pop.	% change	
1901				231	3.0								77584
1910				380	4.1	38.1							92407
1920				645	6.1	47.3							106461
1930				589	4.8	−21.0							123077
1940				699	5.3	10.7							131954
1946	6001	42.8		2434	17.4	228.1	804	5.7		2762	19.7		140054
1950	6402	42.2	−1.6	2117	13.9	−19.8	1057	7.0	21.2	3228	21.3	7.8	151868
1960	8808	48.9	16.1	2421	13.5	−3.5	1527	8.5	21.9	4860	27.0	27.0	179979
1970	13028	63.9	30.5	2881	14.1	5.0	2755	13.5	59.2	7392	36.2	34.2	203984
1980	16213	71.4	11.7	2898	12.8	−9.7	3753	16.5	22.3	9562	42.1	16.1	227225
1990	18369	73.6	3.1	3105	12.4	−2.5	4503	18.0	9.2	10760	43.1	2.4	249623
2000	20876	74.0	0.5	2899	10.3	−17.4	4877	17.3	−4.2	13099	46.4	7.7	282224
2005	21725	72.7	−1.8	2720	9.1	−11.4	5078	17.0	−1.7	13926	46.6	0.3	299000
2011	22156	71.1	−2.1	2854	9.2	0.7	5314	17.1	0.4	13988	44.9	−3.6	311587

Source: Original data from the US Census Bureau, Annual Survey of Public Employment and Payroll, 2011.

205

> government growth and a view of government size that serves the political ends of the prosperous and the powerful, at the expense of those who are not [and] important changes in the world economy and issues at home . . . will be shaped by the rhetorical and political constraints posed by antigovernment sentiment.

It is in this context that American public administration is organized.

Stillman's (1991) discussion of the four different 'contemporary visions' of the American state captures the general tenor of the analysis of American public administration. The underlying question is: how much power can we give to government while preserving individual liberty? One vision is for 'no state', the minimalist vision of a very limited government that is decentralized, its key staff political appointees, with a strong preference for top–down direction. There is a definite split between politics (at the top) and administration. The most important criteria informing administrative actions are economy and efficiency, and there is a strong reliance on the free market as a guidepost for public decision making. In sharp contrast to this is the 'bold-state' vision, where the role of the state in society is broadly expanded. The key staff are career bureaucrats, and governance is bottom–up, with citizens, various interests and public officials all involved in the public decision-making process. Indeed, in this vision there are cooperative relations between politics and administration, and the strongest criteria for action are those favoring managerial effectiveness.

The other two visions fall in between. A 'pre-state' envisions government serving as a balance wheel, with the different levels of government doing what is necessary to meet society's needs. The key staff in this vision are from the three branches of government and administrators, who bargain, negotiate and fix their way through problems, actions and influences that arise from all sides. Relations between politics and administration are complex and indefinable. Governance is guided by pragmatism, and muddling through is the best way to describe the criterion for action. The fourth vision is a 'pro-state'. Here the role of government is global and all-encompassing. The key staff are specialized experts whose professional expertise guides policy at all levels of government. There is no relationship with politics, as technocracy rules and technical rationality and expertise determine the criteria for action. While these four visions might seem to be mutually exclusive, we can argue that they always are present, in varying degrees and at different times, in American public administration and governance. Indeed, these four visions get to the root of the administration challenge: how should the administrative state be organized?

In sum, the earliest notions of public administration drew on the separation of politics and administration, and a concentration on organizing implementation to meet externally established political and policy goals. The visions of the organization of the American administrative state tend to follow this line of thinking. The conceptual separation of politics and administration collapsed after World War II, particularly under the critique of administration leveled by Herbert Simon (1946). In its place, the central role of decision making refocused attention on public administration's organization, and it renewed the concern over the relationship between the people and the government, but this shift toward governance raised the stakes for public administration as traditional hierarchical forms of organizing policy implementation gave way to the changing landscape of challenges facing government decision makers.

FROM GOVERNMENT TO GOVERNANCE

A number of structural and contextual elements make it difficult to even think about a centralized administrative state in the USA. The American federal system evolved as a multilevel governance system, where the scope of conflict over specific policy issues can be shifted nationally to the federal level, regionally to the state level, or locally to the city, county or special districts that overlay American communities (Schattschneider, 1960). In large part, this is in response to the type of government that Americans favor: a limited government, with consent of the governed, a consistent rule of law, and where change is possible but should be difficult to achieve. Governance responsibility is shared between the national and subnational levels, but there is an uneasy 'national supremacy' that is often tied to expenditures of funds for public purposes (and court decisions on the limits of power), and an equally uneasy 'maximum of local self-control' that is tied to each of the political traditions in each of the 50 states. At the national level, there has evolved since the 1960s an extensive grants-in-aid program that leans heavily toward categorical grants (giving the grantor maximum authority over the grantee, and sometimes even over the Congress; see Anagnoson, 1982) over block grants in most functional areas of assistance. Many of these grants require matching funds or other resources from recipient governments or agencies, and there are often other conditions attached to the funding. In addition to funding, there is technical assistance that can be provided to support implementation. However, there is often bargaining and negotiation that occurs in relation to how the funding level can achieve policy and program priorities, effectively shifting power to subnational levels. At the subnational level there is a tension between state control and local 'home rule' that provides local jurisdictions more authority in the states that have a more permissive stance toward local governance authority. In either case, it is at the local level that the effects of service delivery are experienced most acutely.

In this dynamic environment of widely distributed power and cooperative and competitive relations that rely on bargaining to achieve results, there are a number of benefits and dysfunctions that characterize the governance process (Wright, 1988). These are expected when process and human relationships are emphasized in governance, and both governmental and nongovernmental agencies are involved, and the results of decision making often are not 'zero sum' (Agranoff, 2007). Chief among the benefits are flexibility in decision making, encouraging innovation and fostering competition, which leads to responsiveness and efficiency, preventing management overload, coping with conflict and fostering participation (Nice and Frederickson, 1995). There are also several challenges, or dysfunctions, in governance, including the neglect of externalities, coordination problems, unresponsiveness, inequalities, various localistic and professional biases, the loss of accountability, and even the evasion of responsibility. Multilevel governance in the USA (often called 'intergovernmental relations') increasingly requires the management of these horizontal intersectoral approaches, including public–private partnerships, as well as the more traditional vertical relations. This is due in part to the influence of the reinventing government phenomenon in the USA (described in the next section), which propelled interest in devolving governmental authority and responsibility from the national level to levels of government that were closer to the issue, and possibly privatizing the production of services, or perhaps contracting them out for more efficient results. Although the growth of intergovernmental networks was clear in the expansion of federal grants in aid during the 1960s, network management became an issue as a result of the popularity of reinventing government. The boundary-spanning behavior central to the efficacy of intergovernmental and intersectoral approaches is captured by the 'network' metaphor. Here we find a nonhierarchical decision-making environment where uncertainty is a commonly found characteristic, and control issues are confounded by jurisdictional, legal, political, and even professional claims and counterclaims of authority. In this environment, a collaborative strategy for engaging all stakeholders becomes an important requisite to limit the dysfunction (Andranovich, 1995; Vandeventer and Mandell, 2011). Even public–private partnerships are nothing new in the American administrative management landscape (large-scale infrastructure projects have been managed this way), but became more widespread in the administration of national domestic policy objectives after the National Performance Review reinvention initiative launched during the Clinton presidency, and were seen in new arenas since 2001, such as the number of private military contractors in the wars in Iraq and Afghanistan.

Another major change in governance has been in response to globalization. Globalization's effects were widely experienced in the US economy in the 1970s, starting with the OPEC oil embargo in 1973. Although we did not recognize it at the time, and perhaps because of the Cold War's effect on American policy making, the American view of the world was structured around our antagonistic relationship with the Soviet Union instead of growing economic interdependence. The OPEC embargo provided a wakeup call, but one that was not heeded. When the Berlin Wall fell in 1989, the existing 'threat–response mindset' for dealing with international affairs was questioned (Rivlin, 1992, p.27), as was the deployment of US forces and other resources to contain the Soviet Union. In the then-emergent post-Cold War world, power was no longer usefully defined in economic or military terms because the nature of the policy and political challenges changed, almost overnight. Rivlin (ibid., p.29) put it this way: 'In an era when the [USA] can no longer dominate economically, leading by persuasion, example, and coalition building becomes increasingly important'. What this meant, and whether it was a positive or negative outcome, was and remains contested (cf. Wallerstein, 2003; Fukuyama, 1992). Underlying these events, however, are the much more subtle effects of technological advances. In 1990 the USA was struggling to separate domestic and foreign affairs, and manage them differently; in 2013 the arenas are clearly interdependent and the USA is struggling to provide a rationale for managing them differently and finding limited success. From commerce to finance, technology has led to increased global interdependence. Interdependence has introduced, or perhaps 'imposed' is more accurate, new performance standards in the economy and for politics and administration. Interdependence also has introduced new social and cultural influences into the mix, and these have had their own effects – sometimes unclear or misunderstood, but rarely easily resolved – on governance. It seems evident that these impacts are still being sorted out, as the continuing fallout from the Snowden revelations about NSA metadata collection efforts will show.

The task of governance and public administration's role in it in the USA begins with the issue of the relationship between government and society, and with the people's expectations of their government. As the size of the national government has shrunk, expectations for public action have not. One result has been the rise of indirect support for a variety of programs, or what Mettler (2011) has called the 'submerged state'. Her analysis of student aid, tax relief and health care in the USA demonstrates how the changed politics has led to a shift in program benefits (from direct benefits to various types of indirect subsidies). During the several decades of more conservative and polarized politics since 1980, a trend that saw its origins in earlier times flourished: using administrative simplicity as a rationale, public benefits were shifted into indirect categories (e.g. tax breaks). After all, it is easier to rationalize a tax break than to initiate a spending program with direct benefits in the current political environment. The new indirect subsidies benefit the more well-to-do in the economy, particularly those in fast-growth sectors – finance, insurance and real estate, for example – that performed much better than the economy as a whole over the past decades, and certainly better than average workers in the USA. The political power of the actors representing the interests of these sectors is daunting, and it is unchecked in the policy-making process. Rather than shrinking the size of government (size defined in budgetary terms rather than the number of federal workers), governance is complicated by the large expenditures invisibly subsidizing wealthy corporate interests while redistributive programs for the people are on the cutting board. These sorts of cynical political moves have continued the trend of Americans distrusting their government, and the last few US Congresses (111th, 112th and 113th sessions) have seen the trust deficit rise in terms of how the American people perceive the national government (Pew Research Center, 2013). However, federal agencies are viewed favorably compared to the US Congress.

REFORM IN PUBLIC ADMINISTRATION

The issue of trust in government provides a sense of the challenges in discussing reform in public administration and governance. As political science research has shown, the issue of trust is complex. For our purposes, the argument put forth by Stillman (1991) on the stateless origins of American public administration theory – that the debate on the founding principles for our government sought to limit government power to prevent abuses and tyranny, and focused on issues of representation and the separation of powers, not administration – serves to orient our discussion of reform, and to locate it in this broader, American cultural current of limited government, based in notions of natural law and individual liberties, republicanism, popular sovereignty, majority rule and slow, deliberate change. Stillman (1991, p. 32) summed it up best: 'Taken together, these elements serve to continuously pulverize administrative effectiveness and to negate possibilities for any consistent administrative design. State building would prove always to be a tricky business in America because of these foundations of quicksand'. As if to verify this, Light (2006) found

177 different laws containing administrative reform measures enacted in the period 1945–2002.

The history of reform in public administration, then, is best understood in the broader context of two challenges for government in American politics: how much power should be centralized, and are 'they' to be trusted with this power? Light's outstanding overview (1999, 2006) of the 'tides' of reform illustrates the challenges for reformers. For Light (1999), there are four general approaches to administrative reform, each stemming in part from the political times and cultural values ascendant in those times. One is a structural reform approach; the others are process reforms. These approaches are scientific management (structural reform), the war on waste, the watchful eye and liberation management. Unlike in European nations, the history of a formal administrative state begins almost 100 years after the founding of the USA, with the passage of the Pendleton Act in 1883, and in Wilson's (1887) essay, 'The study of administration'. Following the assassination of President Garfield by a disgruntled patronage job seeker, Congress acted to establish a formal merit-based civil service to replace the patronage-based government service that existed since the Jackson presidency in the 1820s. The shift toward a professional public service was a major tenet of the Progressive Reform movement in the USA; this movement saw politics as corrupt and inefficient, and took the values of administrative efficiency and political accountability as its guideposts. Scientific management (following Frederick Taylor's 'one best way') became the mechanism for fighting corruption and inefficiency because it provided a rationale for establishing certain rules and procedures that would permit power to be centralized, but limited through formal rules. Scientific management is well known to students of public administration in the USA through the application of the administrative management principles known as POSDCORB (planning, organizing, staffing, directing, coordinating, reporting and budgeting), which also fed into the Brownlow Commission Report in 1937 calling for new administrative capacity in the president's office (Gulick, 1937). Stillman (1991, p. 117) points out that these recommendations to strengthen the presidency, despite F.D. Roosevelt winning an unprecedented landslide reelection at the height of public popularity for his New Deal programs, were called 'the dictator bill' and became part of the controversy and conflict over the 'court packing scheme' before eventually being partially implemented in the 1939 Reorganization Act. Scientific management reforms characterized the period from the 1930s to the 1960s, when the USA developed a more centralized administrative state apparatus to implement the policies and programs of the New Deal and the Great Society. Today, the Office of Management and Budget reflects the reform approach where there is trust in centralized power, as does the recent restructuring of the federal government to meet the Homeland Security function.

The war on waste and the watchful eye provide two more views of reform. Light points out that these reforms are often coupled with other reforms and are brought about to fix perceived problems, and both became more prevalent after the Watergate break-in during the 1972 presidential election campaign, when the public's trust in government fell. The war on waste became significant during the Reagan administration's years in office in large part because of the rhetoric of candidate and then President Reagan. By 1980, and the election of Reagan to the American presidency, the conservative rhetoric that emerged in reaction to the politics of inclusion of the Great Society years, and the feelings of being let down by Watergate, led to a major shift in governance: the role of the administrative state went from being problem solver to becoming the problem itself. For those who sought a more decentralized solution to the problem, the watchful eye became the reform approach of choice. Both of these approaches gained traction as the USA moved to the right in terms of public opinion, and retrenchment and anti-government rhetoric became the norms in political conversations. In terms of governance, this shift toward neoliberal values privileging market principles in all aspects of people's lives meant that, practically speaking, government agencies no longer were seen as a force of social progress directly delivering public services through agencies that were accountable to elected officials; instead, government agencies would better serve the public by following the market principles and seek nongovernmental partners to do the work of providing services – to steer and not to row, as Osborne and Gaebler (1992) famously put it. By the early 1990s this neoliberal turn was cemented when Democrat Bill Clinton, then a candidate for the presidency, adopted this market-based perspective as well and, after he won office, 'restructuring public bureaucracies into high performance organizations' became a governmental objective, while governance focused on setting organizational missions and streamlining decision processes so that 'customer accountability' and 'decentralized decision making' marked the shift in values and the uncoupling of public administration from its political underpinning. This is what Light terms liberation management, his third process approach.

In the USA, this new public management agenda was more politicized than elsewhere, and some have argued that its consequences were felt more in managing public services than seen in a sharp change in the structure of governance (Denhardt and Denhardt, 2011, p. 19). As Kettl (2002, p. 93) notes, it focused on management rather than social values; on efficiency rather than equity; on mid-level managers instead of elites; on generic approaches rather than tactics tailored to specifically public issues; on organizations rather than processes and institutions; and on management rather than political science or sociology.

In her testimony before the US Congress on 18 June 2013, Elaine Kamarck, the Clinton administration's point person implementing the National Performance Review's (NPR's) 1993 recommendations under the direction of Vice President Gore, made the following points that illustrate how the different reforms come together. During the two terms of the Clinton presidency, the size of government decreased by 426 600 persons, including 78 000 managers, making the federal government smaller than at any time since the 1950s. In addition, some 2000 field offices were closed and some 250 programs were eliminated. $136 billion was saved by following up on the NPR's recommendations. Among the most important contributions to these savings were cutting some 640 000 pages of internal agency rules and changing procurement policy government-wide for small purchases. Kamarck (2013) noted that the 'reinventing government movement' in the federal government was premised on three 'revolutions': the performance revolution; the customer revolution; and the innovation revolution. She directed a staff whose job was to reinvent the federal government, and who were not part of any existing agency.

The 'performance revolution' started with the Government Performance and Results Act of 1993, which required each federal agency to set a mission and develop a strategic plan to achieve it, including annual performance targets and annual reports on performance. The process was pilot-tested in 28 agencies beginning in 1994, and then rolled out across the federal government in 1999. The program was changed by the Bush administration, which adopted program-level assessment (Program Assessment Rating Tool; for more details, see Breul and Kamensky, 2008; Moynihan and Lavertu, 2012). In addition, the performance revolution included a focus on the 1.1 million civil servants who were in front-line positions, interacting with the public (this was Vice President Gore's definition of 'high impact' in the NPR), and included agencies such as the Internal Revenue Service, the Food and Drug Administration, and the Social Security Administration, to find out what was working, and what was not (Kamarck, 2013, pp. 2–5).

The 'customer revolution' started in three agencies – the Internal Revenue Service, the Social Security Administration, and the Postal Service. The idea was to determine what services customers needed by asking them (via surveys), and then to develop service plans and standards to meet those needs. Other rules ('red tape') were not justified and could be cut. This initiative was set up to increase trust in government, then at an all-time low of 21 percent (Kamarck, 2013, p. 5). The focus on customers ultimately led to the development of 4000 standards across 570 different federal organizations by 1998. A 'hammer' award was also created to recognize federal workers who reinvented their operations (named after the $700 hammer purchased through fixed-cost defense contracts, and a symbol of what was wrong with government). One of the most significant changes in agency practice as a result of using this approach was the electronic filing of tax returns, implemented by the IRS in 1998 and now a common practice, after surveys showed that electronic filers were more satisfied with the process (Kamarck, 2013, p. 6).

The 'innovation revolution' had two premises: front-line workers knew what worked, and it was critical to bring information technology into government operations. NPR staff developed 'reinvention labs' to encourage federal workers to think more broadly about their work, and to experiment with different approaches (for more on this, see Thompson, 1999). The NPR staff also worked cooperatively with the various employee unions through a National Partnership Council to ensure that all employees were given a stakeholder position in reinventing government. Finally, in terms of integrating information technology in government operations, in 1997, when only 25 percent of Americans were on the Internet, the NPR staff issued a report of how information technology would change the relationship of people with their government ('the internet would be used to bring information to the public on its terms'; Kamarck, 2013, p. 8).

In sum, Kamarck (2013, pp. 9–10) pointed to five lessons from the NPR that ought to be considered in any administrative reform effort: (i) there are two ways to cut government spending – across the board, or selectively differentiating what is efficient from what is wasteful; (ii) it is not always easy to differentiate programs without looking at their authorizing legislation; (iii) 'show me an inefficient, obsolete, or wasteful practice or program and I can promise you that someone in the private sector is making money off of it'; (iv) calculating efficiency means finding benchmarks, which means providing context (e.g. when calculating waste, fraud and abuse); and (v) career bureaucrats know best what works and what does not, and they need to be part of any administrative reform efforts.

CHALLENGES TO MANAGING IN THE TWENTY-FIRST CENTURY

The twenty-first century has clarified that many fundamental problems of administration in the USA remain unresolved. For the public service, the result of the 9/11 attacks – where deficiencies across a number of responder agencies that were not capable of acting as a network compounded initial security lapses and intelligence failures – was a growth in American bureaucracy unmatched historically except for the period just before and during World War II, only this time much of the activity was outsourced to the private sector (Priest and Arkin, 2010). The federal government's response to Hurricane Katrina in 2005 again raised questions about the ability of government to function as an 'emergency manager' in the face of a large-scale natural disaster, as did the governmental response to Hurricane Sandy in 2012. And a series of high-profile large projects – so-called 'megaprojects' – often accomplished and implemented only after initial failure and the expenditure of a great deal of resources under emergency conditions, raised questions about the government's ability to accomplish its goals, manage under outsourced conditions and raise sufficient resources. Each of these has both a political and an administrative dimension.

Governments have always had some outsourced activities. Even in ancient times, they did not perform even the most basic functions themselves or make all of their own weapons and supplies; nor did they fight all of their own wars. Today, however, the question of outsourcing, which means the provision of what might otherwise be a government program by an outside private or nonprofit sector organization, has become more important because the distinction between what we often think of as 'public' and 'private' has become blurred under the influence of neoliberalism. Many outsourcing decisions look questionable in retrospect, and the justification for outsourcing has changed significantly over time.

In the USA, the original colonial charters mixed public and private functions (Novak, 2009, p. 28). During the nineteenth century, most new American infrastructure, such as roads, bridges, canals and railroads, was constructed with partnerships that enabled state governments, which had few resources, to promote needed development. In the late twentieth century, the attitude toward the public and private sectors reversed, with the private sector looked on by many, in particular political conservatives, as the superior way to provide services. Connected with this is the predominant ideology of the late twentieth century concerning administration, 'New Public Management' (NPM), in which contracting out, the separation of service provision from service production, and privatization are central aspects.

The Reagan administration was the first in the USA to embody this new philosophy, in which the public sector and public provision of services are deemed inherently inferior to private sector provision, almost no matter what the private sector costs, and President Reagan ordered agencies to contract out a certain portion of their activities. During the Clinton administration, the Federal Activities Inventory Reform (FAIR) Act of 1998 required that agencies produce lists of commercial activities that could be contracted out. These were not to be 'inherently governmental' activities. Defining 'inherently governmental' activities is still an issue in the Obama administration, which began with regulations issued on 'inherently governmental' and an effort to '*in*source' some activities, but quickly ran into complications in 2011, and the effort appears to have become bogged down (Clark, 2011; Federal News Radio, 2012). Since the 1990s, the federal government has relied on 'large-scale integrators' to bring together the talent needed for large-scale, often computer-related, projects, according to Kettl (2009). This approach has major disadvantages from the standpoint of accountability.

The Obama administration reduced the amount of contracting, according to its administrator of the Office of Federal Procurement Policy, who left office in January 2013 noting, according to the *Washington Post*, that federal contract spending had fallen from $539 billion in 2011 to $460 billion in 2013 (Davidson, 2013). Still, Bump (2013) noted that, in October 2012, the number of people with security clearances – then over 5 million – was substantially more than the number of federal civil servants.

The major study of the extent of outsourcing is Paul Light's several studies of 'The true size of government' (Light, 1999, 2000, 2003). Light makes the case that the true size of government is not the approximately 2 million civil servants who work for the federal government, but an additional 900 000 postal workers, 1.4 million military personnel, 2.5 million grantee workers, and 5.6 million contractor employees. When he adds employees at the state and local levels of government who work under federal mandates, he arrives at approximately 16 to 17 million people, a far cry from the 1.8 million civil servants often discussed.

Although the number of federal civil servants has fallen over time, Light makes the case that the total numbers working directly or indirectly for the federal government have risen. Light calculates some 8 million contractor employees are working for the federal government, supervised by some portion of the 1.8 million federal civil servants. Light's analysis, however, according to Soloway and Chvotkin (2009), includes goods as opposed to services. Soloway and Chvotkin conclude that both direct and indirect employment is included in Light's figures, and that the real figures are less than generally assumed because of contractor overhead, spending on equipment and so forth, but they do not offer a specific figure. Thus the 5.6 million contractor employees may be a smaller number, but no one is arguing that it is as small as 1.8 million actual civil servants.

Kettl (2009) notes that the extent of contracting is such that 19 of the 20 programs most vulnerable to fraud, waste, abuse and mismanagement, according to the Government Accountability Office, are contracted out in intricate public–private partnerships. Public–private partnerships are substantially more difficult to manage than government agencies, and the challenge facing government agencies to be the senior partner remains on the table. In a classic case of management difficulty, the *New York Times* noted that, in 2007, a State Department investigation of its contract in Iraq with Blackwater was terminated after Blackwater's top manager there issued a threat: 'that he could kill' the government's chief investigator and 'no one could or would do anything about it' (Risen, 2014).

Recent controversies over the number of contractors and the federal government's ability to supervise them have arisen not only in the national security area, but over the development of the Obama administration's website for the Affordable Care Act (Obamacare), www.healthcare.gov, the federal government's lack of knowledge as to how many contractors there actually are, and the cost of these contractors. Regarding the last, the Project on Government Oversight (POGO) released a study in 2011 showing that contractors cost the federal government an average of 83 percent more than regular government employees doing the same jobs (Project on Government Oversight, 2011).

The second challenge is one of the reasons contractors are hired to such an extent: the inflexibility of the civil service rules, which favor contractors over internal employees. Many agencies have caps on the total number of employees overall, in spite of the growth of both the population and the economy in the last two to three decades. The top pay for federal employees is substantially less than the most skilled managers can earn in the private sector. While the caps are politically popular, they also lead, as Pearlstein (2014) points out, to a government where the best talent is in the contractor community. The government, then, has a cap on the salaries of those who work for it directly, but pays the higher salaries its caps are designed to avoid through hiring contractors, who not only get the higher salary, but the government pays for the company's overhead and contributes to its profits as well. For a federal manager, contractors represent the flexibility that is lacking in the federal civil service system: employees can be terminated quickly, hired quickly, reassigned to different projects with ease, and the like. So the typical agency in Washington and around the country has both contractors and regular government employees in the same building, sometimes in the same offices, keeping the same hours and so forth. And reforming the civil service has become a partisan issue, with Republicans supporting reforms and Democrats defending the existing system.

The existing federal civil service system was built in the years following World War II, some 65 or more years ago. Max Stier, president of the Partnership for Public Service, was quoted in the *Washington Post* (2014) saying, 'Name an organization that is succeeding largely under the same system that it had in 1949. It does not exist.' The *Washington Post* editorial points out that that the system is cumbersome, does not 'recruit or compete for talent and does not reward top performers or punish poor ones'.

The third challenge is in developing large projects, whether for physical infrastructure or computer software. These are multi-billion-dollar, multi-year, multiple levels of government, private sector or combinations thereof projects that simply are much larger than the 'normal' governmental endeavor. Examples include the new San Francisco–Oakland Bay Bridge, the high-speed train in California, President Obama's healthcare. gov website, the 'Big Dig' freeway project in Boston, and other large transportation and public projects around the USA.

American government is particularly ill designed to pursue such projects. Historically these projects have tended to cost many times the initial estimates, take many times the proposed construction period to build, and to have continued quality problems over the long run during implementation. While most public sectors are ill equipped to deal with long-term threats such as earthquakes, floods or other disasters, American government, with its strong bias toward the status quo, is particularly ill equipped, and there seems little appetite among the American public for a wholesale revision of such cherished doctrines as the separation of powers or 'checks and balances', or for revising the presidential system toward a parliamentary system.

Complex government websites and software development projects are the subject of the Standish Group's database of several thousand such projects, most of which had problems of one kind or another (Standish Group, 2014). The Standish Group is a consulting firm that deals with the performance of major software projects. The sorts of problems evidenced by healthcare.gov, rolled out in the fall of 2013 to handle enrollments on the federal health exchange for the states that chose not to build their own exchanges, are unfortunately typical. Indeed, experts claim that the speed that healthcare.gov was fixed is unusual: healthcare.gov is to be used by middle-class clients and users, and was fixed relatively quickly. For similar websites developed for the poor, such as those for food stamps or unemployment insurance, the fixes can take many years (Robles, 2014; Klein, 2014). For many American states, the cumulative effect of years of budget cuts, the inability to hire information technology personnel with high skill levels, and low wages for those who administer programs for the poor has left these states in situations difficult to remedy without the expenditure of what, for them, are substantial amounts of new funds. Of course the difference in political power and remedies is striking between the poor and middle- and upper-middle-class citizens and probably accounts for much of the difference.

A 2014 analysis of the new bridge connecting San Francisco and Oakland indicated substantial problems of management in California's state government. The analysis, published in the *Sacramento Bee*, indicated that the state agency chose a Chinese contractor that had never built parts for a bridge before to fabricate the steel structure of the bridge. The contractor ignored quality requirements built into the contract and fell behind schedule, necessitating the expenditure of hundreds of millions of dollars above the contract level. The result was a bridge that was years behind schedule, costing more than twice the original price, and with substantial doubts about its quality (Piller, 2014).

Among the most extensive analyses of megaprojects are those of Flyvbjerg and his associates, who maintain that the only way to pursue megaprojects rationally, given the poor history of past projects with overruns and lack of demand, is to have extensive institutional reforms (Flyvbjerg et al., 2003, 2009; also see Flyvbjerg, 2014). These would ensure that the public sector is not both the promoter of the project and the guarantor of its financing, and that private sector financing, without any government guarantee, is included in every megaproject. Needless to say, many megaprojects would not be feasible under such conditions, and the political support to make such changes is certainly lacking in the USA.

Flyvbjerg found that megaprojects present a paradox in that larger ones are being built around the world in spite of their poor performance records in terms of cost, environmental impacts and public support. Both psychological delusion and political deception occur in underestimating, sometimes by huge amounts, the costs of such projects (Ansar et al., 2014). Environmental impacts in practice are costly; these costs carry financial risk in that they are underestimated at the time the project is being planned and emerge only as projects are being implemented, when it may be difficult politically to cancel them. Government, in Flyvbjerg's view, cannot both promote a project and act as the 'guardian of the public interest' for environmental, safety and financial risks. Another problem is that many political systems allow so much interest-group involvement that groups are able to guarantee themselves 'a piece of the pie'. Flyvbjerg recommends that public sector involvement be weakened to keep interest groups from rent-seeking opportunities.

One frequent recommendation heard in reviews of megaproject development is that the numerous environmental and regulatory hurdles that such projects typically face be eliminated. This has been attempted in several nations; the New Zealand experience from the 1970s is negative. While regulations and sign-offs can be simplified or eliminated, the underlying problems recurred at later stages of the process (Anagnoson, 1985).

Another type of megaproject that has occurred frequently in recent years in the USA is the public sector response to a major natural disaster. Kettl (2009) contrasts the federal government's performance responding to Hurricane Katrina, clearly a 'mega-disaster', with its performance administering Medicare and Medicaid. He finds that the 'system' that administers Medicare and Medicaid functions largely on its own and is effective, but the disaster responsiveness system largely failed with Hurricane Katrina. Of course, there is a big difference between the system for senior citizens, which operates at a constant level of demand through a single agency (the Centers for Medicare and Medicaid Services), and the system for disaster responsiveness, which requires both a long-term multilevel planning process as well as a drastic short-term increase in multilevel response planning and implementation capacity focused on certain geographic locations affected by sudden disasters.

The administrative response improved from the dismal debacle in the aftermath of Hurricane Katrina (2005) to the somewhat improved environment where aid was sent relatively quickly to New York and New Jersey in the wake of Hurricane Sandy (2012). Compounding the response to Hurricane Katrina was the philosophy of the George W. Bush administration, which adhered to a traditional federalism in which the federal government would limit itself to supplementing individual states as needed (and requested). Still, in each instance the response process was very political, which complicated the administrative efforts that could best be characterized as lacking in strategic capacity (McGuire and Schneck, 2010); with the effects of climate change seemingly more evident on the seasonal calendar, the role of government and the processes of governance will continue to be challenged in complex ways.

Several of the problems we have discussed could be called 'wicked'; that is, they span the jurisdictions of different government agencies, departments and networks, and they require the expenditure of substantial amounts of money through time and across many different agencies and contractors, making them particularly difficult to manage effectively. American government at both the federal and state levels offers few examples of effectiveness and efficiency in attacking such problems, and numerous examples of poor implementation.

CONCLUSIONS

Given all of this, what are the factors that define the crucial, central features of American public administration and its role in governance?

- High public expectations about the functioning of the executive branch, combined with reluctance to see that government grow 'large' by historic American standards, and reluctance to provide administrators with the resources and flexibility required to achieve those expectations.
- Enormous complexity and non-standardization, so much so that management challenges seem almost insurmountable, and any management effort faces opposition from parts of Congress as well as from interest groups that benefit so strongly from the amount of outsourcing. The complexity has grown so much since World War II that Roosevelt's administrators would scarcely recognize the contemporary American administrative state. The wide distribution of power, both down to the states and out to various interests, has made management even more difficult. The increased significance of the 'submerged state', characterized by indirect subsidies, contributes to the complexity.
- Many agencies have significant portions of their portfolios outsourced. These pose significant management challenges.
- The level of distrust of government and its institutions is high and has increased in the wake of the Iraq and Afghanistan wars and the NSA spying revelations.
- The trend toward increasing centralization and power in the federal government has continued, and recent Supreme Court cases have assisted states not agreeing with the national majority in continuing their divergent levels of services.
- Governance has become characterized by large expenditures that subsidize corporate and wealthy individuals relatively invisibly while redistributive programs for low-income persons are on the cutting board every year.
- The role and view of public agencies in the USA changed drastically during the Reagan administration (1981–89), from agencies accountable to elected officials delivering public services, to agencies that followed market principles and used nongovernmental partners to deliver services.

It seems clear to us that the reasons why the public sector is not functioning well in the USA are not fundamentally administrative – they are political. With the country roughly equally divided between Republicans and Democrats, between those seeking a significantly smaller government with fewer services as opposed to a larger government with a significant array of services, public administrators and executive branches are caught in the middle. The conservative onslaught on big government includes denigrating the civil service work and keeping from it the resources needed to perform its functions, and clearly that attack over time has had a significant impact. Agencies do not plan for an ambitious future; instead, they cut costs relentlessly and try to keep the damage from spreading while performing their core functions. The liberal impulse has not helped either, as liberals have tried to expand government, add functions to agencies that are already unable to perform effectively, and reinforce the public sector unions in making the workforce less flexible and responsive (Zakaria, 2013).

The role of public administration in governance will need to address capacity building, and we see administrative, organizational and political consequences stemming from this role. Administratively, developing the capacity to manage complexity – including contractor employees and network relations – has become 'Job No. 1'. Organizationally, managing the mission and engaging with the community and in the organization's environment are evolving needs, and these require both a long-term perspective and short-term energy because, as pressing as today's needs are, the calendar marches onward. The administrative and organizational imperatives facing public administration require applications of the knowledge and skills of management, and here we face the challenge of market principles surging into public practice over the past 35 years. Therefore, politically, it will be important to 'speak truth to power' and uphold democratic values while addressing the issues of the day, whether in giving policy advice or engaging in implementation activities. What is to be done? We return to our colleagues, Dvorin and Simmons, who had the following advice for public administration education and practitioners (1972, p. 50):

> It is suggested that the essence of the public is that individual who, in joining with others in a body politic, creates the broader community. The essence of the interest of that broader community is the dignity of each individual within it. Only by a fundamental and searching reevaluation of its role in the community of man can public administration become morally relevant. Unless the bureaucracy 'throws its hat into the ring' of public controversy as an active participant which believes strongly in moral choices of its own derivation, it cannot justify its exercise of power. It is the absence of the commitment to moral relevance, as distinguished from relevance of action, that must be redressed.

REFERENCES

Agranoff, R. (2007), *Managing within Networks: Adding Value to Public Organizations*, Washington, DC: Georgetown University Press.

Anagnoson, J.T. (1982), 'Federal grant agencies and congressional election campaigns', *American Journal of Political Science*, **26** (3), 547–61.

Anagnoson, J.T. (1985), 'Can an industrialized society accelerate the processing of important energy projects? New Zealand's National Development Act', *Energy Systems and Policy*, **9** (3), 249–70.

Andranovich, G. (1995), 'Achieving consensus in public decision-making: applying interest-based problem solving to intergovernmental collaboration', *Journal of Applied Behavioral Science*, **31** (4), 429–45.

Ansar, A., B. Flyvbjerg, A. Budzier and D. Lunn (2014), 'Should we build more large dams? The actual costs of hydropower megaproject development', *Energy Policy*, **69** (March), 43–56. http://dx.doi.org/10.1016/j.enpol.2013.10.069 (accessed May 2014).

Breul, J.D. and J.M. Kamensky (2008), 'Federal government reform: lessons from Clinton's "reinventing government" and Bush's "management agenda" initiatives', *Public Administration Review*, **68** (6), 1009–26.

Bump, P. (2013), 'America's outsourced spy force, by the numbers', *The Atlantic Monthly*, 10 June.

Clark, C.S. (2011), 'OMB announces final guidance on inherently governmental functions', *Government Executive*, 9 September, http://www.govexec.com/oversight/2011/09/omb-announces-final-guidance-on-inherently-governmental-functions/34878/ (accessed 30 May 2014).

Davidson, J. (2013), 'Top contractor official leaves as contracting out falls and contracting officers increase', *Washington Post*, 19 January.

Denhardt, J.V. and R.B. Denhardt (2011), *The New Public Service: Serving, not Steering*, 3rd edn, Armonk, NY: M.E. Sharpe.

Dvorin, E.P. and R.H. Simmons (1972), *From Amoral to Humane Bureaucracy*, San Francisco, CA: Canfield Press (Harper & Row).

Federal News Radio (2012), 'Inherently governmental guidance never made it off launch-pad', Washington, DC, 20 September. http://www.federalnewsradio.com/1011/3021045/Inherently-governmental-guidance-never-made-it-off-launchpad (accessed 30 May 2014).

Flyvbjerg, B. (ed.) (2014), *Mega-Project Planning and Management: Essential Readings, Vols. 1–2*. Cheltenham, UK and Northampton, MA, USA: Edward Elgar Publishing.

Flyvbjerg, B., M. Garbuio and D. Lovallo (2009), 'Delusion and deception in large infrastructure projects, two models for explaining and preventing executive disaster', *California Management Review*, **51** (2), Winter, 170–93.

Flyvbjerg, B., N. Bruzelius and W. Rothengatter (2003), *Megaprojects and Risk, An Anatomy of Ambition*, New York: Cambridge University Press.

Fukuyama, F. (1992), *The End of History and the Last Man*, New York: Free Press.

Gulick, L. (1937), 'Notes on the theory of organization', in L. Gulick and L. Urwick (eds), *Papers on the Science of Administration*, New York: Institute of Public Administration, pp. 191–5.

Gulick, L. and L. Urwick (1937), *Papers on the Science of Administration*, New York: Institute of Public Administration.

Kamarck, E. (2013), *Lessons for the Future of Government Reform*, testimony before the US Congress, House of Representatives Committee on Oversight and Government Reform, accessed 29 December 2013, at http://www.brookings.edu/research/testimony/2013/06/18-reinventing-government-future-reform-kamarck.

Kettl, D.F. (2002), *The Transformation of Governance: Public Administration for Twenty-First Century America*, Baltimore, MD: Johns Hopkins University Press.

Kettl, D.F. (2009), *The Next Government of the United States, Why Our Institutions Fail Us and How to Fix Them*. New York: Norton.

Klein, E. (2014), 'Obamacare's launch was bad. But many programs for the poor are worse', *Washington Post*, 7 January.

Light, P.C. (1999), *The True Size of Government*, Washington, DC: Brookings Institution.

Light, P.C. (2000), 'The true size of government and the next president's challenge', Brookings Institution Policy Brief 65, October.

Light, P.C. (2003), 'Fact sheet on the true size of government', Washington, DC: Brookings Institution, Center for Public Service. http://wagner.nyu.edu/light (accessed 26 May 2014).

Light, P.C. (2006), 'The tides of reform revisited: patterns in making government work, 1945–2002', *Public Administration Review*, **66** (1), 6–19.

McGuire, M. and D. Schneck (2010), 'What if Hurricane Katrina hit in 2020? The need for strategic management of disasters', *Public Administration Review*, **70** (S-1), S201–7.

Mettler, S. (2011), *The Submerged State: How Invisible Government Policies Undermine American Democracy*, Chicago, IL: University of Chicago Press.

Moynihan, D.P. and S. Lavertu (2012), 'Does involvement in performance management routines encourage performance information use? Evaluating GPRA and PART', *Public Administration Review*, **72** (4), 592–602.

Neiman, M. (2000), *Defending Big Government*, Upper Saddle River, NJ: Prentice Hall.

Nice, D.C. and P. Frederickson (1995), *The Politics of Intergovernmental Relations*, 2nd edn, Chicago, IL: Nelson-Hall.

Novak, W.J. (2009), 'Public–private governance: a historical introduction', in J. Freeman and M. Minow (2009), *Government By Contract, Outsourcing and American Democracy*, Cambridge, MA: Harvard University Press, pp. 23–40.

Osborne, D. and T. Gaebler (1992), *Reinventing Government: How the Entrepreneurial Spirit is Transforming the Public Sector*, Reading, MA: Addison-Wesley.

Patterson, J.T. (2012), *The Eve of Destruction: How 1965 Transformed America*, New York: Basic Books.

Pearlstein, S. (2014), 'The federal outsourcing boom and why it's failing Americans', *Washington Post*, 31 January.

Pew Research Center (2013), 'Trust in government nears record low, but most federal agencies are viewed favorably', Washington, DC: Pew Research Center for the People and Press. http://www.people-press.org/files/legacy-pdf/10-18-13%20Trust%20in%20Govt%20Update.pdf (accessed 4 July 2014).

Piller, C. (2014), 'Bay Bridge's troubled China connection', *Sacramento Bee*, 8 June 2014.

Priest, D. and W.M. Arkin (2010), 'A hidden world, growing beyond control', *Washington Post*. http://projects.washingtonpost.com/top-secret-america/articles/a-hidden-world-growing-beyond-control/ (accessed 4 July 2014).

Project on Government Oversight (2011), 'Bad business: billions of taxpayer dollars wasted on hiring contractors', Washington, DC: Project on Government Oversight. http://www.pogo.org/our-work/reports/2011/co-gp-20110913.html (accessed 6 June 2014).

Risen, J. (2014), 'Before shooting in Iraq, warning on Blackwater', *New York Times*, 30 June.

Rivlin, A.M. (1992), *Reviving the American Dream*, Washington, DC: Brookings Institution Press.

Robles, F. (2014), 'Faulty websites confront needy in search of aid', *New York Times*, 7 January.

Schattschneider, E.E. (1960), *The Semisovereign People*, New York: Holt, Rinehart, and Winston.

Simon, H. (1946), 'The proverbs of administration', *Public Administration Review*, **6** (1), 53–67.

Soloway, S. and A. Chvotkin (2009), 'Federal contracting in context, what drives it, how to improve it', in J. Freeman and M. Minow (eds), *Government By Contract, Outsourcing and American Democracy*, Cambridge, MA: Harvard University Press, pp. 191–238.

Standish Group (2014), 'Big bang boom, why large projects fail', http://www.standishgroup.com/ (accessed 6 June 2014).

Stillman, R.J. (1991), *Preface to Public Administration*, New York: St Martin's Press.

Taylor, F.W. (1911), *Principles of Scientific Management*, New York: Harper & Brothers.

Thompson, J.R. (1999), 'Devising administrative reform that works: the example of the reinvention lab program', *Public Administration Review*, **59** (4), 283–92.

Vandeventer, P. and M. Mandell (2011), *Networks that Work: A Practitioner's Guide to Managing Networked Action*, 2nd edn, Los Angeles, CA: Community Partners.

Wallerstein, E. (2003), *The Decline of American Power: The US in a Chaotic World*, New York: The New Press.

Washington Post (2014), 'The true VA scandal is shared across the federal government', Editorial, 26 May.

Wilson, W. (1887), 'The study of administration', *Political Science Quarterly*, **2** (2), 197–222.

Wright, D. (1988), *Understanding Intergovernmental Relations*, 3rd edn, New York: Wadsworth.

Zakaria, F. (2013), 'Why Americans hate their government', *Washington Post*, 21 November.

10. Public administration in Brazil: structure, reforms, and participation
Ricardo Corrêa Gomes and Leonardo Secchi

INTRODUCTION

The Brazilian experience on governance and government is presented in this volume as Brazil has the fifth-largest territory, the fifth-largest population and the seventh-largest economy in the world (CIA, 2013). The public sector is large and still growing. To date, government spending represents 18.2 per cent of gross domestic product (GDP) (Government of Brazil, 2013b). In Brazil, tax revenue as a percentage of GDP is around 35 per cent, and the public sector absorbs 10.3 per cent of the Brazilian labour force (OECD, 2010). Brazil is a federative republic, with a presidential regime and a multiparty system. There are 32 political parties in Brazil, 23 of which are represented in the Congress (Senate and Lower Chamber).

In the last 50 years, Brazil has experienced important political changes. In 1964, a military junta took control of the country; in 1985, democracy was re-established; in 1988, the current Federal Constitution was promulgated; in 1989, the first democratic election for president took place after roughly 30 years; from 1990 to 1995 three presidents took office with a primary goal: to tackle the skyrocketing inflation. President Fernando Henrique Cardoso managed to bring it down to plausible rates; in 2002, the left-wing President Lula da Silva took office and managed to implement redistributive social policies and brought the country back on track in terms of economic growth. Regarding public administration, the last 50 years have seen plenty of initiatives to inject new management tools inspired by both new public management (NPM) and other domestic innovations relating to citizens' participation and public governance.

The aim of this chapter is to present an overview of the Brazilian public administration, its structure, historical background, and the shifts of public administration models (administrative reforms). Brazil is depicted as a mosaic of public administration models in which patrimonial administration, traditional rational–legal administration, NPM and public governance coexist in varied degrees across the complex Brazilian federative structure. This chapter stresses the main feature of the current

Brazilian public administration – participation – achieved through the use of a handful of civic engagement tools for public decision making.

The chapter is structured as follows. The next section presents the current administrative structure of the country. The third section deals with the series of reforms intended by Brazilian governments from a historical perspective. The fourth section is an overview of governance in order to provide a discursive explanation of Brazilian government efforts to ensure public participation in government decisions. Finally, the conclusion presents an analysis of the rich mosaic of Brazil's evolving public administration and participatory governance in a diverse and growing society.

THE CURRENT STRUCTURE OF THE BRAZILIAN PUBLIC ADMINISTRATION

In 1822, an Act of Peter I declared the country independent from Portugal and adopted the monarchy form of government. The first republican constitution set down in 1824 indicated that the country had assumed the federative scheme of regional administrative structure. Brazil became a Republican state from 1889, when the royal Portuguese family returned to Portugal. Since then, the country has been a federation of relatively autonomous states, and each state is composed of municipalities. To date, Brazil has 26 states, one federal district and 5569 cities (Government of Brazil, 2011).

To explain the complexities of government and governance in Brazil, we will briefly describe the structure of the public administration, outlining the powers of government and their relationship with each other and with the central government.

Administrative Structure

The 26 states in Brazil are scattered across five regions. This does not denote an additional administrative structure, but rather a means for understanding cultural, economic and social issues. The regions are:

- North, comprising the states of Acre, Amapá, Amazonas, Pará, Rondônia, Roraima and Tocantins;
- Northeast, comprising the states of Alagoas, Bahia, Ceará, Maranhão, Paraiba, Pernambuco, Piaui, Rio Grande do Norte and Sergipe;
- Centre-west, comprising the states of Goiás, Mato Grosso, Mato Grosso do Sul and the federal district in which it is located: the capital of the country – Brasília;

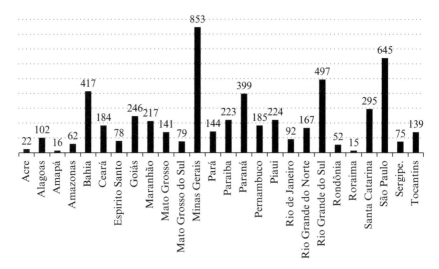

Figure 10.1   Brazilian states and the number of municipalities

- Southeast, comprising the states of Espírito Santo, Minas Gerais, Rio de Janeiro and São Paulo; and
- South, comprising the states of Paraná, Rio Grande do Sul and Santa Catarina.

Municipalities are the smaller administrative units that form each state. Since the 1988 Federal Constitution, the process of creating more municipalities was no longer under state government control, and is now determined by public consultation (referendum) with the involved local population. This has raised the number of municipalities to a great extent (Tomio, 2002) – from 3964 in 1980 to 5565 in 2010 (Government of Brazil, 2011). To date, Minas Gerais has the greatest number of municipalities: 853 units, followed by São Paulo (645 municipalities), and Rio Grande do Sul (497 municipalities). Figure 10.1 shows the distribution of municipalities, totalling 5569 (Government of Brazil, 2013a). We now turn attention to how public administration is structured in each of the three levels of government, namely federal, state and municipal.

The Powers of Government

Drawing on Montesquieu's definition of power (Claus, 2005), there are three powers in Brazil: the executive, the legislative and the judiciary. In theory, they are by definition autonomous and independent from each other, and they have to accept each other's decisions in order to maintain the balance of power.

Executive power is exercised by an elected politician who is in charge of the whole decision-making process of public administration, composed of ministries (federal government) or secretaries (state/municipality), and public agencies in all policy sectors.

The executive mandate is for a four-year term, with the possibility to run for re-election. It is worth mentioning that the law forbids a stay in power of more than eight years, but this does not apply when periods of administration are not consecutive. Executive power is present in the three spheres of government with different denominations, namely president for federal government, governor for state government, and mayor for municipality administration. Each of these positions has a deputy, a politician elected along with the executive head, who takes control in the case of absence, resignation or death of the first person. The president is both head of government and head of state.

Elected politicians compose legislative power, and there are no obstacles to successive mandates. As long as they are re-elected, they can participate in new legislation. Legislative power is also presented in the three spheres of government. In the federal government, there are two houses that represent the people: the Chamber of Deputies and the Senate. In state government, there is only the Legislative Assembly; representatives are called 'state deputies'. In municipal governments, legislative power resides in the Municipal Chamber – the representatives are known in Brazil as *Vereadores* (rough translation of 'aldermen').

Judges are formally appointed by the executive power and approved by the legislative power, and they are in charge of the judiciary power in Brazil. In contrast to the other positions, as soon as a judge is appointed to head the Tribunal, s/he is entitled to stay *in situ* for all his/her professional life up to retirement (at the age of 70). Also, in contrast to the other powers, there are tribunals only at federal and state governments. The administrative structures, as well as competencies, are dealt with as follows.

Competencies and Administrative Structures of the Three Powers

The whole set of competencies for the three powers is set down in the 1988 Federal Constitution (Government of Brazil, 1992). One main difference between public and private administration in Brazil is that public managers are expected to do only things that are formally defined by law. To this end, a federal constitution regulates the federal government, a state constitution regulates the states, and a municipal constitution (called Lei

Orgânica) regulates municipalities. It is worth mentioning that, according to the legal hierarchy, both state and municipal constitutions must comply with the rules set down by the Federal Constitution (Pietro, 2013). The next subsection outlines each power, describing how it works in each of the spheres of government.

Executive power

The federal government   The president, the vice president and the ministries, who work as a staff for the president, compose the executive power in the federal government. The president and his/her ministries comprise the so-called direct public administration, which has this label to denote all the administrative functions directly subordinated to the executive power (Pietro, 2013). Alongside the direct administrative structure, the legislation allows the creation of other entities to help administer services and policies to society. These organizations perform decentralized activities according to their juridical nature. They have a president, who is appointed by the president of Brazil and approved by the Senate, and boards for overseeing finances and approving their strategic plans. In Brazil, to date, there are four types of organizations involved in indirect administration: public enterprises; public foundations; autarchies; and joint-stock corporations. While all these are managed according to the same legal framework as for the direct administration, there are some differences in the way they operate. For instance, joint-stock corporations, of which Petrobras is an example, have the right to attract investments from the markets by selling shares.

In terms of competencies, the 1988 Federal Constitution laid down that it is in the federal government remit to manage issues related to Brazil as a nation; that is, for example, to sign a peace treaty or to engage in war, to ensure national security, to have oversight over the money supply and to manage the whole set of financial activities, and to control the media, among other competencies, as stated in Article 21 of the Federal Constitution. In order to ensure coverage of its expenditures, the federal government is entitled to collect money from several sources, the most important being the individual revenue tax, which is a percentage of gross salary,[1] and the industrial production tax, which is a percentage of every product sold in the country.

State governments   State governments have the same administrative structure as the federal government. They have a governor and a vice governor, who is an elected citizen in charge of general decision making for a period of four years, with the opportunity to be re-elected for an equal period. The vice governor is entitled to substitute for the governor in his/her absence. The governor can appoint secretariats for staff, which can be as numerous as needed and are approved by the Legislative Assemblies. States also have the power to create organizations to deal with the indirect administration of the state; these organizations must follow the same legal framework as those in the federal government.

The state is responsible for several activities within its territory; the most important of these are: security, including police and fire services; secondary education (the federal government is responsible for higher education by funding public and regulating private education); some participation in health services, mainly in terms of hospitals; and so on. States are entitled to collect some tax in order to meet expenditures; the most valuable revenue stream is the circulation of goods and services tax.

Municipal governments   Elected mayors and their vice mayors are head of the municipal government. They are also entitled to appoint secretariats as staff. There is no limit to the number of secretariats, as long as they are approved by the Municipal Chamber. The mayor is responsible for a set of public services, such as primary education, social assistance, urban planning, waste collection and disposal, road maintenance, environment and housing, among others. In Brazil, the municipal constitution is called the 'Organic Law'; it defines the whole general legal framework regulating municipal matters. Municipalities are entitled to collect local taxes; the most representative are property and service sales tax in order to meet expenditure at local level. As in the other spheres of government, municipalities are entitled to create indirect organizations for the provision and control of public services.

Legislative power
The legislative power has the responsibility to create the legal framework under which the whole set of activities of public administration must be carried out, and to oversee the executive power. Laws are created by proposal of the representative, or by initiative of the executive power (Pietro, 2013). However, in both cases the legislative power has the final word on approval of the laws.

Legislative power at the federal government level   At the federal government level, the legislative power is exerted by the National Congress, composed of the Chamber of Deputies (lower house) and by the Senate. The first is the assembly that sends representatives for each state according to their population size. The minimum number of representatives is eight, and the maximum is 70 (Government of Brazil, 1992). Three senators for each state and for the federal district compose the Senate. Some matters are discussed by the National Congress as a whole, which is the case for presidential impeachment, declaration of war, and some other issues defined by Article 49 of the 1988 Federal Constitution. Other matters, such as federal laws, are discussed and approved first in the Chamber of Deputies and then in the Senate for final enactment by the president. The legislative power has the prerogative to control government activities and procedures, and it has the Federal Court of Accounts that oversees federal government (direct and indirect bodies) accountability.

Legislative power at the state government level   The legislative power works in the same way in the state as in the federal government. It is in charge of approving laws and plans, as well as holding state government accountable to the legal framework. For this task, the Legislative Assemblies also have accountancy tribunals to which documents and records are sent for assessment and accountability.

Legislative power at the municipal government level   In terms of operation, the legislative power works in the same way as at the local level, but there is no tribunal to ensure accountability of the municipal administration. The states accountancy tribunal carries out this activity.[2] The Municipal Chamber (Câmara de Vereadores) has the role of approving local laws, plans and regulations, as well as enforcing the Organic Law. It is also in charge of approving the municipal administration accounts as the first instance.

Judiciary power
As stated earlier, judiciary power resides in the federal and state government spheres, but not in the municipal government sphere. The highest court of judgment is the Federal Supreme Court (Supremo Tribunal Federal – STF) as the court of last instance and the guardian of the Federal Constitution (Government of Brazil, 1992). Besides the STF, several courts of justice compose the judiciary power: the Superior Court of Justice, Regional Federal Courts and their federal judges, Work Relations Courts and their judges, Electoral Courts and their judges, Military Courts and their judges, State Courts and their judges and, finally, the Federal District Court. Next, the roles and competencies of the courts are described.

Judiciary power at the federal government level   Although there is no hierarchy in municipal, state and federal governments, the judiciary process must follow the hierarchy of the law, and every appeal finishes when it reaches the STF. Another important institution in the Brazilian judiciary system is the Superior Court of Justice (STJ). Both the STF and the STJ are courts of last instance of appeal; the main difference between them is that the former is the court of last instance for issues related to the Federal Constitution and the latter for other situations. But, in the end, the judges of the STF make the final decision.

As stated earlier, the STF is entitled to judge offences perpetrated by the president, vice president, ministries of state, senators and federal legislators, while the STJ has the power to judge states and the federal district governors. However, even governors and mayors are also entitled to appeal to the STF, if they claim that their individual rights have been offended according to Article 5 of the Federal Constitution (Moraes, 2013).

The federal courts have the competence to judge appeals in which the federation and the direct and indirect administration are involved. The other superior courts, namely electoral, work relations and military, are courts of last instance in matters of their competencies. But, again, the STF is likely to be invoked where individual rights and the Federal Constitution requirements are not fully followed.

Judiciary power at the state government level According to the 1988 Federal Constitution, state tribunals must be regulated by states constitutions. They are formed by judges and they have the competence to judge appeals against decisions made by the first-instance judges. As stated earlier, municipalities do not have courts, but they do have a judge to cover justice in their territories. These judges are subordinated to state courts and their decisions can only be revoked by decision of the higher bodies. Some small municipalities (in terms of population size) share the same judge with other, also small, municipalities; this judge is in charge of civil, criminal and electoral matters.

The Prosecution Service and its Roles in the Three Levels of Government

According to the 1988 Federal Constitution, the Department of Public Prosecution (Ministério Público) is an essential and permanent institution for ensuring the defence of the juridical order, the democratic regime and social and individual interests. To do this, the public prosecution system is structured into federal and states attorneys. In the federal sphere, Public Prosecution is composed of the Federal Public Attorney, the Work Relations Public Attorney, the Military Public Attorney, and the Federal District Public Attorney. In accordance with the judicial system, each state also has its own Department of Public Prosecution.

In overall terms, the Public Prosecutor holds competency for promoting public penal actions in order to ensure civil rights, the right to access public services as well as ensuring their quality, to ensure that the Federal Constitution is fully obeyed, and to exert external control over federal, state and municipal authorities. This institution is very important for the health and functioning of the public institutions, and public attorneys have the following rights ensured by the 1988 Federal Constitution: tenure in the exercise of the function after two years; not be removed from jurisdiction unless required by the public institutions; and irreducibility of remuneration. Any decision contrary to what is stated in the Constitution must be approved by the full collegiate of the last instance within the public attorney system (Government of Brazil, 1992).

In this chapter so far, we have presented the legal and administrative framework that guides the Brazilian public administration. The main aim of the chapter is to depict the whole system of rules and authorities that govern the country in the three spheres of government. In the next section, we discuss emerging values in Brazilian public administration and efforts to engage citizens in government policy and public service delivery.

ADMINISTRATIVE REFORMS IN BRAZIL

Administrative reform is a perennial exercise in Brazilian public administration (see Figure 10.2). Since 1938, when President Getúlio Vargas undertook the first major initiative of rationalization and organization of the Brazilian Federal Public Administration, virtually every federal

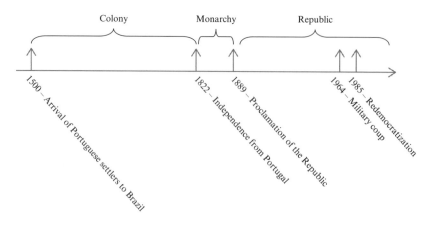

Figure 10.2   Timeline of milestones in Brazilian history

government attempted to push forward administrative reforms (Lustosa da Costa, 2008).

'Administrative reform', however, is a term that may have various connotations. Throughout Brazilian history, administrative reform has meant formalizing procedures, cost reduction, simplification of procedures and privatization. Some politicians have also used the term 'administrative reform' to mean changes in the functions of departments or ministries, or even to suggest an overall change in the composition of the cabinet.

To ensure understanding, the term 'administrative reform' is used here to refer to changes in public management policies and in the design of programmatic organizations, bound by a reasonable degree of coherence in values and rhetoric. This definition is based on the theoretical contributions of Barzelay (2000, 2001), and Hood and Jackson (1991). In other words, an administrative reform is an attempt to change a management model based on some kind of value (equity, efficiency, effectiveness or resilience) in order to change practices in human resource management, financial management, information and communication technology (ICT), marketing, procurement, organization design, participation, privatization, marketization and inter-organizational implementation of public policies. Using this concept, the Brazilian federal government witnessed only two attempts at administrative reform, detailed below.

1. Administrative reform of Getúlio Vargas in 1938 – transition from patrimonial form of administration to progressive public administration (PPA)

As seen earlier, Brazil has long been held hostage to pre-bureaucratic forms of administration inherited from the Portuguese Crown. The characteristics of this patrimonial model are confusion between public and private property, patronage, nepotism and gerontocracy (March, 1961). On taking power in 1930, President Getúlio Vargas imposed measures to rationalize public administration. To this end, in 1938 the Department of Public Service Administration (DASP) was created as a federal agency to design and implement public management policies in the areas of human resource management, financial management and budgeting. DASP was also expected to review the administrative structures and working procedures in the federal government (Bresser-Pereira, 1996). These initiatives were based on the Weberian rational–legal model and were also known as progressive public administration – PPA (Hood, 1995). The rhetoric related to this administrative reform was consistent with the group of theta values, are related to equity, fairness, mutuality, neutrality, accountability and avoidance of abuse by the agent (dishonesty, carelessness) (Hood and Jackson, 1991).

It can be argued that the PPA model had its big push forward in the Vargas era, but is still being implemented at the time of writing (2013). Measures for *ex ante* control of public agents, and for the promotion of the administrative efficiency, can be observed at all levels of direct and indirect government. Recent examples of the adoption of this Weberian bureaucratic model are measures such as the Regime Júridico Único dos Servidores, which guarantees job stability for agents in indirect administration; the 1993 Law 8.666, which restricted procurement procedures in the public sector; and the 2000 Fiscal Responsibility Law, which reduced the autonomy of elected officials in public expenditure decisions (mainly for raising expenditures to meet the cost of personnel). Even today, state and municipal administrations throughout Brazil use the legal–rational mindset, which becomes a management model, to implement new restrictions, to impose neutrality, and to avoid abuse by public agents.

2.   Administrative reform of Luiz Carlos Bresser-Pereira in 1995 – transition from PPA model to NPM

Throughout the twentieth century, Brazil sought to reject pre-bureaucratic forms of administration. While adopting PPA, bureaucratic dysfunctions became evident (Merton, 1949). Initiatives to reduce red tape were taken in 1967 and in 1980, during the dictatorship government (Abrucio, 2007). However, the great effort towards administrative change started in 1995, during Fernando Henrique Cardoso's administration, in which Luiz Carlos Bresser-Pereira took charge of the creation of the Ministry of Administration and Reform of the State (MARE) and the Master Plan for State Reform. Bresser-Pereira imported the New Public Management model as a solution to replace 'a bureaucratic public administration, slow and inefficient, for a managerial public administration, decentralized, efficient, dedicated to responding to the demands of citizens' (Bresser-Pereira, 1996, p. 26). The rhetoric of the managerial reform conducted by Bresser-Pereira was related to the group of sigma values related to efficiency, rational allocation of resources and simplicity (Hood and Jackson, 1991) (see Figure 10.3).

Among the measures that have been included in the Master Plan for State Reform were the privatization of public enterprises, contracting out public services to non-profit organizations, strengthening strategic-level careers (policy analysts, financial managers), fiscal adjustment, simplification of procedures, performance measurement (Bresser-Pereira, 1996; Resende, 2002; Abrucio, 2007; Lustosa da Costa, 2008).

The general assessment of Bresser-Pereira's reform is controversial. Privatization in sectors such as communications, mining and energy was

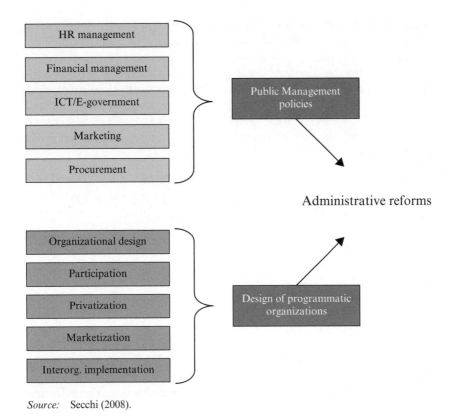

Source: Secchi (2008).

Figure 10.3 The components of the administrative reforms

undertaken. The strengthening of strategic careers in the federal government and contracting out to social organizations for the implementation of public services also achieved relative success. However, hopes for fiscal adjustment, for reducing red tape and for improving decision-making autonomy were not fulfilled.

The subordination of institutional changes to the most pressing issues of economic development, and the subsequent election of President Lula, who had little sympathy for managerial reforms, meant that Bresser-Pereira's reform had limited impact on the federal administration (Abrucio, 2007; Resende, 2002).

One of the great spillovers of the reforms, however, was the strengthening of knowledge and debate in the field. As a result, the theme has received attention from the public and from academia; undergraduate and graduate courses in public administration have proliferated throughout Brazil;

academic and practitioner conferences are now continually organized to discuss 'administrative reform' and 'innovations in the public sector'.

Consequently, public management policies became an important issue for political leaders' arguments and actions. Candidates for state governments, such as Minas Gerais, São Paulo, Pernambuco and Santa Catarina, emphasized public management policies and the design of programmatic organizations. Bresser-Pereira mostly failed in his endeavour, but 'administrative reform' has been an issue on the public agenda as never before in Brazilian history.

PARTICIPATION: THE CORE COMPETENCE OF BRAZILIAN PUBLIC ADMINISTRATION

Brazil is recognized, in the international literature, as a living experiment on participation mechanisms (Abers, 2000; Avritzer, 2008). Participation refers to the involvement of non-state actors in the policy-making process. In other words, participation means the involvement of civil society in identifying public problems, designing alternatives, making decisions, and implementing and evaluating public policies.

Initiatives to increase civil society involvement in public matters have no single root, or single entrepreneur. Several initiatives were taken by the Congress and by the federal government, and also by state and municipal governments. They are implemented to varying degrees. The diffusion of participation as a policy design mechanism is a case of multicentric experimentalism.

The generation of this competence was a product of the following context:

- The military dictatorship that ruled the country from 1964 to 1985 had an impact on the centralization of power (at the federal level), and on the concentration of power in the hands of the ruler.
- The lack of reliability of representative democracy and the bad image of the Congress, politicians and political parties (Almeida, 2007) fostered hopes that direct democracy would increase the legitimacy of decisions.
- Organized civil society is active in Brazil. Civil society was long responsible for an important share of public services, such as public health, education, environmental protection, culture and assistance to the poor, before the state started to increase its participation.
- Church-related charities, non-governmental organizations, unions

and business federations have claimed their positions in designing public policies at all three levels of government since democratization in 1985.

Since 1985, and after the 1988 Federal Constitution, several mechanisms for civic engagement in the elaboration of public policies have proliferated. Among them are policy councils, national conferences, participatory budgeting, and participation in the construction of urban master plans (*planos diretores*). They are briefly presented as follows.

Policy Councils (*Conselhos de Políticas Públicas*)

The 1988 Federal Constitution institutionalized this type of participatory body at all levels of government, to define and evaluate public policies in several areas. At the same time, it gave non-state actors the opportunity to discuss and decide public policies along with government officials. The most visible policy councils are Education, Health, Social Assistance, Child and Youth, Culture, Economic Development and Environment. Virtually every ministry at the federal level has a policy council attached to it. The same logic applies to municipalities and state government: the executive body headed by the municipal (or state) secretary is advised by policy councils to define the general policy and evaluate its outcomes.

The composition and power of policy councils varies from case to case. In general, they are formed by representatives from government (mainly bureaucrats or appointees), and representatives from society, mainly users/citizens, unions, universities and NPOs. Some policy councils have deliberative status, and their decisions are mandatory on the executive body. Others are merely advisory, making recommendations to government. Their composition and power depend on the regulation by which the body at the local, state or federal level has been created.

Some policy councils are mandatory for subnational levels of authority. According to the Brazilian legislation, municipal governments must create policy councils on Health, Education and Social Assistance. If not, the federal government can stop the transfer of money for some specific programmes.[3]

Policy councils increase participation and social accountability. At the federal and state levels, and in larger cities, council members represent important sectors of society. They are in charge of the policy issues at hand. They are experienced managers, and they collaborate effectively in the decision-making process. In smaller cities, policy councils vary in participation and effectiveness. Studies have identified some critical aspects that inhibit the policy councils' goals, such as a low participation culture among the population, lack of information and expertise to make a difference at meetings, and the capture of the policy council by high demanders or 'preference outliers' (Allebrandt, 2003; Secchi, 2006). Even in small towns, a positive spillover effect is the creation of co-responsibility and mutual learning in council meetings, and the rise of technical debate in frequently politicized arenas.

Participatory Budget (*Orçamento Participativo*)

Participatory budget is a decision-making mechanism that some cities employ for deciding investments. It has been created and disseminated in cities controlled by the Workers' Party. The most visible experiment took place in Porto Alegre, with a population of 1.5 million, the capital of Rio Grande do Sul – a southern state. It mixed a historically engaged community with the sympathy of a left-wing party towards participatory mechanisms (Avritzer, 2008).

Basically, the mechanism works as follows: city officials organize forums in every district or neighbourhood to determine top priorities for infrastructural investments – building new schools, streets, health centres and other public services. The resident population is invited to participate in regional forums. The community proposes or rejects the alternatives, and there are no restrictions or barriers to citizen participation. After a first round at the regional forums, the Executive Commission for the Participatory Budget organizes a second round of discussions (the City Assembly) in order to collate all the demands, aiming to balance the investment options chosen by different neighbourhoods, and avoiding duplication of investment for the next fiscal year.

The participatory budget has no influence on matters such as salaries and benefits, administrative costs and tax revenues. The advantage of participatory budgeting is the access to decision making (Fung, 2006). A significant part of the municipal budget is decided within the community, shifting the power from behind closed doors in City Hall. Another gain is the sense of belonging. After two decades of dictatorship, and even with discredited legislative power, the citizenry feel that they finally have a voice in public decision making. This is not a trivial breakthrough in Brazil. The main criticism of participatory budgeting is the lack of discussion of overall policies and public services to the citizenry. Big investments that could benefit the whole city are not subject to the mechanism. Vaz (2002, pp. 276–7) claimed that the mechanism 'does not take into consideration the great investments, administrative costs of the public service and public policies'.

Despite some limitations, participatory budgeting is considered a benchmark to increase public governance and co-production. More than 150 cities in Brazil have adopted the mechanism, and today it is one of Brazil's most discussed and exported examples of innovation in public decision making.

Urban Master Plan (*Plano Diretor*)

The *plano diretor* is the urban master plan that every municipality has to develop in order to map preservation, residential, commercial areas and spaces for urban expansion. It serves as the territorial zoning plan for the municipality. The participatory outlook is mandatory since a federal law was enacted in 2001 (the so-called Estatuto da Cidade), which states that the formulation of the *plano diretor* must be built with the participation of community.

The origins of the *plano diretor* go back to Movimento Nacional pela Reforma Urbana (National Movement for Urban Reform), which, since the 1960s, has gathered non-profit organizations, unions, local associations and professional associations to push for regulation of land use, recovery of degraded urban areas (*favelas*) and the preservation of the urban environment (Avritzer, 2008). This movement was able to influence the agenda during the formulation of the 1988 Federal Constitution and Estatuto da Cidade in 2001, which included the *plano diretor* as the major urban planning mechanism.

After 2001, all cities with more than 20 000 inhabitants started a participatory process to formulate, through public hearings, their *plano diretor*. Public hearings are held in order to understand community problems, to elaborate policy alternatives, and to take final decisions on land use. All citizens are invited to participate, but the more affluent actors are community associations, non-profit organizations and, naturally landlords, developers and realtors. The wave of participation in designing each *plano diretor* started in 2001 and reached more than 1000 municipalities, affecting more than 120 million inhabitants. It is regarded as one of the largest experiments in direct participation ever undertaken.

National Conferences (*Conferências Nacionais*)

National conferences (*conferências nacionais*) are initiatives taken by the federal government to consult the population on several public policy areas. National conferences happen from the bottom, from municipalities, to states, and then up to the federal level. They are organized in policy areas such as health, education and public safety, or in many specific policy issues such as racial equality, fisheries and aquaculture, or health care for the indigenous population.

National conferences have taken place in Brazil since the time of Getúlio Vargas. Health was the first policy area to organize national conferences in the 1940s. Since Fernando Henrique Cardoso (1995–2002) and, especially with Luiz Inacio Lula da Silva (2003–10), national conferences have become a constant channel for building dialogue with civil society for proposing national policies. Since then, more than 100 national conferences have been held (Avritzer, 2012). National conferences happen as follows. The ministry of any area (health, safety, environment etc.) creates an organizing committee for the national conference in that policy area. Representatives of the government and from civil society comprise this committee. The committee is expected to design the conference statute, including deadlines, regulation for electing representatives and the participatory methodology. Each municipality voluntarily organizes a conference and elects the representatives. At the state level, the municipal representatives gather to discuss common problems, to build policy proposals, and to elect state representatives who will attend the national conference. Finally, the state representatives gather at the national conference for a few days, preparing the Final Report. This document is the main product of the national conference. It has no legal value, but serves as a policy report for congressmen, and for the executive branch of the federal government itself to develop its policies.

The discussion is deliberative; reasons and arguments are put forward in an attempt to build a consensus among the various actors. Studies have shown that national conferences are very effective. The knowledge generated by the deliberative rounds at the local, state and national levels is absorbed as input for the formulation of national policies (Pogrebinschi, 2010; Avritzer, 2012).

CONCLUSION: THE BRAZILIAN MOSAIC

Presenting an overview of the prevailing public management model in Brazil is a hard task. Brazil is a large and diverse country, with many forms of public administration. The heterogeneity is such that the 'management model' employed in the Ministry of Finance or Ministry of Planning, which has a numerous and highly skilled workforce, is totally different from that of the Ministry of Health, or that of the Ministry of Education, which does not have a consolidated bureaucracy and relies on specialized and decentralized structures in states and municipalities.

If it is difficult to draw a synthesis of management models in ministries that are located within a mile of each other in Brasília, to compare the public administration of São Paulo – a city with over 10 million inhabitants – with Quixadá – a city with 80 000 inhabitants located in the impoverished hinterland of Ceará (northeastern of Brazil) – is like comparing oranges to apples.

The picture is even more complex if we widen the discussion to other powers, such as legislative and judiciary in various states of the federation. All organs of indirect administration, such as the federal public university with over 50 000 students, the highly professional public bank system in Brazil and the poorly structured utility companies, live in completely different worlds, so to speak.

The synthesis of this canvas is a mosaic. Brazil is a mosaic and its public administration is a consequence of that. What management model predominates in Brazilian public administration? In order to address this question, we have to look at the specific organ, to the specific power, to the specific region or state of the federation.

In general, poorer and smaller municipalities are still hostages to old clientelistic practices, and they are currently undergoing an effort to adopt PPA, and banning patrimonialism. This effort is imposed by federal regulation, such as the Regime Júridico Único dos Servidores, the 1993 Law 8666, and the 2000 Fiscal Responsibility Act. This shift is also an outcome of a maturing society that has been slowly realizing that government officials must be held accountable.

In the federal government, and in some states, such as Minas Gerais and Pernambuco, and even in some cities, such as Curitiba and São Paulo, NPM tools have been adopted, in the form of more autonomy for managerial decisions, performance-related pay and privatization. Public governance initiatives, on the other hand, are present at all levels of government. It can be said that the image of Brazilian public administration is public governance, co-production, policy networks and citizen participation.

Values and doctrines of public governance are present in mechanisms for citizen participation as mentioned: policy councils, national conferences, participatory budgeting and participation in the construction of urban master plans. These participatory mechanisms focus on the process of formulating and evaluating public policies. As for the implementation of public policies, examples are the participation of civic organizations in the delivery of education, environment and health care services. Other examples of implementation are public–private partnerships as a way of sharing risks and benefits in the construction of highways, railways and soccer stadiums for the FIFA World Cup 2014. In Brazil, inter-organizational implementation of policies is a necessary means for facing the state's inability to cope alone with the growing and diverse demands of society.

The most interesting phenomenon in Brazilian public governance has been happening inductively, through innovative experimentation in municipalities, in states and at the federal level. Unlike what happened with the adoption of the PPA after the 1930s, or with the adoption of NPM since 1995, the Brazilian public governance model is *sui generis*. It was born and raised during different initiatives of political parties, different levels of government, and has had to cope with the pressure of a civil society jaded by centralism and illegitimate representativeness.

The Brazilian participation experiences are unique – born, tested and improved locally. There was no inspiration from foreign literature or foreign experiences of public governance, or policy networks or co-production (Rhodes, 1997; Börzel, 1998; Whitaker, 1980). What happened is a combination of what was empirically experienced in Brazil in the last 20 years, and the rise of a normative international literature of public administration arguing for less hierarchical, and more participatory and collaborative elaboration of public policies.

Some countries have attempted to apply deductively the concepts of public governance. In Brazil, the process goes the other way round: an experimentation that goes upwards, synchronized with the lack of legitimacy of public administration and representation.

The symbolic and practical value of participation had such force in Brazil that it has led to 'democratitis' – a pejorative term used to denote excessive participation in all technical and political decisions, which can lead to slow decision making as a result of repeated and ineffective discussions. Democratitis is the inability to make managerial decisions, and the inertial tendency to bring any kind of discussion to the general public.

Despite this participatory fame, the predominance of the public governance model is not the reality in Brazilian public administration. Again, the better image of Brazilian public administration is the mosaic: patrimonialism, PPA, NPM and public governance stand side by side. In some places, the amount of patrimonialism may be greater. In other areas, such as consolidated public administrations (Ministry of Planning, Ministry of Finance), in indirect administration, and in the judiciary, the PPA model stands out. The NPM was applied to the federal government, and in some states and city governments enchanted with its rhetoric of efficiency, effectiveness and streamlined management. Public governance, co-production and participation are also applied variously throughout Brazilian public administration, depending on the political party in office, the strength of civil society and the size of the political community.

NOTES

1.   People whose salary is under R$1637.11 (£460/month), are exempted from this tax.

2. The only exceptions are the cities of São Paulo and Rio de Janeiro, the two largest cities. They have their own municipal account tribunal, linked to the legislative power of the city.
3. Due to an intricate fiscal system, the majority of Brazilian municipalities depend heavily on transfers from upper-level governments. Larger cities rely mostly on their own property and service taxes, but the smaller municipalities are, the higher their dependence on transfers.

REFERENCES

Abers, R.N. 2000. *Inventing Local Democracy: Grassroots Politics in Brazil*. Boulder, CO: Lynne Rienner Publishers.
Abrucio, F.L. 2007. Trajetória recente da gestão pública Brasileira: um balanço crítico e a renovação da agenda de reformas. *Revista de Administração Pública*, Edição Comemorativa Especial 1967–2007, 67–86.
Allebrandt, S.L. 2003. Conselhos municipais: potencialidades e limites para a efetividade e eficácia de um espaço público para a construção da cidadania interativa. *Proceedings. XXVII Encontro Nacional de Pós-Graduação e Pesquisa em Administração*, Atibaia – São Paulo.
Almeida, A.C. 2007. *A Cabeça do Brasileiro*. São Paulo: Record.
Avritzer, L. 2008. Instituições participativas e desenho institucional: algumas considerações sobre a variação da participação no Brasil democrático. *Opinião Pública*, **14**(1), 43–64.
Avritzer, L. 2012. Conferências nacionais: ampliando e redefinindo os padrões de participação social no Brasil. Texto Para Discussão 1739, Rio de Janeiro: Ipea.
Barzelay, M. 2000. The New Public Management: a bibliographical essay for Latin American (and other) scholars. *International Public Management Journal*, **3**, 229–65.
Barzelay, M. 2001. *The New Public Management: Improving Research and Policy Dialogue*. Berkeley, CA and New York: University of California Press/Russell Sage Foundation.
Börzel, T.A. 1998. Le reti di attori pubblici e privati nella regolazione Europea. *Stato e Mercato*, **54**(3), 389–432.
Bresser-Pereira, L.C. 1996. Da administração burocrática à gerencial. *Revista do Serviço Público*, **47**(1), 7–40.
CIA (Central Intelligence Agency). 2013. The World Factbook, Available at https://www. Cia. Gov/Library/Publications/The-World-Factbook/ (retrieved 4 August 2013).
Claus, L. 2005. Montesquieu's mistakes and the true meaning of separation. *Oxford Journal of Legal Studies*, **25**, 419–51.
Fung, A. 2006. Varieties of participation in complex governance. *Public Administration Review*, December, Special Issue, 66–75.
Government of Brazil. 1992. *Constituição da Republica Federativa do Brasil: Promulgada em 5 de Outubro de 1988*, São Paulo: Saraiva.
Government of Brazil. 2011. Sinopse do Censo Demográfico de 2010. In: Estatística, Instituto Brasileiro de Geografia e Estatística Brasília.
Government of Brazil. 2013a. Ibge Cidade@ [Online]. Brasília: Ibge. Available at http://www.Ibge.Gov.Br/Cidadesat/Index.Php?Lang=_En (accessed 6 August 2013).
Government of Brazil. 2013b. Resultado Fiscal do Tesouro Federal. Secretaria do Tesouro Nacional. Ministério da Fazenda.
Hood, C. 1995. The 'New Public Management' in the 1980s: variations on a theme. *Accounting, Organizations and Society*, **20**(2/3), 93–109.
Hood, C. and M.W. Jackson. 1991. *Administrative Argument*. Aldershot and Brookfield, VT: Dartmouth Pub. Co.
Lustosa Da Costa, Frederico. 2008. Brasil: 200 anos de estado; 200 anos de administração pública; 200 anos de reformas. *Revista de Administração Pública*, **42**(5), 829–74.

March, R.M. 1961. Formal organization and promotion in a pre-industrial society. *American Sociology Review*, **26**(4), 547–56.

Merton, R.K. 1949. *Social Theory and Social Structure: Toward the Codification of Theory and Research*. Glencoe, IL: Free Press.

Moraes, A.D. 2013. *Direito Constitucional*, São Paulo: Editora Atlas.

OECD. 2010. Human Resource Management, Country Profiles: Brazil, available at http://www.Oecd.Org/Gov/Pem/Oecd%20hrm%20profile%20-%20brazil.Pdf (retrieved 4 August 2013).

Pietro, M.S.Z.D. 2013. *Direito Administrativo*, São Paulo: Editora Atlas.

Pogrebinschi, T. 2010. Conferênciais nacionais, participação social, e processo legislativo. In Serie Pensando o Direito, No. 27, available at http://Participacao.Mj.Gov.Br/Pensandoodireito/Wp-Content/Uploads/2012/12/27pensando_Direito.Pdf (accessed 4 August 2013).

Resende, F.C. 2002. Por que reformas administrativas falham? *Revista Brasileira de Ciências Sociais*, **17**(50), 123–42.

Rhodes, R.A.W. 1997. *Understanding Governance: Policy Networks, Governance, Reflexivity, and Accountability*. Buckingham and Philadephia, PA: Open University Press.

Secchi, L. 2006. Agenda building in Brazilian municipalities: when and how citizens participate. In Jochen Franzke (ed.), *Making Civil Societies Work*, Potsdam: Potsdam University Press.

Secchi, L. 2008. Public management reforms at the municipal level: multi-case study in Barcelona, Boston and Turin. PhD Thesis, Graduate School in Social, Economic and Political Sciences, University of Milan.

Tomio, F.R.D.L. 2002. A criação de municípios após a Constituição de 1988. *Revista Brasileira de Ciências Sociais*, **17**, 61–89.

Vaz, J.C. 2002. Desafios para a incorporação da transparência em um modelo de gestão municipal. In P. Spink, S. Caccia-Bava and V. Paulics (eds), *Novos Contornos da Gestão Local: Conceitos em Construção*, São Paulo: Pólis/Fgv-Eaesp.

Whitaker, G.P. 1980. Coproduction: citizen participation in service delivery. *Public Administration Review*, **40**(3), 240–46.

11. Public administration in Latin America: adaptation to a new democratic reality
Guillermo M. Cejudo

INTRODUCTION

In recent decades, Latin America has experienced drastic changes in its political landscape: countries in the region have moved from authoritarian rule to democracy, and in the process have transformed their public sector to respond to this new reality. However, each country has responded differently to these processes: whereas some countries have gained institutional capacity and administrative sophistication, others remain unresponsive and ineffectual. This chapter offers an analysis of these changes and an explanation for the different trajectories. In doing so, it addresses contemporary debates on trajectories of public sector reform, on administrative capacity building in developing countries and on the sources of change and continuity in the public sector.

THE EFFECTS OF DEMOCRACY ON THE BUREAUCRACY

For decades, it was widely assumed that the reason behind the poor performance of Latin American governments was the absence of democratic elections that could create incentives for politicians to improve their bureaucracies and to refrain from corrupt practices. The argument was that the quality of government could not be improved as long as authoritarian regimes remained in power because it was in the interest of non-democratic political elites to have a government that functioned on the basis of clientelism (in order to obtain support) and corruption (in order to obtain rents). Yet, at the same time, several scholars have shown that democratic elites do not find it easy to promote reforms aimed at improving the performance of public bureaucracies because either they did not want to lose the patronage opportunities or because any reform would face considerable resistance and could endanger their survival as elected leaders or the stability of the new democratic regime (Grindle, 1977; Arellano Gault and Guerrero, 2003; Geddes, 1994; Ames, 1990;

Oszlak, 1986). Yet change has occurred. Of course, each country has experienced a different trajectory of reform, and with different results: whereas some countries have gained institutional capacity and administrative sophistication, others remain unresponsive and ineffectual. Some nations have experienced greater decentralization towards subnational units, but others have reverted to their initial decentralizing attempts. Finally, some countries have reduced the role of the public sector in the economy, while others have increased dramatically its weight and influence.

In contrast with previous democratic episodes, some "third-wave" democracies in Latin America – those that emerged after the 1970s – have been relatively more successful in transforming their governments by creating more professional bureaucracies, promoting freedom of information initiatives, strengthening external audit agencies, and transforming organizational structures and practices through administrative reforms (Grindle, 2001; Heredia and Schneider, 2003; Longo, 2005; Zuvanic and Iacoviello, 2005; Marcel and Toha, 1998; Barzelay et al., 2003). However, not all democracies have been equally successful in this area; some unlikely candidates have carried out significant reforms whereas other strong democracies have been unable to do so. This new situation of bureaucratic reform within democratic regimes poses a new question: why – despite the tradition of democratic regimes unable to transform their bureaucracies – have some democratic countries, but not others, been able to do so?

The argument of this chapter is that the activation of constraints on the executive, and particularly the interest and capacity of Congress to impose restrictions on the discretionary authority of presidents over the bureaucracy, facilitates administrative reforms that tend to improve the quality of governments. This combination of interest and capacity explains both variation over time (why third-wave democracies have been able to reform their public bureaucracies, but previous democratic regimes have not) and across countries (why some democratic governments have done it, but others have not). If the executive is subject to oversight by other institutional actors and by restrictions imposed by a legislature, if it has to follow certain procedures to appoint and dismiss bureaucrats, and if it is required to apply rules in the daily operation of government, then the quality of government will improve.

These restrictions are rarely self-imposed. As many students of new democracies have found out, new democratic leaders prefer to be free from these constraints in order to be able to appoint people at will, to obtain illegal rents and to implement clientelistic policies. This is the politician's dilemma studied in Geddes's (1994) famous book: if democratic politicians reform their administration, they lose electoral support; if they do not, the regime loses legitimacy:

> [A]lthough a democratic political system should ideally provide politicians with good reasons for supplying public goods desired by citizens whose votes they need to stay in office, in reality the combination of the information asymmetry and the influence asymmetry between members of internal and external constituencies gives politicians an incentive to respond to the particular interests of some politically useful citizens rather than to the general interests of the public as a whole.
>
> Administrative competence is an especially costly form of collective good to most politicians because, as detailed above, politicians in unreformed systems rely on access to state resources to build their support organizations, and administrative reform threatens such access. Effective reforms establish merit as the criterion for employment, price competition as the criterion for awarding contracts, and impersonal rules for determining who received government benefits – thus depriving politicians of important resources.
>
> Politicians who might otherwise consider offering reforms as a strategy for attracting support will not be able to afford the cost in lost political resources as long as they compete with others able to use such resources in the struggle for votes. This is the politician's dilemma. (Ibid.: 41–2)

In the last three decades, Latin American countries have moved from authoritarian (mainly military) regimes, in which electoral competition was banned (or at least restricted), to democratic regimes, which (albeit still imperfect) allow political contestation and protect basic liberties (Mantilla and Munck, 2013). Following these transitions, and despite the fact that the new democratic politicians faced the same dilemma as previous governments, some changes have occurred. Latin American countries have experienced substantial changes in their public bureaucracies: from the managerial reform in Chile during the 1990s, to the transformation of the civil service in Uruguay, the Weberian reforms in Brazil in the 1980s and the managerial reaction to them in the 1990s, the creation in Mexico of a career civil service in the federal bureaucracy, and freedom of information legislation in several countries in the region. These reform episodes challenge those accounts that see bureaucratic reforms in new democracies as heroic acts of politicians going against their immediate interests of reelection or support building, as policy spillovers from economic decisions, or as simple impositions by international organizations.

Indeed, once established, a democracy must face, sooner or later, the challenge of bringing about change in a bureaucratic apparatus that was moulded by the needs and preferences of the authoritarian regime (Cejudo, 2011). This is so because, when trying to implement a government agenda, any regime – authoritarian or democratic – will have a strong interest in aligning administrative institutions to its political

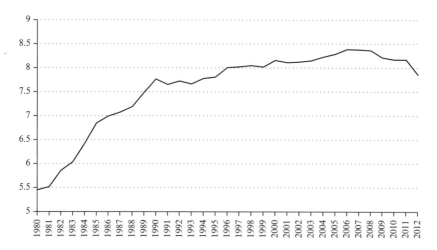

Note: This figure measures Democracy using variable *fh_ipolity2* in the Quality of Government Standard Dataset. The scale ranges from 0 to 10, where 0 is least democratic and 10 is most democratic. The variable is an average of Freedom House political rights and civil liberties scores transformed to a scale 0–10 and Polity IV scores transformed to a scale 0–10. It has imputed values for countries where data on Polity are missing by regressing Polity on the average Freedom House measure. Countries considered are: Antigua and Barbuda, Argentina, Bahamas, Barbados, Belize, Bolivia, Brazil, Chile, Colombia, Costa Rica, Cuba, Dominica, Dominican Republic, Ecuador, El Salvador, Grenada, Guatemala, Guyana, Haiti, Honduras, Jamaica, Mexico, Nicaragua, Panama, Paraguay, Peru, St Kitts and Nevis, St Lucia, St Vincent and the Grenadines, Suriname, Trinidad and Tobago, Uruguay, and Venezuela.

Source: Teorell et al. (2013).

Figure 11.1   Latin America democracy, 1980–2012

project. The process of political change also brings about new demands from an active electorate and new constraints from institutions created (or strengthened) to oversee the executive, which, we might expect, reduces opportunities for corruption, and limits the amount of resources available for clientelism and patronage. Moreover, elites in post-transition democracies want to adjust the bureaucratic structure inherited from the pre-transition regime to reflect their own priorities. As their authoritarian past was left behind, Latin American democratic governments had to respond with strategies to adapt their public sectors to a new environment (see Figure 11.1).

THREE EXAMPLES OF ADAPTATION (AND RESISTANCE) TO THE DEMANDS OF DEMOCRATIZATION

In this section, I analyse the process of public sector reform in three new democracies in Latin America that emerged after a long-lasting authoritarian episode: Mexico, Chile and Argentina (for the evolution of their democracy levels, see Figure 11.2). Improvements in the quality of their public bureaucracy (if any) came not directly from the new democratic status of the regime but from the activation of constraints in the executive, particularly legislative constraints.

Mexico

Mexico's road to democracy was longer than in other Latin American cases (with political liberalization starting in the 1970s and the first presidential electoral defeat of the Institutional Revolutionary Party (PRI) in 2000). A long series of electoral reforms and a gradual increase in the number of local and state elections won by opposition parties led, in 1997, to the first Congress in modern Mexico not dominated by the PRI. Subsequently, in 2000, the opposition National Action Party (PAN) won the presidency (before losing to the PRI in 2012).

In 1997, when the PRI lost the majority in the lower chamber, institutional constraints that were enacted in the Constitution but were dormant under the PRI regime became active. Congress became involved in public sector reform and introduced legislation that continuously stripped the presidency of its almost total autonomy in dealing with the federal bureaucracy. Opposition parties in Congress called for reducing the lack of accountability in the public sector, and discretionary spending in the executive. This was coupled with the budgetary reform proposed by the previous government, which gave legislators more instruments for monitoring government performance. Congress was also the main actor behind one of the last institutional changes under the PRI regime: the creation of the Federal Audit Office (*Auditoría Superior de la Federación, ASF*) in 2000. A constitutional amendment and a new audit law were passed to create a relatively autonomous institution (but under the control of the lower chamber) (Apreza, 2004). This decision not only modified bureaucratic behaviour (because public officials were now under supervision from an external body), but also gave Congress a new instrument to control and oversee the executive, not only in the annual revision of public accounts, but also when Congress decided to initiate special audits. Later, in 2008, this Office would be further strengthened.

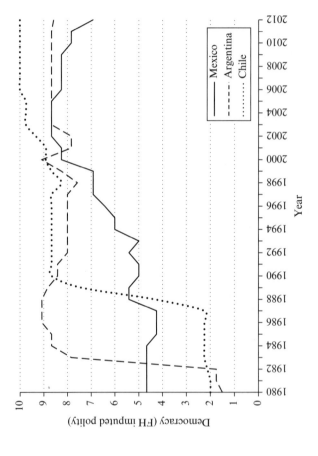

Note: This figure measures Democracy using variable *fh_ipolity2* in the Quality of Government Standard Dataset. Scale ranges from 0 to 10, where 0 is least democratic and 10 is most democratic. The variable is an average of Freedom House political rights and civil liberties scores transformed to a scale 0–10 and Polity IV scores transformed to a scale 0–10. It has imputed values for countries where data on Polity are missing by regressing Polity on the average Freedom House measure.

Source: Teorell et al. (2013).

Figure 11.2   Changing democracy levels in Mexico, Chile and Argentina, 1980–2012

Given the long process of political liberalization, when Vicente Fox (2000–2006) came to power after the first democratic presidential transition in Mexican history, he did not find a bureaucracy that was completely unfamiliar with the pressures of democratic governance. Even before Fox took office, the bureaucratic apparatus had already faced the pressure of an opposition-dominated Congress (Klesner, 2001) and had been open to some extent to congressional oversight and media scrutiny (Guerrero, 2002). Moreover, the bureaucracy was not as clientelist and disorganized as it had been years before. Even if not all the reforms of the 1980s and 1990s were successful, some of them had a real impact on the bureaucracy.

It is not surprising that one of Fox's priorities was to change the public administration's long-standing patterns of clientelism and lack of professionalism, and to introduce modern mechanisms (mainly from private sector practices, to which he had been exposed as a former businessman) to reduce inertia and align the bureaucracy with his ambitious agenda, and to face the high expectations generated during the electoral campaign. Originally, the overall plan of the government was summed up in a document called *Strategic Model for Government Innovation* (Oficina de la Presidencia para la Innovación Gubernamental, 2001), which tried to foster the introduction of managerial practices into the public sector. Two years into Fox's term, the government strategy was further specified in the *Presidential Agenda for Good Government*, which put forward six goals: a government that costs less; a quality-oriented government; a professional government; a digital government; improved regulation government; and honest and transparent government (Muñoz, 2004; Pardo, 2007). Officials in different agencies were assigned responsibility over each of these goals, and the results were mixed. There was greater use of information technologies throughout the government, and several managerial initiatives were implemented (such as citizen charters and prizes for innovation), but most changes were introduced without any structural modification of the public administration towards further decentralization, and the promise to increase managerial autonomy was not fulfilled. So, even if, rhetorically, there had been some similarities with other cases of managerial reform, this strategy did not modify the centralized and hierarchical character of the administration.

All these limited efforts to improve the quality of government after the transition shared a similar origin: presidential decisions, without congressional involvement. And they also shared similar objectives: strengthening the executive's control over the bureaucracy, without reducing its autonomous authority. In the same period, other initiatives from Congress were not only more ambitious but also had greater potential in reducing corruption and improving the performance of the federal bureaucracy.

The first was a campaign to guarantee access to government information. In July 2002, Congress approved a Freedom of Information Law (*Ley Federal de Transparencia y Acceso a la Información*), which has been a useful mechanism for deterring corruption in the federal bureaucracy and for giving citizens the opportunity to obtain information about governmental activities and expenditures. This law has been praised as one of the most advanced freedom of information laws in the Latin American region, and its provisions are enforced by an autonomous organism (the Instituto Federal de Acceso a la Información, IFAI). In a brief period of time, all federal agencies created offices dedicated to processing citizens' enquiries and web portals where basic budgetary and personnel information are posted and updated regularly; and the agencies have also modified rules and procedures to guarantee access to government information (López Ayllón et al., 2010). In 2014, a constitutional amendment transformed IFAI into an autonomous body with jurisdiction over Mexico's three levels of government.

A second important change in the public administration has been the creation of a career civil service system. The Civil Service Law, passed with no opposition in Congress in 2003, charged the newly created Ministry for Public Administration with the responsibility of regulating and implementing the career system. Secondary regulation was issued in March 2004 (and replaced in 2007), and recruitment has started to take place through competitive examinations (severely questioned by some experts). The long-term impact of the law is yet to be seen, and some of its provisions have been short-circuited by "temporary" appointments under both Fox and his successor Felipe Calderón (2006–12) (Méndez, 2010). The Ministry of Finance is resisting loss of power over personal payment decisions, and in some ministries there have been obstacles to the effective operation of the committees in charge of the implementation of the career system (Arellano Gault and Klingner, 2004; Pardo, 2004; Martínez Puón, 2011). Similarly, there have been some questions about the quality of the recruitment process. However, the system is already operating in several parts of the government (Merino, 2006).

Congress has also promoted two additional initiatives aimed at improving the performance of the federal bureaucracy. In 2003 it passed a bill on social development (*Ley General de Desarrollo Social*) that set the basis for creating a policy evaluation regime for all social programs. This law created a National Council of Evaluation of Social Policy (Coneval) in charge of coordinating performance and impact evaluations of all social programs (Maldonado, 2009). Social programs (such as *Oportunidades*, a conditional cash-transfer program) are now routinely evaluated by external agents coordinated by the Council, and there are administrative procedures aimed at making sure that agencies take into account the recommendations of external evaluators (González, 2010). More recently, in 2007 and 2008, a series of constitutional amendments reinforced the emphasis on a results-oriented public administration, a more autonomous and powerful external audit institution, and greater transparency (López Ayllón, 2009; Dussauge, 2010).

Not all these initiatives have been wholly successful. In particular, the civil service law has faced significant resistance from many quarters. During the Fox administration, ministries complained about the centralized design of the system and delayed its implementation. In the Calderón administration, the civil service was regarded with suspicion by ministers and political appointees, and they have effectively avoided following the civil service rules by making repeated use of exception clauses for temporary appointments (Martínez Puón, 2011; Dussauge, 2011). Transparency, evaluation and external control also face several challenges: from their lack of articulation (several institutions, processes and responsibilities are not articulated into a coherent system) to the lack of effective sanctions for public officials (pointed to regularly as the source of corruption and impunity in Mexico) (López Ayllón et al., 2010).

Yet, although not all initiatives were successful, it is clear that Congress has been a key factor in trying to improve the quality of the public bureaucracy. A slow process of democratization and the activation of political constraints on the executive set in motion new dynamics in the Mexican bureaucracy, even if not all of them were deliberately aimed at improving the quality of government (but rather part of political strategies aimed at constraining the power of the president).

Chile

Chile's democracy emerged from a long-lasting authoritarian episode characterized by strong centralization and absence of checks on the authority of the dictator Augusto Pinochet. None the less, the Chilean democratic governments made significant improvements in the public sector in the years following the transition. The Concertación governments (an alliance of Socialist and Christian Democrats) have created in the last two decades a more professional and honest bureaucracy, with reforms that have been emulated by its neighbors, that has contributed to a success story of economic and social development.

Historically, the Chilean bureaucracy has always been more professional and competent than the public administration in other Latin American countries. Yet the legacy of Pinochet's authoritarian regime in the area of public administration was double: the government carried out comprehensive reforms in the structure and size of the bureaucracy, which resulted in a much smaller public sector (from 45 percent of GDP in 1973 to 17 percent in 1989), functionally separating policy-making ministries and implementation agencies. At the same time, however, the long-standing attack on the public sector led to a public administration that was inefficient and demoralized (and underpaid), and lacked resources and capacity to work effectively (Marcel and Toha, 1998; Garretón and Cáceres, 2003).

The rapid democratization of the Chilean regime activated institutional constraints that were either ineffective or non-existent under Pinochet: the 1980 Constitution established a clear separation of powers, and the legislation inherited from the authoritarian period prescribed rules that shaped decisions on labor relations, budget allocation and external control of the bureaucracy. At the same time, when the first Concertación president Patricio Aylwin took power, he faced numerous constraints imposed by the previous regime. The new government opted for a strategy of political and economic stability. This approach was also reflected in the government's position regarding the bureaucracy. The government acknowledged that the public administration lacked the resources and capacity to operate effectively in the new democratic context. However, a radical reform was ruled out from the beginning (Ramírez Alujas, 2001).

By 1993, it was clear to policy makers that the bureaucracy was not performing well and, despite significant increases in the funds allocated to public programs, the outcomes had not improved accordingly (Marcel, 1999). Consequently, there was change in the reform strategy. Instead of pursuing comprehensive reforms in the whole government, the Budget Directorate in the Ministry of Finance, working within the existing legal restrictions inherited from the Pinochet era, initiated a program of gradual improvement in the management of public agencies. It undertook several pilot projects in selected public organizations, based on managerial doctrines of strategic planning and performance evaluation. Each agency in the pilot program would sign a performance contract with the president, specifying measurable objectives and deadlines. This approach was also adopted by the second president of the post-authoritarian period, Eduardo Frei (1994–2000), who, like Aylwin, was a member of the Concertación alliance.

It was only in 1997 that the government formulated a more comprehensive strategy for reform: the *Strategic Plan for Public Management Modernization*. The plan assumed the gradual approach of the previous years and did not include any attempt to modify the bureaucracy in a significant way. Most of the policies were the usual suspects in New Public Management style reforms (Hood, 1991): red-tape simplification, citizen charters, prizes for innovation and quality in the public sector, IT-based procurement systems (ChileCompra), e-government initiatives, and performance evaluation (Waissbluth, 2005). It was, despite its flaws, and with no congressional involvement, one of the most ambitious programs of managerial reforms in Latin America (Bresser-Pereira, 2001).

In this process, the role of Congress was very limited. According to the constitutional design of the Chilean political system – which created a strong executive – the president enjoyed a monopoly of decision making in relation to public administration. Regarding the actual capacity of the legislature to oversee the performance of the public administration, Siavelis (2000: 74) has argued that there is a problem of "disconnected fire alarms and ineffective policy patrols", and that the mechanisms "to investigate, control, and punish corruption and inefficiency are woefully inadequate". More importantly, the opposition in Congress showed no interest in reforming the administration; its interest lay not in reducing the discretionary authority of the president over the bureaucracy, but in defending the *status quo*, because it saw the bureaucracy (and other institutions related to the functioning of government, such as the comptrollership) as authoritarian legacies to be defended, rather than reformed.

It took a combination of a sense of crisis and congressional involvement to initiate the first attempt to go beyond the gradual approach of managerial reforms. When the third president of post-authoritarian Chile took office in 2000, it was expected that new attempts at introducing more ambitious reforms would be made. Ricardo Lagos (2000–2006) was the first Socialist member of the Center–Left coalition to run for president and, even though he won by a small margin, the political context had changed. After two successful administrations, the threat of an authoritarian regression had diminished; and, after Pinochet's detention in London in 1998 on charges of human rights abuses and his prosecution in Chilean courts (before his death in 2006), his influence on national politics was reduced.

Lagos's initial approach to public administration reform was to maintain the moderate changes introduced by Frei. His program on State Modernization and Reform (*Programa de Reforma y Modernización del Estado*), announced in 2000, was a continuation of Frei's managerial policies, with an emphasis on performance assessment, improvement in service quality and customer orientation.

This approach would change after 2002, when major corruption scandals involving illegal payments to politicians and public officials from the government's discretionary "reserved funds" (*gastos reservados*) (Santiso, 2007) and irregularities in public infrastructure projects (Pliscoff, 2004) challenged the view that Chile's public administration was immune to corruption and that gradual managerial reforms had been enough to adapt the bureaucracy to the new democratic context. In response to these scandals, the executive and the opposition parties in Congress signed in January 2003 a series of agreements to reform the administration.[1]

It was the first time since the transition that Congress had become involved in administrative reform (although the pact was brokered by party leaders before submitting it to legislators). Congress and the executive agreed to push for several reforms in the structure and functioning of the bureaucracy, including institutional reorganization (some ministries were merged), administrative simplification, and changes in procurement policies, human resources and financial management. Political parties committed themselves to quickly approve the necessary legal reforms in Congress, which involved amending several laws dating from the Pinochet era.

In these agreements, the rightist opposition pushed for a reform of the appointment process of high-level civil servants that would lower the number of presidential political appointees and create a new career track for top officials (*Sistema de Alta Dirección Pública*) in order to reduce the politicization of the elite bureaucracy (Aninat et al., 2004). The role of the opposition was particularly important for changing the reform strategy because right-wing parties no longer saw the bureaucracy as an enclave from the past that needed to be protected from new democratic elites. Given the changing role of the opposition parties (trying to promote a more future-oriented platform, instead of focusing on the authoritarian past), it made sense for them to introduce reforms that would impose constraints on the government's ability to appoint party loyalists to top positions in the bureaucracy. Furthermore, these changes were "supported by opposition parties in part because of an expectation that the new system would provide them with more opportunities for their partisans in government" (Grindle, 2010: 18).

But the most important reforms were those aimed at transforming the traditional career patterns in the bureaucracy, characterized until then by immovability of public officials and promotions based on tenure rather than on merit. Congress passed a new civil service law (*Ley de Nuevo Trato Laboral*) that eliminated many of the rigidities inherited from the authoritarian regime (such as restrictions in inter-agency mobility) and created a unified legal framework for the civil service. A new personnel management office was created (Dirección de Servicio Civil), in charge of implementing the new career civil service, which incorporates merit and performance as the most important determinants of an official's career, based on regular evaluation and training (Longo, 2005; Pliscoff, 2004). The results of this law were soon evident: "When President Michelle Bachelet took office in 2006, she was allowed to appoint just 800 officials (out of a total of 160,000 in the central government administration), a quarter of the number appointed six years earlier by her predecessor, Ricardo Lagos" ("Chile: not so shiny", *The Economist*, 2008).

Years later, under the presidency of Lagos's successor Michelle Bachelet (2006–10), a similar trajectory of reform (in this case regarding a freedom of information initiative) occurred when, after two high-profile corruption scandals in September and October of 2008, Congress finally passed a Transparency Law (Law 20,285 on transparency of the civil service and access to information on the state administration), which became effective in 2009. This law established a Consejo para la Transparencia (Council on Transparency), an autonomous agency with members appointed by the president with Senate's consent.

Argentina

The development of Argentina's public sector mirrors that of its Latin American neighbors: after a turbulent nineteenth century plagued by elite conflict and the difficulties of state formation, it experienced a significant expansion during most of the twentieth century, with strong intervention in the economy and growing activity in social policies. The bureaucracy, under both civilian and military governments, failed to develop effective mechanisms for merit-based recruitment and was prone to corruption and clientelism.

When, after almost eight years of authoritarian rule, the military junta dictatorship collapsed amidst military defeat and widespread economic crisis, Argentine voters chose Raúl Alfonsín (1983–89) of the Unión Cívica Radical as new president in 1983. The new government faced enormous political and economic challenges. Regarding the public sector, Alfonsín encountered two immediate problems: a demoralized and disorganized bureaucracy; and a budgetary deficit that severely limited the available alternatives. The new government set out comprehensive goals: to control fiscal deficits; to effectively train public officials at all levels; to make public government information; and to create *ex ante* control mechanisms to review legality and rationality in public decisions (Roulet, 1988). However, in practice, "[T]he Alfonsín administration designed an administrative reform policy that was gradual and difficult to be implemented" (Ghio, 1999: 3). Instead of far-reaching reforms that modified legislation and created new institutions, the government opted for incremental changes aimed exclusively at an internal reorganization of the bureaucracy and the training of public officials. At least two reasons explain why Alfonsín opted for an incremental reform. In the first place, legislative legacies from the past impeded any drastic change: from the constitutional provision that granted stability to public employees (that he chose to respect, in contrast to previous governments), to the already chaotic labor relations regime, which he did not want to modify in the first years in order to avoid alienating the already demoralized bureaucracy. A second, and powerful, reason was the critical economic situation, which limited the available resources for any reform and also led him to ignore calls to dismiss significant numbers of employees, thus avoiding the impression that government caused further unemployment.

Eventually, all these attempts to reform the bureaucracy were soon overshadowed by the worsening economic situation. By 1987, it was clear that the economic strategy was not working: hyperinflation was not controlled and economic growth had not resumed. In the 1988 elections, the Peronist candidate Carlos Menem won easily. Carlos Menem's government (1989–99) faced the enormous task of dealing with an economic crisis that seemed out of control. The situation of the public administration, inherited from the Alfonsín years, was no better. Public employment had grown considerably; salaries for public officials had decreased considerably; and the career system had been overshadowed by political appointees and organized in several incoherent regimes.

Menem's initial response to the dramatic economic situation was more radical than Alfonsín's. Soon after taking office, Congress passed the 23,696 State Reform Act and the 23,697 Economic Emergency Act (August 1989), which opened the door for the drastic shift in economic policy that took place under Menem's presidency. The most important consequences of these laws were the large-scale privatizations that took place under Menem, which marked a dramatic shift in the economic role of the state (by which Argentina would became a poster child of international organizations promoting the Washington Consensus).

The government declared a state of emergency in the national public administration and, as part of the powers that Congress had delegated, Menem obtained authority to eliminate or reduce state agencies and to reorganize the public sector in order to deal with the economic crisis. As Llanos (2002: 84) explains:

> The government's proposal for state reform made it clear that it was the executive and its cabinet which would be controlling the process of restructuring the public sector, rather than Congress, for the simple reason that the urgency of the moment did not allow time to discuss each privatization case individually.

As part of the economic restructuring initiated by those emergency decrees, the government suspended any new recruitment for public positions, both in the central administration and in public enterprises. Moreover, executive decrees 435/90 and 1757/90 reduced the number of top civil officials (*secretarías* and *subsecretarías*), forced the early retirement of civil servants and the dismissal of all non-permanent staff, and imposed controls on government purchases and contracting.[2] The number of public sector personnel decreased considerably (although the most significant reduction occurred because of the decentralization of education and health services to the provinces). Despite these decisions, the results obtained through the initial downsizing efforts of the early 1990s were counterbalanced by increases in organizational structures and personnel in the following years. By 1995, the number of top posts surpassed that of 1990, before the initial reductions. Moreover, "[w]hile the number of employees in the Federal public sector dropped (genuinely) as a result of privatizations and (only nominally) decentralization, the number of employees in political areas rose not only in relative but also absolute numbers" (Orlansky, 2000: 2), mainly in areas such as the Office of the Presidency, the Ministry of Interior, Ministry of Economy and the Office of the Chief of Staff.

Menem used his political clout to neutralize institutions that – if effective – could have served as a check on the executive. In 1990, he dismissed members of the Tribunal de Cuentas de la Nación and replaced them by loyal members headed by his brother, and later transformed the Court into a new National General Audit. Menem had already successfully "packed" the Supreme Court, through legislation to deal with the opposition's objection to expanding the number of judges from five to nine, positions that were filled with Menem loyalists (Levitsky, 2000; Helmke, 2004). Similarly, Menem replaced the Fiscal Nacional de Investigaciones (a supposedly autonomous prosecutor) when he initiated investigations regarding corruption allegations against the government. When Menem's own appointees to the Sindicatura General de Empresas Públicas and the Inspector General de Justicia criticized the lack of transparency in the privatization process, the president replaced them as well. In sum, early in his term Menem "short-circuited . . . institutions of horizontal accountability" (Blake and Lunsford, 2007: 14).

By the end of his first term in office, Menem had accomplished important changes in the economic role of the Argentine state and had created a powerful political machine that would serve to gain him re-election and to maintain a Peronist majority in Congress. His government, however, had failed in its attempts to reform the federal public administration, which remained corrupt, demoralized and expensive. This lack of success in public sector reform, combined with new economic pressures by the beginning of Menem's second term, led to a renewed effort of reform, called the Second Reform of the State. The trajectory of this new reform effort was similar to the first one: delegation of legislative powers to the president and the initial emphasis on organizational restructuring replaced by a mere downsizing program.[3] By the end of the Menem administration, corruption remained untamed (Menem and many of his close associates would be prosecuted after leaving office for numerous corruption allegations); the civil service was chaotic, and the rule of law an exception. His successor (from the Unión Cívica Radical), Fernando De la Rúa (1999–2001), tried, again, to introduce some reforms. The rhetoric was similar: the goals of this new process of reform would be to achieve fiscal balance, to fulfill the promise of a professional career civil service, and to eradicate corruption. The new government created an Anticorruption Office (replacing the Office for Public Ethics), charged with investigating allegations against the previous government and preventing bad practices in the new one.

The government also announced an initiative to introduce more flexibility in the public sector, with a managerial strategy following the Chilean experience (Plan de Modernización del Estado, 2001). However, in practice, as in all preceding and subsequent administrations, De la Rúa's government wanted to exercise direct control over the bureaucracy, and existing regulations were an obstacle to that purpose. For even his limited efforts came to a halt when a new economic crisis hit Argentina in 2001. Successive governments – from the short-lived ones after De la Rúa's fall to the long-lasting presidency of Néstor and Cristina Kirchner – had to deal with the economic crisis or were relieved by the commodities boom and had little time for administrative concerns. Congress has failed in its attempt to impose controls or to enact legislation (e.g. Freedom of Information) to limit the executive discretionary power over the bureaucracy. Thus, more than two decades after transition to democracy, the Argentine public sector remained plagued by patrimonialism, corruption and a lack of professionalization.

PUBLIC SECTOR CHANGE: THE LOGIC OF CONGRESSIONAL INTERVENTION

The experience in Mexico and Chile shows that administrative reforms are more likely to succeed when political actors different from the executive (particularly Congress) promote them to limit the discretionary authority of the president over the bureaucracy. In the Argentina experience, this intervention did not take place. Reforms were initiated and promoted by the executive; Congress had a reactive role (if any) but did not activate any mechanism of effective oversight or control of the president's discretionary authority over the bureaucracy.

Like other countries with a relatively stable democracy (e.g. Uruguay, or, to a lesser extent, Colombia), Chile has managed to reform its bureaucracy, introducing changes to the civil service system and making it more accountable and responsive to politicians' priorities. In Mexico, as in Brazil and Peru, initial changes seem to point in the same direction; however, there were limited improvements in corruption control and the professionalization of the bureaucracy has not been completed. Argentina failed in several attempts, and three decades after its most recent democratization, its bureaucracy is still plagued by corruption scandals, an extremely politicized civil service, and a lack of effective controls, just like most countries in the region. The trajectories followed by the political elite in the post-transition period have differed widely among these three countries and reflect broader trends in Latin American countries (Ruhl, 2011; Bohn, 2012; Grindle, 2012; Longo, 2008; Ramió and Salvador, 2008; Panizza and Philip, 2005). These cases allow us to detail the type of decisions that these countries have made when trying to improve the quality of their bureaucratic apparatuses. There are some decisions that point at important institutional constraints, such as civil service legislation aimed at reducing the power of presidents to appoint and dismiss bureaucrats at will, increasing transparency and access to information laws, and strengthening external audit institutions.

These are the types of restrictions imposed by Congress that, while constraining the discretionary authority of presidents, lead to improved quality of government. It is a case of "enabling constraints": restrictions that, by tying the hands of specific politicians, increase the quality of the bureaucracy under their control. Civil service reform, which in many new democracies means creation of a professional career civil service, places merit on personal loyalty or political patronage as the main criteria for decisions about recruitment and promotion. Transparency and access to government information legislation limit the discretionary power of bureaucrats and give citizens access to information; this component has, at least, two effects on governments. First, it improves their archival practices, and makes them more interested in showing effectiveness; second, because it increases the risk of exposure and, thus, respect for laws and regulations, this legislation is a strong check on corruption. The capacity and independence of external audit institutions, finally, is related to improved performance standards and less corruption, because it means that there is effective external oversight and that corrupt or unlawful practices are more likely to be detected and punished. These enabling constraints limit the discretionary authority of a politician, but they improve the capacity of government as a whole. They reinforce the idea of bureaucracy as the executor of democratic decisions, rather than of the spoils system often commanded by some politician's discretion.

OTHER INCENTIVES AND DETERRENTS TO CHANGE

Democracy has not been the only reason behind the changes in Latin America's public administrations. Just as democratization was taking place, many countries in the region also went through processes of political, fiscal or administrative decentralization that have realigned the relationship between national and subnational actors and have modified the instruments available for national public officials to carry out policies (Díaz Cayeros, 2006; Falleti, 2010; Gibson, 2004; Cabrero and Zabaleta, 2009). In recent years, however, some countries (Ecuador, Venezuela) have shifted back towards centralization (Eaton, 2013). But decentralization has not lived up to the expectations it raised in the 1990s, when it was presented as a solution to an overgrown state, with little capacity to identify local needs. On the contrary, as Eaton (2012: 646) argues, "decentralization has made the State in Latin America more fragmented, incoherent and internally divided".

In economic terms, whereas some Latin American governments have abandoned the idea that development will come from internal industrialization with a big role for the public sector and, instead, have embraced the notion that international trade, low government intervention and free markets will be the foundation for development (Chong and Zanforlin, 2004; Bunce, 2001; Przeworski, 1991; Hagopian, 2004), others have opted for a reinvigorated role of the state, with a big, interventionist public sector (Weyland et al., 2010). In any case, the region's openness to trade has increased (not only because of the commodity boom of the past decade, but also because some countries have increased their exporting capacity in manufacturing), and government expenditure in the region has grown significantly, as shown in Figures 11.3 and 11.4.

CONCLUSION

Latin American public administrations have experienced important transformations, following dramatic changes in the political, economic and social reality of the region. Their reform trajectories cannot be explained by simplistic mentions of the Washington Consensus or the New Public Management. They cannot be assumed to be just reactions to economic restructuring. And they cannot be dismissed as mere window dressing to please foreign donors. This chapter has shown that public sector change is directly linked to the process of democratization, which has transformed

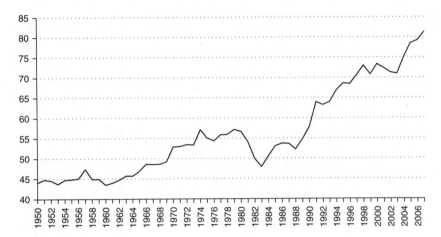

Note: This figure measures Openness to Trade using variable *pwt_openk* in the Quality of Government Standard Dataset, which equals Exports plus Imports divided by real GDP per capita. Countries considered are: Antigua and Barbuda, Argentina, Bahamas, Barbados, Belize, Bolivia, Brazil, Chile, Colombia, Costa Rica, Cuba, Dominica, Dominican Republic, Ecuador, El Salvador, Grenada, Guatemala, Guyana, Haiti, Honduras, Jamaica, Mexico, Nicaragua, Panama, Paraguay, Peru, St Kitts and Nevis, St Lucia, St Vincent and the Grenadines, Suriname, Trinidad and Tobago, Uruguay, and Venezuela.

Source: Teorell et al. (2013).

Figure 11.3 Openness to trade

the incentives of politicians and has placed new demands on the public bureaucracies of the region.

Yet these transformations cannot be considered completed or successful. In some cases, democracy has not been enough to push for meritocratic recruitment, access to government information or accountability. Even in those countries where some positive changes have taken place, a new agenda – again, linked to political processes – is being shaped: a renewed interest in institutional capacity for effective governance, a growing concern for corruption and lack of accountability, and a powerful impetus for building monitoring and evaluation systems across the region. This will not be the last step in the process of administrative change: political transformation and economic demands will continue to shape bureaucratic reforms in the region. The public administration in Latin America is still addressing old problems (from lack of proper meritocratic recruitment in government to accountability institutions that remain ineffective) while being challenged by new ones (the demands from a more tech-savvy

266   *The international handbook of public administration and governance*

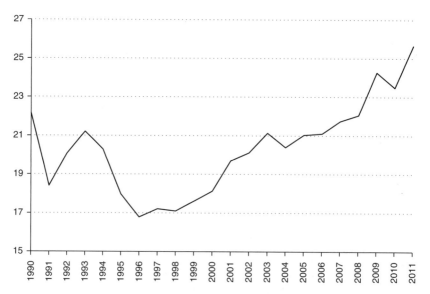

Note: This figure measures Government expenditure as a percentage of GDP using variable *wdi_ge* in the Quality of Government Standard Dataset. Expense is cash payments for operating activities of the government in providing goods and services. It includes compensation of employees (such as wages and salaries), interest and subsidies, grants, social benefits, and other expenses such as rent and dividends. Countries considered are: Antigua and Barbuda, Argentina, Bahamas, Barbados, Belize, Bolivia, Brazil, Chile, Colombia, Costa Rica, Cuba, Dominica, Dominican Republic, Ecuador, El Salvador, Grenada, Guatemala, Guyana, Haiti, Honduras, Jamaica, Mexico, Nicaragua, Panama, Paraguay, Peru, St Kitts and Nevis, St Lucia, St Vincent and the Grenadines, Suriname, Trinidad and Tobago, Uruguay, and Venezuela.

Source: Teorell et al. (2013).

Figure 11.4   Government expenditure as percentage of GDP in Latin America

citizenry, less toleration to corruption, widespread mistrust of government, and the effects of the 2008 financial crisis). Administrative reformers have to cope with these challenges within the democratic institutional setting, which makes reforms less likely to achieve quick results, but more likely to be effective in the long run.

NOTES

1. *Acuerdos político-legislativos para la modernización del Estado, la transparencia y la promoción del crecimiento.*

2. These decrees also suspended the Work Collective Agreements and established that they were to be renegotiated on the basis of these new priorities of fiscal restraint.
3. In 1995, after his re-election, he created the Office for Public Ethics, "an executive branch vehicle for gathering personal financial statements that might identify conflicts of interest and illicit enrichment" (Blake and Lunsford, 2007: 14). Again, this was an executive decision; legislative controls remained weak.

REFERENCES

Ames, Barry (1990), *Political Survival: Politicians and Public Policy in Latin America* (California Series on Social Choice and Political Economy). Berkeley, Los Angeles and London: University of California Press.

Aninat, Cristobal, John Londregan, Patricio Navia and Joaquín Vial (2004), *Political Institutions, Policymaking Processes, and Policy Outcomes in Chile.* Mimeo: Research Department, Inter-American Development Bank.

Apreza Reyes, Martha (2004), "La Auditoría Superior de la Federación: una mirada desde los Órganos Constitucionales Autónomos". In *Cuarto Certamen Nacional sobre Fiscalización Superior y Rendición de Cuentas.* Mexico City: Auditoría Superior de la Federación.

Arellano Gault, David and Juan Pablo Guerrero (2003), "Stalled administrative reforms of the Mexican State". In Blanca Heredia and Ben Ross Schneider (eds), *Reinventing Leviathan. The Politics of Administrative Reform in Developing Countries.* Miami, FL: North–South Center Press.

Arellano Gault, David and Donald E. Klingner (2006), "Mexico's professional career service law: governance, political culture and public administrative reform". *International Public Management Review*, **7** (1): 20–41.

Barzelay, Michael, Francisco Gaetani, Juan Carlos Cortázar Velarde and Guillermo Cejudo (2003), "Research on public management policy change in the Latin America region: a conceptual framework and methodological guide". *International Public Management Review*, **7** (1): 20–41.

Blake, Charles H. and Sara Lunsford (2007), "Contemporary corruption in Argentina: the dawn of a new era or business as usual?" Paper presented at Congress of the Latin American Studies Association, Montréal, Canada.

Bohn, Simone R. (2012), "Corruption in Latin America: understanding the perception–exposure gap". *Journal of Politics in Latin America*, **4** (3): 67–95.

Bresser-Pereira, Luiz Carlos (2001), "New public management reform: now in the Latin America agenda, and yet . . . ". *Revista Internacional de Estudos Políticos*, **9**: 117–40.

Bunce, Valerie (2001), "Democratization and economic reform". *Annual Review of Political Science*, **4**: 43–65.

Cabrero, Enrique and Dionisio Zabaleta (2009), "¿Cómo construir una mística interguber-namental en la política social? Análisis de cuatro experiencias latinoamericanas". *Revista CLAD (Centro Latinoamericano de Administración para el Desarrollo)*, **43** (1): 1–22.

Cejudo, Guillermo M. (2011), *Constraining the Executive: How Democracy Improves the Quality of Government.* Boston, MA: UMI.

Chong, Alberto and Luisa Zanforlin (2004), "Inward-looking policies, institutions, auto-crats, and economic growth in Latin America: an empirical exploration". *Public Choice*, **121** (3): 335–61.

Díaz Cayeros, Alberto (2006), *Federalism, Fiscal Authority, and Centralization in Latin America.* Cambridge, MA: Cambridge University Press.

Dussauge, Mauricio (2010), "Combate a la corrupción y rendición de cuentas: avances, límites, pendientes y retrocesos". In José Luis Méndez (ed.), *Políticas Públicas.* Mexico City: El Colegio de México, pp. 207–52.

Dussauge, Mauricio (2011), "The challenges of implementing merit-based personnel policies in Latin America: Mexico's civil service reform experience". *Journal of Comparative Policy Analysis*, **13** (1): 51–73.

Eaton, Kent (2012), "The state of the State in Latin America: challenges, challengers, responses and deficits". *Revista de Ciencia Política*, **32** (3): 643–57.

Eaton, Kent (2013), "Recentralization and the left turn in Latin America: diverging outcomes in Bolivia, Ecuador, and Venezuela". *Comparative Political Studies*, **20** (10): 1–28.

The Economist (2008), "Chile: not so shiny. How an excess of political stability can get in the way of good government". 17 May, p. 48, http://www.economist.com/node/113 76951?story_id=11376951.

Falleti, Tulia G. (2010), *Decentralization and Subnational Politics in Latin America.* Cambridge, MA: Cambridge University Press.

Garretón, Manuel A. and Gonzálo Cáceres (2003), "From the disarticulation of the state to the modernization of public management in Chile: administrative reform without a state project". In Blanca Heredia and Ben Ross Schneider (eds), *Reinventing Leviathan. The Politics of Administrative Reform in Developing Countries.* Boulder, CO: North–South Center Press, pp. 113–49.

Geddes, Barbara (1994), *Politician's Dilemma.* Berkeley, CA: University of California Press.

Ghio, Jose M. (1999), "The politics of administrative reform in Argentina". Paper prepared for the Conference of the Politics of Administrative Reform in Developing and Transition Countries. Washington, DC, 15 July.

Gibson, Edward L. (2004), "Federalism and democracy: theoretical connections and cautionary insights". In Edward L. Gibson (ed.), *Federalism and Democracy in Latin America.* Boston, MD: Johns Hopkins University Press, pp. 1–28.

González, Javier (2010), "La evaluación de la actividad gubernamental: premisas básicas y algunas anotaciones sobre la experiencia mexicana". In José Luis Méndez (ed.), *Políticas Públicas.* Mexico City: El Colegio de México, pp. 143–75.

Grindle, Merilee S. (1977), "Patrons and clients in the bureaucracy: career networks in Mexico". *Latin American Research Review*, **12** (1): 37–66.

Grindle, Merilee S. (2001), "Despite the odds: the political economy of social sector reform in Latin America". Faculty Research Working Paper Series, John F. Kennedy School of Government.

Grindle, Merilee S. (2010), "Constructing, deconstructing, and reconstructing career civil service systems in Latin America". Harvard University, HKS Faculty Research Working Paper Series, RWP10-025.

Grindle, Merilee S. (2012), *Jobs for the Boys: Patronage and the Politics of Public Sector Reform.* Cambridge, MA: Harvard University Press.

Guerrero, Eduardo (2002). "La reinvención del gobierno en la transición democrática: rendición de cuentas en la administración pública de México". Paper presented at the VII International Congress on State Reform and Public Administration, Centro Latinoamericano de Administración para el Desarrollo, Lisbon, 8–11 October.

Hagopian, Frances (2004), "Authoritarian legacies and market reforms in Latin America". In Katherine Hite and Paola Cesarini (eds), *Authoritarian Legacies and Democracy in Latin America and Southern Europe.* Notre Dame: University of Notre Dame Press, pp. 85–158.

Helmke, Gretchen (2004), *Courts under Constraints: Judges, Generals, and Presidents in Argentina.* Cambridge: Cambridge University Press.

Heredia, Blanca and Ben Ross Schneider (eds) (2003), *Reinventing Leviathan. The Politics of Administrative Reform in Developing Countries.* Miami, FL: North–South Center Press.

Hood, Christopher (1991), "A public management for all seasons". *Public Administration*, **69** (1): 3–19.

Klesner, Joseph L. (2001), "Divided government in Mexico's presidentialist regime: the 1997–2000 experience". In Robert Elgie (ed.), *Divided Government in Comparative Perspective.* Oxford: Oxford University Press, pp. 63–85.

Levitsky, Steven (2000), "The normalization of Argentine politics". *The Journal of Democracy*, **11** (2): 57–69.

Llanos, Mariana (2002), *Privatization and Democracy in Argentina. An Analysis of President–Congress Relations.* Basingstoke: Palgrave.

Longo, Francisco (2005), "Diagnóstico institucional comparado de sistemas de servicio civil: informe final de síntesis". Paper presented at the V Reunión del Diálogo de Gestión y Transparencia de la Política Pública', Banco Interamericano de Desarrollo – Inter-American Development Bank, Washington, DC, 17–18 March.

Longo, Francisco (2008), "Quality of governance: impartiality is not enough". *Governance*, **21** (2): 191–6.

López Ayllón, Sergio, Mauricio Merino and Guillermo Cejudo (2010), "La estructura de la rendición de cuentas en México". México: CIDE – Instituto de Investigaciones Jurídicas.

López Ayllón, Sergio (2009), "El acceso a la información como un derecho fundamental: la reforma al artículo 6° de la constitución mexicana". Mexico City: Instituto Federal de Acceso a la Información Pública.

Maldonado, Claudia (2009), "La evaluación de programas sociales en México. Reflexiones sobre un sistema emergente". *Buen gobierno*, **7**: 23–34.

Mantilla Baca, Sebastián and Gerardo L. Munck (2013), "La calidad de la democracia: perspectivas desde América Latina". Quito: CELAEP Centro Latinoamericano de Estudios Políticos: Fundación Hanns Seidel.

Marcel, Mario (1999), "Effectiveness of the state and development lessons from the Chilean experience". In Guillermo Perry and Danny Leipziger (eds), *Chile: Recent Policy Lessons and Emerging Challenges.* Washington, DC: World Bank, pp. 265–325.

Marcel, Mario and Carolina Toha (1998), "Reforma del estado y de la gestión pública". In René Cortazar and Joaquín Vidal (eds), *Construyendo Opciones: Propuestas Económicas y Sociales para el Cambio de Siglo.* Santiago: Dolmen, pp. 575–633.

Martínez Purón, Rafael (2011), "Directivos versus políticos. La importancia de la función directiva en las administraciones públicas". Mexico City: Miguel Ángel Porrúa.

Méndez, José L. (2010), "El servicio profesional de carrera en la administración pública federal". In José Luis Méndez (ed.), *Políticas Públicas.* Mexico City: El Colegio de México, pp. 179–206.

Merino, Mauricio (ed.) (2006), *Los desafíos del servicio profesional de carrera en México.* Mexico City: CIDE – Secretaría de la Función Pública.

Muñoz, Ramón (2004), "Experiencia mexicana en la construcción de un servicio profesional de carrera". Paper presented at the IX International Congress on State Reform and Public Administration, Centro Latinoamericano de Administración para el Desarrollo, Madrid.

Orlansky, Dora (2000), "Silent innovations in federal civil service. Argentina 1989–1999". Paper presented at IPSA XVII World Congress, Quebec City.

Oszlak, Óscar (1986), "Public policies and political regimes in Latin America". *International Social Science Journal*, **38**: 219–36.

Panizza, Francisco and George Philip (2005), "Second generation reform in Latin America: reforming the public sector in Uruguay and Mexico". *Journal of Latin American Studies*, **37**: 667–91.

Pardo, María del Carmen (2004), "Propuesta del gobierno Fox para reformar la administración pública". Paper read at IX Congreso Internacional del CLAD sobre la Reforma del Estado y de la Administración Pública, Madrid.

Pardo, María del Carmen (2007), "La gerencialización de la administración pública". *Foro Internacional*, **190** (4): 895–925.

Pliscoff, Cristian (2004), "Public management reform in Chile 1990–2003: advances and drawbacks". Santiago, Unpublished paper.

Przeworski, Adam (1991), *Democracy and the Market Political and Economic Reforms in Eastern Europe and Latin America.* Cambridge: Cambridge University Press.

Ramió, Carlos and Miquel Salvador (2008), "Civil service reform in Latin America: external referents versus own capacities". *Bulletin of Latin America Research*, **27**: 554–73.

Ramírez Alujas, Álvaro (2001), "Modernización de la gestión pública. El caso chileno (1994–2000)". Santiago: Universidad de Chile.

Roulet, Jorge E. (1988), *El estado necesario*. Buenos Aires: Fundación Jorge Esteban Roulet, Centro de Participación Política.

Ruhl, Mark (2011), "Political corruption in Central America: assessment and explanation". *Latin American Politics and Society*, **53** (1): 33–58.

Santiso, Carlos (2007), "Eyes-wide shut? The politics of autonomous audit agencies in emerging economies". http://papers.ssrn.com/sol3/papers.cfm?abstract_id=982663.

Siavelis, Peter M. (2000), *The President and Congress in Postauthoritarian Chile. Institutional Constraints to Democratic Consolidation*. University Park, PA: The Pennsylvania State University Press.

Teorell, Jan, Nicholas Charron, Stefan Dahlberg, Sören Holmberg, Bo Rothstein, Petrus Sundin and Richard Svensson (2013), The Quality of Government Dataset, version 20Dec13. University of Gothenburg: The Quality of Government Institute, http://www.qog.pol.gu.se.

Waissbluth, Mario (2005), "La reforma del estado en Chile 1990–2005. Diagnóstico y propuestas de futuro". Santiago: Universidad de Chile, Working Paper Serie Gestión No. 76.

Weyland, Kurt, Raúl L. Madrid and Wendy Hunter (eds) (2010), *Leftist Governments in Latin America: Successes and Shortcomings*. New York: Cambridge University Press.

Zuvanic, Laura and Mercedes Iacoviello (2005), "Informe de situación del servicio civil en Chile". In Koldo Echebarría (ed.), *Informe sobre la Situación del Servicio Civil en América Latina*. Washington, DC: BID.

12. Administrative developments in India
Krishna K. Tummala

INTRODUCTION

Fully cognizant of the greater possibility of errors of omission rather than commission and possible sweeping generalizations, this chapter attempts to provide a brief narrative about Indian administration within the context of an 'ecological study' as advocated by Fred W. Riggs (1961 and 1964), himself inspired by John M. Gaus (1947). Riggs further proposed that it is not enough to study the environment of administration, but must also dwell on the 'context'. The Waldovian (Waldo, 1948) tradition that public administration is political philosophy is also followed here. Administrators do not act in a vacuum but within a given political/ ideological setting. Given that, this chapter starts by providing the Indian setting, then dwells on the political and administrative arrangements, and concentrates on three relevant aspects: 'reservations', administrative behaviour and the more insidious and ubiquitous corruption.

THE SETTING

India, by any criterion, is large, diverse and complex, often challenging generalizations and defying easy emulation. It accounts for more than 17 per cent of the world population but covers only 2.4 per cent of the earth's surface. Spanning nearly 3 287 263 square kilometres of territory divided into 28 different states and union territories,[1] it has a population of 1.2 billion people with a growth rate of 17.6 per cent during the last decadal census (2000–2011). There is an uneven sex ratio of 940 females for every 1000 males. There is a predominant urban–rural divide with nearly two-thirds living in rural areas (Government of India, 2013). Among them, Indians speak 22 constitutionally recognized languages, besides English (not to mention myriad dialects, some of which do not even have written scripts).[2] It is noteworthy that India does not have a national but only an official language, Hindi. However, when the Centre (the commonly used expression to denote the federal government) communicates with any state, the Hindi communication is accompanied by a translation into the language of the state concerned. It is also a multi-religious society with a predominant Hindu population (over 82 per cent), with nearly 13 per cent Muslims (the third-largest congregation in the world).

India can also claim other distinctions. It is a nuclear power (without being a signatory to the Non-Proliferation Treaty), and very much part of the space age, having launched a probe to Mars in November 2013. Its economy is the fourth largest in the world, and the third largest in Asia (next to China and Japan), but with a per capita annual income of only $1527.00 (*The Hindu*, 2012). Yet 71 in 100 Indians have a cellphone. It is a power house of information technology (IT). More importantly, being the largest working democracy in the world, it is often held up as a beacon of democratic developing society. Its political institutions are well established, and work, even if intermittently. It regularly holds elections, which are more or less fair and with not much violence. Unlike its neighbours Pakistan and Bangladesh, India is also politically stable.

Given its diversity, India has a federal form of government. Paul Appleby (1957: 54) commended it as 'extremely federal', inasmuch as the Centre has to depend largely on the state governments for the administration of developmental projects. Yet it is called a 'union of states'. Considering the several fissiparous tendencies at the time of independence, the constitution-makers wanted to make sure that the country would not be balkanized. To that effect they provided some extraordinary features that enables it to be turned into a near unitary form. Three provisions are most important here. First, under Article 3, the Parliament can redraw the boundaries of states by merging some together, or dividing an existing one. Second, and most controversial, are the 'Emergency Powers', in particular Article 356, which permits the president to dismiss any duly elected government of a state and suspend its legislature, on the advice of the governor of the state, who is appointed by the Centre, and take over its administration (Tummala, 1996: 373–84). The third, most importantly for this chapter, are the All-India Services, where the top administrators are moved between the Centre and states. Given these mixed features, Alexandrowicz (1957) described the Constitution of India as *sui generis*.

India also preferred to retain a parliamentary from of government, the foundations of which were laid during the British regime. It has a president at the national level, a ceremonial head similar to the British monarch, except that the president is elected by a rather complex electoral process. With a multi-party system, after regular elections the majority party is invited to form a government headed by the prime minister, who in turn picks his/her cabinet, governed by the principle of collective responsibility. Similar arrangements are made at the level of each of the states, headed by a governor, appointed by the Centre, and an elected chief minister. At the beginning, the Congress Party headed a majority government at the

Centre and most of the states as well (except the state of Kerala, which has the distinction of having the world's first duly elected communist government). But since the late 1960s, with the rise of regional parties, the norm has been to have coalition governments at the Centre, at times formed by as many as 19 political parties coming together to form a majority. Coalition governments tend to have two consequences. One is their short term in office, with one lasting no more than 13 days, when one or more of the coalition partners pull out by withdrawing support for various political or ideological reasons. And the other is a consequent policy paralysis, with the several coalition partners pulling in different directions, pushing their own regional, partisan and even personal political agendas (Tummala, 2009: 323–48).

PHILOSOPHICAL UNDERPINNINGS

Indian politicians subscribed to socialism with its own indigenous character. It is called 'Indian socialism', not 'socialism in India' (Tummala, 1994: chs II and III). The Congress Party itself in its confabulations always added qualifying adjectives. The first prime minister of India, Jawaharlal Nehru, impressed as he was with developments in Russia since its Revolution, did not subscribe to the violence involved. Largely influenced by Fabian but not Marxian socialist thinking, he sought an evolutionary, but not revolutionary, socialism. This was of course the credo, as advocated by Mahatma Gandhi, who himself studied several Western writers such as Thoreau, Tolstoy and Ruskin. In fact, Gandhi translated John Ruskin's *Unto the Last* into *Sarvodaya* ('Upliftment of all'). Independent India's Constitution also made no mention of socialism initially when it emphasized in its preamble only a 'Sovereign Democratic Republic'. As a consequence of Prime Minister Indira Gandhi's militancy, the expression was changed by adding in 1976 the new language of the 42nd Amendment, which read 'Sovereign Socialist Secular Democratic Republic'.

Following the above credo, India launched its five-year plans, and sought to capture the 'commanding heights of the economy'. Almost all private enterprise was restricted, and had to be licensed. Almost all major industries came under state control. Very few imports were permitted in an attempt to help develop and protect indigenous business and industrial establishments. There was also a great proliferation of state-initiated and fully controlled industrial and commercial establishments known as 'public enterprises'. Consequently, the economy experienced what was derogatorily known as 'Hindu growth' at about 2–3 per cent annually. These developments conferred a great deal of power on the bureaucracy, whose permission in the form of licences was needed to start even the smallest enterprise:

> Four different reasons were given for this debacle: the constraints imposed on the manufacturing sector; domestication of the financial sector to suit the whims of the states; poor trade policy; and an obsolete tax system. All this led to what John Kenneth Galbraith described as 'post office socialism'. (Tummala, 2001: 52)

This situation was also stated as one of the main reasons for corruption (Tummala, 2002: 43–63). Time was thus ripe to change direction, which in a sense was inaugurated by Prime Minister Rajiv Gandhi with the launching of a technological revolution, in particular in the dissemination of information technology.

The 1990s had seen a sea change. Because of the dire balance of payments, a major financial crisis occurred, forcing the government to guarantee first 20 tons of gold to raise $200 million, and then another 40 tons to raise $600 million more. The rupee was devalued and left to float. The 'New Economic Policy' (NEP) of 1990 was launched during the prime ministership of P.V. Narasimha Rao, under the tutelage of the then finance minister, and the later prime minister, Manmohan Singh. Following the new public management (NPM) precepts stemming from the belief that the private sector is more efficient and hence the public sector should emulate it, several steps were taken to free the economy from the shackles of government. Markets were liberalized. Now, the private sector, not the state, would act as the center of focus for economic development. Several structural changes were duly made, giving more or less a free hand to the private sector in the development of the nation, and providing it with several contracts. This in itself invested a different kind of power in the hands of the state and in the hands of the administrators – power to award contracts, leading to further corruption as an outcome of the market economy and globalization, as argued by writers such as Rotberg (2009). Thus the current regime may be characterized as 'contract *raj*', replacing the former 'licence *raj*'. A new consumer society, in place of the old largely hoarding one, has been unleashed. Accumulation of wealth, which of course was built into the Hindu system of life (among its four stages, acquiring *artha* – wealth, is the second), became the new watchword. It should also be noted that, among the plethora of gods/goddesses, Lakshmi, the goddess of wealth, occupies a predominant place in Hindu worship. It is claimed that India has now over 103 billionaires, sixth largest in the world (*Indiatoday*, 2013). However, as Jean Dreze and Amartya Sen (2013: viii–ix) point out, the narrative of 'the growth process is biased':

Over this period of growth, while some people, particularly among the privi-
leged classes, have done very well, many more continue to lead unnecessarily
deprived and precarious lives. It is not that their living conditions have not
improved at all, but the pace of improvement has been very slow for the bulk of
the people, and for some there has been remarkably little change. (Ibid.)

Urban areas are becoming enriched. An exodus from the impoverished
rural areas is occurring, resulting in the neglect of agriculture, which still
accounts for a large percentage of national wealth. Unable to meet their
debt burden, several thousand farmers annually commit suicide.

ADMINISTRATIVE ARRANGEMENTS

Pre-independent India did indeed have a well-organized and effective
administrative apparatus, which Prime Minister Lloyd George called the
'steel frame of India'. The mainstay of this system was the Indian Civil
Service (ICS), which was neither Indian, nor civil, much less of service to
India. Generally ill suited to development administration as we understand it now, it served the colonial masters well in terms of collection of
revenues and maintenance of law and order. It also left an administrative
culture which can be still observed.

When India became independent, a debate ensued as to what to do with
an administrative apparatus that was identified as a tool of the colonial
master. The hard choice was either to abolish this abomination altogether
and start afresh, or create something entirely new that would fulfil the
new nation's aspirations. Given the absence of a new model, and the lack
of time to even experiment, inherited services were retained by the Indian
Independent Act, 1947. But in an effort to 'nativize' them according to the
new ethos, Home Minister Sardar Vallabhai Patel observed:

I need hardly emphasize that an efficient, disciplined and contented service is
a *sine qua non* of sound administration under a democratic regime even more
than under an authoritarian rule. The service must be above party and we
should ensure that political considerations either in its recruitment or in its
discipline and control are reduced to the minimum, if not eliminated altogether
. . . In an All-India Service, it is obvious, recruitment, discipline and control
etc., have to be tackled on a basis of uniformity and under the direction of the
Central Government which is the recruiting agency. (Quoted in Shiva Rao,
1966: 332–3)

Accordingly, two All-India Services – the Indian Administrative Service
(IAS), and the Indian Police Service (IPS) – were created with the provision that other new services might be created by the Parliament of India.

Patel and the new services faced major initial challenges. The first was to cope with the largest transmigration of people between the two independent countries of Pakistan and India consequent to the partition of the subcontinent. As many as 10 to 12 million people crossed the borders, although many a Muslim chose to stay back in secular India instead of moving to the Islamic state of Pakistan. The second was to integrate several independent states into the Indian union. As the British left, as many as 565 native rulers, who enjoyed their own rule within India (except for minor, but important, controls by the British), were left behind, pock-marking the length and breadth of India. These needed to be integrated as part of the new nation. And Patel, who was known as the 'steelman', succeeded, except in two cases: Kashmir and Hyderabad. While the latter was integrated by the use of force, the former opted to join the union only when threatened externally, and continues to be a source of irritation even today with a part of the territory still a bone of contention between Pakistan and India.

The third challenge stemmed from the new economic doctrine of democratic socialism, as already explained. The Government of India, in pursuing planned development, began following five-year plans (the latest being the 13th). This came in as a major test for the prevailing administrative apparatus. Created for, and adept at, securing law and order and collecting revenues, it now had to serve a government that decided to control the 'commanding heights' of the national economy, and herald a new equal and just society.

Formidable as the challenges appeared, the Indian administrators rose to the occasion. Tributes were paid by no less a person than Paul H. Appleby. In his report of 1953, commissioned by the Government of India, he said: 'I have come gradually to a general judgment that now would rate the government of India among the dozen or so most advanced governments of the world' (Appleby, 1957: 8). The compliment was well deserved. We now turn to examine the Civil Service in India in detail.

The effort to nativize and shape the administration to suit the needs of the altered state saw several reform attempts. Reports in this regard are so numerous that even to provide a succinct list would take several pages. Yet the attempts were disappointing, as seen by no less than the Chairman of Administrative Reforms Commission II, K. Hanumanthaiah (1970: 1), who said:

> Several studies and inquiries were made of the administrative problems during the last 15 years after independence. These attempts were, however, limited in scope, sporadic and uncoordinated. The effort was largely diffused and its pace uneven. There was no comprehensive and coordinated examination of the whole administrative machinery.

At least such was the case until 1966.

The Government of India in 1966 announced the appointment of the Administrative Reforms Commission (ARC), modelled after the Hoover Commission in the USA. There were also suggestions that some of the recommendations, particularly those related to the civil service, were in fact inspired by the 1968 Fulton Commission report in the United Kingdom, a suggestion denied by both the chairman and secretary of the ARC. In any case, the output of ARC was monumental. In four years' time it presented 20 reports making some 680 recommendations (based on the work of 33 study teams and working groups). Despite all the laborious work by the ARC, it should be noted that the administrative structure itself remained more or less intact.

The Government of India, however, had to deal with the new reality of the 1990 NEP, as the purpose of the state changed once again. This required another serious look at the capacity and expertise of administration. The result was the appointment of a second ARC in 2005. It produced 18 reports (Singh, 2013: 135–53). A Group of Ministers (GoM) was constituted to consider the recommendations and review their pace of implementation. But nothing substantive has come of this to date, as the government seemed to be more preoccupied with fighting to stay in office, with the numerous pressures coming from its several coalition partners. Also to be noted is the resistance of what is known as the 'IAS establishment', as the incumbents object to any radical changes affecting their services. There now follows a detailed examination of the civil service in India.

THE CIVIL SERVICE IN INDIA

While each state has its own cadre of civil servants, the Centre has what is known as Central Services (over 20, in all), divided into Groups A, B, C and D. Then there is the unique cadre known as the All-India Services, which serves both the Centre and the states. Article 312 of the Constitution provides for the All-India Services, two of which are recognized: the Indian Administrative Service (IAS) and the Indian Police Service (IPS). A very small group from among the former may opt to belong to the Indian Foreign Service, IFS. The same article also permits the creation of more All-India Services on the recommendation of a two-thirds majority of the Rajya Sabha (the Council of States, the upper chamber of Parliament). In 1955, the Sates Reorganization Commission (SRC) recommended the creation of several more. But as the states resented the creation of more of these services (arguing that the federal structure would be adversely affected), only the Indian Forest Service was added in 1966. For some time there has been a debate on creating a judicial service, but nothing has so far come of this. There is not scope in this chapter to go into details about all these services; only the All-India Services are dealt with here, given their importance.

As emphasized by the Estimates Committee of Parliament:

> In a vast country like India, with different religions, languages and customs, All-India Services play a vital role. They provide administrative stability, national solidarity, and continuity in administration. They also act as invisible catalytic agents in strengthening national integration. With their broader outlook, these services also provide a bulwark against the forces of disruption, parochialism and regionalism. (Katyal, 1980: 4)

There is further justification, thus:

- As on 1 January 2010, with an authorized strength of 5,689 of which 4,534 were filled, the IAS is the elite corps, at the top of all administration.
- As direct recruits from all over India, and promotees from the State cadres, they occupy the highest administrative positions at policymaking level while heading the various administrative apparatus of various Ministries and Departments.
- As District Collectors, they head the administration at the sub-State level. They also chair the Committees of *Zilla Parishads* (elected bodies at that local district administration level).
- At times they are posted to head public enterprises and other statutory bodies. Of late, some are appointed to head Universities.
- Along with the IPS (who serve as heads of police, among other positions), they serve a crucial role in the successful functioning of all national development and integration activities.
- As elite and permanent employees, they are indispensable in not only advising the transient, elected Ministers in policymaking, but also crucial in administering all developmental projects.
- They set the tone for the entire administration in the country. There in fact is an all pervasive influence of the IAS culture, which at times termed as 'the IAS lobby' (not necessarily as a compliment), but reflective of their strength and importance.
- Most every Indian child is goaded by the parents to aspire for the IAS, although of late the private sector jobs are more attractive and preferred for fat pay and not subject to the continuous pin-pricks inflicted by the elected Ministers and other politicians. But none comes closer to the IAS for prestige and elan. (Tummala, 1994: 157)

Established by Article 315, the Union Public Service Commission (UPSC) serves as a staff agency. Its powers are elaborated in Article 320. It is in charge of recruitment and selection of personnel to both the All-India

Services and a whole host of non-technical Central Services to fill the annual need as requested by various ministries and departments. There are other staff selection commissions in each of the ministries controlling the lower-level and other technical services personnel. Article 316 similarly empowers the governor of each state to appoint a State Public Service Commission. It must be noted, however, that only the state legislatures and the union parliament are empowered (Article 309) to regulate recruitment and other service conditions of civil servants; the respective governments (i.e. the executive) cannot amend or supersede the legislative decisions. At the state level the entire civil service cadre is headed by a chief secretary, who is invariably an IAS officer, just as most other administrative heads of ministries are. At the Centre, the cabinet secretary is the most senior IAS officer. All ministries and departments are also headed by IAS officers.

Members of the UPSC (varying in numbers from time to time) are appointed by the president of India. To uphold the UPSC's integrity and protect its independence, each member is appointed for a six-year term, or until the age of 65 years (whichever comes first). While the members are eligible for appointment as chair (during their term of office), the chair and the members are not eligible for appointment for any other office of the government once they leave the UPSC. The president of India alone can remove the chair or any member when adjudged insolvent, or engages in any outside paid employment during the term of office, or is in the opinion of the president unfit to continue in office by reason of infirmity of mind or body (Article 317). Removal for misbehaviour by the president may occur only after an inquiry by the Supreme Court.

Despite a few lapses (leakage of examination questions, or entertaining undeserved candidates with false birth certificates), the UPSC is known for its integrity to the extent that one of its former secretaries, P.C. Hota (2010: 189–201) observed that 'even the worst critics of the higher civil services would concede that the competitive examination and interview based selection process for the AIS (All-India Services) is fair and merit based'.

Initially, age limits were set for taking these examinations. A candidate must be 21 years and not more than 24 years. The number of attempts to take the examinations was restricted to two. Given the largely generalist nature of the Civil Service, and also as candidates would be coming from different academic backgrounds, two guidelines are set: first, catch the candidates while they are young and still in learning mode, so that they can all be trained further; and, second, a candidate taking the examinations more than twice might get used to the examination process, and the result might not necessarily reflect academic accomplishments. Over time this view had changed. At the time of writing (2013), candidates taking the examinations must have a university degree, and must be aged at least 21 years but not exceeding 30 years. Given their inability to compete with the general category of candidates, due to their uneven education and also the policy commitment to improve their lot, the upper age limit for Scheduled Castes/ Scheduled Tribes (SC/ST) candidates is set at 35 years, and for the Other Backward Classes (OBCs) 33. (The current Narendra Modi government is reviewing the age limits with a view to bringing them down.) Within the given age limits, general category candidates may take the examinations four times, while the OBCs are allowed seven, with no limits for the SC/ST candidates. However, once selected, those failing to get placed in that year may have to start all over again, as the roster of selected candidates relates to the year in question.

The examinations conducted for the higher civil service (IAS) consist of three parts. Given that numerous applicants keep opting to take the examinations, with an enthusiasm that surpasses their credentials, Part I is designed to eliminate the not-so-serious candidates. As an aptitude test in a multiple-choice mode, it consists of two papers of 200 marks each in general studies. Those who pass this phase take Part II, written essay tests: one general essay; two papers on general studies; and two optional subjects (from among the long list of subjects normally taught in any university). Each candidate is also tested in two languages of choice (picked from among the 22 mentioned above). A candidate who does not pass these two will not progress any further, as no other tests are evaluated. Part III consists of the 'personality' test, which takes the form of an oral examination (*viva voce*). Candidates are selected based on cumulative scores.

Coming as they do from varied educational backgrounds, all those selected will be further trained together for a short time and individually according to service: the IAS at the Lal Bahadur Shastri Academy, Mussoorie, and the IPS in the Police Academy, Hyderabad. As the training processes are elaborate, they are omitted here. Instead, three different areas affecting the service are further dealt with briefly: 'reservations', administrative behaviour and corruption.

'Reservations'

'Reservations' connotes preferential provisions for admission into public service designed for those deemed to be socially backward because of eons of social discrimination resulting in economic deprivation as well. This subject is extensively dealt with elsewhere (Tummala, 1994: ch. IX; 2015), and only a panoramic picture is given here. Intent on preventing the scourge of the caste system (if not abolish it altogether), the Indian Constitution talks only about 'classes'.

However, tension was apparent right from the beginning of the Republic between preferential policies and constitutional dictates. The Constitution provides equality before the law, non-discrimination on the basis of religion, race, caste, sex or place of birth, and equal opportunity for all (Articles 14, 15 and 16 respectively). Yet the government set preferential quotas for the three classes. Such set-asides were immediately challenged in the famous case of *Champakam Doairajan* v. *State of Madras* (1951) as violating the equality principle of the Constitution. The Supreme Court agreed with the complainant. Committed as they were to equality on one hand and the uplift of the backward on the other, the government found itself on the horns of a dilemma that was resolved by adding the very first amendment to the Constitution by inserting Clause (4) to Article 15, allowing special preferences to the socially and educationally backward classes, notwithstanding the equality principles.

Such preference was originally designed to cover initial appointments, but later extended to promotions as well, consequent to the 1962 *General Manager* decision of the Supreme Court (by adding Clause 4 [a] to Article 15). Accordingly, among annually available public service slots, 15 per cent would go to SCs and 7.5 per cent to STs. Initially preference for OBCs was left for the states to decide. But the Centre also joined them in 1990 by following a decade-old recommendation made by the Mandal Commission, and setting a 27 per cent reservation quota for them. Keeping in view that Article 335 of the Constitution stipulated that efficiency in administration be ensured, the Supreme Court in its 1963 *Balaji* judgment restricted the overall preference to no more than 50 per cent of the total. This decision also maintained that caste could only be one criterion among others while defining eligibility for preference.

Several troublesome issues have emerged in the implementation of these preferential provisions. The first and foremost is the result of 'competitive populism', whereby successive governments expanded the gamut of reservations to include more and more castes (note, not classes), particularly in the OBC category, when the various political parties and governments try to get electoral advantage by promising, and in fact including, more and more caste groups. Second, contrary to the academic arguments that seeking preference denigrates the applicant (Rudolph and Rudolph, 1967: 150; Steele, 1990: 33, 118), several castes, even those traditionally considered forward, keep demanding inclusion as backward. Third, although preferential provisions are only 'enabling', they tended to be seen as 'entitlements'. Fourth, in an apparent effort to have the political will prevail over constitutional principles, whenever the Supreme Court (following the constitutional provisions meant for equality) put its foot down, the government of the day resorted to constitutional amendments to neutralize the Court's objections, such as the 77th in 1995 (to include promotions), the 81st in 2000 (to carry forward places not filled in one year due to the paucity of qualified candidates), the 82nd in 2000 (to relax standards to fill the quota), the 89th in 1999 (to protect seniority), the 93rd in 2006 (to include institutions of learning, both public and private) and so on. Fifth, sadly, and worst of all, most of the preferences tended to be based on caste, despite the fact that the Constitution talks of 'classes', as already seen. It must be noted in this context that, while caste does not determine class, class does mitigate caste distinctions. And finally, the consequent rancor of the so-called forward castes that their own opportunities are being circumscribed by expanding the number of castes for purposes of reservation continues unabated, just as the demands for inclusion by several castes increases.

Into this miasma of confusion, some uniting principles are provided by the Supreme Court (at least, so it was thought!) in 2007, while upholding the 93rd Amendment: (a) making reservations in state-maintained and state-aided educational institutions does not violate the 'basic structure' of the Constitution, but the issue of 'private unaided' schools is left open to be decided in appropriate cases; (b) identifying 'backward classes' on the basis of caste is valid; (c) while prescribing no time limit (for preference) is valid, a periodical review every five years can be made to see the effectiveness of 'reservations'; (d) the 27 per cent reservations announced for OBCs is valid; (e) Article 15 (5), dealing with unaided institutions, does not contradict Article 15 (4) dealing with aided institutions, as the former has language, 'whether aided or unaided'; and (f) the exclusion of minority educational institutions from the purview of these reservations does not violate Article 15 (4).

Other observations by the Court in this context are also worth noting. If reservations are perpetuated, the entire object of ensuring equality will be defeated, and as it is only an enabling provision, it has to be time-bound. At some point of time, reservations have to be terminated. '[P]eriodic examination of a backward class could lead to its exclusion if it ceases to be socially backward or if it is adequately represented in the services. Once backward, always backward is not acceptable.' The Court further observed:

> There is no deletion from the list of other backward classes. It goes on increasing . . . [I]s it that backwardness has increased instead of decreasing? If the answer is yes, as contended by the respondents (Center and other pro-quota parties), then one is bound to raise eyebrows as to the effectiveness of providing reservations or quotas.

Justices Arijit Pasayat and C.K. Thakker added:

> The inequalities are to be removed. Yet the fact that there has been no exclusion raises a doubt about the real concern to remove inequality . . . If after nearly six decades the objectives have not been achieved, necessarily the need for its continuance warrants deliberations . . . It is to be noted that some of the provisions were intended to be replaced after a decade but have continued. It directly shows that backwardness appears to have purportedly increased, and not diminished.

This is the subject of continued debate. Besides all these controversies, it should be noted that in a multi-religious society, preference is accorded only within the context of the Hindu and Sikh religions. And women are not considered in this regard (although some proportion of seats in the local governing bodies are set aside for them). For the first time the Bombay High Court ordered a disabled quota of 3 per cent IAS, both for initial appointment and promotions in December 2013. Prime Minister V.P. Singh, who in 1990 implemented the Mandal Commission report in fulfillment of his electoral promise extending preference to the OBCs, was reported to have said that he could rest at peace. The country, however, does not seem to be at peace with this policy of preference.

Administrative Behaviour

The proper relationship between the government (the political masters) and civil servants has always been a point of contention and debate. The departure from the timeworn policy–administration dichotomy and the recognition that civil servants not only administer but in fact do participate in the policy-making process by virtue of their expertise and also their proximity to the political decision makers (who tended to be largely less than experts, even less educated) make for some interesting relationships. Those few administrators who stick to rules of procedure have come to regret their professionalism. Others who became fellow travellers by being part of the political, business and criminal nexus, prospered, resulting in some of the worst corruption cases. Either way, the morale of the administrators is shattered. Not only a policy paralysis but also administrative failure can be observed. The following phenomena are illustrative.

First is the harassment meted out to the higher administrators, either to shield the criminal activities of the political masters, or as a sort of punishment for not complying with their often illegal demands. It has long been known that the political masters – the ministers who head the cabinet departments – try to face down strong-willed civil servants by the simple expedient of frequent transfers under the pretext that it is not punishment but only a matter of administrative imperative and/or convenience. The most recent case in this regard is that of one Ashok Khemka, who held the position of director general of Land Consolidation and Land Records, and inspector general of Registration for a period of only 80 days in the state of Haryana. During that time he unearthed a case in which Robert Vadra, the son-in-law of the president of the ruling Congress Party, Sonia Gandhi, was supposed to have made huge sums of money in land scams by doing nothing more than lending his name to a real-estate outfit – DLF. Khemka was not only transferred quickly but also investigated. To add insult to injury, he was charge-sheeted by the government of Haryana, claiming that he insulted Vadra, and sought an explanation in December 2013. This upright civil servant has the dubious distinction of having been transferred nearly 44 times in his 32-year career, so far. The other was that of Durga Shakti Nagpal, who met the same fate on an allegation that she nearly created communal tensions by demolishing a wall around a mosque in the state of Uttar Pradesh (UP). The reason behind her suspension was alleged to be the tough stance she took against illegal miners who lend support to the government. She was not only transferred quickly, but in fact suspended, only to be reinstated later after a demonstration in her support. In all, UP is (in)famous for transferring 800 IAS officers during 2012–13!

It is not simply the incumbent administrators but also retired officials who are harassed in an effort to shield political bosses from their past criminal activities. P.C. Parakh, former secretary of the Coal Ministry (retired December 2005), known as the whistleblower in the coal allocation scam, was himself booked, alleged to have conspired in the same deal. In his turn, he famously responded that the prime minister, Manmohan Singh, who was then in charge of coal, must also be booked if there was a conspiracy as he, as secretary, was after all acting under the minister's orders. Parakh was known for his integrity, and it was he who recommended open competitive bidding for coal blocks to make allotment transparent. Also, he was willing to testify before the Public Accounts Committee (PAC) of parliament, which was investigating the coal scam, but was not invited as a witness. Investigation by the Central Bureau of Investigation (CBI) is continuing.

Second is the flip side of the coin, where civil servants learned the lesson of cooperating with political bosses, thus not only earning peace, but also amassing huge sums as part of the ill-gotten gains. Any number of cases can be provided in which higher civil servants are either the co-accused in political corruption cases, or on charges of disproportionate assets. The mining scandals in Karnataka and Andhra Pradesh provide good examples.

Third, several civil servants also found out that it is in their best interests to be in the good books of the government so that on retirement they find some remunerative and prestigious positions outside the civil service establishment. For example, Nitish Kumar, former director of the CBI (which was often criticized as being a handmaiden of the government – see below), got an appointment as governor of a state. The same government felt no compunction in appointing the Secretary of Defense, S.K. Sharma, immediately after his retirement as Comptroller and Auditor General, despite the several defense expenditure irregularities that are being investigated.

The NEP led to the creation of several regulatory commissions. Most of these are now headed by former higher-level bureaucrats after their retirement. It is reported that, of the 12 economic regulators, nine are retired bureaucrats, and in 20 of the 28 states the chief information commissioner is the state's former chief secretary. When the retired commerce secretary, Dipak Ghosh, was appointed chair of the Competition Commission created in 2003, the appointment was challenged; it was argued that a bureaucrat cannot be appointed to a quasi-judicial position (as the Commission is to supervise competitive practices). The then Chief Justice of the Supreme Court of India, V.N. Khare, was quoted as saying indignantly: 'At this rate, a day would come, maybe after 20 years, when the 26 judges of the apex court would be replaced by bureaucrats' (Sriram, 2013: 28).

Fourth, very unprofessional conduct is observed among some senior officials trying to indulge in politics. Worse, they were formerly in charge of agencies endowed with the power of force – the army and the police. The former is the behaviour of the retired chief of the army, General V.K. Singh. For example, he went all the way to the Supreme Court seeking a change of his date of birth, which would have given him an additional ten months in office and certainly changed the line of succession. When criticized for this unseemly behaviour, he claimed that he was fighting for his honour! He lost his case and had to apologize to the Supreme Court for remarks he made against it. He is now a minister in Modi's Cabinet!

The latter involves the director general of police (DGP) in the state of Andhra Pradesh, V. Dinseh Reddy, who was reported to have expected continuation of office after retirement. The chief minister of the state did not oblige. In turn, the DGP came out with wild charges that his boss (the CM) actually fomented the law-and-order crisis in the state which is burning (as of this writing) after the decision to divide it. During the last year, the Election Commission thrice suggested to the government some cooling-off period for bureaucrats to join politics/political parties after retirement. The Government of India, however, has not acceded so far.

To alleviate some of the harassment, and protect the higher civil servants for acting on oral orders (and not written), 83 retired bureaucrats (including a former cabinet secretary, a former ambassador, former chief election commissioner) approached the Supreme Court on a Public Interest Litigation (PIL). They sought a Writ from the Court to order an end to oral orders by the political masters, who tended to feign innocence when caught, as there is no written evidence. On 13 October 2013, the Court gave its verdict in *T.S.R. Subramanian*, suggesting (at para 17, 6.20 iii) that 'the civil servants are not having stability of tenure, particularly in the Sate Governments where transfers and posting are made frequently, at the whims and fancies of the executive head for political and other considerations and not in public interest'. Thus it recommended a minimum tenure (para 30) by observing: 'Fixed minimum tenure would not only enable the civil servants to achieve their professional targets, but also help them to function as effective instruments of public policy . . . Minimum assured service tenure ensures efficient service delivery and also increased efficiency'. To fix responsibility and ensure accountability (para 33), they said:

> [W]e are of the view that the civil servants cannot function on the basis of verbal or oral instructions, orders, suggestions, proposals, etc. and they must also be protected against wrongful and arbitrary pressures exerted by the administrative superiors, political executive, business and other vested interests . . . [T]here must be some records to demonstrate how the civil servant has acted, if the decision is not his, but if he is doing on the oral directions, instructions, he should record such directions in the file.

If implemented, this should go a long way to alleviating some of the anxiety of the higher civil servants. But past experience with a decade-old similar order regarding the police establishment is not reassuring.

Corruption

Of the 177 countries surveyed by Transparency International (TI) in 2013, India was ranked 94th (TI, 2013). This is not without reason (Tummala, 2013: 167–87). Reports of massive corruption are daily news. But to provide a few samples, to start with: (a) in 2012, of the 543 Indian Parliament members, 158 were found to have pending criminal charges, some even with murder; (b) the Commonwealth Games, which were originally estimated by the Indian Olympic Association in 2003 to cost about $300 million, eventually cost an estimated $11 billion. As much as $1 to $1.7 billion was lost because of alleged malfeasance of the chief of the games, Suresh Kalmadi, who is also a Rajya Sabha member of the governing

Congress Party, and its one-time general secretary. He is on bail; (c) the Adarsh Housing Scheme in Bombay, where apartments built for heroes of the Kargil war (with Pakistan) and army widows were allotted at cut-rate prices to several politicians, including some high-ranking army officers and the then chief minister of Maharashtra, Ashok Chavan (who was forced to resign); (d) the black market, or underground economy, is estimated to be worth nearly $640 billion – about half the annual Indian GDP of $1.3 trillion; (e) land scams involving forceful eviction of poor farmers by paying a pittance of compensation, in the name of 'development' and creation of Special Economic Zones (SEZs), by governments such as West Bengal and UP, led to alleged personal fortunes made by influential political personalities; (f) the 2G spectrum case in 2010, and another commonly known as 'coalgate' came out in 2012. Allocation of coal blocks to companies arbitrarily and without verifying their credentials during 2004–11 alone is said to have led to a loss of nearly $210 billion to the exchequer. The list goes on, with more and worse scandals being unearthed daily.

The obvious questions then are: why such a sea of corruption, and why cannot it be controlled? The simple answer to the first is twofold: need and greed. Need could be addressed by generous pay and benefit packages, which of course is a function of the economy, available human resource skills and competition for the same personnel between the public and private sectors. But, even in the presence of generous emoluments, there is neither a guarantee nor evidence from other countries that corruption could be eradicated. Certainly, the temptation to take a bribe is far greater for a person whose pay is below subsistence level. Greed, a matter of character, is in itself a product of tradition and societal norms. This is where the importance of laws and institutions to fight greed comes in, and the political will of the government of the day to go after the accused, regardless of party affiliation and/or social stature.

The fight against corruption is the domain of two major institutions: the Central Vigilance Commission (CVC) and the Central Bureau of Investigation (CBI). The CVC was created in 1964. The Supreme Court of India in the *Vineet Narain* judgment (18 December 1997) was highly critical of its working, and asked the Government of India to come up with legislation to strengthen it. Consequently an ordinance was issued, and the CVC got a statutory base further to an Act of Parliament in 2003 (Tummala, 2002: 43–69).

Created in 1963, the CBI is a police force investigating both serious crimes and corruption. As an organization, it is an administrative nightmare, serving multiple masters. The Ministry of Home Affairs has to clear the cadre of the commissioners. For funds, it depends on the Ministry of Personnel, Training and Public Grievances, and reports to it on day-to-day working. For hiring of all officers above the rank of superintendent of policy, the Union Public Service Commission's approval is needed. For all corruption cases, it faces the supervision of the CVC. The Ministry of Law and Justice pays the salaries of prosecutors arguing cases of corruption for the CBI. Given its poor budget (a total of about $720 million), and authorized strength of 6526 positions, of which 1379 were vacant for the year 2011–12, the CBI is not expected to be very efficient. Moreover, it came under severe criticism not only for its inactivity when high dignitaries are concerned, but also for the fact that it became a political pawn in the hands of the government of the day. Given the latter, a former director general of police of Haryana, who served with the CBI, raised the not so rhetorical question: 'Who owns the CBI?' (Lall, 2011). The Supreme Court recently observed that the CBI is a 'caged parrot' serving many masters, and demanded that the Government of India should come up with legislation by 10 July 2013 insulating the CBI from political pressures (Nayyaar and Sriram, 2013: 32–4). No action has been taken as of this writing. Having found out that the CBI and other police investigators had not performed their primary duties, the Supreme Court previously observed in its *Vineet Narain* decision (cited above), that '[i]nertia was the common rule whenever the alleged offender was a powerful person'.

Punishment following a trial is accorded by the courts. The Indian court system operates notoriously slowly, with the cumbersome jurisprudence and case overload. It is estimated that there are about 30 million pending cases, and at the present rate of disposal it would take about 300 years to clear such a backlog (i.e. without taking on any new cases). On average, a court case takes about 15 years to be cleared (Vittal, 2012: 148, 154). The already-clogged and slow judicial process is made worse since the inauguration of Public Interest Litigation (PIL), using which anyone can drag anyone to the court on the flimsiest cause, or no cause at all – just to be vindictive, or a nuisance, or to settle past scores. T.S. Tulsi, a Supreme Court lawyer, suggested that hardly 6 per cent of cases lead to conviction in the Indian courts (quoted in Vittal, 2012: 52).

Courts and judges are generally held in esteem and considered less corrupt. Nonetheless, there are several former Supreme Court judges and other justices of the High Courts of States who are being investigated for misconduct. The most current is an accusation by an intern that a former judge of the Supreme Court, A.K. Ganguly, indulged in sexual misconduct with her. Immediately following the break of the story in November 2013, the then chief justice convened a three-judge investigative panel that found out that there is a *prima facie* case against the judge, but did not wish to take any action as the judge is retired and the intern was working in a private capacity. The case, however, is being investigated by the police. Moreover, the courts are accused of being 'active', and one cannot but notice that they can, by their various decisions, be seen to be entering the policy-making arena.

Into this bleak picture a little bit of sunshine appeared under the leadership of Anna Hazare, who went on a fast to death demanding the establishment of a *Lokpal* (an ombudman) at the Centre. The idea itself is not new. As far back as 1968, the Lok Sabha passed a bill to provide for a *Lokpal*, but it did not clear the Rajya Sabha. In response to Hazare's fast, after a very convoluted discussion, a rather weak bill was passed in December 2011 by the Lok Sabha, much to the dismay of Hazare and other activists. The Rajya Sabha did not clear the bill when its session ended on 30 March 2012. Neither was it taken up during the following monsoon session, which ended in mid-2013. In the winter session a watered-down *Lokpal* Act was indeed passed, and Hazare, who had opposed the bill tooth and nail, finally accepted it. The government promised to introduce seven other supplemental bills, but passed only the Whistleblower Protection Act. However, the position of *Lokpal* had not been filled: the first two who were offered the position declined, protesting that the government still wanted to control that office, which was supposed to be independent. Meanwhile the government lost the 2014 election. No party got enough votes to be regarded as the Oppposition. Efforts are now (late 2014) under way to change the law, but the Opposition parties are opposing the legislation.

As Vittal (2012: 5) observed, there was a 'multiple organ failure'. First, time and again, it is argued that corruption is a British legacy. But the British left India over 67 years ago! As already seen, since independence in 1947, first the 'permit *raj*', and then the 'contract *raj*' facilitated corruption. Second, criminalization of politics and politicization of criminals resulted in turning the 'lawmakers' into 'lawbreakers', as the Election Commission (EC) observed. Third, there has been one coalition government after another, the last being the United Progressive Alliance (UPA II) led by Prime Minister Manmohan Singh of the Congress Party. Coalition governments, which are often dubbed as 'unholy alliances', some lasting as little as 13 days, turned out to be less effective due to all sorts of pressures and accommodations among the several partners (Tummala, 2009). Coalition partners pursuing separate agendas, and the government depending upon their support for its very survival, precluded any concerted action. Fourth, both the CVC and the CBI failed in performing their duties. Fifth, the very insistence on rule of law itself seems to have become an impediment. Article 311 of the Indian Constitution protects civil servants from *mala fide* actions of government, and provides security in the job by stating that no civil servant can be 'dismissed or disciplined by an authority subordinate to that which (s)he was appointed'. It is no secret that a minister would not let his/her employee be indicted easily, which also means politicization of cases. Sixth, the recent appointment of P.J. Thomas to head the CVC in 2010, despite charges pending against him on a Pamolein import scandal while he was the secretary in Kerala, did not inspire much confidence in the sincerity or seriousness of the government. Lastly, the one movement that showed some promise also failed, in that Hazare and his team had shown chinks in their armor. They suffered many a setback, some self-inflicted. The 'Team Hazare' (as the group came to be known) consisted of several followers with their own personal agendas to pursue using this movement, thus resulting in the hazards of 'cooptation' (Selznick, 1949). Some of these, in fact, found themselves under a cloud. Kiran Bedi, who was the first female Indian Police Service (IPS) officer (since retired or forced out, whoever is to be believed), was shown to have charged first- or business-class fares when she went on lecture tours, but travelled only in economy. (She explained that she was saving money for her own NGO.) Another, Arvind Kejriwal, a former tax official, was himself charged with tax evasion (since paid). He distanced himself from Hazare eventually, and started a political party, Aam Aadmi, wanting to fight corruption on his own. The feud between him and Hazare continues. Hazare himself proved that he is not entirely above politics, as he went on canvassing in state elections against the Congress Party and Prime Minister Singh. He was charged as lending support to the opposition BJP/ RSS combination. Thus was lost a momentous occasion, when the masses seem to have been mobilized and marched in lock-step with Hazare.

The current *Lokpal* Act is but the latest in the contemplated control measures; nor will it be the last. It would be a folly to believe that a simple creation of a *Lokpal* in itself would be a panacea. It might in fact add yet another layer of bureaucracy were it not to function properly. For that matter, it might be noted that there are the *Lok Ayuktas* (state-level ombudsmen) with rather patchy records, which do not inspire much confidence. Could the working of *Lokpal* be any different?

As already noted, several incumbent Members of Parliament (MPs) face criminal charges. By some estimated at over 1400, other legislators nationwide are under the cloud. On 10 July the Supreme Court in its *Lily Thomas* (2013) decision invalidated Section 8 (4) of the Representation of People Act, 1951 (which allowed convicted MPs and members of legislative assemblies to hold office while an appeal is pending) and stated that all legislators convicted of crimes shall lose their seats immediately, contrary to the prevailing practice of holding on to their seats as the slow appeals process grinds on, seemingly forever. Not only the government but also all parties panicked. With so many in parliament and government coming under this category, the Government of India wanted to neutralize the decision and to restore the *status quo ante*, and passed an ordinance (as the parliament was not in session) and sent it to the president for his assent. The president kept silent. Rahul Gandhi of the Nehru–Gandhi dynasty, vice president of the ruling Congress Party, who is being showcased as possibly the next prime minister of India, in his youthful exuberance or indignation barged into a press conference of a different cabinet minister, convened for an altogether different purpose, and called the ordinance 'nonsense', demanding that it be trashed. The prime minister, who was attending the UN session in New York, was caught by surprise with this stinging rebuke, and had to withdraw the ordinance.

The courts themselves seem to be flexing their muscles. A case in point is that of Lalu Prasad Yadav. He was the chief minister of one of the poorest states – Bihar. Folksy and colorful, he is a proven crook. The case became public in 1996 in the 'fodder scam', when nearly $9.5 billion was siphoned off from funds meant to buy cattlefeed. Yadav appealed as a case was filed against him. But in a supreme fit of arrogance, he brazenly installed his rustic wife as the chief minister, and ran the state by proxy. The good people took it all in their stride. And then the coalition government of the United Progressive Alliance (UPA I), led by the Congress Party at the federal level, needed all the support it could get. Among others, with a handful of MPs, Yadav came to the rescue. In return, he was made the minister for Railways for some time. Finally, on 3 October 2013, a day after the nation celebrated the 144th birth anniversary of Mahatma Gandhi, the Court handed down a five-year rigorous imprisonment and about $40 000 fine to Yadav, along with another former chief minister of Bihar and 44 other accused. Yadav will likely appeal. But, for now, justice is served, even if it took nearly 17 years.

CONCLUSION

The above analysis shows that, although India's administration did serve reasonably well, several reform attempts have not been very successful. Part of the blame lies with the governments of the day and the resistance of the 'IAS lobby'. Now the bureaucracy is under severe stress. Abundant and ubiquitous corruption and the inability to combat it turn out to be major disasters for the development of the country. The political atmosphere, largely due to the coalition government phenomenon, and lack of political leaders who rarely, if ever, talk in a national idiom, but prefer personal, local and regional narratives, corrupt to the core along with the criminalization of politics, is not helping much. But not all is lost. There are reasons, though mixed, for optimism.

- Economic liberalization, which undid past state controls, also led to numerous media outlets, followed by aggressive reportage by outfits such as Aaj Tak and tehelka.com. But it also saw several other private and partisan outlets – in both print and television, each grinding its own personal axe, exposing real or feigned corruption. Currently, the editor of *tehelka*, who in his time exposed several corrupt politicians, is under arrest on sexual assault charges brought by a colleague.

- The Right to Information Act (RTI), 2005, led to such to an active, even zealous, media that several journalists have been killed for relentlessly pursuing unsavory stories of the high and mighty. The nation itself is yet to come to grips with the fundamental issue of protecting the whistleblower. However, it is now rather difficult for the government to hide behind the Official Secrets Act of 1923.

- Several NGOs have emerged, such as the Hazare movement. These civil societies, while raising their own issues of accountability, do expose some of the rottenness.

- The judiciary, which has been held up as the only bulwark of integrity, but not without its own foibles, has become more active of late in going so far as to give numerous directions to various governments, some of which in the normal process have a policy-making flavor. The slow court system, however, needs to be speeded up.

- The new instrument called Public Interest Litigation (PIL) allows anyone to approach a court on any issue, thus helping the courts to step in. Although these suits do serve (or are meant to serve) the public interest, on occasion they tend to be not only frivolous but also vindictive (to settle old scores), while also clogging the already overburdened and slow court system. This needs to be checked. For, by the time cases come to a court to be judged, the lapse of time plays havoc as memories fade, evidence is lost or destroyed, and witnesses are bought and sold.

- Perhaps a more important phenomenon is the progressive disappearance of the mystique and awe of government. The common citizen who was in the past reluctant, or afraid, to approach a public servant with a complaint, is of late ready to confront to the point of ignoring some important traditional taboos. India always showed respect, almost to the point of deference or even subservience, to elders and authority figures. Now, it is not uncommon to throw *chappal* (common footwear) at them, which tradition considers disgraceful and disgusting. Yet the government has been brought down to earth, in a way.

Thus one can see some hope, a hint of optimism, that one day India will emerge at its best, sooner or later, and preferably sooner.

NOTES

1. The number of states needs some explanation. Although Delhi is listed as a union territory, it has its own legislative assembly and government – almost like any other state, except it is not officially designated as such. Also, in 2013 a decision was made by the ruling Congress Party to divide the state of Andhra Pradesh into two. Legislation to this effect was expected to be introduced in the winter 2013 parliamentary session.
2. There were only 18 recognized languages originally, but the 71st Amendment in 1992 added other languages, such as Nepali, making the current total of 22.

REFERENCES

Alexandrowicz, C.H. (1957). *Constitutional Developments in India and its Contradictions.* Princeton, NJ: Princeton University Press.
Appleby, Paul (1957). *Public Administration in India: Report of a Survey.* New Delhi: Government of India.
Balaji v. *State of Mysore*, AIR 1963 SC 649.
Champakam Dorairajan v. *State of Madras*, 1951, SCR 525.
Dreze, Jean and Sen, Amartya (2013). *An Uncertain Glory: India and its Contradictions.* Princeton, NJ: Princeton University Press.
Gaus, John M. (1947). *Reflections on Public Administration.* Alabama: Alabama University Press.
General Manager v. *Rangachari*, AIR 1962 SC 36.
Government of India (2013). Ministry of Statistics & Programme Implementation. *Statistical Year Book.*
Hanumanthaiah, K. (1970). 'Foreword to a brief survey', *The ARC and its Work*. New Delhi: Government of India.
The Hindu (15 March 2012, online).
Hota, P.C. (2010). 'The civil service: past, present and future', *The Indian Journal of Public Administration* **LVI** (2).
Indiatoday (2013). Online, indiatoday.intoday, 7 November
Katyal, K.K. (1980). 'Catalytic agents for national integration', *The Hindu International Edition*, 23 August.
Lall, B.R. (2007). *Who Owns the CBI? The Naked Truth.* New Delhi: Manas.
Lall, B.R. (2011). *Free the CBI.* New Delhi: Manas.
Lily Thomas v. *Union of India* (2013). Writ Petition (Civil), No. 449 of 2005.
Nayyaar, Dhiraj and Sriram Jayant (2013). 'Nowhere to hide', *India Today.* 20 May.
Riggs, Fred W. (1961). *The Ecology of Public Administration.* Bombay: Asia Publishing House.
Riggs, Fred W. (1964). *The Theory of Prismatic Society.* Boston, MA: Houghton Mifflin Co.
Rotberg. R. (2009). *Corruption, Global Security, and World Order.* Baltimore, MD: Brookings Institution Press.
Rudolph, Lloyd and Susanne (1967). *In Pursuit of Lakshmi: The Political Economy of the Indian State.* Chicago, IL: Chicago University Press.
Selznick, Philip (1949). *TVA and the Grassroots: A Study in the Sociology of Organization.* Berkeley, CA: University of California Press.

Shiva Rao, B. (1966). *The Framing of India's Constitution: Select Documents, Vol. I*. New Delhi: Indian Institute of Public Administration.

Singh, Mahendra Pratap (2013). In Meghna Sabharwal and Evan Berman (eds), *Public Administration in South Asia: India, Bangladesh and Pakistan*. Boca Raton, FL: CRC Press.

Sriram, Jayant (2013). 'Revenge of the Babus', *India Today*. 7 October

Steele, Shelby (1990). *The Content of Our Character: A New Vision of Race in America*. New York: St Martin's Press.

Transparency International (2013). http://cpi.transparency.org/cpi2013.

T.S.R. Subramanian & Ors. v. *Union of India & Ors*. Writ Petition (Civil), No. 28 of 2011 and No. 234 of 2011 (2013).

Tummala, Krishna K. (1994). *Public Administration in India*. Singapore: Times Academic Press.

Tummala, Krishna K. (1996). 'The Indian Union and emergency powers', *International Political Science Review*, **17**(4).

Tummala, Krishna K. (2001). 'The Indian administrator in the new millennium', *Asian Journal of Political Science*, **9**(1).

Tummala, Krishna K. (2002). 'Corruption in India: control measures and consequences', *Asian Journal of Political Science*, **10**(2).

Tummala, Krishna K. (2009). 'Coalition politics in India: 2004–2009', *Asian Journal of Political Science*, **17**(3).

Tummala, Krishna K. (2013). 'Can India combat corruption?', in Jon S.T. Quah (ed.), *Different Paths to Curbing Corruption: Lessons from Denmark, Finland, Hong Kong, New Zealand and Singapore*. Bingley, UK: Emerald Publishers.

Tummala, Krishna K. (2015) *Politics of Preference: India, United States and South Africa*. Boca Raton, FL: CRC Press.

Vineet Narain et al v. *Union of India et al*, AIR 1998 SC 889.

Vittal, N. (2011). *India Today*. 10 January.

Vittal, N. (2012). *Ending Corruption: How to Clean up India*. New Delhi: Penguin Books India.

Waldo, Dwight (1948). *The Administrative State*. New York: The Ronald Press.

13. The *Tao* of governance: public administration reform in China
Zhichang Zhu

Public administration (PA) in China is under continuous reforms along-side the country's recent economic transformation and in coincidence with the global New Public Management/Good Governance movements. The interesting questions are: what are being reformed, how do the reforms proceed, who engage in reforms, what are the outcomes, what would further reforms look like and what, if any, are the links between the China experience and global trends? This chapter investigates these questions in China's own terms, informed by indigenous rationales and historical patterns.

LEGACIES AND CONDITIONS

As the birthplace of the modern state (Fukuyama 2011), China has been a 'permanently bureaucratic society' (Balazs 1965). This leaves distinctive imprints on the country's modern administration and its reforms, the most significant of which we present below.

Centralized Authoritarianism

Over the past two millennia, China was governed largely by a single authority. The first emperor, Shi Huangdi (260–210 BC) of the Qin Dynasty (221–206 BC), unified the nation, set up a central government, standardized written language, currency, and length, capacity and weight measures. Since then, there has been only one unified *chaoting* ('court'), no separated 'houses'. Centralized ruling was carried on by means of *fa* – power-oriented punishment, which was formulated by, among others, Shen Buhai (420–337 BC), Shang Yang (390–338 BC), Lü Buwei (290–235 BC) and Han Fei (281–233 BC), and *li* – virtue-oriented persua-sion, which was promoted chiefly by Confucius (552–479 BC), Mencius (372–289 BC), Dong Zhongshu (179–104 BC) and Zhu Xi (1130–1200) (Tan 2011). Foreign invasions and internal rebellions interrupted but did not destroy the central authority. Instead, they nurtured an enduring desire for it. Deep in the Chinese consciousness, an enlightened and powerful ruler was a blessing (Wu 2013). There was, and still is, a tendency in the Chinese to expect the government to deliver order and prosperity (Jacques 2009, pp.198–9). 'We should trust and obey the government, for in the final analysis it serves our interest', the modern public insists (Nathan 2003, p.13). The encounters with foreign powers since the Opium Wars further deepened such a tendency. The Chinese call the painful experience *bainian guochi* (100-year national humiliation), out of which emerged a consensual, single-minded search for *fuguo qiangbing* (rich state, strong army) (Bays 1976). After the collapse of the last empire there was a period of contestation between various political ideas and proposals introduced from abroad. Yet China quickly settled for a Leninist party state under the nationalist generalissimo Chiang Kai-shek, followed by the communist leader Mao Zedong. Ironically, the neoliberal rhetoric since the fall of the Berlin Wall only heightens in China the social-Darwinist sense of national vulnerability. *Yousheng liebai* (survival of the fittest): in the inescapable competition between nations, national power is above everything else. 'Development is the hard truth', 'Staying backward is to be beaten', or so the Chinese believe. While fully committed to opening up the country to foreign capital and embracing the market economy, the 'chief architect' Deng Xiaoping set a stark boundary for China's reforms: national stability guaranteed by the party state (Wu 2013). In China's 'New Long March' towards peace and prosperity, the state continues to be looked to for solutions, not regarded as problems; it is to be strengthened, not weakened.

Blurred Spheres

The role of the government in China had no boundaries (Grieder 1981; Shambaugh 2008). From the very beginning, statecraft was defined broadly as *zhiguo* – governing the state. In practice this allowed, indeed demanded, the government to engage in the full complexity of real-politik, to fulfil both public policy and administration duties (Cheung 2012a, p.211). The combination of technocratic undertaking and political manoeuvre was taken as 'naturally so'. This is in contrast with the long Western discourse since the ancient Greeks that evolves slowly from public 'management' (*guanli*) to 'administration' (*xingzheng*) and only recently to 'governance' (*zhili*) (Hood 2005, pp.8–12). The Wilsonian conception of public administration being a neutral servant untamed by politics made no sense to the Chinese. Seen as the solution instead of the problem, the government in China was expected to intervene in all affairs of people's life: social, culture, economic as well as political (Faure

2006, p. 67). Whereas the state's function in the economic sphere is, in the Anglo-American paradigm, confined to the 'night watchman' role, in China the state's function was, legitimately, to own businesses and control the economy (Wu 2013; Pye 1988, p. 89). While there was no lack of reform programmes, from Guan Zi (725–645 BC) to Sang Hongyang (152–80 BC) and Wang Anshi (AD 1021–86), the debates were firmly focused on how, never on whether, to do it. Consecutive governments either directly ran, or authorized selected social groups to run, its rightful interest in strategic sectors: salt, iron, forests, silk, wine, tea, sugar, cigarettes and so on. In ancient times, *The Book of Song* (11th–7th century BC) read: *putian zhixia, mofei wangtu* (No land under heaven does not belong to the king); in the modern era, Sun Yat-sen (1866–1925) instructed: *tianxia weigong* (All under heaven belongs to the public (as opposite to the private)). Hence, when ruling Mainland China the Guomindang government nationalized the entire banking sector, controlled 90 per cent of steel and iron output, and owned absolute majority stakes in key industries, while the subsequent Mao regime eliminated the private sector altogether (Wu 2013). As the polity and the economy deeply interwove into the governance fabric, 'in China, market and administrative reforms are very much interdependent processes' (Caulfield 2006, p. 254; Xue and Zhong 2012, p. 285). When Deng started the post-Mao reform, there was only one massive, all-encompassing national syndicate, no markets or firms (Lindblom 1977; Wu 2010). China's reformers needed to tackle two tasks simultaneously: state-building and market-building. In this light, the tremendous challenges and the sea changes brought by China's reforms make the Reagan–Thatcher 'Rolling back the state' programmes look almost like sideshows.

Meritocratic Bureaucracy

To maintain central control, the emperor Wudi (185–87 BC) of the Han Dynasty (202–220 BC) sanctioned Confucianism as the state ideology. Wudi founded an imperial academy for training *shidafu* (scholar-officials). The Tang Dynasty (618–907) further institutionalized the national civil-service examination system, gradually dispensing with nepotic 'recommendation' and 'sponsorship' practices. Training and examination were based on Confucian classics that covered history, literary, ethics, political thought, law and official conduct, but left most minutiae of office duties to be learned from experience (Kracke 1964, p. 325). Wang Anshi (1021–86), a chancellor in the Song period (960–1279), when launching large-scale socioeconomic reforms, systematically consolidated the selection, motivation and evaluation of state officials (Drechsler 2013). Such a Weberian bureaucracy of premodern times ensured that the state not only enjoyed the best possible professional functionaries, but also firmly controlled the ideas of society, both fundamental to effective governance of the vast empire. The Tang emperor Taizong (589–649) commented on the civil-service system, 'All the heroic and the capable under heaven are now in my pockets'. This being achieved, 'the exclusion of the people from government was regarded as a positive virtue' (Jacques 2009, p. 207). Thanks to the capable and disciplined bureaucracy, the authority of the state had no rivals; the 'Western concern' of the state, formally sharing power with the Church, the nobility, the merchant class or civil society, was in the Chinese eyes intellectually irrational and ethically wrong (Shambaugh 2008). There was, however, a limit to the bureaucracy's rule. Markedly different from the European tradition of the 'divine right of kings' and the Japanese belief in an unbroken line of rulers, in China, when an emperor behaved badly he would lose the *Tianming* (Mandate of Heaven), and be replaced, even legitimately killed (*Mencius*, 2/8; Perry 2001, p. 164; Tan 2011, p. 472). To serve the 'Son of Heaven' properly, therefore, scholar-officials had a moral duty to criticize the ruler's policies even at the risk of their own lives. Kracke (1964) comments: 'The longevity of China's political system must be credited in significant degree to the power and vigilance of the Censorate' (p. 321). Competence and virtue are hence the two legs of China's imperial bureaucracy.

Inherent Tensions

We focus on two key tensions and begin with intra-state relationships. China is a continental-size country with a huge population and significant climatic and geological variety (Naughton 2007, ch. 1). Governing such a country had to rely on a tall governmental hierarchy. The first emperor Qin Shi Huangdi's *junxian* (prefecture-county) administrative system (see Greel 1964) survived for over 2000 years because it was fit for purpose.[1] Nevertheless, 'the mountain is high and the emperor is far away': the centre's control weakened as it reached downward to lower levels. This generated the opportunity for local elites to advance agendas that might or might not converge with the centre's interests (Tipton 2007, pp. 114–21). The trouble was that, without the local elites, China was ungovernable, to such an extent that the state was 'comprised of competing levels of authority' (Rowe 1983, p. 76). Handling the central–local tensions had thus been a teething problem for all China's rulers, not least for those since the late-imperial era who pursued reformist agendas for the enhancement of national power (Cohen 1988). Then there was the tension between the market economy and state monopoly. China was, until the late Qing era (1644–1912), the most advanced economy in the world, an economy based on specialized households and workshops, vibrant merchant undertakings and competitive markets, supported by functioning commercial–financial institutions (Hamilton 2006; Morck and Yang 2010; Naughton 2007, ch. 2; Tipton 2007, ch. 4).[2] The coexistence of a vibrant market economy and a powerful state sector was enabled by the Chinese instinct for family security via wealth generation (Redding and Witt 2007, ch. 4), on one hand, and the state's tolerance, however reluctant, towards private business in order to heal society (Wu 2013), on the other. The coexistence was, however, unstable, which laid bare the challenge facing China's rulers at all times – governing the relationship between state and society. The sudden global popularity of the 'governance' discourse in the 1990s serves only to invest the challenge with new urgency (Sigley 2006, p. 496).

Pragmatic Mindscape

Confucianism is a naturalist sociopolitical philosophy. The Master was not primarily concerned with otherworldly affairs; instead, he committed himself and persuaded the rulers to solve here-and-now social (governance!) problems by civilized means (Ames and Rosemont 1998; Li 1985). Confucius famously said: '*Dao bu yuanren*' (*Tao* is not far from man) (*Zhongyong*, 13); '*weineng shiren, yanneng shigui*' (Before serving the human, how can one serve the spirit?) (*Analects*, 2/11). While knowledge is highly valued, it is to be generated through this-worldly practice. Ban Gu (32–92), a Han Dynasty scholar, wrote: '*shishi qushi*' (seeking truth from facts). The purpose is not to gain knowledge *per se* but to act on it wisely (Nonaka and Zhu 2012, pp. 26–9). Lin Yutang (1895–1976), a popular writer, compared the West-East ways thus: when come across an unknown animal, to a Westerner the instinct question was 'what is this?' whereas to a Chinese that would be 'how to cook it?' (Lin 1935). Solving real-world problems, the wise do not begin with abstract necessities, absolute principles or proven models: *zi juexi* (The Master was free from four things: preconceptions, predeterminations, obstinacy and egoism) (*Analects*, 4/10). Instead he would start with situated particulars that were taken to be forever transitional. Standing on the riverbank, The Master sighed: *shizhe ruxi fu* (Isn't life's passing just like this, never ceasing day or night!) (*Analects*, 9/17). Living in a world with *wurong wuze* (no fixed shapes nor settled rules) (*Huannanzi*, 9/1/2), flexibility, adaptability and tolerance to ambiguity are great virtues, and one needs to embrace diversity, seize upon opportunities, invent unorthodox means and adjust objectives (Nonaka and Zhu 2012, ch. 6). Confucianism is an ideology without ideological obsessions; historically it has enriched itself by incorporating Taoist and Buddhist teachings (Fung 1948, ch. 1). Such a pragmatic mindscape has great political significance. Kracke commented decades ago: 'Doctrinal ambiguity thus allowed scope for experiment and adaptation without fatal damage to ideals that might be unrealisable immediately' (1964, p. 317). It is the enduring Confucian practical philosophy that Deng and his reformist alliance skilfully turned into a powerful weapon so as to combat the Maoist ideology that still enjoyed status as official doctrine (Heilmann 2008a, 2008b; Pye 1988).

In the next section, we shall, based on the above legacies, explore a 'home-grown rationale' and a 'longer temporal perspective' (Li 2014, p. 11), which will allow a better-informed analysis of China's contemporary reforms.

RATIONALE AND TENDENCY

Following Redding (2002), we use the term 'rationale', taken as a core component of a culture, to encompass the purposes that give a society a set of reasons for doing things (on the basis that the lens through which a people sees reality implicit in it) with shared ideals of action and models of institution (see also North 1990).

In the Confucian conception, humans live in a dynamic web of relations: with the world, with the mind and with others.[3] We may call the triadic relations *wuli*, *shili* and *renli* respectively, abbreviated to WSR. As elaborated in the *Daxue* (*Great Learning*), a chapter in a classic *Liji* (*Book of Rites*), the sages governed the triadic relations beneficially through 'eight exemplary doings'. The 'doings' are usually grouped by modern writers into three clusters: *gewu* (investigating things), *zhizhi* (extending knowledge); *chengyi* (being sincere), *zhengxing* (rectifying the mind), *xiushen* (cultivating character); and *qijia* (managing the family), *zhiguo* (governing the state), *pingtianxia* (pacifying the world) (see, e.g., Chan 1963; Chen 1986; Cheng 1972).[4]

Li as a noun denotes texture, pattern, reason, and so on, which can be actual as well as virtual, for example the texture of jade, methods of inquiry or patterns of conduct. As a verb it means to engage, care, order, manage, serve, govern and so on. In the 'highly suggestive' Chinese tradition (Fung 1948, p. 14), the openness and richness of the meaning of *li* is not unusual. This also applies to *wu*, *shi* and *ren*. In the following we explore in a constructive mode the implications of WSR to governance.[5]

Wu means things, objects and structures that constitute 'the world', that is, differentiated from and interacting with human agents. *Wu* are 'actual' and 'objective' in the sense that, natural or man-made, once in place they facilitate or frustrate our actions irrespective of varied interpretations until we have the chance and ability to change them. Accordingly, *wuli* are the mechanisms that underpin the working of *wu*. *Wu* and *wuli* can be resources or constraints on human actions, depending on circumstances and our skills. Dealing with *wuli*, we act on technical rationality in order to achieve efficiency. In the search for good governance, an obvious task is hence to build (or enhance) a robust PA infrastructure, which usually involves reconfiguring bureaucracy structures, transforming government functions and establishing (or improving) rational–legal institutions.

Shi denotes human engagement with 'the world'. Accordingly, *shili* is about our capacity to act, about the habits and tendencies in which we cope with life's problems. It concerns worldview, learning ability and professionalism. Public administrators are not robots whose only role is to execute instructions; they are problem-solvers who need to interpret unfolding particulars, make situated judgements, mobilize usable resources and generate workable solutions so as to get jobs done amid usually conflicting goals and unstable conditions. Governance with *wuli* infrastructure alone in the absence of *shili* competence is like running an engine without oil in it: however well the engine is designed, it will not work properly. In light of *shili*, reforming PA aims to enhance the governance capacity of the public as well as the administrators.

Ren is about human relations. At the heart of Confucianism is how to act properly in the web of expectations, obligations and reciprocities. *Renli* concerns values, ideals and ethics, and highlights the moral aspect of human life. It is about responsibility and accountability, trust and legitimacy, that is, the 'Mandate of Heaven'. In light of *renli*, good governance demands that *wuli* infrastructure and *shili* competence be geared to serve the higher purposes of the society. At the individual level, good governance relies on public administrators' discipline, honesty and integrity. At the supra-individual level, there must be high-standard responsibility and credible accountability of governments. Over and above 'How to manage?' we must ask 'To what end?'. It is good *renli* that gives the administration machinery a worthwhile purpose and grants it legitimacy.

WSR is not intended to consist of rigorously separated categories that capture the essence of the universe. Instead, it is better understood as heuristic pointers to structure our investigation of what has been done in the search for good governance, how it was done and why, as well as ideal directions. As indicated in Figure 13.1, between *wuli, shili* and *renli* there are complex mutual interactions. For example, *wuli* rational–legal institutions may help to nurture clean and effective government (as the World Bank once assumed); yet it can be used as a convenient tool by self-seeking rulers to round up dissenting activists and political rivals, or by the rich and powerful to protect their wealth of dubious origins (as still happens

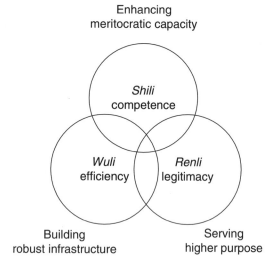

Figure 13.1   WSR as a rationale for good governance and public administration reform

around the world). Another example is transparency. Transparency is obviously at the core of *wuli* institutions, but even in 'mature' societies politicians and social 'servants' can still obscure transparency with skilled cover-ups. Without good *renli*, transparency remains elusive. To grasp the complex effects of *wuli* reforms we need to look at the matter from *shili* and *renli* perspectives, and vice versa. Differentiation and interaction are the two sides of the WSR coin.

If we consider the historical process, we can see that since Guan Zi configured a state-dominant economy for the Qi state (eleventh century–221 BC), there were numerous reforms in China. In a broad perspective, what lessons can be learned from history? Wu's (2013) research draws attention to two inert tendencies and a cyclical pattern.

The first tendency is *jiquan* (concentration of power). From Guan Zi's statism within a small kingdom in the seventh century BC to Qin Shi Huangdi's grand unification in 221 BC and after, political power in China moved steadily towards the state through continuous experimentations, refinements and sophistications. Totalitarian state power was supported by four distinctive institutions: a *junxian* (prefecture-county) system by which the state controlled the entire bureaucracy personnel; a *zunru* (Confucianism worship) system that maintained the state's total domination in ideas; a *keju* (civil-service examination) system that co-opted the best talents to serve the state; and a *guoyou zhuanying* (state-monopoly) system that ensured that the state owned and controlled strategic sectors. Thanks to these four institutional pillars, the concentration of state power had obtained near perfection and become, according to the modern reformer Liang Qichao (1873–1929), a *gongli* (truth) in Chinese governance (cf. Wu 2013, p. 6).

The last institutional pillar, state-monopoly system, led to another enduring tendency: *yishang* (restraining business, more precisely 'restraining *non-state* business'). In Chinese governance, business is always political and *yishang* ensures that no capital in private hands be significant enough to challenge state domination. The rationale is to maintain national unity and stability. Without referring to *yishang*, 'government-function transformation' has little meaning. As a state policy, *yishang* effectively turned the government into an economic organization, institutionally *yumin zhengli* (competing with the public for profit). Four 'classic predicaments' followed. First, an institutionalized boundary between state and public, with the former controlling strategic upstream resource sectors and the latter struggling in downstream markets. Second, public interests were granted by the ruler's goodwill, not protected by laws, whereas the state's legitimacy to rob the public was beyond question.[6] Third, monopolistic state enterprises gave rise to a persistent *guanshang* (official-businessman) model characterized by rampant rent-seeking and extreme wealth concentration, in which economic assets failed to grow via technological innovation, only to be appropriated via state-controlled distribution. All this led to the fourth predicament: private businesses lacked incentives for reinvestment, and business profits tended to be used for hedonic consumption.

These two tendencies have underpinned the history of Chinese governance, no matter what ideology or polity the regimes adopted, from the imperial to the republican to the nationalist and the communist. But there was always, and still is, an inherent tension: although useful for maintaining national unity, exclusive state power is incompatible with political independence and business autonomy of the public, which are fundamental to sustained economic development. The rulers' governance over this inherent tension had been largely similar, resulting in decentralizing/loosening–(re)centralizing/tightening cycles. To begin with, compelled by the need to heal the economy in the aftermath of internal rebellions, foreign invasions or natural disasters, rulers loosened control so that businesses could be revitalized from below. This quickly brought an economic boom and generated wealth. Before long, local elites became too powerful *vis-à-vis* the state. In the name of stability, the state then reconcentrated power and tightened control. The result was a 'strong' state, a weakened society, but also a deteriorated economy. Societal instability and crisis followed. This completed a full cycle, and the next round began. How to break away from such a fatal pattern remains a fundamental challenge to China's reformers.

EFFORTS AND CHALLENGES

In China's official narrative post-Mao, PA has undertaken six rounds of reform, and scholars have used varied schemata to analyse the reform agendas. For example, Ngok and Zhu (2007) discern three stages: institutional reconfiguration; functional transformation; and reshaping government's response to globalization; Xue and Zhong (2012) focus on four aspects: government function; organizational structure; personnel management; and operations management; Cheung (2012b) presents five elements: restructuring and downsizing; cadre management and civil-service system; fiscal reform; decentralization; and anti-corruption. Based on and moving beyond these views, we structure the reforms in accordance with the WSR rationales. Table 13.1 is a brief summary of the official agendas, with the far-right column indicating a tentative WSR mapping of the rationales that underlie the agendas (i.e., is a specific agenda intended to improve rational–legal *wuli* institutions, to enhance administrators' *shili* capacities, to redefine state–society *renli* relations, or some form of combination?). Table 13.2 then groups the reform efforts under WSR headings in order to investigate why the agendas are chosen, what has been gained and what is missing, as well as problems and challenges.

Without claiming to be strictly scientific, the WSR mapping presented in Tables 13.1 and 13.2 displays significant inroads in terms of the triadic WSR rationale. The six rounds of reform demonstrate China's determined experimentation to 'establish a market-based economic system, to separate government from specific economic activities, and to facilitate China's integration with the global economy' (Xue and Zhong 2012, pp. 299–300). As an overall outcome, China has in the past decades (re)built an effective administration machinery, evidenced by the state's increasing abilities to maintain order, generate wealth, improve living standards, respond to disasters, co-opt non-state agencies and project national power.

However, the mapping also reveals considerable imbalance. To begin with, *wuli* efficiency and managerialism appear to feature heavily in each and every reform round: restructuring the state apparatus; downsizing bureaucracy personnel; rationalizing government functions; setting up e-government channels; passing a great number of laws; and strengthening enforcement bodies (Cheung, 2012b; Christensen et al. 2008; Ngok and Zhu 2007; World Bank 2012; Xue and Zhong 2012; Zhang 2009). In itself the insistent *wuli* effort is understandable given the tremendous task

Table 13.1   *Major efforts in China's post-Mao public administration*
reforms

Rounds of reform	Reform agendas		WSR mapping
Round 1: 1982–	1.1	Downsizing (e.g. State Council organs reduced from 100 to 61)	W
	1.2	Streamlining	W
	1.3	Reorganizing	W
	1.4	Increasing professionalism of public servants; imposing an age limit on government positions	S
	1.5	'Fiscal contracting' system	W–R
Round 2: 1988–	2.1	Downsizing (e.g. State Council organs reduced from 72 to 65)	W
	2.2	Government function reorientation	W
	2.3	Envisioning separation of the party apparatus from the government	W–R
	2.4	Envisioning separation of the government from enterprises	W–R
	2.5	Envisioning separation of 'professional officers' from 'political officers'	S–R
	2.6	Setting up Ministry of Personnel in charge of cadre system	S
	2.7	Setting up Ministry of Supervision in charge of cadre performance	S
Round 3: 1993–	3.1	Merging and downgrading of State Council organs (from 86 to 59)	W
	3.2	Reducing central government personnel by 20%	W
	3.3	Reducing number of specialized economic ministries and departments	W
	3.4	Setting up Provisional Regulations of State Civil Servants	S–R
	3.5	'Tax-sharing' system	W–R
	3.6	Establishing Company Law	W–R
	3.7	Enterprise corporatization	W–R
	3.8	'Grasping the large, letting go the small' restructuring	W–R
Round 4: 1998–	4.1	Streamlining, downsizing and merging (State Council organs reduced from 59 to 53; constituent departments from 40 to 29)	W
	4.2	Number of central-level civil servants halved	W

Table 13.1   (continued)

Rounds of reform	Reform agendas		WSR mapping
Round 1: 1982–	4.3	Strengthening macro-control ministries (e.g. renaming State Planning Commission as State Development and Planning Commission with reduced focus on long-term development planning and macro-management functions)	W
	4.4	Eliminating the 15 industrial ministers	W
	4.5	Further corporatization	W–R
	4.6	Strengthening law enforcement/supervision departments and reinforcing their functions	W
	4.7	Functional reorientation	W
	4.8	Enhancing role of government in social security and services (with establishment of Ministry of Labour and Social Security)	W–R
	4.9	Rural 'tax for fee' fiscal reform	W–R
Round 5: 2003–	5.1	Transforming government's role from micro-management to macro-management	W
	5.2	Strengthening state assets management system (establishing State Assets Supervisory Commission)	W-R
	5.3	Improving macroeconomic control and regulatory regime (establishing State Development and Reform Commission)	W
	5.4	Unifying domestic trade and foreign trade regime (establishing Ministry of Commerce)	W
	5.5	Stepping up food safety and production safety regulatory regime in light of outbreak of SARS and food and production safety scandals (establishing State Food and Drugs Supervisory Administration and upgrading the State Production Safety Supervisory Administration)	W
	5.6	Promulgating Civil Service Law	S
	5.7	Abolishing agricultural tax	R

Table 13.1 (continued)

Rounds of reform	Reform agendas		WSR mapping
Round 6: 2008–	6.1	Separating government function into decision-making, execution and supervision	W
	6.2	Adopting 'super-ministry' model (reducing ministries and ministry-level organs to 27)	W

Source: Adopted from Cheung (2012b); Dong et al. (2008); Ngok and Zhu (2007); Xue and Zhong (2012).

Table 13.2 *Mapping WSR rationale, official rhetoric and reform efforts*

Rationale	*Wuli* efficiency Building robust infrastructure	*Shili* competence Enhancing meritocratic capacity	*Renli* legitimacy Serving higher purpose
Official rhetoric	*Tizhi gaige* (reconfiguring structures) *Jingjian jigou* (downsizing structures) *Zhengfu zhineng zhuanhuan* (transforming government functions) *Yifa zhiguo* (governing by law)	*Tigao zhizheng nengli* (enhancing governance capacity) *Tigao zongti suzhi* (increasing overall quality) *Gongwuyuan de gao sushi* (social servants' high quality)	*Yiren weiben* (people first) *Hexie shehui* (harmonious society) *Kexue fazhan* (scientific development) *Guotui minjin* (the state retreats, the public advances)
Reform efforts	1.1, 1.2, 1.3, 1.5, 2.1, 2.2, 2.3, 2.4, 3.1, 3.2, 3.3, 3.5, 3.6, 3.7, 3.8, 4.1, 4.2, 4.3, 4.4, 4.5, 4.6, 4.7, 4.8, 4.9, 5.1, 5.2, 5.3, 5.4, 5.5, 6.1, 6.2	1.4, 2.5, 2.6, 2.7, 3.4, 5.6	1.5, 2.3, 2.4, 2.5, 3.4, 3.5, 3.6, 3.7, 3.8, 4.5, 4.8, 4.9, 5.2, 5.7

facing the reformers – to (re)build a Weberian PA on the debris of Mao's total destruction of the state bureaucracy. The official rhetoric (listed in Table 13.2 under the *wuli* heading) clearly reflects the ruling elites' sense of urgency, and the determined efforts have produced impressive PA efficiency that China can showcase with justifiable pride.

Meanwhile, *shili* and *renli* reforms have been problematic. In the early years, under the slogan of *jiefang sixiang* (emancipating the mind), the Chinese leadership appeared to favour all-embracing reforms, which quickly gained wide support from the society (Ma and Ling 1998; Yang 2007). This allowed the then Party General Secretary Zhao Ziyang to pronounce at the 13th Party Congress in 1987 an ambitious agenda: separating the party from government; separating government from enterprises; and separating government from society (Agendas 2.3, 2.4 and 2.5; see Table 13.1). Zhao's agenda suffered a prompt rupture due to the Tiananmen Square Incident in 1989. In the shadow of *wending yadao yiqie* (stability over everything else), PA reform since then has experienced twists and turns (Cheung 2012b, pp. 265–6; Xue and Zhong 2012, pp. 293–4). On the *shili* front, in the early 1980s Deng Xiaoping introduced the *sihua* (four modernizations) criteria for cadre selection: revolutionary (reform-minded); younger; better educated; and professionally competent (Zhong 2003, p. 109); and if Zhao succeeded, 'professional officers' (career bureaucrats) would be separated from 'political officers' (politicians) and be appointed based on professional qualities, not party loyalty (Burns 1989). Post-Tiananmen politics put all this on hold (Chan 2010). The promulgation of the Provisional Civil Service Regulations in 1993 (Agenda 3.4) reaffirmed the *dang guan ganbu* (party managing cadres) principle, replaced the separation between politicians and bureaucrats with the division between 'leadership' and 'non-leadership' positions. Then the Civil Service Law (passed in 2005, effective 2006) (Agenda 5.6) finally institutionalized the bureaucracy's royalty to the Party, according to which social servants

> shall conform to the guidance of Marxism-Leninism, Mao Zedong Thought, Deng Xiaoping Theory and the important thought of Three Represents, follow the basic line of the primary stage of socialism, observe the line and policies of the Communist Party of China on cadre matters and adhere to the principle that the Party exercises leadership over cadre matters. (Civil Service Law, Article 4)

In theory and in practice, therefore, the imperial meritocracy of 'competence and virtue' is transformed into a peculiar form of technocracy: 'professionally competent and politically obedient to the party' (Cheung 2012b, p. 266). Despite the official rhetoric (listed in Table 13.2 under the *shili* heading), *shili* enhancement is largely symbolic (Chou 2004) and leaves a 'governance-capacity deficit' (Wang 2003, p. 41). It is a reversal, instead of an advancement, of the internationally envied Chinese bureaucracy tradition. This reflects a fundamental tension in the leadership's handling of *renli*: legitimacy in terms of what? Supposing a well-trained and disciplined PA indeed emerges from the reforms, to whom should it be accountable: the society or the one-and-only party? In imperial times the answer was relatively clear; in the era of 'modernization' it is less so. At the 13th Party Congress in 1987, the China leadership appeared to engage with these critical questions (Agendas 2.3, 2.4 and 2.5), and in the early 1980s Deng Xiaoping envisaged wider and deeper political reforms.[7] But since then reluctance and ambivalence have prevailed. The timid appearances of official *shili* and *renli* agendas skim the surface of the no-go area and limits of the current reforms. In a popular phrase in contemporary Chinese political discourse, this is the *shenshuiqu* (deep-water zone) that the current reformers will be unable to avoid for long.

In retrospect, post-Mao reform has gone through two distinct phases, with the mid-1990s as the turning point (Huang 2008; Wang 2003; Wu 2010; Wu 2013). Viewed from a broad historical perspective, the trajectory conforms to the decentralizing/loosening–(re)centralizing/tightening grand cycle along the *jiquan* (concentration of state power) and *yishang* (restraining non-state business) historical tendencies. This is evident in fiscal-taxation reforms and industry restructuring.

In the early phase, a *caizheng baogan* (fiscal-contracting) system was adopted in the 1980s (Agenda 1.5) that allowed local governments to retain revenues after reaching an agreed target. Incentivized by the system, local governments rapidly increased their revenue by promoting local economies and 'off-budget revenue' measures. Meanwhile, the centre's fiscal revenue declined steadily, down from a 34 per cent budgetary share of GDP in 1978 to 10.8 per cent in 1995. Then, in the second phase, a sweeping fiscal-taxation reform in 1994 replaced the revenue remittance mechanism with a *fenshuizhi* (tax-sharing system) (Agenda 3.5). The new system assigned different categories of taxes between the central and local governments so that the centre first collected the bulk of revenues and then shared it with the locals. This dramatically boosted the centre's share of revenue: within one year the central fiscal revenue jumped from RMB95.7 billion yuan to 290 billion yuan, while local revenue dropped from 339 billion to 231 billion (Chen and Chun 2004, pp. 93–4). The centre now controls over 50 per cent of all revenues, and leaves local governments waiting for rebates (Naughton 2007, pp. 430–36). This puts the central government in a strong position *vis-à-vis* locals, and hence completes a decentralization–(re)centralization cycle along *jiquan* (Wu 2013).

In 1995, according to State Council data, over 40 per cent of state enterprises were in the red, with an average debt rate of 78.9 per cent; the 2600-strong core state enterprises possessed 264.4 billion yuan of assets while accumulating 200.7 billion yuan debt. Since then, the situation has changed beyond recognition. By the end of 2012, the 120 *yangqi* (state enterprise under the State Assets Supervisory Commission) with 31.2 trillion yuan assets realized 22.5 trillion yuan revenue. To put the performance in perspective, the figures for the private sector are 10.9 million enterprises, 31.1 trillion yuan of assets and 20.1 trillion yuan of revenue. It is a game of one state enterprise versus 100 000 private enterprises, and the state appears to be winning: of all the assets of the *Chinese 500* enterprises in 2006, the state owns 98.36 per cent (Wu 2013, p. 226). State enterprises today are not just powerful; they are extremely profitable, with return on assets increasing from 0.7 per cent in 1998 to 6.3 per cent in 2006 (*The Economist* 2012, p. 4). The five state banks alone earned a profit of 1 trillion yuan in 2012, twice that of the top 500 private enterprises as a whole (Wu 2013, p. 226); 'By profit, Chinese banks take the top four places in the global league tables' (*The Times* 2013).

The change of fortune is the result of dedicated *yishang* agendas in the second reform phase: the establishment of the Company Law in 1994, the subsequent *gongsihua* (corporatization) programme, the *zhuada fangxiao* (grasping the large, letting go the small) policy in 1997 and the establishment of the State Assets Supervisory Commission in 2003 (Agendas 3.6, 3.7, 3.8, 4.5 and 5.2). These powerful means enable the central government to focus attention on the largest state firms, bundle them into even larger enterprise groups, and refinance them with domestic and overseas capital while keeping them firmly under state control. Under the somewhat misleading *guotui minjin* (the state retreats, the public advances) rhetoric (see Table 13.2 under the *renli* heading), state firms withdrew from competitive downstream sectors while consolidating their domination in upstream 'commanding heights'. This allowed the state to control the economy without competing directly with the private sector. Meanwhile, in 'letting go the small', local authorities were given free rein in closing down and selling off loss-making state enterprises. As the reform proceeded, private enterprises found themselves blocked from entering profitable sectors while struggling for knife-edge margins in downstream markets. To achieve such 'profitable state monopoly' (Huang 2008, p. 240), a price had to be paid: state firms laid off 40 per cent of the workforce and tens of billions of foreign reserves were used to fill the state-sector black holes (Naughton 2007, p. 301; Wu 2013). The state does not retreat; it merely regroups (Sigley 2006).[8] The thousands-year-old *yishang* tendency is in full play. If the early reforms were propelled mainly by *tizhi wai* (outside the system) innovation and growth (Wu 2010), the second phase reversed the market-promoting process, allowed the state to regain some sort of initiative and strengthen its capacity to 'govern the market'.

And what are the consequences? Despite the vast changes made in 'modernizing' the Leninist-Maoist state, China today is facing serious problems: extreme inequality; rampant corruption; total destruction of the moral bottom line; large-scale pollution; and alarming social unrest. National unity and stability, and the rulers' 'Mandate of Heaven',[9] are under severe test. Across the political spectrum in China there are no longer arguments about the problems; disagreements are squarely on solutions (Ma 2012). The critical question is: as official reforms have so far proved unable to pursue a WSR-balanced agenda while succumbing to *jiquan-yishang* tendencies, is it possible that governance in China will ever break away from the fatal historical cycle and, if so, where is the driving force?

AGENCY AND PROCESS

That the Chinese expect the government to take the lead is well known; less noticed is the fact that a similar mentality dominates the study of Chinese PA reforms. Official agendas and state politics occupy almost the entire research attention, whereas actions at the local level, if mentioned at all, are treated as implementing or resisting state directives. In the perceived zero-sum game, the state is the principal; below it are the agents. Should the locals comply fully, the centre's master plan would have succeeded. Here we have an agency deficit (Li 2006a; Zhu 2008). While it is quite true that in China 'the party act[s] as both the driver of reform but also the largest counterweight to more fundamental transformation' (Cheung 2012b, p. 277), ignoring the contribution of non-state agencies will leave our understanding of reform incomplete and a break from historical cycles unimaginable.[10] To illustrate this, the rural fiscal reform and the abolition of agricultural tax (Agendas 4.9 and 5.7) constitute a good case.

The official narrative runs like this. Due to Mao's industry-centred fiscal legacy, and as the country edged away from central planning in the 1980s, rural administration and public services were left unfunded. County and township finance in the 1990s deteriorated further when township–village enterprises were restructured into private enterprises, on the one hand, and the 1994 'tax-sharing' system greatly reduced the local portion of tax collected, on the other. How bad was the situation? A 1996 State Council Research Centre report estimated that 63 per cent of county governments were in debt; a 2001 Ministry of Civil Affairs report showed that the average township debt was 4 million yuan, while at that time a normal township annual budget was merely 1 to 2 million yuan. And the gap was growing: between 1986 and 1995, township government expenditure grew by 22.5 per cent per year, far exceeding the 15.6 per cent growth of budgetary income (Yep 2004, p. 56). Rural governments were steadily 'hollowing out' (Heimer 2004; Kennedy 2007).

To make ends meet, local governments resorted to *yusuanwai shouru* (extra-budgetary revenues). Subnational fees and surcharges collected as a percentage of GDP jumped from 2.6 per cent (23.3 billion yuan) in 1985 to 8.8 per cent (600 billion yuan) in 1996. By 1997, the total number of local fees reached 6800; a marriage registration, for example, would charge over 20 kinds of fee (Chen and Chun 2004; Yep 2004, pp. 46–7). At the same time, local governments minimized public services. Despite paying all the taxes and fees, peasants had to pay out of pocket for health services, some village schools were closed, and social welfare, water irrigation and public transport were depleted (Huang 2004; Li 2008, p. 260).

In these circumstances the rural *fei gai shui* (tax-for-fee) reform was the centre's strategy to discipline local officials and to reduce the peasants' burden. In September 1998 Party General Secretary Jiang Zemin realized the need to tighten controls on local extraction; in October the Party Central Committee Plenum endorsed rural fiscal reform as a national policy. In the same year, Premier Zhu Rongji announced a plan to allocate 20–30 billion yuan annually to finance the reform. A formal reform package was promulgated in 2000 and adopted nationwide from 2002–03. The package was designed to abolish the majority of rural fees, downsize township bureaucracy and rationalize public services. At the same time, agricultural tax was raised from 3 per cent to a cap of 7 per cent in order to compensate townships for their loss of fee/surcharge incomes. Central subsidy for township-bureaucracy downsizing was 24.5 billion yuan in 2002, increasing to 54.6 billion in 2004 and 78 billion in 2006. As local governments failed in their service duties, the central government had to step in: in the 2006 national budget, 340 billion yuan was allocated to rural public services; in 2007 and 2008 the figures climbed to 430 billion and 562 billion respectively (Li 2008, p. 260). In 2003 the Hu Jingtao–Wen Jiabao leadership announced the decision to phase out the tax on agriculture in five years. As the Chinese economy developed fast and the national financial situation improved, in 2006 the central government abolished agricultural tax and launched a *jianshe shehui zhuyi xin nongcun* (construct a socialist new countryside) campaign. Despite ups and downs, the centre was able to dismantle local distortions and steer the rural fiscal reform steadily to completion. Premier Wen Jiabao described the achievement as 'a result of central government's planning' (Li 2006b, p. 90).

There can be, however, other narratives. Chen and Chun (2004), for example, draw our attention to earlier events and local levels. The story begins with a humble man, He Kaiyin. When he was a young student in Beijing Agriculture University in 1957, Kaiyin was labelled a 'rightist' and packed to the far north. He worked on a farm for 20 years until returning to his birthplace, Anhui (a key agricultural province), after Mao's death. Instead of retreating into a mode of victimhood, Kaiyin committed himself to the first wave of reform. In those exciting days he befriended the prefecture party secretary Wang Yuzhao, who took a great risk to support the peasants' *dabaogan* (contracting farming to household) experiment, which eventually decollectivized rural China. When Wang was promoted to be the governor of Anhui, Kaiyin became a researcher in the provincial government. Then Wang was further promoted to be a rural-policy leader in Beijing. In 1988, Wang informed Kaiyin of a forthcoming national essay competition to commemorate a full decade of rural reform. Kaiyin was encouraged because he had things to say. After ten years, the liberating effect of *dabaogan* had diminished and rural China was in trouble. The waves of *nongmingong* (immigrant peasant workers) in (and since) the late 1980s signalled the magnitude of the problems: farming no longer generated income due to high price inputs; peasants became poorer because of proliferating local fees; and as youth labour left the land, agricultural output and productivity declined. Kaiyin submitted an essay to the competition, analysing the problems and arguing for further reforms. The essay won an 'excellent paper' award.

Then, in 1989, the political climate changed. Once a 'rightist', always a 'rightist', however: Kaiyin further turned his analysis into a proposal that would consolidate all rural taxes, fees and surcharges into a standardized agricultural tax, of which a certain portion would be used to finance local administration and beyond which no one could charge the peasants a penny. Kaiyin regarded this as a second *dabaogan*. He prepared to submit his proposal to the Central Rural Policy Research Centre where his friend Wang Yuzhao was vice director, only to be told that the Centre had been scrapped shortly after the Tiananmen Square Incident. He was also warned of criticism in Beijing against his award-winning essay.

Undeterred, Kaiyin determined to appeal directly to the centre. He sent his proposal to the Anhui Bureau of the Xinhua News Agency. Xinhua had a dual role in reporting news publicly and collecting intelligence for senior leaders. Kaiyin's proposal was reported in February 1990 in Xinhua's 'internal reference reports' and *People's Daily*'s 'internal supplements', and subsequently appeared in the State Council's 'reference bulletin'. In the aftermath of Tiananmen, however, no official would say a single word about it. Then, one year later, in February 1991, Kaiyin was called into Zhongnanhai, the headquarters of the party state in Beijing, to be informed that Premier Li Peng was interested in the proposal and suggested that Kaiyin put forward operable programmes. When Kaiyin asked for a written document or note, he was told that it would not be appropriate because that would turn the premier's vision into an official campaign. Kaiyin was encouraged to conduct pilot projects in Anhui. Three months later, he submitted to the Anhui government a refined proposal of ten detailed programmes. In the subsequent months Kaiyin received confusing signals from provincial leaders, simply unable to put his proposal into practice. He was merely a humble researcher, with no power to initiate experiment anywhere.

Deng Xiaoping's 1992 'Southern tour' changed that. That year, at a local meeting in Anhui, Kaiyin met the heavyweight rural policy advocate Du Runsheng, and passed to him his tax-for-fee proposal. Du was deeply impressed, but due to full engagements he introduced Kaiyin to Party Secretary Wang Zhaoyao of the Fengyang Prefecture. It was a historical coincidence: in 1978 it was the 18 Xiaogang village peasants in Fengyang who kicked off China's reform by secretly dividing farming between households. Wang took Kaiyin one level down the administrative hierarchy – the counties – to look for reform volunteers. Wang persistently distanced himself from any decision, but his appearance together with Kaiyin spoke volumes. They went to Yongshang and Woyang counties. In both places Kaiyin's proposal divided the county leadership sharply. Open-minded leaders enthusiastically embraced the proposal, whereas critics firmly rejected it. The critics had good reasons. The proposal was incompatible with existing laws and there were clear disapprovals from much higher authorities. China's taxation law was established in the heyday of Mao's Great Leap Forward in the 1950s, yet it was still the policy foundation in the 1990s despite the changes that had occurred since 1978. While reform is by definition changing the *status quo*, it is a risky undertaking until the *status quo* gets changed, and the absence of consensus increases immensely the risk of local-level reformers, particularly in circumstances where centralized authoritarianism is deep and strong. The Yongshang and Woyang experience reminded Kaiyin once again who he was, where he was and what he was doing.

Just as the county meetings ended in controversy, a breakthrough occurred below this level. In Xinxing Township, Secretary Liu Xingjie and Mayor Li Peijie worked out a simplified way to collect revenue through a one-off collection of combined taxes and fees. As township leaders, Liu and Li dealt directly with the peasants; they had long been troubled by the task of collecting numerous fees from the peasants, on the one hand, and the daily deepening plight of the villages, on the other. 'Risk?' Liu said to his colleagues. 'I am the son of a peasant and was born in Xinxing. If I only collect money and do nothing good, how can I look in the eyes of my parents and fellow villagers?' Liu and Li did not know Kaiyin; their work plan was inspired by the experience in Hebei Province and a report in *Nongmin Ribao* (*Peasants' Daily*). Led by Liu and Li, Xinxing officials presented their plan to the peasants. With their enthusiastic response, Liu and Li turned to county leaders for support. County Secretary Wang Baoming and Director Wang Binyu, who failed to gain consensus at the county level, lent their support to the Xinxing experiment. In November 1992 Xinxing People's Congress approved Liu and Li's plan, and on 1 January 1993 Xinxing embarked on a township-wide tax-for-fee reform.

The road ahead was still rocky and painful. Not long afterwards, Xinxing's reform was ordered to stop; other similar experiments faced the same fate. Kaiyin experienced repeated ups and downs. He was a reform hero on day one, a trouble-maker on day two, and would be listened to again on day three. He missed deserved salary increases and housing-reform benefits. In the low times, he began to drink and smoke; he was tortured by a burning concern for rural China on the one hand and his powerlessness to make a real difference on the other. In the end, the peasants' action spoke loudest. When Taihe County gave Kaiyin's proposal a try in 1994, the 300 000 peasant households in the 31 townships across the county completed paying tax within just five days, a phenomenon not seen in the history of the People's Republic. Before the reform, cadres had to chase for taxes and fees door to door, some using force, while even the cadres themselves were confused by the numerous taxes and fees. Now the peasants queued up at the township doors to pay their tax. Some cadres were moved to tears; they regained a sense of honesty, integrity and moral purpose: 'It is really a second liberation since *dabaogan.*' The effect: the peasants' burden decreased and the tax collected increased. By the end of 1994, tax-for-fee practice, still illegal, spread over 50 counties in seven provinces. After further setbacks and frustrations, on 30 December 1996 the Party and the State Council jointly issued the famous Document No. 13 that paved the way to making rural fiscal reform official. The rest appeared to be history. Since Kaiyin submitted his award-winning essay in 1988, 15 years had passed until his idea was adopted as a nationwide practice; as to the abolition of agricultural tax, 18 years.

Kaiyin was not alone. The stories of Yang Wenliang, a policy researcher in the Hebei provincial government, and Song Yaping, the party sec-retary of Xian'an District in Hubei Province, are as enlightening as Keiyin's (Fewsmith 2010; Li 2008). Former township Party Secretary Li Changping's open letter 'Telling the Truth to the Premier' and the two rural reporters' article, 'A survey of the Chinese peasants', shocked society: 'The peasants are really suffering, the countryside is really poor, and agriculture is really in danger.' A young peasant, Ding Zuoming, was beaten to death by local cadres because he dared to report to the authority corrupt fee-and-surcharge practices in the village; that was on 21 February 1993 in Lixin County of Anhui Province. Ding Zuoming's death touched society's conscience and put the peasants' plight in focus (Chen and Chun 2004). Before the central government decided to abolish the agricultural tax, in 2002 Shunde District in Guangdong Province chose to adopt the lower official rural tax rate; Anhui did the same, across the whole province. Guangdong went further in 2003, suspending the officially allowed 20 per cent surcharge on agricultural tax. These collective bottom-rate choices from below effectively made the centre's tax cap redundant, induced the centre to make frequent *post hoc* endorsements and eventually to abolish agricultural tax (Li 2006a).

So, who led the rural fiscal reform and who abolished the agricultural tax? The above narrative does not deny the role of the elites at the centre. Indeed, the reform bears the fingerprints of all the leaders at the highest level. Without their final approval, tax-for-fee would not have become an official policy with nationwide effects. More importantly, the elites' tolerance, and sometimes encouragement, allowed policy innovations to emerge, be refined and show beneficial effects. Seeking truth from the facts, between ideology and pragmatism the elites had made a wise choice. Unknowingly, they acted according to the Confucian practical tradition.

The point is that reforms are no longer the exclusive property of the elites. Without a master plan, the tax-for-fee reform emerged from the contingent interactions of the dispersed agency of the individual as well as collective actors across the societal hierarchy.[11] Recall Kaiyin, his met and unmet comrades, the kind and not-so-kind leaders, the officials at different ranks across regions, the writers and reporters who 'just did their job', the voiceless farmers, including Ding Zuoming, and the concerned public. Driven by different interests and motives, equipped with different experiences and resources, actors engaged in the reform at different places and different times. Their levels of commitment and attitudes towards risk also varied. Not surprisingly, their contributions differed dramatically. Nevertheless, it is their divergent, seemingly unconnected efforts that collectively moved the reform forward, not by design but contingently. Put another way, the reform invited the dispersed agency into action at different junctures and in different ways. While no one can design detailed outcomes by a magic stroke, the micro, flowing interactions of dispersed agency generate macro, consequential patterns. As actors were 'embedded' in 'legacies', for example the existing laws and the actors' experiences, the process was path-dependent and displayed continuity; yet the contingent twists and turns along the way allowed the actors to experiment, to innovate, to initiate changes and create new paths. Despite unforeseeable uncertainty and challenges ahead, it is from such a perspective of dispersed agency and contingent process that we see the possibility of breaking away from fatalistic historical cycles and of the emergence of good governance. In the end, Mao is right: the people, and only the people, are the driving force of history.

CONCLUSION: GOVERNANCE WITH CHINESE CHARACTERISTICS?

> if we want socialism to achieve superiority over capitalism, we should not hesitate to draw on the achievements of all cultures and to learn from other countries, including the developed capitalist countries. (Deng 1994, pp. 361–2)

Deng's prescription signals, at least to the Chinese, that the added value of the abstract convergence–divergence debate is diminishing. The interesting question now becomes: in what respects should PA follow common patterns or display continuing differences, and how? The WSR rationale may be a useful tool to construct hypotheses for empirical investigations. Since good governance cannot be based on inefficiency, rational–legal *wuli* imperatives are likely to generate similar agendas across countries. As to the *renli* aspect, convergence might be more complicated because societies differ in their ideal social models. But, even here, the *renli* rationale in itself may have global implications. The debt-ceiling deadlocks that paralyse Washington and the timid banking-sector reforms since 2008, for example, may reveal a *renli* deficit: governance in the world's most 'advanced' societies has lost its moral purpose. Furthermore, as Dong et al. (2008) illustrate, 'learning from the West' can be highly innovative. As post-NPM becomes less preoccupied with mergers and restructuring, in 2008 the elites in China sold the *dabuzhi* ('super-department' model) as 'latest international best practice' to the public and established it as the core agenda in the latest round of reform. Whether 'super-departments' actually deliver efficiency is a matter for empirical investigation; intriguing here is the skilled manufacturing of international solutions to locally perceived problems. Dong et al. call this 'biased contextualisation'. But is 'bias' always a bad thing, why does it occur, how should it be judged, and on what grounds? PA and governance should expect more, better-refined experimentation and inquiry.

Informed by historical legacies (first section), this chapter presents a home-grown rationale and a broad process perspective that allows us to analyse China's reform on its own terms (second section). Our analysis illustrates that, while momentous changes have occurred in post-Mao governance, official reforms largely fell short of efficiency–capacity–legitimacy balanced agendas while tending to conform to inert historical tendencies (third section). We can nevertheless be hopeful because reforms are no longer the exclusive property of the elites, and good governance will probably be the outcome of contingent interactions of dispersed agency actors (fourth section). China's reform has displayed historical continuity as well as skilful learning from the West, which will probably continue. We conclude this chapter with the idea that 'convergence' to a single model, of whatever kind, even if possible, will do humankind no good since, in an uncertain world, 'The society that permits the maximum generation of trials will be most likely to solve problems through time' (North 1990, p. 82).

NOTES

1. When China embarked on the recent reforms, under the central government there were 30 provinces and municipalities, most of which are bigger than an average European country, around 340 districts and cities, 2600 counties, and 48 000 communes (now townships).
2. Faure (2006) contents that it is 'almost exactly' these same institutions that proved inadequate for handling the scale of operations of modern enterprises therefore unable to grow the Ming-Qing Chinese 'sprouts of capitalism' into fruition, a view echoed by Redding and Witt (2007).
3. The 'last great Confucian', Liang Shuming, used a slightly different frame: relations with the world, with the self and with others (see Liang 2008).
4. The *Eight Exemplary Doings* is elaborated in Section 2 of the Preface of the *Great Learning* thus:

    The ancients who wished to illustrate illustrious virtue throughout the kingdom, first ordered well their own states. Wishing to order well their states, they first regulated their families. Wishing to regulate their families, they first cultivated their persons. Wishing to cultivate their persons, they first rectified their hearts. Wishing to rectify their hearts, they first sought to be sincere in their thoughts. Wishing to be sincere in their thoughts, they first extended to the utmost their knowledge. Such extension of knowledge lay in the investigation of things.
    Things being investigated, knowledge became complete. Their knowledge being complete, their thoughts were sincere. Their thoughts being sincere, their hearts were then rectified. Their hearts being rectified, their persons were cultivated. Their persons being cultivated, their families were regulated. Their families being regulated their states were rightly governed. Their states being rightly governed, the whole kingdom was made tranquil and happy.

5. For the WSR rationale in corporate and reform strategy see Nonaka and Zhu (2012); Zhu (2007).
6. For this point, see also Cohen (1988, p. 520); Goldman (1983, pp. 111–12); Kirby (1995); Nathan (1986, p. 114).
7. See, e.g., Deng's famous speech (13 December 1978), 'Emancipate the mind, seek truth from facts and unite as one in looking to the future' (http://english.peopledaily.com.cn/dengxp/vol2/text/b1260.html).
8. The nature of 'state retreat' is made clear insistently in Chinese government documents, public media and academic publications, such as the following:

> Any attempt to weaken government power and function is very dangerous. In the process of establishing a socialist market economy the function of the government must be strengthened. Of course the kind of strengthening that takes place must accord with and satisfy the demands of the market economy. (Zhang 1996, p. 19)

9. The Chinese Communist Party claims a self-granted *lishi shiming* (mandate of history) – the quasi-religion of Marxist historical materialism into which the developmentalist economic growth and global capitalism have in recent times been shrewdly incorporated (Nitsch and Diebel 2007, p. 977).
10. Compared with PA reform, non-state agencies are studied more keenly in relation to economic reforms; see, for example, Kelliher (1992); Nee and Opper (2012); Zhou (1996); Zhu (2008).
11. Garud and Karnøe (2005) use a slightly different term, 'distributed agency'. Considering that 'distributed agency' can be interpreted as being distributed by some specific actors, I choose to use the term 'dispersed agency' in order to avoid misunderstanding. 'Dispersed agency' is in my view closer to Hayek's (1945) 'knowledge in society' without distributor(s).

REFERENCES

Ames, R.T. and H. Rosemont (1998), *The Analects of Confucius: A Philosophical Translation*, New York: Ballantine Books.

Balazs, E. (1965), *Chinese Civilisation and Bureaucracy: Variations on a Theme*, New Haven, CT: Yale University Press.

Bays, D. (1976), 'Chang Chih-tung after the "100 Days": 1898–1900 as a transitional period for reform constituencies', in P.A. Cohen and J.E. Schrecker (eds), *Reform in Nineteen-Century China*, Cambridge, MA: Harvard University, East Asian Research Centre, pp. 317–25.

Burns, J.P. (1989), 'Chinese civil service reform: the 13th Party Congress proposals', *China Quarterly*, **120**, 739–70.

Caulfield, J.L. (2006), 'Local government reform in China: a rational actor perspective', *International Review of Administrative Science*, **72** (2), 253–67.

Chan, H.S. (2010), 'Envisioning public administration as a scholarly field in 2020: the quest for meritocracy in the Chinese bureaucracy', *Public Administration Review*, **70** (Special Issue), S302–S303.

Chan, W.T. (1963), *A Source Book in Chinese Philosophy*, Princeton, NJ: Princeton University Press.

Chen, G. and T. Chun (2004), 'A survey of the Chinese peasants', *Dangdai*, No. 6. (in Chinese).

Chen, L.F. (1986), *The Confucian Way: A New and Systematic Study of 'The Four Books'*, London: KPI.

Cheng, C.Y. (1972), 'Chinese philosophy: a characterisation', in A. Naess and A. Hannay (eds), *Invitation to Chinese Philosophy*, Oslo–Bergen–Tromso: Scandinavian University Books, pp. 141–66.

Cheung, A.B.L. (2012a), 'Public administration in East Asia: legacies, trajectories and lessons', *International Review of Administrative Science*, **78** (2), 209–16.

Cheung, A.B.L. (2012b), 'One country, two experiences: administrative reforms in China and Hong Kong', *International Review of Administrative Science*, **78** (2), 261–83.

Chou, B.K.P. (2004), 'Civil service reform in China, 1993–2001: a case of implementation failure'. *China: An International Journal*, **2** (2), 210–34.

Christensen, T., L. Dong and M. Painter (2008), 'Administrative reform in China's central government – how much "learning from the West?"', *International Review of Administrative Science*, **74** (3), 351–71.

Cohen, P.A. (1988), 'The post-Mao reforms in historical perspective', *Journal of Asian Studies*, **47** (3), 519–41.

Deng, X. (1994), *Selected Works of Deng Xiaoping*, Vol. 3: (1982–1992), Beijing: Foreign Language Press.

Dong, L., T. Christensen and M. Painter (2008), 'A case study of China's administrative reform: the importation of the super-department', *American Review of Public Administration*, **40** (2), 170–88.

Drechsler, W. (2013), 'Wang Anshi and the origins of modern public management in Song Dynasty China', *Public Money and Management*, **33** (5), 353–60.

The Economist (2012), 'Special report: State capitalism', 21 January.

Faure, D. (2006), *China and Capitalism: A History of Business Enterprise in Modern China*, Hong Kong: Hong Kong University Press.

Fewsmith, J. (2010), 'Institutional reforms in Xian'an', *China Leadership Monitor*, No. 33.

Fukuyama, F. (2011), *The Origins of Political Order: From Prehuman Times to the French Revolution*, New York: Farrar, Straus and Giroux.

Fung, Y. (1948), *A Short History of Chinese Philosophy*, New York: Free Press.

Garud, R. and P. Karnøe (2005), 'Distributed agency and interactive emergence', in S. W. Floyd, J. Roos, C. D. Jacobs and F.W. Kellermanns (eds), *Innovating Strategy Process*, Oxford: Blackwell Publishing, pp. 88–96.

Goldman, M. (1983), 'Human rights in People's Republic of China', *Daedalus*, **112** (4), 111–38.

Greel, H.G. (1964), 'The beginning of bureaucracy in China: the origin of the *hsien*', *Journal of Asian Studies*, **23**, 155–84.

Grieder, J. (1981), *Intellectuals and the State in Modern China: A Narrative History*, New York: Free Press.

Hamilton, G.G. (2006). *Commerce and Capitalism in Chinese Societies*, London: Routledge.

Hayek, F.A. (1945), 'The use of knowledge in society', *American Economic Review*, **35** (4), 519–30.

Heilmann, S. (2008a), 'Policy experimentation in China's economic rise', *Studies in Comparative International Development*, **43** (1), 1–26.

Heilmann, S. (2008b), 'From local experiments to national policy: the origins of China's distinctive policy process', *The China Journal*, No. 59, 1–30.

Heimer, E.M. (2004), 'Taking an aspirin: implementing tax and fee reform at the grassroots', paper presented at the Grassroots Political Reform in Contemporary China Conference, Fairbank Centre, Harvard University, 29–31 October.

Hood, C. (2005), 'Public management: the word, the movement, the science', in E. Perlie, L.E. Lynn and C. Pollitt (eds), *The Oxford Handbook of Public Management*, Oxford: Oxford University Press, pp. 7–26.

Huang, Y.S. (2008), *Capitalism with Chinese Characteristics*, Cambridge: Cambridge University Press.

Huang, Y.Z. (2004), 'Bringing the local state back in: the political economy of public health in rural China', *Journal of Contemporary China*, **13** (39), 367–90.

Jacques, M. (2009), *When China Ruled the World: The Rise of the Middle Kingdom and the End of the Western World*, London: Penguin.

Kelliher, D. (1992), *Peasant Power in China: The Era of Rural Reform, 1979–1989*, New Haven, CT: Yale University Press.

Kennedy, J.J. (2007), 'From the tax-for-fee reform to the abolition of agricultural taxes: the impact on township governments in north-west China', *The China Quarterly*, **189** (March), 43–59.

Kirby, W.C. (1995), 'China unincorporated: company law and business enterprise in twentieth-century China', *Journal of Asian Studies*, **54** (1), 43–63.

Kracke, E.A. (1964), 'The Chinese and the art of government', in R.C. Dawson (ed.), *The Legacy of China*, London: Oxford University Press, pp. 309–39.

Li, L.C. (2006a), 'Differentiated actors: central–local politics in China's rural tax reforms', *Modern Asian Studies*, **40** (1), 151–74.

Li, L.C. (2006b), 'Working for the peasants? Strategic interactions and unintended conse-quences in the Chinese rural tax reform', *The China Journal*, **57** (January), 89–106.

Li, L.C. (2008), 'State and market in public service provision: opportunities and traps for institutional change in rural China', *The Pacific Review*, **21** (3), 257–78.

Li, L.C. (2014), 'Multiple trajectories and "good governance" in Asia: an introduction', *Journal of Contemporary Asia*, http://dx.doi.org/10.1080/00472336.2013.871836.

Li, Z. (1985), *Commentary on the History of Ancient Chinese Thought*, Beijing: People's Press (in Chinese).

Liang, S. (2008), *An Overview of Oriental Scholarship*, Nanjing: Jiangsu Literature and Art Publishing House (in Chinese).

Lin, Y. (1935), *My Country and My People*, New York: Reynal & Hitchcock.

Lindblom, C.E. (1977), *Politics and Markets: The World's Political-Economic Systems*, New York: Basic Books.

Ma, L. (2012), *Eight Social Thoughts in Contemporary China*, Beijing: Social Sciences Academic Press (in Chinese).

Ma, L. and Z. Ling (1998), *Cross Swords: Documentary of the Three Thought-Liberations in Contemporary China*, Beijing: Contemporary China Press (in Chinese).

Morck, R. and F. Yang (2010), 'The Shanxi banks', Working Paper 15884, NBER Working Paper Series, Cambridge, MA: National Bureau of Economic Research.

Nathan, A.J. (1986), *Chinese Democracy*, Berkeley and Los Angeles, CA: University of California Press.

Nathan, A.J. (2003), 'Authoritarian resilience', *Journal of Democracy*, **14** (1), 6–17.

Naughton, B. (2007), *The Chinese Economy: Transitions and Growth*, Cambridge, MA: MIT Press.

Nee, V. and S. Opper (2012), *Capitalism from Below: Markets and Institutional Change in China*, Cambridge, MA: Harvard University Press.

Ngok, K. and G. Zhu (2007), 'Marketisation, globalisation and administrative reform in China: a zigzag road to a promising future', *International Review of Administrative Science*, **73** (2), 217–33.

Nitsch, M. and F. Diebel (2007), '*Guanxi* economics: Confucius meets Lenin, Keynes, and Schumpeter in contemporary China', *RAP Rio Jeneiro*, **31**, 959–92.

Nonaka, I. and Z. Zhu (2012), *Pragmatic Strategy: Eastern Wisdom, Global Success*, Cambridge: Cambridge University Press.

North, D.C. (1990), *Institutions, Institutional Change and Economic Performance*, Cambridge: Cambridge University Press.

Perry, E.J. (2001), 'Challenging the mandate of heaven: popular protest in modern China', *Critical Asian Studies*, **33** (2), 163–80.

Pye, L.W. (1988), *The Mandarin and the Cadre: China's Political Cultures*, Ann Arbor, MI: Centre for Chinese Studies, The University of Michigan.

Redding, G. (2002), 'The capitalist business system of China and its rationale', *Asia Pacific Journal of Management*, **19**, 221–49.

Redding, G. and M.A. Witt (2007), *The Future of Chinese Capitalism: Choices and Chances*, Oxford: Oxford University Press.

Rowe, W. (1983), 'Hu Lin-i's reform of the grain tribute system in Hupeh, 1955–1858', *Ch'ing-shi wen-t'i* (*Issues of Qing History*), **4** (10), 33–86.

Shambaugh, D. (2008), *China's Communist Party: Atrophy and Adaptation*, Berkeley, CA: University of California Press.

Sigley, G. (2006), 'Chinese governmentalities: government, governance and the socialist market economy', *Economy and Society*, **35** (4), 487–508.

Tan, S.-H. (2011), 'The *Tao* of politics: *Li* (rituals/rites) and laws as pragmatic tools of gov-ernment', *Philosophy East and West*, **61** (3), 468–91.

The Times (2013), 'China's banks put the rest in the shade', 1 July, p. 38.

Tipton, F.B. (2007), *Asian Firms: History, Institutions and Management*, Cheltenham, UK and Northampton, MA, USA: Edward Elgar Publishing.

Wang, S. (2003), 'The problem of state weakness', *Journal of Democracy*, **14** (1), 37–42.

World Bank (2012), *China 2030: Building a Modern, Harmonious, and Creative High-Income Society*, Washington, DC: World Bank.

Wu, J. (2010), *Understanding and Interpreting China's Economic Reform*, Shanghai: Far East Publishers (in Chinese).

Wu, X. (2013), *The Gains and Lost of Economic Reforms in China's History*, Hangzhou: Zhejiang University Press (in Chinese).

Xue, L. and K. Zhong (2012), 'Domestic reform and global integrations: public administration reform in China over the last 30 years', *International Review of Administrative Science*, **78** (2), 284–304.

Yang, K. (2007), 'China's 1998 administrative reform and new public management: applying a comparative framework', *International Journal of Public Administration*, **30**, 1371–92.

Yep, R. (2004), 'Can "tax-for-fee" reform reduce rural tension in China? The process, progress and limitations', *China Quarterly*, **177** (March), 42–70.

Zhang, K (1996), 'Establishing a socialist market economy requires strong government', *Chinese Administration and Management*, **2**, 17–23 (in Chinese).

Zhang, M. (2009), 'Crossing the river by touching stones: a comparative study of administrative reforms in China and the United States', *Public Administration Review*, **70** (Special Issue), 582–7.

Zhong, Y. (2003), *Local Government and Politics in China: Challenges from Below*, New York: M.E. Sharpe.

Zhou, K.X. (1996), *How the Farmers Changed China: Power of the People*, Oxford: Westview Press.

Zhu, Z. (2007), 'Reform without a theory: why does it work in China?' *Organisation Studies*, **28**, 1503–22.

Zhu, Z. (2008), 'Who created China's household farms and township-village enterprises: the conscious few or the ignorant many?', in G.T. Solomon (ed.), *Academy of Management Annual Meeting Best Paper Proceedings*, Washington, DC: George Washington University.

14. Capacity, complexity and public sector reform in Australia
John Halligan

INTRODUCTION

Developing government capacity to address complex and intractable problems has become increasingly a priority for Australian central government. The propensity to address complex capacity questions depends on the extent to which governments engage directly in institutional design and support its successful implementation. A public service system consists of different types of capacity, which may be utilized depending on government goals. Capacity for complex issues is a more specialized matter because it generally involves multiple actors and cross-boundary arrangements.

Capacity and reform are directly related, as invariably a major reform agenda encompasses capacity elements. However, different emphases have been accorded to capacity in reform agendas. In order to explore the emergent options, two narratives are identified. The first follows the trajectory of public sector reforms, and is both state-centric and inclined towards greater collaboration, even though the results have been underwhelming. A neoliberal narrative envisages a smaller role for government and greater reliance on third parties, and will dominate the immediate future.

The chapter examines several types and elements of capacity and how they relate to reform. A range of instruments is employed for basic coordination and collaboration to address complex problems. Narratives of reform suggest different ways of handling the design of the public service, with significant implication for capacity and complexity.

CAPACITY AND REFORM

Capacity is essentially the ability to organize and manage resources for making and implementing decisions, and has several elements: strategic focus and direction; system steering and integration; and capability (e.g. provision of expert staff and the means for implementation). Policy capacity can be seen as marshalling the appropriate resources to make decisions about strategic directions for allocating public resources, whereas administrative capacity addresses human and physical resources needed for delivering government outputs (Painter and Pierre 2005).

Capacity pertains to public organizations, public service systems and external relationships with third parties. The obvious agencies to both lead reform and to respond to complexity issues are those at the centre of government with responsibilities for policy, finance and human capital across the public service. At this system of macro-level frameworks, guidelines and cross-boundary leadership are important, including the overall capability of public officials. Under the Australian devolved system the department is highly important within portfolios, and interaction occurs within policy fields, and involves different forms of relationships and networks both inside the Australian public service (APS) and externally (Edwards et al. 2012).

Four variations on capacity can be distinguished, involving different aptitudes, and are employed for different purposes. For analytical purposes they are basically mutually exclusive, although in practice they may be used in combination. They vary according to whether capacity is being sought by strengthening the internal system or by an external-centred approach that relies on levering off third parties.

A focus on internal capacity essentially addresses management improvement and strengthening staff capability. A second approach concentrates on steering and features machinery of government, and particularly central agencies, departments of state and effectiveness questions. An external approach seeks to reduce dependence on internal capacity either by relying on external expertise through substituting third parties or relinquishing responsibilities outright, with efficiency objectives being prominent. A fourth approach, collaboration, involves inter-agency and inter-sector arrangements that enlarge and improve capacity.

Basic roles for supporting a reform agenda have been identified as system capacity, and capability and culture, as well as strategic direction and systemic performance. Fundamental failures in major reform of a public service system derive from the lack of sophisticated strategic focus and investment in capacity and cultural change, and the necessary management of system performance (Barber 2007: 337, 339).

AUSTRALIAN CONTEXT

Australian central government operates within a federal system where the main service delivery occurs at the state and territory level. This has major implications for how capacity is organized because of the mixture of autonomy (the state operates its own systems) and interdependence (most revenue flows through the Commonwealth). The national system remains a two-track one, with the state government accounting for the bulk of the expenditure, particularly in the major sectors (apart from defence), while the federal government combines national policy, some delivery and transfers.

Australia is one of the anglophone countries with an administrative tradition that readily adapted to a public management approach. The distinctiveness of the anglophone administrative tradition was reaffirmed during the reform era beginning in the 1980s, when Australia adhered more to precepts of new public management (NPM) than other OECD countries (OECD 1995; Pal 2012). The emergence of this distinctive set of reforms was facilitated by instrumentalism and pragmatism, which are features of this administrative tradition. It also reflected patterns of interaction that accorded legitimacy and relevance to initiatives within the group (Halligan 2010). Endogenous communication patterns have been influential through networks based on relationships developed between Britain and its former colonies, which have included staff exchanges and regular meetings of networks. The specialized networks are a prime source for the circulation of ideas and documentation of experience. For Australia, the long-standing relationship with the UK, which continues to furnish its head of state, is the most important source of reform ideas. Policy transfers may produce convergence of public sector reforms and isomorphism within the group, although the pattern is inconsistent and contextual factors usually intervene (Halligan 2013; Pollitt 2013). A recent example is the UK's system for capability review, which was adopted in a modified form by Australia (and New Zealand).

The latest Australian reform process was unusual in that it occurred amidst the international financial crisis, but was not essentially a product of it. The impact of the fiscal crisis on the Australian public sector was less than for other OECD countries, but was still highly significant for the budget. At the national level the consequences for dimensions of governance (central steering, leadership and capacity) and the evolution of public management were more far-reaching. The medium effect of Australia's superior trading position affected the private sector, lowered government revenue and guaranteed deficits for the foreseeable future. Under a government committed to reducing the role of the state while confronting budget issues, there are major implications for capacity to address complex problems.

Capacity in Reform

The Australian trajectory can be summarized with reference to phases of reform. Managerialism (Halligan 2007) best reflects the first phase in which management became the central concept and reshaped thinking as part of a paradigm change. This was succeeded by a phase that for a time came close to the mainstream depiction of new public management (NPM) (Hood 1991), in which the market element was favoured and features such as disaggregation, privatization and a private sector focus were at the forefront. Variations on state-centric governance became apparent in the 2000s through the renewed focus on modes of coordinating and control that were designed to confer greater coherence and central capacity on the public sector (Halligan 2006).

Management capacity
The initial period of reform in the 1980s, managerialism, displaced traditional administration with a package of reforms based on management and an emphasis on results rather than inputs and processes (Halligan and Power 1992). The main elements of the reform program focused on the capacity of the core public service (including the senior public service), new forms of management (e.g. financial), decentralization, commercialization and corporatization. The focus on results, outcomes and performance-oriented management dates from this time, although the emphasis was on program budgeting and management. There was also a major reorganization of the machinery of government that produced mega-departments in order to improve capacity.

Externalizing capacity
A strong commitment to neoliberal economic reforms in the 1990s led the public service to become highly decentralized, marketized, contractualized and privatized. The new agenda was centred on competition and contestability, outsourcing, client focus, core business, and applying the purchaser/provider principle. The private sector and market forces were closely related: the exporting of responsibilities to the private sector and/ or making the public sector subject to market disciplines; and the importing of business techniques combined with attempts to replicate market conditions internally. The agenda also covered a deregulated personnel system; a core public service focused on policy, contestability of the delivery of services with greater use of the private sector, and a new financial management framework that included outputs and outcomes reporting, and extended agency devolution to budget estimates and financial management.

Reducing central capacity
The devolution of responsibilities from central agencies to line departments and agencies was highly significant in the late 1990s, with a diminished role for central agencies being one consequence (Halligan 2006). The Public Service Commission's role was modest, while the Department of the Prime Minister and Cabinet interventions were constrained and were no longer providing overall public service leadership. The role of the Department of Finance also contracted substantially. The ascendancy of neoliberal reforms and NPM reached its apogee.

Strengthening internal capacity
A change in trajectory emerged in the 2000s, with an emphasis on state-centric and integrating governance, which had an impact on relationships within, and the coherence of, the public service, delivery and implementation, and performance and responsiveness to government policy. Four dimensions were important: resurrection of the central agency as a major actor with more direct influence over departments; whole of government as the stronger expression of a range of forms of coordination; central monitoring of agency implementation and delivery; and departmentalization through absorbing statutory authorities and rationalizing the non-departmental sector (Halligan 2006).

An underlying element was control: the use of programs to improve financial information for ministers; greater emphasis on strategic coordination by cabinet; controlling major policy agendas; the abolition of agencies and bodies as part of rationalization and integration; and monitoring the delivery and implementation of government policy. These measures increased the potential for policy and program control and integration using the conventional machinery of cabinet, central agencies and departments, as well as other coordinating instruments. The intensity of the Australian reassertion of the centre and the ministerial department resulted from both system shortcomings and environmental uncertainty and threat favouring the stronger centre. Underlying change was a state-centric focus on sorting out the architecture and processes of the system to provide for more effective government.

Refining internal and third-party capacity
A major reform agenda was instigated in 2010 with a new 'blueprint' plus a supplementary agenda on financial accountability. They represented both responses to capacity issues that emerged in the wake of previous reform, particularly in the late 1990s, and a basis for moving the overall agenda forward. Both have strong capacity elements. The review, *Ahead of the Game: Blueprint for the Reform of Australian Government Administration*,

raised significant questions about coordination and governance of agencies. The actual diagnosis suggested lack of capacity and accountability, performance weaknesses, and creeping bureaucratization and compliance issues (AGRAGA 2010). The other significant inquiry, the Commonwealth Financial Accountability Review (DFD 2012a), ranged widely over financial and related matters, including governance. The imperative for greater attention to capacity and capability weaknesses was underscored, and the rhetoric intensified about the need for collaborative governance with third parties.

Components of Capacity

Central agencies

Of the anglophone countries, Australia has emphasized a strong prime minister's department and enhancing the resources of the political executive. Although several models have been evident during the reform era (Halligan 2011), the long-term trend has been towards strengthening central steering to cope with greater complexity, but how effectively that potentiality is utilized depends on the political leadership.

As the key organizations in this realm, the central agencies have as their mandate whole-of-government and systemic responsibilities that cross the public service: the Department of the Prime Minister and Cabinet for policy, the Treasury for economic policy, the Department of Finance and Deregulation for financial management, and the Australian Public Service Commission (APSC) on human capital. Each has distinctive and complementary roles and is presided over by the source of power and policy direction in the machinery of government, the Department of the Prime Minister and Cabinet, although the Prime Minister's Office has assumed greater significance.

A strong central drive with implications for capacity has been based on the concept of 'One APS' to counter the devolution of responsibilities to departmental secretaries and to propagate the APS values. This devolution of responsibilities to line departments after 1999 had the effect of 'balkanizing' the APS as different conditions of service became prevalent and the identity of an employee's department was more important than their identification with the public service (AGRAGA 2010).

With this corrosion of system identity, 'One APS' resurfaced as a centrepiece for reconstructing consciousness and identity at the APS level (MAC 2005), and via the reform blueprint (AGRAGA 2010). The question of public service coherence and consolidation was strongly expressed through the mantra of 'One APS'. The lament across the service – the reasons differing between location and level – was of the limitations of a devolved agency structure. Chief executives and departmental secretaries had control over conditions of employment, which produced substantial variations in salary packages. The then head of the public service, Terry Moran (2009), asserted that there was 'one-APS, and . . . we need to bring more meaning to that statement. The APS is not a collection of separate institutions. It is a mutually reinforcing and cohesive whole.' The mobility of APS officers needed to be enhanced to enable movement across departments without loss of pay or conditions. This position was endorsed by the reform review through a recommendation to clarify and align employment conditions. This also informed the recommendation that departmental secretaries needed support from a unified APS-wide leadership group (AGRAGA 2010: 22).

A related dimension focused on collective action in pursuit of the reform agenda. The *Ahead of the Game* report identified a need to enhance leadership, talent management, and learning and development across the Australian public service (AGRAGA 2010). The responsibilities of the APSC in the reform process were strengthened and repositioned to take a leadership role for the APS and, as a central agency, engage in the provision of 'expertise, guidance, performance monitoring and some centralized services to agencies'. This would entail developing options for a common approach that included leadership and learning and development, with responsibilities including work-level standards, employment conditions and greater consistency across the APS (AGRAGA 2010: x). The APSC has worked to achieve greater commonality in terms and conditions across agencies, and to reduce disparities in order to facilitate mobility across the APS. The Commission oversaw the department bargaining of enterprise agreements to ensure consistency, which would also increase commonality of terms and conditions across the APS (APSC 2012: 14–15).

In addition, the Secretaries Board (comprising heads of departments) has been exercising the responsibility of stewardship with regard to the need to increase capacity and One APS (APSC 2012: 7). Central agencies have risen in significance, with stronger central roles and responsibilities for standards and guidelines. There is greater emphasis on collaboration with line departments. The Department of the Prime Minister and Cabinet has shifted its approach to working with departments on projects. Finance has also been exploring more sympathetic approaches, and conducted a highly consultative review of financial management accountability (DFD 2012b).

Departments of state: systemic coordination (at the macro level)
In the architecture of public organization, a significant trend has been the swing back to a more comprehensive ministerial department (Halligan

2006). This agenda for enhancing the department was given formal recognition through a review of corporate governance. The solution was to force all non-departmental agencies to operate according to one of two templates, a board model or a non-board structure. Ministerial departments acquired more direct control over public agencies in part to deal with the extent of non-departmental organizations, and questions about their governance. The emphasis on the department was expressed through rationalizing statutory authorities and extending control of agencies with hybrid boards that failed corporate governance prescriptions. The long-term result was a reduction in the number of agencies in the outer public sector (114 to 85 between 2003 and 2013) and an expansion in the number in the core public service (84 to 103).

The drive for the ministerial department was exemplified by the demise of Centrelink (see below). The largest department outside Defence was the Department of Social Security, a monolithic and functionally integrated organization that combined policy and implementation. In 1996, a new type of service delivery agency was created based on delivering services that accounted for about 30 per cent of Commonwealth expenditure. The Centrelink concept was of an agency that would merge the two networks for social security and unemployment acquired from departments that became its two major clients. Centrelink's mandate became that of a one-stop shop delivery agency providing services to purchasing departments (Halligan 2008). Centrelink was subsequently subsumed within a new parent department, the Department of Human Services, created to improve service delivery for six agencies. Centrelink was subsequently formally integrated within the department. The natural tendency of the Commonwealth has been to focus on the ministerial department, and this is entrenched as the default position. Accordingly, the cycle moved over 15 years from integrated department to multipurpose delivery agency to an integrated department. The circular process was complete in 2011 when Centrelink's absorption meant that it was reduced to a badge for customers.

Questions have also been raised about capability at the department and agency level. There are now systematic assessments from 17 departments' capability reviews, each based on an independent review panel of former senior public servants and consultants with a rating system that combined traffic lights and back-up judgements.[1] One of the most significant capability and performance gaps for the senior executive service (SES) and the SES feeder group was people management (AGRAGA 2010: 53). Also, surveys of employees have indicated low satisfaction with senior leaders as a continuing trend (JCPAA 2012: 14–15).

From the Australian capability review program of departments, the results across dimensions of leadership, strategy and delivery provide insights into strengths and weaknesses. For leadership, 76 per cent of agencies were 'well placed' (or better) in terms of motivating people, but 71 per cent were ranked as a development area (or worse) for developing people. These and other results indicated considerable variations in departmental assessments. The category 'staff performance management' ranked poorly in the assessments, with three-quarters of reviews rating agencies below the required level (APSC 2013: 215).

A significant clarification of the departmental secretary's role was the introduction of the stewardship function. According to the blueprint for reform (AGRAGA 2010), APS-wide stewardship was a core role of the secretary, and one that was 'discharged in partnership with other secretaries and the APS Commissioner'. Politicians' lack of strategic focus and 'short-termism' indicated that an alternative was needed to relying heavily on political direction. The stewardship role was designed for the public service to have 'the capacity to serve successive governments. A stewardship capability must exist regardless of the style of any one Minister or government.' Stewardship covered 'financial sustainability' and efficient resource management, as well as 'less tangible factors such as maintaining the trust placed in the APS and building a culture of innovation and integrity in policy advice' (AGRAGA 2010: 5).

Vertical and horizontal: Inter-agency: Horizontal management

The Australian system displays tensions between the strength of vertical accountability on the one hand, and the increasing scale of existing horizontal relationships on the other. Departments and FMA agencies have continued to have

> traditional structures with an emphasis on clear organisational boundaries and vertical hierarchical accountability. While it establishes some overarching whole-of-government principles, the current framework has a strong-willed focus on the operations of individual entities. The roles and responsibilities of chief executives . . . relate to the particular entities they are appointed to run, and do not directly consider concepts such as joint operations. (DFD 2012a: 36)

Nevertheless, views continue to be expressed that support horizontal approaches, collaboration and collective action, in particular by the major reform report *Ahead of the Game* (AGRAGA 2010), whose recommendations were endorsed by the government.

Independently of this impetus at the centre, a continuing momentum towards cooperation and coordination has been apparent, particularly as agencies sought solutions to delivery problems. There are over 1800 inter-agency agreements for 21 departments (i.e. all departments of state, plus two large agencies), 'signifying a breadth of cross agency activity and interdependencies' (ANAO 2010: 30). Of the 1800 cross-agency agreements in Australia, three types of services were provided by one agency for another. The first type was delivery services to the public (e.g. on behalf of a policy department, best exemplified by Centrelink). Second, there was provision of advice or data to another department (e.g. data collection and provision; expert advice to Murray–Darling Basin Authority). Third, there were shared services between two agencies (e.g. the provision of corporate services by one department to another; ICT services provided by DFAT to other agencies' overseas posts) (adapted from ANAO 2010: Table 1.1).

Then there were relationships that are of more relevance here: joint program implementation (e.g. shared oversight for delivering international climate change adaptation initiatives); and border security support (e.g. national security coordination between agencies whose roles are interdependent or complementary, such as border security functions by customs and DAFF) (ANAO 2010). Only one of the governance agreements (which take various forms, including memoranda of understanding, and service level and partnership agreements) is obviously closer to collaboration; the 'collaborative head agreement' defines 'high-level principles and obligations for a collaborative relationship between two or more agencies' (ANAO 2010: Table 2.1). For the purpose here, the survey of types of agreements does not go far enough in terms of specification of the collaborative relationships focused on accountability and outcomes. There is a shortage of evidence about the incidence and types of collaboration and what cases contribute in practice.

Capacity through collaboration and shared outcomes

Collaboration has been in vogue for some time but the term has been employed loosely and aspirationally by practitioners, and the results are modest (O'Flynn 2007). An incipient approach to sharing outcomes emerged from the review of Australian government administration (AGRAGA 2010), which recommended the introduction of shared outcomes across portfolios focusing on priority areas. Several elements were proposed for establishing shared outcomes involving the allocation of roles and responsibilities across portfolios based on high-level inter-agency agreements; and a transition process for moving from output structures to shared outcomes. Accountability for achieving shared outcomes would be through budget reporting against the outcomes, and monitoring by the Department of the Prime Minister and Cabinet's Cabinet Implementation Unit (AGRAGA 2010). However, it was unclear whether accountabilities and risks were also to be shared, and through what mechanisms. These issues needed attention if align-ment were to occur between collaboration, accountability and shared governance (Edwards et al. 2012: 235).

The sharing of outcomes in horizontal arrangements is handled in several ways. The standard set of distinctions between communication, cooperation, coordination and collaboration has been used for types of sharing, each successively denoting an elaboration of the relationship. Such a developmental perspective can also be represented by a range of informal and formal collaborative mechanisms and other characteristics of the relationship (ANAO 2007: 49). There are important distinctions between relationships where tasks are performed by one agency on behalf of another, and the application of what ANAO terms 'whole-of-government', which represents a significant step up (ANAO 2007: 48, 49). In confronting the question of sharing accountability and outcomes, the assumption is made that partners are involved as peers and that the focus is on outcomes. Shared accountability can be conceived of as the arrangements for specifying responsibilities and accountabilities within a collaboration based on a formal partnership. If a whole-of-government approach is envisaged, it is 'broader, involving collaboration at multiple levels, shared outcomes and a culture that values government priorities over those of a single department' (ibid.: 48–9).

The Department of Finance and Deregulation recognized the need for dual and multiple accountabilities, and for legislation that accommodates collective responsibility and multi-party accountabilities (DFD 2012b: 26). Partnering arrangements that involve individuals or organizations working towards shared objectives were advocated where the arrange-ments were among equals and entailed shared accountability. In contrast to standard contractual arrangements, partners have collective respon-sibility and each partner would have several accountability obligations, both horizontal and vertical (DFD 2012b: 26–7).[2]

The subsequent legislation, Public Governance, Performance and Accountability, has been critiqued for dealing with collective responsibil-ity and multiple accountabilities in a limited manner (ANAO 2013b: 8). The cautious legislative approach was regarded as failing to be ambitious and was therefore a missed opportunity.

A comprehensive system of shared accountability for system-wide results would require a recasting of aspects of governance as we know it. Without fundamental change, a durable systemic focus on shared results and accountability is unlikely. The main consideration is of course to institutionalize within governments principles and practices that provide for shared accountability based on outcomes. Within that framework,[3] different types of partnership can operate, providing of course that they are reflected at the political level and through parliamentary reporting and accountability.

There is therefore some evidence of movement towards collaboration, and some institutionalization, but this has yet to be capitalized on in terms of systemic action. In order to look more closely at incipient collaboration, three recent cases provide an illustration of processes in train and yet to be realized.

The first case, Project Wickenby, is a cross-agency exercise that has been depicted as providing a model for future taskforce projects (ANAO 2012a; DFD 2012a). It was established in 2006 as a cross-agency taskforce 'to protect the integrity of Australia's financial and regulatory systems by preventing people from promoting or participating in illegal offshore schemes' (ANAO 2012a: 10). Tax evasion crosses the boundaries of the responsibilities of many government agencies. Rather than individual agencies being responsible for key project tasks, the focus has been on enabling agencies to work together to achieve project outcomes. A joint taskforce was regarded as more likely to produce results, as more effective use could be made of agency expertise and capacities. Project governance and assurance processes and structures were designed by the taskforce to enhance collaboration and joint decision-making, and their formalization shaped the taskforce approach. Each agency also has its own agency-specific framework for delivering taskforce outputs. The Australian Taxation Office (ATO) is the lead agency for the project, and responsible for handling governance and assurance arrangements for the eight agencies.[4] The taskforce's work includes civil audits and risk reviews, criminal investigations, prosecutions and other legal action (ANAO 2012a: 92).

The second case is about coordinating whole-of-government arrangements for Indigenous services and programs. A major government commitment is to 'close the gap' in Indigenous disadvantage. The case shows the role of the Department of Families, Housing, Community Service and Indigenous Affairs operating within a coordination framework when the broader environment of ideas and practice has moved towards collaboration.[5]

The delivery of programs and services to Indigenous people involves complex networks and several thousand funding agreements, and requires 'an unprecedented level of cooperation and coordination . . . to integrate and improve service delivery for Indigenous people as well as the need for collaboration between and within Governments at all levels, their agencies and funded service providers'. Since multiple agencies have been involved in policy and delivery, an explicit lead-agency role was needed to ensure information was shared 'across agencies, to coordinate service delivery on the ground, to provide consolidated advice to Government and to address any systemic issues in a timely manner' (ANAO 2012b: 44). The enunciation of collaboration did not ensure that practice conformed where politics was involved. The department agreed to move from an approach centred on sharing information (coordination) towards one that drives whole-of-government, innovative policy development and service delivery; and involves collaboration, greater integration, and accountability that addresses outcomes (ANAO 2012b: 29, 45).

The third case involves the employment program, Working Age Payments, which covers income support delivered through a partnership between Department of Education, Employment and Workplace Relations (DEEWR) and the Department of Human Services (DHS). In 2012–13, DHS delivered an estimated \$19.8 billion of payments for programs administered by DEEWR (ANAO 2013a: 1–2). What is described as a partnership between DEEWR and DHS has been supported by a formal agreement. Cross-agency agreements are an important mechanism for supporting collaboration and coordination between agencies, where they provide a framework for governance and operations by establishing individual and joint roles and responsibilities; outlining agreed structures and processes; and providing for transparency and accountability of administration and outcomes. DEEWR has had several cross-agency agreements since 1998 for the delivery of employment programs. In 2009, DEEWR and Centrelink entered into a partnership arrangement, which replaced the previous purchaser–provider arrangement between the agencies and provides for direct appropriation by the Department of Human Service of most funding of service delivery (ANAO 2013a: 13). The partnership approach means that departments must 'negotiate and agree service delivery strategies that meet the intended outcomes of the BMA and acknowledge each department's operational priorities'. In order to realize a more collaborative approach, DEEWR and DHS resolved to apply agreed outcomes and work practices on a consistent basis (ANAO 2013a: 15–16).

TWO REFORM NARRATIVES

Two reform narratives are distinguished. The public service reform narrative has a lineage that encompasses a series of reform documents and agendas across 40 years. It is essentially a state-centric perspective that perceives change in terms of modifications to the existing public service system. Given this is one of the anglophone countries closely associated with public management reform, the changes may be substantial (Halligan 2007). In terms of capacity, they emphasize the internal and steering approaches, which in recent times can be traced to joined-up and whole-of-government responses.

Picking up the development of the narrative more recently, the most significant, and typical, event was the review of the Australian government administration, discussed earlier (AGRAGA 2010). The report's recommendations covered leadership and strategic direction, and public sector workforce capability with reform areas including a strengthened APSC for driving change, strategic planning and expectations for agencies (agility, capability, effectiveness and efficiency). Specific recommendations addressed the roles and responsibilities of secretaries, strengthening leadership and assessing the senior executive service. They also reflected the emerging importance of collaborative relations internally, as well as with other levels of government and non-governmental actors.

Ahead of the Game gives the idea of collaborative governance a possible foundation in public governance. At the very least, collaborative governance requires wider societal accountability, shared intra- and intergovernmental governance accountabilities, and participatory governance (Edwards et al. 2012).

In Australia, as elsewhere, the question of articulating the future public service has been problematic. In this case the lack of a distinctive and unifying core issue or theme added to the mixed acceptance of the reform agenda overall within and beyond the public service. Without an 'urgent, politically "hot" reform trigger, the Moran group clearly found it difficult to weave a coherent narrative that holds the disparate activity clusters together' ('t Hart 2010). Nevertheless, the agendas derived from *Ahead of the Game* were pursued, and official claims were subsequently made that the recommendations were either implemented or in progress (JCPAA 2012).

The continuing expressions of the narrative have come from two former heads of the public service, Terry Moran (2013) and Peter Shergold (2013). One is grounded in the needs of public service, while advocating greater devolution and some external (community) engagement. The other seeks to redefine the public service role in terms of oversight of third-party activity.

The architect of *Ahead of the Game*, Moran (2013), envisages the APS as being

> on the threshold of the next stage of public sector reforms . . . The real benefit is that they have the potential to unlock a range of outcomes, similar in scale to the benefits that flowed from the economic reforms of the 1980s and 1990s.

The groundwork for reform was laid by *Ahead of the Game*, but a broader framework was required to support and direct reform (Moran 2013: 1).

Five major reform directions provide the basis for this framework: strategic direction setting (in particular long-term strategy, joining up service delivery, consolidation); reforming government structures (intergovernmental roles and relationships and localization); rationalizing public administration (core business of levels of government, smaller agencies); improving accountability processes of department heads, agencies and ministerial advisers; and increasing organizational readiness (improving internal capacity of the public service, public sector management, staffing and skills).

The variation on this narrative locates the public service more explicitly within a broader governance framework. Shergold's conception of partnering also envisages a strong public service, but one with redefined roles where it comes to dealing with delivery and external relationships. His position is clearly differentiated from Moran's:

> public administration . . . is becoming harder. The complexities of public policy are becoming progressively more 'wicked' . . . To tackle more effectively these and similar conundrums requires a different type of public service, not just an improved version of what already exists. (Shergold 2013: 8)

Five of his six elements of reform are externally focused: a market for delivering public goods; delivery through third parties; empowering experience; co-production of public services; and reinvigorating democratic engagement. (The sixth envisages sharing the development of public policy through increased competition, particularly with political advisers – Shergold 2013: 10).

The origins of the neoliberal narrative are international and date from the rise of conviction politicians in the UK and the USA and associated economic philosophy in the 1980s (Pollitt 1990). The ideas also have a considerable lineage in Australia and with elements that cross political parties, but the most complete position was taken by the first Coalition government to take office in the reform era. It was articulated most explicitly under the Howard government and in particular through its Commission of Audit (1996), elements of which have been reproduced by a successor Commission of Audit in 2013–14 under another Coalition government.

The Commission of Audit has been resurrected by the Abbott government, with reporting to occur in 2014. The National Commission of Audit's terms of reference cover, *inter alia*, scope of government (current split of roles and responsibilities between the levels of government and whether continuing a Commonwealth activity can be justified). A second element, efficiency and effectiveness of government expenditure, covers options for greater efficiencies, such as: contestability of services, technologies and service delivery; consolidation of agencies and boards and support functions; flattening organizational structures and streamlining lines of responsibility and accountability; and asset privatization. Other elements are the adequacy of budget controls and disciplines, Commonwealth infrastructure and public sector performance and accountability (NCA 2013). These were similar to those of the 1996 audit.

Both narratives involve reducing central government. Of the two, public service reform directly engages with complexity and intractable problems. The two variations either anticipate greater collaboration and/or devolution. However, it has yet to be convincingly applied in practice, despite opportunities. In contrast, the neoliberal narrative focuses primarily on questions about the scope and roles of government, expenditure matters (e.g. contestability and privatization) and performance. It does not directly address capacity questions except in so far as pressures on capacity may be relieved by transferring responsibilities to the private sector. The narrative is closely associated with the current government and will dominate both reform and capacity for the short to medium term.

The capacity is inherent in the machinery, but this is dependent on how it is used for steering and engagement. The medium-term future is budget driven, combined with neoliberal agendas (which will be clearer once the Commission of Audit has reported and the government has responded in 2014). The impact on capacity is expected to be threefold: heavy reduction of public service staff; movement of some capacity outside the public sector; and greater use of third sector organizations. There is already one exception, with Indigenous management and delivery being integrated under the Department of the Prime Minister and Cabinet, and further capacity development is possible where it is efficiency-based, the precedent being Centrelink (discussed earlier, which entailed efficiency through the merger of two delivery networks). It is unclear whether other forms of integration, such as back office management and IT, have much to offer the handling of complexity.

CONCLUSION

Australian public sector reform has invariably addressed questions of capacity, and has a range of instruments that can be deployed. Increasingly the emphasis has shifted towards collaboration because the need for effective inter-agency, inter-sectoral and inter-jurisdictional initiatives is well established. Despite the existence of a range of intractable problems that require decentralized and cross-boundary solutions and interfacing with non-government actors, the arrangements for sharing responsibilities remain underdeveloped. The preconditions for a greater commitment to collaboration appear to be undermined by the prevailing focus on the budget deficit and reconfiguring the capacity and role of government.

NOTES

1. The main sources are the APSC, http://www.apsc.gov.au/aps-reform/current-projects/capability-reviews and APSC (2013); there were 17 Australian reports at the end.
2. Joint ventures were also supported for a range of circumstances, including the use of a responsible lead agency, and interdepartmental committees or taskforce working on a complex issue. There is a need to recognize a range of options for structures that facilitated greater collaboration and collective responsibility (DFD 2012b: 27).
3. The DFD paper (2012a: 37–9) indicates a range of ways in which the rigidities of the current Australian appropriations can be modified to accommodate collaborative approaches.
4. The other main agencies are: Australian Crime Commission, Australian Federal Police, Australian Securities and Investments Commission, Commonwealth Director of Public Prosecutions (Attorney-General's Department).
5. Collaboration entails agencies sharing risks, responsibilities and rewards, whereas coordination focuses on sharing information and agencies that adjust activities in response to interaction (ANAO 2012a: 59).

REFERENCES

AGRAGA (Advisory Group on the Reform of Australian Government Administration) (2010) *Ahead of the Game: Blueprint for the Reform of Australian Government Administration*, Canberra: Commonwealth of Australia.
ANAO (Australian National Audit Office) (2007) *Whole of Government Indigenous Service Delivery Arrangements*, Audit Report No. 10, Canberra: ANAO.
ANAO (Australian National Audit Office) (2010) *Effective Cross-Agency Agreements*, Audit Report No. 41, Canberra: ANAO.
ANAO (Australian National Audit Office) (2012a) *Administration of Project Wickenby*, Audit Report No. 25, Canberra: ANAO.
ANAO (Australian National Audit Office) (2012b) *Australian Government Coordination Arrangements for Indigenous Programs: Department of Families, Housing, Community Service and Indigenous Affairs*, Audit Report No. 8, Canberra: Commonwealth of Australia.
ANAO (Australian National Audit Office) (2013a) *Cross-Agency Coordination of Employment Programs: Department of Education, Employment and Workplace relations, Department of Human Service*, Audit Report No. 45, Canberra: Commonwealth of Australia.
ANAO (Australian National Audit Office) (2013b) Submission 008 to Joint Committee of Public Accounts and Audit, *43rd Parliament: Report 438: Advisory Report on the Public Governance, Performance and Accountability Bill*, Canberra: House of Representatives, Parliament of Australia.
APSC (Australian Public Service Commission) (2012) *State of the Service Report 2011–12*, Canberra: APSC.
APSC (Australian Public Service Commission) (2013) *State of the Service Report 2012–13*, Canberra: APSC.
Barber, M. (2007) *Instruction to Deliver: Tony Blair, Public Services and the Challenge of Achieving Targets*, London: Politico's.
DFD (Department of Finance and Deregulation) (2012a) Is less more? Towards better Commonwealth performance, Commonwealth Financial Accountability Review Discussion Paper, Canberra.

DFD (Department of Finance and Deregulation) (2012b) Sharpening the focus: a framework for improving Commonwealth performance, Commonwealth Financial Accountability Review Position Paper, Commonwealth of Australia, Canberra.
Edwards, M., J. Halligan, B. Horrigan and G. Nicoll (2012) *Public Sector Governance in Australia*, Canberra: ANU Press.
Halligan, J. (2006) 'The reassertion of the centre in a first generation NPM system', in Tom Christensen and Per Lægreid (eds), *Autonomy and Regulation: Coping with Agencies in the Modern State*, Cheltenham, UK and Northampton, MA, USA: Edward Elgar Publishing, pp. 162–80.
Halligan, J. (2007) 'Reintegrating government in third generation reforms of Australia and New Zealand', *Public Policy and Administration*, **22**(2), 217–38.
Halligan, J. (2008) *The Centrelink Experiment: Innovation in Service Delivery*, Canberra: ANU Press.
Halligan, J. (2010) 'The fate of administrative tradition in anglophone countries during the reform era', in M. Painter and B.G. Peters (eds), *Tradition and Public Administration*, Basingstoke: Palgrave Macmillan, pp. 129–42.
Halligan, J. (2011) 'Central steering in Australia' in C. Dahlström, B.G. Peters and J. Pierre (eds), *Steering from the Centre: Strengthening Political Control in Western Democracies*, University of Toronto Press, pp. 99–122.
Halligan, J. (2013) 'The role and significance of context in comparing country systems', in C. Pollitt (ed.), *Context in Public Policy and Management*, Cheltenham: Edward Elgar.
Halligan, John and John Power (1992) *Political Management in the 1990s*, Melbourne: Oxford University Press.
't Hart, P. (2010) 'Lifting its game to get ahead: the Canberra bureaucracy's reform by stealth', *Australian Review of Public Affairs*, July, http://www.australianreview.net/digest/2010/07/thart.html
Hood, C. (1991) 'A public management for all seasons?' *Public Administration*, **69**(1), 3–19.
JCPAA (Joint Committee of Public Accounts and Audit) (2012) *Report 432: APS – Fit for Service*, Parliamentary Paper 205/2012, House of Representatives, Parliament of Australia, Canberra.
Management Advisory Committee (MAC) (2005) *Senior Executive Service of the Australian Public Service: One APS–One SES*, Commonwealth of Australia, Canberra, http://www.apsc.gov.au
Moran, T. (2009) Speech on Challenges of Public Sector Reform, Institute of Public Administration Australia, 15 July, Canberra.
Moran, T. (2013) 'Reforming to create value: our next five strategic directions', *Australian Journal of Public Administration*, **72**(1), 1–6.
National Commission of Audit (1996) *Report to the Commonwealth Government*, Canberra: Australian Government Publishing Service.
National Commission of Audit (2013) Terms of Reference.
OECD (1995) *Governance in Transition: Public Management Reforms in OECD Countries*, Paris: OECD.
O'Flynn, J. (2007) 'Elusive appeal or aspirational ideal? The rhetoric and reality of the "collaborative turn" in public policy', in J. O'Flynn and J. Wanna (eds), *Collaborative Governance: A New Era of Public Policy in Australia*, Canberra: ANU E Press, pp. 181–195.
Painter, M. and J. Pierre (eds) (2005) *Challenges to State Policy Capacity*, Basingstoke: Palgrave.
Pal, L. (2012) *Frontiers of Governance: The OECD and Global Public Management Reform*, Basingstoke: Palgrave Macmillan.
Pollitt, C. (1990) *Managerialism in the Public Service: The Anglo-American Experience*, Cambridge, MA: Basil Blackwell.
Pollitt, C. (ed.) (2013) *Context in Public Policy and Management: The Missing Link* Cheltenham, UK and Northampton, MA, USA: Edward Elgar Publishing.
Shergold, P. (2013) 'My hopes for a public service for the future', *Australian Journal of Public Administration*, **72**(1), 7–13.

15. Australia: building policy capacity for managing wicked policy problems
Brian W. Head and Janine O'Flynn

INTRODUCTION AND BACKGROUND

Governments in Australia, as in many other countries, have wrestled since the late 1970s with a series of structural reforms in the public sector, intended as the foundation for improving governmental efficiency and effectiveness, and thereby contributing to national economic productivity. While these broad goals and directions of public sector reform have been widely shared among the liberal-democratic countries, the methods and pace of change were quite different, depending on the administrative traditions, local leadership and political ideologies prevalent in each country (Pollitt and Bouckaert 2011). This public sector reform process, designed broadly in accordance with neoliberal principles of new public management (NPM), was initially directed towards deregulating the economy, redefining core roles for government, and enhancing efficiency in the delivery of public services (Dunleavy and Hood 1994). These reforms were initially focused on structures and managerial processes within the public sector (e.g. divestment of 'non-core' functions, restructuring, and skills development to enhance managerial efficiency), but the reform process soon moved on to promote market-based approaches to service delivery by non-government providers. Relationships with external service providers were developed and shaped through competitive tendering in many areas, with new forms of performance-based service contracting.

By the early 2000s, contestability was well entrenched in most OECD countries, and performance metrics were widely used in program management both within and beyond the core public sector (Bouckaert and Halligan 2008). Australia was widely regarded as among the front-runners in terms of implementing NPM principles of economic rationalism, competition and outsourcing of service delivery. In recent years, the capacity of the redesigned system in Australia to deliver efficient and effective policy solutions and reliable public services has been repeatedly tested. Four areas of political, economic and governance challenges have been especially important.

First, national elections delivered political changes in 1996, 2007 and

2013, leading to stocktakes, audits, organizational restructuring and new policy priorities driven by an incoming government. Changes in the machinery of government have required renegotiation of how key public agencies perform their core tasks and how they monitor and oversee the work of third parties engaged in service delivery. The leadership group in the Australian Public Service (APS) has generated a series of reviews and new strategies that have focused on the capacities and flexibilities required to deal with rapid change. Second, the international economic environment has been somewhat turbulent during the last two decades, including robust trade competition, exchange-rate adjustment pressures, and repeated external economic shocks (the Asian financial crisis in the late 1990s, and the global financial crisis and economic recession ongoing since 2008). These external shocks and challenges have put pressure on public budgets through reduced revenues and demands for compensatory expenditures. Third, Australian governments have increasingly attempted to address complex social and environmental policy challenges since the late 1980s, some of which are discussed in more detail below. The need to address several large and complex issues simultaneously has placed the decision-making and policy advice systems under great pressure, and has required innovative thinking both in relation to policy design and implementation mechanisms.

Fourth, within the Australian federal system of government, many of these complex challenges are not resolvable simply through the decisions of the federal government acting alone. While the federal government has undisputed authority in matters of international trade, finance, national economic management and social security payments, the picture is less clear-cut for many key areas of service delivery (Fenna and Hollander 2013). For example, the federal and state levels have shared roles in education, health, housing and Indigenous services. In these policy areas, it has become standard practice for policy and service agreements to be negotiated between the federal government and the six states and two territories. In such cases, policy and program settings are a product of bargaining in a multi-level system. Moreover, in important social policy areas where the service delivery capacities of non-government actors have become vital, the capacity to move forward requires multisectoral collaborative solutions and raises a range of boundary challenges in practice (O'Flynn 2014).

The complex economic, social and environmental problems faced by contemporary Australia have demanded policy and governance innovation. These have stretched the capacity of political and administrative leaders to design, implement and evaluate new approaches and to identify and manage new risks. This chapter considers the evolution of recent attempts to increase the capacity of Australian government to manage complex policy challenges. We examine the institutional and network mechanisms developed for these purposes, the performance management frameworks used to clarify goals and accountabilities, and the impediments to innovation in a federal system. We also consider the inherent trade-offs between innovation and risk management, the evidence base for policy development, and the extent to which the wider availability of research evidence and program evaluations in some key areas has assisted in this quest for better performance. Finally, we consider the ongoing challenges faced by government leaders who attempt to address wicked problems using traditional policy instruments delivered through functionally based bureaucratic organizations.

PUBLIC SECTOR REFORM: OVERVIEW OF TRENDS, CHALLENGES AND RESPONSES

The substantial reforms in Australian public administration over recent decades were directed at (i) reshaping the structures, roles and managerial efficiencies of public organizations, (ii) improving their capacities and skills to undertake new roles, (iii) promoting competition and reducing business regulation to increase productivity, and (iv) forging new relationships with the business and community sectors for providing publicly funded services. While these four directions have proceeded in parallel, the initial focus on reshaping the functions of public agencies entailed a far-reaching and time-consuming work program. The strong critiques of the public sector (as ponderous, rigid, monopolistic, unresponsive and expensive) were increasingly accepted through the 1980s, and an alternative narrative of public sector reform emerged in the 1990s. Henceforth, agencies responsible for service delivery were expected to become more responsive and flexible, ensuring value-for-money services in a contestable environment. They were given more devolved authority to manage their operations, and these managerial expectations were reinforced by new funding mechanisms (e.g. results-based budgeting) and performance management systems. Agencies were required to outsource many of their program services through competitive tendering (Industry Commission 1996), and they invested in performance monitoring systems to demonstrate the efficiency and effectiveness of their programs (Halligan and Power 1992; Clark and Corbett 1999).

Public regulatory agencies and compliance/enforcement agencies were formally separated from agencies that were providing services to citizens and stakeholders. Business regulation was reduced, and government-owned business enterprises were sold to the private sector. Superfluous public bodies were abolished, and service delivery departments underwent processes of consolidation (e.g. the creation of 'mega'-departments in 1987). Major agencies retained a capacity to provide policy advice to their minister, but alternative sources of advice were increasingly available from business associations, consultancy firms, lobbyists and think tanks. The policy coordination role of the central policy agencies (Prime Minister and Cabinet, Treasury, and Finance) was strengthened in order to steer the reform agenda.

The scale of reform increased as leaders moved beyond the efficiency agenda in individual public agencies. In particular, government leaders moved to tackle the perceived systemic barriers and regulatory obstacles to national economic productivity (Forsyth 1992), and they also began to promote more effective delivery of human services programs through competitive tendering (Davis and Weller 2001). Commercialization, privatization and market-based approaches were strongly favoured despite some resistance from established public sector providers. The reform process was conducted separately in each governmental jurisdiction (the federal government, the six states and two territories), but a very high level of policy transfer and institutional mimicry was evident, and there was a noteworthy trend towards policy convergence on the main features of market-based reform.

Microeconomic reform principles, based on economic rationalism, were applied to a wide range of regulatory challenges, especially public utilities and public infrastructure in each jurisdiction (Forsyth 1992). The reform agenda was elevated by Prime Minister Hawke in mid-1990, when he announced a series of special premiers' conferences to tackle nationwide issues of efficiency and productivity. After some important reform agreements, widely attributed to the new processes of 'cooperative federalism', this intergovernmental forum was redesignated as the Council of Australian Governments (COAG), and given the task of addressing major issues of national importance. The development of a national competition policy framework, and its endorsement by all jurisdictions during 1993–94, was a landmark COAG achievement (Carroll and Painter 1995; Painter 1998). The scale and significance of the problems had prompted fresh strategic thinking about the institutional mechanisms needed for driving this new agenda in a coordinated way. However, the states remained unhappy that their fiscal dependency (i.e. their reliance on transfer payments from the dominant federal government) was not recognized as a public sector capacity problem.

The strength of the COAG reform process arose from top–down coordination through a powerful network of central agencies (Weller 1996), facilitated and strengthened by political support from senior ministers.

Subject to such support, central agencies became bolder in identifying key issues requiring national attention. This powerful political–bureaucratic reform alliance had been prompted by the perceived urgency of microeconomic reform. Over time, the agenda was broadened to consider complex issues in human services delivery and sustainable development that required agreements between the levels of government. In particular, central agencies began to use national forums selectively to reshape major social program areas and to negotiate settlements in areas of conflict between environmental protection and resource development agencies. This approach occurred alongside the more market-based reforms, organizational disaggregation and the adoption of new performance regimes that focused agencies more narrowly, setting the scene for the next era of reform.

An important lesson drawn from this period was that institutional innovation and capacity-building were necessary to support major reforms with broad impacts (APSC 2003; Lindquist et al. 2011). The level of political appetite for tackling 'big issues' was unusually robust among leaders in the late 1980s and early 1990s. Hence the underlying challenge for policy bureaucrats was how to enhance strategic policy capacity and coordination capacity across the federation. Chaired by the prime minister, the Council of Australian Governments provided political and administrative impetus for reforms that required the cooperation, or at least acquiescence, of the states. The formal legislative powers of the federal government were considerable but were insufficient to deal with many issues. A wider range of policy instruments became necessary, including financial incentives for state compliance with competition policy reforms in the public utilities sector, and a large number of federal/state agreements in human services (e.g. health, education, training, housing, disability services and Indigenous services). These agreements stipulated shared policy objectives and performance indicators, and were tied to large financial transfer payments.

It had become clear by the 1980s and 1990s that many policy goals transcended the boundaries of individual departmental responsibilities. The rhetoric of 'joined-up government' in the UK was complemented by the rhetoric of 'whole-of-government' coordination in Australia (O'Flynn et al. 2014). This cooperative agenda within the public sector became widely discussed, at two levels – line agencies within each jurisdiction (e.g. within the Australian Public Service) were encouraged by central agencies to cooperate more fully to achieve shared objectives; and at the nationwide or systemic level, the intergovernmental strategic policy agenda was pursued through the COAG process. Paradoxically, much of the impetus for building better capacity for problem-solving had its origins in the efficiency and market-oriented directions of NPM, but the collaborative instruments chosen for achieving better integration extended across wide areas of policy, raising expectations that narrow top–down solutions were unlikely to be effective. A related wave of enthusiasm for consultative and stakeholder-oriented governance models emerged in the late 1990s and began to influence the rhetoric of responsive and customer-focused service provision.

THE PUBLIC SERVICE INNOVATION AGENDA

A range of major reports released throughout the 2000s reflected these concerns, mapping out the various drivers for change and calling for a range of solutions – with collaboration, innovation and engagement all becoming central to the task of transforming government. At the centre of these manifestos was a theme of building capacity in the APS to address these increasingly complex demands. In *Connecting Government*, published by the Management Advisory Committee of senior officials (MAC 2004), a more joined-up approach was positioned as central to how government would operate with a clear aspiration to develop a collaborative culture across the APS. Introducing the report, the Secretary of the Department of the Prime Minister and Cabinet argued that 'whole of government is the public administration of the future . . . [the means] to face the governance challenges of the 21st century' (Shergold 2004). The *Connecting Government* report was focused on the importance of driving fundamental change in structures, systems, skills and cultures to build the capacity to work in a more collaborative, joined-up fashion: 'The report does not believe that effective solutions lie in moving around the deckchairs of bureaucratic endeavor. Rather it reinforces the need to continue to build [a] culture that supports, models, understands and aspires to the whole of government solutions' (MAC 2004: v). The political–bureaucratic commitment to the collaborative project was strong: Cabinet processes were amended to encourage a more whole-of-government approach, new interdepartmental structures were developed, COAG was reinvigorated, new coordinating units were established in the Department of the Prime Minister and Cabinet, and new attempts at integrated service delivery were fashioned (O'Flynn et al. 2011).

In 2007, the APSC released two major reports of relevance. The first, *Changing Behaviour* (APSC 2007a), focused on how government could influence the behaviour of citizens in an attempt to overcome barriers to effective policy implementation. The rise of increasingly complex issues, it was argued, demanded new approaches that combined traditional instruments with behavioural insights; this reflected the acceptance that government could not solve these complex, often wicked, problems alone. The need to address rising rates of obesity, the need to reduce tobacco use, and the need for cooperative approaches to improved management of natural resources were used as examples of how more nuanced policy measures were required to deliver outcomes. These new, potentially more sophisticated approaches to policy design and implementation, however, would demand cooperation across boundaries, increased engagement with stakeholders, and the development of new types of skills in the APS. The capacity to operationalize a more behaviourally focused approach was an important part of the recommendations and conclusions.

In the same year, the APSC released its *Tackling Wicked Problems* report (APSC 2007b). This built on the joined-up agenda from the *Connecting Government* (MAC 2004) agenda, but specifically emphasized those policy issues that Rittel and Webber (1973) had famously characterized as 'wicked' or intractable. The report pointed to the importance of working across boundaries, including those between agencies within the APS sector, and between the federal government and the states. There was also attention to further devolving governmental authority, better engaging stakeholders, and the development of new skills that public servants would require in these challenging contexts. Collaboration and innovation were seen as critical tools in tackling these wicked problems, and there was a greater emphasis on addressing capacity issues by showing how the current ways of operating and the current skill sets of public servants constrained the ability of the APS to address these wicked issues.

By the late 2000s the Australian government was looking to technological solutions and released its report *Engage* (Government 2.0 Taskforce 2009), which set out a blueprint for how agencies and public servants could use Web 2.0 tools to connect with each other and with communities, and potentially to transform policy and service delivery. These potential achievements, however, required culture change, the freeing up of information, and a movement away from the traditional hierarchical model – all aspirational goals indeed.

A major blueprint for reform of the APS, *Ahead of the Game* (AGRAGA 2010), was published soon after. Emerging from a thorough review of the APS, the report was the most comprehensive manifesto for public service change that had been produced for some time in Australia. Key themes identified in the previous reports were prominent – collaboration, joining up, engagement, innovation and capacity-building all featured. The report was introduced as

an ambitious and interlinked reform agenda that seeks to improve services, programs and policies for Australian citizens. Above all, it recognises that to be strong, the APS must make the most of the talents, energy and integrity of its people. The proposed reforms therefore seek to boost and support the APS workforce and leadership, and to embed new practices and behaviour into the APS culture. (AGRAGA 2010: xi)

At the centre of the report was the notion of a 'high performance public service' which would: meet the needs of citizens through high-quality, tailored public services and engage them in design and development of policy and services; contain strong leadership and have a strategic direction; be reliant on a highly capable workforce; and operate efficiently and consistently at a high standard. Nine report themes were identified to underpin this transformation, ranging from more client-centred services, more open government, enhanced policy capacity, and developing agency agility, effectiveness and capability. *Ahead of the Game* (AGRAGA 2010) exhibited an increasingly familiar mix of behavioural change, capacity-building and culture change, and an emphasis on joining up, co-production and engagement. The blueprint had echoes of previous reform agendas and manifestos, most of which had been proposed in isolation, with limited success. Bringing these together in a macro-level blueprint may have been considered novel and powerful (Lindquist 2010; 't Hart 2010; Moran 2013), but the fundamental obstacles to the various reforms remained firmly embedded.

In the same year as *Ahead of the Game*, a complementary report on *Empowering Change* (MAC 2010) was released. This report, steered by the Management Advisory Committee, set out a blueprint for fostering innovation in the APS, drawing on international literature, and building on key ideas from *Ahead of the Game* (AGRAGA 2010) connected to the notion of a 'high-performing' public service. In the introduction to the report it was argued that major changes were needed to the APS, 'both how it thinks and how it operates', and that the 'red tape and siloed thinking' of the past would have 'no place in the high performing APS our citizens expect and deserve' (MAC 2010: iii). Recommendations from the report focused on familiar themes – strategy and culture, information flows, technology, leadership, structural barriers, funding, technology and collaboration.

This series of reports through the 2000s points to the considerable attention the APS was directing towards the range of challenges confronting it, the increasing complexity of the policy challenges it faced, and the need to increase policy capacity to deal with this. Throughout that decade new ways of operating were promulgated, and much was written and said of the need for innovation, for cultural change, for new modes of leadership, for changing the basic structures and systems, and for developing new capacity based on twenty-first-century skills and capabilities. However, the practical implementation of these reforms has fallen far short of the aspirations. Whilst identifying and addressing the barriers to each of the big ideas contained within them, the reports appear to have had little impact on the standing arrangements that, as they rightly pointed out, constrain their ability to deliver on these aspirations. Major tensions emerged between these new, highly desired, ways of operating and the embedded approaches. For example, the report on *Connecting Government* (MAC 2004) had advocated large-scale structural and cultural change to enable collaboration and a whole-of-government approach, but little was done to change the existing architecture of government: budgets, programs, departments, performance regimes and so on, remained internally focused.

The tensions between the new and old frameworks have persisted throughout recent decades. These tensions are very clear in two major policy domains discussed below, namely, (i) the federal government's response to Indigenous disadvantage, and (ii) the federal government's responses to pressing challenges in natural resource management and climate change. Both of these policy domains are key examples of 'wicked' problems, understood as major policy issues exhibiting high levels of system complexity, stakeholder diversity, knowledge uncertainty and ongoing change (Rittel and Webber 1973; APSC 2007b; Head 2008, 2010; Head and Alford 2015).

In the following section we provide a background to each of these policy areas, set out the policy architecture that has been created and adapted to deal with them, and draw out outcomes and implications for discussion. These cases highlight both a commitment to reconfiguration to address these wicked problems but also the challenges that are confronted in attempts to do so.

RESPONDING TO INDIGENOUS DISADVANTAGE

Background

The federal government has a long, and mixed, experience in responding to Indigenous disadvantage. The challenges are numerous, with the full range of socioeconomic indicators pointing to the substantial disadvantage experienced by Indigenous Australians. There is wide acceptance that these issues are interconnected, complex and resistant to the numerous interventions that have been attempted over several decades; in this sense this issue is a classic 'wicked' problem (Rittel and Webber 1973). We focus specifically on developments since the early 2000s, as this has represented an era of substantial experimentation, political–bureaucratic transformation, and strategic intergovernment agreements that accept this wickedness, yet have attempted to establish strategies to address it.

Despite decades of policy experimentation to address chronic disadvantage, persistent and significant gaps remain between the Indigenous and non-Indigenous populations of Australia. This remains persistently true regardless of the substantial expenditures that have been made (see Altman et al. 2008 for an alternative view on progress). In a major report of the Australian National Audit Office (ANAO 2007), it was estimated that the federal government alone spent $A3.5 billion in 2007–08 in attempts to address this. Another report, this time by the Productivity Commission (2012), examined Indigenous expenditure in Australia and identified a combined spend of some $A25.4 billion in 2010–11 (all governments); this represented 5.6 per cent of total direct government expenditure for 2.6 per cent of the Australian population. Of this expenditure, $A11.5 billion was spent by the federal government and $A13.9 billion by state and territory governments; and of this total, $A25.4, $A5.5 billion was on Indigenous specific services – the remaining $A19.9 billion was embedded in 'mainstream' services. The report estimated that this translated into expenditure of $A44 128 per head for Indigenous Australians compared with $A19 589 for non-Indigenous.

Socioeconomic indicators across a range of areas continue to paint a bleak picture, and the focus on these has continued to spur governments in Australia into action, in particular over the last decade or so. Specific estimates/indicators vary, but broadly we know that: life expectancy at birth is 20 years lower for Indigenous Australians; infant mortality rates are double those for the non-Indigenous population; Indigenous primary school students have lower levels of numeracy and literacy, secondary school students have lower completion rates and university enrolments are around half those of the broader population. Labour force participation rates trail, with unemployment rates triple those for the non-Indigenous population, while rates of suicide, homicide, hospitalization for assault, and incarceration all exceed the broader population (Prime Minister of Australia 2010; Steering Committee for the Review of Government Service Provision 2003). Whilst there is bipartisan agreement on the wickedness of the issue, the challenge of responding to disadvantage cannot be underestimated. However, in a report by newly elected Prime Minister Tony Abbott (Prime Minister of Australia 2014: 2), he noted:

> No one should be under any illusion about the difficulty of swiftly overcoming two centuries of comparative failure. Nevertheless, it would be complacent, even neglectful, to not address, from day one, the most intractable difficulty our country has ever faced.

Indeed, where work has been done to estimate the time required to 'close the gap' between Indigenous and non-Indigenous Australians, the scale and scope of the challenge becomes formidable. In their report, Altman et al. (2008) indicate that convergence between these population groups may, in reality, take several generations to address.[1] Based on these estimates, closing the life expectancy gap will take more than 100 years for men and around 47 years for women; more than 100 years to close the home ownership gap; 94 years to address the gap in median weekly incomes; 44 (25*) years to overcome the differences in post-school qualifications for adults; and 100 years (*) or more to converge on equal rates of degree or higher qualifications. This bleak picture has fuelled increasing policy experimentation and positioned addressing Indigenous disadvantage as a wicked problem in government discourse, and one that requires new approaches. In launching the *Connecting Government* report, the Secretary of the Department of the Prime Minister and Cabinet singled out this issue for attention:

> Now comes the biggest test of whether the rhetoric of connectivity can be marshaled into effective action. The Australian Government is about to embark on a bold experiment in implementing a whole of government approach to policy development and delivery . . . and the embrace of a quite different approach to the administration of Indigenous specific programs and services. (Shergold 2004)

Similar sentiments were also expressed in the *Tackling Wicked Problems* report:

> Indigenous disadvantage is an ongoing, seemingly intractable issue . . . The need for coordination and an overarching strategy among the services and programs supported by the various levels of government . . . is also a key ingredient. (APSC 2007b: 2)

Responding to the wickedness of Indigenous disadvantage is complex and there has been considerable stock placed in the power of joined-up approaches over the last decade in Australia. This mirrors broader attempts discussed above to engage in more collaborative, whole-of-government ways of working. It also reflects an acceptance that past attempts have been largely unsuccessful. Such frustration spurred new approaches through the 2000s that have required large-scale transformation of the political and bureaucratic architecture. Attempts to do this, as will be discussed, were hampered by embedded modes of operating and the challenges that permeate both bureaucratic and political domains.

The Policy Architecture

Attempting to address the breadth and depth of the challenges faced by Indigenous people has occupied governments across Australia for decades. Here we focus specifically on the changing policy architecture since the early to mid-2000s because this period captures a series of experiments requiring radical reconfiguration of both the policy and bureaucratic architecture and relationships with Indigenous Australians. We focus on four main stages that reflect the trajectory of how the federal government has attempted to respond to Indigenous disadvantage: the COAG trials; the new Indigenous Affairs Arrangements; the creation of Indigenous Coordination Centres (ICCs); and the development and implementation of the Closing the Gap agreement between the governments of Australia.

1.   The Council of Australian Government trials
The election of the Liberal–National government in 1996 signalled the start of a new approach to responding to Indigenous disadvantage in Australia; however, it took several years to broker the bipartisan political support needed to enact this large-scale change. In 2002 the 'new deal' in Indigenous affairs began with agreement, via COAG, to run a series of trials in a new way of working. These 'COAG trials' took place in eight sites across Australia and they relied on governments working together more collaboratively and new forms of engagement with communities. The trials incorporated Shared Responsibility Agreements (SRA), essentially a quasi-contract between communities and governments based on the principle of mutual obligation. These agreements attracted considerable public debate and were a controversial part of the new government's plan to transform Indigenous affairs in Australia. One that attracted considerable attention was the Mulan SRA, struck between the Mulan Aboriginal Community in the Kimberly region of Australian and federal and West Australian governments. In the agreement, community members agreed, among other things, to daily showers for children, washing their faces twice a day, school attendance and keeping houses clean; the federal government agreed to install petrol bowsers that could deliver non-sniffable petrol; and the West Australian state government agreed to review the adequacy of health services to the community (see McCausland 2005 for more).

The rationale for the COAG trials was that they provided an opportunity to be innovative, experiment with new ways of working, develop approaches more tailored to community needs, and cut through the red tape that constrained government's ability to address this wicked problem. The COAG trials were, not surprisingly, incredibly controversial and there was widespread critique (see Collard et al. 2005 for example); the influence of the trials was, however, substantial in setting out the next era of architectural change in this policy area.

Whilst it is important to recognize the influence of the trials, it is also important to reflect on the formal evaluations at the time, which shone a light on to the embedded barriers to more joined-up approaches and the inherent challenges in this policy area. These reviews pointed to some success but placed attention on the entrenched barriers to scaling up this model. Several important requirements for joined-up success (see O'Flynn 2014) were missing; for example, shared objectives and priorities, skills for cross-boundary working, and new leadership styles (Morgan Disney & Associates 2006). The trials, then, gave designers of a new approach to responding to Indigenous disadvantage plenty of indication as to the challenges that would be faced as they sought to redesign the policy and delivery architecture through the mid-2000s and beyond.

2. The new Indigenous Affairs Arrangements

Despite being elected in 1996, it took the Liberal–National government considerable time to garner the bipartisan support it needed for the radical transformation of Indigenous affairs. This included both political and institutional transformation. In 2004 the massive reforms to institutional arrangements and policy were laid out in the Indigenous Affairs Arrangements (IAAs), which sought to 'provide high-level stakeholder involvement through a Ministerial Taskforce, a framework for departmental collaboration . . . and on-the-ground through a network of Indigenous Coordination Centres' (ANAO 2007: 12).

A controversial part of the transformation was the dismantling of the Aboriginal and Torres Strait Islander Commission (ATSIC),[2] the peak representative body for Indigenous Australians. This statutory authority was created in 1990 to ensure that Indigenous people were involved in the governance activities that affected their lives. ATSIC comprised 35 regional councils and a national board of commissioners, and, in addition to being the peak representative body, it had developed considerable responsibility for the delivery of programs to Indigenous Australians. ATSIC was disbanded in 2005 following the passing of the ATSIC Amendment Bill, which also abolished regional councils, effectively removing political representation for Indigenous Australians.

The political and bureaucratic reforms set out in the IAAs sought to transform the way in which responses to Indigenous disadvantage were developed and implemented. In the political domain, the Ministerial Taskforce on Indigenous Affairs was created to ensure ongoing commitment to tackling disadvantage. All ministers with day-today responsibility for programs and services that focused on Indigenous Australians were members of the taskforce, which was required to focus on setting long-term strategic policy goals in this area. The taskforce connected with the bureaucratic domain via the Secretaries' Group on Indigenous Affairs (SGIA), which was charged with supporting ministerial goals and implementing decisions of the taskforce. The Secretaries' Group had formal responsibility for driving reforms related to the IAAs and the group stated early on in its term that reform success rested on an ability to work in a more collaborative, joined-up fashion (SGIA 2005). The Secretaries' Group was supported by the Indigenous Communities Coordination Taskforce, which was given responsibility for leading the required coordination across various departments and jurisdictions, and also the Office of Indigenous Policy Coordination (OIPC), with responsibility for whole-of-government coordination, community engagement strategies, overseeing intergovernmental relationships and monitoring performance (see KPMG 2007).

As this political and bureaucratic transformation took place, the COAG trials were under way, throwing up examples of inspiration and frustration in terms of the ability of governments to experiment, innovate and work more collaboratively, but also how to work with Indigenous communities. As mentioned, the evaluation of these trials was mixed, with some evidence of innovation, but plenty of acknowledgement of the entrenched barriers to new ways of working. There is no doubt, however, that they provided the first major test of operationalizing a more joined-up approach to tackling Indigenous disadvantage in Australia.

3.   The creation of Indigenous Coordination Centres

The COAG trials were the genesis for the next major stage in tackling Indigenous disadvantage, the creation of Indigenous Coordination Centres (ICCs). These were intended to be permanent hubs for policy coordination, service delivery and community engagement, operating across Australia and encapsulating key learning from the COAG trials. The ICCs were considered the front line of the bold experiment in responding to Indigenous disadvantage in Australia (Shergold 2004) and were to be the vehicle for 'local responsiveness, community-based innovation and negotiation' (SGIA 2005: v).

Thirty ICCs were established beginning in 2004, with locations across urban, rural and remote Australia. The centres drew together multiple departments/agencies from across government and created 'portals' into government for Indigenous Australians. A process of mapping where staff were working in areas related to Indigenous issues was undertaken to identify the relevant organizations to be represented and, by 2006, there were some 562 Commonwealth public servants located in the ICCs, which were overseen by the Department of Families, Housing, Community Services and Indigenous Affairs (FaHCSIA). In some cases, state and territory government also had representation. Staff in the centres carried out three main roles: program administration; solution brokering to provide a bridge between community needs and the various programs offered by departments; and developing SRAs with local communities (ANAO 2007).

The ICCs were seen as the face of the transformation of the political and bureaucratic architecture. However, despite the boldness of this experiment, there is limited empirical work that has evaluated its success or otherwise. In their study, O'Flynn et al. (2011), who examined the functioning of ICCs as representations of joined-up government approaches, found that generally the model underperformed against its intentions. This was mainly due to embedded barriers to collaboration. In particular, they pointed to three factors: the failure to design a supporting architecture that could undergird a more joined-up approach – including authority structures, training and development, financial arrangements; the continued programmatic focus, which created vertical–horizontal tensions; and centralized decision-making. Where they identified success it was centred on deep relational capital and a craftsmanship style of leadership that enable some centres to prosper, despite the embedded barriers. They warned, however, that it was unrealistic to build ways of operating that could produce these outcomes until these entrenched barriers were addressed.

A series of evaluations of ICCs supports the findings of O'Flynn et al. (2011), but also strongly echo the review of the COAG trials. These reports (ANAO 2007; KPMG 2007; Morgan Disney & Associates 2006) indicated that barriers identified in the trials had not been addressed, and remained a major impediment to the success of the ICC model. The evidence to date shows that the ICCs were not able to fulfil their bold ambitions in practice.

4. The Council of Australian Governments 'Closing the Gap' agreement

A major redesign of the policy architecture, building on the previous three stages, emerged in 2007 with the election of the Labor government. One of the first acts of the new government in 2008 was to offer an apology to Indigenous Australians and to push forward with an intergovernmental strategy to 'close the gap'. Late in 2007 it was announced that COAG had settled on a new approach and this was formalized via the National Indigenous Reform Agreement (NIRA) in 2008 (COAG 2008). The NIRA, which was known as 'Closing the Gap', set out the new architecture – a range of objectives, outcomes, outputs, performance indicators and benchmarks against which progress could be tracked, and a range of new funding partnerships was announced. Most of the attention came to bear on the targets that were agreed as part of the NIRA and against which the prime minister agreed to report annually. The ambitious targets, agreed by all governments across Australia, covered important socioeconomic indicators that reflected the entrenched disadvantage experienced by Indigenous Australians. Closing the Gap committed the various governments to the following aims:

- close the gap in life expectancy within a generation (by 2031);
- halve the gap in mortality rates for Indigenous children under five by 2018;
- ensure access to early childhood education for all Indigenous four-year-olds in remote communities by 2013;
- halve the gap in reading, writing and numeracy achievements for children by 2018;
- halve the gap for Indigenous students in Year 12 (or equivalent) attainment rates by 2020;
- halve the gap in employment outcomes between Indigenous and other Australians by 2018.

To achieve these, a series of eight 'building blocks' or areas for action were agreed, each seen to contribute to the Closing the Gap targets: early childhood; schooling; health; economic participation; healthy homes; safe communities; and governance and leadership. Alongside this, governments committed to major investments across these areas, including $A4.6 billion in Indigenous specific funding for the following decade. Again there was focus on the need for a new approach, recognition of the entrenched disadvantage of Indigenous Australians and a focus on a more collaborative, joined-up approach as the means to address this wicked problem.

> An unprecedented level of cooperation and coordination between the Commonwealth and State and Territory Governments is needed to deliver on this commitment to Close the Gap. The Commonwealth, State and Territory Governments are committed through COAG to the Closing the Gap agenda and this partnership, underpinned by effective engagement with Indigenous Australians, establishes a genuinely national approach. (COAG 2008: A-17)

As mentioned earlier, the modelling undertaken on how long it might take to close the gap between Indigenous and non-Indigenous Australians showed that this would require a long-term commitment (Altman et al., 2008). The targets set out in the NIRA, therefore, were bold and ambitious when compared to these estimates. Part of the agreement was to report annually on progress, and the series of reports subsequently released has played an important role in cataloguing the range of activities focused on improving the lives of Indigenous Australians, tracking performance against the targets, and areas where attention is needed. By 2013 good progress had been recorded on some targets: in the 2013 report it was announced that the early childhood target would be achieved, that the infant mortality target was on track and that the Year 12 educational achievement target was ahead of schedule (Prime Minister of Australia 2013). Yet it was also accepted that some of the targets would be extraordinarily difficult to achieve, with closing the gap on life expectancy and employment outcomes the most challenging.

In addition to the prime minister's reports, which were mainly about cataloguing activity, the COAG Reform Council also reported on performance progress annually. These reports provided much more detailed analysis of the performance against targets, and pointed to success and risks. For example, in its 2013 report (COAG Reform Council 2013), the council noted that there had been little improvement in Indigenous reading rates and that there had been decreases in numeracy rates across the board. Further, it was reported that the gap in employment, labour force participation and unemployment had widened in the period 2006–11. Little progress was reported on closing the gap in rates of death; indeed, in some states it was reported that this had not changed significantly since 1998.

The election of the Liberal–National government in 2013 signalled more change in the policy architecture. Whilst the 'Closing the Gap' approach remains in place, arrangements to deliver on Indigenous disadvantage were changed. One of the first acts of the new prime minister was to centralize the administration of more than 150 Indigenous programs from across eight federal government departments into the Department of the Prime Minister and Cabinet on the basis that this would allow for a major overhaul of administration, remove duplication and enable a simpler approach. He also made it clear in his first Closing the Gap report that he wanted to shift the focus from what government is doing (i.e. his view of the government's reporting on Closing the Gap) to how Indigenous people were living (Prime Minister of Australia 2014). In his report, the prime minister lamented that progress had been too slow, or non-existent in some areas, that there has been too much attention to spending and government activity, and too little attention to outcomes. He announced that there was still bipartisan support for Closing the Gap, but that he would refocus attention on three main areas: getting children into school; getting adults into work; and safer Indigenous communities.

Outcomes and Implications

There can be no doubt that responding to Indigenous disadvantage is one of the most challenging policy areas confronting governments in Australia. The previous decade has seen major experimentation with approaches and, in particular, with how government organizes itself to confront this wicked problem. The evidence on its success, however, is mixed. Organizationally, governments have struggled to work together more collaboratively due to a series of embedded barriers that seem resistant even to the most enthusiastic political and bureaucratic leadership (O'Flynn et al. 2011). Throughout the 2000s the stages of architectural change have focused more and more on partnership, collaboration and innovation, without enough attention to the fundamental barriers that permeate government operations (O'Flynn 2014), and the outcomes for Indigenous people have not yet been realized to the extent that has been intended.

Part of this is a reflection of the inherent wickedness of the challenge, part the failure of governments to confront their own organizational dysfunctions. Combined, this means that a decade of radical change and substantial investments has so far not produced major shifts in the most critical socioeconomic indicators – those that will reflect a transformation in the position of Indigenous Australians in society. The time frames for Closing the Gap are aspirational in many cases, and the outcomes desired may take generations to be achieved. The building blocks may be in place, but the challenge in all of this, of course, is how to maintain the commitment of political and bureaucratic actors to goals that they will not be able to claim as their own achievements.

RESPONDING TO NRM AND CLIMATE CHANGE CHALLENGES

Background

The federal government has become increasingly involved since the 1980s in developing policy responses to pressing challenges in natural resource management (NRM) and climate change. Historically these issues have been matters of state-level responsibility in the federation. However, the federal government has become more active in seeking better solutions for the major ongoing challenges in land, water and resource management and other aspects of environmental planning (Dovers and Wild River 2003). The range of issues is substantial and diverse, reflecting the wide variety of landscapes, resource endowments and patterns of urbanization across a vast continent.

The national *State of the Environment* report (Department of Environment 2011) summed up the major ongoing issues identified by expert panels in environmental science: greenhouse gas emissions; urban air quality; ecosystem health of inland waterways; adequate water resources for urban and industrial uses; quality of land and soils; destruction of biodiversity; marine ecosystems protection; natural and cultural heritage protection; and planning for intensively populated coastal areas. In short, Australia faces similar types of environmental and NRM stress as other countries, but the mix and intensity of issues in Australia entail several unique challenges. General drivers for change have been enlivened by emergent crises, such as the increased awareness of pollution threats to marine water quality in the Great Barrier Reef, rising understanding of soil salinity issues in many agricultural regions, and extensive problems for inland river systems and irrigated agriculture stemming from the long drought that commenced around 2000. Underlying issues that had remained politically dormant sprang to life in response to these crises and challenges.

Such major policy challenges can be seen as 'wicked' because the NRM and environmental processes are interconnected, with complex chains of causality; and while the problems have now been well documented through scientific inquiry, their scope and significance remain deeply contested by stakeholder interests. Moreover, viable solutions may require diverse actors to work effectively together for the first time; and, as problems continue to evolve, program designs may require constant adjustment along with a changing mix of policy instruments. Natural resources problems generally require adaptive management within an overall framework of sustainability principles and key desired outcomes (Adger and Jordan 2009).

Approaches to environmental and natural resources policy have evolved not only in response to these substantive problems, but also in response to changing fashions and capacities in public policy and governance arrangements (Head 2009). Early attempts to address these issues were focused on setting and enforcing regulatory standards (most notably, concerning hazardous chemicals and waste materials). While governments initially saw this as politically risky, regulatory standard-setting gained legitimacy and community support over time. However, it was soon evident that other big issues would need different approaches. For example, in relation to landcare and catchment management on a regional scale, it became clear that involving local landholders in sustainable management practices would be essential. Traditional approaches had failed to correct the long history of subsidization and over-allocation of scarce water resources. Hence, from the late 1990s, the NPM principles of efficiency and user-pays were increasingly applied to valuable natural resources such as water. The large issues, however, were continually bound up in administrative and legal tangles arising from the division of powers in a federation, and embedded in ongoing disputes about the appropriate roles of government, private businesses, consumers and expert advisers.

The Policy Architecture

Environmental and NRM policy issues have achieved increasing prominence since the 1970s, and state-level legislation began to incorporate standards and objectives for environmental protection. The states have had the main policy responsibilities but little funding to implement effective frameworks. By contrast, the federal government has had large financial resources but limited constitutional powers over environmental matters (federal environmental responsibilities are codified in the Environment Protection and Biodiversity Conservation Act 1999). Depending on its political will to intervene, the federal government can expand its policy influence through four mechanisms: political–administrative leadership through chairing intergovernmental councils and forums; financial leverage via conditional grants to other levels of government or to business organizations; regulatory leverage through its constitutional powers over corporations; and strategic policy leverage through its external affairs and treaty-making powers (hence, for example, the federal government intervened in 1983 to declare a World Heritage conservation area in the state of Tasmania despite opposition from the state government).

The states have continued to develop policies, programs and administrative structures to address local and sub-regional issues, but many of the large environmental challenges in Australia extend across state and regional boundaries. From the 1980s the federal government strengthened its roles in providing strategic environmental policy leadership and financial incentives for improved natural resource management. Three examples are briefly outlined to illustrate how the financial, legal and political levers available to the federal government were deployed to tackle issues that the states acting alone could not have resolved.

1.   Water resources in the Murray–Darling Basin
Occupying one-seventh of Australia, this major river basin extends across several jurisdictional borders. Businesses and natural resource use have been subject to the regulatory and developmental policies of four states (New South Wales, Victoria, Queensland, South Australia) and the

Australian Capital Territory. The intergovernmental Murray–Darling Ministerial Council, which also included the federal government, oversaw the political–administrative governance of cross-border issues for several decades but was unable to deal with tough issues. In particular, the states had difficulty, individually and collectively, in addressing three major issues: the trade-off between water use for industry (irrigated agriculture) and environment (river health and biodiversity); the introduction of full-cost pricing for extracted water; and the introduction of a water trading market to facilitate buy-backs and retirement of water extraction licences. During the long drought of 2001–08, the pressures for concerted action intensified (Hussey and Dovers 2007; Crase 2008). The federal government asserted its political, legal and financial strength to negotiate agreements under which the states ceded the legal powers necessary for a single federal authority to be established, to undertake integrated water planning. Additional federal legislation also established a market for irrigation water in the Basin, and statutory powers to reserve water for environmental flows (Quiggin et al. 2012). This strategic policy solution involved elements of collaborative governance, market-based instruments and traditional regulatory authority to change the paradigm for water management in the Basin. There was a reasonable degree of bipartisan support in the federal parliament for the reform process, allowing breakthroughs to be achieved despite the complex local politics concerning water targets and trade-offs in each sub-region. The scientific evidence concerning the need for action and the scope for significant change was insufficient to convince many local stakeholders that the socioeconomic impacts could be readily managed.

2. Regional NRM planning

Natural resource management issues in Australia have focused on rural industries: their use of land and coastal resources for farming, forestry, mining and fisheries, and the impacts of these activities on the long-term sustainability of natural resources and environmental assets. In the late 1980s and early 1990s, the federal government began to encourage 'ecologically sustainable' approaches to rural industries in order to avoid further degradation of land and water resources. Owing to the inherent conflicts between economic development lobbies and environmental advocacy groups, the federal government invested in science initiatives to strengthen the information base for impact assessment, and for determining reasonable limits for resource extraction (e.g. forestry assessment processes were established to facilitate sustainable harvesting while protecting 'old-growth' forests). Landholders were also encouraged to take responsibility for improved management of their properties. Governments could not compel the adoption of better farming techniques, but they were able to encourage local landholder groups to champion new approaches. State-level landcare initiatives were provided with additional federal funds (Campbell 1994; Curtis and Lockwood 2000), and new federal programs encouraged NRM planning and assessments at a 'regional' scale appropriate to the bio-physical scale of landscape issues (AFFA 1999). For this purpose the federal government negotiated 56 regional planning regions with management capacity to undertake evidence-based NRM planning and to identify key priority projects for funding. These well-intentioned federal programs had mixed results owing to governance confusion and duplication of state efforts. While the federal audit office (e.g. ANAO 2008) emphasized the need to specify more tightly how federal funds were expended, the federal programs were essentially complementary to state efforts and did not attempt to integrate with them. Funding uncertainties and periodic shifts in federal priorities undermined local morale and effective collaboration (Head 2009; Robins and Kanowski 2011).

3.   Greenhouse gas reduction and climate change response
Awareness of greenhouse gas reduction as a strategic policy issue for national action was slow to develop in Australia. The issue has remained contentious in recent years despite Australia's willingness to accept international obligations under both Labor and Conservative governments. State governments also developed a range of measures to assist in reduction of greenhouse gases, such as restrictions on massive land clearing in rural areas and incentives to reward energy efficiency. However, the main policy levers to influence corporate behaviour always resided with the federal government. A prescriptive and regulatory approach had no political support, so the policy instruments selected were a mix of direct incentives and market-based mechanisms. Given the prominent role of the coal-mining sector in Australia, both for domestic power generation and for lucrative exports into the rapidly growing Asian economies, Conservative governments tended to favour subsidies to industry for switching to energy-efficient practices. The federal government of Prime Minister Howard (1996–2007) also developed a grants program to encourage adaptation to climate change, with an emphasis on robust infrastructure and better emergency management in response to climate variability and extreme weather events. The main debate from 2007 was about the role of a carbon pricing scheme to encourage new investment in alternative energy sources. Howard appointed an expert taskforce that recommended a trading scheme in 2007, and the new Labor government of Prime Minister Rudd established a major review by economist Ross Garnaut, modelled in part on the UK's Stern Report, which had argued for the benefits of early action. The Garnaut review recommended an emissions

trading scheme (Garnaut 2008) and a bill was passed in the lower house of parliament in 2009 but blocked in the Senate by an unlikely combination of Conservatives and Greens. The fragile bipartisanship concerning a market-based mechanism for carbon pricing collapsed in 2009, although a revised legislative scheme was passed in 2011 for implementation in 2012 (Beeson and McDonald 2013). A new Conservative government in 2013 abolished the federal agencies focused on climate change, and abolished the emissions trading scheme entirely, while maintaining a grants program for energy efficiency. The scientific evidence base, identifying the scope of climate change problems and related needs for policy change, was quickly discounted in the partisan politics that were rekindled after 2009.

Outcomes and Implications

The Australian government's attempts to address these major policy challenges in environmental and natural resource management required an increased commitment to strategic policy intervention in these areas. The federal role began, first, by attempting more systematic coordination across levels of government and across departmental boundaries; and, second, by providing greater investments in scientific research and systems for monitoring and evaluation. Over time, the government explored other options – grants programs, high-level inquiries and market-based trading instruments. The timeframes for influencing NRM and environmental outcomes are long term, and the five-yearly *State of the Environment* report indicates few, if any, matters of measurable improvement over the last two decades. The difficulties of reversing such trends in NRM systems are well known and widely understood. In the specific case of climate change policy, greenhouse gas reduction targets have been modest and the achievements over the last two decades are more akin to stabilization rather than transformative new directions.

Nevertheless, some of the building blocks have been put in place to enable future progress in a number of NRM and environmental fields. The extent of progress will depend on several factors. Political leadership is necessary, to provide authorization and encouragement for the public bureaucracy to seek creative and collaborative solutions, as envisaged in the various APS innovation documents outlined above. Ideally, the processes and forums for developing long-term approaches would allow bipartisan support to consolidate broad directions and lessen the risk of chaotic policy switches. Collaboration across agencies and across levels of government is necessary for developing and implementing the broad packages of goals and programs to tackle the wicked problems of NRM. Processes to allow pools of shared funding, with shared goals and accountabilities, have been envisaged (DFD 2012) but progress in implementing such arrangements in risk-averse cultures has been glacial.

CONCLUSIONS: BUILDING POLICY CAPACITY AND GOOD GOVERNANCE

The task of reforming the machinery of the public service, improving the capacities of the workforce, and simultaneously rethinking the strategic frameworks necessary for tackling major long-term policy challenges, has constituted a massive contemporary tension at the heart of APS governance. With the increased contestability in sources of policy advice that emerged as part of the NPM reforms, and an associated risk that the policy capacities of core departments would be undermined, some additional sources of policy capacity and review have been built alongside the standard advisory activities of the core public service agencies. As in other countries, there have been some limited moves to reassert central steering on major policy issues (Dahlström et al. 2011). In the Australian case this was exemplified when the newly elected federal government in 2013, as one of its first acts of governing, pulled all Indigenous programs into the Department of the Prime Minister and Cabinet.

An example of this return to central steering has been the use of special taskforces, generally steered and coordinated by central agencies such as the Treasury or the Department of the Prime Minister and Cabinet. These taskforces have investigated long-term structural issues, and led to a number of valuable reports, for example, on the implications of an ageing population (Department of Treasury 2010), the challenges of Australia's future prosperity within the Asia-Pacific region (DPMC 2012), and a major review of taxation (Henry 2010). Unfortunately, these strategic documents tend to be seen as associated with the government of the day, and are often devalued by an incoming government with different priorities and preconceptions.

A second important strategic policy option for the federal government has been to refer a number of key issues each year to the Productivity Commission. Formed in 1998 from an amalgamation of policy research entities, the Productivity Commission is a statutory public body dedicated to undertaking strategic policy inquiries as requested by the government (Banks 2010). The value of such a body lies in a combination of factors that underpin its unique status: its professional reputation for strong analysis; its open inquiry and submissions process; and its hard-won enjoyment of bipartisan support within the national parliament. The Commission has produced a large number of reports covering key topics on economic productivity, social policy reform and better management of environmental assets (Productivity Commission 2013). It has also provided invaluable support for two COAG steering groups on comparative services provision and on Indigenous strategies for 'closing the gap'.

A third source of strategic direction has focused on better performance monitoring in the complex field of intergovernmental services agreements. A large part of public expenditure is covered by such agreements, which include reporting requirements in relation to agreed performance benchmarks. The COAG Reform Council was established in 2004 to provide oversight of progress in the implementation of policy reforms and programs agreed by the prime minister and the premiers. The Reform Council focuses on the outcomes and performance benchmarks specified in national agreements, offering critical commentary on an ambitious and sometimes overcrowded agenda of policy changes to improve service efficiency and effectiveness (COAG Reform Council 2014). The Reform Council's reporting against Closing the Gap has been a prime example of its ability to weigh up the successes and challenges of intergovernment agreements that attempt to address wicked policy challenges. The COAG Reform Council was disbanded in 2014 by the Abbott federal government.

As we have shown here, building the capacity for addressing wicked problems is a complex business. Through exploring two cases we have highlighted that, whilst government may seek more collaborative and cooperative approaches both within its own boundaries but also across them into other sectors and with the community, its ability to do so is limited by seemingly immovable commitment to operating in a programmatic and bureaucratic fashion. Report after report has pointed to these tendencies as impediments to new ways of working, yet they persist and constrain attempts to address wicked policy challenges. It is difficult to see how substantial progress can be made without serious attempts at structural and cultural transformation of the model of governing in Australia. Our cases show, however, that incremental change is possible in some areas of these policy domains. Moving attention to the next stage, and fast-tracking progress, however, requires a fundamental rethinking of the way in which governments operate within and across their boundaries.

NOTES

1. Altman et al. (2008) present two sets of estimates: one for convergence based on long-run trends since 1971, and another for convergence based on post-1996 trends (see p. 13). We present estimates from the 1971 set unless indicated otherwise (*). They assume no radical change in policy settings. It is important to note that, whilst they acknowledge severe data issues, they work with the best-case scenarios.
2. For more information see http://www.atns.net.au/agreement.asp?EntityID=618.

REFERENCES

Adger, W.N. and A. Jordan (eds) (2009), *Governing Sustainability*, Cambridge: Cambridge University Press.

AFFA (Agriculture Fisheries and Forestry Australia) (1999), 'Managing natural resources in rural Australia for a sustainable future'. Discussion Paper, Canberra: AFFA.

AGRAGA (Advisory Group on the Reform of Australian Government Administration) (2010), *Ahead of the Game: Blueprint for the Reform of Australian Government Administration*, Canberra: Department of the Prime Minster and Cabinet.

Altman, J., N. Biddle and B. Hunter (2008), *The Challenge of 'Closing the Gap' in Indigenous Socioeconomic Outcomes*, Canberra: Australian National University, Centre for Aboriginal Economic Policy Research.

ANAO (Australian National Audit Office) (2007), *Whole of Government Indigenous Service Delivery Arrangements*, Audit Report No. 10, Canberra: ANAO.

ANAO (Australian National Audit Office) (2008), *Regional Service Delivery Model for the Natural Heritage Trust and the National Action Plan for Salinity and Water Quality*. Audit Report No. 21, Canberra: ANAO.

APSC (Australian Public Service Commission) (2003), 'The Australian experience of public sector reform', Occasional Paper 2, Canberra: APSC.

APSC (Australian Public Service Commission) (2007a), *Changing Behaviour: A Public Policy Perspective*, Discussion Paper, Canberra: APSC.

APSC (Australian Public Service Commission) (2007b), 'Tackling wicked problems: a public policy perspective', Discussion Paper, Canberra: APSC.

Banks, G. (2010), *An Economy-Wide View: Speeches on Structural Reform*, Canberra: Productivity Commission.

Beeson, M. and M. McDonald (2013), 'The politics of climate change in Australia', *Australian Journal of Politics and History*, **59**(3), 331–48.

Bouckaert, G. and J. Halligan (2008), *Managing Performance: International Comparisons*, London: Routledge.

Campbell, A. (1994), *Landcare: Communities Shaping the Land and its Future*, Sydney: Allen & Unwin.

Carroll, P. and M. Painter (eds) (1995), *Microeconomic Reform and Federalism*, Canberra: Federalism Research Centre, Australian National University.

Clark, C. and D. Corbett (eds) (1999), *Reforming the Public Sector: Problems and Solutions*, Sydney: Allen & Unwin.

COAG (Council of Australian Governments) (2008), *National Indigenous Reform Agreement (Closing the Gap)*, Canberra: Council of Australian Governments.

COAG Reform Council (2013), *Indigenous Reform 2011–12: Comparing Performance across Australia*, report to the Council of Australian Governments, Sydney: Council of Australian Governments.

COAG Reform Council (2014), *COAG Reform Agenda*, at https://www.coagreformcouncil. gov.au/agenda.

Collard, K.S., H.A. D'Antoine, D.G. Eggington, B.R. Henry, A.C. Martin and G.H. Mooney (2005), 'Mutual obligation in Indigenous health: can shared responsibility agreements be truly mutual?', *The Medical Journal of Australia*, **182**(10), 502–4.

Crase, L. (ed.) (2008), *Water Policy in Australia: The Impact of Change and Uncertainty*, London: Earthscan.

Curtis, A. and D. Lockwood (2000), 'Landcare and catchment management in Australia', *Society & Natural Resources*, **13**(1), 61–73.

Dahlström, C., B.G. Peters and J. Pierre (eds) (2011), *Steering from the Centre: Strengthening Political Control in Western Democracies*, Toronto: University of Toronto Press.

Davis, G. and P. Weller (eds) (2001), *Are You Being Served? States, Citizens and Governance*, Sydney: Allen & Unwin.

Department of Environment (2011), *Australia State of the Environment 2011*, report of the independent SOE committee, Canberra: Department of Environment. http://

www.environment.gov.au/topics/science-and-research/state-environment-reporting/
soe-2011.
Department of Treasury (2010), *Intergenerational Report 2010*, Canberra: Treasury.
DFD (Department of Finance and Deregulation) (2012), 'Sharpening the focus: a framework
for improving Commonwealth performance', Commonwealth Financial Accountability
Review Position Paper, Canberra: DFD.
Dovers, S.R. and S. Wild River (eds) (2003), *Managing Australia's Environment*, Sydney:
Federation Press.
DPMC (Department of the Prime Minister and Cabinet) (2012), *Australia in the Asian
Century: White Paper*, Canberra: DPMC.
Dunleavy, P. and C. Hood (1994), 'From old public administration to new public manage-
ment', *Public Money & Management*, **14**(3), 9–16.
Fenna, A. and R. Hollander (2013), 'Dilemmas of federalism and the dynamics of the
Australian case', *Australian Journal of Public Administration*, **72**(3), 220–27.
Forsyth, P. (ed.) (1992), *Microeconomic Reform in Australia*, Sydney: Allen & Unwin.
Garnaut, R. (2008), *Report of the Garnaut Climate Change Review*, Canberra: Climate
Change Review. http://www.garnautreview.org.au/2008-review.html.
Government 2.0 Taskforce (2009), *Engage: Getting on with Government 2.0*, Canberra:
Department of Finance and Deregulation.
Halligan, J. and J. Power (1992), *Political Management in the 1990s*, Melbourne: Oxford
University Press.
't Hart, P. (2010), 'Lifting its game to get ahead: the Canberra bureaucracy's reform by
stealth', *Australian Review of Public Affairs*, July, online at http://www.australianreview.
net/digest/2010/07/thart.html.
Head, B.W. (2008), 'Wicked problems in public policy', *Public Policy*, **3**(2), 101–18.
Head, B.W. (2009), 'From government to governance: explaining and assessing new
approaches to NRM', in M.B. Lane, C. Robinson and B. Taylor (eds), *Contested Country:
Local and Regional Natural Resource Management in Australia*, Melbourne: CSIRO
Publishing, pp. 15–28.
Head, B.W. (2010), 'How can the public sector resolve complex issues? Strategies for steer-
ing, administering and coping', *Asia Pacific Journal of Business Administration*, **2**(1), 8–16.
Head, B.W. and J. Alford (2015), 'Wicked problems: implications for public policy and man-
agement', *Administration and Society* (available online 28 March 2013).
Henry, K. (2010), *Australia's Future Tax System. Final Report* (chair Ken Henry), Canberra:
Department of Treasury.
Hussey, K. and S.R. Dovers (eds) (2007), *Managing Water for Australia: The Social and
Institutional Challenges*, Melbourne: CSIRO Publishing.
Industry Commission (1996), *Competitive Tendering and Contracting by Public Sector
Agencies*, Canberra: Industry Commission.
KPMG (2007), *Evaluation of Indigenous Coordination Centers: Final Report*, Canberra:
KPMG International.
Lindquist, E. (2010), 'From rhetoric to blueprint: the Moran Review as a concerted, com-
prehensive and emergent strategy for public service reform', *Australian Journal of Public
Administration*, **69**(2), 115–51.
Lindquist, E., S. Vincent and J. Wanna (eds) (2011), *Delivering Policy Reform: Anchoring
Significant Reform in Turbulent Times*, Canberra: ANU e-Press.
MAC (Management Advisory Committee) (2004), *Connecting Government: Whole of
Government Responses to Australia's Priority Challenges*, Canberra: Department of the
Prime Minister and Cabinet.
MAC (Management Advisory Committee) (2010), *Empowering Change: Fostering Innovation
in the Australian Public Service*, Canberra: Department of the Prime Minister and Cabinet.
McCausland, R. (2005), 'Shared responsibility agreements: practical reconciliation or pater-
nalistic rhetoric?', *Indigenous Law Bulletin*, **6**(12), 9–11.
Moran, T. (2013), 'Reforming to create value: our next five strategic directions', *Australian
Journal of Public Administration*, **72**(1), 1–6.

Morgan Disney & Associates Pty Ltd (2006), *A Red Tape Evaluation in Selected Indigenous Communities: Final Report for the Office of Indigenous Policy Coordination*, Canberra: Office of Indigenous Policy Coordination.

O'Flynn, J. (2014), 'Crossing boundaries: the fundamental questions in public management and policy', in J. O'Flynn, D. Blackman and J. Halligan (eds), *Crossing Boundaries in Public Management and Policy: The International Experience*, London: Routledge, pp. 11–44.

O'Flynn, J., D. Blackman and J. Halligan (eds) (2014), *Crossing Boundaries in Public Management and Policy: The International Experience*, New York: Routledge.

O'Flynn, J., F. Buick, D. Blackman and J. Halligan (2011), 'You win some, you lose some: experiments with joined-up government', *International Journal of Public Administration*, **34**(4), 244–54.

Painter, M. (1998), *Collaborative Federalism: Economic Reform in Australia in the 1990s*, Cambridge: Cambridge University Press.

Pollitt, C. and G. Bouckaert (2011), *Public Management Reform: A Comparative Analysis*, 3rd edn, Oxford: Oxford University Press.

Prime Minister of Australia (2010), *Closing the Gap: Prime Minister's Report 2010*, Canberra: Commonwealth of Australia.

Prime Minister of Australia (2013), *Closing the Gap: Prime Minister's Report 2013*, Canberra: Commonwealth of Australia.

Prime Minister of Australia (2014), *Closing the Gap: Prime Minister's Report 2014*, Canberra: Commonwealth of Australia.

Productivity Commission (2012), *2012 Indigenous Expenditure Report*, Canberra: Productivity Commission.

Productivity Commission (2013), *Annual Report 2012–13*, Canberra: Productivity Commission. http://www.pc.gov.au/__data/assets/pdf_file/0008/128438/annual-report-2012-13.pdf.

Quiggin, J., T. Mallawaarachchi and S. Chambers (eds) (2012), *Water Policy Reform: Lessons in Sustainability from the Murray–Darling Basin*, Cheltenham, UK and Northampton, MA, USA: Edward Elgar Publishing.

Rittel, H.W.J. and M.M. Webber (1973), 'Dilemmas in a general theory of planning', *Policy Sciences*, **4**(2), 155–69.

Robins, L. and P. Kanowski (2011), '"Crying for our country": eight ways in which "Caring for our country" has undermined Australia's regional model for natural resource management', *Australasian Journal of Environmental Management*, **18**(2), 88–108.

SGIA (Secretaries' Group on Indigenous Affairs) (2005), *Annual Report on Indigenous Affairs 2004–05. Canberra, Australia: Office of Indigenous Policy Coordination*, Department of Immigration and Multicultural and Indigenous Affairs, Canberra: Commonwealth of Australia.

Shergold, P. (2004), 'Connecting government: whole of government responses to Australia's priority challenges', speech to launch the report of the Department of the Prime Minister and Cabinet, 20 April.

Steering Committee for the Review of Government Service Provision (2003), *Overcoming Indigenous disadvantage: Key Indicators 2003 Overview*, Canberra: Commonwealth of Australia.

Weller, P. (1996), 'Commonwealth-state reform processes: a policy management review', *Australian Journal of Public Administration*, **55**(1), 95–110.

16. The state and perceptions of public sector reform in Europe

Dion Curry, Gerhard Hammerschmid, Sebastian Jilke and Steven Van de Walle

INTRODUCTION

As in most other areas of the world, the public sector in Europe has undergone significant reform in the past two decades, shaped in part by a broader new public management (NPM) paradigm, but one that also introduces a unique European flavour. Whilst NPM and public administration in Europe share similarities with other cases, differing starting points and the EU layer provide interesting insights into the nature of public sector reforms from a broader comparative perspective. This chapter will draw on a large-scale survey of top European executives in central government in order to develop a more comprehensive and comparative picture of NPM reforms and their effects over the last five years. Focusing on a cross-section of nine EU countries plus Norway, the chapter will present findings on reform initiatives, relevance of different reform trends and their general success and impact within the case countries.

The chapter will first provide a general overview of the state of public administration and the public sector in the European countries under study before turning to how the public sector and its reform are perceived by top executives. This latter investigation will focus on key trends in public sector reform in terms of both NPM and post-NPM reforms such as outcome/result orientation, downsizing, contracting out, cutting red tape, transparency and openness, cooperation, digital/e-government, citizen participation and others. The chapter will look at the importance of these trends in the selected countries before examining the nature of these reforms. Finally, the perceived success and overall impact of these reforms will be assessed, along with a brief examination of the impacts of the fiscal crisis on reforms in Europe. Throughout, the chapter will explore similarities and differences in these issues across the European countries under study, before providing some conclusions about the state of the public sector, its reform and prospects for its future from a European perspective.

PUBLIC ADMINISTRATION AND THE PUBLIC SECTOR IN EUROPE: A GENERAL OVERVIEW

The public sector in Europe has always drawn on a diverse set of starting points in terms of ideals, wealth and breadth. NPM-style reforms have also moved at different times, paces and extents through Europe. While the UK was at the forefront of such reforms, countries on the continent, especially southern European countries and the post-communist states, were slower to adopt change. In all countries, these changes came about through various combinations of necessity, learning and innovation, ability and will. At the base of any public sector reform in Europe lie different and often competing traditions of public administration. Napoleonic traditions in many of the southern European countries (Ongaro, 2009) come from a very different starting point from the former communist states in terms of both what the public sector should do and how it should do it. Anglo-Saxon and Scandinavian models also add to the mix. The EU has also acted to shape the nature of reform, especially through accession criteria for new member states. Reforms to these traditions have then been driven by political will or a lack thereof, with some countries having politicians with clear and distinct driving ambitions for the public sector, whereas in other countries reforms have been more piecemeal and less ideologically driven. Political will is often also shaped by the power of the trade unions representing the public sector, which in turn affects the nature and extent of reform. Finally, the economic boom of the 1990s and the current economic crisis have necessitated changes in direction and approach.

While classic NPM issues are still relevant to any discussion of the state of the public sector and its future reform, in recent years other factors have risen in importance. Questions of civic engagement through forms such as digital and e-governance have become more important with technological and ideational shifts (Dunleavy et al., 2006). Along with this, there is more emphasis on making public management more transparent and accountable, potentially opening it to new public and private actors. At the same time, within the public sector there has been an increasing prevalence of cooperation and collaboration in many different directions (O'Leary and Blomgren Bingham, 2009). A more bottom–up approach has been championed in some public sector approaches as either a positive way to engage governments and citizens 'on the ground', or as an attempt to download services and costs to lower levels of government. There has also been a consolidation of public services as a way of improving efficiency and streamlining public services. These factors all create a complex stew of factors that act differently in diverse country contexts to both drive and impede reform in European countries.

THE CASE COUNTRIES

The case countries cover a broad swathe of European countries and provide a comprehensive picture of how public sector reforms have taken root in different European contexts. The sample is drawn from countries of varying economic, social and political conditions, as well as covering both traditionally 'West' and 'East' countries, and both northern and southern European countries. The case countries include Austria, Estonia, France, Germany, Hungary, Italy, the Netherlands, Norway, Spain and the UK.

Administrative reform in Austria has been an integral part of most government programmes over the last decades and frequently described as a never-ending story. The influx and rise of a more managerial agenda started in the late 1980s/early 1990s (1989–1993) with a relatively comprehensive public management reform project that was later succeeded by administrative innovation programmes with a similar managerial emphasis (Hammerschmid and Meyer, 2005). These programmes included a commitment to efficiency and cost-saving, corporatization, customer orientation, modern personnel management, management instruments and performance measurement mostly implemented in the form of small-scale projects. With a fundamental political change in 2000 that brought a nearly 60-year period of social-democratic government involvement to an end, public sector reforms strongly gained momentum. A large number of corporatizations, in addition to civil service system reforms and other restructuring of the machinery of government, played an important role in this phase, which culminated in a prominent 'Austrian convent' (2003–2005) for fundamental state and administrative reform. However, this had only very modest outcomes in administrative practice. More recent years have been marked by far-reaching budgetary reform in 2007 and a strong e-government agenda that has put Austria in a top position in the EU e-government benchmark. The budget reform resulted in a government-wide change towards outcome-based budgeting and accrual accounting, as well as other key elements of a performance management logic that came into force in 2013.

In Estonia, reforms started after the country regained its independence from the Soviet Union in 1991. There were three main periods of public sector reform. In the first period after transition (1991–96), broad reforms were carried out and privatization, regulation and de-monopolization all occurred. In the lead-up to EU accession (1996–2004), more specific reforms took place to meet EU accession criteria and address issues such as transparency, accountability and accessibility of services. Post EU accession (2004 to the present), Estonian public service reform has been disjointed, although some NPM-style reforms have taken place, such as harmonizing public and private working conditions. In general, Estonia has been amenable to NPM reforms, and regularly uses tools such as contracting out and performance-based indicators. It is also widely recognized for its e-government reforms (Savi and Metsma, 2013).

In France, public service reforms have occurred slowly and have been relatively resistant to NPM-style reforms (Rouban, 2008; Pollitt and Bouckaert, 2011). France's limited application and slow roll-out of NPM public administration reforms in the 1980s and 1990s have given it a considerably different outlook on the role and values of public administration compared to other countries in the study. However, France's approach to public administration did evolve, but more incrementally and selectively than in other countries. This may be due in part to the Napoleonic traditions still valued in France, and the high degree of centralization of the French state. In the 1980s, reforms in France first favoured decentralization over efficiency or managerial reform, but did address some NPM issues such as service quality, user concerns and various management reforms. Throughout the 1990s, NPM policy instruments and tools were increasingly used in the French public service. The main reforms were in the area of budgetary processes, introducing tools such as programme-oriented budgets, an increased emphasis on performance management and new accountability measures. Under Sarkozy in 2007, there was also a General Public Policy Review intended to look at efficient use of objectives, instruments and implementation, again drawing from NPM-style ideas. This led to rather far-reaching reforms under Sarkozy's government, which have substantially altered the French public service, moving it away from Napoleonic ideas of centrality and uniformity and introducing more performance management techniques. In contrast, approaches such as agencification have occurred to a much lesser – and less systematic – extent in France (Bezes and Jeannot, 2013).

In Germany, public administration reform has been a recurring phenomenon in which different strands or waves have been identified (Jann, 2003). While Germany in the 1960s espoused an 'active' state emphasizing state planning and intervention as drivers for social and economic progress, this shifted in the 1980s and 1990s to a 'lean' state model stressing privatization and public sector downsizing in line with NPM ideas. Since the late 1990s, this shifted to the idea of an 'activating' state built on new ways of engaging with society where the state guarantees public services, but engages with private and third sectors for financing and delivering these services. The government reform programmes initiated since 1998 clearly resemble both NPM and neo-Weberian ideas such as a professional and flexible HRM, better public management based on modern management instruments, structural changes (e.g. shared services, task reduction, process orientation, customer service) and e-government. While many of the reforms have taken up NPM ideas, Germany is considered as a late-comer and is at a rather early stage of building a managerial state system (Bouckaert and Halligan, 2008). The overall hesitant stance towards administrative reform is due to several institutional factors. First, the highly federalized nature of the German state severely limits the imposition of centralized administrative reforms. This is coupled with a decentralized power structure, functionally divided policy-making and implementation, and a pronounced legalistic Rechtsstaat tradition with a deeply ingrained civil service identity and ethos emphasizing formal processes, rules and stability. Recent reform initiatives have now started to move towards newer post-NPM ideas such as transparency and network-based solutions (Pollitt and Bouckaert, 2011), but these are still very much an evolution of previous reforms, rather than a complete break into something new (Hammerschmid et al., 2013b).

Hungary has also significantly reformed its public administration since the fall of communism. A unitary state, it makes extensive use of both ministries and agencies, with the former largely responsible for policy-making and the latter responsible for implementing these policies. Since 1990, Hungary has undergone significant agencification, but these agencies largely lacked any overarching structural or legal framework until 2006, when a law was enacted that set out the basic requirements of these agencies as part of the larger government apparatus. Local governments were responsible for a large amount of public service delivery as well, but in 2011 many services, including health and education, were centralized. A combination of a strong legislature responsible for many executive functions, a high, two-thirds vote threshold for the change of many laws, a strong system of checks and balances, a separate judicial administration and a strong network of ombudsmen created a system of 'regulatory impotence' (Hajnal, 2010) that placed limits on what policy-makers could do. Wide-sweeping administrative change has been undertaken since 2010 when the Viktor Orbán government secured a two-thirds majority in Cabinet and thus was able to undertake significant reforms. These changes have removed many of the checks and balances that previously directed public administration in the country, and strengthened political and hierarchical control over most facets of administration, partly as a way of dealing with the financial crisis at the time. Ministries were overhauled and replaced by eight 'superministries', regional agencies have come under tighter central control, local government power has been reduced and bureaucratic recruitment is now controlled more hierarchically (Hajnal, 2013).

In Italy, the administrative systems and structures have been relatively unstable over the last 20 years. New and old structures have been introduced or changed in a sometimes overlapping fashion without improving their stability. The administrative situation has also been affected by the changing political landscape, with centre–right and centre–left coalitions treating administrative needs differently, and the installation of a technical government in 2011/12. Italy's attitudes towards Europe have altered the administrative landscape in both normal and austerity-era politics and policy. Whilst the centre–left largely abided by EU standards, the centre–right coalition was more willing to break from these, but the debt crisis in the country has pushed EU institutions into playing a more prominent role in public management reform in the country. While Italy has long displayed some patterns of 'southern' public administration, such as clientelism and a certain absence of an administrative elite, reform in the early 1990s has allowed for the development of a more autonomous administrative body and the introduction of NPM-style ideas. Relations between government and the bureaucracy were brought more in line with the private sector in terms of employment conditions and performance management measures were introduced. Many reforms related to public service employment conditions, with further reforms increasing transparency of contracts and introducing further performance assessment measures. However, other issues have remained relatively unchanged, including political appointments to middle-level civil service positions and the centrality of trade unions in issues related to public service employment practices. Interestingly, NPM-style reforms have taken place in one policy area – health care – to a much greater extent than in any other policy area (Ongaro et al., 2013).

In the Netherlands, the central government is mostly responsible for policy-making tasks, with executive and implementation tasks undertaken by agencies or local levels of government (although financed centrally). Dutch politics is consensual, and, as a result, ministries are relatively open to hearing external viewpoints from opposition parties, science and industry, but ministers retain ultimate responsibility for decisions. Although it has a unitary system, the Netherlands mostly avoids centralized government, and this is reflected in administrative reforms. For the most part, these reforms have aimed to slim down central government by devolving more tasks to agencies and local levels. NPM-type reforms such as results-based budgeting and performance measurement have been used, with a move to private sector style approaches undertaken in the 1980s. This slowed in the 1990s due to an easing of financial pressures and a desire to return to the 'primacy of politics' (Pollitt and Bouckaert, 2011, p. 291). Under the second Balkenende government starting in 2003, reforms were also undertaken at the state level, focusing on quality of services, savings on overhead costs and reducing the administrative burden of governments (Van Twist et al., 2009, p. 32). At the central level, there was also a push to reduce the administrative burden and bureaucracy, improve organization, clarify central government tasks and develop e-government approaches (Pollitt and Bouckaert, 2011, p. 296). While efficiency was a goal of this reform, it was more focused on reducing budgets and not on reducing the size of the civil service. Since 2007, reforms have focused on the central level of government, again looking to improve efficiency by promoting cooperation between departments and reducing fragmentation, but now also by reducing staff (Luts et al., 2008, p. 41; Van de Walle et al., 2013).

Norway features a large civil service due mainly to its universal welfare state, and trust in government has been high while the effects of the financial crisis have been small. Although it is a unitary state, there is some political and administrative decentralization. There are two ministerial levels in the country, with relatively powerful sectoral ministries and weaker supra-ministries that mainly play a coordination role between ministries (Christensen, 2003). There is a strong local level of government, and this level both develops and implements local-level policy and implements centrally decided policy. While economic strength and political and administrative culture have largely dampened the effects of NPM reforms in Norway, some changes have occurred in line with international waves of NPM reform. In the mid-1980s there were moves to reform the central level along some NPM-style lines, with more reform in the 1990s under pressure from the OECD to pursue further change. However, these reforms have not been consistent over time and tend to be piecemeal in nature. They have focused mainly on efficiency aspects within the public administration and have largely avoided other reforms such as privatization or downsizing the state. There has also been a shift towards developing more autonomous agencies, with a move since the 1990s to create more autonomous state-owned companies in many sectors, along with a greater focus on NPM reforms within these bodies, such as performance measurement and results-based budgeting. While these changes have increased vertical coordination, there is little horizontal coordination across sectors. In addition, the current government has attempted to roll back some of these NPM reforms. However, there is disagreement within the governing coalition about the state of the administration, resulting in a rebalancing rather than transformation of NPM reforms already implemented. This has created a layered and hybridized form of public administration combining old and new ideas (Christensen et al., 2007; Christensen and Lægreid, 2011; Lægreid et al., 2013).

Public administration reform in Spain has been undertaken both to get rid of Franco-style public administration ideals and also as an attempt to modernize the public sector. Starting from a broad Napoleonic tradition, Spanish reform in the late 1970s focused on reducing bureaucracy and red tape by reorganizing administrative and ministerial bodies. In the 1980s, the focus shifted to decentralization with the creation of regional governments and regulation of local governments. A greater emphasis was placed on modernization in the 1990s as a way to improve relations between the administration and citizens. This included NPM-type ideas such as treating the citizen as a customer, streamlining administrative procedures and increasing the focus on efficiency, effectiveness and quality of services. However, there was some resistance from senior executives to certain NPM objectives, such as managerial autonomy, management by objectives and a results-based focus, which limited the actual reform that took place in the country. Since the late 1990s, Spain has had a clear reform agenda with an NPM focus, aiming for a flexible and efficient organizational structure, reform of administrative courts, new regulatory frameworks for recruitment, efficiency and quality in service delivery, and the incorporation of new technology in the process (Torres and Pina, 2004). Other post-NPM reforms have started to appear in the 2000s, such as efforts to improve transparency and cooperation and collaboration among different public bodies. Since the crisis, most reforms have been driven by budgetary restrictions (Alonso and Clifton, 2013).

Finally, public administration reform has been a persistent theme in the UK, albeit one that ebbs and flows. The extent of changes and the focus on many private sector ideals in public administration have generally led the UK to be seen as the 'purest' and most extensive form of NPM in Europe. While this is true, the differences between the UK example and other European cases should not be overstated (Pollitt and Bouckaert, 2011). After the establishment of the welfare state and a gradual professionalization of the civil service, in the 1970s the focus moved to improving efficiency and effectiveness of public institutions, including a drastic reorganization and reduction of local governments in 1974. After the economic crises of the 1970s and the election of Thatcher in 1979, significant NPM-style reform of the public sector was undertaken. Key goals were to reduce the size of the public sector, open it to market forces and run it more like a private sector business. The civil service, previously under its own department, was put under control of the Treasury and business-like arrangements such as target-based management and, in some cases, performance-based pay were introduced. Compulsory competitive tendering was launched at the local level, along with further competition in providing public services. Tony Blair's election in 1997 marked the beginning of a 'Third Way' approach to balance the market, state and civil society in providing services. This approach retained business-inspired ideas such as performance measures and contracting out, while attempting to balance this with a top–down focus on continuous improvement and target-based planning, along with a post-NPM aim to strengthen relationships and coordination between the various actors in delivering public services. This 'Third Way' approach left a public service driven largely by the market and NPM-style public administration coupled with a wilful effort to 'steer' the management of these disparate actors at the central governmental level. Since the election of the Conservative/ Liberal Democrat coalition in 2010, the focus of public administration reform has been clearly on reducing costs and the size of the public sector (Andrews et al., 2013).

FACTORS AFFECTING REFORM: GOAL AMBIGUITY AND PUBLIC SECTOR AUTONOMY

The Survey

In 2012, a 31-question survey was sent electronically or via post to over 21 000 high-ranking civil servants in ten European countries. The survey's aim was threefold: (1) to capture perceptions on the current status of management, coordination and administration reforms; (2) to gauge the effects of NPM-style reforms on performance, values/identities, coordination and social cohesion; and (3) to examine the impact of the financial crisis on public administration. The survey was sent to the entire population of top- and medium-high-level civil servants in both ministries and agencies in each country, translated into each country's national language. The overall response rate for the survey in the first ten countries was 23.7 per cent, with individual country response rates varying from 11.4 per cent (UK) to 36.5 per cent (Austria). While the overall response rate is somewhat low, it is consistent with other surveys of executives and in each country at least 300 responses were recorded, with total responses numbering 4814.[1]

As outlined above, many factors affect the ability of public sector reform to be introduced, and in turn the success of these reforms hinges on the public service's ability to undertake them in an effective manner. Two factors that have an impact on how easily managerial or NPM-type reforms are implemented are the existence of clear and measurable goals, and the autonomy of public sector executives or 'managers' in making these and related changes without political interference.

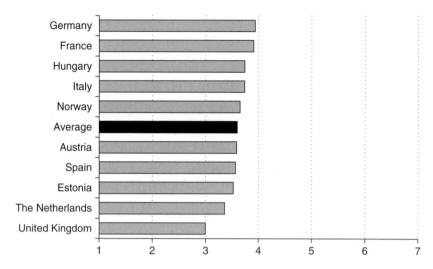

Note: Aggregate mean for four items per country: 1 = low goal ambiguity, 7 = high goal ambiguity.

Figure 16.1   Perceived goal ambiguity and measurability

Goal Ambiguity

Performance management and NPM-type reforms are best executed when goals are limited, clearly stated and communicated, and easy to observe and measure (Rainy and Jung, 2010). Based on the executives' perception of these four factors,[2] a rather uniform and moderate degree of goal ambiguity is evident in all countries (see Figure 16.1). A slightly lower degree of goal ambiguity is perceived in the UK, the Netherlands and Estonia, indicating a somewhat greater openness of these countries to performance management reforms. In contrast, Germany and France show a slightly higher degree of goal ambiguity. As to be expected, managers of agencies reported less goal ambiguity than managers in ministries.

There was also some variation between countries. Especially in Germany, the Netherlands, Norway and the UK, executives had a much more favourable view of whether their goals were clearly stated and communicated to staff, but that it was not so easy to observe and measure activities related to these goals. While this existence of goal ambiguity poses a challenge for many executives, the overall rather low degree does not seem to make it a major barrier to introducing management tools and concepts into public sector practices.

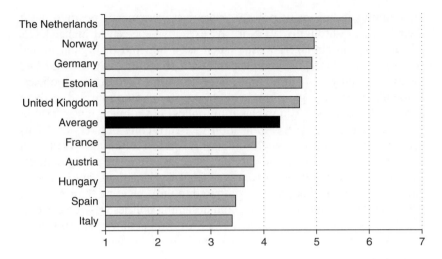

Note: Aggregate mean for eight items per country: 1 = very low autonomy, 7 = very high autonomy.

Figure 16.2   Perceived degree of management and policy autonomy

Autonomy of Public Sector Executives

Increasing the autonomy of the public sector *vis-à-vis* political institutions – in other words, letting the managers manage – has been a major focus of NPM-type reforms and has an impact on the nature and quality of reform. Autonomy consists of both managerial autonomy (the ability to make organizational and structural changes, as well as decisions on personnel, budget and contracting out) as well as policy autonomy (to design, decide on and implement policies), and the extent to which public sector institutions can make technical decisions free from political interference will have an effect on reform. While some country executives felt they had a high degree of autonomy (the Netherlands) with regard to these factors, others felt a low degree of autonomy to manage or make decisions freely (Italy) (see Figure 16.2).

In different countries, different types of autonomy were noted as being either stronger or weaker by public sector executives. For instance, in the UK, all forms of autonomy were perceived as higher than average, but especially in allocating budgets, organizational structuring and implementation of policies. Autonomy of the public sector in the Netherlands was perceived as high, and this applied across the board. Autonomy was seen to be highest in managerial tasks and implementing policy, but, even in designing and choosing policies, executives were mostly positive about their levels of autonomy. In Norway, executives perceived higher levels of autonomy in managerial issues such as hiring staff or organizational structure, as well as policy implementation. However, they felt they had lower autonomy in contracting out or choosing or designing policies. Estonian executives perceived a high degree of autonomy in making personnel decisions and implementing policy, but a much lower level in terms of structuring the organization or contracting out services. This was similar in Hungary, where the lowest level of autonomy was felt in contracting out services, and the highest level in implementing policies. Interestingly, in Germany, executives felt they had more autonomy in choosing and designing policies compared to implementing these policies. While their autonomy in choosing and designing policies was perceived as significantly higher than average in the European countries studied, their control over implementing the policies as well as management autonomy was actually lower (Hammerschmid et al., 2013b).

In France, in contrast, where perceptions of autonomy were below average, civil servants felt they had very little autonomy over recruitment, budgeting decisions and, especially, firing staff. On the policy side, French executives felt little autonomy in deciding on public policy decisions, but more autonomy in implementing them. Different groups of executives also felt different levels of control. While agency directors reported a high level of autonomy, directors of interministerial units at the *département* level felt they had little autonomy in most areas (Bezes and Jeannot, 2013).

Autonomy was perceived as particularly low in Italy and Spain. In Spain, executives felt they had a low level of autonomy almost across the board in both policy and managerial senses. Spanish results were well below the European average in choosing and designing policies, implementing policies, organizational structures, contracting out and allocating budgets, and were particularly low in promoting, hiring or firing staff. Italian executives perceived little autonomy over managerial decisions such as hiring and dismissing staff, partly due to a heavily unionized public sector, but on other measures of autonomy – budget reallocation, contracting out, organizational and structural design and effecting policy formulation and implementations – Italian executives perceived a level of autonomy higher than the European average. There was a significant sectoral difference in Italy, with those in the health care sector feeling they had significantly greater autonomy across the board. Overall, though, Italian executive autonomy was well below the European average (Ongaro et al., 2013).

In addition to the degree of autonomy, another indicator of managers' freedom in reform is the degree of politicization of the public sector. This

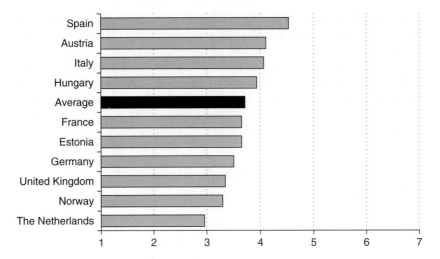

Note: Aggregate mean per country: 1 = low degree of politicization, 7 = high degree of politicization.

Figure 16.3   Perceived degree of politicization based on three items

was measured with questions about whether politicians respect the technical expertise of the administration, whether they try to influence senior-level appointments and whether they interfere in routine activities. When aggregated, these factors of politicization show some variation across Europe (Hammerschmid et al., 2013c) (see Figure 16.3).

Figure 16.3 shows that, unsurprisingly, those executives who felt they had higher autonomy also perceived a lower degree of politicization. In general, agency executives felt more autonomy than their ministry counterparts. With regard to country differences, executives in the Netherlands perceived the lowest level of politicization, with less interference from political levels, non-politicized senior-level appointments and more political respect for the technical expertise of executives. Executives in Norway and the UK also showed a relatively positive perception of their autonomy, particularly in regard to the respect politicians have for the technical expertise of the administration, which was significantly higher than the European average. Also, Estonia was found to have a relatively low level of politicization of the public sector, which is in line with previous research that shows that Estonia has among the lowest level of political interference in the civil service among the new Central and Eastern European EU countries (Meyer-Sahling, 2011). As a new democracy, the political parties in the country have not yet developed the capacity to steer public administration or become overly involved, and the small size of the country also means that there is less capacity to develop overlapping political and bureaucratic functions (Randma-Liiv, 2002).

In contrast, countries such as Spain, Italy and Austria showed a rather high level of politicization. Spanish executives had the highest perception of political interference, especially in influencing senior-level appointments and in instigating reforms, whereas executives at the same time do not feel that politicians interfere with day-to-day activities.

KEY TRENDS IN EUROPEAN PUBLIC SECTOR REFORM

As the countries analysed are rather diverse, it is interesting to note both similarities and differences in public sector reform across national contexts. NPM as a rather broad label encompasses several ideas and concepts, such as performance measurement, results orientation or contracting out and privatization. In addition, in recent years post-NPM ideas such as transparency, e-government and collaboration have also begun to take root in different national contexts. The relevance of these different facets of NPM and post-NPM reforms were assessed by top public executives and provide interesting insights into how well NPM is performing and has taken hold in various countries and Europe as a whole. It also provides an understanding of whether these NPM reforms have been increasingly supplanted or replaced by post-NPM ideas, as often argued in public administration literature.

The next three sections of this chapter will examine the perceptions of top public executives of public sector reform in their policy field over the last five years. First, it will examine perceptions on the importance of these reforms, before looking at the nature of these changes in terms of their approach. Finally, assessments of the success of these reforms will be examined. General trends can be observed, but specific examples will also be drawn from the case countries.

IMPORTANCE OF DIFFERENT TYPES OF REFORM

Public administration reform trends address different issues and have very different goals and trajectories. While traditional NPM reforms focus on issues such as contracting out, privatization and performance management, post-NPM ideas have placed greater emphasis on factors such as coordination and cooperation, transparency and citizen participation.

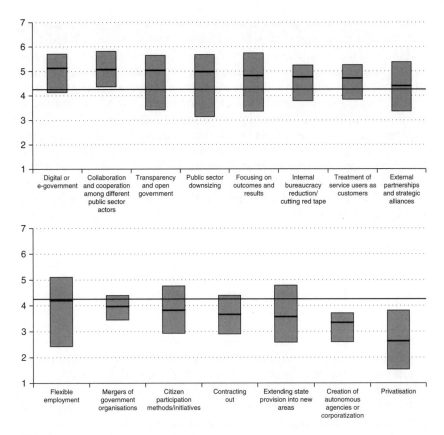

Notes:
Q: How important are the following reform trends in your policy area? 1 = Not at all, 7 =
To a large extent.
The graph depicts overall average plus highest/lowest country average; the solid line
indicates the average for all reform trends.

Figure 16.4   Importance of reform trends

After 20 years of NPM in the public eye, perceptions of NPM-style
reforms still differ on whether these reforms are, in fact, necessary, and
how important they are; the focus of public sector modernization over the
last 20 years has also shifted and now often incorporates post-NPM ideas
as well.

The results of the survey are revealing in showing an increased relevance of post-NPM reforms, while many NPM-style reforms have lost
relevance (see Figure 16.4). Overall, digital/e-government, public sector

collaboration and cooperation, transparency and open government are currently the most important reform trends. The main wave of NPM-type reforms such as privatization, agencification/corporatization or contracting out seems to be over and increasingly superseded by a new agenda of partnership- and network-oriented government arrangements and reforms. The effects of the fiscal crisis are clearly visible in European public administration, with a high relevance of public sector downsizing, outcome and result orientation and the reduction of internal bureaucracy.

In certain areas there was significant variation between countries. This was especially true in relation to public sector downsizing, a significantly important trend in countries such as the UK, France, Estonia and the Netherlands, but least important in Norway, where executives rated it a full point less important than the next-lowest country (Italy). There was also a large difference in how important a focus on outcomes and results was in each country: it was much more important in more managerial countries like the UK and the Netherlands, but less important in Spain, France and Italy. Flexible employment, privatization and transparency and open government also see significant cross-country variation. Transparency and open government are important throughout, although France remains somewhat of an outlier, with French executives rating it as much less important than executives from all other countries. Digital/e-government, collaboration/cooperation among public sector actors and customer orientation are all seen as important and show high consistency across countries.

In specific countries, there was also some variation in the comparative importance of these trends. Norwegian officials are mostly in line with the overall assessment and tend to see higher relevance in post-NPM reforms, often to a greater extent than the overall average. Transparent and open government and e-government are seen as most pertinent, but a focus on outcomes and results is also regarded as important. Although these officials saw collaboration and cooperation among different public actors as important, this was not reflected as clearly in actual practice, as vertical coordination is strong but horizontal coordination remains weak in Norway (Fimreite and Lægreid, 2009). The largest differences between Norway and the rest of the Europe were in the area of public sector downsizing, where only 25 per cent of Norwegian executives saw this as important compared to 70 per cent of the overall population (Lægreid et al., 2013).

The Netherlands also shows a mix in perceived importance between NPM and post-NPM reform trends. Collaboration and cooperation and transparency and open government are both seen as highly important, as is a focus on outcome and results. Privatization was seen to be the least important reform factor, along with agencification. Although the country pursued these strategies in the past, these are now seen as less important. In the UK, a focus on outcomes and results, public sector downsizing, e-government, transparency and external partnerships all received high scores in terms of importance. Privatization, agencification and the extension of state provision were deemed the least important in terms of reform. Transparency and open government and especially the development of external partnerships were more important in the UK than in Europe on average, while the extension of state provision was lower than average.

In Germany, NPM-style reform trends are not seen as overly important, with a majority finding reforms such as privatization, contracting out and agencification to be of low importance. However, some NPM-related trends were seen to be more relevant, with downsizing perceived as the most important, followed by a focus on outcomes and results, customer orientation and the cutting of red tape. Post-NPM trends such as e-government and transparency & open government were all seen as important by a majority of executives. In general, the German case was in line with other European countries, though, which belies the conception of Germany as lagging behind other countries in terms of public sector reform (Hammerschmid et al., 2013b).

French executives had a different perception of reform trends compared to other countries in many areas. Transparency, open government and citizen participation, along with flexible employment, contracting out and external partnerships, were all seen as relatively less important. While the relevance of downsizing measures and organizational mergers were seen as high, this was not equated to privatization, where only 9 per cent of executives felt this was highly relevant. Hungarian executives saw rather low relevance of many NPM-style reforms, most notably privatization, but also agencification and contracting out. However, downsizing was seen as one of the most relevant types of reform, along with a focus on citizens as customers. The importance of NPM reforms was also somewhat less developed in Spain, especially as regards agencification and customer orientation, which were lower than the European average. The reforms seen as most important were public sector downsizing, e-government and transparent and open government.

In Italy, the perceptions of importance of various reform trends were quite different from actual government priorities in these areas. Executives perceived that e-government, enhancing transparency and open government and citizen participation were important reform initiatives, but these had not been singled out at the governmental level. The importance of privatization and contracting out was also significantly higher in Italy than in Europe on average. This was even higher in the health sector, showing that NPM-style reforms have probably hit that sector the most (Ongaro et al., 2013).

THE NATURE OF REFORM IMPLEMENTATION

Overall views on the success of public sector reform are obviously important. Executives were asked their perceptions of reform dynamics based on ten different scales, as depicted in Table 16.1.

While some factors – such as top–down reform and an emphasis on cost-cutting and savings versus service improvement – were confirmed in nearly all countries, interesting differences were also noted in some countries. Executives in Norway tended to have a more positive view of reforms across the spectrum, seeing them as more consistent, comprehensive and substantial than the average. In addition, they saw them as more bottom-up, less contested by unions and more open to public involvement. The situation was clearly more negative in France, where most executives felt that the reforms were too demanding, contested by the unions, driven by the crisis and mainly implemented without public involvement. In Germany, more public sector executives than the European average felt that reforms were not demanding enough, which fits with previous research on Germany's incremental approach to public sector reform. This is also supported when compared to results in other countries. German executives perceived reforms to be more inconsistent, partial and symbolic than other countries, indicating more reticence to fast and comprehensive reform (Hammerschmid et al., 2013b). However, perceptions

Table 16.1   Public sector reforms

Public sector reforms in my policy area tend to . . .		
Be too demanding	←———→	Be not demanding enough
Be unsuccessful	←———→	Be successful
Have no public involvement	←———→	Have high public involvement
Be about cost-cutting and savings	←———→	Be about service improvement
Be contested by unions	←———→	Be supported by unions
Be substantial	←———→	Be symbolic
Be crisis and incident driven	←———→	Be planned
Be driven by politicians	←———→	Be driven by senior executives
Be comprehensive	←———→	Be partial
Be consistent	←———→	Be inconsistent
Be top–down	←———→	Be bottom–up

of success of these reforms were quite similar in Germany compared to most other countries.

Several of these factors deserve to be singled out. Executives in all ten countries were asked, in general, not just how successful public sector reform was, but also whether the reform was too demanding, or not demanding enough. On these two factors, little cross-country consensus or clear pattern was observed, as the groups cut across traditional north/south and east/west divides. Whilst the reform trends in most countries tend to be assessed as too demanding (especially in France, the Netherlands, Estonia, Hungary and the UK), executives in Austria, Germany and Norway see an overall need to speed up reforms. We also see that reforms in Norway, Estonia, Germany and the Netherlands are considered rather successful, whereas the reforms in Spain, France and Italy are regarded more critically. This suggests an uncoupling between types of reform undertaken (which more closely mirrors traditional groupings) and perceptions of whether these reforms were undertaken in an appropriate manner.

There was significantly more consensus between countries on whether the reforms were about cutting costs or improving services, but more variance on whether they had been successful or unsuccessful. Spanish executives were an extreme case in feeling that the reforms were clearly about cost-cutting but mostly unsuccessful.

Executives were also questioned about whether the reforms were conducted from the top down or from the bottom up. Here, executives in none of the surveyed countries felt that the reforms were conducted from the bottom up, and no clear pattern connected the top–down reforms with level of success. There were also few cases where executives felt that the reforms were conducted with significant public involvement, except in Hungary and Norway. The data gave a slight indication that reforms that involved the public were seen to be moderately more successful though (Hammerschmid et al., 2013a).

SUCCESS OF PUBLIC SECTOR REFORMS

Overall Impact

Of course, these reforms are aimed at improving the general situation of public administration in the case countries. After assessing the importance given to different facets of reform that public administration executives have experienced over the past five years, and the nature and reasoning behind these reforms, we now look at whether these reforms were perceived to be effective and successful.

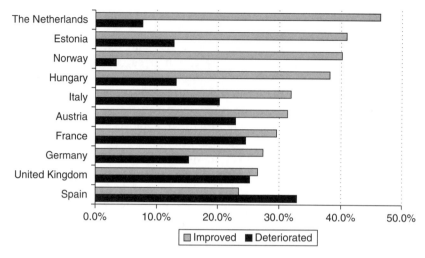

Notes:
Q: Compared with five years ago, how would you say things have developed when it comes to the way public administration runs in your country?

Figure 16.5   Overall PA assessment

Public executives were asked overall whether they had a positive or negative opinion of the situation of public administration in their country compared to five years ago. Here, there is significant variance between countries in whether their assessment of public administration had improved or deteriorated (see Figure 16.5). Spain was the only country where more respondents felt that the situation had deteriorated more than improved. Views were decidedly mixed in France and the UK, whereas Norway, Estonia, Hungary and the Netherlands all had high perceptions of improvement and low perceptions of deterioration. Concerning the impact of reforms, the survey aimed for a more nuanced perspective regarding different performance dimensions such as quality, costs, transparency or citizen trust in government.

All in all, there is relatively high stability with only moderate changes in these dimensions over the last five years. Also, there was not significant variation from country to country on many of these dimensions (see Figure 16.6). There was a perception that more managerial factors such as cost and efficiency, service quality and innovation all improved slightly, as did external transparency and openness, fair treatment of citizens and ethical behaviour among public officials. In contrast, there were perceptions of a slight deterioration in areas such as social cohesion, staff motivation and attractiveness of the public sector as an employer. Citizen trust

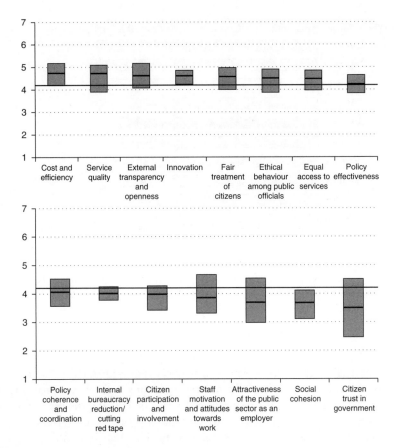

Notes:
Q: Thinking about your policy area over the last five years, how would you rate the way public administration has performed on the following dimensions? 1 = Deteriorated significantly, 7 = Improved significantly.

Figure 16.6   Different performance dimensions

in government was seen, on average, to be the aspect that had deteriorated to the highest degree over the last five years. In certain issues such as internal bureaucracy reduction/cutting red tape and innovation, there was little variation between countries in their assessment of these characteristics. In other areas, most noticeably citizen trust in government, but also in attractiveness of the public sector as an employer and staff motivation and attitudes towards work, there was more variation between countries in the relative success/deterioration in these qualities.

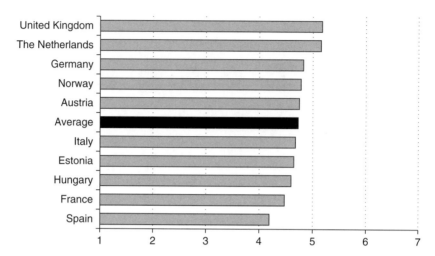

Notes:
Q: Thinking about your policy area over the last five years, how would you rate the
way public administration has performed on the dimension 'cost and efficiency'? 1 =
Deteriorated significantly, 7 = Improved significantly.

Figure 16.7   Cost and efficiency

Cost and efficiency was the most positively assessed outcome of public
sector reforms overall, with all countries reporting a general improvement
compared to five years ago (see Figure 16.7). The UK and the Netherlands
assessed this most positively, with Germany, Norway and Austria also
having an above-average view of success in this area. In contrast, Spain
was the country that reported least success in this area, although even
there the assessment was generally slightly positive.

At the other end of the spectrum, citizen trust in government was seen as
the least successful outcome of reform trends (see Figure 16.8). This trend
also showed significant variation between countries. Norway was the only
country to feel that citizen trust had modestly improved in the past five
years, with all other countries feeling that it had deteriorated. By some
margin, Spain was the country that felt this aspect had deteriorated the
most, with France, Italy and the UK also having fairly pessimistic views of
citizen trust compared to five years ago.

Each country had slightly different areas in which they felt there was
the most improvement. Situations were generally felt to have improved
in almost all areas in Norway, especially in service quality, cost and efficiency and innovation. Only in internal bureaucracy reduction/cutting of
red tape was there a relatively strong feeling that things had deteriorated,

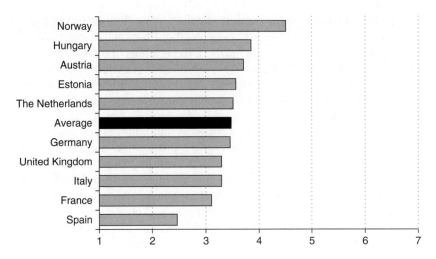

Notes:
Q: Thinking about your policy area over the last five years how would you rate the way public administration has performed on the dimension: citizen trust in government?; 1 = Deteriorated significantly, 7 = Improved significant

Figure 16.8   Citizen trust in government

but even here a larger proportion felt that it had improved. Results were significantly more positive in all areas apart from innovation when compared to the overall European perception, with service quality, transparency and citizen trust in government showing the biggest gap between Norway and the rest of Europe (Lægreid et al., 2013).

In Estonia, fair treatment of citizens, equal access to services and social cohesion were perceived to have improved more than in other European countries. Ministerial executives found more improvement in policy effectiveness and policy coherence and coordination, while, at the agency level, equal access to services and fair treatment of citizens were seen as the areas in which things were better than five years ago (Savi and Metsma, 2013). Improvements in the UK were mostly perceived in managerial functions such as cost efficiency, innovation, service quality and policy effectiveness, while citizens' trust in government and attractiveness of the public sector as an employer were seen by a majority of respondents to have deteriorated.

Dutch perceptions seem to have been shaped by recent issues in that country, with citizen trust in government and ethical behaviour among public officials rated rather low, corresponding to Dutch media stories about a 'Dutch dip' in public trust and numerous ethical scandals that were revealed within politics and the public service. In managerial areas, however, the Dutch were mostly positive about the quality compared to five years ago (Van de Walle et al., 2013). In Germany, managerial aspects of reform were also most positively assessed, with a majority of respondents seeing improvements in service quality, innovation and cost and efficiency. In policy-related fields, there was more sense of deterioration, with overall negative assessments of citizen trust in government, policy coherence and coordination, social cohesion and policy effectiveness.

In France, most reform outcomes were rated rather negatively, with cost and efficiency and innovation seen as most improved. In contrast, it was felt that social cohesion and citizen trust in government had declined the most, but citizen participation, staff motivation, attractiveness of the public sector as an employer and cutting of red tape were also seen to deteriorate. Views on most of these issues were more favourable for executives from the economic and financial sectors, especially as regards quality of service. In Hungary, ethical behaviour among officials was seen to be most improved, but this figure was still significantly below the European average. In general, Hungarian attitudes towards improvement were below the European average, with the least improvement seen in areas such as attractiveness of the public sector as an employer, citizen trust in government and the cutting of red tape.

Although the Spanish case was the most pessimistic compared to five years ago, there were certain areas where greater improvement was perceived. Ethical behaviour of civil servants, equal access to services and fair treatment of citizens were perceived as relatively improved, and service quality, innovation and transparency and openness also had some positive perceptions. However, over half felt that citizen trust in government had deteriorated, and public sector motivation and desirability as an employer were also perceived negatively. The perception of the public sector as an employer was actually more positive than the European average.

A few other employment-related factors were also measured in all countries. Job satisfaction was moderately high in all cases (more positive than negative), being highest in Norway, the Netherlands, the UK and Italy. For organizational commitment we found that in all countries executives showed a rather positive commitment to their organization. Commitment was especially high in Hungary and Italy, and lowest (but still positive) in Norway and the Netherlands. On the other hand, work stress showed fairly significant country variation. Stress was perceived as high in Spain (more stressful than not), while all other countries found their job to be less stressful than stressful. Stress levels were particularly low in Austria and Germany.

IMPACT OF THE FISCAL CRISIS

The financial crisis that has gripped Europe starting in 2008 has had an impact on the nature of the public sector and its reform in the countries under study. Only Norway was a significant outlier and barely affected by the financial crisis. Therefore a majority of respondents in this country did not perceive any cost-cutting measures. The nature of cuts differs across countries and can be assessed both in where these cuts took place and the way in which they were implemented. At an organizational level, most cutbacks in Estonia were realized through personnel savings. It was felt that the largest proportion of the cuts were made across all areas, whereas a somewhat smaller proportion of cutbacks were achieved through targeted cuts. The opposite was true in the Netherlands, where a somewhat higher proportion felt cuts were targeted, but a significant proportion still felt that cuts were across the board. Most cuts in that country came about through hiring freezes and cuts to programmes. In France, a main effect of the crisis has been an adjustment downwards of public servants' benefits to come into line with the private sector, along with a hiring freeze. There was no clear consensus on the nature of these cuts, with almost equal numbers feeling they were across the board, targeted or achieved through productivity gains. However, staff cuts and pay cuts are seen as unimportant in France: although a hiring freeze was in place, this did not result in cutting of staff. Meanwhile, there was a feeling that the budget crisis had increased the powers of the Ministry of Finance and centralized decision-making.

UK reforms in public administration were greatly affected by the downturn, which hit the country significantly. The current coalition government has made large cuts to the public sector as a response to the crisis. A majority of respondents felt that these cuts were targeted, but over one quarter felt that they were across the board and almost 20 per cent felt they were efficiency savings. In comparison to the rest of Europe, a larger proportion of UK executives saw some form of cutbacks, and these were more likely to be a result of pay freezes or staff cuts in the UK. The fiscal crisis also hit Spain hard, as it moved from above-average growth rates to significant decline and unemployment. The cuts were perceived by a large majority to be mostly targeted cuts. Proportional cuts across the board were the next-largest perceived cut. Many of these savings came from cutting personnel costs, with hiring freezes, wage freezes and pay cuts being seen as the most significant, along with cuts to new and existing programmes. The fiscal crisis hit Italian public administration as well, but was somewhat mitigated by the fact that Italy had been trying to rein in public spending before the crisis. The most significant cuts were across the board, and were significantly higher than the European average, whereas targeted cuts and efficiency savings were lower than average.

German public administration reform responses to the fiscal crisis have been evaluated as quite successful. Most executives responded that they had faced some sort of cutbacks. Compared to other countries, however, a much higher proportion saw these cuts as targeted, with fewer seeing across-the-board cuts. As in France, these cutbacks could not be realized through layoffs or even pay cuts, with savings brought about more through programme cuts and hiring freezes. Cutbacks in Hungary were fairly equally seen to be across the board and targeted, with mainly across-the-board cuts in delivering services, but targeted cuts at the ministerial level. Although the government in Hungary explains cutbacks as a move to make the public service more efficient, interestingly less than 2 per cent of respondents felt that cuts came from productivity and efficiency savings. Hiring freezes were seen as the most-used approach to cost-cutting, but staff cutbacks also represented a higher-than-average level of cost-cutting in Hungary compared to other European countries.

CONCLUSIONS

While public administration reforms – both NPM and post-NPM types – have taken place in all the countries under study in Europe, the nature and extent of these reforms vary greatly. Some of these differences follow traditional European North/South and East/West divides, but, especially since the fall of communism and the rapid extension of the EU, this has become more blurred. Even more interestingly, the perceptions by those undertaking the reforms of the nature and success of these reforms do not split along traditional lines.

The countries can be divided along the lines of NPM/post-NPM-style reforms, as well as the level of success of these reforms (see Table 16.2). In the Netherlands and Estonia, reforms were mostly seen as positive, and often followed an NPM-like trajectory. The UK was the only country that followed an NPM trajectory but had negative views about these reforms. Other countries focused more heavily on post-NPM reforms, or had few reforms overall along NPM lines. Some of these still felt that the reforms were successful, such as Norway, Hungary and to a lesser extent Germany, while others – most notably France and Spain and to a lesser extent Austria – had overall negative views of reform that has taken place (Hammerschmid et al., 2013c).

Some conclusions can be drawn from the above results. First, context

Table 16.2   Views on NPM-style and non-NPM-style reforms

	NPM-style reforms	Non-NPM-style reforms
Positive view	Netherlands Estonia	Norway Hungary Germany
Negative view	UK	Spain Italy France Austria

does matter, as there is some differentiation based on the starting points of each country. However, this is not as strong an indicator of types of reform as might be expected. Countries with a Napoleonic tradition of public administration tended to fare poorly in implementing NPM-style reforms and have a negative view of these reforms, but other groupings were less clear-cut. While the UK has the longest and strongest history of NPM-style public administration, it had a negative view of reforms undertaken, which could possibly be a result of its longer history with NPM. The two Eastern-bloc cases under consideration – Hungary and Estonia – have responded differently after their democratic transition and entry into the EU, with Estonia embracing NPM-style public administration, whereas Hungarian reform has been more reticent to adopt these processes. However, both countries saw any reform that took place as positive. The different clusters presented by this research point to the great reforms undertaken in the past 20 years (and even in the past five), and the fact that these reforms, while sometimes having an NPM-style base, have followed different trajectories that do not always accord with public administration traditions.

Second, to a great degree reforms depend on public sector autonomy and politicization. Autonomy was high and politicization low in countries such as the Netherlands, the UK and Norway, but not in Spain and Italy. While there was not perfect correlation, in general those with higher autonomy and less politicization perceived reforms as being more successful. The level of goal ambiguity had a less clear effect on the relative success of reforms, as all countries perceived their goals to be more ambiguous than not, with less cross-country difference.

Third, in almost all countries under study, NPM-type reforms such as privatization, contracting out or agencification have become less important in the past five years, often supplanted by post-NPM-style reforms based on e-government, transparency, citizen engagement and coordination.

Privatization was seen as the least important trend, but some NPM-style reforms remained important, such as a focus on outcomes and results, and treating citizens as customers.

There was a significant level of cross-country similarity on the dynamics of implementing these reforms. All countries perceived these reforms as rather top–down, and all countries apart from Norway felt that these reforms were undertaken to cut costs rather than to improve services. Likewise, all countries apart from Norway and Hungary felt that these reforms were made with little public involvement. There was less cross-country consensus on factors such as whether these reforms were driven mainly by politicians or senior executives, or whether these reforms were contested by unions.

Countries were split on whether reforms – regardless of their type or dynamic – were successful or not, and there was no clear pattern determining this perception of improvement or deterioration. There was no significant variation on different dimensions of success either, with the average perception of most executives being clustered around a neutral view, indicating neither success nor failure. Cost and efficiency, service quality, transparency and openness, innovation and fair treatment of citizens were rated relatively positively, but, worryingly, citizen trust in government was seen to have deteriorated – albeit to a moderate degree – over the past five years.

Finally, the financial crisis has been seen as an impetus for strengthening reform in recent years in all countries apart from Norway. It has not hit the countries to the same extent, and strategies for cost-cutting have differed across countries, but few felt that it has not affected reform. Taken together, these factors illustrate the complexity of public service reform in Europe and the forms it may take. In some aspects, it also shows a lack of a coherent European-wide pattern of public sector reform and whether they have been a success. While there is some convergence on the importance of factors such as e-government and collaboration, in other areas countries are split on the relevance of reforms, and this is also reflected in the reforms that have taken place, and their perceived success. However, there seems to be relatively clear consensus that public administration has moved beyond a straightforward NPM-dominated pattern of reforms (if such a thing ever existed in the first place), with most countries now embracing post-NPM reforms in response to some of the challenges and differences the continent has faced.

ACKNOWLEDGEMENTS

The research leading to these results has received funding from the European Union's Seventh Framework Programme under grant agreement No. 266887 (Project COCOPS), Socio-economic Sciences & Humanities.

NOTES

1. For a more detailed outline of the survey methodology and process, see Hammerschmid et al. (2013a).
2. See Hammerschmid et al. (2013a) and Hammerschmid et al. (2013c) for a more detailed description of scales and questions.

REFERENCES

Alonso, J. and Clifton, J. (2013). 'Public sector reform in Spain: views and experiences from senior executives'. COCOPS Work Package 3 Country Report.

Andrews, R., Downe, J. and Guarneros-Meza, V. (2013). 'Public sector reform in the UK: views and experiences from senior executives'. COCOPS Work Package 3 Country Report.

Bezes, P. and Jeannot, G. (2013). 'Public sector reform in France: views and experiences from senior executives'. COCOPS Work Package 3 Country Report.

Bouckaert, G. and Halligan, J. (2008). *Managing Performance: International Comparisons.* Abingdon: Routledge Taylor & Francis.

Christensen, T. (2003). 'Narrative of Norwegian governance: elaborating the strong state', *Public Administration*, 81(1): 163–90.

Christensen, T. and Lægreid, P. (2011). 'Complexity and hybrid public administration: theoretical and empirical challenges', *Public Organization Review*, 11(4): 407–23.

Christensen, T., Lie, A. and Lægreid, P. (2007). 'Still fragmented or reassertion of the centre?' In T. Christensen and P. Lægreid (eds), *Transcending New Public Management*. Aldershot: Ashgate, pp. 17–42.

Dunleavy, P., Margetts, H., Bastow, S. and Tinkler, J. (2006). 'New public management is dead – long live digital-era governance'. *Journal of Public Administration Theory and Practice*, 16(3): 467–94.

Fimreite, A.L. and Lægreid, P. (2009). 'Reorganization of the welfare state administration: partnerships, networks and accountability'. *Public Management Review*, 11(3): 281–97.

Hajnal, G. (2010). 'Failing policies or failing politicians? Policy failures in Hungary'. *World Political Science Review*, 6(1): Article 13.

Hajnal, G. (2013). 'Public sector reform in Hungary: views and experiences from senior executives'. COCOPS Work Package 3 Country Report.

Hammerschmid, G. and Meyer, R.E. (2005). 'New public management in Austria – local variations of a global theme?'. *Public Administration*, 83(3): 709–33.

Hammerschmid, G., Oprisor, A. and Štimac, V. (2013a). 'COCOPS executive survey on public sector reform in Europe: research report'. COCOPS Work Package 3 Report.

Hammerschmid, G., Görnitz, A., Oprisor, A. and Štimac, V. (2013b). 'Public sector reform in Germany: views and experiences from senior executives'. COCOPS Work Package 3 Country Report.

Hammerschmid, G., Van de Walle, S., Andrews, R., Bezes, P., Görnitz, G., Oprisor, A. and Štimac, V. (2013c). 'Public administration reform in Europe – views and experiences from senior executives in 10 countries'. COCOPS Work Package 3 Cross-National Report.

Jann, W. (2003). 'Administration and governance in Germany: competing traditions and dominant narratives'. *Public Administration*, **81**(1): 95–118.

Lægreid, P., Dyrnes Nordø, Å. and Rykkja, L. (2013). 'Public sector reform in Norway: views and experiences from senior executives'. COCOPS Work Package 3 Country Report.

Luts, M., Delbeke, K., Hondeghem, A. and Bouckaert, G. (2008). 'De efficiënte overheid geanalyseerd: synthese & aanbevelingen'. SBOV II Synthesis Report. Leuven: Bestuurlijke Organisatie Vlaanderen.

Meyer-Sahling, J.-H. (2011). 'The durability of EU civil service policy in Central and Eastern Europe after accession'. *Governance*, **24**(2): 231–60.

O'Leary, R. and Blongren Bingham, L. (eds) (2009). *The Collaborative Public Manager: New Ideas for the Twenty-First Century*. Washington, DC: Georgetown University Press.

Ongaro, Edoardo (2009). *Public Management Reform and Modernization: Trajectories of Administrative Change in Italy, France, Greece, Portugal and Spain*. Cheltenham, UK and Northampton, MA, USA: Edward Elgar Publishing.

Ongaro, E., Ferré, F., Galli, D. and Longo, F. (2013). 'Public sector reform in Italy: views and experiences from senior executives'. COCOPS Work Package 3 Country Report.

Pollitt, C. and Bouckaert, G. (2011). *Public Management Reform: A Comparative Analysis*. Oxford: Oxford University Press.

Rainy, Hal and Jung, Chun Su (2010). 'Extending goal ambiguity research in government: from organizational goal ambiguity to programme goal ambiguity'. In Richard M. Walker, George A. Boyne and Gene A. Brewer (eds), *Public Management and Performance. Research Directions*. Cambridge and New York: Cambridge University Press, pp. 34–59.

Randma-Liiv, T. (2002). 'Small states and bureaucracy: challenges for public administration'. *Trames*, **6**(4): 374–89.

Rouban, L. (2008). 'Reform without doctrine: public management in France'. *International Journal of Public Sector Management*, **21**(2): 133–49.

Savi, R. and Metsma, M. (2013). 'Public sector reform in Estonia: views and experiences from senior executive'. COCOPS Work Package 3 Country Report.

Torres, L. and Pina, V. (2004). 'Reshaping public administration: the Spanish experience compared to the UK'. *Public Administration*, **82**(2): 445–64.

Van de Walle, S., Jilke, S. and van Delft, R. (2013). 'Public sector reform in the Netherlands: views and experiences from senior executives'. COCOPS Work Package 3 Country Report.

Van Twist, M., Van der Steen, M., Karré, P.M., Peeters, R. and Van Ostaijen, M. (2009). *Vernieuwende verandering: continuiteit en discontinuiteit van vernieuwing van de rijksdienst*. Den Haag: NSOB.

17. Government challenges in Slovenia at a time of global economic crisis and austerity measures

Stanka Setnikar Cankar and Veronika Petkovšek

INTRODUCTION

The global economic crisis has led to a decline in economic activity in Slovenia and a deterioration in its fiscal position. A system of economic governance within the context of the so-called 'European semester' has been in place since 2011; it is aimed at strengthening fiscal discipline and introducing more wide-ranging economic supervision and control. Under this scheme, Slovenia is obliged to follow the public finance situation more closely and to take the necessary steps to remedy its position.

Slovenia has made progress towards fiscal consolidation, with the government adopting an ambitious fiscal consolidation package that emphasizes the cutting of expenditure. Positive effects are also expected from the pension reform measures adopted in 2012 and the labour market reforms carried out in 2013. While Slovenia's budget deficit is expected to fall further, public debt will still rise, which is why fiscal consolidation should continue. Policy decisions in Slovenia have mostly relied on temporary measures, cuts to the public wage bill and reductions in discretionary expenditures. More structural reforms and measures are needed, in addition to the pension and labour market reforms carried out (OECD, 2013).

In 2013 the European Commission made recommendations for bringing an end to Slovenia's excessive government deficit. As part of these recommendations, Slovenia is to abolish the present excessive deficit by 2015, with a deficit target of 4.9 per cent of GDP in 2013, 3.3 per cent of GDP in 2014 and 2.5 per cent of GDP in 2015. Slovenia is also required to rigorously implement the measures already adopted to reduce the public sector wage bill and social transfers, and to increase mainly indirect tax revenue. These measures should be complemented with the new structural consolidation measures necessary for correcting the excessive deficit by 2015 (Institute of Macroeconomic Analysis and Development, 2013a).

IMPACT OF THE GLOBAL ECONOMIC CRISIS ON THE SLOVENIAN ECONOMY, PUBLIC FINANCES AND ECONOMIC COMPETITIVENESS

The sharp deterioration in the fiscal position is inhibiting economic recovery. Borrowing costs are increasing, while limited access to the financial resources of the state is further eroding private sector borrowing conditions; this is affecting competitiveness and reducing the potential for further economic development. Fiscal policy decisions in the coming years therefore need to balance two challenges: one is to implement a credible fiscal consolidation programme; and the other is to pay sufficient regard to the state of the economy and the adverse effects of fiscal policies on aggregate demand (OECD, 2012; Setnikar Cankar and Petkovšek, 2013a).

Economic Activity in Slovenia at a Time of Global Economic Crisis

From the beginning of the economic crisis, the decline in economic activity in Slovenia was among the highest in the EU. The sharp fall in GDP in 2009 (–7.8 per cent) was followed by modest growth (1.2 per cent) in 2010 and 2011 (0.6 per cent); however, GDP fell once again in 2012 (–2.3 per cent). Following a significant decline in economic activity in 2009, the recovery in Slovenia was slower than the EMU and EU average (see Table 17.1) (Setnikar Cankar and Petkovšek, 2013a). Slow economic recovery in the EMU in general was the result of poor business and consumer confidence, and of uncertainty in the financial markets. Measures to consolidate public finances are a further reason for the slowdown in economic activity. These measures will have a short-term negative impact on economic activity; on the other hand, they are essential if funding is to be restored to allow economic recovery in the years to come (Government of the Republic of Slovenia, 2012). In Slovenia in 2012, household consumption fell by 2.9 per cent and government consumption by 1.6

Table 17.1   Real GDP growth rate, 2008–13 (% of GDP)

	2008	2009	2010	2011	2012	2013*
Slovenia	3.4	−7.8	1.2	0.6	−2.5	−2.7
EMU	0.4	−4.4	2.0	1.4	−0.7	−0.4
EU	0.3	−4.3	2.1	1.5	−0.4	0.0

Note: * Forecast.

Source: Eurostat (2013b).

per cent. The forecast for 2013 shows a 2.7 per cent decline in GDP in Slovenia, mainly due to the anticipated deterioration in the situation in the international environment and a further decline in final consumption. Poor labour market trends, restrictive payments in the public sector and the further rationalization of public spending will all lead to a decline in household and government demand in the next few years (Government of the Republic of Slovenia, 2013a).

The factors inhibiting recovery come mainly from the domestic environment, particularly in relation to the situation in construction and related activities, along with access to sources of financing, fiscal conditions and trends in the labour market; taken together, these are not creating conditions for the recovery of private consumption. The tight fiscal situation, deterioration in the financial environment in which businesses are operating and deterioration in competition are all factors that will, in the coming years, have a dominant influence on the subsequent relatively slow recovery of the Slovenian economy. This shows the necessity of structural changes and reforms that will increase the potential for growth (Institute of Macroeconomic Analysis and Development, 2012a; Setnikar Cankar and Petkovšek, 2013a).

Public Finances in Slovenia at a Time of Global Economic Crisis

The public finance situation in Slovenia has worsened since the onset of the economic crisis. Trends in public finances have been downward since 2008, with the public finance deficit remaining at around 6 per cent of GDP in recent years and, in 2012, reaching its lowest level (4 per cent of GDP) since the beginning of the crisis. Government debt has been increasing rapidly since 2008. Without radical short- and long-term structural measures, Slovenia will be unable to improve its fiscal balance. The need to balance public finances is justified primarily in terms of providing a stable and sustainable domestic macroeconomic environment, but also of meeting EU requirements (Institute of Macroeconomic Analysis and Development, 2013a; Setnikar Cankar and Petkovšek, 2013a).

The public finance deficit increased sharply to 6 per cent of GDP in Slovenia in 2009. There was no significant shift in 2010, but in 2011 the state of public finances worsened still further, with the deficit reaching 6.4 per cent of GDP. Up to 2010, Slovenia had a lower public finance deficit compared to the eurozone and EU averages (see Table 17.2). In 2011, with a deficit of 6.4 per cent of GDP, it recorded a higher deficit compared to those averages, but in 2012 Slovenia's deficit fell to 4 per cent, which was similar to the EU average. Due to past excessive deficits that exceeded the permitted upper limit of 3 per cent of GDP, the European Commission

Table 17.2   Public finance deficit (PFD) and public debt (PD) in selected EU countries, 2007–12 (% of GDP)

	2008		2009		2010		2011		2012	
	PFD	PD	PFD	PD	PFD	PD	PFD	PD	PFD	PD
Slovenia	−1.9	21.9	−6.0	35.0	−5.7	38.6	−6.4	46.9	−4.0	54.1
EMU	−2.1	70.1	−6.4	79.9	−6.2	85.6	−4.1	88.0	−3.7	90.6
EU	−2.4	62.5	−6.9	74.8	−6.5	80.2	−4.5	83.0	−4.0	85.3

Source: Institute of Macroeconomic Analysis and Development (2012a); Eurostat (2013a).

launched an excessive deficit procedure for Slovenia at the end of 2009 (Government of the Republic of Slovenia, 2012).

On the other hand, Slovenia is still recording a significantly lower public debt (as a percentage of GDP) compared to the eurozone and EU averages. Slovenia's debt reached 46.9 per cent of GDP in 2011 and 54.1 per cent of GDP in 2012 – still below the upper limit of 60 per cent of GDP permitted under the Stability and Growth Pact. However, in the 2009–12 period public debt in Slovenia increased relative to the eurozone and EU-27 averages (Institute of Macroeconomic Analysis and Development, 2012a).

Competitiveness of the Slovenian Economy at a Time of Global Economic Crisis

The macroeconomic imbalance indicators show that economic competitiveness is one of the problems faced by Slovenia. In the years leading up to the economic and financial crisis, the imbalances were indicated by strong growth in house prices and private sector borrowing. In addition to the level of competitiveness in 2009 and 2010, a mild imbalance was seen in Slovenia's net financial position and, in 2008 and 2009, in the current account deficit (Setnikar Cankar and Petkovšek, 2013a).

The IMD *Competitiveness Yearbook* placed Slovenia 52nd of the 60 countries assessed for overall competitiveness in 2013 (see Table 17.3). In 2013 Slovenia fell significantly down the competitiveness rankings in terms of economic performance (from 43rd place in 2012 to 51st place in 2013), with business efficiency also worsening (from 57th place in 2012 to 58th place in 2013). Government efficiency and infrastructure remained in the same position as the year before. Considerable dissatisfaction with the current situation and with the opportunities for doing business in Slovenia

Table 17.3   Slovenia's national competitiveness, 2008–13

	2008	2009	2010	2011	2012	2013
			Rank*			
Overall performance	32	32	52	51	51	52
Economic performance	25	21	42	43	43	51
Government efficiency	43	38	53	53	53	53
Business efficiency	32	39	57	56	57	58
Infrastructure	29	27	34	31	33	33

Note: * The report included 55 countries in 2008, 57 countries in 2009, 58 countries in 2010, 59 countries in 2011 and 2012, and 60 countries in 2013.

Source: Setnikar Cankar and Petkovšek (2013a); Institute for Management Development (2013).

continues to dominate, as in previous years. Slovenia's key competitive advantages are, in particular, the high level of education and a reliable labour infrastructure; on the other hand, international competitiveness is inhibited by an inefficient legal system and inefficiency in the workings of government (Setnikar Cankar and Petkovšek, 2013a; Institute for Management Development, 2013).

In the IMD's assessment, Slovenia's economic performance deteriorated sharply from the onset of the economic crisis, ranking it 51st of the 60 countries in 2013. The deterioration in economic performance was most strongly detected in the fields of international trade, domestic economy and employment. According to the survey results, businesses are continuing to think about moving services, R&D and production abroad, which suggests difficulties with exports and cost-competitiveness. The decline in these areas is reflected in the deterioration in the business environment. In the field of business efficiency, Slovenia has declined considerably during the crisis, being ranked 58th of the 60 countries covered in the 2013 IMD report. This low ranking is partly the result of low labour productivity, with one major obstacle to business being the area of corporate finance. In this area, the main problems are high corporate indebtedness and poor access for the corporate sector to financial resources, which have fallen in recent years (Setnikar Cankar and Petkovšek, 2013a; Institute for Management Development, 2013).

The efficiency of the state, which is responsible for ensuring the proper functioning of the economy, is low compared to other countries (53rd of 60 countries in 2013). Since the beginning of the crisis, the state of public finances has deteriorated. The sharpest fall in the country's ranking in 2013 was mainly due to a deterioration in the institutional framework, where the IMD highlights business dissatisfaction with the inability of government policies to adapt to changes in the economy and with the poor implementation of government decisions. The area of business law, particularly as regards the rigidity of labour legislation, scored poorly. Slovenia's highest ranking is in the field of infrastructure (33rd of the 60 countries surveyed in 2013), which in recent years has also fallen back, mainly due to lack of technological infrastructure and a legislative and regulatory environment that lacks support and is poor at promoting R&D, innovation and technological development (Setnikar Cankar and Petkovšek, 2013a; Institute for Management Development, 2013).

Other international competitiveness reports also show how Slovenia's competitiveness has declined during the economic crisis. As observed in the WEF *Global Competitiveness Report,* Slovenia's institutional competitiveness has fallen in recent years. The fall in Slovenia's ranking and evaluation in the post-crisis period has been noted in most international comparisons of competitiveness indicators, with most ranking its institutional competitiveness at a much lower level than in other comparable European countries; this is largely due to the delay in institutional changes to adapt to global challenges, a lack of enforcement of the regulations adopted, and a deterioration in social relations and values. The economic survey results show a strong dissatisfaction with the functioning of institutions, particularly government and the central bank, as well as with the poor implementation of government decisions and an increase in bureaucracy and corruption. Eurobarometer also shows that confidence in government, parliament and political parties has fallen in Slovenia since the crisis, and is much lower than in other EU countries. Political uncertainty and low confidence in institutions have had a major effect on the results of a number of key structural reforms rejected in popular referendums. People are acknowledging the urgency of measures to consolidate public finances; at the same time, they do not believe the government is able to take appropriate and fair measures. According to polls, the need for economic and social reforms that could improve the country's competitiveness has gained very low public acceptance, which has also led to the failure of a number of key structural reforms. A similar picture of decline in Slovenia's competitiveness is also reflected in the World Bank Governance Indicators, as Slovenia's ranking has fallen in most areas examined, particularly in relation to corruption. The number of instances of suspected corruption and other irregularities has greatly increased. According to the World Bank's 'Doing business' survey, Slovenia's main obstacles are the time-consuming procedures for obtaining documents and licences, as well as the number and length of tax payment procedures (Setnikar Cankar and Petkovšek, 2013a).

PUBLIC SECTOR REFORM AND AUSTERITY MEASURES IN SLOVENIA

Public Sector Reform in Slovenia before the Global Economic Crisis

In Slovenia, public administration represents part of the broader public sector and consists of state administration, municipalities, and other holders of public powers and functions. Public administration reform in Slovenia constituted a systematic set of strategies and activities implemented from the country's independence in 1991. Public administration reform in Slovenia can be divided into four steps: 1991–96, when the country gained independence, established administrative structures and reformed local government; 1996–99 and 2000–2004, when reforms of public administration related to EU integration (legislative reform and other measures towards new public management) took place; 2003–08, when further modernization through specific policies continued; and post-2008, when adjustments to cope with the economic crisis were made (Kovač, 2011).

New public management (NPM) was the key element in the modernization of the development of public administration in Slovenia. The aims of the reform processes were rationalization of structures and resources, user orientation, the development of e-government and quality management. Even if certain reforms were driven by the NPM model, NPM in Slovenia implies merely organization (i.e. not political theory as an ideology of governance). All the public administration reforms implemented in Slovenia can be seen as successful in terms of methodological and technical progress, for example the rationalization of structures, the optimization of processes, user-friendly services, e-government and so on. However, the reforms were less successful with regard to processes disputable in terms of interests, such as local government and the wages system (Kovač, 2011).

Public Sector Reform in Slovenia at a Time of Global Economic Crisis and Austerity Measures

In times of economic crisis, public administration takes on a much greater role; this is because it has to carry out more regulatory tasks, engage in more direct regulation in decision-making, provide incentives for the economy and so on (Kovač, 2011). Radical structural interventions and structural reforms are needed if public finances are to be sustainable. These solutions must include rationalization of the public sector, with structural measures to increase efficiency, and restructuring that focuses on strengthening the role of development expenditure in order to promote competitiveness and ensure long-term sustainability. Most measures to consolidate public finances aim to reduce government expenditure (streamline the public sector, freeze or reduce employment in the public sector, reduce public sector pay, reduce social transfers and pension transfers etc.). At the same time, measures are required on the revenue side, mainly through the raising of taxes and the introduction of new ones (Institute of Macroeconomic Analysis and Development, 2012a). In the short term, austerity measures are a necessary step for reducing the deficit below 3 per cent of GDP. At the same time, these measures do not provide for a sustainable reduction in the government deficit, as they can, in certain segments, lead to a deterioration in the quality of public services in the medium term (Setnikar Cankar and Petkovšek, 2013b).

In November 2008 the Slovenian government formed a group of key ministers tasked with combating the economic and financial crisis. This group has created two packages of measures to alleviate the effects of the financial and economic crisis. In the first set of measures, adopted in December 2008, the government tried to increase the liquidity of the banking system, provide additional incentives for economic growth, reduce public spending resources and preserve jobs. The second package of measures was drawn up in February 2009 and was slightly more development-oriented. Additional measures were adopted in the field of finance and company liquidity, covering the labour market, lifelong learning and social security, incentives for sustainable development, and measures to improve the use of cohesion funds (Setnikar Cankar and Petkovšek, 2013a, 2013b).

In response to a worsening of the situation in Slovenia, the government began to address the need for structural measures. In October 2009 the government adopted structural adjustments for 2010 and 2011; and, at the beginning of 2010, it also adopted the Slovenian Exit Strategy 2010–13. The main objective of the exit strategy is long-term sustainable economic growth, to be achieved by economic policy measures, structural measures and institutional adjustments. The consolidation of public finances by cutting spending and not raising the tax burden is the guiding principle in the formulation of economic policy. While ensuring fiscal sustainability, the social situation of the most vulnerable improves, the competitiveness of the economy strengthens, jobs and skills are created, and innovation is promoted. The key task of the strategy is to ensure the consistency of short-term stimulus measures with long-term structural changes. Major adjustments to the pension and healthcare systems are among the structural changes being introduced. Institutional adjustments bring changes that allow markets and public asset management to function better. Adjustments are also needed in transport and energy infrastructure to bring about an effective environmental and climate policy. With measures to remove administrative barriers and simplify administrative procedures, Slovenia can improve its economy, which will be reflected positively in competitiveness and investment (Republic of Slovenia, Government Office for Development and European Affairs, 2010; Setnikar Cankar and Petkovšek, 2013a).

In March 2012 Slovenia adopted a package of proposed austerity measures to balance public finances. These measures related to internal savings in the public sector, as well as various programmes and policies. The proposed internal savings measures included organizational measures to streamline costs, along with other rationalization measures. The proposed public sector measures included adjustments to the functioning of the public sector and to civil servants' salaries. The proposed measures relating to programmes and policies covered investment, subsidies and programmes, labour market policy and social security policy. Through organizational measures, the government sought to optimize public spending. The measures included the abolition of certain government bodies and the transfer and redistribution of tasks to existing government bodies. Through rationalization, the government aimed to merge and transform a number of public institutions, as well as reduce budget funding (Government of the Republic of Slovenia, 2012).

Due to the continuing worsening in the economic and financial situation, and despite the measures taken, in May 2012 the government adopted the Balancing of Public Finances Act, which aimed to achieve the following objectives: ensure sustainable public finances; provide a legal framework for the effective management of public finances; ensure macroeconomic stability; provide for the sustainable and stable development of the national economy; and establish rules for greater fiscal discipline. The Act pursued the principles of prudent use of resources and the achievement of maximum impact in the implementation of specific tasks using minimum resources. One general solution introduced by the Act was a reduction in public expenditure, with measures to reduce expenditure in all areas (Balancing of Public Finances Act, 2012).

Measures and challenges in relation to civil servants
Under the Balancing of Public Finances Act, the government has made larger cuts to the salaries and other benefits of civil servants. The basic salaries of civil servants have been progressively reduced by 8 per cent and

protected salaries abolished. Performance-related pay for increased work-load in 2012 and 2013 was not to exceed 20 per cent of basic salary. The Act also restricted promotion to a higher pay grade and more senior job title, determined the payment of the salary bonus for 2012 and a reduction in the bonus in 2013, and set a reduction in travel expenses, meal expenses, long-service awards, social assistance, severance pay and mileage and so on; it also reduced daily subsistence allowances and limited the duration of service contracts. A maximum number of days of annual leave was also determined (Setnikar Cankar and Petkovšek, 2013a).

If the 3 per cent deficit limit was to be achieved, an intervention in wages and other employee benefits in the public sector could not be avoided. Due to the measures implemented in the second half of 2012, the gross wages of legal entities in the public sector in 2012 fell by approximately 1.5 per cent compared to 2011 (Government of the Republic of Slovenia, 2013a). In addition to measures affecting the salaries of civil servants, the government has also had to take measures to change conditions and to reduce a number of work-related and other benefits in order to bring down the budget deficit and establish greater sustainability of public finances. This should also help to achieve the objective of standardizing work-related and other receipts from employment, which have so far been arranged differently for different entities (Government of the Republic of Slovenia, 2012). In any case, a reduction in labour costs is a sensible measure in the consolidation process. The challenge is to create more permanent employ-ment solutions and a more incentivizing wages policy in the public sector, which could contribute to greater efficiency (Institute of Macroeconomic Analysis and Development, 2013a).

Measures and challenges in the field of welfare
The increase in unemployment, a reduction in wages and a lack of liquid-ity, as well as the current method of adjusting pensions, have given rise to additional transfers from the state budget to the pension fund. Measures in the field of welfare are designed to reduce the period of receipt of unem-ployment benefit for recipients who are over 50 years old and for those who are over 55 years old and who have an insurance period of 25 years. The percentage of the baseline from which the benefit amount is deter-mined is to be reduced to 70 per cent of the baseline in the first two months and 60 per cent of the baseline in the third month, with the maximum amount of benefit also being reduced. The Act also abolishes sick leave for benefit recipients, lowers parental benefits to 90 per cent, and increases the parental allowance. The general government subsidy for student con-sumption has been abolished (Balancing of Public Finances Act, 2012; Institute of Macroeconomic Analysis and Development, 2013b).

Some of the measures covering social transfers were temporary, such as freezing the indexation of social transfers and tying eligibility for annual allowances for pensioners to the pension amount. The challenge in the field of social transfers is to provide a more target-based approach and to improve the transparency and efficiency of the system (Government of the Republic of Slovenia, 2013a; Institute of Macroeconomic Analysis and Development, 2013a).

Pension reform and its challenges
Pension-related measures provide for the harmonization of pensions and other pension and disability insurance benefits so that, by the end of 2014, pensions and other benefits will no longer be indexed, and pension supplements will be temporarily reduced (Government of the Republic of Slovenia, 2013a). In December 2012 Slovenia adopted a new Pension and Disability Insurance Act aimed at reforming the pension system; this came into force in January 2013. New pension legislation envisages the adjustment of the existing pension system to the new demographic and economic circumstances, ensures its long-term fiscal sustainability and stability, and provides for decent pensions for current and future generations of pensioners. Among the other changes, the new pension legislation brings in a gradual increase in the retirement age to 65 by 2020 (up to now the retirement age has been 58 for men and 57 for women) (Government of the Republic of Slovenia, 2013b; Institute of Macroeconomic Analysis and Development, 2013b).

Pension reform was necessary in order to achieve financial sustainability on the part of the pension fund and to prevent further reductions in pensions. With these changes, Slovenia has established a fairer, more reliable and financially more efficient pension system (Government of the Republic of Slovenia, 2013a). The challenge remains, however, as the new pension law does not ensure long-term sustainability; this is because of the rapid increase in the share of the elderly population, which will increase age-related expenditures (pensions in particular). Recent changes to the pension system will only have a short- and medium-term positive impact on fiscal sustainability (Institute of Macroeconomic Analysis and Development, 2013a).

Labour market reform
Measures relating to the labour market will focus on the development of the concept of 'flexicurity', which will give companies the opportunity to adapt to market conditions more effectively. Various measures and incentives are designed to promote the formation and development of jobs that are adapted to the needs of the elderly, have no adverse health

consequences and contribute to sustainable development. All types of employment should be promoted, with a particular emphasis on a change from more flexible employment to permanent employment. Labour market reforms were adopted in March 2013 with the main objective of reducing segmentation and increasing labour market flexibility. With a new labour law, the government wishes to ensure flexicurity by providing more adequate protection for workers, reducing administrative costs and levies on businesses, and introducing effective control of violations of legal requirements. The new solutions will contribute to a higher proportion of permanent employees (Government of the Republic of Slovenia, 2013c). Since the new labour legislation came into force in April 2013, its impact on segmentation in the labour market, flexibility and labour court proceedings has been monitored, which will serve as a basis for possible further amendments. The new Act encourages employment of the elderly. In this sense the Act retains the long-service bonus as a compulsory constituent of pay. The right is determined by the Act, but the conditions for its acquisition and the amount are determined by the collective bargaining agreement for the activity in question. In terms of enhancing flexibility, the new Act regulates in more detail the possibility of giving workers other work during their employment; in terms of reducing labour market fragmentation, the Act limits the conclusion of fixed-term employment contracts and also introduces measures regarding the payment of employer contributions (Government of the Republic of Slovenia, 2013a; Institute of Macroeconomic Analysis and Development, 2013b).

Tax-related measures and measures to promote economic activity and competitiveness

In addition to the cost-saving measures adopted in various fields, there is also a need for measures designed to increase state revenues. These measures are connected to raising taxes that have no direct negative impact on the competitiveness of the Slovenian economy. The Balancing of Public Finances Act introduces a tax on profits generated by a change in land use (imposed on the sale of land), an additional tax on boats and an additional tax on motor vehicles. The Act also introduces an additional fourth income tax class for 2013 and 2014, and raises the rate of taxation on all income from capital from 20 per cent to 25 per cent (Setnikar Cankar and Petkovšek, 2013a). In 2013 VAT rates were also raised by two percentage points to 22 per cent, with the reduced rate being raised one percentage point to 9.5 per cent (Institute of Macroeconomic Analysis and Development, 2013a).

To promote economic activity, measures are planned that will eliminate administrative barriers and payment indiscipline, attract foreign investors, and provide relief to companies in the form of tax incentives. Tax relief will be focused chiefly on measures to promote the formation of new businesses and jobs, investments in funds, and investment in knowledge and development (Setnikar Cankar and Petkovšek, 2013a).

Future Steps and Challenges Regarding Public Sector Reform and Austerity Measures in Slovenia

Slovenia needs further structural changes in order to revive the economy. The changes and reforms should be directed towards: (1) further fiscal consolidation, where more radical structural interventions on the expenditure side are needed, along with measures on the revenue side; (2) improvements in labour market efficiency, where other flexicurity components need to be strengthened alongside flexibility (e.g. active employment policy, lifelong learning), as well as the construction of a system for monitoring the needs of employers and the needs of labour market; (3) the creation of a business environment that fosters enterprise (an emphasis on reducing the administrative burden and creating an encouraging tax environment); (4) improvements in the institutional framework that enable development changes and the implementation of these changes, and that ensure effective functioning of the legal, economic and political system; (5) stabilization of the banking system, permanent adjustments to the pension system, adjustments to the health and long-term care systems, and an increase in the added value of goods and services (Institute of Macroeconomic Analysis and Development, 2013b).

Under the National Reform Programme 2013–14, Slovenia is continuing with further measures to limit public sector labour cost volume, as well as expenditures on pensions and social transfers. Expenditures on investment will also be limited. The government is also aiming to implement a policy of reducing the number of employees by 1 per cent per year. The revenue side also receives some attention alongside the expenditure side, particularly in terms of measures to improve the efficiency of tax collection and to reduce the size of the informal economy. Measures for 2013 and 2014 to manage economic imbalances in Slovenia are divided into three pillars: institutional changes; measures for the short-term revival of the economy; and measures to improve competitiveness and sustainable growth in the long term (Government of the Republic of Slovenia, 2013a).

In addition to changes to the economic structure, one very important obstacle to overcome is the existing institutional framework in Slovenia. It is essential that the rule of law be improved and the efficiency of regulatory and supervisory functions be secured; the withdrawal of the government from the economy is also needed in order to prevent its direct intervention in the decision-making of economic entities (Institute of Macroeconomic Analysis and Development, 2013b).

PUBLIC SECTOR CAPACITY AT A TIME OF GLOBAL ECONOMIC CRISIS

A government plays a series of significant roles – as legislator, owner, entrepreneur, customer, promoter, facilitator and revenue manager – and requires an international representative. Public administration therefore plays an important role in providing frameworks and conditions for the functioning of the economy. Long-term economic success can be achieved with high-quality government institutions. At a time of economic crisis in particular, and in order to aid recovery, government institutions play a crucial role, as the appropriate institutional environment will lead to a better business environment, which is vital for the operation of businesses, for domestic and foreign investments, and for the creation of economic activity (Petkovšek, 2012; Slabe Erker and Klun, 2012).

A sharp economic downturn can reduce public sector capacity as governments make sharp cutbacks to the public sector. If savings were made entirely by cutting programmes and activities, this would not affect the capacity of the public sector because it would mean that the government was asking the public sector to perform fewer tasks. Usually, however, savings are made in other ways as well, such as cutting capital spending, trimming non-wage operating budgets to the bone, freezing wages and so on. Each of these savings limits the capacity of the public sector. Particularly steep declines in real wages can be very damaging as they lead to a loss of qualified staff and to breakdowns in organizational discipline (Polidano, 2000).

Slovenia's institutional competitiveness has fallen in recent years; in the post-crisis period, this has largely been due to a delay in implementing the institutional changes required to adapt to global challenges, a lack of enforcement of adopted regulations, and a deterioration in social relations and values. For example, the WEF economic survey results show strong levels of dissatisfaction with the functioning of institutions, particularly government and the central bank, as well as with the poor implementation of government decisions and an increase in bureaucracy and corruption. Political uncertainty and low confidence in institutions have had a major effect on the results of a number of key structural reforms, rejected in popular referendums. People are acknowledging the urgency of measures to consolidate public finances; at the same time, they do not believe the government is able to take appropriate and

Table 17.4   *Number of employees employed by legal entities on the basis of hours worked*

	2008	2009	2010	2011	2012	2013 (February)
No. of employees	155935	157252	159297	160868	159214	157534

Source: Buzeti and Stare (2012); Government of the Republic of Slovenia (2013a).

fair measures (Institute of Macroeconomic Analysis and Development, 2012b).

If we consider the role of the public sector and the public finances that the government has at its disposal in the public sector, one important factor is whether the public sector is organized in order to be as cost-effective as possible and to offer the highest possible quality. In this respect, the question regarding the most suitable number of public sector employees is also important (Buzeti and Stare, 2012).

The number of employees in the public sector began to fall following the implementation of the Balancing of Public Finances Act and its measures in 2012 (see Table 17.4). Before the Act came into force, the number of employees had been falling since 2006 only in the administrative sections of the public sector; in the service sections, by contrast, it had been increasing. The number of public sector employees began to fall in June 2012 with the implementation of the Act (Government of the Republic of Slovenia, 2013a).

CONCLUSION

The global economic crisis has exposed critical weaknesses in the Slovenian economy and its development. These include an inflexible labour market, problems in the financial system, and an insufficiently competitive business environment. Immediate radical structural reforms were needed, and are still needed, if Slovenia is to emerge from the crisis and lay strong foundations for sustainable economic growth, competitiveness and prosperity.

The macroeconomic stabilization of the Slovenian economy is urgently required. Significant shifts in this direction were made in 2012 in the area of fiscal consolidation. In addition to the restructuring of the banking system, fiscal consolidation is the key economic policy challenge that will improve macroeconomic stability. The consolidation process requires an economic policy mix that provides a sustainable reduction in the deficit but also has a less damaging impact on economic growth. Measures to reduce expenditure must play the central role, while a higher tax burden in the form of indirect taxes should be only an auxiliary measure for fiscal consolidation. Discretionary expenditure-related measures are focused on limiting employee compensation and social transfers; some of these are temporary. The key challenge of economic policy will be to put in place permanent measures on the expenditure side that will head off the need to introduce a crisis tax. A crisis tax would swing the policy mix for deficit reduction strongly towards the revenue side (Institute of Macroeconomic Analysis and Development, 2013a; Institute of Macroeconomic Analysis and Development, 2013b).

Because of the existing structural weaknesses in the Slovenian economy and the changes in the demographic structure of the population, it is impossible to achieve fiscal consolidation without larger systemic adjustments in pension, labour market, healthcare and long-term care policies. The measures adopted to restore public finances are defined as a necessary first step – one that needs to be followed by measures to create jobs and employment opportunities for the unemployed and first-time jobseekers. Governments need to allocate additional resources to the promotion of self-employment and enterprise by offering assistance in starting a business, investing in the necessary infrastructure and financing new projects. Financing new projects for existing companies through the banking system must become a common form of business.

REFERENCES

Balancing of Public Finances Act (Zakon za uravnoteženje javnih financ) (2012). *Official Gazette of the Republic of Slovenia*, No. 40/2012. Available at http://www.vlada.si/fileadmin/dokumenti/si/projekti/2012/varcevalni_ukrepi/ZUJF_precisceno.pdf.

Buzeti, J. and Stare, J. (2012). Mednarodna primerjava kot vodilo za opredelitev racionalnega števila zaposlenih v javnem sektorju. In P. Pevcin and S. Setnikar Cankar (eds), *Razumen in razumljen javni sektor v Sloveniji*. Ljubljana: Faculty of Administration, pp. 141–56.

Eurostat (2013a). Government deficit/surplus, debt and associated data. Available at http://appsso.eurostat.ec.europa.eu/nui/submitViewTableAction.do.

Eurostat (2013b). Real GDP growth rate. Available at http://epp.eurostat.ec.europa.eu/tgm/table.do?tab=table&init=1&plugin=1&language=en&pcode=tec00115.

Government of the Republic of Slovenia (2012). *Draft Balancing of Public Finances Act (Predlog zakona za uravnoteženje javnih financ)*. Ljubljana: Government of the Republic of Slovenia.

Government of the Republic of Slovenia (2013a). *National Reform Programme 2013–2014*. Ljubljana: Government of the Republic of Slovenia.

Government of the Republic of Slovenia (2013b). New pension legislation *(Nova pokojninska zakonodaja)*. Available at http://www.vlada.si/teme_in_projekti/arhiv_projektov/nova_pokojninska_zakonodaja/.

Government of the Republic of Slovenia (2013c). *Changes in labour legislation (Spremembe delovne zakonodaje)*. Available at http://www.vlada.si/teme_in_projekti/arhiv_projektov/spremembe_delovne_zakonodaje/.

Institute for Management Development (2013). *World Competitiveness Yearbook 2013*. Lausanne: IMD World Competitiveness Center.

Institute of Macroeconomic Analysis and Development (2012a). *Economic Issues. Fiscal Developments and Fiscal Policy (Ekonomski izzivi 2012. Fiskalna gibanja in politika)*. Ljubljana: Institute of Macroeconomic Analysis and Development.

Institute of Macroeconomic Analysis and Development (2012b). *Development Report 2012 (Poročilo o razvoju 2012)*. Ljubljana: Institute of Macroeconomic Analysis and Development.

Institute of Macroeconomic Analysis and Development (2013a). *Economic Issues 2013. Fiscal Developments and Fiscal Policy (Ekonomski izzivi 2013. Fiskalna gibanja in politika)*. Ljubljana: Institute of Macroeconomic Analysis and Development.

Institute of Macroeconomic Analysis and Development (2013b). *Development Report 2013 (Poročilo o razvoju 2013)*. Ljubljana: Institute of Macroeconomic Analysis and Development.

Kovač, P. (2011). The public administration reform agenda in Slovenia – two decades of challenges and results. *Hrvatska I komparativna javna uprava*, **11**(3), 627–50.

OECD (2012). *OECD Economic Outlook: 2012/2*. Paris: OECD Publishing. Available at http://dx.doi.org/10.1787/eco_outlook-v2012-2-en.

OECD (2013). *OECD Economic Surveys: Slovenia 2013*. Paris: OECD Publishing. Available at http://dx.doi.org/10.1787/eco_surveys-svn-2013-en.

Petkovšek, V. (2012). *Primerjalna analiza vpliva javne uprave na konkurenčnost gopodarstev Slovenije, Avstrije in Italije s poudarkom na čezmejnem sodelovanju*. Master's thesis. Ljubljana: Faculty of Economics.

Polidano, C. (2000). Measuring public sector capacity. *World Development*, **28**(5), 805–22.

Republic of Slovenia, Government Office for Development and European Affairs (2010). *Slovenian Exit Strategy 2010–2013 (Slovenska izhodna strategija 2010–2013)*. Available at http://www.arhiv.svrez.gov.si/si/teme_in_projekti/izhod_iz_krize/slovenska_izhodna_strategija_20102013/.

Setnikar Cankar, S. and Petkovšek, V. (2013a). Slovenia's national competitiveness during the economic crisis and the role of public finance. In *Regionalisation and Inter-regional Cooperation*. Belgrade: NISPAcee. Available at http://www.nispa.org/files/conferences/2013/papers/201305021329520.Paper_Petkovsek,%20Cankar.pdf?fs_papersPage=10.

Setnikar Cankar, S. and Petkovšek, V. (2013b). Austerity measures in the public sector in Slovenia and other selected European countries. International Conference Europeanization of Public Administration and Policy: Sharing Values, Norms and Practices, 4–7 April 2013, Dubrovnik, Croatia. Available at http://ipsa2013.iju.hr/downloads/downloads-2/files/6_2_Setnikar%20Cankar.pdf.

Slabe Erker, R. and Klun, M. (2012). The contribution of institutional quality to lowering company compliance costs. *African Journal of Business Management*, **6**(8), 3111–19.

18. United Kingdom: government, governance and public administration complexity
Duncan McTavish

INTRODUCTION

This chapter outlines the traditional configuration of public administration in the UK: central government influence, especially in areas of growing welfare state provision within a unitary state, yet an open economy much influenced by the international economic and trade environment, subject to exogenous shock. The ideational and ideological challenges to postwar Keynesianism saw the UK as a particularly strong candidate for new public management (NPM) and related approaches to public administration and government. The chapter analyses the regulatory, inspection, audit and governance-based dimensions, assessing the impacts and limits of government and state activity as well as the outcomes in terms of public and democratic accountability. The final section of the chapter evaluates the UK's public administration–territorial complexity in a multilevel governance environment. Governance of the UK's relationship with the European Union (EU) is examined, as are the patterns of asymmetry within the UK's present devolution arrangements, concluding with comments on the significance of bi-constitutionalism as an explanatory tool for UK government and public administration.

THE LONG WALK TO NEW PUBLIC MANAGEMENT (NPM)

The governmental arrangements and the delivery of public services in the UK from the late 1940s to the late 1970s is conventionally viewed through the lens of a 'traditional' public administration paradigm. The key aspects of this included a focus on the management of inputs (resource allocations), a growing national welfare state, and the prominence of elected politicians in shaping and defining the scope of government and the public sector (Stoker 2011). This of course was underpinned by electoral legitimacy. General election turnout in 1950 was 83.9 per cent, in 1955, 76.8 per cent, in 1964, 77 per cent, in 1974, 78.8 per cent, and in 1979, 76 per cent (Rallings and Thrasher 2007). In the UK, this traditional public administration approach had certain particularities not necessarily found in other democratic polities. There was an especially strong central state direction. Nowhere was this more evident than in the centrally controlled and funded National Health Service (NHS), a key instrument of the welfare state. The central state for much of this period had power over a great deal of the country's economic infrastructure through nationalized industries and utilities. In a more general sense, the state (under both main political parties, Conservative and Labour) saw itself as a key player in a variety of economic and business matters, from rationing in the postwar years, to efforts at indicative planning, and control of prices and incomes in the 1960s and 1970s. Outwith local government, there were no separate elected administrations in other parts of the UK, and the country was not included in the six-member European Economic Community (EEC): the dramatic changes to this landscape, now visible, are addressed in this chapter.

Yet, despite state-centric approaches in the 1950s–1970s, UK governance was not contained within the governmental boundaries of the UK state. Suffice it to say that macroeconomic policy from the 1950s focused on extending sterling convertibility with the underlying assumption of the UK's continued role as a leading world player; and this often led to severe strain on government spending and pay policies (Booth 2000). In no way could the UK's economy be considered isolationist. Even after wartime dislocation, in the early 1950s the UK produced over 30 per cent of the industrial output of non-communist Europe, half of the world's trade was conducted in sterling and it was a major world financial centre (with an overseas sterling area) (Self 2010). Imports, exports and the international trading environment were therefore important to the UK.

The UK economy's high degree of interaction internationally exposed it to a series of exogenous shocks in the 1970s. There was a sustained slowing down of economic growth triggered by a fourfold rise in oil prices in the early 1970s, and a reduction in international trade growth (Kreiger 1986). The UK's economy was hit because of its reliance on international trade, but also due to structural factors: historical reliance on manufacturing industries; low productivity in these sectors partly due to the rise of new competitors; and high trade union density (often in multi-union workplaces) leading to the possibility of cost-push inflation. This economic performance (the UK had an average 2.3 per cent per annum growth in 1960–70 compared to the EEC average of 4.2 per cent – Sanders 1990) and strained public expenditure (which reached 60 per cent of GDP in the mid-1970s) at times led to high government borrowing (borrowing increased by about 40 per cent to £11 billion in one year from 1974 to 1975) and ultimately, due to failed attempts at incomes policies, to very fractious industrial relations, particularly in the latter half of the 1970s. The UK was depicted as the strike-prone sick man of Europe, though in fact by international standards working days lost through strike action was not a peculiarly UK phenomenon (Wrigley 1996).

The predominant ideational/ideological framing in this environment was based on the belief that stagflation (that is, the combination of low or no growth and high levels of inflation – inflation measured by the retail price index peaked at 25 per cent in 1974) was endemic to postwar Keynesian policies and institutional capture in the public sector by vested interests. There was a belief that politics thus practised posed a threat to market forces – so, instead of a market failure narrative, there was one of government failure (Roberts 2010). It was believed that bureaucratic self-interest not only skewed resource allocation but led to market interference (Niskanen 1968); and it was argued that the democratic process itself was prone to inflate public expectations of what governments could or should deliver. This all provided the underpinning of the 'government crisis through overload' thesis (Crozier et al. 1975; King 1975; Rose 1980).

While an ideologically driven – and medium- to long-term – programme in response to this could involve state rollback, large-scale privatizations, the use of market and other non-governmental players in government and service provision, an immediate and practical political initiative was to infuse the public sector with efficiency transferred from the business sector. The UK's Secretary of State for the Environment in 1980 put it thus:

> Efficient management is the key to the national revival – and the management ethos must run through our national life – civil service, nationalised industries, local government, the NHS. (Heseltine 1980, p. 15)

The UK was a particular candidate for such an initiative for two main reasons. First was the dominance of the central state in the expanding welfare and social services. Such centralization – which was not universal throughout Europe, with many countries organizing their welfare systems differently (Blair 2010) – made central government political and policy initiative easier. Second, many features of the UK by the late 1970s seemed to give succour to some of the analysis and ideas provided by public choice theorists, the overloaded state thesis and pro-market thinking. For example, there was a powerful bargaining position used by trade unions in an inflationary environment, which destabilized industrial relations, as unions ran catch-up exercises that further fuelled inflationary pressures; attempts to macro-control this via incomes policies were only sporadically successful. Government borrowing and public finances appeared to be in crisis at times throughout the 1970s. However, again some perspective is required: some of the dramatically adverse borrowing figures upon which the UK's mid-1970s application for an IMF loan were founded were based on Treasury miscalculation ('egregious blunders', as Reece 2010, puts it); and by the late 1970s much of the public finance and spend crisis was under control, with the UK government well committed to a cash limits regime in public financing, and North Sea oil revenues starting to flow, all leading to increased confidence from the markets (Ludlam 1992). There was none the less an undoubted display of policy drift throughout much of the latter half of the1970s in the UK (Sandbrook 2012). This provided the backdrop for an environment that would downplay 'traditional' direct state provision of many services, introduce and privilege market-based and other non-governmental providers and actors in the policy process, thereby presenting a departure from the post-1945 paradigm.

AN ERA OF NPM, REGULATION AND GOVERNANCE

NPM, a conceptual understanding about how the public sector is managed, can therefore be seen as part of a larger picture about the size and role of the state, the privileging of markets and the positioning of key interests and agents in the politico-economic environment. There are various definitions of NPM – some commentators and scholars have noted that the concept is ill defined – including those that focus on managerial, market and organizational dimensions; others on entrepreneurial and innovative government; yet others on consumerism and governmental reform (for a good account of these, see Van de Walle and Hammerschmid 2011). Most, however, would acknowledge detail on management, standards and performance measures, output controls, disaggregation and fragmentation, competition, prioritizing of private-sector-styled management, resource and cost control, and separation of political decision making from direct management (Hood 1991).

While discussion of NPM has had considerable prominence in scholarly and academic circles, actual hard empirical evidence on the uptake, impact and effectiveness of NPM is relatively sparse. Studies undertaken in the UK have shown some increased efficiency in the health sector but the situation is rather less clear cut in other sectors (Boyne et al. 2003); some aspects of NPM have been seen to have positive impacts in terms of performance in English local government (Andrews et al. 2006).

Key to the NPM agenda has been the process of agencification designed to deal with departmental efficiencies, involving the transfer of responsibilities from departments to agencies alongside strengthening agencies' financial and managerial autonomy. Between 1988 and 2001, 173 agencies were set up, employing staff ranging in number from 30 to 86000. While some individual agency performance was improved, there were performance problems where agencies were involved in extensive joint working with other public bodies (e.g. welfare payments) (James 2003).

Several vital issues should be considered when evaluating NPM. First, cost, economy and efficiency have been key concerns of NPM; some indicate these to be essential qualities (Christensen and Lægreid 2007; see also Hood and Dixon 2013). As such, recent empirical research indicates that in UK central government in the 1980s and 1990s, cost cutting under NPM regimes fell far short of what was planned (Hood and Dixon 2013). Second, agencification has been an important instrument of NPM; in part this was to bring in managerial practice (and personnel at senior level) from the private sector. Recent research on UK executive agencies from 1989 to 2012 (which covers the key 'next steps' period) has found that, in terms of the overall stock of chief executives in central government agencies, the majority are from inside the civil service and the vast majority from the public sector in general (Boyne et al. 2013). This does not tell us about managerial practices carried out by such individuals within these agencies, which could of course be much influenced by private sector practice – this has yet to be researched. Added to this is the fact that there has been a marked trend towards de-agencification (e.g. the UK Border Agency, college funding in Wales, aspects of social housing in Scotland). None the less, a return to the *status quo ante* is unlikely; we should expect, rather, a reassertion of some powers to the core government but with continued delegation elsewhere (Bouckaert et al. 2010). Third, the introduction of private–public funding partnerships, contractual and other arrangements may in fact contradict value-for-money and efficiency goals, apparently central to NPM. There has been a profusion of off-balance-sheet methods of financing major economic infrastructure, often involving balance-sheet treatment and retiming of expenditure and financial engineering. Such policy innovations (e.g. private finance initiative (PFI)/public–private partnerships (PPP)) are not always assessed on their contribution to value for money but on scoring against financial reporting or national accounts standards. Problems here are compounded by complex and long-term contractual arrangements that often exceed political decision-making time frames (Heald and Georgiou 2011). Finally, the political–ideational underpinnings of NPM appeared seriously wounded in the aftermath of the global financial crisis given that (a) the market-privileging neoliberal policies could be seen to have played a part in the financial crash and subsequent crisis, and that (b) the short-term response (especially in the UK and USA) was counter-recessionary and Keynesian in tone. Yet much of the thinking and policies behind NPM have remained untouched for a variety of reasons: globalization and international trading means that competitiveness of the national economy is dominant in governments' thinking and that competitiveness means state spending is constrained – especially given the long-term hangover cost of bank bailouts; international regulatory and governance frameworks are important and individual state action (in the UK or elsewhere) is thereby delimited, particularly if the ruling paradigm in this environment remains neoliberal and NPM dominant; and there is limited political pressure to alter this, given the conflation between the main political parties and state structures (Hardiman 2012).

Another emphasis can be put on NPM. Whereas the cost, efficiency and transferability of managerial practices were key concerns in the early phases of NPM ('phase one'), through much of the 1980s there was a somewhat different (though complementary) tone used by John Major ('phase two'). This approach recognized the importance of public services to the population and society as a whole; Major himself attributed his views in part to his personal background:

> When I was young my family had depended on public services – these personal experiences left me with little tolerance of the lofty views of well-cosseted politicians, the metropolitan media or Whitehall bureaucrats who made little use of the public services in their own lives and had no concept of their importance to others. They may have looked down on the public sector and despised it as second rate but many of them knew nothing of the people who worked there or the manifold problems they faced. (Major 1999: 246–7)

Performance orientation was to be the focus; more user orientation and accountability to the citizen–consumer were key to much of Major's approach, for example the Citizen's Charter. Later the focus was on 'joined-up government', 'whole-of-government' approaches to integrate some of the fragmentation resulting from earlier reforms and also in recognition of the fact that complex problems often traversed governmental, sector and organizational boundaries (Hood 2005; Mulgan 2005). It is clear that the governance of such arrangements is vital to managing the delivery of public services rather than traditional mono-bureaucratic processes. Considine and Lewis (2003) wrote of this in a comparative study that examined the UK some ten years ago.

The inspection and regulation of performance and governance in NPM 'phase two' is strongly underpinned by an audit and regulatory environment. It should be noted, of course, that phases one and two were not discrete but overlapped: the Audit Commission was created under Thatcher in 1983 to combine the auditing of health and local government spending, but it also had a remit to focus on enhancing performance. However, the regulatory–performance improvement environment has travelled considerably from the 1980s and 1990s to the present and has throughout displayed tension. Concern for regulation and inspection has tended to create a profusion of initiatives and agencies. Interestingly, two major spikes in this regard occurred under Major (who, as noted, had some empathy for public services) and Blair, who, as a prime minister of a left-of-centre party could be expected to have some public service orientation. Under Major, the Citizen's Charter was launched and this used comparative performance data 'to inform the public how their local services compared with those of other areas' (Burton 2013: 234). Major also invested heavily in separating inspection regimes from service delivery, best typified by the creation of the Office for Standards in Education (Ofsted). Under Blair, these initiatives were in the main continued or extended in the field of health care (Healthcare Commission), social services (Commission for Social Care Inspection), housing and more, underpinned by National Service Frameworks and other policy instruments such as Comprehensive Performance Assessments and Public Service Agreements (Burton 2013). In some areas there was undoubted regulatory and inspection overload, with a National Audit Office report in 2009 instancing 35 regulators, inspection and accrediting agencies with a healthcare remit (National Audit Office [NAO] 2009a).

Currently what can be observed is something of a tension or 'divide' on the role of regulation and inspection. There is a view that emphasizes the centrality of direct regulation and inspection, expressed by the NAO:

> Regulation – including guidance, inspection and reporting – is central to the delivery of effective public services and provides accountability for public funds and essential protection for citizens. Regulation also plays an important role in delivering improvements to services. For example, inspections and reporting can have a critical role to play in highlighting examples of good and bad performance and variations in public service. (NAO 2010)

On the other hand is the ambition to decentralize power from the centre, with the state 'instead of seeking to run services directly ... [moving towards] **overseeing** [author's emphasis] core standards and entitlements' (HM Government 2011).

The UK coalition government in 2010 abolished the Audit Commission and its performance monitoring regime; part of this policy initiative was to stipulate all items of local government expenditure above £500 to be published online, with 'armchair auditors' filling in part of the void left by the Audit Commission. This philosophy has been extended to central government. For example, with regard to the Treasury *Business Plan*:

> By publishing a wide range of indicators, we will enable the public to make up their own minds about how departments are performing. We will use transparency to facilitate the choice and democratic accountability which will replace top down targets and micromanagement. (HM Treasury, cited in Burton 2013: 238)

The managerial and regulatory environment has an impact at individual organizational level; this is not usually captured when analysing overall political, policy and governance frameworks. A key accompaniment of managerialism and regulation has been an 'audit explosion', often leading to 'rituals of verification', dysfunctionalities of performance regimes (including gaming and other strategies), the practice of measuring what can be measured rather than what public bodies and principals actually want measured and so on (see Power 1997).

A number of authors have indicated that the expansion of monitoring and auditing has generated 'spirals of distrust' within organizations (Djelic and Sahlin 2012: 750; see also Power 2004; Moran 2002; Hood et al. 1999). According to this line of thinking, 'responsibility spirals' (Djelic and Sahlin 2012: 751) can occur in organizations where regulatory and inspection regimes disperse responsibility. Such dispersal is intensified and accentuated where varying degrees of external (e.g. governmental) monitoring are devolved or delegated to institutional level – for example 'earned autonomy' from more frequent or intrusive audit or inspection (as in healthcare) or institution-led enhancement or improvement (as in higher education). It is also accentuated with risk management regimes (prevalent in public and private sector organizations) seeking to calibrate and control risk within the organization. Such dispersal, which usually internalizes much monitoring activity at the local level, leads to a culture of defensiveness, with people gaming to avoid responsibility (Power 2004). In complex multi-agency environments dealing with 'wicked policy problems' and much dependent on street-level bureaucrats with considerable discretion, the scope for responsibility avoidance is immense, especially when the policy area has high political salience. Sometimes this can have a devastating impact, as several high-profile child protection cases in the UK and elsewhere have shown (see, e.g., Marinetto 2011).

CAPACITY, CONTROL AND COMPETENCE: IS GOVERNMENT STILL THE KEY PLAYER?

Some interesting analogies and metaphors are used to address this question. For example, it has been said that under NPM there is a sense of standing back from the system, treating it as a black box, choosing output criteria or providers to effect change. Governance, on the other hand, involves a stepping into the system, interacting and steering/controlling to influence matters (Klijn 2012). There has been much debate – which continues – on the extent to which government's powers are reduced in this environment or whether government can actually extend its reach through processes of metagovernance (Fenwick et al. 2012; Robichau 2011; Bell and Hindmoor 2009; Jessop 2004). However, in this environment government has to occupy and share a space with other actors and agents, so metagovernance opens up the arena that distributes and perhaps relocates governmental power, leading it to interact in a way not seen as a conventional way of doing government.

The argument is nuanced, with evidence pointing in several directions. There is evidence that the role of government is somewhat diminished in the managerial, market-driven and governance environments. A 2008 study calculated that the UK public sector market built around public services was worth 6 per cent of GDP, second only to the USA and with a turnover approaching £80 billion (Julius 2008). It is recognized that there may be a regulatory deficit here. According to the NAO (2012):

> When markets are used to deliver public services, the government typically retains a reversionary interest if services fail, yet it has much less ability to intervene than when it delivers services directly.

Government has had to use this backstop on a number of occasions, including in the rail industry and during the 2012 Olympics, when private contractors failed to provide security and other services (the military had to step in at large cost). Of particular significance has been government loss of control of major IT contracts: with much of this outsourced to the market, departments have been stripped of their supervisory capacity. The NAO report on major government projects (2009) indicated that only half of the departments had sound commercial expertise, with special weaknesses identified in contract management, commissioning, management of advisers and business acumen. Much of this was attributed to staff turnover and loss (NAO 2009b).

There can also be knowledge asymmetries, making it difficult for governments to effectively control, supervise or regulate. In areas of banking and financial services, the expertise required to effectively regulate resides in the sector rather than in the government, though one must be somewhat sceptical of this view given the seeming incapacity of leading bankers to act at crucial stages in the banking crisis, contrasted with the rescue work carried out by government, especially the UK Treasury (Darling 2011). Often in major technical and/or environmental disasters (e.g. BP's Gulf of Mexico crisis) the technical resources and knowledge to handle and manage the crisis reside not within government or its regulatory arm, but with the major companies involved – this was indeed the case with the BP crisis, even though the US Minerals Management Service was severely criticized.

Various formulations of the state crisis thesis would lend support to the idea of government diminution. It has been argued that the overloaded state of the 1970s (see above) resolved its crisis through economic restructuring and transformation, underwritten by neoliberalism and expanding markets. In reality, many states and their governments have 'bought peace' by relying on cheap money and low interest rates, fuelled by rapid internationalization of finance and significant build-up of private leveraged debt based on asset price inflation (Lodge 2013; Streeck 2012). However, this has been accompanied by the 'complexification' of public services and political decision making (Hood 2011). Citizens find it difficult to articulate political blame in the complexity of co-production and co-governance networks, resulting in a hollowing out of accountability. The UK *Audit of Political Engagement* (Hansard Society 2013) shows that, consistently since 2003, UK citizens have been disappointed by and have become disengaged from formal politics, not actively engaged in its regular processes. This contrasts with the (admittedly narrower definition of electoral) legitimacy in the period 1945–79 highlighted at the beginning of this chapter. So the message is this: government power is diminished from outwith conventional governmental institutions by market-based and other players in the governance environment; added to this, government's legitimacy from below, from citizens, is diminished too.

But one must view this state depletion thesis, the idea that the UK state has lost capacity in this governance environment, with some care and circumspection. The fact that governments move things to independent or semi-independent bodies who then become part of a governance network, operating with some autonomy from government, may not necessarily be evidence that government is losing power or control. Governments may wish to take actions that are politically contentious and have negative consequences within the electoral cycle. For example, there can be negative political consequences for governments directly setting interest rates, but giving independence to a central bank with authority to do just that, within broadly defined objectives set by the government, enables a stable monetary environment over a period not circumscribed by short-term electoral considerations. This does not represent a downplaying of the state.

There is a range of evidence to suggest that there is no loss of state power in key strategic decision making. At the height of the global financial crisis, the UK Financial Services Authority did not permit Barclay's proposed purchase of US-owned Lehman Brothers, fearing the excessive exposure to risk, much to the dismay of US policy makers. It is undoubtedly the case that strong and direct government intervention to shore up the banking sector, especially in the USA and UK, prevented collapse of much of the sector in the immediate aftermath of 2008. Strong state action was also witnessed in muscular counter-recessionary policies and initiatives that saw, for example, the nationalization of key parts of the banking sector in the UK and USA, and especially in the latter's massive injections of support to key industries (e.g. auto manufacture). There are also numerous examples of the use of state power in key policy sectors like education and skills development (Wilson 2012).

Rather than the loss of state power, it is more meaningful to talk of a depoliticization of state activity. For example, the wide use of regulatory impact assessment, particularly in the UK, places considerable emphasis on 'objective' technocratic criteria for the widespread use of a cost–benefit analysis threshold (rather than, say, political criteria) before proceeding (Radaelli 2004, 2005). Bodies such as the UK Competition Commission (UKCC) value political independence and their depoliticized role; however, governments have no difficulty using state power to override decisions and recommendations when they consider such veto action to be in the national interest – as for example when the Brown-led government encouraged the Bank of Scotland–Lloyds TSB merger in 2008 against UKCC advice. However, such depoliticization, if not a sign of loss of state or governmental power, may come at a democratic cost, implying a democratic deficit; this will be observed in the following section when analysing aspects of EU monetary and fiscal stabilization policies.[1]

In a UK context, other, somewhat different questions can be asked about the capacity of governments in terms of institutional design and competence. Governments often fail to achieve policy objectives – or at least do not optimize policy outcomes – due to a relative lack of resource or capacity at the centre of government. Prime ministers do not have the scope of resource of their Cabinet colleagues who head up government departments; there is no prime-ministerial responsibility for a government department (except for the relatively small Cabinet Office). Attempts have been made from time to time to strengthen the centre. Though such attempts occurred before New Labour, Blair's governments drove this with some force, overseeing the appointment of special advisers ('spads') and the creation of centrally controlled units with a remit to drive and coordinate government policy and action through the whole of government (e.g. policy unit – though this pre-existed Blair, it was strengthened by the following: strategic communications unit; research and information unit; social exclusion unit; performance and innovation unit; prime minister's forward strategy unit later combined in the strategy unit; delivery unit). As recent literature has indicated, this did not prevent serious failures, including tax credits and plans to issue the public with identity cards, to name only two (King and Crewe 2013). As King and Crewe point out, heads of government in almost every European country have much more significant staff support than the UK prime minister.

In fact there is an issue of institutional design and configuration at play. In the UK the increased concentration of power at the centre – in effect in the hands of the prime minister – can be viewed negatively (see, e.g., Aucoin 2012), running counter to traditional processes and resource capacities that have seen much policy and service delivery emanating from departments rather than the centre. But while the case has been made for the paucity of resourcing and capacity at the centre vis-à-vis international comparators, criticism can also be made of departmental capacity. There is considerably shorter tenure and more regular reshuffling of departmental ministers than occurs in comparable democracies (Huber and Martinez-Gallardo 2004) and a range of evidence that indicates the adverse impact of such on government and departmental performance (Riddell et al. 2011; Public Administration Select Committee 2008). The departmental capability reviews were first established in 2005, with subsequent evaluations, giving an indication of governmental performance. While many of the reviews and their subsequent follow-up showed substantial improvement – some sceptics may say inevitably so, since the focus was internal management improvement – the NAO in 2009 indicated that the information collected could not prove a link between departments' actions and improved performance, that common weaknesses were poor skills, leadership and understanding delivery models. The NAO's conclusion was:

> it will be possible to determine value for money only when departments demonstrate that specific improved outcomes, including better public services, are linked to actions taken in response to Capability Reviews. (NAO 2009c)

So UK government seems to have an institutional configuration less than optimal: a rather weakly resourced centre and a less than efficient or effective departmental infrastructure. This, despite adverse impact on governmental competence, does not amount to state depletion.

UK GOVERNANCE AND TERRITORIAL COMPLEXITY

The UK is firmly embedded within a system of multilevel governance. The European Union (EU) is the key external dimension to this; but important too is the (increasingly) complex governance arrangement within the UK at the level of devolved polities and local government. It is outwith the scope of this chapter to address non-governmental organizations in the governance framework – agencies, collaborative bodies, private public and third sectors – but these bodies too are significant in the UK's governance map. The EU will be considered. Within the UK, the main devolved polity focus will be Scotland, since this is the most powerful of the devolved administrations and since its independence referendum in 2014 has high political salience.

The UK government's relationship with the EU is in some senses puzzling. While the dominant coalition partner (Conservatives) is ambivalent if not hostile, in many areas of macroeconomic policy there is congruence between UK policy and the direction of EU policy. The pro-market, liberal approaches to address the post-financial crash are founded on budget deficit reduction, not unlike the aims of the UK coalition government. Institutions of the EU, ranging from the European Commission (EC) to the European Central Bank (ECB), with the support of international bodies like the International Monetary Fund (IMF), have been particularly forceful in this regard when providing support to seriously indebted – at risk of default – nations such as Portugal, Ireland, Cyprus, Greece; financial support from the European Stability Mechanism is based on strong public spending cuts and privatization. However, the trend has been towards a depoliticization and technocratization of economic policy management by the 'Troika' composed of functionaries from the EC, ECB and the IMF led by the EC's Director General for Economic and Financial Affairs (Olli Rehn). The Troika has a particular locus on EU support (bailout) packages; however, in parallel, Rehn's office has been given responsibility for setting annual targets for all member states, and these budgets must be submitted to Rehn's office before going before parliaments with countries considered 'at risk', facing fines of up to 0.2 per cent of GDP; Rehn must also be consulted about other commissioners' initiatives if they affect government spending (Watkins 2013). Although much of the Troika's work pertains to the eurozone, and so does not directly involve the UK, the nature of the EU within a system of multilevel governance is considered by some scholars to require an almost exceptional definition of democracy – to encompass 'indirect, elitist, depoliticised insulated and non-participatory' conceptualizations (see Flinders

2010: 282) – and this often requires a complex working out of multilevel governance arrangements between EU and national governments; such is a key challenge for the practice of public administration.

Nowhere is this more so than in the UK, outside the eurozone and with a semi-detached commitment to the EU. Supranational oversight of national banking by the ECB (as proposed by the EC) is relatively non-controversial throughout Europe, except that the UK government is opposed to this measure, presumably seeing competitive advantage to the UK in being outside any European regulatory arrangements. Complexities are compounded when we observe the shifting dynamic within the EU. Aspects of the supranational banking oversight are opposed by Germany, which is resisting an EU-wide deposit insurance scheme and oversight plans that include the power to take over failed German banks. Beyond the banking case there appears to be division of thinking over the long-term governance of the EU that will affect the UK government's approach to the EU. There are intergovernmental visions of national governments coordinating budgetary and macroeconomic policies (led by Van Rompuy, President of the European Council); but also supranational approaches for more explicit coordination in the eurozone alone, focusing on the EC as the key policy institution with different variants of this supranationalism favoured by Schauble, Germany's Finance Minister and Barroso, when EC President (Watkins 2013). How the UK government responds in this multilevel governance environment is yet to be seen, though presumably it will engage with the intergovernmental approach more positively. The political dimension to this may be the most significant on two counts. First, substantial new powers for supranational or intergovernmental bodies would require another treaty, entailing referendum processes in a number of countries, whose outcome at this stage is difficult to predict. Second, within the UK, a referendum on EU membership ('in or out') has been promised by the Conservative Party by 2017, should it form the next government. There is added complexity when one considers that a Labour or Labour-led coalition post-2015 is unlikely to hold a referendum. So it can be clearly seen that the EU dimension to territorial complexity contains several fault lines with difficult-to-predict outcomes.

The public administration and governance within the UK is well summed up by the phrase 'asymmetric devolution', with the attendant complexities, continuities and disjunctures that this involves. The background to devolution has something of a variable geometry. In Scotland, an unsuccessful referendum for a devolved parliament in the late 1970s (despite a small majority voting in favour), followed by episodic peaks of SNP electoral support in the 1980s and 1990s, steady, almost uninterrupted, decline of the Conservatives and a stronger commitment to devolution from Labour/New Labour, along with an articulation of support for self-government from civil society, all led to a clear majority for devolution in the 1997 referendum. Wales had a wafer-thin majority for devolution in 1997, but clear support to extend the Welsh Assembly's powers in the 2011 referendum. Northern Ireland's devolved government is very much a creature of the peace process, based on consociational principles (until its suspension in 1972 it was different, more an instrument of the loyalist majority). Scotland, with around 9 per cent of the UK population, has a government with primary legislative powers and an annual spend in devolved areas of around £30 billion (Scottish Government 2013); Wales, with under 5 per cent of the UK population, has recently increased its powers to include primary legislative competence in '20 devolved areas' with an annual spend just under £15 billion (Welsh Government 2013); Northern Ireland has primary legislative powers in devolved areas, a population under 3 per cent of the UK's and an annual spend of £11 billion (Northern Ireland Executive 2013). There is an elected mayor and separate elected assembly in London (which has over 12 per cent of the UK population), with powers over policing/fire services and transport. The combined expenditure of these two areas of responsibility at over £10 billion approximates the Northern Irish devolved budget (Mayor of London 2013; Shawcross 2013). There are major paradoxes and anomolies in this asymmetry. For example, while devolution aims to bring some measure of transparency and accountability closer to the electorate, the mayor of London has been criticized for opacity in decision making, particularly over transport (Shawcross 2013). The funding of devolved bodies (for Northern Ireland, Scotland, Wales) is historically (rather than needs) based on the Barnett formula and is not related to fiscal capacity. And, London notwithstanding, there is no devolved government for England, which comprises about 83 per cent of the UK population.

Complexities arise due to overlapping responsibilities that may spill over and cut across various areas of policy. One such example is the Scottish government's (then titled Scottish Executive) introduction in 2002 of free personal care for the elderly. Those receiving this at home were therefore no longer eligible for Attendance Allowance ('reserved' rather than devolved, and administered through the UK government's Department for Work and Pensions). The subsequent saving to the UK Treasury was not passed back to the Scottish government, leading it to claim that this money was lost and so had to be found within existing Scottish resources. Another example is the issue of Barnett consequentials. Since the funding for devolved governments is a formula based on UK government spend authorized by the UK Parliament, it may mean that funding for, say, major transport infrastructure will have a consequential effect on moneys allocated to Scotland, Wales and Northern Ireland – the governments there can then spend this in any devolved areas of expenditure. Arguably this breaks an important principle of democratic governance – the principle of accountability for money spent and the concomitant responsibility for raising this money; in fact the entire devolution funding package could be criticized thus – since there are elected representatives in the devolved institutions spending moneys they are not accountable for raising: in effect, representation without taxation. The Scotland Act 2012, implemented from 2015, only partially addresses this – and only for Scotland – by giving the Scottish Parliament a degree of constrained fiscal autonomy (though in November 2013, the UK prime minister offered similar arrangements for Wales after a referendum there).

The final section of the chapter will examine the robustness, resilience, continuities and disjunctures in the existing pattern of territorial governance in the UK. Substantial study of the post-1997 period when New Labour introduced the current Westminster-devolved polity settlement provides the contextual foregrounding (e.g. Flinders 2010; Bogdanor 2009; Hazell 2008). Despite the devolution policies introduced in the New Labour years, there was a considerable strengthening of 'traditional' Westminster model-type arrangements with strong centralizing around the executive. Even where there were aspects of a 'consensus' rather than a 'majoritarian–Whitehall' model developing (to use Lijphart's terminology – Lijphart 1999), this was accompanied by strong reserve powers maintained at executive level (e.g. with the independent central bank, the Freedom of Information legislation, incorporation of the European Convention on Human Rights – see Flinders 2010). It is also the case that changes to local government governance introduced intensification of the Westminster system with the widespread adoption (prescribed through legislation) of Cabinet-style organization in councils, allied of course to strong central government leverage via funding, much of which came from the centre and was not raised locally. Post-New Labour, in the current Conservative–Liberal Democrat coalition there is some evidence of a shift away from strong executive–central focus, with ministers like Gove (education), Pickles (local government) and Boles (planning minister) enthusiastic about bypassing established governmental structures (e.g. local education authorities) and planning regulatory procedures in pursuit of a localism agenda. It must be stressed, though, that it is far too early to assess the long-term impact of current coalition government actions.

A key issue to be explored is the impact on UK government and governance of the post-1997 devolution settlements, driven particularly by the experience in Scotland. Based on a more participatory and consensual model of democracy (using, for example, a partially proportional electoral system with some aspects of institutional design differing from Westminster), this is said to coexist with the national (UK) system still largely undisturbed. Such hybridity has been termed 'bi-constitutionalism' (Flinders 2010). There are resulting impacts and consequences for the government of the UK. First, devolution has not been 'normalized' as a framework for UK government (see Parry 2013); this is dramatically displayed in the absence of any electorally based regional devolution in England – in fact with New Labour, the instigator of devolution settlement in Scotland, 'conniving at the heavy loss of the North East [of England] referendum in 2004' (Parry 2013: 3). So, while the key purpose of granting some devolved power to Scotland was to facilitate constitutional stabilization (see McTavish 2014) giving firmer grounding to Scotland's position within the UK – hence the statements from John Smith, Labour leader before Blair, that devolution 'was the settled will of the Scottish people' and George Robertson, when Secretary of State for Scotland, that 'devolution would kill Scottish nationalism stone dead' – the argument is made that this bi-constitutionalism is always likely to be unstable within a Westminster-styled unitary state (Flinders 2010). This of course is quite distinct from further instability with the possible enhanced powers for the Scottish Parliament in the future and/or knock-on effects in Scottish MPs' representation and curtailed voting arrangements in the UK Parliament.

There is some evidence of a nascent instability. One may read the lack of enthusiasm for electorally based devolution in England as a form of satisfaction or tolerance of existing arrangements, with the devolved governments' (in particular Scotland's) existence and operation accommodated within prevailing arrangements. However, current evidence based on public surveys shows a growing feeling of inequity in England regarding government funding and aspects of political representation (especially *vis-à-vis* Scotland). Although the reality (especially regarding public spending and fiscal transfers) may be more complex, there is none the less a potential link between perceptions of inequity and a sense of grievance on the one hand and instability with current constitutional arrangements on the other.[2] The sense of inequity is indicated in Tables 18.1 and 18.2.

Second, there is the possibility that the devolution anomalies or perceived lack of equity might self-correct, but this assumes that, over time, the constitutional changes made to accommodate devolution in the first place (i.e. the bi-constitutional arrangements) will transfer back through attitudinal or cultural change to the heart of the existing Westminster-centred system itself, thereby countering the destabilizing effects of bi-constitutionalism (this argument is outlined by Flinders, 2010: 305). There is scant evidence of constitutional or policy learning in this way post devolution. Studies have shown that, while there are instances of policy trans-

Table 18.1   English attitudes towards Scotland's share of public spending

Year	2000	2001	2002	2003	2007	2008	2009	2010	2011	2012
	%	%	%	%	%	%	%	%	%	%
More than fair	21	24	24	22	32	41	40	38	44	52
Pretty much fair	42	44	44	45	38	33	30	29	21	18
Less than fair	11	9	9	9	6	3	4	4	4	4
Don't know	25	23	22	25	22	23	25	28	31	35
n	1928	2761	2897	1917	859	982	980	913	1507	3600

Note: Cited in McKay Commission (2013); for 2000–2010 based on British Social Attitudes Surveys; for 2011–12 based on FoES.

Sources: FoES (2012); Ormston (2012); Wyn Jones et al. (2012).

Table 18.2   Respondents in England agreeing with statements

Scottish MPs no longer vote on English laws	81%
Scottish Parliament to pay for services from own taxes	78%
Scotland gets more than fair share of public spend	52%
Don't trust UK government to work in England's interests	62%
n	3600

Note: Cited in McKay Commission (2013).

Source: FoES (2012).

fer and learning from centre (UK, often England) to periphery, there are precious few examples of periphery-to-centre transfer or learning, and the same can be said of periphery to periphery (see Nutley et al. 2012); there are indeed examples of initiatives designed in devolved polities so that their transfer elsewhere is limited (e.g. Moon's analysis of 'made in Wales' policies under Morgan's period as first minister – Moon 2013).

Third, the instability thesis can be viewed differently. It can be seen in terms of how diverse or uniform arrangements are in reality between devolved polity and UK-centred approaches.

The devolved institutional design is in some senses very different from Westminster. Scotland's multi-party system, facilitated by its additional member proportional-based electoral system, is considered an example of moderate pluralism (signified by three to five relevant parties not separated by intense ideological difference – see Sartori 2005; Bennie and Clark 2003). Only the current Scottish government is an outright single-party majority; all previous administrations have been coalitions or minority governments. The period of minority government in particular (2007–11) in theory empowering Parliament vis-à-vis the executive conceptually provides a strong contrast with Westminster. However, the impact of this must not be exaggerated: although that minority government could not implement a small number of flagship initiatives due to lack of parliamentary support (e.g. plans for a local income tax and for a referendum on independence), its legislative output was little different from preceding majority coalition governments (Lundberg 2013). Other areas of difference should perhaps be viewed with some caution. While there are areas of policy divergence (NHS institutional design, higher education fees regime, organization of elderly care to name a small number), and evidence that, over time post devolution, there has been greater divergence as policy capacity and confidence increase (Keating et al. 2012), what should also be recognized is that policy goals and paradigms may be quite commonplace across the UK, though the policy instruments and tools used may differ. For example, the desire to have greater partnership working to provide more integration and coherence of public service provision is commonplace throughout the UK, though in Scotland there is a greater role for local authorities in this through the use of 'single outcome agreements'. It is well recognized that policy ideas and goals travel more readily than policy instruments and tools (e.g. Radaelli 2005).

Similarities are not insignificant. There are procedural and institutional design features that differ from those in Westminster, but the executive's power, as in Westminster, is significant; there are examples of a strong centralization of policy initiatives in some areas (e.g. the creation of single unified Scottish police, and fire and rescue services, centrally driven mergers in the college sector, and the 'voluntary' freezing of local council tax since 2008). The adversarial approaches to accountability of government in the Scottish Parliament are similar to those in Westminster; the at-times hostile nature of interaction between government and main opposition party is equal to that in Westminster (and in the run-up to the referendum vitriolic). There is evidence to support Mitchell when he states:

> The Scottish Parliament is one of the Westminster family of legislatures . . . the more proportional electoral system used for Holyrood has given rise to limited changes in its operation compared to Westminster. The multi party nature of Scottish parliamentary politics . . . has not altered the fundamentally adversarial nature of Scottish politics . . . nor executive dominance of Parliament. (Mitchell 2010: 114)

Finally, there is the intriguing irony of a Scottish National Party (SNP) government acting as an exemplar of traditional Westminster-system values in the practice of public administration. At the UK level the coalition government's Civil Service Reform Plan has led to concerns about the introduction of politicization of the senior civil service (see Pyper 2013); no doubt the government's plans are the result of UK ministers' frustration regarding the advice and service they are receiving. SNP government appears to have no such problem, with the civil service giving the impartial advice the government desires; apparently in Scotland 'politicians and officials have found a mutual interest in the old model' (Parry 2013). Added to this is a robust defence of the traditional 'British' delivery model of public services outlined at the start of this chapter – but outlined here by Nicola Sturgeon, Cabinet Secretary for Health and Well Being when the speech was delivered, and from November 2014 Scotland's First Minister.

> There will be no privatisation of the NHS in Scotland . . . unlike its counterpart in England, NHS in Scotland will remain a public service, paid for by the public and accountable to the public . . . in the past the Union would have been seen as not just the creator but also the guarantor of the values and vision of the post war Welfare State . . . independence will give us the power not only to protect Scotland from policies that offend our sense of decency and social cohesion. (Glasgow University Law School, 5 March 2012, cited in Massie 2012)

CONCLUSION

The UK makes an interesting country case in any analysis of public administration and governance. It adopted a traditional public administration paradigm with a strong central state directing and assuming overall responsibility for the growing provision of public services, accountability ultimately residing with elected government ministers. There were high levels of state activity in industrial sectors and utility provision, with day-to-day operations distanced from politicians but final authority controlled by government. Alongside was a traditionally strong internationalization of the UK economy. The result was that shocks from the international economy, and increased difficulties in making the postwar Keynesian politico-economic framework operate with stability, occurred in the context of a UK state directly placed as the central power source holding the key fiscal, spending and delivery instruments to effect change.

As has been well documented, the UK's adoption of this change – NPM – was more systemic and thorough than in other countries, and the ideational and ideological drive was clear: the accentuation of management, often transferred in from the business sector; cost control and discipline;

competition; privatization and use of market mechanisms; efficiency and modernization leading to a separation of policy and management of delivery through agencies and arm's-length bodies. The extant research evaluating the success of these approaches has been sporadic and somewhat sparse: many NPM-type 'value-for-money' initiatives have not borne fruit; cost control, the key driver in many NPM policies, has had limited success. But much of the underlying paradigm has remained intact and shown remarkable resilience since the global financial crash (for an account of this internationally, see McTavish 2013).

Given the performance improvement and modernization aspects of NPM, an inspection and regulatory environment developed, leading to a proliferation of players beyond direct government. Over time the balance has shifted from direct regulation (which saw two spikes in regulatory activity under Major and Blair in the 1980s and 1990s) towards an aspiration of 'overseeing' core standards and so on. Low-key, 'light' or self-regulation has had mixed success (successful in some areas of professional or peer-controlled regulation, spectacularly not in parts of the financial services sector), but in many circumstances very adverse impacts on organizational culture, creating 'spirals of distrust'. It remains to be seen if the aspiration of governments and other regulators to oversee rather than directly supervise standards will hold – for example, there will be political demands for greater direct regulation in highly salient areas like health care.

Viewed in chronological perspective, NPM, public management reforms and policies influenced by this paradigm have clearly given us a landscape of governance rather than government. In an era of governance, governments share the stage with other, non-governmental actors, public and private. In a complex and interdependent world there are asymmetries of power. Where governments rely on institutions beyond their immediate locus, complex co-production and co-governance arrangements may lead citizens to feel that there is a lack of accountability (with a subsequent delegitimization of the political system) and an increase in technocratization and bureaucratization of policy and decision making. But this is far from saying that government is an off-stage actor with very limited power or capacity. The chapter shows instances in the UK of government choosing to distance itself from direct political control; and also cases where government has taken very direct and effective action when major national or economic interests are at stake. This is not in contradiction to (but is compatible with) the notion that competence and capability of government can be lacking at times and could be much improved: the chapter certainly gave evidence of this.

Finally, of immense significance to the UK government and

governance is the territorial complexity of the UK government's field of action and control. For the study and practice of public administration this raises challenges as significant as those seen in the post-1945 decline of empire. The chapter examined the UK's governance relationship outside the UK, to the EU; and within, the link with devolved polities, in particular Scotland. The fundamental irony with regard to Europe is the policy objective congruence between the UK government and the EU, though running alongside this is an unenthusiastic commitment to the EU from the main partner in the UK coalition. The parameters of complexity of the EU–UK multi-level governance relationship were examined with reference to the trend towards depoliticization of economic policy management in the EU, the UK's hostility to EU banking supervision (seeing competitive advantage for the UK if outside these arrangements), division in thinking about future EU governance between intergovernmental and supranational alternatives and the UK's (especially the Conservatives') particular issues with the EU ('in' or 'out') referendum.

Devolution within the UK is differentiated, the most powerful polity being Scotland, but with no devolution in England other than the limited autonomy of London's Mayor and Assembly. A key feature of the UK's territorial governance system is very limited fiscal autonomy: spending authority without the responsibility to raise significant levels of revenue, a democratic-accountability gap. It has been argued that the devolution settlement has contributed to a bi-constitutionalism, with devolved governments departing from the dominant executive-controlled Westminster model. A range of instabilities and disjunctures that this presents to the unified UK system of government was examined, balanced by an analysis of similarities and continuities between devolved polity and centre. The final fundamental irony is that, in contrast to proposals for civil service reform by the current UK government (and civil service norms, it should be remembered, are considered a fundamental component of the Westminster system), the SNP-led Scottish government, whose aim is an independent Scotland outside the current UK, exhibits a relationship with the civil service much more aligned to traditional UK Westminster-styled civil service norms; and the stated position of the SNP government on public service delivery makes complimentary and positive reference to traditional UK unionist approaches that, according to the SNP, have been abandoned by the current UK government.

NOTES

1. An interesting concept is that of negative power, that is the power of prevention, surveillance and evaluation, which it is claimed has substantially increased. The negative power has 'the ability to claim the legitimacy to veto political decisions in the name of supposedly neutral and even natural rules' (Stein 2006, cited in D'Eramo 2013: 24). The thesis claims that the prevailing conventional, neoliberal thinking underwritten by an increasingly powerful range of international financial institutions such as the IMF, the World Bank, the World Trade Organization and the European Central Bank provides an institutional conduit for such negative power; and this is politically underpinned by a narrow political choice ('essentially the same') from centre-centre-right to centre-centre-left. Thus a former governor of the German Bundesbank, Hans Tietmeyer, in 1998 praised national governments for preferring 'the permanent plebiscite of global markets to the plebiscite of the ballot box' (D'Eramo 2013: 25).
2. This of course gives an ironic and historic twist to the quotation from P.G. Wodehouse: 'It is never difficult to distinguish between a Scotsman with a grievance and a ray of sunshine'.

REFERENCES

Andrews, R., Boyne, G.A. and Walker, R.M. (2006) Strategy content and organisational performance: an empirical analysis, *Journal of Public Administration Review*, **66**(1), 52–63.

Aucoin, P. (2012) New political governance in Westminster systems: impartial public administration and management performance at risk, *Governance: An International Journal of Policy, Administration and Institutions*, **25**(2), 177–99.

Bell, S. and Hindmoor, A. (2009) The governance of public affairs, *Journal of Public Affairs*, **9**, 149–59.

Bennie, L. and Clark, A. (2003) Towards moderate pluralism: Scotland's post devolution party system, 1999–2002, *British Elections and Parties Review*, **13**(1), 134–55.

Blair, A. (2010) *The European Union Since 1945*, 2nd edn. Harlow: Longman.

Bogdanor, V. (2009) *The New British Constitution*. Oxford: Hart Publishing.

Booth, A. (2000) Inflation, expectations and the political economy of Conservative Britain, *The Historical Journal*, **43**(3) 827–47.

Bouckaert, G., Peters, B.G. and Verhoest, K. (eds) (2010) *The Co-ordination of Public Sector Organisations: Shifting Patterns of Public Management*. Basingstoke: Palgrave Macmillan.

Boyne, G.A., James, O., Moseley, A. and Petrovsky, N. (2013) When do public organisations recruit outsiders? Paper presented at Public Administration Committee Conference, Edinburgh, 11 September.

Boyne, G.A., Carrell, C., Law, J., Powell, M. and Walker, R.M. (2003) *Evaluating Public Management Reforms*. Buckingham: Open University Press.

Burton, M. (2013) *The Politics of Public Sector Reform. From Thatcher to Coalition*. Basingstoke: Palgrave Macmillan.

Christensen, T. and Lægreid, P. (eds) (2007) *Transcending New Public Management*. Aldershot: Ashgate.

Considine, M. and Lewis, J. (2003) Bureaucracy, network or enterprise? Comparing models of governance in Australia, Britain, the Netherlands and New Zealand, *Public Administration Review*, **63**, 131–40.

Crozier, M., Huntington, S.P. and Watanuki, J. (1975) *The Crisis of Democracy: Report on the Governability of Democracies to the Trilateral Commission*. New York: New York University Press.

Darling, A. (2011) *Back From the Brink. 1000 Days at Number 11*. London: Atlantic.

D'Eramo, M. (2013) Populism and the new oligarchy, *New Left Review*, **82**, July–August, 5–28.

Djelic, M.-L. and Sahlin, K. (2012) Reordering the world: transnational regulatory governance and its challenges, in D. Levi-Faur (ed.), *The Oxford Handbook of Governance*. Oxford: Oxford University Press, pp. 745–58.

Fenwick, J., Miller Johnston, K. and McTavish, D. (2012) Co-governance or meta bureaucracy: perspectives of local governance 'partnerships' in England and Scotland, *Policy and Politics*, **40**(3), 405–22.

Flinders, M. (2010) *Democratic Drift. Majoritarian Modification and Democratic Anomie in the United Kingdom*. Oxford: Oxford University Press.

FoES (2012) *Future of England Survey*. Edinburgh University and Cardiff University: IPPR.

Hansard Society (2013) *Audit of Political Engagement 10: The 2013 Report*. London: Hansard Society.

Hardiman, N. (2012) Governance and state structures, in D. Levi-Faur (ed.), *The Oxford Handbook of Governance*. Oxford: Oxford University Press, pp. 228–41.

Hazell, R. (2008) *Constitutional Futures Revisited*. Basingstoke: Palgrave.

Heald, D. and Georgiou, G. (2011) The substance of accounting for public–private partnerships, *Financial Accountability and Management*, **27**(2), 217–47.

Heseltine, M. (1980) Ministers and management in Whitehall, *Management Services in Government*, **35**, 61–8.

HM Government (2011) *Open Public Services White Paper*. Cabinet Office.

HM Treasury (2010) *Business Plan 2011–2015*. London: HM Treasury.

Hood, C. (1991) A public management for all seasons?, *Public Administration*, **69**(1), 3–19.

Hood, C. (2005) The idea of joined up government. A historical perspective, in V. Bogdanor (ed.), *Joined Up Government*. Oxford: Oxford University Press, pp. 19–42.

Hood, C. (2011) *The Blame Game*. Princeton, NJ: Princeton University Press.

Hood, C. and Dixon, R. (2013) A model of cost cutting in government? The great managerial revolution in UK central government re-considered, Public Administration **91**(1), 114–34.

Hood, C., Scott, C., James, O. and Travers, T. (1999) *Regulation Inside Government*. Oxford: Oxford University Press.

Huber, J.D. and Martinez-Gallardo, C. (2004) Cabinet instability and accumulation of experience: the Fourth and Fifth Republics in comparative perspectives, *British Journal of Political Science*, **34**, 37–41.

James, O. (2003) *The Executive Agency Revolution in Whitehall: Public Interest versus Bureau Shaping Explanations*. Basingstoke: Palgrave Macmillan.

Jessop, B. (2004) Multi level governance and multi level meta governance, in I. Bache and M. Flinders (eds), *Multi Level Governance*. Oxford: Oxford University Press, pp. 49–74.

Julius, D. (2008) *Public Services Industry Review. Understanding the Public Services Industry: How Big, How Good, Where Next?* Department for Business Enterprise and Regulatory Reform.

Keating, M., Cairney, P. and Hepburn, E. (2012) Policy convergence, transfer and learning in the UK under devolution, *Regional and Federal Studies*, **22**(3), 289–307.

King, A.S. (1975) Overload: problems of governing in the 1970s, *Political Studies*, **23**, 284–96.

King, A.S. and Crewe, I. (2013) *The Blunders of Our Governments*. London: Oneworld.

Klijn, E.H. (2012) Public management and governance: a comparison of two paradigms to deal with modern complex problems, in D. Levi-Faur (ed.), *The Handbook of Governance*. Oxford: Oxford University Press, pp. 201–14.

Kreiger, J. (1986) *Reagan, Thatcher and the Politics of Decline*. Cambridge: Polity Press.

Lijphart, A. (1999) *Patterns of Democracy: Government Forms and Performance in Thirty Six Countries*. New Haven, CT: Yale University Press.

Lodge, M. (2013) Crisis, resources and the state: executive politics in the age of the depleted state, *Political Studies Review*, **11**(3), 378–90.

Ludlam, S. (1992) The gnomes of Washington: four myths of the 1976 IMF crisis, *Political Studies*, **40**, 713–27.

Lundberg, T.C. (2013) Politics is still an adversarial business: minority government and mixed-member proportional representation in Scotland and New Zealand, *British Journal of Politics and International Relations*, **15**(4), 609–25.

Major, J. (1999) *The Autobiography*. London: HarperCollins.

Marinetto, M. (2011) A Lipskian analysis of child protection failures from Victoria Climbie to 'Baby P', *Public Administration*, **89**(3), 1164–81.

Massie, A. (2012) Nicola Sturgeon: we must kill Britain to save Britain. *Spectator*, 6 March.

Mayor of London (2013) *MOPAC Budget Submission 2013–2014*. Mayor of London, Office for Policy and Crime.

McKay Commission (2013) *Report of the Commission on the Consequences of Devolution for the House of Commons*. www.tmc.independent.gov.uk, accessed 30 October 2013.

McTavish, D. (2013) 'Who's responsible for the state we're in?' Government and public sector accountability: accountability and responsibility in an era of crisis and austerity, in J. Diamond and J. Liddle (eds), *Looking for Consensus: Civil Society, Social Movements and Crises for Public Management*. Bingley: Emerald, pp. 3–23.

McTavish, D. (2014) Debate: Scotland, the United Kingdom and complex government, *Public Money and Management*, **34**(1), pp. 4–8.

Mitchell, J. (2010) The narcissism of small differences: Scotland and Westminster, *Parliamentary Affairs*, **63**(1), 98–116.

Moon, D.S. (2013) Rhetoric and policy learning: on Rhodri Morgan's 'clear red water' and 'made in Wales' health policies, *Public Policy and Administration*, **28**(3), 306–23.

Moran, M. (2002) Understanding the regulatory state, *British Journal of Political Science*, **32**, 391–413.

Mulgan, G. (2005) Joined up government: past present and future, in V. Bogdanor (ed.), *Joined Up Government*. Oxford: Oxford University Press, pp. 175–95.

NAO (2009a) *Reducing Bureaucracy for Public Sector Frontline Staff*. London: National Audit Office.

NAO (2009b) *Commercial Skills for Complex Government Projects*. London: National Audit Office.

NAO (2009c) *Assessment of the Capability Review Programme*. London: National Audit Office.

NAO (2010) *Taking the Measure of Government Performance*. London: National Audit Office.

NAO (2012) *Delivering Public Services Through Markets: Principles for Achieving Value for Money*. London: National Audit Office.

Niskanen, W. (1968) The peculiar economics of bureaucracy, *American Economic Review*, **58**(2), 293–305.

Northern Ireland Executive (2013) *Budget and Economic Strategy* http://www.northernireland.gov.uk/index/work-of-the-executive/pfg-budget-economic-strategy.htm, accessed 30 October 2013.

Nutley, S., Downe, J., Martin, S. and Grace, C. (2012) Policy transfer and convergence within the UK: the case of local government performance improvement regimes, *Policy and Politics*, **40**(2), 193–209.

Ormston, R. (2012) *The English Question: How is England Responding to Devolution?* National Centre for Social Research.

Parry, R. (2013) The odd couple: civil servants and nationalists in devolved government, Paper delivered to Public Administration Committee Conference, Edinburgh, 10 September.

Power, M. (1997) *The Audit Society. Rituals of Verification*. Oxford: Oxford University Press.

Power, M. (2004) *The Risk Management of Everything. Rethinking the Politics of Uncertainty*. London: Demos.

Public Administration Select Committee (2008) *Good Government*, HC 2008–09, 97-11, Ev. 37, 39.

Pyper, R. (2013) The UK coalition and the civil service: a half term report, *Public Policy and Administration*, **28**(4), 364–82.

Radaelli, C.M. (2004) The diffusion of regulatory impact analysis: best practice or lesson drawing? *European Journal of Political Research*, **43**(5), 723–47.

Radaelli, C.M. (2005) Diffusion without convergence: how political context shapes the adoption of regulatory impact assessments, *Journal of European Public Policy*, **12**(5), 924–43.

Rallings, C. and Thrasher, M. (2007) *British Electoral Facts 1832–2006*. Aldershot: Ashgate.

Reece, D. (2010) Economic forecasters are often even less reliable than the weathermen, *Daily Telegraph*, 18 May. http://www.telegraph.co.uk/finance/economics/7734421/Economic-forecasters-are-often-even-less-reliable-than-the-weathermen.html, accessed 30 October 2013.

Riddell, P., Gruhn, Z. and Carolan, L. (2011) *The Challenge of Being a Minister: Defining and Developing Ministerial Effectiveness.* London: Institute for Government.

Roberts, A. (2010) *The Logic of Discipline: Global Capitalism and the Architecture of Government.* Oxford: Oxford University Press.

Robichau, R. (2011) The mosaic of governance: creating a picture with definitions, theories and debates, *Policy Studies Journal*, **39**(1), 113–31.

Rose, R. (1980) *Challenge to Governance: Studies in Overloaded Politics.* Beverly Hills, CA: Sage.

Sandbrook, D. (2012) *Seasons in the Sun. The Battle for Britain 1974–79.* London: Allen Lane.

Sanders, D. (1990) *Losing an Empire, Finding a Role: British Foreign Policy Since 1945.* London: Macmillan.

Sartori, G. (2005) *Parties and Party Systems: A Framework for Analysis.* Colchester: ECPR Press.

Scottish Government (2013) *Budget Statement* www.scotland.gov.uk.publications.2013/09/9971, accessed 29 October 2013.

Self, R. (2010) *British Foreign and Defence Policy Since 1945. Challenges and Dilemmas in a Changing World.* Basingstoke: Palgrave Macmillan.

Shawcross, V. (2013) Boris Johnson and TfL must commit to greater transparency. *Open Government London 2013.*

Stein, B. (2006) In class warfare guess which class is winning? *New York Times*, 26 November.

Stoker, G. (2011) Was local governance such a good idea? A global comparative perspective, *Public Administration*, **89**(1), 15–31.

Streeck, W. (2012) Markets and peoples, *New Left Review*, **73**, 63–71.

Van de Walle, S. and Hammerschmid, G. (2011) The impact of the new public management: challenges for co-ordination and cohesion in European public sectors, *Halduskultuur – Administrative Culture*, **12**(2), 190–209.

Watkins, S. (2013) Vanity and venality, *London Review of Books*, 29 August.

Welsh Government (2013) *Draft Budget 2013–14*, www.wales.gov.uk/ funding/budget/draft budget1314/, accessed 30 October 2013.

Wilson, G. (2012) Governance after the crisis, in D. Levi-Faur (ed.), *The Oxford Handbook of Governance.* Oxford: Oxford University Press, pp. 372–86.

Wrigley, C. (1996) 'Trade unions strikes and the government', in R. Coopey and N. Woodward (eds), *Britain in the 1970s. The Troubled Economy.* London: Routledge, pp. 261–79.

Wyn Jones, R., Lodge, G., Henderson, A. and Wincott, D. (2012) *The Dog That Finally Barked: England as an Emerging Political Community.* London: IPPR.

Conclusion
Karen Johnston

INTRODUCTION

The first decade of the new millennium has revealed unprecedented global problems in scale and scope. These include the economic and financial crisis, rapid social and demographic changes, technological advancements, and the global geo-political and governance landscape continuing to exist in a state of change. Nation states that have emerged from autocratic regimes have embraced the principles of democracy and the challenge of reforming government during a transitional period in the new political and socioeconomic 'order'. Increasingly it may be observed that countries around the globe are embracing democracy and reforming the institutions of the state. This is evident in countries in Africa, the Middle East, South America and Asia, which are removing the vestiges of authoritarian rule. Yet a challenge for transitional as well as advanced democratic polities is to build the institutional, policy and service delivery capacity of a government in order to deal with rapid and increasingly complex policy problems. We live in a world that is experiencing rapid change and, with it, dynamic challenges for governments. As the chapters in this book have illustrated, there have been ebbs of crisis, followed by change and the inevitable and seemingly intractable challenges that these present for government and society in general.

PUBLIC ADMINISTRATION, DEMOCRACY AND GOOD GOVERNANCE

In the first part of this book Bouckaert provides a discursive interpretation of governance, with its cornucopia of definitions, but usefully analyses governance into a typology of a 'span of governance'. In his review of governance he argues that democracy and good governance are integral to the effectiveness of the state. Furthermore, an inclusive state with a participatory and democratic environment with open and transparent political systems, facilitating free and open communication, and resulting in citizen input in political and administrative decisions, has better prospects for success in its administrative effectiveness. Thus Bouckaert argues that democracy is about participation, transparency, open society, due process in decision making, responsibility and accountability, legitimacy and trusting systems, which are key words that define the concept of governance.

Bouckaert refers to Fukuyama's (2013) conceptualization of governance as 'government's ability to make and enforce rules, to deliver services'. Fukuyama (1992) argued that the spread of liberal democracies and capitalism fashioned after Western values signalled the end of a sociocultural evolution, with most countries abandoning authoritarian forms of government and embracing democracy. He viewed democracy as the final form of government in humanity's evolution. This assessment was based on the collapse of communism. The USSR imploded and countries once part of the Soviet bloc and supported by the USSR during the Cold War abandoned communism and moved towards capitalism. This trajectory was not smooth and had severe implications for the orphans of the Cold War. In many parts of the world, particularly in Africa, which was emerging from centuries of colonialism, countries were part of a Cold War game of chess played by ideological rivalries between the USA and the USSR. Countries embroiled in this proxy war, such as Afghanistan and Somalia, remained scarred, recovering from civil wars and lawlessness. Similarly in Europe, the end of the Cold War ignited a civil war in the Balkans. Even more recently, in Syria and the Ukraine we see old Cold War ideologies and allegiances in play. But Fukuyama underestimated the latent and atavistic conflicts held in check by the Cold War: religion, race, ethnic jealousies and a welter of vicious regimes funded by crime, especially narcotics and corruption (see Huntington, 2002). There are many promising developments, however, such as regime changes in Burma and the embryonic democratic developments in North Africa. Arguably, we have not seen the end of history, but rather we are witnessing history in humanity's slow march towards democracy and good governance. According to the International Foundation for Electoral Systems (2013), an international independent body that monitors elections, there has been an increase in democratic elections, reaching a peak in 2011.

The increased democratization of states around the globe shows promise, in terms of expanding the practice of good governance, but equally presents challenges. The overhaul and reform of political systems and institutions requires, in equal measure, reform of public administration in order to achieve good governance and provide better socioeconomic outcomes for society. As interventions in Iraq and Afghanistan have demonstrated, the failure to build the capacity of public administration had tragic consequences for the population. Many governments in more advanced economies have been challenged by the economic crisis and have had to reduce public expenditure while at the same time maintaining social welfare service provision as in the case of Greece. The chapter on Slovenia by Cankar and Petkovšek (Chapter 17) demonstrates this point. The situation there tested the public administration capacity to balance population needs in a period of austerity, often requiring innovative policy solutions and forms of public service delivery.

This book has given a historical account of the socioeconomic, political and administrative changes in various countries. Often, in response to a crisis, governments have made structural and functional changes to the administrative apparatus of the state. They have struggled and will continue to struggle to meet dynamic challenges, but the capacity to deal with complex policy problems appears limited. The book has explored the capacity of developing and developed countries to address what are often termed 'wicked policy problems' (Rittel and Webber, 1973; see Chapter 15 by Head and O'Flynn). Wicked policy problems are problematic social situations where:

1.   there is no obvious solution;
2.   many individuals and organizations are necessarily involved;
3.   there is disagreement among stakeholders about the solutions; and
4.   desired behaviour changes are part of the solution. (Rittel and Webber, 1973).

The problems include, for example, poverty, social exclusion, inequalities, climate change, pollution, terrorism, ethnic rivalry and a range of intransigent and often perennial issues.

The capacity of governments to address these is integral to good governance. For example, as evident in the chapters on China, Brazil and India (Chapters 13, 10 and 12), these countries are experiencing rapid urbanization. Some outcomes of rapid urbanization are slums and endemic poverty, with poor housing and sanitation, and an increase in diseases and mortality (particularly child mortality) (Davis, 2007). People who live in these areas are often not treated as citizens, but are socially excluded; governments usually respond by demolishing slums and destroying communities (Saunders, 2010). Saunders (2010) argues that the social and economic vitality of these rising mega-cities is often met with inadequate and draconian government policies, demonstrating governments' weak policy capacity to integrate demographic changes and a growing urban population, which could contribute to the gross domestic product and economic growth of a country. In advanced economies such as the USA there are also questions about the capacity of governments, at various levels, to deal with wicked policy problems. Andranovich and Anagnoson, in their chapter on US public administration (Chapter 9), provide numerous examples, such as Obamacare, various crises such as Hurricane Katrina and megaprojects disasters, to illustrate the various levels of governments' ineffectiveness, inefficiency and poor implementation. As Andranovich and Anagnoson highlight, the root of the public administration challenge is how the administrative state should be organized to achieve the collective public good.

The capacity of governments to address wicked policy problems and societal problems in the new millennium is challenged by the contributing authors to this book. Indeed, there is a conundrum involved in reforming the state in order to address complex policy challenges: the exact institutions, the administrative apparatus of the state, that invariably formulate reform policies are their implementing agents as well. As Cameron (Chapter 6) argues, the case of South Africa illustrated the abolition of apartheid required change and the overhaul of the public administration, while concurrently implementing public sector reforms and more progressive development policies. The capacity of the state was tested by addressing the complex legacy of apartheid policies while simultaneously reforming its public administration. In countries such as India, the trajectory from colonialism to independence saw an overhaul of colonial administrations, with the challenge of reforming and modernizing public administration institutions, while addressing complex societal issues such as religious and caste divides, poverty, inequality and economic development. As Tummala (Chapter 12) argues, India is still grappling with modernizing and reforming institutions of the state, addressing corruption and professionalizing the civil service.

Most anglophone and Commonwealth countries have adopted the Westminster form of government, as discussed in this book (see Chapter 4 by Rhodes and Tiernan), with party-political neutrality, impartiality and objectivity in civil service culture with the aim of serving the elected government of the day. Yet, as the contributing authors have observed, the bureaucracy is not value free and in some countries such as India and Egypt the extreme is evident, with endemic corruption. Moreover, countries that experience a political transition, particularly those that move from autocratic forms of government to democratic polities, rely on a civil service that may be biased towards the values of the previous political regime. These states are often scarred by conflict and authoritarianism, but are dependent precisely on the institutions of the state to rebuild the country. How do you instil good governance when the public administration is not accustomed to the principles of democracy, public service to all, equality, transparency, accountability, openness, anti-corruption and so on? As Afghanistan and Iraq have demonstrated, change in a political regime towards democracy is not sufficient for good governance. The capacity of government and institutions of the state to deliver essential services and infrastructure is important to democratic development, to adherence to progressive constitutional principles, and to fulfilling people's aspirations for a peaceful and prosperous existence. This is often what most citizens live in hope for and justifiably expect from their government. These traits do not simply materialize. They need institutional support and protection; training and socialization are required for officials to broadly serve the public interest according to the principles of good governance. Andranovich and Anagnoson (Chapter 9) argue for public administration that has 'commitment to moral relevance'.

Good governance is more than adoption of democracy by political actors; it is about state and non-state actors practising a civic duty, a public service ethos, and serving the citizen (irrespective of race, class, gender, ethnicity, religion, tribal and caste allegiance) to their utmost for the common good of society. Public administration is central to good governance and the sustainability of democracy. For if citizens feel aggrieved because of corruption, or if their expectations of the state are not realized, then democracy stands a very slim chance. People will lose faith in the institutions of government and their legitimacy. As many contributing authors to this book have illustrated, trust in and legitimacy of government are essential tenets of good governance (see Bouckaert, Chapter 2). The administrative apparatus of the state plays an important role in governance: it is the bureaucracy that provides politicians with advice in the formulation of policy; and is responsible for policy implementation and delivery of public services.

Pyper, citing the United Nations Economic and Social Commission for Asia and the Pacific (2006), argues in Chapter 1 that good governance involves the principles of accountability, orientation in consensus, efficiency and effectiveness in public services, equitability and inclusiveness, participation, respect for the rule of law, responsiveness and transparency. The European Commission's *White Paper on Governance* (2001), as a guiding principle to improve governance within Europe, proposes: citizen involvement, openness and transparency; better policy, regulation and delivery; performance improvement of public administration; and policy coherence. Cameron (Chapter 6), citing the South African National Planning Commission, lists themes of good governance in public administration. This list is worth summarizing as it resonates with the themes of the book: a public service focused on development and serving the public; free from political interference; instilling the principles of accountability and transparency; improving human resource capacity; and maintaining a professional career civil service. There is sufficient empirical evidence for a link between good governance on measures of government and public administrative effectiveness, low levels of corruption, quality of legal system and rule of law with measures of economic growth and quality of life (Rothstein, 2012). Thus good governance and public administration effectiveness are integral to socioeconomic development, democracy and political stability.

A recurring theme in the book is the reform of public administration over the decades and, furthermore, the effects that these reforms have had on the structure, function and ethos of the administrative apparatus of the state. We turn our attention in the next section to this central theme, as well as to further issues that reforms have generated, and the implications for the capacity of the state to address complex policy problems and effect good governance.

PUBLIC ADMINISTRATION REFORMS

Many countries have, over the decades, embarked on successive waves of public sector reforms. In Chapter 1 Pyper argues that this was first in response to the post-World War II demands for development and modernization, and then in response to the recession of the 1970s. The latter period saw governments reforming the administrative apparatus of the state by embracing neoliberal reforms of the public sector. These public sector reforms were in later years termed new public management (NPM) (Hood, 1991). They were structural and managerial, and extended beyond Anglo-Saxon countries. Many countries often borrowed NPM reforms introduced in the UK under Prime Minister Margaret Thatcher. There were nuances in the transferability of NPM. The chapter by Curry, Hammerschmid, Jilke and Van de Walle (Chapter 16) showed that even in Europe there were convergences and divergences in the application of reforms (see also Halligan, 2011). There was a general adoption of performance management, results-orientated service delivery, contracting out and privatization. But even in Europe there was variation in the application of public sector reforms. In the UK, France, Estonia, the Netherlands and Slovenia (see Chapter 17 by Cankar and Petkovšek) there was downsizing of the public sector, but in Norway to a lesser extent. Transparency and open government were more prominent in many European countries, but in France these were less important. In Spain, especially with regard to agencification and customer orientation, NPM was less evident. Italy, however, had higher levels of privatization and contracting out than other European countries. Curry et al. in their chapter found that, in the implementation of reforms, public sector executives felt that the reforms were top–down and there were significant variations in the perception of their success.

In the USA, reinventing government, introduced by the Clinton administration, also adopted NPM-type reforms with a reduction in red tape, and a performance, customer and innovation orientation. Yet, despite the reforms of federal and other levels of government, Andranovich and Anagnoson argue that American public administration and its role in governance have resulted in enormous complexity, large expenditures, outsourcing and private sector contracting, high levels of distrust, divergent levels of services, a 'submerged state' and high public expectations.

Thus, in general, the neoliberal-type reforms included the privatization of public sector services and state enterprises, deregulation, contracting out of services to the non-state sector, agencification of government departments, and the adoption of private sector management techniques (see McTavish, Chapter 18). Savoie in Chapter 8 provides a good illustration in a table of the contrasts between public administration and NPM. The reforms were isomorphically adapted, but Pyper (see Chapter 1), Halligan (2011 and Chapter 14, this volume) and even Hood (1995) question the ubiquity and universality of NPM. As this book has illustrated, neoliberal public sector reforms did not necessarily travel well. In some countries the sheer complexity of public administration systems and structures led to poor implementation of reforms. In other countries the socio-economic and political context led to unintended outcomes. For example, in Brazil we see a complex mosaic of patrimony, progressive public administration, NPM and public governance at various levels of government. In the USA, as well, the privatization and contracting out of services to the non-government sector has in fact increased public expenditure and has also increased the complexity of public service delivery.

NPM as a global paradigm is contested, and it is hoped that this book, by providing country perspectives, adds to this debate by exploring public administration systems and reforms in the countries studied. It is not the intention of this concluding chapter to summarize the arguments of each chapter of this volume; rather we discuss the consistent themes evident in the reform of various countries' public administration. We make some tentative arguments about public administration and good governance, and challenges that governments face. We argue that government, in order to address increasingly complex socioeconomic challenges and wicked policy problems, should orientate public administration reforms towards achieving good governance rather than managerial and structural tinkering. We argue that reforms of the state and its public administration institutions should include due regard, *inter alia*, to:

- coordinating governance;
- political and administrative relations;
- performance and accountability;
- policy and administrative effectiveness;
- the value of bureaucracy; and
- a public service ethos.

COORDINATING GOVERNANCE: CENTRALIZATION AND DECENTRALIZATION

As Halligan argues (Chapter 14), there have been two narratives of public sector reforms in anglophone countries: the neoliberal retraction of the state in the provision of social welfare services; and the more centralized control of reforms, with the state playing a steering role. This centralization and decentralization of reforms in the public sector is a consistent theme in the book. The reform of the public sector from a centralization perspective has seen the rise of top–down reforms with limited input from street-level bureaucrats (see Chapter 16 by Curry et al.). The outcome is often poorly implemented reforms, with middle managers and street-level bureaucrats showing little enthusiasm, understanding and inclusion in the state's reform agenda (see Chapter 14 by Halligan). Rhodes and Tiernan (Chapter 4) refer to this as a central capability *vis-à-vis* an implementation puzzle where central government capacity is focused on tools used by political leaders to coordinate and regulate the government environment, which is increasingly becoming pluralized, fragmented and contested.

This puzzle is perhaps magnified in countries where there is limited capacity of the central state apparatus to include and build a consensus on public sector reforms through various stakeholders. Thus a consequence of more centrist public sector reforms is the rise of performance management systems, metrics and a bureaucracy to collect and analyse the performance data. As many of the contributing authors to this volume have argued, performance management has had unintended outcomes, such as game-playing, bureaucratic rivalry and fragmentation, demotivation and even corruption. In countries such as South Africa, where there is poor capacity to capture the public sector performance data make the implementation of reforms a moot exercise. Yet in other countries performance management has enhanced the delivery of services, accountability and transparency (see, for example, Chapter 16 by Curry et al.). This reminds us of the importance of deploying a skilled workforce to gather and analyse data.

The decentralization theme of public sector reform may have empowered local and regional public agencies as well as non-state actors, but here too are challenges of fragmentation, coordination, duplication, 'postcode lottery' and variant public service provision. Thus we argue, as does Halligan, and Rhodes and Tiernan, that the challenge for any government is the capacity for vertical and horizontal coordination. There are two dimensions of governance in the capacity of governments for vertical and horizontal coordination of policy and public services. The vertical dimension is what Hooghe and Marks (2003) termed the Type I form of governance. Type I governance is the distribution of authority across jurisdictions with a limited number of territorial levels (ibid.). The vertical coordination across jurisdictions and multi-levels of governance is evident in the EU, and in states with federal political architecture such as the USA, Canada and Brazil. Even in the UK, a seemingly unitary state, McTavish (Chapter 18) argues that the UK polity struggles with the implementation of policy across an increasingly divergent decentralized system of governance.

The horizontal dimension of coordination refers to what Hooghe and Marks (2003) termed the Type II form of governance. There is no defined jurisdiction, with a fluidity of state and non-state actors operating across boundaries in policy specific areas (ibid.). According to Rhodes (1996, 2000), governance involves interactions between various network actors. He argues that

> these networks are characterised, first, by interdependence between organisations. Governance is broader than government, covering non-state actors . . . Second, there are continuing interactions between network members, caused by the need to exchange resources and negotiate a shared purpose. Third, these interactions are game-like, rooted in trust and regulated by rules of the game . . . Finally, the networks have significant degree of autonomy from the state. Networks are not accountable to the state; they are self-organising. (Rhodes, 2000: 61)

Thus, as Curry et al. observed in Chapter 16, NPM-type reforms such as privatization and contracting out appear to have been superseded by a new agenda of partnerships and network governance. We therefore see an increasingly complex environment of service provision by state and non-state actors in various horizontal network arrangements. Andranovich and Anagnoson also make the observation that there is increased complexity, with multiple scales (from supranational to local levels) involving the public sector, contractors, private and non-governmental institutions working through markets and networks to deliver public services. The accountability of non-state actors such as the private sector in the provision of services poses challenges in horizontal coordination.

Thus, joining up and coordinating government and agencies across the vertical and horizontal dimensions of governance requires the reconciliation of Rhodes and Tiernan's puzzle, that is, formal and informal coordination. They argue in Chapter 4 that governments confront two broad tasks in such multi-organizational systems: managing individual networks; and managing a portfolio of networks. This, they argue, requires collaborative leadership, which in turn requires government leaders to be integrative, facilitative, hands-off and diplomatic rather than directive, hands-on, and command and control in style. However, as various contributing authors to this volume have observed, the top–down and directive style of leadership is more evident. This control-and-command style of leadership, and indeed public sector reforms, are principally the function of a political environment with a demand for results-based service delivery and accountability. In the coordination of governance across increasingly complex vertical and horizontal dimensions, governments face a paradox of coordination. As discussed in this volume, governments face demands by citizenry and subnational levels of government for the decentralization of policy and public service delivery to satisfy the needs and democratic demands of the local population, or in some cases to shape bureaux at subnational levels of government. Yet there is a need for policy and public service provision to be coordinated from a central level, to ensure equality in the provision of services and accountability of public administration performance to the electorate.

Accountability for performance of government is integral to good governance and democratic ideals. Thus coordinating governance in terms of reconciling the centralization and decentralization of policy and public services requires capacity-building and training to effect collaboration among government departments at and across various levels, as well as with non-state actors involved in service delivery. The term 'joined-up government' has become a cliché, but was a response to increased fragmentation as a result of neoliberal reforms. The poor operationalization of collaboration is partly due to a reluctance to share financial and human resources between government departments and the streamlining of procedures, lines of accountability and managerial systems. Neoliberal managerial performance and accountability processes entrenched bureaucratic organizational silos rather than encouraged coordinated and collaborative governance.

POLITICAL AND ADMINISTRATIVE INTERFACE: ACCOUNTABILITIES AND PERFORMANCE

The capacity for collaborative leadership within network governance is mediated by a political environment with an electorate that requires accountability, transparency and responsiveness (principles of good governance). In most Western democracies, citizens ultimately hold politicians accountable for public policy and public services, irrespective of the delivery agent. The political context of public administration is a recurring theme of many chapters.

Neoliberal reforms and network governance, as many authors in this volume have argued, far from enhancing accountability, had unintended outcomes. Many contributing authors have observed the fragmentation of accountability. Marketization and networks resulted in the authority of public service delivery being dispersed across vertical and horizontal dimensions of governance. Rhodes and Tiernan in Chapter 4 observed the anomaly of a 'web of accountabilities'. Accountability is often tested in a time of crisis. Questions emerge over which government agency, network or contracted organization is responsible and who should be held accountable when public service delivery goes awry. The recent banking crisis provided an insight into the complex web of regulation (or perhaps the lack thereof), the public and private sector interface, and national and international networks. Even in geographically localized crises such as flooding in the UK or Huricanne Katrina in the USA, disputes among various levels and agencies of government were played out in the media, with a frustrated citizenry demanding responsiveness and accountability. At a global level, accountability for more complex crises and problems such as the banking crisis becomes an enigma. 'Who should be held accountable for what' becomes opaque in modern society, with an increasingly complex web of policy formulation and implementation. This is perhaps an accusation from which the EU, as a multi-level system of governance, suffers. An erosion of accountability and transparency alienates the citizenry and makes the disaffected public question governance and the legitimacy of state institutions (Rothstein, 2012).

Savoie, in Chapter 8, argues that the NPM reforms of the Canadian public service saw the politicians attacking the bureaucracy for inefficiencies and red tape, and for introducing results-based accountability and private sector principles. Politicians wanted the public service to reflect a bottom line of performance and be held accountable, but the capacity of government departments to measure is inadequate. This is true for the South African case as well, where public sector reforms were implemented in an erratic and inconsistent manner, with high levels of political interference. In South Africa, NPM did not actually improve performance, nor did it address complex socioeconomic problems and the legacy of apartheid. The success of NPM reforms in South Africa is therefore questionable. In the USA, Andranovich and Anagnoson (Chapter 9) argue that many of the public administration reforms were politically motivated and, moreover, 'the reasons why the public sector is not functioning well in the USA are not fundamentally administrative – they are political'.

The link between measuring public service performance and accountability is desirable, but often problematic for a number of reasons. First, the public service, given the political context and, as Savoie argues in Chapter 8, has its own intrinsic characteristics and cannot be measured according to the bottom line of a profitability benchmark. The public service for the most part delivers services that are often intangible and socially beneficial in nature, making measurement difficult. For example, measuring the progression rates of students passing a level of examination does not measure their educational gains; and the number of patients on a hospital waiting list may provide some evidence of the efficiency of the hospital, but does not measure long-term health benefits and outcomes. Robert McNamara (2003), whose career started in the Ford Motor Company as a statistician, and who later became the US Secretary for Defense, reflecting on the Vietnam War, stated that the 'body count' provided data on the number of enemy combatants killed, but it did not imply that the outcome was a US victory in South-East Asia. As Savoie notes, 'Efforts to borrow management practices from the private sector overlook the reality that public and private sectors are fundamentally different in both important and unimportant ways.'

Second, performance management may not necessarily enhance accountability and the principles of good governance. To the contrary, as many contributing authors to this volume observed, there has been gameplaying and corruption. The chapter on South Africa is illustrative of this point. Third, the political–administrative relationship becomes fraught with blame-shifting between politicians and bureaucrats. McTavish in Chapter 18 cites Djelic and Sahlin (2012), who describe regulatory, performance and inspection regimes dispersing responsibility and creating 'spirals of distrust'. The result is often accountability falling between the cracks, and the neutrality of the administrative apparatus of the state being tested by political interference. In Chapter 8, Savoie describes the case of the Chief Statistician for Canada, Munir Sheikh, who resigned after ministerial interference cast doubt on his integrity and that of Statistics Canada.

Politicians ultimately wish to provide the electorate with evidence of the delivery of electoral promises, and do so vicariously through the administrative apparatus in order to be re-elected. This pressure is manifested in the political–administrative interface. Public administrators play an important role here. They not only provide policy advice on the formulation involved in the implementation and on occasion the evaluation of policy, but importantly the administrative arm of government plays a mediating role in political excesses (see Page and Jenkins, 2005; Peters, 2001). As the case of India illustrates, the convergence of roles between politicians and administrators leads to corruption. The separation of powers and roles between politicians and administrators is important to the preservation of democracy. The hybridization of political and administrative roles (see Aberbach et al., 1981) is not desirable. The party-political neutrality and impartiality of public administration is fundamental to good governance.

Finally, holding politicians and administrators accountable for government performance is essential to good governance, but it should be a means to an end and not an end in itself. The performance measurement of government activity is complex, given the qualitative factors and outcomes of the public policy environment. According to Dunleavy and Carrera (2013), measuring the productivity of government is difficult, although not insurmountable, given the dynamic political environment, with consequent policy shifts, policy demands and variations, a lack of domestic and international comparative benchmarking data, poor data collection and standardization, changing data specifications, and resistance to measurement from political and public officials. Measuring the performance of a government department is a managerial tool and should be considered alongside other measures to enhance accountability. It can have positive and negative outcomes, as discussed earlier; performance and accountability systems can erode collaborative efforts. Chapter 17 by Cankar and Petkovšek, for example, demonstrates performance management as applied in Slovenia, which had the positive result of improving fiscal prudence, but had negative effects of eroding staff morale. Performance management and targetization can never address complex socioeconomic and wicked policy problems. This requires joined-up, collaborative, innovative thinking of policy solutions to increasingly challenging socioeconomic problems rather than bureaucratic organizational rivalries and target-chasing bureaucrats appeasing the whims of political masters.

IN PRAISE OF BUREAUCRACY

Du Gay's (2000) book entitled *In Praise of Bureaucracy: Weber, Organisation, Ethics*, makes the case for the contribution of bureaucracy against an onslaught of neoliberal reforms and political managerialism. Bureaucracy has often been associated with inefficiency, ineffectiveness, red tape, over-regulation, risk-aversion and so on. Administrators are often caught in a puzzle of embracing private sector principles of risk-taking, providing choice, responsiveness and efficiency gains versus compliance with the rule of law, service provision on an equitable basis, responsiveness to a broader populace with varying needs (as opposed to a narrowly defined clientele), and making efficiency gains within the context of decreasing public finances (particularly in this period of financial crisis and austerity measures) and increasing public demands for services (given demographic changes and political electoral promises). Many of the authors in this volume have made the case for the pervasiveness and persistence of bureaucracy. Bouckaert, Perri 6, Drechsler and Savoie, for example, in their contributions to this volume, remind us of the Weberian ideals of bureaucracy. The rule, merit-based and communitarian organization provides a positive contribution to government. Indeed, Pyper notes that good governance prescriptions by organizations such as the World Bank, the EU and the United Nations stress the importance of Weberian-orientated government with, *inter alia*, 'precise and unambiguous rules; merit-based recruitment; . . . public officials less susceptible to bribery; and a transparent system of responsibility' (see Pyper, Chapter 1 in this volume, citing Pierre and Rothstein, 2011: 409). Weber viewed bureaucracy as a rational and efficient form of organization mediating arbritarianism and corruption, with a fixed jurisdictional area of authority ordered by laws, hierarchically ordered officialdom and based on meritorious careers and promotion (see Mommsen, 1974; Du Gay, 2000; Meier and Hill, 2005). This, Weber believed, was imperative for the stability of democratic political systems (Mommsen, 1974; Du Gay, 2000).

Some of the authors of this book have argued that the values of bureaucracy have been eroded by neoconservatism and neoliberalism. Indeed, it appears that some public sector reforms such as agencification have reduced the policy and administrative capacity of government; marketization and contracting out have fragmented service delivery with resultant accountability and transparency complexities; fixed contracts and declining salaries have reduced staff morale and made the public sector seem a less attractive career. Governance and networks as described above have had their own unintended, negative outcomes. Perri 6, however, questions the theory of governance and raises the debate about hierarchy and networks. He argues in Chapter 3 that the theory of governance is a myth and suffers from 'stretch'. Moreover, he argues that hierarchy is an underlying institutional ordering that encompasses hierarchical bureaucracy, which remains a pervasive form of institution. Perri 6's view is that the centrality of government and bureaucracy remains, with the 'hollowing out' of the authority of the state overstated. The state remains prominent through regulation and policy instruments in managing networks. Fenwick et al. (2012) also argue that the authority of the state is not being eroded through governance networks, but rather extended through bureaucracy involving non-state actors and organizations in a meta-bureaucracy.

The policy and administrative capacity of government to deal with complex, wicked policy problems depends on the extent to which governments engage directly in institutional design and support successful implementation (see Halligan, Chapter 14). Yet many government reforms are focused at best on internal capacity to improve managerialism, and the external focus tends to be on reducing dependence on internal capacity by relying on external expertise through third parties or non-state actors and relinquishing responsibilities to 'spirals' and 'webs' (see chapters by Halligan; McTavish; Rhodes and Tiernan). Perri 6 (see also Chapter 4 by Rhodes and Tiernan) argues that public administration requires institutional analysis to understand the positive and negative dynamics of institutional change. Thus, if neoliberalism has eroded the values of bureaucracy and has unintended outcomes such as fragmented accountabilities and corruption in some countries, has eroded the policy capacity of public administration, has created anomalies or puzzles, and has provided inadequate instruments to effectively and innovatively deal with increasingly complex, global wicked policy problems, what could this volume contribute to debate on postmodern public administration and governance? We believe that public administration should establish a public service ethos to achieve public administration effectiveness and good governance.

PUBLIC SERVICE ETHOS

Neoliberal public sector reforms have swung the pendulum towards the intrinsic values of private sector consumerism and competition, with, as discussed above, unintended outcomes. Barberis (2011) argues that NPM and private sector values have undermined the principles of a public service ethos. Indeed, public administration and bureaucracy became synonymous with an anachronistic, monolithic form of organization: rule-bound, inefficient, rigid and so on (see Peters and Pierre, 2003). Proponents of NPM who hailed the death of bureaucracy and hollowing out of the state may have been premature in their analysis. As many authors in this volume have stated, government and its administrative/ bureaucratic apparatus is still prominent and central to any political system. In any democratic system, politicians operate within a turnstile of electoral cycles, but the permanency and political neutrality of the public administration is a value to society, and therein lies its power. As with any arm of government, this power, in terms of a good governance narrative, should be monitored and held accountable. Politicians, through various policy instruments and reforms, have sought to do this with varying success, as illustrated in the chapters of this book. Irrespective of various attempts at institutional changes across the decades, as described by the contributing authors of this volume, and although various public admin-istration scholars over the decades have debated, coined and contested the terms and theories of NPM, governance and new public governance, fundamental to values of public administration must be a public service ethos.

Simply, a public service ethos is the principle of serving all of the public as opposed to personal, political, tribal or other self-interests and preju-dices. A public service ethos includes the ethical conduct that Kernaghan (1993: 6) describes as 'principles and standards of right conduct . . . not only with distinguishing right from wrong and good from bad but also with the commitment to do what is right or what is good' for the public.

O'Toole (1993) describes public service ethos as the setting aside of personal interests; working altruistically, anonymously and collegially for the collective public good of others; and conducting oneself with integrity and professionalism to deal with diverse problems that need solving if the public good is to be promoted.

As Drechsler argues in Chapter 5, contrary to neoliberal reforms, public administration should instil a public service ethos that incorporates high standards of ethical and meritorious conduct. Drechsler (citing Jones, 1998) argues that public administrators should adopt Confucianism, which promotes harmony over individual freedoms, consensus over choice, and communitarianism over individualism. Indeed, Drechsler questions the orthodoxy of neoliberal Western-style public sector reforms, and points out, as do other contributing authors to this volume, that these reforms have reduced the noble profession of achieving common goals of the collective public good for all. He goes on to make the case for explor-ing non-Western paradigms of public administration and governance. For example, the Five Pillars of Islam speaks of communitarianism, self-sacrifice, and public service and charity to others. The Chinese historically viewed public service as prestigious, and Savoie in Chapter 8 calls for a return to viewing public service as a noble profession incorporating an *esprit de corps*. Andranovich and Anagnoson in Chapter 9 cite Dvorin and Simmons (1972), who believe that the struggle to achieve better gov-ernance cannot be found in the routine application of existing models of public administration, but that bureaucracy should be grounded in concerns for human dignity with morally relevant public administration.

Many scholars, commissions and supranational organizations have listed principles of ethical standards, features of a public service ethos and good governance for those in public office (see O'Toole, 1993; Pratchett and Wingfield, 1994; Nolan, 1995; Barberis, 2001; IMF, 2007). Thus a core set of values of public service should include, *inter alia*: accountability and transparency; honesty and impartiality, selflessness; serving the public; altruistic motivation; loyalty to the community, organization, profession and the public; rejecting corruption and the appropriation of public office for personal gain; and respect for the rule of law. As Bouckaert argues, these are key tenets of democracy and good governance.

In an age of modernity and postmodern public administration we believe these normative values hold true, but are worth restating and, indeed, as Du Gay (2001) argues, public administration and Weberian bureaucratic values need to be reasserted. He states:

> in the field of public administration this can be undertaken by describing practical ways in which actual existing bureaucratic practices function as institutional manifestations of a conscious effort to create responsible, accountable government by ensuring discretion is not abused, that due process is the norm and not the exception, and undue risks are not taken that undermine the integrity of the political and administrative system. (Du Gay, 2001: 4)

A footnote to this discussion of a public service ethos is that the integrity and functioning of political and public administration institutions will increasingly be questioned. Governments will face escalating public scrutiny in an age of modernity and technological advancement to capture and disseminate knowledge of public service functionality and delivery. Particularly in an era of social media, there are increasing networks of scrutiny and calls for open government. Andranovich and Anagnoson in Chapter 9 on the USA illustrate the pervasive nature of technology in public administration. Blame-shifting, game-playing, poor public value and service provision, and fragmented diffusion through webs of accountabilities or spirals of responsibilities will not be tolerated by an ever-demanding and expectant public.

The electoral promises by the political class and introduction of neoliberal-type reforms in the public sector with promises of choice, responsiveness, consumerist values and private sector standards have opened a Pandora's box of expectations. The public will no longer, through the lens of an information age and increased awareness, tolerate mediocrity. As Ahmed Badran in Chapter 7, describing the Arab Spring, demonstrates, frustration with corruption and poor public service delivery can destabilize a political system. Increasingly, whether in countries in Africa, Asia, Europe, North or South America, societies are holding government to account through social media and becoming active co-governors in the delivery of services. Thus, as does Barberis (2001), we add to the list of principles of a public service ethos: ethical conduct in the provision of quality public services for the common, public good to achieve good governance.

CONCLUSION

In conclusion, we argue that, for public administration to adhere to the principles of good governance requires:

- an inclusive, democratic political and administrative environment;
- a public service ethos;
- resource investment to improve policy making and administrative capacity rather than institutional managerial reforms or tinkering;
- preserving party-political neutrality of administrative institutions without political interference;
- continuous improvement towards prudent and effective delivery of quality public services;
- collaborative and coordinated accountability and governance; and
- innovative policy capacity to address wicked policy problems.

Neoliberal public sector reforms will, at best, if implemented correctly, create organizational efficiencies and, at worst, create anomalies, but will not necessarily provide the administrative capacity to address wicked policy problems and achieve good governance. Moreover, to improve the administrative and policy capacity of civil servants to formulate and implement innovative policies requires educational programmes and knowledge exchange in public policy and public administration. Good governance and a public service ethos should be at the core of the curriculum and knowledge exchange, and should include a collaborative effort among practitioners and scholars to learn the lessons and formulate innovative policy solutions. Governments' capacity to deal with complex problems requires not merely management training, often reinforcing neoliberal-type reforms, but instillation of a public service ethos. Public administration according to Confucian doctrine should be viewed as a noble profession consisting of an *esprit de corps*, serving the public and solving wicked policy problems for the common and collective good with due regard to human dignity. It is hoped that this volume has made some contribution to this exchange of knowledge of the various countries' public administration and governance reforms, lessons, challenges and how they are addressing crisis and wicked policy issues. Developing the policy capacity of civil servants will be key to addressing the global challenges that we face in this new era.

REFERENCES

Aberbach, J.D., Putnam, R.D. and Rockman, B.A. (1981) *Bureaucrats and Politicians in Western Democracies*, Cambridge, MA: Harvard University Press.

Barberis, P. (2001) 'Civil society, virtue, trust: implications for the public service ethos in the age of modernity', *Public Policy and Administration*, **16**(3), 111–26.

Barberis, P. (2011) 'The Weberian legacy', in Andrew Massey (ed.), *International Handbook on Civil Service Systems*, Cheltenham, UK and Northampton, MA, USA: Edward Elgar Publishing, pp. 13–30.

Davis, M. (2007) *Planet of Slums*, London: Verso.

Djelic, M.-L. and Sahlin, K. (2012) 'Reordering the world: transnational regulatory governance and its challenges', in D. Levi-Faur (ed.), *The Oxford Handbook of Governance*. Oxford: Oxford University Press, pp. 745–58.

Du Gay, P. (2000) *In Praise of Bureaucracy: Weber. Organisation. Ethics*, London: Sage Publications.

Du Gay, P. (2001) *The Politics of Bureaucracy*, Abingdon: Routledge.

Dunleavy, P. and Carrera, L.N. (2013) *Growing the Productivity of Government Services*, Cheltenham, UK and Northampton, MA, USA: Edward Elgar Publishing.

Dvorin, E.P. and R.H. Simmons (1972), *From Amoral to Humane Bureaucracy*, San Francisco, CA: Canfield Press (Harper & Row).

European Commission (2001) *White Paper on Governance*, COM(2001) 428, Brussels: EC.

Fenwick, J., Miller Johnston, K. and McTavish, D. (2012) 'Co-governance or meta-bureaucracy? Perspectives of local governance "partnerships" in England and Scotland', *Policy & Politics*, **40**(3), 405–22.

Fukuyama, F. (1992) *The End of History and the Last Man*, London: Penguin Group.

Fukuyama, Francis (2013) 'What is governance?', *Governance*, **26**(3), 347–68.

Halligan, John (2011) 'NPM in Anglo-Saxon countries', in T. Christensen and P. Lægreid (eds), *The Ashgate Companion to New Public Management*, Farnham: Ashgate.

Hood, C. (1991) 'A public management for all seasons', *Public Administration*, **69**(1), 3–19.

Hood, C. (1995) 'Contemporary public management: a new global paradigm?', *Public Policy and Administration*, **10**(2), 104–17.

Hooghe, L. and Marks, G. (2003) 'Unravelling the central state, but how? Types of multi-level governance', *American Political Science Review*, **97**(2), 233–43.

Huntington, S.P. (2002) *The Clash of Civilization and the Remaking of the New World Order*, London: Free Press.

IMF (International Monetary Fund) (2007) *Manual on Fiscal Transparency*, http://www.imf.org/external/np/pp/2007/eng/051507m.pdf, accessed January 2014.

International Foundation for Electoral Systems (2013) http://www.ifes.org/, accessed November 2013.

Jones, D. (ed.) (2008), *Confucius Now: Contemporary Encounters with the Analects*, Chicago and La Salle, IL: Open Court.

Kernaghan, K. (1993) 'Promoting public service ethics: the codification option', in R.A. Chapman (ed.), *Ethics in Public Service*, Edinburgh: Edinburgh University Press, pp. 15–30.

McNamara, R. (2003) *The Fog of War*, E. Morris (director), Sony Pictures.

Meier, K.J. and Hill, G.C. (2005) 'Bureaucracy in the twenty-first century', in E. Ferlie,

L.E. Lynn Jr and C. Pollitt (eds), *Public Management*, Oxford: Oxford University Press, pp. 51–71.

Mommsen, W.J. (1974) *The Age of Bureaucracy: Perspectives on the Political Sociology of Max Weber*, Oxford: Basil Blackwell.

Nolan (1995) *First Report of the Committee on Standards in Public Life – Vol. 1: Report*, Cm 2850 – I, London: HMSO.

O'Toole, B.J. (1993) 'The loss of purity: the corruption of public service in Britain', *Public Policy and Administration*, **8**(2), 1–6.

Page, E.C. and Jenkins, B. (2005) *Policy Bureaucracy. Government With a Cast of Thousands*, Oxford: Oxford University Press.

Peters, B.G. (2001) *The Politics of Bureaucracy*, Abingdon: Routledge.

Peters, B.G. and Pierre, J. (eds) (2003) *Handbook of Public Administration*, London: Sage.

Pierre, J. and Rothstein, B. (2011) 'Reinventing Weber: the role of institutions in creating social trust', in T. Christensen and P. Lægreid (eds), *The Ashgate Companion to New Public Management*, Farnham: Ashgate, pp. 405–16.

Pratchett, L. and Wingfield, M. (1994) *The Public Service Ethos in Local Government: A Research Report*, London: Commission for Local Democracy.

Rhodes, R.A.W. (1996), 'The new governance: governing without government', *Political Studies*, **44**(4), 652–67.

Rhodes, R.A.W. (2000) 'Governance in public administration', in J. Pierre (ed.), *Debating Governance: Authority, Steering and Democracy*, Oxford: Oxford University Press, pp. 54–90.

Rittel, H.W.J. and Webber, M.M. (1973) 'Dilemmas in a general theory of planning', *Policy Sciences*, **4**, 155–69.

Rothstein, B. (2012) 'Good governance', in D. Levi-Faur (ed.), *Governance*, Oxford: Oxford University Press.

Saunders, D. (2010) *Arrival City*, London: Random House.

United Nations Economic and Social Commission for Asia and the Pacific (2006) *What is Good Governance?*, www.unescap.org/huset/gg/governance.htm, accessed January 2014.

Index

Abbott, Tony 350
Abdülhamid II 121
accountability 41, 52, 235, 265, 333, 338, 451
  collective 82
  democratic 106
  mechanisms 173
  political 81, 93
  shared 333
  webs of 81, 88, 93, 452
administrative management principles
  planning, organizing, staffing, directing, coordinating, reporting and budgeting (POSDCORB) 211
Afghanistan 445–6
  Operation Enduring Freedom (2001–14) 69, 200, 221, 443
  presence of private military contractors during 209
African National Congress (ANC) 5, 138, 141
  Cadre Policy and Deployment Strategy (1997) 141
Albania 122
Alfonsín, Raúl
  administration of 259–60
  electoral victory of (1983) 259
Algeria 177–8
Andrews, Matt 107
Appleby, Paul 272
  Report for Government of India (1953) 276
Argentina 6, 251, 262
  bureaucracy of 259–60, 262–3
  democratic reform in 259
    Anticorruption Office 262
  managerial reform in
    23,696 State Reform Act (1989) 260
    23,697 Economic Emergency Act (1989) 260
    Second Reform of the State 261–2

National Reorganization Process (1976–83) 259
  public sector of 259–60
Aristotle 110
Asian Financial Crisis (1997–9) 342
Association of Education Committees 68
Australia 4, 7, 17, 25, 96, 337, 341–2, 351, 365
  Australian Capital Territory 361
  Australian National Audit Office (ANAO) 333, 350
  Australian Public Service Commission (APSC) 328–9, 336
    Changing Behaviour (2007) 346–7
    Tackling Wicked Problems (2007) 347
  Australian Taxation Office (ATO) 334
  Centrelink 335, 338
    closure of 330–31
  Council of Australian Governments (COAG) 344–5, 352
    Closing the Gap program 355–8, 365
    National Indigenous Reform Agreement (NIRA) (2008) 355–7
    Reform Council 357, 365
    trials (2002) 352–4
  Department of Education, Employment and Workplace Relations (DEEWR) 335
  Department of Families, Housing, Community Service and Indigenous Affairs (FaHCSIA) 334–5
  Department of Finance 327–8, 333, 344
  Department of Human Services (DHS) 330, 335